The Hidde~~~
the Historic Fu~~~amentalists,
1933–1948

Reconsidering the Historic Fundamentalists'
Response to the Upheavals, Hardships, and
Horrors of the 1930s and 1940s

Jim Owen

University Press of America,® Inc.
Lanham · Boulder · New York · Toronto · Oxford

Copyright © 2004 by
University Press of America,® Inc.
4501 Forbes Boulevard
Suite 200
Lanham, Maryland 20706
UPA Acquisitions Department (301) 459-3366

PO Box 317
Oxford
OX2 9RU, UK

Library of Congress Control Number: 2004108486
ISBN 0-7618-2896-6 (hardcover : alk. ppr.)
ISBN 0-7618-2897-4 (paperback : alk. ppr.)

In memory of two outstanding Fundamentalist scholars – Herbert Hotchkiss and Marchant King – who loved the Lord their God with all their hearts and minds, and taught their students to do likewise.

TABLE OF CONTENTS

FOREWORD

In this present age there exists one minority group whose members and their views may be disparaged with abandon and no one will rise to defend them or charge the attacker with bigotry or incivility. That group is fundamentalism. What fundamentalism actually means is usually in the eye of the beholder, but you can rest assured that it is bad. One can safely get away with insensitive, negative, and even pejorative comments about those who identify with it or who are accused of being fundamentalists.

Although the term originated in the conflict within North American Protestantism in the early twentieth century, it has over the years been expanded to include virtually any kind of traditionalist, conservative, or extremist movement in all the world's religions. This is best illustrated by the five large volumes that resulted from the Fundamentalism Project, a multiyear, interdisciplinary enterprise sponsored by the American Academy of Arts and Sciences and funded by the John D. and Catherine T. MacArthur Foundation, which set the benchmark for fundamentalist scholarship.[1] I am sure, however, that many of the groups that were treated as "fundamentalist" in this extraordinary scholarly endeavor would not accept that label, but the venture epitomizes how elastic the concept has become in the present world.

In the United States context, the term first gained currency with the publication between 1910 and 1915 of a series of twelve volumes known as *The Fundamentals*. The ninety essays contained in them testified to the truth of traditional Protestant orthodoxy. As the controversy between liberals and conservatives heated up after World War I, a Baptist journalist, Curtis Lee Laws, in 1920 applied the label "fundamentalism" to the movement which by then had become a self-conscious grouping within American Protestantism. Its spokespeople had a clear sense of the orthodox beliefs that must be defended and a well-defined enemy— "modernism." Although the media of the time paid considerable attention to their activities, it lost interest after the fundamentalists failed in their effort to halt the teaching of evolution in the public schools or to gain control of the major denominations—especially the Northern Baptist Convention, and the Presbyterian Church in the U.S.A. With the onset of the Great Depression, media attention focused on the unparalleled crisis that had beset the nation. Although now out of the public eye, the fundamentalists quietly developed an extraordinary institutional structure—an interlocking network of small denominations and independent churches, Bible institutes and seminaries, magazines and publishing firms, radio broadcasters, Bible camps and conference grounds, urban rescue missions, evangelistic ministries, and foreign mission agencies. At the end of World War II they emerged organizationally stronger and more aggressive in their evangelistic and missionary work than ever before.

However, a rift in the fundamentalist front became evident as a new generation of "evangelicals" called for greater engagement with the culture and a wider role in public life. Through the remarkable evangelistic ministry of Billy Graham, the organizing skill of Harold John Ockenga, the intellectual leadership of Carl F. H. Henry, and the variety of publishing enterprises, especially the journal *Christianity Today* (founded 1956) and the books produced by the William B. Eerdmans Company and Baker Book House, the new evangelicals reentered the mainstream of American Christianity. The gulf between them and the fundamentalists who chose not to follow their lead became increasingly wider as the years passed. In the eyes of the mainline Protestant leaders and many of the new evangelicals, the continuing fundamentalists were relegated to an outer darkness of ignorance, narrow-mindedness, obscurantism, and bigotry. Still, the rise of the television evangelists, the appearance of the new religio-political right, and the conservative victories in the Lutheran Church-Missouri Synod and Southern Baptist Convention denominational struggles made it patently clear that fundamentalism was as alive and vigorous as ever.

Although people in the media and scholarly world alike ridiculed and belittled fundamentalists, some now began to pay serious attention to the phenomenon. Among these were Louis Gasper, *The Fundamentalist Movement,*[2] Ernest R. Sandeen, *The Roots of Fundamentalism: British and American Millenarianism, 1800-1930,*[3] C. Allyn Russell, *Voices of American Fundamentalism,*[4] and above all, George M. Marsden, whose seminal works *Fundamentalism and American Culture: The Shaping of Twentieth Century Evangelicalism 1870-1925*[5] and its sequel *Reforming Fundamentalism: Fuller Seminary and the New Evangelicalism*[6] brought fundamentalism to the fore in the considerations of American church historians. Joel A. Carpenter, *Revive Us Again: The Reawakening of American Fundamentalism,*[7] examined the years it was out of the public eye and showed how the resilient movement quietly built its institutional structure. A veritable avalanche of scholarship on fundamentalism has occurred in the past quarter century, and the books and articles continue to flow unabated from both scholarly and religious presses.

Although most fundamentalists focused their attention on evangelism and church growth, a few scholars in their own ranks sought to provide an alternative account of the movement. Among the most noteworthy examples are George W. Dollar, *A

History of Fundamentalism in America[8] and *The Fight for Fundamentalism*,[9] David O. Beale, *In Pursuit of Purity: American Fundamentalism since 1850,*[10] and Paul Tassell's history of the General Association of Regular Baptists.[11] George Dollar's work is especially noteworthy because of the attention he gives to southern fundamentalism. The line of argumentation in these books is encapsulated in a comment by Dollar: "Historic fundamentalism is the literal interpretation of all the affirmations and attitudes of the Bible and the militant exposure of all non-biblical affirmations and attitudes."[12] Thus many of the fundamentalist writers are not particularly interested in cultural or sociological explanations of their movement; they see themselves as setting forth the record of the work of God, one that was carried out in an uncompromising fashion. Interestingly enough, Owen does not draw on these works but instead looks to the primary literature to expand our understanding and appreciation of urban fundamentalism. And, he does not hesitate to point out sloppy scholarship on their part, even as he critiques from the other end of the religio-political spectrum for half-baked judgments about the fundamentalists.

It is reasonable to say that the fundamentalist scholars, as much as they might disagree with one another—and they can be quite acerbic in their judgments of fellows whom they feel have gone astray in their actions—are not generally known for their "civility." After all, they are dealing with the Truth, the whole Truth, and nothing but the Truth. Unfortunately, "militancy for the truth," a hallmark of the movement, has left us with the unflattering stereotype of the "fighting fundamentalist." As one who came to Christ in a fundamentalist church and has a deep appreciation for the strong biblical teaching that I received in my youth, I have some sense of empathy for the firm, uncompromising approach of fundamentalists. At the same time, it helps me to understand why they tend to regard their "evangelical" cousins as having missed the boat spiritually when they identified with the broader church and historic Christianity. Fundamentalists have particular problems with evangelicals who entered the scholarly world, because it seems to them that the latter were seeking to be "respectable" and accepted in the academy and that they now subscribed to "liberal" views on societal issues, politics, and economics.

It should not be surprising that fundamentalist writers are ignored by mainstream academics. Their providential explanations of historical developments cannot be accepted because, according to the standards of modern scholarship, they are unverifiable. Their pugnacious approach to those in the evangelical realm who are reasonably sympathetic to their concerns usually ends up becoming a case of shooting one's own friends. Critics maintain that the conservative political thrust of their literary works is as ideological driven as the works of those liberal scholars whom they so deeply dislike.

Should their writings be banned from the marketplace of ideas? I would say, absolutely not. In this post-modern and multicultural age, the fundamentalists have as much a right to be heard as anyone else. If one accepts the idea of "diversity," then fundamentalists may not be excluded from the conversation. Professor Owen's work is a good example of my point. Just because his approach to those with whom he disagrees is not particularly "civil" is beside the point. Other ideologues, whether they are animal rights advocates, environmentalists, supporters of gay rights, or anti-abortion (pro-life) militants, pursue their agendas in a fashion that is just as militant and uncompromising. I don't go along with a great many of Owen's contentions and regard some of his critiques of evangelical scholars as unfair or at least off the mark, but the First Amendment, which I love and cherish, insures that he has the right to espouse his views. Of course, by taking that step of entering the public forum, he exposes himself and his ideas to criticisms from other scholars and I suspect these may turn out to be rather harsh.

All in all, the most valuable part of the book is his detailed descriptions of what fundamentalists actually were doing in the political and social realms in the 1930s and 1940s. He forces us to reconsider our assumptions about their alleged non-involvement and to nuance our assessments of their work. They may have been doing the right things for the wrong reasons, but they certainly were not passive or indifferent to human needs. To be sure, their political activities revealed their own political conservatism, but this foreshadows the massive shift to the right that occurred in fundamentalist/evangelical circles in recent years and helped to make the current Republican majority possible. In spite of what some may think, fundamentalism is not a marginal feature of American life, a historical curiosity that can be viewed clinically and then discarded as hopelessly passé. Rather it is a force that is very much a fact of contemporary life. Scholars need to consider whether it might even be a viable alternative to post-modernism. One thing is for certain: fundamentalism is not going to go away.

Dr. Richard V. Pierard
Beverly, Massachusetts
January 2004

[1] Martin E. Marty and R. Scott Appleby, *The Fundamentalism Project. Fundamentalisms Observed* (1991), *Fundamentalisms and Society: Reclaiming the Sciences, the Family, and Education* (1993), *Fundamentalisms and the State: Remaking Politics, Economics, and Militancy* (1993), *Accounting for Fundamentalisms: The Dynamic Character of Movements* (1994), and *Fundamentalisms Comprehended* (1995), all published by the University of Chicago Press.

[2] The Hague: Mouton, 1963.

[3] Chicago: University of Chicago Press, 1970.

[4] Philadelphia: Westminster Press, 1979.

[5] New York: Oxford University Press, 1980.

[6] Grand Rapids: Eerdmans, 1987.

[7] New York: Oxford University Press, 1997.

[8] Greenville, SC: Bob Jones University Press, 1973.

[9] Sarasota, FL: Daniels Publishing Co., 1983.

[10] Greenville, SC: Unusual Publications,

[11] *Quest for Faithfulness: The Account of a Unique Fellowship of Churches* (Schaumburg, IL: Regular Baptist Press, 1991).

[12] *Fight for Fundamentalism*, p. iii.

FOREWORD

For decades American fundamentalists have been the object of derision most certainly from secular and mainline church historians but unfortunately also from evangelical historians who owe much of what they claim to believe from these faithful fundamentalists of the first half of the twentieth century. Professor Owen has written a much needed corrective to this one-sided critique. Hopefully, this book will reopen the need for a more serious, even handed evaluation of American fundamentalism.

One of the greatest challenges in the research of this movement is the inability to recognize its many different strains. The reason for this is that unlike the Federal Council of Churches with its mainline denominations consisting of their hierarchical organizational structures, American fundamentalism was highly constructured consisting of numerous independent churches and organizations thus making quality research a difficult task.

There is also no question as to Professor Owen's presuppositions. Unlike many who before have written on this subject with veiled contempt, Owen makes no attempt to veil his; in fact, this book is written from the viewpoint that American fundamentalism indeed contributed much to the political and social context of the period. Using extensive primary documentation he shows that their pastors and leaders were active in confronting many issues of that day from poverty and unemployment to the predicament of Jews in pre-war Nazi Germany. Owen also makes clear that within the movement there were varying views both to the causes and solutions to these problems.

Another area where Owen takes issue with most critiques of American fundamentalism is their failing to take seriously fundamentalists activities in the above areas due to their "excessive supernaturalism." But should not those who took the Bible seriously reflect openly on what they saw were the "momentous spiritual realities" that under laid much of that period? How can one seek to explain why millions of ordinary citizens became willful accomplices to the mass killings of Jews without mentioning the word "sin" or "evil"? Obviously today American fundamentalists will not fair well in an era of political correctness where peoples' sin and spiritual rebellion are non issues.

The most important issue for Owen in relation to the critiques of American fundamentalists is what he sees as a lack of fairness. With this as the overall issue, he proceeds to challenge much of the conventional historiography done by Christian historians as they deal with the fundamentalists political and social involvement during the 30's and 40's.

Professor Owen's greatest contribution is his scholarship in building the case for the fundamentalists positive support for European Jewry within the broader context of American indifference during the pre World War Two years. This is in stark contrast once again to views held by many Christian historians.

With great detail Owen delves into the many accusations and debates that were ongoing in the 30's concerning the role of fundamentalists in relation to anti-Semitism. Within these chapters is also a strong defense of dispensational theology and how it has been unfairly treated in much historical analysis.

Whether one agrees with Professor Owen's critique of those who have written on this subject or not, one will find this book lively and engaging. The detailed scholarship concerning the fundamentalist world of the 30's and 40's is reason enough to give this book a careful reading.

Dr. John P. Stead
Santa Clarita, CA
January 2004

PREFACE

Twenty-five years is a long time, especially when you are writing a book. And double that "especially" when it is one you believe will radically modify the historical interpretation of a particular event or movement. However, that is about how long this book has been waiting to be written. In fact, it was the basis of my Master's thesis, which was written in 1979. Even then I was troubled over the way scholars, including evangelical scholars, were portraying the historic fundamentalists of the 1930s and 1940s. It seemed excessively denigrative and one-sided—i.e., the historic fundamentalists of that era had made a mess of things spiritually, biblically, politically—you name it and apparently they were guilty of it. There seemed little effort to move in among them and get to know them. Excoriate them, yes! Really try to understand them—no!

Now, I will confess to some exaggeration (perhaps) but not by much. What I was reading did not seem to be in continuity with what limited primary research I was able to do in my undergraduate program, nor with my own personal understanding of what being a Christian constituted.

Although I had been baptized at the age of 13 (by J. Frank Norris, no less), I really did not enter into a true Christian life until the age of thirty-four as—let all know who read this book—a full-fledged bible-believing, premillennial dispensational, evangelical. (And thank God my wife entered with me.) At age thirty-eight, I went back to college—yes, a most conservative one; Los Angeles Baptist College (LABC), now The Master's College—pursuing my life-long passion, history. I graduated at age 40. After a brief pause, next came the slow pursuit of a Master's degree, slow because even as I pursued it, I was asked to teach American history at LABC. One of the first courses I initiated was one on American church history (then a semester course, now a two-semester course).

Between the research I did for the class and the research I did for my Master's thesis, under the encouraging hand of Dr. Donald MacPhee, I become more convinced than ever that the historic fundamentalists were being short-changed by historians who presented them as theologically "challenged," politically indifferent, socially uncaring, and economically only one small step above a Social Darwinian Neanderthal. They were portrayed as a people who cared not a wit about the world's woes and miseries because they were obsessively self-focused on personal piety, extreme ecclesiastical separation, and wild prophetic speculation. But this was a very one-sided description of the historic fundamentalists I was uncovering in my research. Something was amiss.

I must admit to a certain frustration at the time because the information offsetting the negativism noted above was so obvious and so easily obtainable. Surely, I thought, someone will pick up on this and the historic fundamentalists will receive a more objective(?), balanced(?), fair(?) (one is unsure what word is acceptable in a post-modern academy), treatment in future histories. Alas—no one did that I know of and I must admit my own complicity in this regard. As the years wore away, I found myself involved in a number of activities outside the field of history: outreach ministries, as evangelicals like to call them (or in a more postmodern idiom, service to "the other")—from a chaplaincy to gang-bangers in a couple of juvenile facilities, to their older counterparts in drug and alcoholic rehabilitation centers and prison. I even pastored for a decade during the 1990s.

However, Mark Noll's highly acclaimed, *The Scandal of the Evangelical Mind* (1994), a book that ignored the universal motherly advice that if you can't say something nice don't say anything at all, loudly served notice that those sources which would modify extreme criticism of the historic fundamentalists still remained "hidden," perhaps even assumed non-existent, perhaps ignored. Thus I began to haunt library archives, assemble data, write—and rewrite, and rewrite again. Joel Carpenter's well-written and well received, *Revive Us Again* (1997), a work that in all fairness tries to find the Jekyll residing within the notorious fundamentalist Hyde, and commendably somewhat succeeds—though not in areas where I believed revision was most crucially needed—provided an additional spur to finish a project too long delayed. Hence, *The Hidden History of the Historic Fundamentalists 1933-1948*. It is not your usual history book, either in style or content—which means I am probably in trouble.

For I make no attempt to disguise my consternation at, and criticism of, some of the serious shortcomings seemingly inherent among historians when it comes to the writing of histories of the historic fundamentalists. Nor do I apologize for giving way at times to a passionate, even intense (perhaps even colorful), style of writing or to passionately expressed editorials or interpretations. History should not always have to be written in polite academic monotones nor does it have to read that way. (Even my breakfast cereal is more exciting than some academic history books I study.) I am not a biologist studying the spastic movements of an amoeba. My subject is my fellow evangelicals who were living in, and interacting with, immense difficulties and even more immense evil both personal and cultural. By any measure, life during the 1930s and 1940s was intense and passionate, and for many soul crushing. For others, it was unspeakably worse. Intensity and passion, then, should not be absent if the historian truly hopes to convey to today's evangelical the traumatic dynamics of such a past. For this past impinges upon his or her life and thoughts whether he (or she) realizes it or not. However, willful ignorance is a sin.

That does not mean one is excused from diligent research or judicious evaluation of the evidence in one's possession. But in fact, if I may commit the unforgivable historiographic sin, it does seem now and then "that the facts do speak for themselves"—or come so very close that it is extremely difficult to tell when they do not. I simply cannot buy into the politicized, contextualizing, radical subjectivism that pervades so much of my discipline.

Still, the reader will decide for himself or herself how much leeway will be yielded to me in this matter. Not every one will appreciate the way I have written this book. The first Foreward, written by Dr. Richard Pierard,* is an example of those who may take strong exception. Briefly surveying the scholarship of the fundamentalist movement over the last forty years, he classifies me as a tried and true son of the movement. He believes my book is too polemic in nature (and uncivil in tone), in the way I take to task some fellow historians whose interpretations of the historic fundamentalists I believe are unnecessarily one-sided and unfair. This will, he believes, cause my book to be harshly received if not ignored. On the other hand, while he makes it clear he disagrees with many of my contentions, he does acknowledge that I have indeed uncovered sloppy research and biased opinions, and that the information I have assembled should cause historians to rethink the way they portray the historic fundamentalists' politically and socially. That which has been hidden will be hidden no more.

In the second Foreward, Dr. John Stead,** who has for thirty years been the iron that sharpens my heart and mind, and over that span has discussed and argued with me issues of time and eternity (and considers me a throwback to the 1890s' Populous Party for siding with the government in its suit against Microsoft), gives barely a mention to the issue of critiquing my peers and focuses instead on the necessity of my book as a corrective that off-sets the too often one-sided histories of the historic fundamentalists. In addition, he notes how the considerable use of primary sources reveals a side of fundamentalism that not only has been hidden but is highly commendable.

Dr. Pierard is likely right, though, I probably will be handled roughly by some who will not take kindly to being reminded that they too are all too human, and thus their history can at times reflect more their prejudices than what the people they are writing about actually were like. Inadvertently, then, controversy looms (and all I wanted to do was set the record straighter); the lions roar, the arena beckons. (But as I strap on my armor, I reflect on the rules: is it permissible for any one "fundamentalists" to slay any one lion?)

Certainly I do not consider *The Hidden History of the Historic Fundamentalists 1933-1948* without blemish or the final word. There is a plethora of material to be researched and articles and books to be written. I hope especially evangelicals will do so, for it is their heritage, and unfortunately they have been too often taught to disdain it. And, in fact, time permitting (literally), I already have in mind a follow-up book. Even the secular scholar would benefit from researching this material for it gives additional insight into how the Great Depression and Roosevelt's New Deal were viewed by a particularly influential and numerous (ten million) religious group. In addition, one would learn about their awareness of and opposition to Stalin's communism, Hitler's fascism, Franco's war in Spain, Japan's invasion of China, a Catholic church they believed was fascist friendly and too ambitious for power in America, and, of course, the rampant anti-Semitism in Europe—and on a smaller scale in America—and what they knew and how they responded to the Holocaust. Studies in American history could only benefit from their inclusion.

Finally, I will close with a personal note. There is a certain joy in rummaging through whatever parts of the past that are available to us, desiring not only to understand previous cultures and institutions, but also to briefly walk with the people. And the longer we live the more of the past we are. Perhaps that is why history, both in the whole as well as the particular, is so spellbinding. It is, when all is researched and written, very personal. I give my American History survey students three books to read: a generic textbook, a book of speeches and articles giving the pros and cons of important issues from various periods of our sojourn, and a book of excerpts from private diaries and letters covering the span of our nation's story. Almost invariably, the students select the latter book as their favorite. Individually we share much in common with our forebears—both in nature and in circumstances—and the students grasp this commonality as they read the diaries. That is a wisdom we all should acquire.

Jim Owen
Frazier Park, California
January 2004

* Richard Pierard is Professor of History Emeritus, Indiana State University and resident Scholar at Gordon College. A cofounder of the Conference on Faith and History, he has co-authored a number of books on the Christian and politics.

** John Stead is Professor of History and Political Studies at The Master's College. Over the last half-dozen years he has traveled numerous times to Albania under the auspices of the Abraham Lincoln Foundation to present lectures on civil society, education, and democracy to members of the Albanian parliament, and high government officials.

ACKNOWLEDGMENTS

In such a project as this, which takes years to bring to completion, I am indebted to a host of colleagues and friends. Special thanks, though, go to my fellow historians at The Master's College, Dr. John Stead and Dr. Clyde Greer, who read various parts of the manuscript and offered encouraged and helpful advice. Similar thanks for similar reasons also go to Professor Grant Horner of The Master's College English Department, Doug Bookman, pastor of the Trinity Baptist Church in Pasadena, CA and pastor Fred Rose of the Evangelical Free Church in Frazier Park, CA.

Librarians are at the heart of any historical research project and I am indebted to five in particular. Peggy West—interlibrary loan—and Janet Tillman—research—both from The Master's College, were helpful in the extreme and never lost patience with my incessant request (well, almost never). Sue Whitehead and Flo Ebeling, both librarians at Biola University, were also graciously helpful in my many trips to their campus and in answering my numerous emails. Finally, Melinda Howard, a librarian at Cedarville University (Ohio) deserves an emphatic nod of thanks for trusting me (and the U.S. Postal Service) with Cedarville's collection of the Jewish Missionary Magazine. Other librarians, unknown but helpful, at the Southern Baptist Seminary in Louisville, KY, Union Seminary in Richmond, VA, and the Union Seminary in New York City, also deserve thanks.

For the chapters on the historic fundamentalists and the Jews, I am particularly indebted to Wes Tabor, president of the American Messianic Fellowship, and his staff for making available to me *The Jewish Era* which was the monthly publication of the old Chicago Hebrew Mission, Bill Sutter and the staff of Friends of Israel who allowed me to spend a few days on their picturesque New Jersey Campus and gave me unlimited access to their historical records, and Mitch Glazer, president of the Chosen People Ministries, for sending me a copy of his unpublished doctoral dissertation, *A Survey of Missions to the Jews in Continental Europe 1900-1950*. It is a "gold mine" on the effectiveness of Jewish evangelism during the first half of the twentieth century. Thanks goes also to Vera Kuschnir, director of the American European Bethel Mission (in the 1930s the Bethel Mission of Eastern Europe), headquartered in Santa Barbara, CA. She gave me free access to the mission files, especially her grandfather's file, Leon Rosenberg, founder of the mission and rare copies of the *Bethel Witness*. Thanks goes to Vincent Price, Director of the North American branch of European Christian mission for loaning me rare copies of *Europe's Millions* from the 1930s. They provided insights into the life of Europe's lower classes during the Great Depression.

I am grateful to Dr. John Hughes, vice president for Academic Affairs at The Master's College for granting me a semester sabbatical in order to do my research and another semester with only a half load that I might spend time making sense out it. I am also indebted to the Administration for supporting the publication of *The Hidden History of the Historic Fundamentalists, 1933-1948*, believing it would make a valuable contribution to twentieth century American Protestant history. And a very sincere, heartfelt thanks goes to Marjorie Ackerman, administrative assistant to Dr. Hughes, who spent numerous hours reformatting the manuscript and offering me helpful advice. It was a Herculean task she completed with patience and grace.

Many others also assisted me in one-way or another and deserve my gratitude: Kristy Briggs who put together the index, Abby McElwee and Krista Breedveld who helped correct and format the manuscript, and type numerous corrections, edits, and revisions until I am sure they were tired of the project but nonetheless persevered with a smiling and encouraging demeanor. It is not easy to work for a curmudgeon. Cheryl Markowitz should also be mentioned in this regard as she helped in the early phases of the work. A very deep thanks goes to a dear elder sister in the Lord who lives in Haan, Germany. Irmgard Linder not only shared with me what conditions were like for the believing church in Germany during the Great Depression and World War II, but also shared the painful memory of her father's association with the Nazi Party. She has encouraged me in this endeavor.

Others have helped or encouraged and thanks is extended to them also: Jim Lutzweiler of Wake Forest who shared information from his own files, John Hotchkiss, Chair of the The Master's College English Department who was always there for advice and shared information on his father, Dr. Herbert Hotchkiss and Dr. Marchant King, Julie Hershberger and Janine Smith, History Department student TA's, who fetched books, made copies, and even brought me lunch from the cafeteria so I could focus on the book. I am sure there are others who have assisted whose names escape me. I trust they will forgive me for my memory lapse.

I also extend a deep felt thanks to Dr. Richard V. Pierard and Dr. John P. Stead for penning Forewards that help present to the reader "things to come" from very different perspectives.

Finally, I must thank my dear and lovely wife of forty-two years. With loving patience she endured the long and seemingly endless hours putting together this work and encouraged me by reading it and offering helpful suggestions and corrections. And being the tenderhearted woman she is, wept over the injustices and brutalities visited upon Christian and Jew alike during those dark and bloody decades known as the 1930s and 1940s.

Publisher Acknowledgments:

The journal, *Fides et Historia*, for permission to quote from Timothy Weber's, "Finding Someone to Blame," (Summer 1992).

William B. Eerdmans Publishing Co., Grand Rapids, MI, for permission to quote from Mark Noll's, *The Scandal of the Evangelical Mind*, 1994, and for permission to quote from Carl Henry's, *The Uneasy Conscience of Modern Fundamentalism*, 1947.

INTRODUCTION

Over the last quarter of a century or so there has been a renewed interest on the part of scholars, especially evangelical scholars, in the lives and activities of the historic fundamentalists between the two great wars, and the papers, articles, and books have multiplied accordingly. This proliferation of information and analysis has nudged the writings of this much-berated movement's history in what appears at first glance to be an ever so slightly even-handed, though not necessarily friendlier, direction.[1] Appearances, of course, can be deceiving, and certainly it is a worse fate to be "damned by faint praise" than pilloried outright by an enemy. Nevertheless, all this attention has brought the movement somewhat front and center once again. It has always been *the* movement historians can fondly dislike, even loath, or at a minimum, if you are an evangelical, hold at arm's length as you try to find *something* positive to say amid all those obvious liabilities. And if you are the academically aspiring son or daughter of "those people" such a past is an embarrassment to expurgate posthaste.

Joel Carpenter, who, in his *Revive Us Again* (1997), often portrays the historic fundamentalists in a more sympathetic vein (at times they really were very much like us) than historians had previously done, characterizes fundamentalist historiography this way:

> The dominant story line for fundamentalism's career, then, has been declension and dissolution. Fundamentalists' opponents gave them premature burials or banished them to the outer darkness of cultural marginality; fundamentalists gloried in their tribulations; liberal historians passed fundamentalists off as marginal and vestigial; and even historians who rehabilitated fundamentalists as worthy of scholarly attention considered them to be the tattered remnant of a once powerful tradition.[2]

While Carpenter refutes in part such a picture (making his book a welcomed addition),[3] he is not thereby free from some glaring biases and he along with other historians of historic fundamentalism, constantly repeats accusations against them that should have been seriously modified, if not abandoned, long ago.

The Bill of Indictment

If the historical fundamentalists are "guilty" of anything (other than being in the minds of many incorrigible, nasty, mindless, quarrelsome, and militant) it is that under the pressure of modernity and social rejection they turned their backs on the world at large during the 1930s, ignoring pressing social needs and needed political reflection and involvement. Dispirited and defeated, they focused instead on personal piety and bizarre prophetic speculations, thereby "sinfully" yielding social dominance to the secular and quasi-Christian humanist. Yale University historian (and evangelical) Harry Stout claims that in an age of Christian triumph, "they felt and acted like losers who took their fundamentals and ran home, leaving the responsibility of power in a Christian age to other voices."[4] Only with the publication of Carl Henry's *The Uneasy Conscience of Modern Fundamentalism* (1947), did one wing of fundamentalism (slowly transforming itself into neo-evangelicalism), begin to emerge from the "dark-age" of social and political neglect that took it captive during the Great Depression (if not earlier) and rediscover its God-mandated social and political obligations.

The problem with this all-too-common scenario is that it is only marginally accurate at best. This study in part, then, seeks in two ways to redress the misinformation this overly repeated cliché perpetrates. First, sufficient evidence is offered to show that an important segment of historic fundamentalism was vigorously active in seeking to help alleviate the distress and poverty that attended the Great Depression, and was *anything* but politically moribund. In other words, historic fundamentalists were not monkishly withdrawn into enclaves of self-focused piety, obsessively counting down to the tribulation while the world went up (or down) in flames. Piety was important and prophecy was important, but so were the problems of the mundane world around them.

Second, because many historic fundamentalists were involved socially and politically, historians must be questioned as to why they have allowed this important segment of historic fundamentalist's history to be ignored, denied, misinterpreted, reinterpreted or downplayed so that the contributions they did make are never given due consideration. The question is even posed as to whether the critics have the right to judge if the historic fundamentalists' participation (or non-participation) in the social or political affairs of America was what it should have been. This unwillingness to allow the historic fundamentalists to be themselves and speak for themselves constitutes a blatant example of history written with an uncontested bias.

For good or ill, we are experiencing a new and intense reawakening of evangelical political activity and thought. It is a two-fold awakening. On the evangelical right, the goal seems to be the re-Christianization of America. On the evangelical left, the goal is evidently to advance the Kingdom of God on earth through pressing for "social justice" for the poor, the oppressed, and the marginalized, whomever or wherever they may be. Both find their inspirational model in the nineteen century postmillennial evangelical activities and vision of America. Their model of "disinspiration" is, of course, the historic fundamentalists' of the 1930s. However, it is my assertion in this study that this new evangelical political awakening is built on a questionable theological "given" that the church as the church is to be actively involved in molding political and social institutions along biblical lines. (Certainly the historic fundamentalists found much to criticize in such a "given" for this "given" was part and parcel of the Social Gospel theology of the modernist that controlled the Federal Council of Churches.) And as noted, the political and social activities of the historic fundamentalists have been so ignored or misrepresented, and in many instances never even researched, that even historians of this movement seem largely uninformed or even ignorant of what the historic fundamentalists did think or do in these areas. This makes any comparisons blemished at best. Now is a good time, then, to revisit what the historic fundamentalists actually did and said regarding the political and social issues of their day, and the theological rationalizations that safe-guarded, as well as justified, their position. What follows may surprise many, and hopefully lead all evangelicals to a more balanced appreciation of their "fundamentalist" grandparents.

Uncovering a Different Fundamentalism

While delving closely into the data left to us from the historic fundamentalists, I was surprised to find that the clichés so often used to quarantine them seem as more a form of self-justifying dislike than a well founded summary of substance. One finds, for instance, that except for the secular academy, secular media, and insecure, liberal Protestants who were willing to "kill" the God of biblical, historic Christianity to be accepted as modern intellectuals,[5] the historic fundamentalists were not as isolated, or alienated, or lacking in respect in the public arena (even during the 1930s and 1940s) as has often been indicated. Though evidently economically composed of middle class and working class families, like any other group historic fundamentalists housed (or were on friendly terms with) doctors, lawyers, teachers, business executives, college professors, judges, and even local, state and national elected officials, many of whom also possessed a biblically grounded faith.[6] They even performed such social functions as operating orphanages or homes or camps for troubled youth with court or social services approval. No doubt such relationships would bring cries of horror from today's secularized governmental agencies, the press, the courts, academic experts and, of course, the ACLU.[7]

And although not the focus of this book, it still bears commenting that the general, all encompassing rubric of anti-intellectualism does not truly reflect the historic fundamentalists' mind-set. In fact, this whole business of fundamentalists' anti-intellectualism is somewhat one-sided. The phrase, of course, is used pejoratively with little in depth discussion of just what constitutes the "intellectualism" the historic fundamentalists rejected or *why*. (And "why's" are important.) If it means that they were anti-learning, or uninterested in the great questions of the day, or cultural illiterates, then their critics are wrong. (What it usually implies is that they did not accord the secular academy the "authority" it believed was its due.) In addition, if the academy (liberal seminaries included), was willing to be honest about the "assured results" of past scholars, there was a considerable amount of anti-evangelical, not to say generally arrogant, pontificating coming out of the secular academy during the first half of the twentieth century, especially between the great wars.[8] (This was, after all, the new America of eugenically inspired sterilization, of the lobotomy practiced upon the cowed and hapless beneficiaries of the new scientism, the new America of Freudian authorized sexual liberation, and an America in which hundreds of liberal academics found that our constitutional rights and responsibilities paled before the shining epiphany of the Kingdom-come in Stalin's USSR.) Does refusal to honor such secular apologists of genuine evil really constitute anti-intellectualism? The academy, media, and historical/cultural critics of historic fundamentalism, who are hostile to any view that might limit their rational and emotional autonomy, have (joyfully) penned this appellation upon historic fundamentalists and it has stuck. (Admittedly, then, a job well done.) However, scholarly hubris is the other side of the coin of anti-intellectualism, one that can do far more damage to the well-being of the commonweal, and one seldom noted by the academic critics of historic fundamentalism.

Obviously there were those among the historic fundamentalists who were uninterested in intellectual matters (in an academic sense), probably the majority. However, such could be said for the population as a whole at that time. (The opportunities for advanced education and cultural appreciation simply were not as available as they are today.) But even with our present-day advantages, the argument could be made that the same holds true now, if not more so—despite the increase of college educated people—if we consider the state of television programming or the National Endowment for the Arts, or the postmodern, politically correct University which seems in some circles to embrace an anti-intellectualism of its own.[9] Perhaps what one reader of *Books & Culture* wrote to the editor of that journal (a journal which seeks to prove that not all evangelicals chew grass and thump Bibles), would apply equally well to those who write (and wrote) about the historic fundamentalists circa 1930s-1940s:

> The term "fundamentalists" is today no more than a code word that has little descriptive content. It does have, however, a very clear and widely understood illocutionary

force. In good Hofstadterian fashion, it gives the writer a convenient way to assure the reader that he is really quite unlike those embarrassing anti-intellectual country cousins. I hope that *B & C* will not permit the collective inferiority complex of evangelical academics to dictate this kind of rhetorical strategy.[10]

Roger Lundin, in his *The Culture of Interpretation* (1993), is also negative about the historic fundamentalists' appreciation of the various artistic expressions due to what he terms (borrowing from H. Richard Niebuhr), their "Christ against culture" mind-set. According to Lundin,

> they had neither the time nor the inclination to write essays in aesthetic theory. Indeed, when the arts are even mentioned in fundamentalist works from the first half of this century, it is usually for the purpose of calling into question either their use or their value . . . some forms, such as theater, dance, and film, seem by their very natures to belong to this "material realm governed by a principle opposed to Christ," while other forms, including fiction and poetry, appear to waste precious time that might be better spent in pursuing the goals of the kingdom.[11]

Unfortunately, Lundin exaggerates his case. Granted, there are cultural "luddites" in every segment of society (including universities). Granted also, that the historic fundamentalists had little personal love for the modern theater or modern dancing for obvious ethical/moral reasons that they grounded in Scripture. (And it ought to be added that though the critic may not agree with their "reasoning" from Scripture in these matters, that does not mean the critic is right and the historic fundamentalists wrong.) Nor did they think much of the Hollywood film industry, very much for the same reasons its films are being criticized today—too much violence, glorification of the corrupt, and gratuitous sex. In 1942, Dan Gilbert drew attention to the fact that "underworld 'manners,' as well as underworld morals, have come in for glorification by the film industry." This included the physical abuse of women. "The 'beating up' of women is the movie method of demonstrating the 'he-manhood' of its actors," Gilbert wrote, and "the abuse of women" had become "a standard element of many motion pictures."[12] Films are opposed today, if they are opposed, for the psychological harm they can do to young minds. The historical fundamentalists opposed them for the moral/spiritual harm they did to young souls. It is a bit of a stretch to declare, as Mark Noll does, that the historic fundamentalists "made a virtue of their alienation from the world of learned culture."[13] Nor did they appear to have considered fiction and poetry a "waste of precious time" as numerous fictional works were being published by fundamentalist presses (even during the Great Depression), especially for young people.[14] And they loved poetry. They honored the medium of poetry as a favorite means of expressing their religious feelings and thoughts. They read poetry, quoted poetry, wrote poetry, and published it on a regular basis in their journals. Will Houghton,

Max Reich, James Gray, and Lewis Sperry Chafer, to name only four well-known historic fundamentalists, all wrote poetry. (However, the poetry of both men and women graced the pages of these fundamentalist's journals.) *The Sunday School Times* even published an article coaching its readers on how to write poetry the magazine would consider for publication.[15] I would even dare say some of it is of excellent quality.

Nor, evidently, were they unfamiliar, or "uncomfortable," with the ancient classics. For example, in the September 1940 *Moody Monthly*, editor Will Houghton quotes at length from an oration by Demosthenes to show that the "fifth column" activities practiced by Nazi sympathizers in the countries the Nazis intended to invade, had been practiced for centuries. In quoting Demosthenes, Houghton casually remarks (almost apologetically) that it would take his readers "back to high school days to read these extracts from the orations of Demosthenes."[16] One is tempted to ask when was the last time any of us saw a quotation from classic Greek writings used in an editorial to throw light upon current events? Such easy familiarity with classic Greek literature hardly strikes one as anti-intellectual or devoid of a "life of the mind." It also makes one wonder if high school graduates prior to World War II might have been more educated in critical thinking skills than many of today's college graduates.

It is not unreasonable, then, to say that many historic fundamentalists possessed a "life of the mind" (one which seemed to have valued teaching over writing and research).[17] And this life of the mind provided in part the foundation for their interest in things social and political (an interest stimulated also in part by the Great Depression and Roosevelt's precedent fumbling New Deal). As the 1930s progressed, this increasingly included the "Jewish Question." Here again, this has attracted some scholarly interest. And again, it has been largely critical. This is evidently due to the historic fundamentalists' eschatology which promoted the Jews as God's (still) chosen race who, though in this present dispensation of Grace are under His judgment, had a glorious and unique future in the coming millennial kingdom to be established by Jesus Christ at His Second Coming. Such a biblically prophetic view of Israel, especially during the horrendous anti-Semitism of the 1930s and 1940s, was (and is) controversial by its very claims. This has been exacerbated by their additional belief that the Jews would be restored to the land of Palestine prior to the Second Coming. They were then, on theological grounds, among the most dedicated supporters in America for the establishment of a Jewish state many years prior to World War II.[18] Such a theological stance regarding a continuous controversial (and bloody) political issue is bringing criticism upon the already well-pummeled heads of the historic fundamentalists.[19] In addition, despite their well-known support of Israel, these criticisms carry the charge (often by implication) of anti-Semitism against some of historic fundamentalism's most respected leaders. As for the historical fundamentalists as a whole, they are accused of indifference and neglect of the Jews of Europe who were suffering increasing persecution at the hands of the Nazis. Such condemnatory writing requires not only a reevaluation of the historic fundamentalists, but also of the critics accusing them. For this very purpose, three chapters are dedicated to discussing and analyzing the historic fundamentalists' relationship with the Jews in America *and* Europe during the 1930s and 1940s.

Finally, I believe something must be said in response to the criticism that the historic fundamentalists were guilty of "excessively supernaturalism" in their approach to social and political issues, hampering in effect a more educated and rational response and contribution to solutions of these problems by evangelicals. It evidently also hampered the development of an evangelical cadre of academics that could shake off the opprobrium of "fundamentalist" and find acceptance as peers in good standing among secular academics. It is true, of course, that the historic fundamentalists did view history through a "living" biblical grid. God reigned sovereign over the affairs of mankind. History unfolded "according to the plan of him who works out everything in conformity with the purpose of his will" (Eph. 1:11b, NIV). Man would not triumph over God nor would history end with T. S. Eliot's proverbial whimper. Such a view of history may not give social psychologists much to write about in academic journals, but it gave the historic fundamentalists the boldness and incentive to preach the gospel in every byway on the face of the earth. (Which is to say, editorially speaking, that collecting and analyzing the minutia of cultural forces may not be the stuff for building visions and pursuing them.) At the same time, it also gave them courage and willingness to knowingly face and endure great suffering and loss for their Lord's sake. And during the chaos and disintegration of the thirties and forties, suffering and loss were many times their lot. Too often, in our hurry to separate ourselves from our embarrassing forebearers, we turn our backs on an inspiring and humble inheritance. We are the poorer for it, despite our progress in penetrating the secular academy. There has been much talk recently about the "Great Generation" that slugged its way through the Great Depression, defeated the fascists in a hot war and communists in a cold war, thereby making the world "safe for democracy," and, in addition, laid the foundation for today's prosperous, free-market economy. The historic fundamentalists, though this may come as a surprise to many, were an integral part of that generation. Their sons, fathers, brothers and friends died in unfamiliar places along side other Americans during World War II. However, they were great for a far more vital reason. They would not let the gospel be muted, nor distorted, nor destroyed, nor allow themselves to be shamed into silence by a mocking intelligentsia—at times under circumstances hard for us to imagine.

A Time of War Both Spiritual and Carnal

It is not an exaggeration to say that the 1930s and 1940s was also a time of war against evangelical missions worldwide. Wherever communism or fascism came to power, evangelicals suffered and their missions were either destroyed (along with indigenous churches) or deeply impeded. And innumerable evangelicals lost their lives. The same held true in countries where the Roman Catholic Church (e.g., Poland or Spain), or the Orthodox Church (e.g., Romania) dominated and carried both national as well as local political and social influence. Additionally, even in America there were overt attempts by modernists and secularists to discredit biblical, evangelical Christianity, and had they had the political where-with-all, I have no doubt that attempts to limit the historic fundamentalists would have been set in motion.[20] In fact, many of the historic fundamentalists worried about just such a possibility, and were, therefore, strong advocates of civil liberties, especially religious freedom. The same cannot be said for many that were in the academy who helped perpetuate the "Brown scare" with an intensity that matched their later nemesis, Senator McCarthy.

The pressures on the historic fundamentalists, then, were considerable. Their uncompromising belief that God was sovereign over history, and that events simply could not be properly understood apart from this, not only gave them "patient endurance" through some very difficult times both at home and abroad, both at peace and at war, but also gave them the means to interpret events in a way that mitigated despair and made sense of the apparently senseless. Additionally, their belief in the "fallenness" of humanity and the reality of Satan as the father of (and instigator of) all evil allowed them to answer "why" in extra-mundane dimensions (which in turn gave the gospel a dynamic attractiveness), in the face of the unprecedented social and political wickedness of the time. (Here, I believe, by comparison, the academy comes up sterile.) Indeed, in this present era, when even evangelical scholars eschew providential interpretations for more anthropocentric and career satisfying "cultural forces," it is refreshing to read of Christians who unabashedly proclaimed that God is and is in charge, and that if we humbly and diligently look, we, too, might discern the moving finger writing "mene, mene, tekel, parsin."

Admittedly, of course, such a position makes havoc with the necessity of academicians who have garnered "expertise" in their chosen fields by studying motive and behavior and events, and analyzing such with the scalpel of experience and reason. But the embarrassment of the unanticipated collapse of the "Evil Empire" should remind all scholars that they are mere mortals—and that predicting the future course of human events and behavior is an uncertain business at best, as many an over-zealous, prophetically obsessed, foolish looking, "wrong again" premillennialists (and postmillennialists) can attest.[21] Evangelical historians who, in a paroxysm of self-censorship, have abandoned reference to Providence in order to be considered "professional" scholars may be making a poor exchange. The criticism directed at the historic fundamentalists is that their supernaturalism was an obstruction to a "proper" (natural, rationalistic) understanding of the affairs of men, and thus thwarted the development of evangelical (social science) scholars who could contribute to the academy in this regard. It is worth a few pages to evaluate the fairness and wisdom of such an evangelical disdain for, and criticism of, their own heritage.

On the Author's Usages and Biases

In constructing this study, I mainly use the term "historic fundamentalists" and "historic fundamentalism" rather than the familiar "fundamentalists" and "fundamentalism." The distinction seems necessary in light of the differences between the present-day fundamentalists and those of the 1930s when evangelicals were historic fundamentalists and historic fundamentalists, evangelicals. However, in Chapter Five, when discussing Carl Henry's *The Uneasy Conscious of Modern Fundamentalism,* I make an exception to this and use Henry's interchangeable fundamentalist/evangelical and fundamentalism/evangelicalism. The terms are further restricted to the premillennial, dispensational wing of American evangelical Protestantism. Although the terms may be used more broadly, it is difficult to construct a fundamentalist history of the period under consideration that is not dominated by this group. And, of course, this is how they defined themselves. Harry E. Stafford, writing in the *Moody Institute Monthly* in 1935, declared that a fundamentalist was one who first of all was a conservative Christian who held fast to the doctrines of the fall of man, the incarnation, the virgin birth, the crucifixion, bodily resurrection and ascension of Christ into heaven, that the teachings and miracles of Christ happened as recorded in the Scriptures, the atonement of man's sin by His death, and the verbal inspiration of the whole Bible. Such a definition would have included many evangelical groups outside the dispensational circle.

However, Stafford went on to add that a fundamentalist also believes in a personal, visible, imminent return of Christ to the earth that will terminate the present dispensation of Grace. Likewise he will oppose "expectations of a gradual progress of the Church toward complete evangelization of the world in this age." (Stafford is, of course, referring to postmillennial expectations.) Nor will the fundamentalist look for a cessation of war or the triumph of social reform prior to the return of Christ. Finally, the fundamentalist foresees a troubled church as the world becomes more antagonistic to its message, and unwittingly prepares itself for the anti-Christ.[22]

I also admit to an empathy with the historic fundamentalists so defined. My eschatology approaches theirs and my theology can be termed Calvinistic as was theirs. In truth, my research has deepened my respect for them. To a certain extent, then, this work is an apologetic on their behalf. Besides, considering the string of critics who have delighted in excoriating the historic fundamentalists for their sins, real and imagined, a little friendliness is in order. On the other hand, I do not consider myself a fundamentalist as that term is used today. However, as David Wells has pointed out, "The word *evangelical* precisely because it has lost its confessional dimensions, has become descriptively anemic."[23] In other words, it can mean whatever we want it to mean. Humpty Dumpty, perhaps the ultimate deconstructionist, has taught us well.[24] Even so, the options are limited. The choice comes down to either "conservative evangelical" or "liberal fundamentalist." The latter, though, is truly an oxymoron and will never do except with tongue in cheek.

I am not unaware of the historic fundamentalists' *many* sins and foibles, although a case can be made that these have been exaggerated when compared with other disruptive periods of church history, and the nature of the battle they were forced to wage, or when one takes into consideration the historian's antagonism. It should also be noted that sociological or cultural interpretations have taken us about as far as they can—usually, as will be shown, into repeated clichés and predictable conclusions. (Just what are those all-purpose, ever-ubiquitous, middle-class values, anyway?) Being accused of positions they did not hold, or actions they did not execute, or opinions they did not support, or being labeled "wrong" simply because the critic thinks they should have done and thought as he or she is doing and thinking, is not a history that desires to be fair toward those being critiqued. (But all too often this seems to be the subtle thrust of the critics' conclusions when writing about the historic fundamentalists.) At a minimum, the historic fundamentalists should be seen in their own context and judged first as to whether they were true to their own theological beliefs regarding social and political involvement. Something Timothy George wrote on how we ought to approach the reformers should be applied with equal thoughtfulness to the historic fundamentalists:

> Although we shall have occasion for critical assessment, we must not prejudge the validity of the reformers' thought. If F. M. Powicke's dictum, "A vision or an idea is not to be judged by its value for us, but by its value for the man who had it," is not the whole truth, it at least reminds us that we cannot begin to evaluate the significance of earlier Christians, especially the reformers, until we ask their questions and *listen well* to their answers.[25] (Italics added)

One cannot ask for better advice when writing history. However, I am far from convinced it has been heeded when the writing of the history of the historic fundamentalists has been undertaken. What follows will seek to redress this too often tolerated historiographical failing. Not everyone will appreciate what I have to say. Some, in fact, will probably get quite upset with my criticism. But a censorious dislike has been so incorporated into so many historians' narratives of the historic fundamentalists that a corrective is long over do.

In closing, a word needs to be said about the use of notes. The reader will find many of them quite lengthy (as the notes for this introduction attest). My desire has been to keep each chapter as uncluttered and to the point as possible. Therefore a considerable amount of information—supportive or explanatory or correlative material—that will expand upon a point made in the main body is placed in notes. There is, then, for all intense and purposes, two books between the covers of this historical study. When I read an interesting or challenging book (and I am sure others do the same), I find myself engaging in a dialogue with the author ("that is interesting, but have you considered..."), or sometimes arguing with him or her ("I just don't see how you can say that..."), or even now and then exploding ('WRONG! NO WAY!"). The margins often become cluttered with my comments, approval or counter arguments, and my underlines have an emphatic quality to them. Hopefully the lengthy notes will stimulate this process and satisfy those who admit to a like idiosyncrasy, and a hunger for greater detail behind the predilections and emphases of each chapter.

NOTES

1. In a recent article appearing in the *Atlantic Monthly* evaluating the current attempt by evangelical colleges and universities to develop "a life of the mind," the author, Alan Wolfe, seems to hold to a number of out-dated views regarding the historic fundamentalists. For example, Wolfe claims that the historic fundamentalists "emerged in the United States toward the end of the [19th] century, as a reaction against the increasing cosmopolitanism of most American Protestant denominations" (p.56). He also claims *The Fundamentals* were written to enunciate the "strict principles" America had to return to if it was to be saved (pp. 56, 57). Finally, he goes on to write that "while the rest of American religion accepted modernity, and with it freedom of thought, fundamentalists moved backward" (p.58). None of these statements, of course, are historically accurate or defensible.

    Wolfe also accuses evangelical scholars of citing "one another far too often" (p.76). This is, of course, a case of the pot calling the kettle black. Evidently it is extremely difficult for some scholars to set aside their ingrained prejudice against the historic fundamentalists, even when they are dog-eared, yellow with age, and have little to commend them. (Alan Wolfe, "The Opening of the Evangelical Mind," *Atlantic Monthly*, October 2000, 55-76).

2. Joel A. Carpenter, *Revive Us Again: The Reawakening of American Fundamentalism* (New York: Oxford University Press, 1997), 14. Carpenter seems somewhat ambivalent toward the historic fundamentalists. At times he is harsh, even hostile to the point of being unfair, and leans too heavily on sociological and psychological interpretive clichés. On the other hand, at places in his book he appears sympathetic and even supportive of their actions. This ambivalence may reflect his own

evangelicalism.
3.   Carpenter concludes his book by noting that,
     fundamentalists could be bitter, contentious, and spoiling for a fight, but they
     could also be sweet-spirited in yielding to their Lord, to each other, and to the
     call to serve in the world's hard places. Self-righteous militancy and self-
     mortifying piety could coexist, and it often did, to a perplexing degree, in the
     same individuals. (*Revive Us Again,* 246).
     In other words, despite Carpenter's perplexity, the historic fundamentalists were
     like most of us. After all, the ability to balance contradictions seems a perfectly
     normal human trait. Caricatures of the historic fundamentalists may reveal more
     the hostility of their critics rather than a true reflection of those who peopled the
     movement. However, this should not surprise us either. It is interesting to note that
     Vincent Bacote, in the November 13, 2000 issue of *Christianity Today,* while
     eschewing any desire to become a fundamentalist, nevertheless holds an olive branch
     out to them, concluding his editorial by writing that he acknowledges "without
     hesitation that fundamentalists are a part of my Christian family and they deserve
     my understanding and respect." ("The New Scarlet Letter," 98, 99.)
4.   Harry S. Stout, "Reviewer Reviewed," *The Banner of Truth,* March 1995, 10. Of
     course, the historic fundamentalists might have been as amazed as I am to learn that
     the 1930s and 1940s were an age of "Christian triumph."
5.   James Turner draws attention to the fact that the impression exists that "the rise of
     science, and the spread of critical ways of thinking associated with science,
     undermined belief in God." Turner strongly disagrees. "On the contrary," he writes,
     "religion caused unbelief. In trying to adopt their religious belief to socio-economic
     change, to new moral challenges, to novel problems of knowledge, to the tightening
     standards of science, the defenders of God *strangled* him." (Italics added). (*Without
     God, Without Creed* [Baltimore: The John Hopkins University Press, 1985], xiii]).
6.   This is an area that needs, and would benefit from, some intense research and it is
     impossible to go into great detail here. However, one could name Arnold Grunigen,
     Jr., a member of the Executive Committee of the Investment Bankers Association of
     American, California Group, James L Kraft, one of the founders of Kraft Foods, H.
     P. Crowell, head of Quaker Oats Company, Charles M. A. Stine, vice-president of E.
     I. duPont deNemours and Co., Pulitzer Prize winning political cartoonist for the
     Chicago Daily News, Vaughn Shoemaker, William Hazor Wrighton, head of the
     Department of Philosophy at the University of Georgia, and I. H. Linton, a member
     of the District of Columbia bar association and approved to argue cases before the
     Supreme Court, as friends of the historic fundamentalists. In the realm of politics,
     there was Governor Luren D. Dickinson of Michigan who was one of the principle
     speakers at the 1940 gathering of the World Christian Fundamentals Association in
     Chicago ("God and Good Government," *The King's Business,* October, 1940, 363),
     and Governor Frank Merriam of California who was Sunday School superintendent
     of the First Presbyterian Church of Long Beach and president of that church's Men's
     Brotherhood. He wrote a special article for *The Sunday School Times* on the vital
     importance of the Sunday School ("Governor Merriam's Statement," February 23,
     1935, 122). Likewise the Governor of North Carolina, J. M. Broughton, continued
     to teach his adult Sunday School class even after he was elected. (He took office in

January of 1941.) It was a class he had been teaching for over twenty years. He, too, was a member of *The Sunday School Times* family ("A Governor's Letter to William H. Ridgway," April 22, 1944, 302[14]). The Lt. Governor of South Dakota, Robert Peterson, allowed *Moody Institute Monthly* to publish a letter in which he revealed his conversion to Jesus Christ as his Savior and called it "the outstanding event in [his] life." When the Independent Fundamentalist Churches of America held their fifteenth annual meeting in Detroit in 1944, the Mayor invited them to the city hall for a reception and public welcome ("Independent Fundamental Churches' Fifteenth Annual Convention," *The Sunday School Times*, July 22, 1944, 524[12]). Historic fundamentalists such as Dawson Trotman, Paul Rood, Arthur I. Brown, and R. G. LeTourneau spoke to the weekly prayer meetings held by both U. S. Senators and Representatives who professed faith in Jesus Christ ("The Senate Prayer Meeting," *The Sunday School Times,* April 6, 1946, 316[24]).

In perhaps one of the strangest Zionist events in America, Senator Copeland of New York, at a mass meeting of 15,000 Jews in Chicago's coliseum on Armistice Day, 1936, "re-preached" a sermon written by Adam Clarke a century earlier in which Clark had quoted Amos 9:14, 15, verses in which the prophet predicted that Israel would be restored to its Land. Senator Copeland concluded his "sermon" to the audience of mostly Jews by noting that if Clarke "could see Palestine today as I saw it, he would realize that it is the fulfillment of the predictions of Amos, and he would probable say: 'He can do it because He is Jehovah, AND HE HAS DONE IT.'" The author of the article that reported on this event noted that Senator Copeland not only spoke with much conviction, but that he was the only one at the rally who referred to the Bible at all (A. G. Fegert, "The Light of Prophecy at a Zionist Meeting," *The Sunday School Times*, November 6, 1937, 783, 796, 797).

Finally, it is fitting that this note should conclude with the annual Fast Day Proclamation issued by Governor Cross of Connecticut setting aside April 15, 1938 as a day of fasting and prayer. *The Sunday School Times* (April 16, 1938) reprinted Governor Cross proclamation verbatim on its front page, and it reads as follows:

> In remembrance of the day when the world passed through the deep shadow of the Cross toward the coming glorious Resurrection, on the third dawning light, of our Lord and Savior, Jesus Christ, I appoint Friday, the 15th day of April, next, as a day of fasting and prayer.

> I call upon the people of our state to observe this day, in their homes and in public places of worship, and to ponder again the truth taught by the Great Master that for Man and Nature alike there is life in death and that in His service there is perfect freedom for the living.

> It is written: 'God so loved the world, that he gave His only begotten Son, that whosoever believeth in Him should not perish, but have everlasting life.'

(One simply cannot imagine a governor of any state publishing such a proclamation today.) Were the historic fundamentalists really all that isolated and alienated from the common stream of American society? Such a thesis is open to question.

7.   A good example of government/historic fundamentalist cooperation was Camp Midway in Boone County, Iowa. Started by a young minister concerned over the influence the media was having upon young people by glorifying gangsters (yes, even in the 1930s), its purpose was to provide them with a week in the country and

an intense exposure to the gospel. Starting with everything borrowed (including the land the camp was on), the camp was so successful in its first year that county officials help him establish a permanent camp, including $30,000 from the WPA. Camp Midway became a "summer vacation center for all underprivileged young people in the State of Iowa." However, no restrictions were placed on the minister and it remained a camp where young people were clearly and deliberately exposed to the gospel. ("A Christian State Camp," *The King's Business*, July, 1937, 247, 285.)

8.   A "for instance" is found in Wilbur Smith's *Therefore Stand* (Moody Press, 1945) where Smith quotes Kirsopp Lake and John Dewey (as well as others), as saying, to use Smith's quote of Lake as a summary, "In past generations to attain salvation was thought to be the object of existence. It is not altogether surprising that the people who argue in this way contribute little to the improvement of the world" (pages 24 and 25, and endnotes). I submit this is not only anti-Christian rhetoric but also arrogant nonsense.

9.   There has been a veritable flood of books and articles written to expose the corrupting effect of postmodern political correctness on America's universities. New academic societies have been organized (such as the National Associations of Scholars and The History Society), to combat this at the scholarly level. So for now, one brief example will suffice, and that is the "case" of Jared Sakren, famed acting teacher, who was fired by Arizona State University because he refused to distort the plays of Shakespeare by using them "as a pretext for talking about feminism" or any number of multicultural victimizations. In other words, he taught Shakespeare "straight." He failed, according to his department chair, Ms. Lin Wright, to meet the department's goals, which included "Confronting our theatrical heritage. There is a tension between the use of a Euro-American canon of dramatic literature and production style vs. post-modern feminist/ethnic canons and production styles."

Ms. Wright also noted that the [university's] feminists were "offended by the selection of works from a sexist European canon that is approached traditionally." As Gene Veith (author of the article I am using in this note), acidly commented about the new postmodern, politically correct universities: "the great works of the past are 'interrogated,' to use a current critical term that conjures up images of the KGB and gulags, to reveal their political crimes." Mr. Veith also observed that while Mr. Sakren's students were "performing *Midsummer Night's Dream*, his colleagues were having their students put on plays like *Betty the Yeti* an 'eco-fable' about an evil logger who transforms into an environmentalist after having sex with a Sasquatch." (Gene Edward Veith, "Hamlet or Betty the Yeti," *World*, November 21, 1998, 25, 26.)

Now, about the anti-intellectualism of the historic fundamentalists…(many of whom, it should be added, were quite fond of Mr. Shakespeare's plays—read or played "straight," of course).

10. "Letters: Fundamentalism as a Code Word," *Books & Culture: A Christian Review*, September/October, 1997, 5.

11. Roger Lundin, *The Culture of Interpretation: Christian Faith and the Postmodern World* (Grand Rapids: William R. Eerdmanns Publishing Company, 1993), 234. It is of interest to note that Lunden accuses the historic fundamentalists of conforming

to "what Niebuhr terms the 'Christ against culture' position." He even uses Niebuhr's explanation of what is meant by that phrase. In doing so, one gets the impression that this was Niebuhr's conclusion also, that the historic fundamentalists fit into the "Christ against culture" category. However, H. Richard Niebuhr did not hold this view. Rather he placed them within the "Christ for Culture" column, noting "the movement that identifies obedience to Jesus Christ with the practices of prohibition, and with the maintenance of early American social organizations, is a type of cultural Christianity; though the culture it seeks to conserve differs from that which its rival honors." (*Christ and Culture* [New York: Harper & Brothers Publishers, 1951], 102). Douglas E. Herman's *Fides et Historia* review (Winter/Spring 2000, 168-170) of Daniel L Turner's history of Bob Jones University, *Standing Without Apology: The History of Bob Jones University* (1997), takes note of the university's interest in the arts and culture, including a Shakespeare festival, which dated back to the 1930s.

12. Dan Gilbert, *Hell Over Hollywood* (Grand Rapids: Zondervan Publishing House, 1942), 41. Gilbert mentions six films in which well-known actresses are physically abused by their on screen boy friends.

13. Mark Noll, *The Scandal of the Evangelical Mind* (Grand Rapids: William B. Eerdmans Publishing Company, 1994), 211. H. A. Ironside, for instance, wrote:

    How often as one comes in contact with men of most gracious personality, gentlemanly appearance, high spirituality and well trained intellect he finds upon inquiry that they are like John Wesley, "men of one book," and in some instances hardly conversant with the literature of the earth. And in saying this I do not mean to put a premium on ignorance, for as mentioned in the beginning of this address, the knowledge of this world is not under the ban. The Christian may well avail himself of any legitimate means of becoming better acquainted with the great facts of history, the findings of science, and the beauties of general literature; but let him never put human philosophy in the place of divine revelation. If he studies it at all, and there is no reason why he should not do so, let him begin with this—God has spoken in His Son and in the Holy Scriptures. He has given us the last words upon every question that philosophy raises.

    (*Lectures on the Epistle to the Colossians* [Neptune, New Jersey: Loizeaux Brothers, Inc., 1929], 76).

14. *The King's Business, The Sunday School Times,* and *Moody Monthly* all had book review sections that included reviews of evangelical fiction, and *The King's Business* occasionally carried short stories by leading evangelical fiction writers. During the late forties Moody Press, Eerdmans Publishing, and Zondervan all offered large monetary prizes for Christian fiction that would "encourage Christian writers to raise the art of the Christian novel to a new and acceptable level," one that would rival the secular novel in literary quality.

15. "Notes on Open Letters: On Writing Poetry," *The Sunday School Times,* July 2, 1938, 466.

16. "Editorial Notes: Trojan Horse Technique," *Moody Monthly,* September 1940, 4.

17. I could give innumerable examples that have come to my attention as I have informally pursued this topic since the publication of Mark Noll's *The Scandal of the Evangelical Mind* (1994). One will have to suffice for this note. Herbert V. Hotchkiss was a premillennial, pretribulation, dispensational Baptist deeply

influenced by the New Jersey Keswick Bible Conference. From 1953 until his death in 1972, he taught Bible, literature, and history at the fundamentalist Los Angeles Baptist College (now The Master's College). His educational background was quite varied. He received his B. S. degree in engineering from the University of Pennsylvania. Dissatisfied, he went to Cornell where he obtained a B. A. in Literature. Next it was off to Princeton to receive his M. A. He then went to the University of Chicago to pursue his doctorate in Literature. While attending Chicago, he served as an Assistant Professor of English Literature at Wheaton College. (He was then 32 years old.)

Believing himself called of the Lord to the pastorate, Hotchkiss left his studies at Chicago and went to Princeton Seminary in 1928 to study under J. Gresham Machen, a mentor to a goodly number of young historic fundamentalists. He was a part of the first graduating class of Machen's new Westminster Seminary in 1930. He then served as pastor of Philadelphia's Spruce Street Baptist Church for 17 years and taught at the Philadelphia School of the Bible for 13 years. In the late 1940s he came to California to teach at Los Angeles Baptist College & Theological Seminary. At his death, Dr. Carl Sweazy, a past president of the college, wrote, "His has a great hunger for truth and craving for knowledge that kept him awake on the average day until after the midnight hour. He studied on his feet to stay awake."

Did Dr. Hotchkiss have a life of the mind? In 1927, he gave to his students at Wheaton a brief, two-page essay entitled "Raising the Cultural Level." In this handout, he stated that Wheaton College "should set for itself the highest standards not only in Christian faith, but also in education and culture." Culture, Hotchkiss believed, included "accurate knowledge gained through painstaking study...breadth of vision, a sense of the proper proportions and relations of things, and an appreciation of all that is fine and good."

He offered his students four ways to achieve cultural growth. The first way was to make one's "studies...more and more a part of his thoughts, his general conversation and his actions." Next, one must open oneself to a variety of interests that will force the mind to grow. "Sheer indolence of mind" shuts one up in narrow mindedness. Third, one must use one's time profitably and "engage in those activities that give a lasting reward." This would change the "vacant stare" of the sleepwalker into "the lively countenance of the keen observer.... The attention to things worthy develops the appreciation and the sense of proportion in life, which are important elements in culture." Obviously, the final point in cultural development, from Hotchkiss' view-point, was "the careful study and appropriation of the Bible." Nothing has so affected culture as the Scriptures. While "other parts of a college training modify the faculties a man possesses; the Bible changes his very nature." (I am indebted to Dr. Hotchkiss' son, John Hotchkiss [present English Department Chair at The Master's College] for a copy of his father's class handout and other writings.)

Dr. Hotchkiss never departed from the above. He had one "fault," but it was not a lack of "the life of the mind." He eschewed publishing (though often encouraged to do so), in order to devote himself to his true love, teaching. Certainly, though, it is difficult to give credence to Noll's claim that fundamentalism "undercut the possibility for a responsible intellectual life." (*The Scandal of the Evangelical Mind*,

1994, 127.)

18. By the end of World War II, they, along with many non-dispensational evangelicals, Liberals, and non-Zionist Jews, supported the establishment of a Jewish state in Palestine for political reasons. Considering all the Jews of Europe had suffered, they deserved a state of their own that could speak for their interest and offer them a refuge. Palestine was the preferred site because hundreds of thousands of Jews were already there. In other words, a *de facto* Jewish state already existed in Palestine.

19. Mark Noll, among others, is especially critical of the historic fundamentalists' support of Israel based on prophetic Scripture rather "than from contemporary analysis or more general theological reflection on nations, international justice, or the recent history of the Middle East." (*The Scandal of the Evangelical Mind*, 167). Noll considers this evidence of the absolute poverty of the historic fundamentalists' political reflection. (See also Timothy Weber's "How Evangelicals Became Israel's Best Friend," *Christianity Today*, October 5, 1998, 39-49.)

20. There is evidence to support the charge that the Federal Council of Churches of Christ in America did its best to persuade the major radio networks and the government agency licensing radio stations to exclude the "sectarian" fundamentalists during the thirties and forties. (See "A Survey of Religious Life and Thought," item two, *The Sunday School Times, November 18, 1944,* (3) 839; "Freedom of Religion on the Air," *The Sunday School Times*, April 7, 1945, (5) 257; "Around the King's Table: Evangelicals Without Representation," *The King's Business*, April 1942, 123, and "Bible in the News: Christian Radio," *The King's Business*, May 1948, 5. Also see *Revive Us Again* by Joel Carpenter, pages 33, 34, 129, 130.)

   The Federal Council used its influence with government agencies to be "nasty" in other ways. For example, in 1945 the WPB denied three evangelical churches in Detroit the needed materials to build new churches. They were not turned down because of a shortage of materials but because they "were not listed in the directory of pastors and churches published by the Detroit Council of Churches." To procure the needed materials, they were informed that "they must present from the Detroit Council a certificate of compliance with its comity rules before their application could be received" ("Inter-Church: Detroit Council Blocks Church Building Plans," *United Evangelical Action*, August 1, 1945, 16.)

21. Now and then a voice of caution is raised in the secular academy pointing out the unwarranted hubris that resides there. Irving Horowitz, Professor of Sociology and Political Science at Rutgers University, candidly admitted the social science level "of predictability...have been so poor and so porous as to occasion mirth in nonbelievers..."and "have been consistently not much more accurate than random guesswork." ("Are the Social Sciences Scientific," *Academic Questions*, Winter1995/1996, 54).

   Eva Etzioni-Halevy, another sociologist, writing in the mid-1980s, assessed "the socio-political role of intellectuals as part of the (so-called) knowledge class" and concluded that the results were not an increase in "social well being" but rather pictured "the sorcerer's apprentice who is no longer able to control the gush of events that threaten to overwhelm him." Etzioni-Halevy also implied that the increasing influence in recent years of social scientists on public policy "have also been years in which policy failures have been rife and in which a variety of formidable social problems have been multiplying." (*The Knowledge Elite and the Failure of Prophecy*, 5, 43.)

Finally, a lengthy but necessary quote from Neil Postman is in order. Postman is scathing in his criticism of what he labels as (academic) "Scientism:"

> This, then, is what I mean by Scientism. It is not merely the misapplication of techniques such as quantification to questions where numbers have nothing to say; not merely the confusion of the material and social realms of human experience; not merely the claim of social researchers to be applying the aims and procedures of natural science to the human world. Scientism is all of these, but something profoundly more. It is the desperate hope, and wish, and ultimately the illusory belief that some standardized set of procedures called "science" can provide us with an unimpeachable source of moral authority, a supra-human basis for answers to questions like "What is life, and when, and why?" "What is right and wrong to do?" "What are good and evil ends?" "How ought we to think and feel and behave?" . . . Social research can tell us how some people behave in the presence of what they believe to be legitimate authority. But it cannot tell us when authority is "legitimate" and when not, or how we must decide, or when it may be right or wrong to obey. To ask of science, or expect of science, or accept unchallenged from science the answers to such questions is Scientism. (*Technopoly: The Surrender of Culture to Technology*, 1993, 161, 162).

Perhaps, then, if the above critics have pointed-out a festering canker on the body academic, one the academy is reluctant to acknowledge, one can conclude that historic fundamentalists were not necessarily being "anti-intellectual" in building their personal and social moral and ethical foundations on the Scriptures and the Scriptures alone.

22. Harry E. Stafford, "What Constitutes a Fundamentalist?" *Moody Institute Monthly*, February 1935, 276. Interestingly, premillennial dispensationalism was written into the by-laws of The World Christian Fundamentals Association.

23. David F. Wells, *No Place for Truth: Or Whatever Happened to Evangelical Theology* (Grand Rapids: William B. Eerdmans Publishing Company, 1993), 134.

24. In *Alice's Adventure in Wonderland*, Alice and Humpty Dumpty had a discussion on how many "unbirthday' presents one might receive when compared to how many birthday presents. Humpty boastfully declared "that there are three hundred and sixty-four days when you might get unbirthday presents..."

> "Certainly," said Alice.
> "And only *one* for birthday presents, you know. There's glory for you!"
> "I don't know what you mean by 'glory,' " Alice said.
> Humpty Dumpty smiled contemptuously. "Of course you don't—till I tell you. I meant 'there's a nice knock-down argument for you!' "
> "But 'glory' doesn't mean 'a nice knock-down argument,' " Alice objected.
> "When *I* use a word," Humpty Dumpty said, in a rather scornful tone, "it means just what I choose it to mean—neither more nor less."
> "The question is," said Alice, "whether you *can* make words mean different things."
> "The question is," said Humpty Dumpty, "which is to be master—that's all."

(Lewis Carroll, *Alice's Adventure in Wonderland* (New York: Liverwright, Inc. Publishers, nd), 246, 247.)

25.　Timothy George, *Theology of the Reformers* (Nashville: Broadman Press, 1988), 18, 19.

CHAPTER ONE

Historic Fundamentalism and Its Critics:
"It Ain't Necessarily So!"

Like Job's friends, Eliphaz, Bildad, and Zophar who knew before listening the reason for his misery, historians gather around that old derelict, historic fundamentalism, with doleful faces that remind one and all that inevitably sin brings judgment. Surely if it had conducted itself properly no one would be pointing a finger of criticism and censure. And like Job, all historic fundamentalism can do is answer (to use the title of an irreverent song from that era), "it ain't necessarily so." However, it is apparent that the critics are not listening. They have their indictment—posted for all to read. At the top, or quite close to the top, are listed the supposed sins of political and social neglect, cold indifference if you will, even an inexcusable detachment, on the part of the historic fundamentalists during those bleak and tragic years known as the Great Depression and World War II.[1] There is, of course, a certain repetitiveness to the charges no matter who writes up the indictment. For example, consider the following penned by Robert Linder over a quarter of a century ago:

> As a result of the largely negative reactions to evangelical efforts to meet the threat of evolution through political and social action, the fundamentalist wing of evangelical Christianity increasingly withdrew from the mainstream of American life and turned its attention more and more narrowly to a Gospel shorn of its social dimensions.[2]

Other critics (and they are legion), echoing from decade to decade like the song "Johnny One Note," include Louis Gasper, who, in *The Fundamentalist Movement* (1963), charged that the historic fundamentalists "lost interest in humanitarian endeavors" and allowed their concern for applying the "gospel in social welfare to fade and evaporate,"[3] as well as David Moberg, who made a similar charge in his often mentioned and much admired, *The Great Reversal* (1972). He claimed that historic fundamentalists rejected the prophetic aspect of the Christian ministry—that is, calling believers to collective repentance and social reform, and reminding them that service to mankind followed proclaiming the good news.[4]

In *The Gospel in America* (1979), a trio of evangelical critics declared that, "In contrast to Puritan teaching that Christians must build moral principles into society, and to the message of reform in the days of Finney, Fundamentalists began to argue that Christian involvement in society actually denied rather than fulfilled the gospel."[5] According to this trio, the modernist-fundamentalist conflict "fostered a 'siege mentality' among fundamentalists, a brittle defensiveness that often spent more time reacting to evil than proclaiming the good news." If the social gospel characterized the liberal church, "a gospel of individual piety" characterized the historic fundamentalists—a piety that separated the believer from "the evil world" until Christ's return. With such a mindset "mention of concern for the poor raised, for many, a terrible specter—'the poison of the social gospelers.'"[6] George Williams and Rodney Peterson, writing in *The Evangelicals* (1975), accused the historic fundamentalists of being reactionary and holding economically to an "uncritical acceptance of nineteenth-century laissez-faire."[7] This echoed an earlier remark by Robert Miller that "the courtship of the capitalist and the premillennarian was an affair of the purse as well as the heart."[8]

More recently, John Bernbaum and Jerry Herbert of the American Studies Program continued this theme of disengagement by writing:

Most orthodox Protestants retreated from social reform efforts and political involvement in what has been called the "Great Reversal".... During the 1930s and 40s...most fundamentalists concentrated their energies on announcing personal salvation while denouncing the social gospel, communism, and the New Deal.[9]

More extreme is the comment by S. Stephen Thomas that "the mind-set of discontinuity" of the Anabaptist "has come to a fuller, more consistent expression in dispensational theology," resulting, as far as civil government is concerned, in the state being "given freedom from biblical morality. It began by restraining the hand of civil authority in religious matters of minor importance and personal conviction, but it has come to tolerate child sacrifice and other horrors for the sake of personal convenience."[10]

To paraphrase Nathanael's words in the gospel of John, "Historic fundamentalism? Can any thing good come from there?" Joel Carpenter, in his recent *Revive Us Again* (1997), a book that gives surprisingly high marks to the historic fundamentalists for laying the groundwork for the evangelical resurgence that followed World War II, also claims that their worldview "prompted them to remain passive and detached about the world's problems. The world was in a terminal downward spiral; social and political reforms were largely useless," thus their fascination with prophecy pushed them "toward social and political alienation and passivity...."[11]

Predictably, Mark Noll added a few words of his own to the endless decibels of negative criticism. In his highly acclaimed *The Scandal of the Evangelical Mind*

(1994), he writes that in the 1930s "an intuitive uneasiness about the evils of politics nurtured a widespread evangelical quietism."[12] He goes on to charge that William J. Bryan's optimistic view of reform and belief in active government "gave way to a cultural pessimism and a fear of governmental encroachment." The possibility of being involved in politics "was replaced with an almost exclusive focus on personal evangelism and personal piety. Current events evoked interpretations of prophecy instead of either reforming activity or political analysis."[13] Over and over Noll hammers the historic fundamentalists for their supposed desertion of the political marketplace. "Political activism went into an eclipse among evangelicals during the 1930s," he writes, "at the same time that political reflection reached an absolute nadir."[14]

Noll does caustically admit that this non-action, non-reflection was "no more irresponsible and considerably less dangerous than the swooning for Stalinism that infected large swaths of American learned culture in the 1930s."[15] (Like the little boy looking for the pony in the manure pile, somewhere in that sentence is a compliment.) In fact, Noll is willing to admit that the premillinnial dispensationalists "were not entirely wrong" in their stress on the spiritual. "The tumults of the 1930s," he notes, "no doubt reflected momentous spiritual realities; the trends could, in fact, not be analyzed satisfactorily if the spiritual character of human beings was neglected."[16] He is right, of course, but does not pursue this concession. He does not tell us exactly how the spiritual is to be factored in. It would have been helpful had he done so, for he continuously accuses historic fundamentalists of excessive supernaturalism and of negating the "historical process."[17] Despite his obligatory nod to the reality of the spiritual realm, Noll is very much in step with most present-day evangelical historians who hold to the view that we must ignore the spiritual as a factor in historical writing; we cannot be accepted as legitimate scholars if we will not set aside appeals to the providential.[18]

Questionable Generalizations

The citations above are only a sampling of the criticism aimed at the historic fundamentalists. Most of those used are from evangelical sources. A host of others are stored in numerous books and articles patiently waiting on innumerable library shelves to bias the reader. Are these critiques all justified? Were the historic fundamentalists really so obtuse and self-centered? If so, surely we have a movement from the nether region—or at least from a nearby suburb. (And many a critic might be tempted to gleefully highlight this comment.) We are, however, faced with some rather broad and hackneyed generalizations (e.g., just what *are* the "social dimensions" of the Gospel?). The historic fundamentalists did not do this; they ought to have done that. Which ones?—all of them, some of them, a few of them? Is it true, as Robert Linder has charged, that "it has only been in the twentieth century, and especially after 1925, that *large numbers* of evangelical Christians have been *enslaved* by the radical right?"[19] (Italics added).

Now that is pretty strong medicine. Yet in his essay Linder did not define the term "radical right." In the 1930s, though, it might imply silver-shirted fascist leanings, or perhaps a paranoia-driven, irrational anti-communism. Nor did he give a percentage figure for what constitutes "large numbers of evangelical Christians," or even what their "enslavement" might consist of. Nor does he even give us a name or two (such as the *always* mentioned anti-Semitic, Gerald Winrod), that might allow us to place his serious charge in a personal context. Williams and Petersen also claim that "Evangelicals seemed to become politically reactionary and even crypto-fascist and sometimes anti-Semitic in an attempt to defend the Christian faith and the American way of life."[20] These authors, too, fail to offer any substantiation. They simply make the charge assuming, one supposes, that it will be believed because everyone knows it must be so. Such vague generalizations, which border on demagoguery rather than substantiated historical evidence, render many of the charges against the historic fundamentalists open to question and perhaps tainted with scholarly or even personal bias. It would be illuminating to know the political and economic leanings of the critics of historic fundamentalism. Where do they stand regarding extensive state welfare and an activist, intrusive national government such as was emerging in Roosevelt's New Deal? Have their political/economic commitments in any way affected their interpretations of the social and political activities of the historic fundamentalists—or even how the church is to interact with society or the state? (The answer to this question, of course, is an obvious yes!) So, when all is said and written, are the historic fundamentalists being criticized for a glaring scriptural failing, a clear disobedience to a straightforward command of Jesus (e.g. "go out and subdue the culture") or a faulty hermeneutical conclusion (e.g. "do not interpret Scripture literally")? Or are they being criticized for not adhering to the historical critic's view of how the church should engage the world politically and socially? And it should be noted that not all the critics of the historic fundamentalists concur with the above mentioned extremes. Mark Noll, as severely critical as he is, states "most American evangelicals for much of the twentieth century…were as likely to be Democrats as Republicans until sometime in the 1960s." Likewise, Joel Carpenter notes "that relatively few religious fundamentalists have followed right-wing radicals."[21] One could wish they had expounded upon these statements in more depth.

Leo Ribuffo, on the other hand, in his commendable, *The Old Christian Right* (1983), does dispute in some depth the argument that historic fundamentalists were enslaved in large numbers by "crypto-Facists" during the nineteen thirties. According to him, there was no necessary connection between conservative theology and far right activism. Many fundamentalist leaders, largely oblivious to politics, spent the 1930s building seminaries, missionary societies, and publishing houses. And a majority of devout fundamentalists, because they were poor, Southern, or both, voted for Roosevelt. Nevertheless, the convention associating fundamentalism with bigotry and reaction, created during the 1920s, was widely disseminated during the Brown Scare. Following World War II, this convention, combined with surfacing suspicion of "simple folk," would decisively influence interpretations of the far right.[22]

Now charges of political and social indifference or neglect pose additional questions. What constitutes acceptable political activism or political reflection for a Christian? How is the measure determined so that the critic may berate the supposedly political and social failings of the historic fundamentalists? Especially since this is a question that has been debated among Christians for centuries. If they tended to oppose the New Deal programs, does that mean they were politically unreflective, or even "crypto-Fascist?" If they pursued an apolitical course based on their understanding of Scripture, did they thereby become enemies of the poor? There seems to be a "given" among some of the critics of historic fundamentalism that the body of Christ is obligated to be deeply involved in bending the political process, as well as the culture as a whole, toward Christian ends. To oppose such a commitment often brings the accusation that one is holding to a "tradition of dualism, rooted in the neo-platonic subversion of North American pietism...[which]...short-circuits the dynamics of the Gospel by privatizing Christian faith, thereby failing to be grasped by the world-transforming power of a worldview."[23] (Whew!)

Of course, caught in such a dualistic bind one is unable to discern how Scripture addresses "our culture." Therefore, it would seem that not only must the evangelical be involved politically, but it seems, as far as some critics are concerned, he or she must be involved with a particular political orientation—usually activistic and tinted liberal or left of liberal. Very comfortable with such a conclusion, David Moburg declared in *The Great Reversal*, that to "refuse to work for [political] change designed to eliminate evil from society is to perpetuate its organized systems of exploitation, oppression, cruelty and hypocrisy."[24] It seems clear that Moberg has in mind the American capitalist system. To the historic fundamentalist that might point out that all systems are corrupt because man is corrupt, Moberg would answer that the Christian "will not arbitrarily assume that all social, economic, and political revolutions are necessarily evil," and rather than side "with the power structure" he will be open and understanding of the revolution and "declare his sympathy with the oppressed...."[25]

To the historic fundamentalist that might wish to eschew political issues and involvement and concentrate on preaching the gospel and nurturing his congregation, Moberg would answer that "the gospel of individual piety" is an excuse that has "led many selfishly to try to escape from the world and live lazily in separation from it while waiting for Christ's coming instead of working in it until he returns...."[26] Actually, Moberg has only contempt for those who try to remain "neutral." Those taking such a position "indirectly communicate that they believe those vested interests [which oppress the poor] are morally right in social controversies." In other words, one's "refusal to take an active position constitutes a blessing upon the selfishness and covetousness which lie at the root of much political and economic life." As far as Moberg is concerned, "To be neutral usually is to give one's support to evil."[27] (So much for the Salvation Army. In fact, based on Luke 12:13-15, one wonders if Jesus, himself, does not come under Moberg's judgment.)

To those who hold that the [local] church as such should stand aloof from political action and commentary, Moberg reminds them that "The reality of social sin, just as much as the reality of individual sin...demands the attention of churches," even to the point of setting up [political] task forces to keep the individual member informed of the issues and the "politically correct" position to support.[28] For the historic fundamentalists who would dare to think that the present capitalist/free market economy offers the best hope for the poor and marginalized, Moberg points the finger of judgment and accuses him or her of betraying the Lord. "If we honestly are attempting to seek first the Kingdom of God," he roars, "we ought to be the last to adopt sociopolitical positions which are selfishly oriented toward heaping up treasures on earth." He excoriates such people for defending " 'the rights of property' when they clash with the physical, psychological, or intellectual welfare of underprivileged people." Moberg believes that "efforts by Christians to resist changes in basic social institutions and equating of Americanism with Christianity" not only "imply that present social structures are viewed as either God's best for man (or alternatively as so corrupt that "any change is worse than no change"), but also show that those taking this position are involved in a "form of idolatry." "To put socioeconomic or politically loyalties first," Moberg fumed, "and Christian values second is...a type of elevating a false god to the position of God Almighty."[29]

Moberg, of course, is not surprised, given the deplorable "sold-out" state of evangelicalism, that "sensitive youth" reject such hypocrisy. "Evangelicals who defend the wealthy and powerful who 'are grinding the face of the poor' (Isa. 3:15) in a selfish drive for earthly gain are in danger of hearing the judgment curse of the Lord (Matt. 25:41-46) as well as the curses of earthly protest movements."[30] It is obvious Moberg is quite sure what form of activism is acceptable for Christians, but what is not clear is how he arrived at his conclusion beyond some rather vague and questionable appeals to Scripture. It is difficult not to believe Moberg's own political viewpoint colored his criticism of the historic fundamentalists. In fact it is not difficult to read Moberg's, *The Great Reversal,* as a 1960s political tract saturated with the leftist rhetoric of that period. It would be wrong to question his evangelical sincerity, or that his every criticism of fundamentalism/evangelicalism's attachment to the status quo is invalid, because it is not—either in the 1930s, or when he wrote his book (1972), or now. But his own commitment to a leftist liberalism has moved him to create something of a straw-man opponent whom he pummels with abandon but never seriously engages intellectually. And Moberg himself comes across as one wavering between being a public relations advocate for Great Society programs, such as the War on Poverty, or an evangelical consultant to the Students for a Democratic Society.

Postmillennialism Past

Given the above, it ought to be noted that when historians (or sociologist) compare the political involvement of evangelicals of the nineteenth century with the historic fundamentalists of the 1930s and 1940s, they quite often fail to mention that most nineteenth century evangelicals were ardent postmillennialists. They fervently believed that in "Christianizing" the social order they were helping to bring closer God's Kingdom on earth—literally—beginning in America. In their eschatology of the coming kingdom through their efforts, they bought heavily into the idea that continuous progress in every sphere of life—economic, technical, political, cultural and moral (under a Protestant umbrella)—was evidence that the kingdom was even now unfolding. This justified continued, intense evangelical involvement to ensure that it would not be forfeited.

This prevailing view of the majority of evangelicals throughout the nineteenth century was carried over into the early years of the twentieth century despite the increasing influence of premillennial dispensationalism. In fact, this kingdom optimism was embraced and propagated by the liberal-modernist wing of Protestantism well entrenched in the Federal Council of Churches right up into the 1930s.[31] True, the premillennial dispensationalists did oppose this kind of naivete and what they considered to be an unwarranted optimism. However, they disagreed not only because of their prophetic beliefs, but also because they believed biblical anthropology and soteriology were undermined by such a position. From a biblical perspective, nineteenth century postmillennialists put forward a false view of man, sin, society, history, and the gospel. William Jennings Bryan's "support for active government" so admired by Noll was fed by this postmillennialism (and an almost Pelagian view of man's nature) that lined up with the Enlightenment's view of the inevitability of progress "upward" through the application of "unfallen" man's reasoning ability.[32] On the other hand, the historic fundamentalists' "fear of [federal] governmental encroachment" put them in the same school as the Founding Fathers who, though influenced by the Enlightenment, temporarily regained their sanity and wrote the Constitution with a distinctly "Princetonian" understanding of man and a Whig understanding of political power. Rather than being criticized, one would think the historic fundamentalists would be commended for bringing evangelicals back to both political and biblical sanity.

Granted, of course, their opposition to the Pelagian-tinged postmillennialism embraced by a large segment of evangelicalism as well as liberalism did not make many friends for the dispensationalists in either Bryan's time or in the 1930s and 1940s. S. H. Kellogg noted this state of affairs as far back as 1888:

> We thus think it nothing strange that in this age of triumphing and exalting democracy, and most of all in a land like the United States, where people are the most sanguine of being able to work out a satisfactory solution of the problems of self-government, premillennialism should be unpopular.[33]

The reason for its unpopularity was not hard to discern according to Kellogg, "for no type of Christian belief," he noted, "is so intensely opposed to certain of the most pronounced tendencies of our time."[34] (Kellogg's words have a distinctly current ring to them.)

Kellogg was not simply trying to boost his marginalized self-esteem.[35] As late as 1923, despite World War I, the Reverend Alexander Hardie could write, "Most certainly the defamers of the Gospel spread dismay in the ranks of the Church Militant and hinder the extensions of the Redeemer's Kingdom. These pious pessimists are most dangerous enemies to the church."[36] After comparing "these pious pessimists" with German spies who tried to undermine America's war effort, Hardie went on to declare that these pessimists should be called "Satan-sent propagandists. Most assuredly they are betraying the cause of Christ to his enemies."[37]

Hardie, of course, was unabashedly thrashing the premillennial dispensationalists for obstructing the physical unfolding of God's Kingdom on Earth. Hardie, however, was not a modernist. He was an evangelical (Methodist) postmillennialist who passionately believed the crowned and armed rider on the white horse in Revelation, chapter 19, who "'goes forth conquering and to conquer,' is a *beautiful* and *true* symbol of our Holy Christianity, which is conquering, and is destined to conquer, the world in the name of the once crucified, but now glorified Redeemer."[38] Before anyone criticizes the prophetic "headline" interpreting of the historic fundamentalists, they need to check out Hardie's use of current world events to validate his postmillennial triumphantism (a habit, evidently, common to many postmillennialists of his era).[39]

Postmillennialism Present

In retrospect of course, one might ask, "What Kingdom?" One might ask, "Who now has played the fool?" Joel Carpenter notes that, "Fundamentalists frustrated optimistic liberals with their predictions of 'wars and rumors of wars' and their disparagement of hope of moral progress in what liberals envisioned as the 'Christian century.' *But in the end, fundamentalists had the more realistic outlook.*"[40] (Italics added). One cannot resist wondering how many emerging neo-postmillennialists, hoping to give direction to the evangelical community in the opening decades of the twenty-first century and longing for a more active influence for Christ on world affairs through their efforts, would concur with this comment by Hardie: "In the coming decades we may expect leagues of nations that will develop ultimately into a universal Federation of the World which will constitute a vast brotherhood of Christian fellowship...that will be the Golden Age of Millennial rest...."[41] While the emerging neo-postmillennialists have not repeated verbatim (though some come close) their forebears' mistake of identifying the Kingdom with America's democratic "destiny," they seem no less determined to move history in the right (political) direction under the guidance of the church.[42]

Brian Walsh, for example, in his essay, "Worldviews, Modernity and the Task of Christian College Education," envisions a combination (in this writer's opinion) of the old radical Christian socialism with an Earth First! environmentalism in which "dreams of the kingdom must replace the American dream. The biblical worldview must energize us (fill us with the Spirit) so that we can begin to walk in new paths of discipleship," that "would be culturally subversive."[43] Modestly, Walsh admits, "We are not called to bring the kingdom but simply to erect obedient signposts of the kingdom."[44] One might be constrained to ask, however, just what political wording these obedient signposts will have. Inspiring, "biblical" sounding rhetoric such as Welch's may thrill the "radicalized" believer's ears but offer little of substance that can be concretely engaged.

Mark Noll also has no qualms about evangelical involvement in things political and heralds what he considers to be something of a renaissance now taking place in this field. However, he insists it must be done with more scholarly input and less "populist" biblicism.[45] He bemoans the fact that "the evangelical tendency" (inherited, of course, from the historic fundamentalists) "to exalt the supernatural *at the expense of the natural* makes it nearly impossible to look upon the political sphere as a realm of creation ordained by God for serious Christian involvement."[46] (The thought that it might not be is indeed a scandal and an anathema in his sight.) Likewise, he considers that this same evangelical failing, "makes it very difficult to search for norms in this life that combine reverence for God with respect for the variety of political institutions that God has ordained."[47] However, one must admit that it is difficult to "respect" some of the "variety of political institutions" that have been practiced in the twentieth century. While I gladly acknowledge God's sovereignty over nations and history, I will also surmise that some of the political institutions that have arisen in the last century were ordained for purposes of judgment and wrath, thereby turning back those who have ears to hear and eyes to see to the "Judge of all the Earth," but not to respect (let alone participate in) in the sense of esteeming them for how they have benefited mankind or acknowledged the Creator of all the universe.

Hints of this "Kingdom Manifesto" for believers also comes through in a recent editorial by Richard D. Land, President of the Christian Life Commission of the Southern Baptist Convention:

> The Southern Baptist confession of faith, The Baptist Faith and Message affirms a believer's involvement with the world when it states that "every Christian is under obligation to seek to make the will of Christ supreme in his own life and in human society." The confession also says that Christians not only "should oppose, in the Spirit of Christ, every form of greed, selfishness, and vice," but "should seek to bring industry, government, and society as a whole under the sway of the principles of righteousness, truth and brotherly love." These Baptist Faith and Message statements clarify our *responsibilities* as Christians and our *rights* as citizens.[48]

Finally, Bernbaum and Herbert insist "Evangelicals typically fit into the religious tradition that Richard Niebuhr describes as transformational—working toward the eventual reformation or transformation of culture."[49]

Dissenting Voices

Contemptuously disdaining the ghost of fundamentalism past, we now joyfully invoke the shade of Walter Rauschenbusch to hauntingly instruct our present political motions and musings. That classic "social gospeler" could not have said it better than those quoted above. What can be said in response to this resurrection of political postmillennialism in all but name? Throughout history there have been some opponents to this politically intense "here and now" kingdom talk, though those pillorying the historic fundamentalists seldom give them time to speak. Tertullian's famous "what has Athens to do with Jerusalem" still irritatingly resonates in the ears of the cultural mandatists past and present. As does, I am sure, his anti-political confession that "all zeal in the pursuit of glory and honor is dead in us. So we have no pressing inducement to take part in your public meetings. Nor is there anything more entirely foreign to us than the affairs of state."[50] One can only applaud that rasping curmudgeon's longevity. Roger Williams also comes to mind. Any man who would dare approve cutting the cross out of the British flag because he considered such a union blasphemous cannot be completely ignored or completely wrong. Needless to say, he p aid the p enalty for his audacity, f or separating cross and crown, coldly slogging through frosty New England's snowy woods all dark and deep. Long, long before the poet put his wintry thoughts to words, Williams *walked* miles and miles before he slept, pursuing a promise none had ever kept. But God was on his side. (Dare I, did I say that?) And in a place he named "Providence," and his enemies the "sewer of New England," that which was promised was kept. (And OH! what a legacy that incorrigible sectarian has given us.) Regretfully, he is all but forgotten by evangelicals today, and we are beggars for our neglect. As Robert Wilkens reminds us, such neglect "is a great loss, a kind of self-imposed deafness. Where there is no one to answer, we are deprived of a precious intellectual gift—resistance."[51] Williams was a mighty resister of the Christian "political" notions of the M assachusetts Bay Puritans, who, it might be added, were not above hanging those whose theology they *really* detested.

Edwin S. Gaustad, in his biography of Roger Williams, sums up William's view on the Christian and politics with these words:

> The people had the power to create a government. Yet they did not have the power to baptize that government—that is to make it a Christian civil order. Roger Williams...left the Bay Colony in order to show the whole world (if eyes were not tightly shut) that a commonwealth was never Christian: no Christian country, no Christian England, no Christian Rhode Island . . . God redeemed men and women, not empires or dominions. Christendom was still the enemy. But this was not to dismiss government; it was to clarify its purpose and specify its motives. Justice, peace and the common good— these were the charges under which a civil order operated....[52]

In the present evangelical political resurgence, where we plan our strategies to redeem America (or social structures) once more, and willingly embrace new ways to "cooperate" with the state for the social good of all,[53] few seem willing to ask , "Should the church be doing this?" There are a few, of course—voices faintly heard above the neo-postmillennial din—Kurt Schaffer is one. Pointing to the cross, he warns that our embrace of the cultural redemption motif places us "in danger of surrendering the Reformation theology of the cross." He passionately reminds his readers that,

> we are inclined toward every kind of progressive foolishness about our usefulness to the creation, unless we die with Christ and have our confidence shattered; we naturally suffer self-delusions about the grandeur of subduing and being fruitful and multiplying and filling creation mandates, about our ability to function as if there had been no fall, unless Christ first shows us to be what we are: feeble, forgetful pilgrims even on our best days.[54]

Pointing to the consummation of all things, Schaffer reminds us that if we forget Jesus is coming again and that He will set things right, we will be inclined to believe that what we think ought to be done, and how it ought to be done, is what God wants done. We will thus raise "to creedal status our favorite policy option, for w hich our e xpertise is w eak and p assing, and t hus choke o ff inquiry and ultimately embarrassing the gospel."[55]

However, the consequences go even beyond this, for by ignoring the Second Coming, "we risk thinking of Christ as merely one who has bonded with the world, who dislikes violations of its harmonies, rather than as the Transcendent Lord who has atoned for sin by the shedding of His blood."[56] The life of the believer, Schaffer reminds u s, consists of far m ore "than conferring 'redeemed' status on clever mutations of secular ideas."[57]

Schaffer's words cut deep. But politics is an intoxicatingly perfumed whore, and for those who have slept with her, or want to, his words are easily dismissed. Philip Rieff (who c omes from t he "secular" si de b ut n onetheless is a v oice evangelicals need to hear), and has traced the triumph of the Freudian therapeutic mindset in America, and mourned such a misbegotten victory, has also warned us "political cures are always and entirely faithless." (Too cynical?—perhaps—but a wisdom, while ignored by Moberg et al., was not overlooked by many historic fundamentalists.) "The therapeutic politicized," he warned, "is the latest rough beast slouching toward his own imaginary Bethlehem."[58] Sadly, we cannot exclude the evangelical community from this warning, for we have so willingly embraced the therapeutic mindset through our Christianized psychotherapy that we are now part of that "therapeutic politicized."[59] We, too, want our guarantees of self-esteem and cultural well-being; and glibly exchange our "more than conquerors" status for that of the victim in order to profit with the rest from a government and a society and a church more than willing to accommodate our narcissism. The idea of a true pilgrim church, manifested in the local church which is for now the only valid reflection of kingdom life to come (Col. 1:13,14), and that history may indeed be coming to a close with the church neck-deep in faithlessness, are all anathema to a r estless, politically a mbitious, therapeutically a dept, kingdom d reaming, evangelical Christianity.

Of course, it would be unfair to stigmatize all evangelicals with Rieff's thoughtful and provocative heresy. Some are made of sterner stuff and just plain despise dispensationalism. Thus one of historic fundamentalism's more radical critics, S. Stephen Thomas, lashes out at the premillennial dispensationalists, angrily writing:

> Having stood everything on its head, we are dismayed to find that we are not a mighty army storming the gates of hell with the word of God, but rather hapless victims awaiting rescue from the onslaught of the enemy. This eschatology of martyrdom is with us still and bears no resemblance with the Hebrew hall-of-famers we claim as our fathers. We should be ashamed to even think that the return of our Lord is imminent when the kingdoms of this world lie in unbelief and have not yet been realized as the kingdoms of our Lord.[60]

Heady stuff, this new postmillennial militancy (though lacking, it appears, in historical depth). Obviously murmurs of protest or questions of doubt are not welcomed, let alone seriously heeded. Nevertheless, some thoughtful words by Alva McClain, an outstanding premillennial dispensationalist of a previous generation, are worth repeating here:

> Theological confusion, especially in matters which have to do with the Church, will inevitably produce consequences which are of grave practical concern . . . once the Church becomes the kingdom in any realistic theological sense, it is impossible to draw any clear line between principles and their implementation through political and social devices . . . The difference is very great between the Roman Catholic system and modern Protestant efforts to control the state. But the basic assumption is always the same: the Church in some sense is the kingdom and therefore has a divine right to rule.... Thus the church loses its "pilgrim" character and the sharp edge of its divinely commissioned "witness" is blunted. It becomes an *ekklesia* which is not only in the world, but also *of* the world."[61]

There have been, then, many thoughtful believers through the centuries, both sophisticated and unsophisticated (including some historic fundamentalists of the Great Depression era), who would agree to a considerable degree with John Howard Yoder that it is "inappropriate and preposterous...that the fundamental responsibility of the church for society is to manage it."[62]

Has Anyone Bothered to Listen?

Thomas Howard, in *The Christian Vision* (1984), draws attention to the fact that "even when we carry the topic...further than" just political issues, "and include the whole idea of 'culture in the word society,' we get nowhere with the Bible." This silence on the part of Scripture causes considerable distress for those who believe Christians must be cultured "to help counteract the notion that Christianity [is only] for churls and fanatics and revivalists...surely we say, Christianity has been the great fountainhead of western culture."[63] But Howard reminds us that the minute we say this we are brought face to face with Athens and Jerusalem—the earthly city and the City of God—cities "we cannot pretend" are "at peace with each other."[64] This, of course, raises the question of whether we are called to be pilgrims or to infiltrate and subdue.

Some believers, drawing on Scripture, Howard notes, "would stress the fallenness of human nature to the point of outright rejecting, or at least casting grave doubt on, the whole enterprise of human culture and society." Howard, though not in agreement with this position, does not condemn those who do follow such a path, who, as he writes, bear "witness to a vision of things that set very little store by history or its achievements," who "live as simply as possible in the light of the heavenly calling laid upon us by Christianity," holding as of ultimate importance "things above" not the furtherance or glory of societies and their cultures.[65]

Many second-century Christians, Waldenses, Anabaptist groups, and, yes, as noted, even some of the historic fundamentalists were influenced in various degrees by such a "literal" reading of Scripture. George Marsden, in his *Fundamentalism and American Culture* (1980), writes that in the shift from "postmillennial to premillennial views...politics became less important." He goes on to note that few historical fundamentalists went the whole way by embracing the "Anabaptist tradition—that since Satan ruled this age and its governments, Christians should avoid all political action even voting."[66] However, it is quite possible that more than a "few" historic fundamentalists were doing this very "Anabaptist" thing. One of them wrote *The Sunday School Times* the following letter in 1935:

> For years I have seen that a Christian, a born-again soul, like his Lord, is not of this world though in it. If so, is he to have a say in politics, in voting to elect rulers,—most of them men of the world with God left out of their reckoning! I am told that the Word says to pray for the powers that be, for they are ordained of God. Which is true. But it does not say I should help to make those powers. God allows, and overrules all, but Satan is still the Prince. Am I wrong?[67]

Before answering "yes" to the writer's closing query, the editor also added a letter from a pastor in Ohio complaining of those in his area who were of the same mind as the above writer:

> There are ministers and laymen who refuse to vote or do anything toward community improvement except to try to win individuals to Christ. Of course we are to be separated from the world (that is, from worldliness), but should Christians go to the above extreme and cut themselves off from all civic and political opportunities for community, state, and national betterment?[68]

There is no way to establish just how many of these "Anabaptist"-like fundamentalists there were. It is evident they were not in a majority nor did they hold positions of leadership. But there were enough of them that the leadership of historic fundamentalism, which did advocate involvement with political and social issues, had to take note of them and politely "disown" their position. Still, though the leadership believed in participation in politics and society, it was not always of one mind on what that entailed and tended to be charitable when differences were evident.[69]

However, historic fundamentalism is a varied and complex movement (even within the confines of premillennial dispensationalism), which is hardly done justice by clichés grounded in leftist political rhetoric or academic hubris. More is required from the critic, then, than calling the historic fundamentalists border-line heretics, or aficionados of Social Darwinism, or an intellectual black plague, or to look back only to build one's reputation as a scholar by painting unflattering graffiti on their tombs.[70] The critic who judges the historic fundamentalists on the bases of what he thinks they should have done or been is himself open to judgment. The historian does not have to agree with all that the historic fundamentalists did or said or wrote to treat them with all consideration and *fairness,* trying to understand their concerns, asking their questions, and listening with respect to their answers. As J. Gresham Machen, mentor to many historic fundamentalist divinity students, once plaintively requested:

> It is true, I do wish that those persons who do not agree with me might occasionally give me a hearing. It does seem rather surprising that people who pride themselves on being broadminded should take their information about what is called by its opponents "Fundamentalism" from newspaper clippings or from accounts of "Fundamentalism" written be opponents on the basis of newspaper clippings, instead of reading what these so-called "Fundamentalists," these conservatives, these Christians, have published in serious books over their own signatures, or instead of listening to what they have to say when they lecture.[71]

Would not it be profitable, then, after all these decades, to finally accede to Machen's polite request?

NOTES

1.   Of course, far, far less flattering terms have been graffitied across its memory, but we will pass on these. Joel Carpenter has noted that fundamentalism is often equated with "bigotry, fanaticism or anti-intellectualism" and "has been spoken with derisive loathing and, no doubt, some fear in liberal intellectual circles...." (*Revive Us Again,* [1997], 4.) Ernest Sandeen commented over twenty years ago that "the fate of fundamentalism in historiography has been worse than its lot in history" ("The Origins of Fundamentalism," *Religion in American History: Interpretive Essays,* John M. Mulder and John F. Wilson, eds., [Englewood Cliffs: Prentice-Hall, Inc., 1978], 415). Things have not changed much since Sandeen wrote.
2.   Robert D. L inder, "Fifty Years After S copes: Lessons t o Learn, A Heritage t o Reclaim," *Christianity Today,* July 18, 1975, 10.
3.   Louis Gasper, *The Fundamentalist Movement* (The Hague: Mouton and Company, 1963), 122, 123.
4.   David O. M oberg, *The G reat Reversal: E vangelicalism versus Social Concern* (Philadelphia: J. B. Lippencott Co., 1972), 34-38.
5.   John D. Woodbridge, Mark A. Noll, and Nathan O. Hatch, *The Gospel in America: Themes on the Story of America's Evangelicals* (Grand Rapids: Zondervan Publishing House, 1979), 241.

6. Ibid, 242, 243. Some of the charges leveled against the historic fundamentalists are surprising, to say the least. It is almost ridiculous, for example, to charge that they "spent more time resisting evil than proclaiming the good news."

7. George H. Williams and Rodney L. Petersen, "Evangelicals: Society, the State, the Nation (1925-1975)," *The Evangelicals*, David F. Wells and John D. Woodbridge, eds. (Nashville: Abingdon Press, 1975), 219.

8. Robert S. Miller, *American Protestantism and Social Issues, 1919-1939* (Chapel Hill: University of North Carolina Press, 1958), 18. Martin E. Marty, in his *Righteous Empire* (1970), also writes, "fundamentalists restricted their acceptance of Darwinism to the social-economic realms, in support of laissez-faire individualism and competition on 'survival of the fittest' lines" (215).

9. John Bernbaum and Jerry Herbert, "Beyond Self-Interest: Politics, Justice, and Evangelical Faith," *Commentary*, Summer 1990, 4.

10. S. Stephen Thomas, "Culturally Barren," *Credena, Agenda*, Vol. 8, Number 5, 12. One wonders how the persecution of dissenters, including mutilation and death, plus the issue of liberty of conscience, can be casually noted as "religious matters of minor importance and personal conviction." And it does seem reprehensible in the extreme to blame dispensationalists for the Supreme Court's *Roe vs Wade* decision.

11. Joel A. Carpenter, *Revive Us Again: The Reawakening of American Fundamentalism* (New York: Oxford University Press, 1997), 244.

12. Mark A. Noll, *The Scandal of the Evangelical Mind* (Grand Rapids: William B. Eerdmans Publishing Company, 1994), 160.

13. Ibid, 165.

14. Ibid, 168.

15. Ibid, 169.

16. Ibid.

17. Ibid.

18. George M. Marsden, "What Difference Might Christian Perspectives Make?" *History and the Christian Historian*, Ronald A. Wells, ed. (Grand Rapids: William B. Eerdmans Publishing Company, 1998). Marsden writes:

    I also emphasized that Christian scholars need not violate the legitimate rules of the academic game. Rather, as in a court of law, it does no good in the mainstream academy to try to settle an issue by an appeal to a special revelation. We must, instead, argue for our perspectives according to standards of argument and evidence accessible to people from a wide variety of other viewpoints. So in such a setting Christians will not be quoting Bible verses or alleging special providences as means of historical explanation (11).

    See Chapter Ten for a fuller discussion on this subject.

19. Robert D. Linder, "The Resurgence of Evangelical Social Concern (1925-1975)," *The Evangelicals*, 198, 199.

20. Williams and Petersen, 220.

21. Noll, 161 and Carpenter, 4.

22. Leo P. Ribuffo, *The Old Christian Right: The Protestant Far Right from the Great Depression to the Cold War* (Philadelphia: Temple University Press, 1983), 181. Also see Arthur Herman's, *Joseph McCarthy: Reexamining the Life and Legacy of America's Most Hated Senator* (New York: The Free Press, 2000), 172-175.

23. Brian J. Walsh, "Worldview, Modernity, and the Task of Christian College Education," *Faculty Dialogue*, Fall 1992, 26.
24. Moberg, 141.
25. Ibid, 142.
26. Ibid, 37.
27. Ibid, 87, 88.
28. Ibid, 132, 133.
29. Ibid, 40, 41, 97, 43. Also see 145, 138, 95.
30. Ibid, 43. Also see 95. Looking back from the perspective of the century's end, it is difficult to understand why Moberg's, *The Great Reversal*, was so lauded. It lacks depth in its use of history, is sparse in its use of Scripture and lacking in depth in its interpretation of the same, theologically shallow, and rife with generalizations which are never proven. Nor does he really try to understand the fundamentalists' belief in a spiritual church or fear of a political pulpit. He does not seek a constructive dialogue but simply "slams" them. His confidence in sociology is amazing and he makes little effort to evaluate his own presuppositions. It is at best a polemic work.
31. See Sydney E. Ahlstrom, *A Religious History of the American People* (New Haven: Yale University Press, 1972), 779-784. Also see George M. Marsden, *Fundamentalism and American Culture: The Shaping of Twentieth-Century Evangelicalism 1870-1925* (New York: Oxford University Press, 1980), 146, 147.
32. Noll, 162-165.
33. S. H. Kellogg, "Premillennialism: Its Relation to Doctrine and Practice," *Bibliotheca Sacra*, April-June 1888, reprinted in the April-June 1943 issues of the same journal, (308).
34. Ibid.
35. Both Joel Carpenter (*Revive Us Again*, 35, 40) and Harry S. Stout ("Reviewers Reviewed," *The Banner of Truth*, March 1995, 10), claim that the historic fundamentalists yearned for a lost respect. However, this charge is so nebulous and based on current pop-psychology that it is facile at best. From the earliest days of the movement, as Kellogg indicated, they knew they were outside the developing mainstream, not only of society, but of Protestantism as well. They seemed to have accepted this as part of what it meant to stand up for what they believed to be true. What is interesting is how influential they became. Within their own community, as well as outside of it, men such as Torrey, Gray, and Barnhouse were respected. And as mentioned in the Introduction, the historic fundamentalists do not appear to have been as "alienated" and "disrespected" by society as their critics have claimed.
36. Alexander Hardie, *The World Program According to the Holy Scripture* (Los Angeles: Times-Mirror Press, 1923), 17.
37. Ibid, 96, 97. Hardie is evidently alluding to a slur originally promoted by Shirley Jackson Case in 1917 and 1918. Case charged that the premillennial dispensationalists were being financed by German money in an attempt to undermine the American war effort "to make the world safe for democracy." (See, for instance, Marden's *Fundamentalism and American Culture*, 146, 147.)
38. Ibid.
39. As evidence that the Kingdom was just around the corner, Hardie listed, among other items, women's suffrage, the allied victory in the war, Russia and China recently

becoming republics, and the leading countries of the world being led by Christian statesmen. Shirley Jackson Case, in his *The Millennial Hope* (1918), listed a number of other—other than premillennial—interpretations of the Second Coming:

> And who can imagine Mark's feeling had he also been told, in certain modern fashion, that his prediction of Christ's return was to be fulfilled in the Lutheran Reformation, in the French Revolution, in the Wesleyan Revival, in the emancipation of the slaves, in the spread of foreign missions, in the democratization of Russia, or in the outcome of the present world-war.

(quotation in J. Dwight Pentecost's *Things to Come*, 1958 [1970], 19.)

40.   Carpenter, 245. Richard J. Mouw makes a similar observation in his, *The Smell of Sawdust: What Evangelicals Can Learn from Their Fundamentalist Heritage*, writing: "Now I ask: who had a better sense of what was going to happen in the twentieth century? It seems obvious to me that Protestant liberalism was simply wrong in its predictions, whereas much of the dispensationalist scenario was vindicated. Why have we not given the dispensationalists more credit for their insights?" (102)

41.   Hardie, 223.

42.   It hardly needs to be mentioned that a number of conservative Christian organizations have just such a goal in mind. The Family Research Council, the California Restoration Project, The Voice of Vision America, to mention only three, all have aggressive policies toward "re-Christianizing" America. On the left are such evangelical groups as Call to Renewal, Evangelicals for Social Action and the International Justice Mission which are more concerned with "eliminating poverty," promoting "social justice," and guarding "human rights," in a transnational context.

43.   Walsh, 27, 28.

44.   Ibid, 28.

45.   Noll, 221-228.

46.   Ibid, 174.

47.   Ibid.

48.   Richard D. Land, "A Threat to Democracy?" *Light*, March-April, 1996, 2.

49.   Bernbaum and Herbert, 6.

50.   David W. Bercot, ed., *A Dictionary of Early Christian Beliefs* (Peabody, Mass.: Hendrickson Publishers, Inc., 1998), 502.

51.   Robert L. Wilkin, *Remembering the Christian Past* (Grand Rapids: William B. Eerdmans Publishing Company, 1995), 13. My apology to the memory of Robert Frost for borrowing from his touching *Stopping by Woods on a Snowy Evening*. I have always considered him to be America's greatest twentieth century poet.

52.   Edwin S. Gaustad, *Liberty of Conscience: Roger Williams in America* (Grand Rapids: William B. Eerdmans Publishing Company, 1991), 147. One might contrast Williams' view of Christendom with the recent comments of Douglas Wilson of *Credena, Agenda*. Wilson, a Reform neo-postmillennialist, laments the passing of the first Christendom (the last manifestation of the same being the Confederacy). However, he believes, "this means there will be a second Christendom, and if necessary, then a third. The Lord taught us to expect the process to be a gradual one...." According to Wilson, Jesus "told us to disciple *nations*...to pray for the heavenly commonwealth to have an earthly manifestation. We are to pray for Christendom" (*Credena, Agenda*, Vol. 9, Number 1, 12).

53. Faith-based organizations' receiving government funds to do social/welfare work is an excellent example of present day attempts to partnership church and state in helping to ameliorate societal ills. Interestingly enough, there was a considerable amount of historic fundamentalist-local government cooperation during the Great Depression.

54. Kurt C. Schaefer, "Creation, Fall, and What?" *Faculty Dialogue*, Fall 1992, 128.

55. Ibid, 134.

56. Ibid.

57. Ibid.

58. Philip Rieff, *The Feeling Intellect: Selected Writings*, Jonathan B. Imber, ed. (Chicago: University of Chicago Press, 1990), 360. Also see "Editorial," *Antioch Review*, Winter 1998, which notes that Rieff saw "an impoverished society that sought community by asserting the primacy of therapy over old religious orthodoxies" (4), and in the same issue, "The Therapeutic State: The Clarence Thomas and Anita Hill Hearings." Charles Krauthammer lamented that the President's impeachment trial, "the closest a republic gets to regicide," sounded more like "group therapy" as "both parties, the entire political establishment, had succumbed to the politics of feeling" (The Arizona Republic, February 21, 1999, B7).

59. Evangelical theologian David Wells, in *No Place for Truth: Or Whatever Happened to Evangelical Theology* (1993), claims that modern evangelicalism is in serious trouble because it has "increasingly found that the cost of modern relevance has been theological evisceration. And shorn of theology, evangelicalism has become simply one more expression of the self movement." (140) He strongly believes that "the psychologizing of faith is destroying the Christian mind," (183) and astutely observes:

> Modernity obliges us to psychologize life, to look to the states and vagaries of the self for the reality that once was external. For the most part, evangelicals have failed to see that this shift from the objective to the subjective, is invariably inimical to biblical and historical faith. (142)

60. S. Stephen Thomas, 12.

61. Alva J. McClain, *The Greatness of the Kingdom: An Introductory Study of the Kingdom of God* (Chicago: Moody Press, 1959 [reprint 1968]), 438, 439.

62. John Howard Yoder, *The Politics of Jesus* (Grand Rapids: William B. Eerdmans Publishing Company, 1972), 248. The last chapter of Yoder's book, "The War of the Lamb," has some excellent thoughts along this line.

63. Thomas Howard, "Mere Christianity: A Focus on Man in Society," *The Christian Vision: Man in Society*, Lynne Morris, ed. (Hillsdale, Mich.: The Hillsdale College Press, 1984), 19, 20.

64. Ibid, 20.

65. Ibid, 30, 21.

66. George M. Marsden, *Fundamentalism and American Culture: The Shaping of Twentieth-Century Evangelicalism 1870-1925* (New York: Oxford University Press, 1980) 88.

67. "Notes on Open Letters: Should Christians Vote?" *The Sunday School Times*, February 23, 1935, 122.

68. Ibid.

69. As an example, Moody Bible Institute drew-up a loyalty pledge in the Summer of
     1940 which every employee (including faculty) signed. The Pledge read as follows:
     "I solemnly promise, in the sight of God, that I will be loyal to the United States of
     America, and I pledge every necessary personal sacrifice for the defense of its flag,
     its form of government, its constitution, and its territory." However, the
     announcement also included a paragraph acknowledging that not all who worked
     for Moody agreed on the pledge's interpretation. "There was an understanding that
     a few of the company were conscientiously opposed to personal participation in
     war, and they were not asked to violate conscience but to decide for themselves the
     extent of their participation if the nation ever engaged in war." ("A Loyalty Pledge,"
     Moody Monthly, September 1940, 3.)

     Gertrude Himmelfarb disapprovingly comments on the new historical biography
     which she dubs " 'pathography,' " a form of writing "emphasizing the pathological
     or diseased qualities of the subject." Its purpose is not to show that outstanding
     individuals are all too human but nevertheless can still accomplish great things, but
     rather to dishonor and bring down those who have affected the past. "The new
     biographers reveal their vices (or more often follies) to dishonor them—to make
     anti-heroes of them" (*On Looking into the Abyss: Untimely Thoughts on Culture
     and Society* [New York: Vintage Books, 1994], 36, 37).

70. Over sixty years ago, Edward Ulbach wrote that "yet, while we are careful to be
     exact in our statements of facts, and unprejudiced in our estimate of the past, let us
     remember . . . that that is a 'poor and one-sided criticism which delights to expose
     the inconsistencies' and failings of great men" ("The Reformers of the Sixteenth
     Century," *Bibliotheca Sacra*, [July-September 1935], 319).

71. J. Gresham Machen, *The Christian Faith in the Modern World* (Grand Rapids: Wm.
     B. Eerdmans Publishing Co., 1936 [reprint 1970]), 64.

CHAPTER TWO

Historic Fundamentalism and the Great Depression: Seeing It from Their Perspective

Despite the negative evaluations of their critics and despite the fact that there were historic fundamentalists whose concept of "separatism" did not fit the historic activistic expectations of America's postmillennial evangelicals (or their present-day apologists), there is ample evidence to show that many historic fundamentalists do not fit the conventional profile of political or social neglect or indifference. In fact, upon investigation, one is surprised to learn just how civic-minded they were and just how much they resemble present evangelicals in this regard.

It should be remembered that historic fundamentalism was at heart a theological movement defending and proclaiming biblical, historical, Protestant, evangelical Christianity and its gospel. For the most part, its leaders were pastors, Bible teachers and some seminary professors. As such they were not prone to publish political tracts, white papers, books or magazines with a social gospel emphasis, as was the bent of the Federal Council of Churches. The magazines they did publish were religious journals largely given over to devotional articles, sermons, evangelistic appeals, biblical exhortations, prophetic analysis, Sunday School lessons, missionary reports, fundamentalist justifications and editorials designed to help the reader understand proper Christian doctrine, conduct, and the modern biblical issues confronting every believer.[1] The Bible was central to their lives. It was to be an open book, a studied book, a well-marked book, and a well-preached book. In this they reflected a true relationship with their Reformation forefathers. In fact, the rise of premillennial dispensationalism promoted more than a different eschatology. It also held to a more "Calvinistic" view of man, sin, and the atonement than was held by nineteenth century postmillennial evangelicals and twentieth century modernists, both of whom who were inclined toward a democratic, Pelagian interpretation of these doctrines.

Still, throughout the Great Depression, there was a surprising amount of social, economic and political interest and comment by the historical fundamentalists in their religious journals. So much so, in fact, that it seems strange to read such a charge as, "Concern for political involvement was replaced with an almost exclusive focus on personal evangelicalism and personal piety."[2] How such an untenable generalization has become accepted by historians as common fact is something of a mystery. Current events did indeed evoke "interpretations of prophecy" but they also evoked an equal number of jeremiads against national sin and religious apostasy. Many historic fundamentalists, along with their enthusiastic witnessing for Christ, were quite open about their political commitments and their political comments (especially among the movement's leadership)—indeed, at times right in the middle of an article on prophecy. (Which, of course, raises the unexplored possibility that these articles were used, in part, as vehicles for political commentary.) They appear as an alert, concerned people troubled by America's spiritual, moral, political and economic difficulties. They were distressed, not just for what these difficulties portended prophetically, but also for what they meant regarding basic liberties, the nation's relationship with God, its future as a great republic, and its Christian roots and values. Louis Bauman once wistfully commented that he prayed America would hold fast to its heritage, including freedom of worship, "until the Lord Jesus" returned again.[3]

Depression at Home and Abroad

There is no way, of course, to clearly understand historic fundamentalism of the 1930s apart from imaginatively grasping that the religious, political, international, and economic gyrations of that grim decade were being experienced by our parents and grandparents. Too often, great events are measured and understood by the statistics that can be marshaled. Such leaves the soul barren, however, and uneducated. It may be true that twenty-five percent or more of the workforce was unemployed, and millions more feared they would soon join their ranks, and/or found themselves making so little that they could not adequately support their families by themselves. Those are indeed sobering statistics. But for my father, who had a wife and three very young sons to support, and who fell into the latter category, it was a frantic time and bleak beyond my experiences. Within the statistical profiles, then, are the personal narratives of real people whose lives protest the easy convenience that reduces the reality of the past to footnotes in a scholarly article, or casually labeled generalizations that fill out paragraphs in our latest text books. For millions of Americans on a personal basis, it was the worst of times—period.[4] The country seemed inescapably imprisoned by the Great Depression, an economic malignancy that held on tenaciously, defying every attempt by Roosevelt and his frantically experimenting New Deal to end it. For the first time many Americans were made to realize that material progress was not inevitable and that capitalism was a deeply flawed system in the hands of all too mortal "experts." Gone from innumerable minds was any vestige of the hope of the coming kingdom through the Christianizing of the nation's institutions. (Tragically, many of these "kingdom dreamers" turned to communism as their new paradigm of earthly glory.)

So great was the Depression's impact that it permanently altered the way millions of Americans viewed (and still view) the role of the federal government. To this day, my Mother, a Depression born Democrat, has voted for a Republican presidential candidate only twice--both times in a fit of absent-mindedness. And in seeking a solution through massive governmental intervention, monumental constitutional questions were raised and answered that also altered the exercise of federal power:

> Considered in its entirety, the emergency program enacted under Roosevelt's leadership constituted a more far-reaching assertion of federal authority over national economic life than had hitherto been dreamed of in responsible political circles.... Roosevelt's reform program thus inevitably precipitated a tremendous struggle between two opposing conceptions of national authority, a struggle fought out immediately in the courts, but ultimately decided in the arena of politics and public opinion.[5]

It was, then, a major turning point both politically, *and* religiously, in American history. This dual tension needs to be kept in mind (for it was very much in the minds of the historic fundamentalists) as we review the evidence and establish the political and social activities of these public-minded evangelicals.

Three years into the Great Depression—1932—many Americans had gone from anxiety to desperation and some had gone irreversibly beyond even that. "Pessimism," the dispensationalist Louis Bauman had noted the previous year, "seems to have gripped the very vitals of man."[6] A few pessimistic months later, the editor of *The King's Business* commented that Americans were apprehensive, some even wondering if the nation was not fast ripening for revolution. The editor hoped such was not the case, but unless something was done quickly revolution seemed a possibility. "People are worn out physically, depressed mentally, oppressed politically, discouraged economically," and, he noted, so spiritually destitute that they were attempting suicide in unprecedented numbers.[7]

Like other Americans, the historic fundamentalists, too, were caught up in the Great Depression's maelstrom. Discouragement pressed hard against their faith in Christ's provision. Church budgets dropped, pastors went unpaid, unemployed church members found themselves dependent upon their church for help and often the church itself was so poor that little help could be given. Missionary agencies and missionaries struggled to stay afloat and stay on the field.[8] Bible schools teetered on the verge of bankruptcy.[9] These were days of intense strain, *The Sunday School Times* noted: "Everybody feels it; some break under it; some stand it. We need God's help to stand it and he offers it to us."[10] In the spreading impoverishment— impoverishment of the soul as well as the purse—the Christian must do more than talk about Christ. Whatever else happened, the Depression could not take away one's faith in God, one's true friends, or the privilege of loving, unselfish service. The Depression placed a great responsibility upon the believer. *The King's Business* wrote, "The Christian has to show whatever other men have to do, that Christianity is a religion for night, winter, ill health, loss, and discouragement—a religion that comforts, sustains, and animates under deprivations of the severest kind."[11] Along this line, no doubt to encourage the discouraged believer, *The Sunday School Times* periodically published articles which consisted of letters from its readers detailing how God had used the Depression for their good despite the apparent hopelessness that seemed everywhere.[12]

Concurrent with the domestic strain was an international situation that was going from bad to terrible. Stalin's version of communism was devastating the people of Russia and bringing Christians of all denominations under severe persecution.[13] Disturbingly, Stalin's "New World Order," despite its brutality, was finding a sympathetic welcome among American intellectuals, political and labor leaders, as well as the leadership of the Federal Council of Churches.[14] Evidently their anti-capitalist bias and liberal ideology made them easily susceptible to communist blandishments.[15] By the early thirties, another repressive "ism"—fascism—was finding a ready welcome in Italy, which would soon invade hapless Ethiopia, Libya, and Albania (in that order); and in Japan, which would soon invade fractured and famished China. Likewise, in Germany, a new fascist/Nazi paradise, Hitler and his Nazi cronies were beginning to move with seeming demonic compulsion internally against communists, socialists, Jehovah Witnesses, Gypsies, and increasingly the Jews (Christians and the mentally and physically handicapped would quickly follow), while externally threatening central Europe with his military rearmament.[16] What did all this portend politically for the United States and the other Western democracies? Along with their prophetic speculation and their growing alarm over an international missions movement falling rapidly into disarray,[17] this question was as much on the minds of the historic fundamentalists as it was on the minds of other Americans.

As the 1930s progressed, the international question forced itself into the American public's consciousness despite its uncompromising isolationism and overwhelming domestic preoccupations. By 1936, it was evident to the perceptive observer, including many historic fundamentalists, that another European war was inevitable. Will Houghton, who had taken over editorship of *Moody Institute Monthly* after the death of James Gray in September of 1935, wrote a poem expressing his apprehensions following a visit he and his wife made to Belgium. He titled it, "Another Crop on Flanders Fields?" The last stanza reads as follows:

> Oh, tell me, sin-ruled world of men,
> These wars of hatred, can they stop?
> Drive not these boys on fields again
> To mow them down—another crop.[18]

Admittedly, this is not poetry of critical acclaim. But in retrospect its apprehension of another coming apocalypse makes this insignificant. Death rode a pale horse— Houghton saw him coming. Dread colored the ink with which he wrote. Another "crop" *would be* mowed down. It ought not to be necessary to point out that these are hardly the words of one who has turned from a troubled world to become absorbed in prophetic speculation or personal piety.[19]

Interpreting the Times

The historic fundamentalists approached the crisis of the thirties in three ways. One was to try to understand unfolding events in the light of what prophetic Scripture revealed about end-time history. Such was a "given" for the premillennial dispensationalists. Accordingly, a seemingly endless stream of prophetic speculation flowed from their pens. It must be admitted that if modesty becomes one, the historic fundamentalists were not always becoming in this regard.[20] (On the other hand, as Carpenter has commented, if ever a decade lent itself to premillennial prophetic interpretation and curiosity, the 1930s certainly was that decade).[21] Still, considering what the 1930s was "giving" to the world, it is difficult to criticize too severely those who deeply longed for Jesus' appearing and Kingdom. However, critics who would make this the controlling preoccupation of historic fundamentalists regarding "current events" are simply presenting cardboard cutouts of some very intelligent and concerned people.

A second way they dealt with the Great Depression was to try to discern what God was saying or doing in and to America in those troubling times. Today, many evangelicals seem embarrassed by those past attempts to read the times so providentially. Now, like so many others, evangelicals also (only) "read" cultural forces in order to construct an historical narrative. Alas, God, not being a cultural force, cannot be consulted—at least not out loud. However, by doing history in such a secular fashion, today's evangelicals are setting aside something of immense value. By acquiescing in the removal of God from history and the writing of history, they inadvertently surrender the historical uniqueness of Christianity— willfully, it appears, afflicting all of us with an amnesia that will eventually (in the words of Robert Wilken) rob "our lives of depth and direction."[22] Such was not the failing of the historic fundamentalists. God was sovereignly and immediately at hand. In trying to understand events providentially, they were very much in the historic mainstream of American Protestantism. Jonathan Edwards speculated on

God's historic purpose for America through the Great Awakening.[23] Abraham Lincoln (and others such as Horace Bushnell and Philip Schaff) did the same regarding the Civil War.[24] (And Lincoln's second inaugural address is perhaps the greatest example of a providential interpretation of history to ever come from the pen of an American president. To this day, one cannot read it without being moved to nod, if even in involuntary silence, in agreement.) Woodrow Wilson, too, saw millennial hopes in the approval of the League of Nations.[25] In a similar fashion, the historic fundamentalists sought to providentially understand the great and unparalleled falling away within the Protestant church, the rise of brutal, anti-Christian dictators in Europe, and the seemingly inexplicable economic depression overwhelming America. Were these events related? Was God speaking to a nation unwilling to listen? In the most climactic decade in twentieth century American history, they sought, as had their mentors, "to discern the *kairoi*, to sense the significance of the particular moment."[26] Indeed, this was no ordinary moment in God's plan for the ages or for America.

Finally, many historic fundamentalists responded to the crisis of the Great Depression by advocating greater political and social involvement on the part of the believer. Although this goes against the perennial generalization that the historic fundamentalists ignored the social, economic and political crisis of the 1930s and retreated "into fascination with inner spirituality or the details of end-times prophecy,"[27] the evidence is overwhelming in support of the opposite. The problem with the critics of historic fundamentalism is that, too often, they seem as fixated on the premillennialists' fixation on prophecy as the premillennialists were on prophecy itself—and this "fixation" colors how the historic fundamentalists' other interests are interpreted. Needless to say, then, political events were not simply a foil to explain the prophetic text. In fact, James Gray went out of his way to deny that the gospel of "conservative evangelicals" was "too narrow." He insisted that *Moody Institute Monthly* was very interested in political issues and quite willing to give its opinion in such matters. "It is the inspiration," he wrote, "of our not infrequent warnings against the undercurrents of socialism, fascism, or communism in the religious and political life of the nation."[28] And Gray was not the "lone wolf" in saying this.

Interpreting the Historic Fundamentalists

Now, out of this last response, three difficulties arise. They are difficulties because although they were central to historic fundamentalists, they are either ignored by their critics or briefly mentioned before being set aside. First was the historic fundamentalist's understanding of the church as such as a "spiritual church." While discussion of this will be deferred until the next chapter, it needs to be stressed here that this concept was influential in shaping the way in which the historic fundamentalists viewed political involvement.

Second is the central place the local church is to have in the believer's life. For most historical fundamentalists, despite their many para-church organizations, fellowships, and affiliations, the local church and its ministries were of prime importance, one to which many lovingly and voluntarily devoted considerable time. It was not just a place for finding meaning or protection from modernism's assaults. Rather it was a place established by God where, together, they were to worship Him, hear His Word expounded, and serve one another, or go out and serve others. For many, then, it played the central spiritual and cultural role in their lives. Yet this is seldom considered in any depth when they are criticized for their lack of social and political involvement. However, given the "command" between going out and subduing the culture, or serving within or under the auspices of the local church as a Sunday School teacher, youth worker, Rescue Mission volunteer, or even as a missionary, the historic fundamentalist would see the latter, not the former, as conforming to Scripture. This was God's will for him or her in Christ Jesus. This intimacy with a local congregation also shaped the way they might respond to an "outside" political issue or economic and social problem. As far as they were concerned, to be serving God in this way under the umbrella of the local church was to be doing social good. Nor, on the basis of their theological suppositions, are *they* guilty of a "Great Reversal." Such is the interpretive "myth" of their critics. For many historic fundamentalists would have considered the shift away from considerable evangelical involvement in politics and direct cultural molding not as a great reversal, but rather as a "Great Correction," one that put the Church back on its biblically mandated course.

The third difficulty, as mentioned previously, is how terms like "social justice," or "social concern," or "political activism," or "political reflection," are to be defined. If they are to be defined in such a way that no matter what the historic fundamentalists did or said they come up short, then it has to be asked whether the critic has an agenda that *requires* them to be portrayed as political misanthropes. Michael Novak, in a recent article in *First Things* notes how difficult it is define "social justice," that while people write endlessly about the subject, they do so "without ever offering a definition of it." As Novak points out,

> it is allowed to float in the air as if everyone will recognize an instance of it when it appears.... It becomes, most often, a term of art whose operational meaning is, "we need a law against that." In other words, it becomes an instrument of ideological intimidation, for the purpose of gaining the power of legal coercion.[29]

Social justice, then, becomes a utopian goal which can only be imposed from above by an all-powerful "command economy" (i.e., a totalitarian state run by "lovers of power") whose duty is to protect the "victims" of the system, for it "is of the function of 'social justice' to blame somebody else...."[30] And although Novak does not address this directly, the question that would follow is always open-ended; when is "social justice" achieved for the victims and who decides this in a fallen world? (If Christians disagree on this issue, who is in sin and who or what determines this? Who or what is authoritative?)

Interestingly, Novak offers a "definition" of "social justice" that most historic fundamentalists would probably have found points of agreement with, even those of a separatist inclination. Novak "defines" social justice as that which is performed by "free citizens" joining together to do "for themselves [that is, without turning to government] what needs to be done." And what they do by this "giving back" is to benefit the community as a whole rather than any particular individual. "We must rule out," Novak writes, "any use of 'social justice' that does not attach to the habits (that is virtue) of individuals. Social justice is a virtue, an attribute of individuals, or it is a fraud."[31] The historic fundamentalists would have wanted to add the vertical dimension to Novak's equation, without which they could only see it failing.

No doubt Novak's article incurred some vigorous responses. No doubt, also, this is not the view of social justice used to measure the historic fundamentalists' social concerns and actions. They are given little if any leeway to define how they understood these things. Consider the following as an example:

> From the 1920s, with the rise of fundamentalism, through the 1940s, most orthodox Protestants retreated from social reform efforts and political involvement in what has been called the "Great Reversal." Of course, it was true that during this time many evangelicals were involved in activities in their local communities which assisted the poor and underprivileged. During the 1930s and 40s however, most fundamentalists concentrated their energies on announcing personal salvation while denouncing the social gospel, communism, and the New Deal.[32]

Now, at first this statement seems to be an improvement of sorts over those who a decade or so earlier claimed that the thought "of concern for the poor raised for many a terrible specter—'the poison of the social gospelers.' " At least the authors concede that many "evangelicals" showed compassion for those in need and, as we shall see, indeed they did.[33] But despite its concessions, one cannot help viewing its words as precluding any possibility that the historic fundamentalists were doing anything of national political or social significance. Basically what they did, other than help some of the people—who were poor—and preach the gospel to all of the people—who were lost—was (apparently) to unproductively "denounce."

The "No Gospel" Social Gospel

Of course, Bernbaum and Herbert's assertion raises additional questions they do not pursue but no doubt the historic fundamentalists would have and probably have answered as follows: first, based on Scriptures like Luke 24:46-48 or Romans 1:16, 17,[34] is not "announcing personal salvation" to "lost" individuals in bondage to sin and Satan the most important task of the church? Can there be anything more important from an evangelical perspective than men and women find forgiveness of sins and be placed in a right relationship with God through faith in His Son, Jesus Christ? If this is so, then it must take precedence over redeeming cultures. Surely, then, evangelical historians can show a little enthusiasm over the fact that the historic fundamentalists never wavered in this regard. Next, according to Acts 20 where Paul instructs the Ephesian elders to be on their guard because wolves in sheep's clothing would come into the church and destroy it with false doctrine, was it not wise that the leaders of historic fundamentalism opposed the Social Gospel being advocated by the Federal Council of Churches? One of the prime tasks of pastor/teachers is to protect the "flock" of Christ from false teachers (not be political agitators) and this must, of necessity, take precedent over bringing political institutions into an impossible conformity with the Sermon on the Mount. It goes without saying that the Social Gospel was another gospel—one that sought to build a "Christian" civilization devoid of the cross and a resurrected Son of God. Its attempt to pose as the "real" Christianity was unconscionable; its failure, legendary. Nor did the historic fundamentalists just "denounce" it—though certainly that is what it deserved. They clearly explained their opposition based on a careful exegesis of the Scriptures. One would think they should receive high praise for their stand in this area, one devoid of the often implied "but." The thinly veiled criticism they receive in place of commendation is somewhat puzzling. Had they not defended the content of the faith "once delivered," would today's evangelicals be criticizing them for their lack of political astuteness? Would there even be "today's" evangelicals? In other words, in opposing the Social Gospel (no small task), were not the historic fundamentalists doing that which was most essential for the good of mankind? Why do not evangelical historians, at least, write, "Praise God, they opposed the Social Gospel! What an unbiblical deception that was!" Ahh—but no—that is far too blatantly evangelical for the academy and certainly not a scholarly appraisal—even if it is true.

Psychologically Impaired Fundamentalist Anti-Communism

Certainly the same holds true, (if not more so), for the historic fundamentalists' opposition to communism. Under Stalin, the USSR truly did create an "evil empire" of enormous proportions. As Stephane Courtois has noted in *The Black Book of Communism* (1999), "from the 1920s to the 1940s, Communism set a standard for terror to which fascist regimes could aspire." And again, he writes, "as for the Soviet Union of Lenin and Stalin, the blood turns cold at its ventures into planned, logical, and 'politically correct' mass slaughter."[35] Included in this "political correctness" was the deliberate starvation of six million Ukrainian kulaks during the winter months of 1932-33 for resisting Stalin's plans for collectivization.[36] "Here," Courtois writes, "the genocide of a 'class' may well be tantamount to the genocide of a 'race'—the deliberate starvation of a Ukrainian child as a result of a famine caused by Stalin's regime 'is equal to' the starvation of a Jewish child in the Warsaw ghetto as a result of the famine caused by the Nazi regime."[37] As Arthur Herman has poignantly noted, "the scale of Stalin's atrocities in the 1930s might not have been as shockingly obvious as those of Hitler would be, [but] in terms of sheer numbers Stalin's put the Holocaust in the shade."[38] Communism was (and is), then, a political philosophy of death disguised as a "this world" salvation that sought through brute tyranny to bring in the anti-Christian, "New World Order" of Lenin's dark fantasy. Wherever it has been tried millions upon millions have died cruel and inhuman deaths. It is almost incomprehensible that so many English and American intellectuals and religious modernists found the "future" in such a system, and were so willing to compromise their integrity by excusing its horrors.[39] The historic fundamentalists were not ignorant of these things. Does not their opposition to it constitute legitimate spiritual warfare as well as legitimate political activism and commentary?[40] If not, why not?

It is noteworthy that the National Association of Scholars, in a symposium on the philosopher Sidney Hook, could commend him and express thanks to him, because by his devotion "to discovering the truth," and his commitment "to democratic values, he may have done more than any other American intellectual to combat one of the great evils of the twentieth century. Our country and our culture are better for his confrontation with communism."[41] During the same period, the historic fundamentalists were devoted to *defending* the truth and also committed to democratic values. Yet it would appear that their opposition to communism during the 1930s and 1940s is considered (at a minimum) little more than a misguided use of evangelical intellectual energy which probably should have been spent on more appropriate "political involvement" (i.e., supporting the New Deal, perhaps, rather than opposing it).

Others see it in more disturbing psychological dimensions. George Marsden, for example, seeks to explain what he labels the "development of hyper-American, patriotic anti-communism" of the historic fundamentalists (a position he calls "a puzzle and an irony in the history of fundamentalism,") by appealing to historian Richard Hofstadter. Hofstadter believed the historic fundamentalists possessed an "essential Manichean" mindset which viewed the whole culture as a field of warfare between good and evil. Because of this, Marsden claims that the historic fundamentalists "were disposed to divide *all* reality into neat antithesis: the saved and the lost, the holy and the unsanctified, the true and the false." And due to their "common sense philosophical assumptions" they believed they could discern the differences "when they appeared in everyday life." Combine this curvature of mind with their "experience of social displacement...and [their] 'Manichean mentality' becomes comprehensible."[42]

"Given this mentality," Marsden explains, "it is possible to shed some light on the paradox of super-patriotic premillennialism:"[43]

> Like their premillennialism, the political threats could be placed in the framework of the conflict between the forces of God and Satan. The two types of conspiracy theory, the political and the religious, might well have appealed to a single mind-set in such a way as to override the difficulty of reconciling specific details.[44]

This is about as definitive a socio/psychological interpretation of historic fundamentalism as one will find. Their "essential Manicheism," their feelings "of social displacement," their "common sense" presumptions, their lack of political sophistication, along with their predisposition to "conspiracy" which left them "little basis for evaluating these theories [e.g., communism] on their own merit,"[45] evidently moved them to extremism when it came to comparing communism with democracy or contrasting communism with biblical Christianity.

Manicheist or Realist?

Once more, a host of questions come to mind begging answers. For instance, one might ask why an evangelical historian would turn to a neo-socialist, secular historian who was unfriendly toward fundamentalism to find an authority who could "expose" the historic fundamentalist mind? How ironic! (A mind, it might be added, saturated not with the teachings of Manes but of Jesus, Paul, Peter and John, as well as Moses and the Old Testament prophets, and an exegesis that was historical/grammatical not allegorical). What evaluations had Hofstadter done in historical theology or New Testament studies that he could pronounce the historic fundamentalists "essentially Manichean" rather than essentially New Testament Christians? If he did study these, his conclusion does not reflect it. If he had not done any of this, why, then, is he appealed to as an authority on the *theological* mindset of the historic fundamentalists? For to call someone a Manicheist, is to make a theological judgment not a political judgment. It is difficult to avoid the conclusion that "Manicheist" is a bit of name-calling (rather than a realistic appraisal) meant to bias the reader against the historic fundamentalists and place the critic in a position of justifiable superiority.

Next, it might be asked, in what way did the historic fundamentalists' disposition to "divide *all* reality into neat antithesis: the saved and the lost, the holy and the unsanctified, the true and the false" differ from Paul's or Augustine's or Luther's or Edwards' or Charles Hodge's? Clearly the Bible itself encourages Christians to be discerning in this regard on a daily basis. Let us remember they were biblical fundamentalists not liberal relativists who, because of their relativism, would "sympathize with and protect communism's champions and profess to find moral worth in a system of absolute evil."[46] Surely if we are going to substantiate that the historic fundamentalists had a "Manichean mentality" we ought to build our case by offering viable comparisons from Christian history, and a solid exegesis from Scripture, rather than repeating a vitriolic "smear" (for that is what it is) by a hostile historical critic.[47]

In addition, it might be asked why the historic fundamentalists are not allowed to speak for themselves? (It does seem there are times when the criticism of the historic fundamentalists takes on the trappings of a Star Chamber proceeding.) Have they nothing to say that we ought to hear so that we might understand their political concerns and theological justifications? Journals such as *The Prophetic Word, The European Harvest Field, Prophecy Monthly, Moody Monthly, The Sunday School Times,* and *The Baptist Bulletin* were laced with articles that detailed the suffering being experienced by individual believers and congregations under communism.[48] While the realization of the murder of millions of people is almost incomprehensible to the mind, it is well to remember that these millions were millions of individuals loved and valued—wives, husbands, sons, daughters, and friends and neighbors deliberately starved, beaten, arbitrarily shot, or sent to gulags to die from exposure, overwork, disease, or malnutrition—unnumbered thousands simply because they were Christians. Many of those who suffered under the henchmen of Stalin (and it would be the same under Hitler), who screamed and moaned, or went insane while being tortured, or died in their own filth while being treated like dumb beasts in the forced-work camps, or simply disappeared forever into the endless maul of the GPU (which became the more familiar KGB), were not strangers to the historic fundamentalists. Even if not known directly, they were brothers and sisters in Christ whose plight was known and who were prayed for, and assisted whenever and wherever possible. The letters published in the historic fundamentalist's journals were letters from fellow believers that personalized the brutality and hatred of the communist toward Christians. The Russian refugees (again, thousands of whom were believers), that huddled in abject poverty and malnutrition and sickness just inside Poland's eastern border, or the borders of the Baltic states were not merely statistics to the historic fundamentalists.[49] Food, clothing, medical supplies, Bibles and the gospel flowed into these areas from the local churches and homes of the historic fundamentalists in America. (Many of the Hebrew Christian missionaries that would work among the Jewish refugees fleeing from the Nazis were themselves refugees from Russia.) And the tragic end to this "real life adventure" is that when Russia invaded these regions the refugees simply disappeared from historical view, and few, if any, ever reappeared. It is quite evident that the historic fundamentalists were well informed on what was taking place to their fellow Christians and others inside the USSR.

They were equally aware of, and angered, by those men and women in America who admired the "future" unfolding in the USSR, who excused, denied, or looked past the horrors being perpetuated by Stalin, all the while labeling those who criticized Russia, or even the New Deal, as fascist sympathizers who threatened America. (This, of course, included the historic fundamentalists.) As Arthur Herman has noted, as absurd as it may seem, "the historical record reflected again and again the same dismal result of liberals giving the benefit of a doubt to a monstrous political system, or even lying in order to protect it."[50] Herman's book, *Joseph McCarthy: Reexamining the Life and Legacy of America's Most Hated Senator* (2000), over and over reminds its readers that,

> by 1935...progressive intellectuals were embracing the Soviet experiment and its advocates. The result was a strange situation. While old-styled American socialists like Norman Thomas, A. J. Muste, and Sidney Hook were fiercely anti-Communist [and were labeled "fascists and allies of fascists" because of it], many mainstream liberals were convinced that the Communists' professed humanitarian principles were genuine and were prepared to overlook certain "details"—including constant rumors about murderous purges, shootings, and mass starvation in the Soviet Union—in order to arrive at a common understanding.[51]

Nothing seemed too strange for these liberals to swallow. "On their obligatory visits to the Soviet Union," Herman writes, "they displayed an amazing credulity. They were willing to believe literally anything that cast a favorable light on soviet society and a bad light on their own." Thus one witnessed the spectacle of "progressive journalists" praising "the Soviet's strict censorship of the press, pacifists" cheering "their military parades, and churchmen their abolition of Christianity."[52] Herman points out that "the plain truth—that Stalin was a mass murderer who governed through compulsory labor, prison camps, and systematic murder of his own supporters—was ignored, explained, or shrugged away" by fellow traveling liberals.[53]

Historic Fundamentalism Vindicated

It was not, however, "shrugged away" by the historic fundamentalists. Donald Barnhouse, who visited Russia in 1936 and confirmed for himself the depth of Soviet hostility toward Christianity, was frustrated by those [liberal] ministers who were admirers of communist Russia. He wondered aloud why "they do not realize that a movement to the left in the United States would destroy the liberty of religious thought and the freedom of religious meetings, even as it has been in Russia."[54] The fears of the historic fundamentalists were not exactly eased by such men as Oswald Garrison Villard, editor of the *Nation*, a magazine that found in the Soviet Union, according to Herman, a true soul mate and which "argued that New Deal liberalism and communism were not so different from each other after all. Both shared a belief in centralized planning and in social betterment."[55] Villard wrote an article that shocked Barnhouse for in it Villard speculated on what he would do if he were made dictator of America. Among other things, he claimed that he would "close two-thirds of the churches...allowing only those to remain open that were absolutely dedicated to peace at any price..." and which would give their time "over to social endeavors...preaching sermons directly connected with the problems of society...."[56] (If today's evangelicals are inclined to think the historic fundamentalists were over-reacting, they should consider Richard Lands reaction to a 1992 editorial comment by the *New York Times*, which declared that the evangelical involvement in public politics posed "a greater threat to democracy than was presented by communism." [Considering what is now known, this is about as ludicrous a statement as every found its way into an American newspaper]. Land, who is President of the Ethics and Religious Liberty Commission of the Southern Baptist, acidly replied that "it is the narrow secular biases of the nation's social, political and media elite's that pose a grave threat to American democracy, not evangelicals."[57] This is as good a tit-for-tat as any historic fundamentalist might have given.)

As if to dramatize his perplexity and frustration that any one would seriously embrace communism, Barnhouse recalled for his readers his memory of,

> the white, tense look on the faces of two Russian pastors in Moscow when we talked to them in the presence of a member of the Bolshevik party who was there to supervise the interview, though their membership in the party demanded that they be professing atheists, and I knew that our very presence there might mean suffering for them. I do not want anything in America to take us even one step on the road that leads in that direction.[58]

In another article, he noted "in Russia the political leaders have declared war on God." Barnhouse's conclusion was based on an interview with Emillian Yaroslavski, President of the Society of Militant Atheists, who unapologetically admitted, "that he and the Russian government were against all religion." Yaroslavski boasted that "Our slogan is: The struggle against religion is the struggle for socialism."[59] Barnhouse did not take this as an idle boast. To be a member of the communist party one had to be an avowed atheist. And the party controlled the government. The Russian constitution supposedly guaranteed freedom of religion,

Barnhouse noted, but that mattered little. The government simply ignored the constitution. As a result, the church in Russia was under severe persecution.[60] Barnhouse's experience (which was not an isolated one) showed a realistic grasp of communism and its intent (despite the fact, of course, that he was an historic fundamentalist).

Finally, one might ask just what "merit" there was about Stalinistic communism that deserved evaluating (even on its own terms) that the historic fundamentalists, hampered as they were with their "conspiratorially" inclined Manichean minds, missed? There is a witticism that goes, "just because you're paranoid doesn't mean that someone isn't out to get you." While it cannot be denied that some historic fundamentalists accepted political or historical conspiratorial theories, it must also be admitted that Stalin did conspire to do America great harm and sought with great effort to subvert its system of government. With the recent publication of a number of books detailing Soviet espionage in the United States, it is now evident that the Soviet Union had deeply penetrated the United States government during the Roosevelt and Truman administrations.[61] Anna Kasten Nelson, after reviewing some of these books, writes that, "When considering spying within the United States, most reviewers have concluded...that the Cold War red-baiters had it right: There was widespread espionage after all."[62] Combine this exposé with the open and plentiful support many American intellectuals gave to Stalin's regime (even to the point of excusing known evils executed by the Soviets) during the 1930s, while being hypercritical of America's every failing,[63] as well as being contemptuously hostile toward historic fundamentalism, it is no great wonder the historic fundamentalists were anti-communist and fervently appreciative of Constitutional liberties—especially freedom of worship and speech. Marsden labels this "super patriotic premillennialism" but as Keith Brooks noted in mid-1940, "certainly the fact that one has the 'blessed hope' will not lesson his loyalty as a citizen of the United States of America. May every reader...daily seek divine guidance as to how he can most effectively serve his country. Now is the time to prove that Premillennialists are something more than dreamers."[64] Considering when Brooks penned these words, and considering what he knew of communism—and fascism—his words hardly seem "super-patriotic."

Historian Robert Conquest, in his *Reflections on a Ravaged Century* (2000), spends considerable time detailing the betrayal by the American and English intellectual community and draws this conclusion:

> Many whose allegiance went to the Soviet Union may well be seen as traitors to their countries, and to the democratic culture. But their profounder fault was more basic still. Seeing themselves as independent brains, making their choices as thinking beings, they ignored their own criteria. They did not examine the multifarious evidence, already available in the 1930s, on the realities of the Communist regimes. That is to say, they were traitors to the human mind, to thought itself.[65]

And a few pages later he caustically notes:

> On the intellectual level it is revealing to see some of the most respected minds in philosophy, literary criticism, the sciences, falling into the fundamentally simplistic political scholasticism, and in too many cases into the mental idiocy of pure Sovietophilia. This alone is enough to discredit any idea that the notions harbored at any given time by a section of intelligentsia are to be taken seriously, except as symptoms requiring treatment.[66]

Ouch! No doubt were these the words of a historic fundamentalist, they would be considered evidence of anti-intellectualism or the absence of a "life of the mind." (One wonders if it could be said of these university elite's, these intellectuals, that they had no "life of the mind" for they "sold it" to Stalin, and thus they were in the truest sense anti-intellectual?) Nor does one have to be paranoid or Manicheistic to grasp the nature of the political philosophies vying for the minds of Americans during the 1930s. It is just possible that the historic fundamentalists rejected communism (and fascism) on the basis of the information at their disposal; that those who torture or slaughter or brutalize their people and viciously persecute the church, and burn bibles in the name of an "ism", may not be people you want to admire and ally yourself with. In retrospect, in light of what we now know, without denying there were a few extremists among them, one is still justified in asking who had the high ground in this matter, the historic fundamentalists or that part of the American intellectual community enthralled with a regime dedicated to gross evil and a hatred of Christianity? Despite their often glaring failings, in this matter the historic fundamentalists stand vindicated. When all is said and done, it was the historic fundamentalists who valued civil liberties more than those in the American intellectual community who "loved" communism and despised their own birthright.[67] What a bizarre irony. Sidney Hook, though vilified by many intellectuals in the 1930s and 1940s, is commended by his intellectual progeny. On the other hand, historic fundamentalists are considered distracted and almost mentally unhinged by their evangelical offspring for openly and vigorously opposing communism—a true enemy of biblical-historical Christianity. Something does not make sense here.[68]

A New Deal Closing Comment

Bernbaum and Herbert's "triology" of historic fundamentalists' "denunciations" also included the New Deal. And so numerous were their denunciations that the fourth chapter is reserved for their "unpolitical" political activity and thought. But a word is in order here on this subject before closing. After a brief openness toward the New Deal, they did become avid and vocal opponents. Here again, though, their reasons for opposition were well expressed and simply have to fall under the heading of political commentary. Claiming their opposition was "instinctive" is facile at best and does little to help us understand their political reasoning. In the long run, looking back from the perspective of the end of the century, some of the historic fundamentalists' criticisms of the New Deal seem quite perceptive and justifiable. However, whether we agree or disagree with their political opinions, as we shall see, one will not be able to sustain the generalization that they spurned political involvement and reflection. However, it was on their own terms, not those of their critics. A comment Michael Bauman made regarding the critics of early Christianity should apply equally well to the critics of historic fundamentalism:

> We must not, even if we fancy ourselves rather capable philosophers and theologians, establish some standpoint of our own about what they ought to have said, and then reject as inconsequential or marginal in their message whatever does not suit our private predilections.[69]

Yet this is exactly what many of the critics of historic fundamentalism have done.

NOTES

1. The historic fundamentalist magazines used to gather information for this book are *The Sunday School Times, The King's Business, Moody Institute Monthly* (later *Moody Monthly*), *Revelation, Bibliotheca Sacra, Prophecy Monthly, The Hebrew Christian Alliance Quarterly, The Hebrew Christian, The Jewish Era, The Jewish Missionary Magazine, Salvation, The Chosen People, The European Harvest Field, The Prophetic Word, United Evangelical Action, The Baptist Bulletin,* and *Europe's Millions.*

2. Mark A. Noll, *The Scandal of the Evangelical Mind* (Grand Rapids: William B. Eerdmans Publishing Company, 1994), 165. Joel A. Carpenter also lines up with Noll on this matter, commenting "preconditioned by their political instincts toward individualism and populist antielitism, it was relatively easy for fundamentalists to see beast-like tendencies in New Deal planning and to remain alienated from the public arena" (*Revive Us Again: The Reawakening of American Fundamentalism* [New York: Oxford University Press, 1997], 101). Exactly why the historic fundamentalists political positions are instinctive rather than the product of thoughtful conviction is not clear. I must confess that I am not exactly sure what a political "instinct" is or how it shapes a political position. However, this off-hand way of referring to their political opinions does seem to excuse the critic from having to treat the political and social activities of the historic fundamentalists in any depth.

3. Louis Bauman, "The Blue Eagle and Our Duty as Christians," *The Sunday School Times,* September 16, 1933, 584.

4. An excellent, well-written, recent book on the Great Depression that balances the general and statistical with personal narrative is T. H. Watkins' *The Hungry Years: A*

Narrative History of the Great Depression in America (New York: Henry Holt and Company, 1999). Although written from a "leftist" perspective, it is nonetheless well worth reading.

5. Alfred H. Kelly and Winfred A. Harbison, *The American Constitution: Its Origin and Development*, 3rd. ed. (New York: The Dial Press, 1970), 730.

6. Bauman, "There Shall Be Signs," *The King's Business*, March 1931, 102.

7. "The Case for the Depression," *The King's Business*, April 1932, 156; see also "Darkness Deepens," *Moody Institute Monthly*, September 1932, 4.

8. "Notes on Open Letters: Missionaries Shrunken Dollars," *The Sunday School Times*, November 11, 1933, 700.

9. The Bible Institute of Los Angeles (now Biola University) was one such institute. Saddled with a debt that approached a million dollars, Biola was on the verge of foreclosure in 1938. Only the persuasive powers of its President (and pastor of the Church of the Open Door), Louis Talbot, kept the inevitable from occurring. (see G. Michael Cocoris, *70 Years on Hope Street: A History of the Church of the Open Door* [Los Angeles: Church of the Open Door, 1985], 64-66.)

10. "Standing the Strain," *The Sunday School Times*, June 15, 1935, 401. Also see "Alarming World Conditions," *The Jewish Era*, July 1933, 72, 73.

11. "Discouragements," *The King's Business*, August 1932, 344. Also "What to Do in the Times of Depression," *Moody Institute Monthly*, May 1932, 438, and "Stand Fast in the Faith," *The King's Business*, June 1931, 243. See also Carpenter's *Revive Us Again*, 96.

12. "What has the Depression Meant to You?" *The Sunday School Times*, August 22, 1931, 457, 460, and "Why We are Thankful for the Depression," *The Sunday School Times*, November 12, 1932, 584, 585.

13. A number of fundamentalist mission agencies worked with Christians in Russia and Christian refugees from Russia. Three of them were Russia Inland Relief Mission, Russian Christian Relief Society, and All-Russian Evangelical Christian Union. Missionaries or lay-people associated with these agencies, as well as others (such as the American European Fellowship), provided the historic fundamentalists with a steady flow of information on what was taking place in these regions.

14. See for example, "Was Sinclair An Innocent Lamb Led to Slaughter," *Prophecy Monthly*, February 1935, 6-9; "Moscow and Red Terror in the US," *Prophecy Monthly*, September 1935, 17-19; "Democracy—the Pet Theme of Communism," *Prophecy Monthly*, February 1939, 10-12; Col. E. N. Sanctuary, "Communism—Its Heart and Goal," *The Sunday School Times*, October 24, 1936, 697, 698, and Dan Gilbert, "Can Christians Join Forces with Communists," *The Sunday School Times*, July 4, 1936, 455, 456.

15. Arthur Herman, *Joseph McCarthy: Reexamining the Life and Legacy of America's Most Hated Senator* (New York: The Free Press, 2000), 61. "In the minds of many American progressives," Herman writes, "Communists were just 'liberals in a hurry,'…. Communist goals for the Soviet Union seemed to be pretty much the same as those of the New Dealers for America. In the thirties the Soviet Union enjoyed the same sort of intellectual respectability that Mao's China would in the 1970s. The plain truth—that Stalin was a mass murderer…was ignored, explained, or shrugged away."

16. "Before World War II," Stephane Courtois notes, "Nazi terror targeted several groups. Opponents of the Nazi regime, consisting mostly of Communists, Socialists, anarchists, and trade union activists, were incarcerated in prisons and invariably interned in concentration camps, where they were subjected to extreme brutality. All told, from 1933 to 1939, about 20,000 left-wing militants were killed after trial or without trial in the camps and prisons." (Stephane Courtois et al., *The Black Book of Communism: Crimes, Terror, Repression*, trans. Jonathan Murphy and Mark Kramer (Cambridge, Massachusetts: Harvard University Press, 1999), 14.

17. For articles detailing the extent of the problem by the end of the 1930s, see "Shall Our Missionary Front Collapse?" *Prophecy Monthly*, August 1940, 21, 22; "Closed Doors," *Prophecy Monthly*, November 1941, 59, 60, and Herbert Lockyer, "The Lamps Are Going Out," *The King's Business*, May 1941, 174, 175, 198.

18. Will Houghton, "Another Crop on Flanders Fields?" *Moody Institute Monthly*, November 1936, 111. Louis Bauman, writing in *The King's Business* late in 1936 detailed how the countries of Europe, as well as Japan, China, and increasingly the United States, were frantically spending billions on armaments. ("The Cry of 'War,' " *The King's Business*, December 1936, 468-470.)

19. Recently, within a two day span, I heard two evangelical scholars repeat the cliché that the historic fundamentalists retreated into personal piety and abandoned public involvement. Not only is this an inaccurate overgeneralization, but I am finding myself increasingly disturbed by this constant "put-down" of their personnel piety. I find myself asking why a hunger for a deep, personal relationship with Christ is considered a liability? Dr. Marchant King, student and friend of Machen, graduate of Princeton University (MA in Arabic) and Seminary in 1929, and professor at Los Angeles Baptist College (now The Master's College) beginning in 1953, was a man who combined both deep personal piety with a breadth and depth of learning that filled his students with awe and respect. He required of us the highest standards and we willingly gave them. We would have been ashamed to have given him less. To this day he epitomizes my ideal of the Christian scholar.

    As the featured speaker at honors chapel for the graduating class of 1975, he spoke on the topic of "What Value Scholarship," encouraging all of us to pursue this goal, for scholarship was of immense value to the evangelical community. However, he reminded us that scholarship was "a fine servant, but a bad master" (a thought that many of today's young evangelical scholars might want to contemplate). He also reminded us, in closing, that without a corresponding spiritual renewal (i.e., true piety) "scholarship is only a pebble."

20. In mid-July, 1940, fifty leading historic fundamentalists assembled at Moody Bible Institute at the invitation of the institutes' president, Will Houghton. The purpose of the gathering was stated in the preamble of the conferences' ten-point "Statement and Call." "We have assembled," they wrote, "to humble ourselves before our sovereign God, and to seek His will and His message for us and the world in the darkest hour of human history."

    Point four of the "Statement and Call" began by stating that the conferees "deeply deplored both the lack of and abuse of scriptural prophetic teaching today," and concluded by noting that the "prophecies have been given by inspiration to save us from foolish prophesying, speculation, date setting and 'star gazing.' " ("A Significant

Conference," *The Baptist Bulletin*, October 1940, 11, 12. Also see "The Call of a Prophecy Conference," *The Sunday School Times*, November 16, 1940, 924, 925.)

21.   Carpenter, 71. His exact words are, "much of dispensationalism's attractiveness came from the uncanny resemblance of its predictions to the trend of the twentieth century." Carpenter does admit that their interest "in prophecy helped them identify some of the deepest flaws in American life."

22.   Robert Wilken, *Remembering the Christian Past* (Grand Rapids: William B. Eerdmans Publishing Company, 1995), 170. Wilken is commenting on the notion that "to be an intellectual is to loosen the moorings that bind one to a particular tradition or a living religious community." He finds such an approach untenable and notes, "that such ideas could take hold in the academy is evidence of how insular intellectuals can be, even religious ones" (170). However, this seems to be the direction many evangelical scholars wish to go. For example see, Noll's *The Scandal of the Evangelical Mind*, 241-253, "Symposium: God in the Academy," *Academic Questions*, Spring 1996, 10-36, and *Evangelicalism: Comparative Studies of Popular Protestantism in North America, The British Isles, and Beyond, 1700-1990* (New York: Oxford University Press, 1988), 411. Also see David F. Wells, *Losing Our Virtue* (Grand Rapids: William B. Eerdmans Publishing Company, 1998), 9-12.

23.   Robert W, Jenson, *America's Theologian: A Recommendation of Jonathan Edwards* (New York: Oxford University Press, 1988), 130-135.

24.   Sydney E. Ahlstrom, *A Religious History of the American People* (New Haven: Yale University Press, 1972), 686, 687.

25.   Ernest Lee Tuveson, *Redeemer Nation: The Idea of America's Millennial Role* (Chicago: The University of Chicago Press, 1968), 209.

26.   E. Harris Harbison, *Christianity and History* (Princeton: Princeton University Press, 1964), 64. Harbison notes that "from Amos to Reinhold Niebuhr the prophets of the Hebraic-Christian tradition have attempted to read 'the signs of the times,' to discern the *kairoi*, to sense the significance of the particular moment." Futurist have always been among us, especially (now) in the academy. It is interesting that Harbison ignores the premillennialists. It is acceptable to be a prophet in America as long as one is not a premillennial dispensational prophet. Perhaps this is because the dispensationalists took God's pronouncements in Scripture too literally.

27.   Noll, 107.

28.   "Editorial Notes: Human Interest," *Moody Institute Monthly*, August 1935, 553.

29.   Michael Novak, "Defining Social Justice," *First Things*, December 2000, 11.

30.   Ibid, 12.

31.   Ibid, 13. The historic fundamentalists' basic assumption that the conversion of the individual is the best means of changing society (not the "regeneration" of social institutions), and that the financial support and involvement in Christian organizations is based on the concept of "voluntary giving," seems to parallel in some ways Novak's definition of "social justice."

32.   John A. Bernbaum and Jerry S. Herbert, "Beyond Self-Interest: Politics, Justice and Evangelical Faith," *Commentary*, Summer 1990, 4.

33.   However, one wonders why the authors write that "many evangelicals" showed compassion for the poor but that "most fundamentalists" mainly preached "personal

salvation" while denouncing "the social gospel, communism, and the New Deal." During the 1930s, evangelicals were fundamentalists and fundamentalists were evangelicals. Yet the authors seem to be implying there is a distinction. In addition, it is disturbing that no mention is made of the historic fundamentalists' strong opposition to fascism during this same period.

34. Luke 24:46-48 reads, "He told them, This is what is written: The Christ will suffer and rise from the dead on the third day, and repentance and forgiveness will be preached in his name to all nations, beginning at Jerusalem. You are witnesses of these things" (NIV). Romans 1: 16 and 17 reads, "I am not ashamed of the gospel, because it is the power of God for the salvation of everyone who believes: first for the Jew, then for the Gentile. For in the gospel a righteousness from God is revealed, a righteousness that is by faith from first to last, just as it is written: 'The righteous will live by faith' "(NIV).

35. Stephane Courtois et al., 14, 5.

36. Ibid, 9. Also see Herman, 5. Louis Bauman, in an article that appeared in *The Sunday School Times* (June 20, 1940) describes in emotional detail the deliberate starvation of the Kulaks and the persecution of those that survived. "As for Josef Stalin," Bauman wrote, "no more beastly creature ever ruled over man." ("Europe's Triumvirate of Beasts," 581). In the announcement of the formation of the Russian Missionary and Relief Service, the editor of *The Sunday School Times* opened with these words: " 'Religion is the opiate of the nation.' This is the slogan of Lenin, who established Bolshevism in Russia fifteen years ago. 'Today we have the fruits of that principle,' writes a Russian Christian, 'and surely they are most bitter.' Dependable reports describe famine raging in southern Russia, where not only dogs, cats, mice, and tree bark are eaten, but where cases of cannibalism occur. A recent letter tells of parents being afraid to let their children go out alone." ("A New Russian Relief Service," November 18, 1933, 735, 736.)

37. Ibid, 9.

38. Herman, 70.

39. Robert Conquest, in his recent book *Reflections on a Ravaged Century* (New York: W. W. Norton & Company, 2000), list a number of reasons for academics' embracing the Soviet Union during the 1930s. Included on the list is the belief that socialism would bring about a "better and juster social order," that such a system "represented a higher historical level" (116), that those who embraced it were repulsed by the "muddled" and "exhausted" political and economic systems then operating in America (117), that it was fashionable, giving those who embraced it a sense of being more advanced than others (119), and what Conquest labels parochialism ("people could not bring themselves to believe the horrors of Stalin. It was far easier to attribute such stories to reactionary spite...."[120]).

An interesting "Protestant" example of the above was E. Stanley Jones, a popular "modernist" preacher and writer. In his *Christ's Alternative to Communism* (1936), Jones claimed that if the church did not rebuild the social order along the lines of communism—minus the atheism and class hatreds—than "marxian" communism would overcome it. Contending that the gospel has everything to do with this world's politics, Jones (according to *The Sunday School Times* reviewer of Jones' book), invested "Soviet Communism with divine purpose." The reviewer then quotes the following from *Christ's Alternative to Communism*: "When the Western world was floundering in an unjust and competitive order…God reached out and put his hand on the Russian Communists to produce a juster order and to show a recumbent church what it had missed in its own Gospel" (p. 224). And again, "I [Jones] am persuaded that the Russian experiment is going to help—I was about to say *force* Christianity to rediscover the meaning of the Kingdom of God on earth (p. 32)." ("With the New Books: Stanley Jones on Communism," *The Sunday School Times*, June 27, 1936, 443.)

In his later book, *The Choice Before Us*, Jones repeated his unrestrained praise of the Soviet System, calling it "born again" and claiming that it was destined to be the greatest nation on earth. "Why? Because she has hold of a higher principle, cooperation, and it is working out in higher results than we can work out in a lower principle, competition." (Quoted in Brooks' "The Church of Christ in America," *Prophecy Monthly*, February 1948, 17.) Jones' uninhibited admiration for Russian communism, ignoring all the while the decades of wickedness and brutality of Stalin's system is simply inexplicable and inexcusable. Carpenter accuses Charles Trumbull, editor of *The Sunday School Times*, of "relentlessly" attacking "fellow evangelical and holiness advocate E. Stanley Jones for his alleged apostasy," (*Revive Us Again*, 85). But considering Jones fawning over communism, and claiming that God had raised it up to show the church the direction it should go, and considering what an inhuman and evil system it was, it is difficult to see how Jones could be called evangelical and how he could not be called apostate.

40.   The point here is not whether some historic fundamentalists went to extremes in their opposition to communism, but that vigorous opposition to Stalinistic communism in the 1930s and 1940s was a justifiable political response as well as a justifiably biblical one for a historic fundamentalist who sought to be both a responsible American citizen and a faithful Christian.

41.   Harvey H. Klehr, "A Vigil Against Totalitarianism," *Academic Questions*, Summer 1996, 28. In the same issue, John H. Bunzel wrote: "For Sidney, heresy was an inevitable companion of freedom. Conspiracy, on the other hand, crossed the line by violating the rule of law and need not therefore be tolerated by democracy. Many of us as individuals, and our society as a whole, owe him a profound debt for his heroism in defending democracy…." ("The Intellect as a Weapon for Freedom," 36).

The famous movie director, Elia Kazan (*On the Waterfront*), went through a similar transformation. He left the communist party in 1936 "because he had 'had enough of regimentation, enough of being told what to think, say and do, enough of their habitual violation of the daily practices of democracy to which I was accustomed.' " Kazan voluntarily testified before the House UnAmerican Activities Committee in 1952. (Stephen Schwartz, "The Rehabilitation of Elia Kazan," *The Weekly Standard*, February 8, 1999, 22-27.)

One looks in vain for anything resembling even faint praise for the historic fundamentalists from current evangelical historians on this issue.

42.   George M. Marsden, *Fundamentalism and American Culture: The Shaping of Twentieth-Century Evangelicalism, 1870-1925* (New York: Oxford University Press, 1980), 210, 211.

43.   Ibid. As noted in the Introduction, Roger Lunden is another who pastes the Manicheist
      label on the historic fundamentalists. In his *The Culture of Interpretation: Christian
      Faith and the Postmodern World* (Eerdmans, 1993), he writes:

> In the categories employed by H. Richard Niebuhr, the evangelicals of the
> early nineteenth century embraced a "Christ of culture" position because they
> saw America as a Christian nation, . . . Their fundamentalists heirs, however,
> could hardly hold to the "Christ of culture" view in the late nineteenth century.
> As they witnessed what one observer has called "the demise of biblical
> civilization" in the last years of the century, evangelicals came to adopt what
> Niebuhr termed "Christ against culture" position. In the spirit of the modern
> gnosticism we discussed earlier [Manicheism], by adopting this view the
> fundamentalists run the risk of denying the sovereignty of God over the course
> of nature and history (234).

The irony in this, as noted previously, is that Niebuhr included the historic
fundamentalists *under* the "Christ of culture" category. As he noted, "The movement
that identifies obedience to Jesus Christ with the practice of prohibition, and with
the maintenance of early American social organizations, is a type of cultural
Christianity; though the culture it seeks to conserve differs from that which its rivals
honor" (*Christ and Culture,[1951]*, 66). When one reads the literature of the historic
fundamentalists, it is difficult to take Lunden's remarks seriously. (They were, after
all, premillennial dispensationalists.) And, as the endnote below indicates, some of
the historic fundamentalists' critics seem to think they overly stress the evidence of
God's sovereignty over "the course of nature and history." Mark Noll is also a
perfect example of this latter school of critics. Evidently the historic fundamentalists
can be all [bad] things to all of the critics all of the time, even when they contradict
one another. What a remarkably diverse movement!

44.   Ibid. If Lundin thinks the historic fundamentalists are in danger of denying God's
      sovereignty over history, Timothy Weber almost seems to think they give Him too
      much and in the process turn all of history into a giant conspiracy. Weber, who has
      analyzed the premillennial dispensationalists' understanding of the course of history,
      concluded the following:

> This eschatological perspective amounted to a vast conspiracy theory: as the
> end approaches, the forces of evil, under the control of Satan and the Anti-
> Christ, will undertake the deception of the nations, the persecution of the
> saints, and the destruction of the Jews. Such matters were revealed by God
> through the prophets and were certain to come to pass. The course of history
> was already determined by forces completely beyond human control. In the
> end, the nations and all the people in them must conform to a predetermined
> divine plan. Evil forces will operate behind the scenes in their attempt to
> defeat God's people and plan. Eventually, they will fail in their unholy designs;
> but until the ultimate victory of Jesus Christ, the conspiracy will play itself
> out in human history. Nothing can stop it. God's righteous remnant must
> prepare for the worst and not be surprised when things start to fall apart.
> ("Finding Someone to Blame: Fundamentalism and Anti-Semitic Theories in
> the 1930s", *Fides et Historia*, Summer 1992, 41.)

The problem with Weber's "conspiracy" is that it was not the "invention" or the exclusive possession of the historic fundamentalists. They did, indeed, have their own particular version of it, but in general form, and in many specifics, such a view has been common teaching in the church since its inception. Irenaeus, Augustine, Luther, Roger Williams, Jonathan Edwards, and Charles Spurgeon, to name only a very few, would have all agreed with the above "conspiracy." And a number who were not dispensationalists, also believed that the Jews would either be converted at the end, or gathered back to their land and converted (e.g. Owen, Ryle, Edwards, Spurgeon, Hodge). This so-called historical "conspiracy" theory has been pretty standard fare for Christians since Jesus walked the earth.

Possibly in the 1930s, because of the influence of historicism, evolution, postmillennialism, socialism, modernism, and secularism, the historic fundamentalists with their biblical approach to history, stand in stark contrast to those around them. Nor from a Christian/biblical perspective, can Weber's scenario be considered a true-blue conspiracy (if a conspiracy is something plotted in secret by a select few and only revealed when the conspiracy is put into motion). Why is it not? Well—because everybody knows about it (even Weber). The Bible portrays it as an open and well-documented rebellion against God. It is a rebellion everyone knows will not succeed, whose sure defeat was achieved at Calvary, and whose terrible end God has carefully detailed in the Bible.

Now some historic fundamentalists did hold to historical conspiracy theories (e.g., A. C. Gaebelein and Keith Brooks). But blaming their eschatology seems spacious because it cannot account for those who held to conspiratorial theories but did not conform to the same eschatology. On the other hand, it would not be out of line to point out that the Bolsheviks and the Nazis did conspire to overthrow each others government respectively, and that Stalin did conspire with a fair amount of success to damage the American government during the 1930s and 1940s.

45. Ibid.
46. Herman, 307.
47. Mark Noll, in *The Scandal of the Evangelical Mind*, makes an oblique, unflattering comparison between the Medieval Albigenses (or Cathari), a gnostic sect, and the historic fundamentalists. Both were movements that neglected the Christian "life of the mind" (46, 47 & 122-139). But the comparison is invidious at best.
48. See, for example, "A Russian Cry: We are Sinking," *The Prophetic Word*, March 1941, 7; "A Letter from a Suffering Russian Believer," *The European Harvest Field*, January 1931, 31;"Horror of Russian Concentration Camps," *Prophecy Monthly*, September 1934, 11; "Some News from Russia," *Moody Institute Monthly*, November 1935, 132; "An Escape from the Russian Inferno," *The Sunday School Times*, July 22, 1939, 491 (front page); and "Baptists Chief Sufferers in Russia," *The Baptist Bulletin*, April 1939, 12. Literally scores of additional articles could be added to the above.
49. See, for instance, Louis Richard, "When These Things Begin to Come to Pass," *Moody Institute Monthly*, November 1935, 122, 123. Richard's article deals mainly with the wretched conditions of the Russian refugees living on the Polish side of the border with Russia. Also see, "Desperate Conditions in Poland," *Moody Monthly*, May 1941, 530.
50. Herman, 88. As an example, Herman mentions "the *New York Times's* chief Russian

correspondent, Walter Duranty, who had repeatedly lied about the Great Famine in Stalin's Russia in exchange for official favors, and won a Pulitzer Prize"(89). Also see Robert Conquest's *Reflections on a Ravaged Century*, 122-124. Conquest notes that the "announcement of the prize" praised Duranty's correspondence as "marked by scholarship, profundity, impartiality, sound judgment, and exceptional clarity...."(123). The only problem, of course, was that they were blatant lies.

51. Ibid, 66.
52. Ibid, 64.
53. Ibid, 61.
54. Donald Barnhouse, "Tomorrow: Some Observations on Religion in Russia," *Revelation*, December 1936, 498, 530. Also see, "Misguided Pinks in the Pulpit," *Prophecy Monthly*, April 1935, 19-21
55. Herman, 65.
56. Donald Barnhouse, "Hate for the Church," *Revelation* March 1932, 609.
57. Richard D. Land, "A Threat to Democracy," *Light*, March-April 1996, 2.
58. Donald Barnhouse "Tomorrow: Current Events in Light of the Bible—The Decline of Civil Liberties," *Revelation*, 398.
59. Barnhouse, "Tomorrow: Some Observations on Religion in Russia," *Revelation*, December 1936, 498.
60. Ibid, 498, 532. Barnhouse's analysis is supported by a recent book published by Cornell University Press (1998), *Storming the Heavens: The Soviet League of the Militant Godless* by Daniel Peris. (See also "Christian Suffering in Soviet Russia," *The Sunday School Times*, June 28, 1930, 385, and Louis Bauman, "God and Gog and 1937 (?)," *The King's Business,* January 1933, 6, 7. In this article, Bauman asserted that "the Russian state has set itself against every moral and spiritual idea which God's word proclaims" and intended to close every church by 1937.)
61. Three of these books are *The Haunted Wood* by Allen Weinstein and Alexander Vassiliev, *Venona: Decoding Soviet Espionage in America* by Earl Haynes and Harvey Klehr, and the recently published *The Venona Secrets* by Herbert Romerstein and Eric Briendel.
62. Anna Kasten Nelson, "Illuminating the Twilight Struggle: New Interpretations of the Cold War," *The Chronicle of Higher Education*, June 25, 1999, B4-B6. For a more chary perspective of these writings, see Amy Knight, "The Selling of the KGB," *The Wilson Quarterly*, Winter 2000, 16-23.
63. Conquest, 116, 117, 118.
64. "No Tranquility for Our Generation," *Prophecy Monthly*, August, 1940, 11.
65. Conquest, 118.
66. Ibid, 127. Leaving aside for the time being Gaebelein's view on *The Protocols of the Elders of Zion* and his supposed anti-Semitism (these will be dealt with later), it is difficult to fault his exposure of the efforts of the Soviet Union to subvert America's liberties in *The Conflict of the Ages* (1933), 115-140. Barnhouse, in his review of Gaebelein's book noted that "Daily newspapers in some of the great cities of the United States have seen fit to call attention to it on their front pages. For there are chapters in this book which go outside the usual field of Bible study and occupy themselves with sheer counter-propaganda against the world wide movement of Communism and its anti-religious propaganda." ("The Conflict of the Ages,"

Revelation, December 1933, 447).

67. Leo P. Ribuffo details the "Brown Scare" waged by liberals both in and out of government during the late 1930s and early 1940s in an effort to silence even legitimate right-wing and conservative opponents of the Roosevelt administration and leftist liberals. These liberals seemed to believe freedom of speech should apply only to themselves. (Very much like the "politically correct" liberals do today on campuses across America.) No wonder the historic fundamentalists were concerned about possible suppression of freedom of speech and worship. (*The Old Christian Right: The Protestant Far Right from the Great Depression to the Cold War* [Philadelphia: Temple University Press, 1983], 180ff.) Also see Herman's, *Joseph McCarthy*, 80-83 and 172-174.

68. In light of the evidence presented in this chapter, it would have been wiser if Noll had edited out of *The Scandal of the Evangelical Mind* his facetious comment that "the evangelical substitution of apocalyptic speculation for serious political analysis was no more irresponsible and considerably less dangerous than the swooning for Stalinism that infected large swaths of American learned culture in the 1930s" (169). When it came to communism, the historic fundamentalists were anything but irresponsible either as citizens or Christians.

69. Michael Bauman, "Introduction: The Nature and Importance of Religious Historiography," *Historians of the Christian Tradition: Their Methodology and Influence on Western Thought*, Michael Bauman and Martin I. Klauber, eds. (Nashville: Broadman & Holman Publishers, 1995), 2.

Robert Wilken warns against turning our forebears into "footnotes, transforming them into Historical sources invoked for the purpose of documenting an idea or illustrating a theory." Such a procedure, he believes, exiles the people of the past. "No longer welcome as partners in a living dialogue, the lively voices of the dead fall silent as we turn our backs to them. The consequence is not only a loss of depth but also a sacrifice of memory" (*Remembering The Christian Past*, 13).

CHAPTER THREE

Historic Fundamentalism and the Oversight of God: Judgment and Mercy Toward a Prodigal Nation

Even a cursory reading of their literature leaves one with the undeniable impression that the historic fundamentalists passionately believed that God was speaking to America through the Great Depression. How could they have thought otherwise? Considering that America was turning against God was not God turning against America? Considering the rise of godless, popular dictators, was not democracy a tottering wall—even in America? What was God saying to us in the midst of the ever-increasing social and political cacophony of the 1930s? "Why," Kenneth Monroe asked the readers of his 1934 essay, "Biblical Philosophy of History," "have powerful and brilliant civilizations…gradually degenerated?"[1] In answer to this question, Monroe offered two possible "secular" explanations. He identified one as the "psychological interpretation of history because it sought to analyze the 'cyclic development and decline of nations.' " The other was Marx's economic interpretation, which at heart held that the "underlying causes of a community's or a state's or a nation's development and decline may be sought in the field of their economic condition."[2]

But more than secular interpretations were needed if this question was to have a satisfactory answer. So Monroe next turned his attention to a third possibility, the biblical interpretation of history. He began by noting that the "Scriptures are full of the doctrine that the providential government of God extends over all nations and communities of men." He then posed another question: "Do the characters and actions of rulers and people in any way determine God's government of them?"[3] Monroe's "yes" could not have been more emphatic.

Monroe offered the nation of Israel as an example and gave a short biblical review of its history, concluding "that God's providential government extended over Israel's every national event." One might respond that this might have been true for Israel, but what had this to do with the Gentile nations? Did God oversee their history in a similar fashion? Again Monroe answered with an emphatic "yes." "National blessings and adversities of Gentile nations have practically the same philosophy as that behind Israel's life." With this background established, Monroe turned to the present. Did God deal with nations today as He had done in the past? Once more came an unequivocal "yes." "The revelation of God and His will possessed by Christian nations of the world is superior to that of Israel," he noted, implying [thereby] a greater responsibility.[4]

Monroe was now ready to apply his conclusions to America. First, however, he explained his own eclectic philosophy of history, which integrated the economic and psychological with the biblical, noting "the outworking of divine providence must include a working in the minds of men and things material." One does not seek from secular philosophies "ultimate causes." They may be helpful to a point, but they cannot deal with "the basic reasons for change." By the same token, Monroe was not "contending that every historical change has a theological background which, if known, would furnish the master key to the situation." What he was advocating was,

> the recognition of divine providential government as a dynamic in the affairs of men; that we may see Christ as the constructor of the ages;[5] that we may recognize that the way a nation's leaders and citizenry treat Almighty God and sacred things has considerably to do with the permanency and well-being of that nation.[6]

What did this have to do with the America of the 1930s? Monroe noted that America was at the place of prosperity many other civilizations occupied before they began their slide into disaster. Therefore, the question challenging "multitudes of serious-minded intellectuals from every field" was, "Can and will America maintain herself indefinitely in this phase of prosperity?" Monroe denied any personal competency to answer such a question, or to offer any economic panacea that would solve America's depression problems. He did believe the country faced serious internal threats created by problems such as "unemployment, injustice, the unequal distribution of wealth, mercenary crime and lawlessness." But he also believed there were other, more pressing issues endangering the nation when one considered "the fact of divine providential government" and the "question of the relation of America to God and His Sacred things."[7]

Monroe listed seven areas from which he believed America had defected from faithfulness to God and thus brought upon the nation His disapproval.[8]

1. Millions no longer believed God existed in any meaningful way.
2. The authority of the Bible "is denied in history, science, and even in religion." Legions denied "the authority of the Bible in faith and practice."
3. The person and work of Christ was denied. Claims of His deity, His virgin birth, His resurrection "were only figments of disillusioned fishermen." And His teachings were no longer considered relevant.
4. The Ten Commandments were scorned and sin was being reinterpreted as disease.

5. "There is a lack of sin consciousness. Scriptural sin is not 'unsocial conduct' but transgression of divine will."[9]
6. The Sabbath day was no longer considered holy but rather treated as a holiday.[10]
7. Only a few treated Christianity with any seriousness. "At times," Monroe lamented, "we are tempted to ask with Dean Inge, 'is Christianity anything more than the generic name of various religions professed by people with white skin?' "[11]

With the above in mind, Monroe declared:

I am not alone in thinking we are due for a radical change, the end of an era, the beginning of a new epoch. What the future holds for us is highly problematical.... We cannot go back to normality; we must go forward, but to what I cannot answer. Without a doubt economically there must be reorganization, or we shall continue in the throes of class struggle, if there be no supernatural ingression, until revolution is upon us.[12]

As he concluded his essay, Monroe offered up four "possibilities which may soon be upon us:"

1. America may be facing doom—perhaps through internal factors or divine judgment. Those of the "Spenglerian School," Monroe noted, saw civilization waning. He backed up this possibility with a quote from Santayana's *Character and Opinion in the United States*: "Civilization is perhaps approaching one of those long winters that overtake it from time to time.... Romantic Christendom—picturesque, passionate, unhappy episode—may be coming to an end."
2. A dictator would come upon the scene and set all right, cleaning out corruption "and reestablishing on a firm basis our capitalistic order."
3. This may be the darkness before the dawning of a "new and more glorious day, even a supercivilization." However it might not be a capitalist new world order. Paraphrasing Sherwood Eddy's hopes, Monroe wrote, "the ruin and fall of America's capitalistic regime is inevitable before we can begin to build some structure fitted to our new utopian age."
4. Last, there might be some kind of supernatural intervention. A "mighty man of God" may lead America to repentance and "thereby preclude, or at least temporarily check, disaster." Or the Lord Jesus Himself may come back as promised, bringing to an end this present church age.[13]

Monroe did not select any of the four, but left to his readers the right to "prophesy which of these possibilities will materialize before we reach the middle of the twentieth century."[14] It is clear, however, that Monroe was seeking to frame the Great Depression darkness with transcendent meaning, reminding his readers that when we moderns ask of history what it all means, history replies, "ask God." In this regard, Monroe spoke the mind of the historic fundamentalists from the least among them to the greatest.

America's Greatest Depression Problem

However, as good as Monroe's advice was, that is, "ask God," America apparently refused to heed it. And this refusal, according to the historic fundamentalists' endless jeremiads, was the ultimate reason for America's failures and miseries in the 1930s.

The nation had turned from God and the Bible and as a result was now sinking into chaos, revolution and class hatred.[15] Rollin Chafer, editor of *Bibliotheca Sacra*, observing America's growing Depression lawlessness, gloomily noted:

> With the marked decline in the church at large during the last generation, of faith in Christ as Savior and the Scripture as the infallible Word of God, indifference to moral and ethical truth has resulted.... Until America experiences a revival of true Christian faith which will shake the very foundations of our social life, permanent improvement in the crime situation will remain an evanescent dream.[16]

And lawlessness had meaning beyond any individual's criminal behavior. It also had social and political dimensions. For instance, the historic fundamentalists were appalled by the New Deal's wanton destruction of food and animal surpluses in an effort to restore a profitable agriculture market. *The King's Business*, sounding like John the Baptist, roared: "It is insanely inhuman to destroy—on the plea of overproduction—that which would sustain starving multitudes. Yet in our own land in spite of the fact that thousands are suffering the pangs of hunger, a wholesale destruction of foodstuffs is ordered."[17]

This was not God's wisdom but man's foolishness. The question was raised and answered as to whether the drought and dust storms that plagued mid-America in the mid-thirties were not God's reply. The editor of *The Sunday School Times* had no doubts: "Surely," he wrote, "God is judging our nation."[18] (And who knows, perhaps God was.) The editor of the *Jewish Missionary Magazine* called the New Deal's action an "injustice to the poor" as well as "an insult to the Almighty who gave the crops for the benefit of man." "Can he do ought else," he queried, "than reveal his retributive justice?"[19]

The Rev. Reginald Shipley subsumed all of the country's ills under one heading. Writing in *Moody Monthly*, he declared: "God is America's one and only problem. That problem is foundational. All others are relative to it. And when that problem is rightly solved, all questions are answered, the crisis overcome."[20] Five years earlier, the editor of *The King's Business* had sounded a similar theme: "What is the trouble with our nation and the world? We have turned away from God. All our national problems and our local problems are but the inevitable results of our departure from the government of the living God."[21] Repentance then, was desperately needed. The nation must choose between Christ or an ever-increasing disintegration. "We need to get back to God, or we will perish," warned the magazine. Nothing else would heal America or restore its prosperity.[22]

J. Gresham Machen, teacher and mentor to some, but listened to and revered by practically all the historic fundamentalists, was of the same mind. Writing in 1935, he made it clear he believed:

> The relation to God is the all-important thing. It is not a mere means to an end. . . . It is impossible to deal successfully even with these political and social problems until we have come to be right with God. No emergency can possibly be so pressing as to permit us to postpone attention to unseen things.[23]

However, in 1938 when the Rev. Shipley wrote, the Great Depression, which had appeared to be on the wane, had reasserted itself with frightening familiarity. Therefore, he could speak with added weight when he concluded:

> The Depression through which we have passed may have had as its aim our restoration to divine favor and blessing, but because we did not heed its tokens, another is upon us, and others will continue to come, until we face God in national humility and repentance.[24]

This was something the historic fundamentalists deeply longed for America to do—humble itself before God. Both President Hoover and Roosevelt had been asked to call a national day of prayer and both had refused.[25] Congress, too, had been petitioned but "some Congressional leaders have seemed to feel that the Democratic Party can do for America all that is needed," and that it would be disloyal to both the party and the administration "to admit that we need God's help in this crisis." How much more must God judge us, gloomily mused the editor of *The Sunday School Times*, before "the nation turns away from itself, from its political parties, from any human government" and in a national day of prayer ask God to be merciful?[26]

In 1937, because the nation's political leaders would not, the historic fundamentalists called their own National Day of Prayer. Believers were asked to pray that God would spiritually revive America because corruption in government, communism, personal sin, lawlessness, and apostasy in the church all threatened the nation with God's judgment.[27] Throughout the Great Depression their message remained what it had been from the beginning: "If the American Republic is to stand, if the unbearable conditions, which now exist, are to be remedied, there must be a return to God. The Bible must be restored in the belief of men. God not gold must loom large in the thoughts of our citizens."[28]

The great national revival never came; therefore the historic fundamentalists never ceased calling the people of America to repentance. They were God's messengers protesting against national unrighteousness as had the Old Testament prophets, the true church calling an apostate people and a prodigal nation back to its only hope, Jesus Christ. If this were to happen, the economic and political ills that had beset the nation's body politic would find a solution. So pervasive is this theme in the journals of the historic fundamentalists that one finds it difficult to give much credence to the charge that they rejected the prophetic aspect of ministry; that is, calling the American people collectively to repentance.

The Spiritual Church

Bernbaum and Herbert claimed in their essay, "Beyond Self-Interest: Politics, Justice, and Evangelical Faith," that:

> Evangelicals share a common theological heritage and a commitment to the basic doctrines of historic orthodox Protestantism. The belief that Christ transforms culture, as well as saves souls, provides the common ground for evangelicals despite their different emphases on the question of *how* the Christian faith affects political life and a Christian's participation in it.[29]

Many historic fundamentalists would not have found the above comment alien. They readily believed Christianity could not help having an impact on the culture, even if only through converting one person at a time. The apparent difference between the historic fundamentalists and their critics is that the historic fundamentalists usually differentiated between the purpose or duty of the church (understood as a local congregation, agency, denomination, or pastor or pastors association) and those of the individual Christian citizen. In other words, they adhered to an ecclesiology which Mark Noll has classified as "A doctrine of 'the spirituality of the church' which held that bodies of believers in their corporate life should eschew political involvement...." Surprisingly (and perhaps somewhat inexplicably), Noll attributes this doctrine to the "Southern" churches which, through their racial and economic policies, corrupted it "into an escape from social responsibility."[30]

However, it is obvious this was not just a "Southern" church doctrine but one that was widespread among evangelicals as a whole, and particularly among the historic fundamentalists. Fundamentalism's adherence to this standard is clearly seen in a brief editorial penned by the aged James Gray in 1935. Gray was moved to write his comments because a Methodist Episcopal bishop had publicly claimed "that the Church as such has as much right to discuss political questions as any individual." Gray conceded that this may be legally true, but not morally or spiritually true (except when the political question dealt with the church's spiritual calling.)[31]

Gray's main objection was that when the church becomes involved in politics, "its tendency is to go further and, as a contemporary says, attempt to press its will on the government." And, he noted, there was no shortage of pastors "using their church organizations to bring about revolutionary changes in our political and economic order, and in effect, to establish Socialism in the United States."[32] Then there was Father Coughlin, who seemed to have a considerable following among Protestants. Gray had no objection to such people expressing their views as individual citizens, but when they did so in an official capacity, "it was another matter." It caused many to turn away from the church.[33]

Even more serious in Gray's view was that the clergy who became entangled in political affairs were exchanging the Word of God for that "which is not bread" and cannot, then, truly help mankind. "They are transferring their vocation from that of ambassadors of Christ to something far beneath it in scale of values for both time and eternity."[34] As he concluded, Gray pointed out that the church's desire to impose its will on the government invites the government to respond in kind. Neither position is beneficial to the state or the church. It should be remembered that Gray's remarks were made against the backdrop of what was happening in Europe and the heated rhetoric that was ricocheting from one side of America to the other. Nevertheless, Gray was protesting a trend that always has a deadly impact on the spiritual life of the church—the politicizing of the Body of Christ under the leadership of political pastors.

Gray's friend, J. Gresham Machen, was of a like mind. In a radio address given in 1935, Machen queried the ministers in his audience with these words:

> What do you ministers do—if any of you are attending to me now—when you enter into your pulpits on Sunday mornings? Do you tell the people about your religious experiences; . . . do you express to them your views on the great questions of the day...? If these things are what you do, you may have rich rewards, but there is one thing you will miss. You may be great orators, but never will you be ministers of Jesus Christ.[35]

Then, with an eloquence of his own, Machen concluded with these words:

> Oh may God send us ministers of another kind! . . . who are servants of Christ and not servants of men...who as they stand behind the open Bible and expound its blessed words, can truly and honestly say, with Micaiah the son of Imlah, "As the Lord liveth, what the Lord saith unto me, that will I speak."[36]

The main body of historic fundamentalists would have been in agreement with Gray and Machen's reasoning. Interestingly, the sociologists Robert Lynd and Helen Merrell found this position a source of irritation in their follow-up volume on the impact of the Great Depression upon "Middletown." They were critical of the "Middletown" churches' unwillingness to take the [political] lead in a time of "flux" just so they could continue to teach "theological verbal stereotypes inherited from an era in the remote past." Stereotypes, the authors believed, that were "increasingly unreal to Middletown...." The churches continued to barter away (they condescendingly moaned) leadership opportunities in the area of change for the right to be shadow leaders in the "changeless."[37] Although Lynd and Merrell had little respect for evangelical Christianity, they do inadvertently confirm that the "fundamentalist" churches of Middletown stood shoulder to shoulder with Gray and Machen on the spirituality of the church and pulpit.

Considering the importance of this doctrine to the historic fundamentalists, it is surprising how little weight their critics give to it when commenting on their political responses. The focus is almost exclusively on their eschatology. Both Noll and Carpenter tie the historical fundamentalists' lack of political activity to their eschatology.[38] In other words, prophetic speculations and expectations shaped their passive political posture. But this is a flawed analysis. Because they held to the "spiritual church," they simply did not view the church's purpose as that of the primary agent of political change or control, or an agent to make social or political institutions "Christian." Their eschatology might make them skeptical of political solutions promising to alleviate permanently social or political problems (although so would their view of man's nature), or allow them to see analogues to the coming anti-Christ, but this did not make them apolitical. However, the church as such had a spiritual, not a political, task to attend to.[39]

First Things First

The church's main calling, then, was not political activism or political anything, but to teach the inerrant Word and preach the unadulterated gospel; man is ruined in sin and redeemed and restored in Jesus Christ. "For the church the issue is clear," wrote the Rev. I. R. Walls, as the Depression began. "She should not exhaust her powers fighting the battles of democracy at the polls or engaging in crusades in the vain hope of bringing peace." Instead, she should go and preach the gospel and direct the believer in the way of Christian life and service.[40] In other words, the relevance of the church was not in its political position(s) or activism, but in its message—the dynamic of the gospel.

This was becoming something of a formidable task in the 1930s, comparable in some ways to that which faced the early church. The early church went out into a pagan world to share the gospel, an enormous undertaking and seemingly impossible when one studies it. (And by our standards, woefully ill-prepared.) They were ostracized, belittled, scorned, slandered, and now and then slaughtered for their refusal to synthesize or integrate their proclamation of salvation in Jesus' name alone (a monumental offense to the Greek mind), with other religions and philosophies of the day. How intolerant! The hope of the early Christians was, in the words of its archenemy, the pagan Celsus, "the hope of worms." (A view "resurrected" with an indulgent smirk by modernist and humanist intellectuals of the 1930s and 1940s.)

The historic fundamentalists of the 1930s found themselves facing the enormous task of preaching the gospel to a world that appeared in a frenzy to escape it, that detested hearing it (in some places to the point of violence), which seemed in an unseemly rush to "secularize" from the highest levels intellectually to the lowest. Once more Christians were ostracized, belittled, scorned, slandered, and now and then slaughtered for their refusal to synthesize the gospel with the prevailing thought. Small wonder, then, that Wilber Smith was moved to write that "Probably at no time since the beginning of the Christian church could we discover so many powerful forces working together for the creation and deepening of religious skepticism and unbelief as in the last quarter of a century."[41]

Unlike the Protestant modernists, however, the historic fundamentalists did not acquiesce to the "assured results" of questionable scholarly research or "intellectual" intimidation. Certainly it cannot be denied they faced a formidable onslaught from their enemies—from mockery to ridicule to contempt. (But neither can it be denied that it seemed at times as if some of them were more than willing to supply caricatures of themselves which made all fundamentalists look bad and which made their enemies' task a delight.) Nevertheless, they persevered, continuing to preach the everlasting gospel despite being reminded innumerable times that they were not only incorrigible, but also irrelevant. But their critics could not force their silence because "what they outrageously claimed was that they were preaching the *truth*, yesterday, today, and forever."[42] How intolerant! They refused to compromise this eternal message with the philosophical and religious integrationists of the day. Their message was that "You must be born again—not society but you, the individual." As H. A. Ironside wrote in the midst of the Great Depression:

> To take the position, as many who are hailed as "great thinkers" do today, that we are not to be so much concerned about individual salvation as we are to seek social regeneration of the nations, is to be false to our commission, and is a case of sadly misplaced emphasis. Man is made for eternity. . . . It is of all importance to every individual that he be properly oriented to his creator—in other words that he be right with God—then all other necessary things will follow.[43]

In response to a Federal Council of Churches' Depression era supplication (which read in part as follows: "from false notions that by preaching we can save the souls of men, while unemployment breaks their hearts, unbalances their minds, destroys their homes, tempts them beyond measure, visits want and disease upon their children; turns their heart to bitterness, hatred, rebellion, or to hopelessness, despair and death—*Good Lord deliver us*,"), James Gray testily replied:

Did the author of this supplication, or the Federal Council which approved it, mean to imply that preachers of the gospel which saves men are not interested in social welfare? Did they mean to imply that such preachers are not doing all in their power to relieve the present physical distress? Does the Federal Council believe men possess souls as well as bodies? Do they believe that their souls need salvation and if so, do they think it wise for the unemployed who are unsaved to postpone consideration of their eternal interests till they get a job? Do they believe that unsaved men are more likely to harken to the voice of the Holy Spirit in prosperity than adversity? Does either the Bible or the history of evangelism justify this opinion?[44]

Gray was appalled and deeply discouraged by the FCC's message, and concluded his editorial response by despairingly exclaiming, "If the message were the inception and utterance of one man it would be nothing, but the Federal Council of the Churches of Christ in America claims a representation of twenty million! God forbid!"[45]

The historic fundamentalists were convinced, then, with some justification, that if they did not concentrate on the gospel, it would be abandoned by the mainline Protestant denominations altogether. There were ample pundits willing to analyze society, the economy or the culture, but only the church (whether local or universal) could tell the world that God was in Christ reconciling the world to Himself—one on one.

As the Great Depression swiftly merged into World War II, despite the strain of a decade of economic and political turmoil, historic fundamentalists were still of the same mind. The gospel was the only true power that could change the human heart. The church's mission still did not include reforming society or managing history or becoming a special interest bloc. "Her duty was to proclaim a message," wrote John T. Reeve, moderator to the New York Synod of the Presbyterian Church, which would hopefully win people to Christ and then incorporate them into His body. "Let us return to our first love," he wrote, "and make known to mankind that God is love, and that He so loved the world that He gave His only Son for our salvation. Such was the supreme mission of the chuch."[46]

Multitudes of historic fundamentalists agreed. So they went out and preached the gospel on street corners and in parks, at construction sites and WPA projects,[47] in CCC camps,[48] in migrant labor camps,[49] juvenile halls, jails, hospitals,[50] on the wharves and in rescue missions.[51] Bible camps were sponsored that took city children (black and white) into the country for a week or two of recreation and child evangelism.[52] The list could go on and on. No wonder the historic fundamentalists increased in numbers during the Great Depression—they worked at it!

At times such home evangelism was done at great personal sacrifice. *The Sunday School Times* printed the letter of a "home" missionary (name withheld on request) who worked in the mountains of Kentucky. As the Great Depression closed around her, she lost most of her support. Still, she decided to stay where she was and continue her work, which included overseeing two Sunday Schools. Christian friends now and then sent her gifts of money and clothing that she shared with her needy neighbors, encouraging and praying with them. "Today," she wrote, "I have two cents left, some rice and potatoes and half a can of coffee in the cupboard. But I have Him and the joy of preaching the gospel to the poor."[53] Uncommon dedication was a common trait during this period. Nor was her financial situation an uncommon one among Christian workers even in America.

Along with the work of evangelism went the constant plea for believers to pray for a great "God-sent, Holy Spirit" revival that would shake America as had the Great Awakening of 1740 or the Great Prayer Revival of 1857. Oh my, how they longed for those showers of blessings, for the mercy drops round them falling!

Foreign Missions Under Siege

Foreign missions was the other half of this great commission, one the historic fundamentalists were careful not to ignore. In fact, they dare not, for the modernists, who controlled the mainline denominations and their many agencies were seemingly as intent on "defundamentalizing" mission boards and mission fields as they had been regarding America's Protestant churches, schools and seminaries. Nowhere was this better illustrated than in the report published by the Layman's Foreign Missions Inquiry. Released in late 1932, and understood to have been financed by Rockefeller money, it was for all intense and purposes a manifesto to make the mission field the exclusive domain of modernism rather than evangelicalism. Charles Trumbull, editor of *The Sunday School Times*, speaking before a gathering of hundreds of Presbyterian layman concerned over the direction of the Board of Foreign Missions, angrily noted:

> The Appraisal Commission declared...that all religions are ways to God, and Christianity must recognize that it stands on common ground "with the non-Christian faiths of Asia." The heathen are not lost, and no one needs to be "saved" in the Bible meaning of this word: there is no need of any such Savior as Christ claimed to be, and Christian missionaries should be ashamed to conduct Christian schools or hospitals in heathen lands as a means of winning people to Christ.[54] It is a mistake to be concerned about a future life, and the early missionaries were mistaken in supposing that souls would be lost unless the Gospel was carried to them. Buddha, Jesus, Mohammed were all individual founders of missionary religions and had in common the experience of leaving "behind them an impulse which had moved on steadily."[55]

If these "shocking falsehoods" were not enough, the report, in an utterance that "eerily" anticipated the coming "beast" of political correctness, wondered "What has the West done that it should be the teachers of mankind?"[56] The report also suggested that the mission field be restricted to modernist missionaries.

Righteous anger and shock only hint at the response of the historic fundamentalists. Obviously, it was vigorously denounced in their circles as a betrayal of the Great Commission. The Interdenominational Foreign Missions of North America (a consortium of sixteen "faith" missions), acidly commented in a formal response that "to call their scheme un-Christian is to put it mildly. It is positively anti-Christian—a bold and shameful betrayal of Christ by his professed friends."[57]

The venerable Thomas Chalmers, editor of the *Jewish Missionary Magazine*, and Director of the New York Jewish Evangelization Society, prophetically anticipated the ultimate results of the Report's recommendations:

> Put the Lord Jesus Christ on a level with the founders of heathen systems, cast out of God's Word its supernatural elements, teach the heathen and Moslems a spurious culture based on human worthiness and genius, and the results will be the dechristianizing of America, the establishment in due time of heathen systems of worship for the degraded masses and a philosophical syncretism for the educated, the Old Gnosticism of the second Christian century ruling the thoughts and demoralizing the lives of men everywhere. Are The Christian forces of America ready for such a betrayal of Christ?[58]

On April 25, 1933, hundreds of ministers and lay people of various denominations gathered at the Central North Broad Street Presbyterian Church and issued a "remonstrance" against the Layman's Report. Without a doubt it expressed the historic fundamentalists mind-set regarding missions and the negative impact they believed modernism was having. Titled "Declarations of the Philadelphia Mass Meeting," it began by affirming the fundamentals of the faith (eight in this instance) essential to the gospel and then declared it is "our belief that it is the duty of the whole Church of Christ to proclaim the whole Gospel of our Lord Jesus Christ to the whole world, and we heartily approve all missionaries and mission organizations that are holding to uncompromising faithfulness to this duty."[59] Next, the document rejected and repudiated "in its entirety the [Layman's] Report," denouncing its rejection of the Great commission, its rejection of the uniqueness of Christ and condemning its universalism. In effect, the commission had "dishonored and betrayed the name of Christ and had forfeited all right to be heard on any subject related to the Christian missionary enterprise, not only in the field of doctrine, but also in that of method and administration."[60] This second section closed with thanksgiving to God for the thousands of faithful missionaries "laboring in the white fields" and which had been "sent out by practically all of the missionary boards and societies now at work which bear the name of Christ."[61]

In the third part of the remonstrance, those affirming it expressed "deep regret" that many denominational mission boards were sending out modernist missionaries.

They urged these boards, then, "in all earnestness and Christian love," to cease sending such missionaries to the field and recall those who had been sent.[62] "And we further appeal," they wrote, "to the General Conferences, General Assemblies, and other official and legislative organizations of our denominations to take such action for instructing their missionary boards as may be needed to bring this to pass."[63]

In conclusion, the remonstrants "lovingly" reminded their "denominational boards" that the Layman's Report was the "logical and inevitable fruitage" of the modernist doctrines that various boards had been toying with in recent years. They acknowledged that "most of our boards" had "protested against or severely criticized some of the findings of the Commission."[64] However, now more was needed if modernism was to be expunged. "We believe," they concluded, "that a complete and clean break with Modernism's message and methods is demanded on the part of all missionary organizations that really declare to a lost world that 'there is none other name under heaven given among men, whereby we must be saved.' "[65]

In one sense, the "Declarations" were "a day late and a dollar short," as modernism continued to make inroads into denominational mission agencies with disastrous results for the proclamation of the gospel. The Report did act, however, as a spur to redouble both the sending of faithful missionaries and efforts to either clean up existing denomination mission boards, or if that failed (and usually it did), establish their own. It is noteworthy that while mainline denominations under the influence of modernism reduced their missionary forces, the historic fundamentalists increased not only the number of missionaries but also the number of sending agencies.[66]

It is difficult not to sympathize with the historic fundamentalists in their battle with the modernists no matter how poorly they may have handled themselves at times. Not only were modernists reinterpreting biblical, historical Protestant Christianity but they were also sending missionaries to the field who were at heart ecumenical humanists.[67] Like the adulteress in Proverbs 30:20, who "eats and wipes her mouth and says, 'I've done nothing wrong,' " so it was with the modernists. In retrospect, as one studies the mission's conflict of the 1930s and 1940s, one cannot help but be disturbed by the moral rationalizations and lack of intellectual integrity that so marked the modernists' words and thoughts. With the smug arrogance that has so often identified the intellectual of the twentieth century, the modernists were sure they could bring mankind into the Kingdom on the wave of humanist intellectualism, (western liberal) optimism and good intentions. (Evidently the West had something to teach the rest of the world after all.)[68] It was an optimism and good intentions that was unable or unwilling to acknowledge the necessity of the Cross.

Going Into All the World

Impressive is the only word to describe the incredible amount of mission activity supported by the historic fundamentalists and reported in their magazines during the worst depression in American history. No sector of the globe seemed beyond their interest or desire to evangelize if it could be reached. Historian Michael S. Hamilton has written:

> Fundamentalism's passion for global evangelization during the isolationist 1930s is especially noteworthy, and it makes one wonder if fundamentalism was not, in its own particular way, one of the most internationalist segments in all of American society at that time.[69]

"Especially noteworthy" may be something of an understatement. The historic fundamentalists had a story to tell to the nations, and tell it they did during tumultuous times and under unimaginable circumstances. From the isolated, illiterate hollows of the Appalachian mountains to the unspeakable, SS established, Jewish ghettos of Poland, from the undisturbed jungled highlands of Borneo where untouched tribes dwelt to the starving fields of the Ukraine being "harvested" by Stalin's macabre bands, the gospel of Jesus Christ was being preached as twentieth century humanity (seemingly insatiable in its lust for death and blood), tortured and maimed and slaughtered its way through its own [more] deadly version of the Thirty Years War. And the historic fundamentalists, either directly or indirectly, played a part in this worldwide gospel drama.

In China, perhaps the mission field par excellence for the historic fundamentalists, along with famine and petty warlords, communist bands pillaged and burned churches and missionary compounds, killed Chinese Christians (or turned them into pack "animals" for their armies), and often kidnapped or even killed foreign missionaries.[70] When the Japanese invaded China, the process was repeated. Chinese pastors were used for bayonet practice and young Chinese Christian women were dragged out of churches and raped. Mission compounds were frequently and deliberately bombed and missionaries forced to flee or if caught were expelled or interned for the duration of the war, or even killed. Others stayed as long as they could and ministered as long as possible.[71] The Hunan Bible Institute is an example of this. Located in the city of Changsha, it was originally established to train Chinese pastors and evangelistic teams that went into the outlying regions to preach the gospel. However, the war finally forced it to close the school in October 1938. Rather than flee, though, the missionaries and staff converted the compound into a refugee center and hospital. Ultimately, however, the constant bombing, and the fact that the compound was actually occupied for a short time by the Japanese, reduced it to little more than rubble.[72]

The USSR's communist savagery toward Christians has already been noted.

Evangelical pastors, if they did not flee the country, were either deprived of food ration cards (so they and their families could starve), or they were sent to the gulags. Some were killed on the spot while others were arrested by the GPU and never seen or heard from again. As one Russian evangelical plaintively wrote, "the few Christians left are being destroyed."[73] And the situation was no better in fascist dominated countries. As Franco's fascist army subdued Spain, evangelical missionaries were expelled. Spanish pastors were jailed, some tortured, some slain, churches burned and congregations harassed, Bibles confiscated and destroyed—all with the approval of Pope Pius XII who had nothing but praise for Franco's "conquests."[74] When Italy (despite the incompetency of its "legions") finally conquered Ethiopia, Protestant missionaries were forcibly rounded up and expelled, and the Roman Catholic Church brought in. This pattern was repeated in Libya and Albania.[75]

It seems almost unnecessary to speak of the ruthlessness of Nazi Germany it is so well known. The historic fundamentalists closely and sympathetically followed the struggle of the German Confessing Church as Hitler slowly squeezed it to death or into submission with hundreds of pastors ending up in concentration camps, or drafted and sent to the Russian front if they would not bend. And wherever the Nazi's went, both home and foreign missions to the Jews of Europe, which were extremely effective, were strangled. Once Germany declared war on the United States, European missionary organizations such the American European Fellowship, the European Christian Mission and the Belgium Gospel Mission went into more or less suspended animation as their American and/or English missionaries fled and indigenous workers that were not arrested went into hiding. Those Protestant evangelical churches that were allowed to function were under constant Gestapo scrutiny. Their pastors lived precariously, often being jailed or taken away to forced labor, or if they were considered especially suspect, taken away to a concentration camp—a sure death sentence.[76] The Norwegian Lutheran church's "heroic" struggle against the Quisling government and Nazi occupiers also attracted the attention, admiration, and support of the historic fundamentalists.[77]

As Europe prepared to bathe itself in the blood of its young men once again, "to mow down another crop," the editor of *the King's Business* raised the possibility that the question would soon be asked if missions are not more urgently needed in Europe than in Africa, especially in light of the fact that "Europe is a nationalistic madhouse." One only had to look closely at the situation, the editor observed, to note:

> The present aggressor nations are those where Christianity is either completely repudiated or where it is only a cloak of national respectability. Germany's militarism was born out of the neo-paganism and the new Germanic religion which related her to the gods of force and hate.[78]

Of course, this brief survey barely stirs the water. The extensive coverage of missions' repression in the historic fundamentalists' journals worked to make vivid, acute, and personal the international political turmoil that was rapidly enveloping the world, as well as how difficult and even dangerous missionary service had become in the third and fourth decades of the twentieth century. Yet still they went, leaving their families and the "easy life" to love strangers, their numbers ever increasing even during the scarcity and poverty of the 1930s. And those who could not go supported those that could, and when pleas for aid came to their ears they responded with an amazing generosity despite the rigors imposed by their own personal "Great Depression." In war zones (or potential war zones), mission centers became refugee havens where food, medical care, shelter, clothing, and even visas (along with the gospel) were provided for the persecuted and dispossessed fleeing the unreasoning hatred of humanist ideologies. Just who were these fundamentalist "obscurantists" who cared so deeply? Just what was so important about hundreds of millions of human beings whom lived and died in obscurity and poverty and ignorance that they should be sought out by these "anachronites?" Certainly it is worth noting that while the leaders of communism and fascism, in the name of the "New World Order," considered multiple millions unworthy of life and saw to it they were deprived of it, the historic fundamentalists (and those of a like mind around the world) considered these millions as made in the image of God and worthy of hearing God's message of repentance and life. They were even willing to give their own lives that these "expendables" might hear this good news of eternal life. Just what, then, was so subversive about their message that communists and fascists and even American intellectuals feared it and wanted to discredit it, and some even to destroy it or undermine its credibility, and some even to silence permanently those who preached it?

As I have studied the worldwide missionary activities of the historic fundamentalists I admit to being deeply impressed and deeply moved. Why, I wondered, do I never read of *this* in the critical histories of the historic fundamentalists? They were (and are) unsung heroes of the faith when The Faith was under deadly and brutal attack by those who had little use for the message of the cross. Some were killed, some were beaten or placed in wretched concentration camps for years (or suffered both). Others were expelled or forced to flee with little more than the clothes on their backs. Left behind was their life's work shattered and scattered. Left behind were their brothers and sisters in Christ, dear friends who they knew would pay dearly for having identified with them and the Lord Jesus. Theirs is a story (as it is of those believers in the nations where they served) of patient endurance, and suffering, and for some the martyr's death. That we have forgotten them, or never knew of them, that they have been excluded from the history of historic fundamentalism is both a tragedy and a disgrace. They numbered in the thousands, ministering the love and compassion of their Savior to humanity being made monstrous by war and hate. (It was Joseph Alliene, I believe, who wrote in his, *An Alarm to Unconverted Sinners*, that God had made man but little lower than the angels, but that sin had made him little better than the demons. This period of history make his comment seem almost too kind.)

In summary, they offered a word of hope and a cup of cold water in places where hope and kindness had been banished by mind-breaking fear and unrelenting brutality. They of all people deserve a history in the annals of American evangelicalism. To our shame, we have been so busy cataloguing their faults— see how petty and imperfect the historic fundamentalists were, see how many are their sins, see how they have embarrassed us—that we have failed to acknowledge that many of them possessed (mingled with their all too obvious sins), a self-effacing nobility of character and purpose, and a devotion to Christ that humbles those who read their stories.

A Tale of Two Missionaries

Regretfully, the story of all of them cannot be told at this time. But there is time (or room) for two who shall stand in for the rest. One, Trodis Christofferson, a native of Denmark and a 1929 graduate of Biola, went to Poland in 1933 under the auspices of the American European Fellowship there to minister to the Jewish children (and Jewish Christian children) of Warsaw. In 1937, she wrote an article for *The King's Business* detailing the terrible economic and social persecution the Jews of Warsaw were subjected to, as well as their intense poverty. She noted that only a few Protestant missionaries showed any love and concern for them. Miss Christofferson operated a summer camp where Jewish children could escape the ghetto for a week or two in the Polish countryside, and where the gospel would be shared with them. For some of the children, it was the first time in their short lives they had ever been out of the ghetto or had ever received a decent meal, let alone three, in a day. In the spring of 1938, with anti-Semitism increasing, the Polish government refused to renew her visa. With a heavy heart she took leave of the children she had served and loved so unselfishly. She was never allowed into Poland again to visit them except for a brief two-week period the following spring. (The "goodby's" are poignant beyond the telling.) In September of 1939, western and central Poland was overrun by Hitler's blitzkrieg. With Poland's defeat, all foreign missionaries were forced to leave. As for the Jewish children so much a part of Miss Christofferson's heart, she was to never see them again. They were slaughtered—every one of them—by the Nazis.[79]

After being forced out of Poland she went to Paris, and began ministering to the Jewish and non-Jewish refugees from Nazi Germany. When the Nazis defeated France she fled south and continued her ministry in Nice under the Vichy government. When the Nazis took over Vichy France, and she was threatened by the Gestapo with imprisonment if she continued to minister to the Jews, she went into hiding with some of her Jewish and Christian friends until southern France was liberated. Despite the fact that she emerged from the war with her health broken, she took up where she had left off and continued to minister the gospel to both Jew and Gentile. She also provided on the spot relief of clothing, food, medical supplies, and money sent to her from the New York office of the American European Fellowship. Miss Christofferson was, by any measure, a Christian missionary of immense courage, endurance, and compassion.[80]

Dr. Robert W. Hockman did not fare as well. Born to missionary parents stationed in western China, a region that experienced a great deal of war, he determined early in life to become a medical missionary and never wavered in this resolve. He achieved his medical degree with high honors and in 1933 went to Ethiopia as a medical missionary under the United Presbyterian banner. Shortly after arriving he was put in charge of the American Hospital at Addis Ababa. As the article noted, "no operation was begun without a little prayer meeting in the operating room, and no patient got out of the hospital without having heard again and again the story of [Christ's] redeeming love." As the war with Italy approached, Dr. Hockman trained an Ethiopian Red Cross team and assembled equipment for a front line Red Cross field hospital.

When the war did come, Dr Hockman and his Red Cross crew moved as close as possible to the front lines located in Ogaden province. Red Cross units on the Ethiopian side of the war zone were evidently singled out by the Italians, for their planes bombed them frequently. An American Red Cross hospital camp at Dessye received extensive damage. In the south, a Swedish Red Cross camp at Dolo "was all but exterminated, nearly eighty Swedes or natives being wounded or killed...." The Daggah Bur camp, where Dr. Hockman and his crew worked, was bombed again and again "until everything was wiped out." Still the tent hospital persevered in its task. Operating in heat that registered as high as 125 degrees, Dr Hockman worked thirty-six hour shifts. Because newspaper reporters were forbidden from the Ethiopian front, portions of his letters and photographs sent home made their way into the press. Unbeknown to him, he became somewhat of a hero to the American public. And he did more than operate on wounded soldiers. For safety reasons, he also dug up unexploded Italian bombs. He did it once too often.[81]

News of his death in December 1935 was reported in the "Missionary Department" section of the February 1936 *Moody Institute Monthly*. The editor responsible for that section of the magazine was William H. Hockman, Dr. Hockman's dad. The article paid tribute to Dr. Hockman with these words:

> The meager outfit at Daggah Bur contained not only Red Cross supplies, but a goodly stock of Gospels and scriptural tracts as well. In his letters home, the missionary doctor spoke not so much of his surgical feats—though many of them were brilliant—

but of holding the hands of the suffering and dying, and trying to tell them of a Savior's redeeming love. In the midst of this extraordinary setting, Robert Hockman had not the slightest thought of doing anything unusual or dramatic. He did not know that the newspapers of the world were displaying his picture or printing headlines about the "Red Cross Hero of Ethiopia," but with utter simplicity and abandonment of self-forgetfulness was doing just what the love of Christ constrains every true missionary to do.[82]

The roll of the missionaries names from this period is long and often written in their blood.[83] As I worked my way through the missionary writings of the historic fundamentalists from this era of fanatical ideologies, which measured their success in the copious flowing of innocent blood, a very personal and human face of the historic fundamentalists emerges that the emphasis on "cultural forces" can never capture, or even make us aware that such people ever existed. The world might not want to listen and believe the true and eternal gospel, but historic fundamentalists believed without reservation that if it did not, sheer hell would result. They were right—it did. From their perspective, a great, unseen war was being fought in the 1930s, a no-holds barred spiritual war. It spilled with bloody, fleshy savagery into the material world of the everyday. As far as the historic fundamentalists were concerned, then, there could be no abrogation of the Great Commission. It alone could offer hope in a world engaged in a full-dress rehearsal of Armageddon.

The Historic Fundamentalists and the True Social Gospel

Still, despite what one reads, preaching the gospel was not the end of the matter. While the historic fundamentalists opposed the FCC's Social Gospel with good reason, it needs to be made clear that they knew and taught that the gospel had a social dimension. Most of them would have agreed with John T. Reeve's comment:

Inherent in the gospel from the very beginning, have been every consideration of pity and brotherly love, every thought of sympathy and kindness, every desire to help the helpless and relieve the suffering, that the world has ever known or will know. Without these, *the gospel is not.*[84]

The necessity of the new birth was accompanied by a recognition of the necessity to give shelter to the homeless, feed the hungry, cloth the naked, comfort the sick, and visit the prisoner.

Moody Institute Monthly, for example, issued successive appeals to its readers to aid in relief of human suffering. During the bleakest days of the Great Depression, it called upon believers not to allow the work of community social agencies to be impaired. The Federal Government was doing all it could, "but that is not nearly enough." All must pitch in, all had a duty to do what they could. "On the shoulder of each citizen," the editor pointed out, "therefore, rests a responsibility that the essential services in his community shall be kept intact, especially the services of our hospitals, nursing groups, child care and family agencies."[85] As the majority of *Moody's* readers were historic fundamentalists, it was, then, a call for this community to help rescue the broader community's infrastructure of compassionate services. Evidently the editor did not think that its readers were so withdrawn into personal piety or indifferent or alienated from the general commonweal that they could not respond. The following year, 1934, the magazine again appealed to individual charity to pick up a share of providing relief "or the suffering will be catastrophic. May God Himself put this on our hearts."[86] Nor did the magazine restrict its appeals only to America's needs. Starving children in Puerto Rico, famine in war-stricken China, the persecuted church in Germany, among others—all moved *Moody* to ask its readers to share generously with those who were suffering.[87]

Just how extensive the social activities of the historic fundamentalists were is difficult to determine. Unlike the Federal Council of Churches, they did not issue white papers or hold conferences that issued proclamations on what others needed to do—they just did what they believed they were called to do. Now, obviously there were those who called themselves fundamentalists who did not live up to their calling in Christ in this regard—who were selfish and narrow, and withheld their mercy and kindness. But myriads did respond in true Christian compassion and their story, then, is well worth the telling. One thing is certain, the works of those who were true to their faith was extensive, beginning at the most basic of levels, the family. An excellent example of this was the parents of Ernest W. Leferver, founder and senior fellow of the Ethics and Public Policy Center. He wrote about his parents' actions during the Great Depression in the *American Enterprise*. Today, he notes, they would be classified as evangelicals. His father was a foreman in a machine shop, "the Bible reading foreman" as he was called. His mother, an ex-school teacher, loved Dickens and Shakespeare, and read to her children stories from McGuffey's reader "that unashamedly proclaimed Christian virtues." Three books were constantly referred to in the Leferver's household: a Sears Catalogue, the dictionary, and the Bible. Both his parents taught Sunday School.[88]

When the Great Depression came, Leferver's father had to work at half-pay for a couple of years. Twenty dollars a week had to provide for seven people. But "we never thought of ourselves as poor," Leferver notes. And despite the shortage of money his parents tithed because "the first ten percent 'belonged to God.' " His father was in charge of the church's poor fund out of which families in need were given twenty dollars a month. "Beyond his substantial giving to the church, Dad wrote checks for lepers in Nigeria and the Near East Foundation to help the 'starving Armenians.' " The family also skipped "an occasional meal to contribute to the nonpartisan 'Spanish War Relief.' " In addition, his mother canned peaches for the poor and "fed vagrants on our back porch…and for two summers we took in a 'fresh air boy' from Brooklyn." Leferver's parents believed helping those in need "was primarily the duty of the family and the church, not the federal government…despite FDR's New Deal."[89] One suspects Leferver's Bible believing parents would have been called fundamentalists in the 1930s. Nor was their way of life that of an isolated, oddly compassionate, humble family among indifferent millions "fleeing from the problems of the wider world." There's was a Christian compassion performed by historic fundamentalists thousands upon thousands of times across America.

As Leferver mentioned, his father's church established a poor fund to help the unemployed buy food. Other churches did the same. The Church of the Open Door in Los Angeles (then home of Biola), established a Commissary Department in 1932 to provide food for the unemployed and needy families—especially families with children.[90] Felton Williams, who became pastor of the Wesley Memorial Church in Atlanta, Georgia in 1931, opened a mission where the gospel was preached every night. Shortly thereafter an unemployment bureau was established along with a church kitchen where 250 "undernourished women and children" were fed daily. Next, the pastor sought to establish a dormitory for men and the city responded by supplying a building along with cots, blankets and furniture. The dormitory provided sleeping quarters for 126 unemployed men on a nightly basis. "The gas company…contributed gas, the Coal Dealers Association coal, and the Atlanta Laundry Association" provided clean linen and towels.[91]

A former missionary, Miss Turker, "opened an emergency home for homeless women and children." The owner of the house where the shelter was housed gave "use of the building for taxes and the city pay[ed] the taxes." Food, clothing, money, shoes and other necessities were donated in abundance.[92] And so it went in historic fundamentalists' and other evangelical churches across America.

Nor did it stop there. We know from what was written about and advertised in their journals that a wide variety of ministries were freely supported: jail ministries (which reached both the prisoner on the inside and his or her family on the outside), medical missions and clinics, visiting nurse programs, hospitals, vocational schools, Bible institutes and colleges, leper colonies, orphanages, homes for delinquent boys and girls, rest homes for the infirm, and as mentioned, refugee centers for the victims of war or persecution—all these and more found historic fundamentalists involved.[93] Even such evangelistic endeavors as Children's Bible Clubs and rescue missions included a deliberate social dimension. Free summer camps sponsored by Bible Clubs were intended not only to offer Christ to the slum child but also to remove him or her from a slum environment for a week or two of exploring and playing in the country.[94] Likewise, rescue missions found themselves ministering in a new way to "children and families and men out of work," as well as transients who were not alcoholics, by providing food, clothing, medical aid, and shelter, while acting as an employment agency.[95]

Interestingly, one of the best reports on just how essential the rescue missions were during the Great Depression comes not from the journals of the historic fundamentalists, but rather from the authors of *Middletown in Transition*.[96] Though they did not look favorably upon evangelicalism,[97] and were puzzled and frustrated by the way the "meagerly educated" workers clung to their religion,[98] nevertheless the authors of this sociological study were admittedly impressed by the work of the local rescue mission. They found themselves constrained to write that "this mission's relief was conducted throughout the depression with the extreme devotion to the poor that characterize such organizations at their best."[99]

The mission was organized in late 1930 by an ex-bartender and his wife. (Both had been saved at a Billy Sunday crusade.) By the end of the first year, it was serving four to five thousand meals a month plus providing clothing, sleeping quarters and other assistance to transients.[100] Devoted to the principle of "teaching practical religion with relief work," the mission was supported by pennies, dimes and anonymous contributions and "did spectacular relief work all through the depression." Besides housing and feeding transients, it also "begged clothing, shoes and bedding for the poor and night after night shouted the old-time religion at them."[101] When the local Federal Transient Camp closed its gates to newcomers in 1935, the mission became the only agency in town willing to help the overflow. Nightly the police sent an additional 150 to 225 transients to the mission to be fed and housed.[102] By the end of 1935, the mission had served 228,735 meals to the hungry, distributed 135,250 free gallons of milk to poor families, "and furnished clothing, stoves, and spiritual advice to thousands."[103] Multiply this type of rescue mission by the approximately 500 hundred situated in the cities and towns across America, and one cannot help being impressed by the magnitude of social assistance flowing from these most "fundamentalist" of organizations. And we have not included in the above, the work of the Salvation Army, an organization (along with the rescue mission) that Donald Barnhouse believed exemplified the only true form of Christian social work.[104]

It should be noted that the various social works of the historic fundamentalists were largely carried on by freewill offerings and the voluntary service of thousands of individual believers and congregations. It is an incredibly impressive testimony![105] In truth, one of the most encouraging traits of the historic fundamentalists during the Great Depression is the extent of their concern and the service that flowed from it. Along with millions of others, many of the historic fundamentalists found it difficult to support themselves and their families. Nevertheless, despite these difficulties, they helped the needy through countless acts of personal and corporate compassion while continuing to support their churches, Bible institutes and colleges, evangelists, mission agencies (both at home and abroad), rescue missions, colportage associations, and a host of other ministries. The New Testament may say little about a Christian's involvement in politics, but it says a great deal about meeting the needs of the poor and suffering. Multitudes of historic fundamentalists tried to be faithful to the latter.[106]

In Conclusion, A Comparison

It would not be saying too much to note that while the "Social Gospelers" and other political savants sought to find the "political" solution to the social and economic ills besetting America, the historic fundamentalists, in the name of Christ, sought to minister to the individual victims of society's ills and war's horrors—the jobless, the poor, the dispossessed, the persecuted, the neglected and rejected, the drunk, the prostitute, and the criminal, whether overseas, in the slums, in the prisons, or among the isolated mountain folk of Appalachia—with the good news of salvation in Jesus Christ and immediate acts of social compassion.

The historic fundamentalists could point to thousands, even tens of thousands, who had been "washed in the blood of the Lamb" and because of that experience had had their lives transformed permanently, and on a horizontal level became (to use that awful cliché), useful, productive citizens. On the other hand—neither in communist lands, nor in fascist/Nazi domains, nor even in New Deal America—can anyone point to one social or political structure or institution that was "Christianized," redeemed or regenerated for Christ during the same period despite millions of words spoken and printed, conferences called and attended, and ideologies embraced and ruthlessly practiced—and wars, oh so many wars, fought and concluded—but not one of them the war to end all wars.

The social activities described above are hardly the actions of a people that have turned their backs on the needy or forgotten that service to mankind accompanied the preaching of the gospel. The evidence gives the lie to such charges. Why, then, do evangelical historians continue to repeat them? Perhaps some have been lax or indifferent in historical research. As Michael S. Hamilton kindly suggests, "Because we historians have so much to read, perhaps we do not read as closely as we might."[107] Or perhaps, because we have mostly been taught by secularists in advance degree programs, we have inadvertently absorbed their prejudices. This seems to be the point of Robert Lundin's confession when he wrote:

> We [Christian scholars] were trained several decades ago by scholars who had, for the most part, dispensed with the Christian faith. We have embraced their theories and methods and have made them Christian by reading them into the Bible and the traditions of the faith.... The heresy of the day before yesterday becomes the orthodoxy of today.[108]

Or it could be that the compassionate works of the fundamentalists of the 1930s now seem archaic—no longer measuring up to the socially and politically sophisticated and ambitious demands of present day political evangelicals. Whatever the reason, we have been "taught" to see the historical fundamentalists in negative hues, and any hue to the contrary simply does not seem to register. Without painting over their faults, it is not unreasonable to assert that the historic fundamentalists deserve better than they have received from historians, especially evangelical historians. It is time for some "revisionist" history. Consider this chapter a first step in that direction.

NOTES

1. Kenneth Monroe, "Biblical Philosophy of History," *Bibliotheca Sacra*, July 1934, 318. In *The Scandal of the Evangelical Mind*, Noll constantly berates the historic fundamentalists for ignoring or negating the historical process (132-137). However, as Monroe's essay demonstrates, they seemed quite conversant with the historical thinking of their day, as well as current events and commentary. They were willing to consider historical process, but because they were "biblical" Christians, the biblical understanding of time was paramount. It is difficult to fathom why they should be criticized for being consistent with their own belief system just because it does not conform to a "more" secular model of historiography now preferred by some evangelical historians.
2. Ibid, 321.
3. Ibid, 324, 325.
4. Ibid, 330. Neither Monroe nor other historic fundamentalists meant by the term "Christian nation" a theocracy or the postmillennial idea that America had replaced Israel as God's chosen people or that the Kingdom of God would be ushered in through America's political institutions. Rather they had in mind a national culture historically dominated and influenced by a large evangelical Protestant community and the Bible. They saw America as a unique nation in modern Christian history—but it was not immune from judgment because of that. Part of their concern stemmed from what they saw as a disintegration of the family and social structure that had its roots in anti-Christian or evolutionary derived secular thought. Their fears in this regard were not imaginary, as the passing years since the Great Depression have demonstrated.
5. Twenty years later, the dispensationalist, Alva J. McClain, founder of Grace Theological Seminary, made a similar observation:
    But the philosophers have been right in one respect; that is, in believing there *is* a philosophy of history. Age does not follow age in a kind of "fortuitous concourse." There is an orderly arrangement, a plan, in the midst of seeming chaos and confusion. The great periods of history were not ushered in by chance nor are they wound up by the will of men. The Son of God is the maker of the ages, the Father everlasting, the God of history. . . . Here is the trouble: men are trying to understand history apart from Christ.... (*The Greatness of the Kingdom*

[Chicago: Moody Press, 1959 (1968)], 33.)
6. Monroe, 331.
7. Ibid, 332
8. Very few historic fundamentalists would have disagreed with Monroe at this point. They were convinced of America's Christian foundation and that those who founded the nation believed, as Dan Gilbert wrote, "that government should be the expression of the Christian conscience of the people." ("How Can We Combat Atheism in Our Schools," *The Sunday School Times*, August 6, 1938, 551.)
9. If Monroe was worried in the 1930s about Scriptural truths being replaced by self-focused, psychological concepts, he would be horrified today. James Davison Hunter, writing in *Public Interest* magazine (Spring 2000), points out how the psychological concepts of "self-esteem" and "self-love" have replaced biblically moral terminology even in the evangelical community. After reviewing the books of a handful of evangelical Christian psychologists, Hunter offers the following evaluation:
   The premise is that psychology provides the tools that are, by themselves, theologically and morally neutral but useful all the same when linked to the truths of the Christian faith. Yet insofar as popular psychology provides the framing categories for this literature of popular guidance and admonition, *it is the Christian worldview that undergoes a peculiar reworking . . . the cultural incongruities these advice books represent are, from a historical point of view, breathtaking.* (emphasis added.)
   Toward the end of his essay, Hunter concludes:
   Because evangelicals are among the most self-conscious about the preservation of their orthodoxy, it is a bit ironic that they are among the least self-conscious about their embrace of therapeutic categories and ideals . . . the fact that Evangelical Protestantism...is comfortable with a therapeutic understanding of morality and moral development suggests that its resistance to the dominate culture may, in fact, be little resistance at all. ("When Psychotherapy Replaces Religion," http://proquest.uni.com/pdqweb?ts=9.)
10. The breaking of the Sabbath as a reason for God's disapproval of America was a common theme among the historic fundamentalists even in the 1930s. An editorial in *The Sunday School Times* related the keeping of the Sabbath to the survival of America's equilibrium and its people's well-being. "The foes of the Christian Sunday are a menace to our national well-being," the editor wrote. "Perhaps this awful depression would never have come upon this nation," he theorized, "had we only rested each Lord's day and looked to God for wisdom, for calm, and for future guidance." ("The Breakdown of Sunday in America," February 10, 1934, 82.) I must confess this is inconsistent theology from one who was such a fervent dispensationalist, expecting—given worsening conditions in the world—the possible soon rapture of the church and the appearance of the anti-Christ.
11. Monroe, 332-334.
12. Ibid, 334. A decade later, as World War II was tilting in the Allies' direction, Wilber Smith also looked toward the future as he considered the continuing impact of Hume, Kant, Hegel, and Comte:
   Whether European thought, and this includes America, will ever be delivered from the chains of these revelation denying and Christ-rejecting systems, I do

not have the wisdom for predicting. I cannot help but feel that our thinking will be more pagan and chaotic, unless a great revival from heaven falls upon our western world, and men are omnipotently delivered from the power of this darkness. (*Therefore Stand*, 10.)

Basking as we do under the dubious light of postmodernism, Smith was far from wrong in his musings. The very presuppositions that liberated the secular person from the God of heaven and earth have imprisoned him in the mirrored abyss of self from which he is incapable of extracting himself.

13. Ibid, 335, 336.

14. Ibid, 336.

15. Will B. Houghton, "Let's Go Back to the Bible," *The Sunday School Times*, February 4, 1935, 175.

16. Rollin T. Chafer, "Dealing With Crime," *Bibliotheca Sacra*, July-September 1936, 257, 258.

17. "A Modern Joseph Needed," *The King's Business*, September 1934, 298.

18. "Prosperity by Destruction," *The Sunday School Times*, June 6, 1934, 409. See also in the same periodical, "Why the Drought After Prayer for Rain," September 1, 1934, 550. The editor also considered the fact that "this so-called Christian nation" gave diplomatic recognition to atheistic Russia as another reason for the dust storms ("God's Judgment in the Dust Storms," April 27, 1935, 289.) Considering the severe persecution of Christians by the communists, the historic fundamentalists were furious over Roosevelt's recognition of Russia.

19. "Editorial Notes: Governmental Madness," *Jewish Missionary Magazine*, September-October 1934, 129, 130. Also see, Clarence E. Mason, Jr., "The Pearl Harbor Disaster," *The Sunday School Times*, April 18, 1942, 307, for an interesting take on this issue in relation to the bombing of Pearl Harbor.

    With the passing of time, like most other Americans, the historic fundamentalists were not beyond appreciating the biting humor spawned by New Deal fumblings. The following appeared in both *The Baptist Bulletin* and *Prophecy Monthly*, and was attributed to the popular columnist, Dorothy Thompson:

    A friend asked what the difference [was] "between Communism, Fascism and some other present day governmental 'isms' "

    [Answer] If you have two cows the Communist says you have no right to them at all. Your cows belong to the state, so turn them over to the state and you will get a proper percentage of income from all the cows of the state.

    The Fascist says he will protect your cows from the dreaded Communist. You may keep your cows but you must feed them and keep them in good flesh and health, but all the milk belongs to the state.

    The New Deal says you must shoot one cow and keep the other but pour [its] milk down the drain. ("Cows and Government," *The Baptist Bulletin*, December 1938, 24.)

20. R. Shipley, "Can God Meet America's Need in the Present Crisis," *Moody Monthly*, July 1938, 563.

21. "Where is Stability?" *The King's Business*, June 1935, 205.

22. Ibid.

23. J. Gresham Machen, *The Christian Faith in the Modern World* (Grand Rapids: Wm.

B. Eerdmans Publishing Co., 1936 [1970]), 8, 9.

24. Shipley, 563. Also see Bishop Chandler's "God's Purpose in the Flood." Originally published in the *Atlantic Journal* newspaper, it was reprinted in the April 1933, *Moody Institute Monthly*, 410.

25. Donald Barnhouse related an incident (perhaps apocryphal) in which a group of laymen presented President Hoover's office with a petition requesting he "call a national day of humiliation and prayer to God." The petition was refused and one of the President's secretaries stated "that the White House was so widely quoted that any such call for humiliation and prayer might be interpreted to mean that the situation was worse than it really was and that there was no recourse but to divine means." ("What the Church Can Do For the World in Depression," *Revelation*, September 1932, 511.)

26. "Why the Drought After Prayer for Rain," *The Sunday School Times*, September 1, 1934, 550.

27. "A Call for a Day of Prayer," *The Sunday School Times*, October 20, 1934, 661, 662. Also see, "A Day of Prayer for Repentance and Prayer," *Jewish Missionary Magazine,* November-December 1934, 174-176 where a listing is found of all the leaders, pastors and organizations which issued the call.

28. Joseph Taylor Britan, "Is Prohibition to Blame," *Moody Institute Monthly*, September 1932, 13.

29. John A. Bernbaum and Jerry S. Herbert, "Beyond Self-Interest: Politics, Justice and Evangelical Faith," *Commentary*, Summer 1990, 4.

30. Mark A. Noll, *The Scandal of the Evangelical Mind* (Grand Rapids: William B. Eerdmans Publishing Company, 1994), 167, 168.

31. James Gray, "The Church in Politics," *Moody Institute Monthly*, February 1935, 263.

32. Ibid.

33. Ibid.

34. Ibid. When Cal Thomas and Ed Dobson came out with their controversial book, *Blinded by Might: Can the Religious Right Save America* (1999), they advocated a return of the church as the church to the position practiced by the historic fundamentalists. At times they come close to repeating the words of James Gray (see pages, 80, 81, 94, 98, 104, 105, and 109). Perhaps they would be surprised by the connection.

35. Machen, 85, 86.

36. Ibid.

37. Robert S. Lynd and Helen Merrell, *Middletown in Transition: A Study in American Culture* (New York: Harcourt, Brace and World, Inc., 1939), 311.

38. Noll, 164-169 and Joel A. Carpenter, *Revive Us Again: The Reawakening of American Fundamentalism* (New York: Oxford University Press, 1997), 91-109.

39. "Notes on an Open Letter: Should Christians Try to Reform the World?" *The Sunday School Times*, June 29, 1935, 430

40. I. R. Wall, "Christ and Anti-Christ," *The King's Business*, November 1929, 524.

41. Wilber Smith, *Therefore Stand* (Grand Rapids: Baker Book House, 1945 [1972]), 184. Smith was also becoming "more and more convinced..." that "some of the most widely-circulated and highly praised books of our generation, have been

prompted, though their authors do not know it…by evil spirits" (177).

42. John Wilson, "The Secret History of Fundamentalism," *Christianity Today*, December 8, 1997, 48. As Wilson rightly observed, "That is a scandal that even the 'moderating heirs' of these immoderate fundamentalists can't avoid, as long as they continue to preach the gospel."

43. H. A. Ironside, *Except Ye Repent* (Grand Rapids: Zondervan Publishing House, 1937), 181.

44. James Gray, "Labor Sunday Message: Editorial," *Moody Institute Monthly*, September 1935, 5.

45. Ibid, 6.

46. John T. Reeve, "The Supreme Mission of the Church," *Moody Monthly*, January 1938, 248.

47. "Outdoor Ministry," *Revelation*, September 1938, 386. Also see "Vigorous Summer Evangelism in New York City," *The Sunday School Times*, October 30, 1937, 774, 775.

48. "Witnessing for Christ in C. C. C. Camps," *The Sunday School Times*, July 29, 1939, 508.

49. "Missions to the Migrants," *The King's Business*, April 1939, 132.

50. William A. Corey, "The Shadow of the Prison House," *The Sunday School Times*, June 22, 1935, 419.

51. "A World-Wide Ministry to Sailors," *The King's Business*, January 1931, 5, 10.

52. Marion Bishop Bower, "Will Eddie Go to Camp This Summer?" *The Sunday School Times*, June 18, 1935, 436, 437. Also see "Bible Club Camps," *Revelation*, September 1938, 306.

53. "When the Depression Reached Me," *The Sunday School Times*, September 21, 1935, 607. Also see, "What Trust Means," *Moody Institute Monthly*, November 1935, 110, for a similar story from an unnamed female missionary in Hankong, Fukien, China. An excerpt from the letter related that three American Banks had failed in Shanghai on May 24th. "So many Americans have lost life savings. Chinese have lost also. Preachers Aid Funds, Bible Women's Retirement Fund, Hospital and School Funds for Leper Work, and many endowment funds entrusted to banks vanished in a day…."

54. Moberg, in his *The Great Reversal*, (109), sounds very much like a spokesman for the FCC by lashing out at the use of "bait" by evangelicals. He accuses them of using a form of bait and switch with their hospitals, clinics, etc., luring the unbeliever to their facilities only to first make them listen to the gospel. Moberg considers such tactics as ego trips for those engaging in such disreputable practices and a kind of spiritual snobbery that lets the recipient know he was beneath the giver. It is a bitter and hostile judgement.

55. Charles G. Trumbull, "Foreign Missionary Betrayals of the Faith," *The Sunday School Times* March 23, 1935, 196.

56. Joseph Hoffman Cohn, *Beginning At Jerusalem* (New York: American Board of Missions to the Jews, 1948), 80.

57. "Concerning the Laymen's Report on Foreign Missions," *The European Harvest Field*, February 1933, 7, 8.

58. Thomas M. Chalmers, "Editorial Notes: That Appraisal Commission," *Jewish*

Missionary Magazine, January-February 1933, 32.
59. "Declarations of the Philadelphia Mass Meeting," *The Sunday School Times*, May 20, 1933, 338.
60. Ibid. The 1933 meeting of the World's Christian Fundamental Association, meeting in Chicago, passed a similar resolution condemning the Layman's Report. ("Resolutions of the Fundamentalists," *The Sunday School Times*, July 22, 1933, 472.)
61. Ibid.
62. Ibid.
63. Ibid.
64. Ibid.
65. Ibid.
66. Carpenter, 28-32.
67. The following is typical of the type of letters that appeared in the historic fundamentalists' journals complaining of modernist on the mission field:
    Things are not easy here these days, but what makes it hardest is the many Modernist missionaries who are out here receiving good salaries from home boards, living in fine well-built houses and teaching the natives the rankest poison. One of these men has lately come back with his family, came in spite of the protest of the natives sent to the home board while he was on furlough. They did not want his teaching but it made no difference. The Board in the States reckons him a good worker. It takes much effort on the part of true missionaries to overcome these modernistic teachings and explain to the natives that there are Christians in the home field who do not approve such betrayals of the Faith. ("Poison Peddlers," *Prophecy Monthly*, June 1941, 22.)
68. Machen could not resist a little sarcasm regarding the ecumenism of the modernist missionaries. "People say that Western creeds ought not to be forced upon the Oriental mind. The Oriental mind, they say, ought to be allowed to go its own way and give its own expression to the Christian faith. Well, I have examined one or two of those expressions of the Oriental mind, and I am bound to say that they look to me uncommonly like the expressions of the mind of the South Side of Chicago." (*The Christian Faith in the Modern World* (Grand Rapids: Wm. B. Eerdmans Publishing Co., 1936 [1970]), 92, 93.)
69. Michael S. Hamilton, "The Hidden Years of Fundamentalism Revealed," *Evangelical Studies Bulletin*, Winter 1997, 5.
70. See A. B. Lewis, "Three Months in the Hands of Chinese Captors," *The Sunday School Times*, December 27, 1930, January 3, 1931, and February 7, 1931. Also Ernest Gordon, "A Survey of Religious Life and Thought: Contrasts in Hunan and New Haven," *The Sunday School Times*, June 9, 1934, 380; "Missionary Department: The Communist Trail in China," *Moody Institute Monthly*, November 1935, 131; "Our Martyrs," *Moody Institute Monthly*, February 1935, 269. This article relates the news of the death of Betty and John Stam, and Chiang Shusen, an elderly Chinese Christian who pleaded with the communists to spare the young couple's lives. The Stam's martyrdom became well known among the historic fundamentalists in part because their daughter (only weeks old) was rescued by her nurse and eventually brought back to America.

71. See "Bombers Coming! Shriek the Sirens in China," *The Sunday School Times*, March 12, 1938, 189. Also see "Appalling Atrocity," *Moody Monthly*, April 1938, 418; "China's Hour of Anguish: Some Experiences," *Moody Monthly*, September 1939, 22-25; Ernest Gordon, "A Survey of Religious Life and Thought: Medical Missionaries in China," *The Sunday School Times*, February 17, 1940; "China's Miseries," *Prophecy Monthly*, November 1941, 21, 22; Hallet Abend, "Ebb of the Missions," *The European Harvest Field*, December 1941, 13, (this was a reprint from the *New York Times Magazine*, November 9, 1941); Charles A. Roberts, "Machine Guns at the Gate," *The King's Business*, April 1942, 127, 130; Beth M. Lindberg, "Answered Prayer in Wartorn China," *The Jewish Era*, March 1943, 27, 28; " 'The aggregate of systematic bombings of Christian missions in China by the Japanese (more than 800 to date) should go down in history as one of the bloodiest and most ruthless campaigns ever carried out against any comparable number of Christians.' So writes Robert Bellaire (former American newspaper correspondent in Shanghai) in the *Daily Sketch* (London)," "Flashes," [item 7], *Prophecy Monthly*, September 1944, 26. Similar activities by the Japanese took place in Korea, the Philippines, New Guinea, and elsewhere.

72. See "Adjustment to China's War Conditions," *The King's Business*, October 1938, 325; "China Department of the Bible Institute of Los Angeles," *The King's Business*, March 1939, 96, 126; Charles A. Roberts, "Hunan Refusing to Retreat," *The King's Business*, January 1941, 5, 27.

73. "A Russian Cry: 'We are Sinking!' " *The Prophetic Word*, March 1941, 7.

74. See "Protestant Work Paralyzed by Spanish Rebels," *Prophecy Monthly*, June 1937, 28, 29; Ernest Gordon, "A Survey of Religious Life and Thought: The Real Trouble-Maker in Spain," *The Sunday School Times*, March 12, 1938, 191; "Starving Spain," *Prophetic Word*, January 1943, 22-25; Hispanofilo, "Protestantism Under Franco," *Prophecy Monthly*, May, 1945.

75. See "An Ernest Plea from Ethiopia," *Prophecy Monthly*, December 1935, 8; "Sudan Interior Missions Seized by Rome," *Prophecy Monthly*, August 1936, 10; Ernest Gordon, "Daybreak in Abyssinia," *The Sunday School Times*, February 7, 1948, 105(1); Also see "Expulsion of Missionaries from Tripoli by the Italians," *Moody Monthly*, September 1937, 22, 23; "News from Albania," *The European Harvest Field*, November 1939, 7, and "Editorial Notes and Comments," *The European Harvest Field*, December 1939, 3.

76. Hundreds of articles could be listed. The events in Germany and elsewhere in Europe regarding the church, were closely followed in the historic fundamentalists' publications. These listed below must suffice for now. "The Belgian Gospel Mission in Wartime," *The Sunday School Times*, January 6, 1945, 3, 4, 14; "Christian Host to Europe's Refugees," *Moody Monthly*, November 1947, 171-173, 214; "Why Our Workers Left Poland," *The European Harvest Field*, October 1939, 2; "The Past and Present," *The European Harvest Field*, September 1941, 2-5; "Around the King's Table: Modern Martyrs," *The King's Business*, February 1941, 42; Bartlett L. Hess, "Concentration Camp Christianity," *The Sunday School Times*, June 21, 1941, 503; Also see Harvey L. Phelps, *God's Deliverence from Nazi Hands* (Brooklyn, N. Y.: American Bible Institute, 1943).

77. See, "Norway's Revival," *Prophecy Monthly*, February 1943, 24; "Luther's Hymn

in Norway," *The Sunday School Times*, May 9, 1942, front page, and "Suffering for Christ in Norway," *The Sunday School Times*, January 27, 1945, front page.

78. "Missions or Munitions," *The King's Business*, June 1939, 212. Surveying the situation in 1944, Wilbur Smith also concluded "When this war is over we will have a Europe to confront more pagan than Europe has been since perhaps the days of Constantine" (*Therefore Stand*, 106).

79. "Children of Poland for Christ," *The King's Business*, May 1937, 166, 167, 188, 189; "Whither Goest Thou, Oh Israel? *The European Harvest Field*, April 1938, 8, 9; "New Fields to Conquer," *The European Harvest Field*, October 1938, 2; "Past, Present and Future," *The European Harvest Field*, February 1939, 12, 13; "A Faithful Worker With a Saddened Heart," *The European Harvest Field*, December 1939, 7.

80. "With the Jews in France," *The European Harvest Field*, April 1940, 15; "In the South of France," *The European Harvest Field*, October 1940, 4, 5; "Its Steadfast Purpose," *The European Harvest Field*, July-August 1945, 7, 8; "Prisoners of Hope," *The European Harvest Field*, July-August 1948, 10, 11.

81. "Tragedy in Ethiopia," *Moody Institute Monthly*, February 1936, 307.

82. Ibid.

83. One more should be mentioned in this regard. The historic fundamentalists often took note of suffering outside of there immediate camp. In August 1947, *The King's Business* reviewed the book, *We Found Them Waiting*. This book detailed the sufferings of missionaries associated with the American Lutheran Church stationed in New Guinea. "When the floodtide of war in the Pacific overflowed the shores of New Guinea," wrote the reviewer, "it engulfed much of the mission work being done there. The field of the American Lutheran Church was in the very heart of the conflict and the losses were great, both in equipment and missionary personnel. Eleven missionaries, nine men and two women, were martyred" ("Book Notices," 853).

84. Reeve, 249. Also see Joseph Edwin Harris, "Sin, Satan, and the Social Gospel," *Bibliotheca Sacra,* October 1934.

85. "Human Needs This Winter," *Moody Institute Monthly*, November 1933, 96.

86. "Help the Needy," *Moody Institute Monthly*, December 1934, 151.

87. For example, see "Facts About Puerto Rico," *Moody Institute Monthly*, June 1931, 499; "Our Brethren in Germany," *Moody Institute Monthly*, March 1935, 314; "The Famine in China," *Moody Monthly*, September 1938, 4.

88. Ernest W. Leferver, "Charity During the Great Depression," *The American Enterprise*, May-June 1996, 314.

89. Ibid.

90. G. Michael Cocoris, *70 Years on Hope Street* (Los Angeles: Church of the Open Door, 1985, 54, 55.) The Church of the Open Door and Biola were also intimately connected with the Los Angeles Union Rescue Mission.

91. "Truly Christian Relief Work," *The Sunday School Times*, October 14, 1933, 641.

92. Ibid. It is interesting to note how much the city of Atlanta assisted the pastor in his compassionate endeavors.

93. See, for example, "Going Around With the Jail Chaplain," *The Sunday School Times*, June 8, 1935; Ernest Gordon, "Some Southern Presbyterian Schools," *The Sunday School Times*, November 21, 1931, 655; Edwin D. Monroe, "Sister Abigail—A

Woman Who Believed God," *The Sunday School Times*, July 22, 1939, 491, 492; R. Celestia Churchill, "God and the Budget," *The King's Business*, February 1933, 44, 45, 52, (this article deals with a home for girls); H. S. Riley, "Refuge for Boys," *The King's Business*, January 1939, 19-22; "A Christian State Camp," *The King's Business*, July 1937, 247, 285, and Joseph Taylor Britan, "An Appeal for Persecuted Israel," *The Sunday School Times*, December 3, 1938, 874.

94.   Bower, *The Sunday School Times*, 436, 437, and "Bible Club Camps," *Revelation*, 387.

95.   Melvin E. Trotter, "Is Life Worth Living," *The King's Business*, September 1932, 385, 386. Trotter, who became a "household" name among fundamentalists for his rescue missions work, had, himself, been "saved" from a life of hopeless drunkenness in early 1897 at Chicago's famous "skid-row" Pacific Garden Mission. His story is briefly covered in Carl Henry's *The Pacific Garden Mission: A Doorway to Heaven* (Grand Rapids: Zondervan Publishing House, 1942), 47-50.

96.   Robert S. Lund and Helen Merrell, *Middletown in Transition: A Study in American Culture* (New York: Harcourt, Brace and World, Inc., 1939).

97.   Ibid, 311.

98.   Ibid, 316. The wrenching impact of the depression, the authors speculated, may have caused the "meagerly educated" to "swing" back to what "they have been told since infancy is the unfailing Rock of Ages, and the gap between what the intellectual world may call 'religion' and 'reality' may increase with a popular huddling back to fundamentalism...." (With such a condescending academic attitude toward the average working class family and its religious beliefs, is there any wonder that there was an "anti-intellectualism" abroad among many lay historic fundamentalists? Even the "meagerly educated" know when they are being held in contempt.)

99.   Ibid, 141.

100. Ibid, 106.

101. Ibid.

102. Ibid, 141.

103. Ibid, 306. The authors also noted that the Salvation Army carried on a hot lunch program for the school children in the poorer section of town.

104. Donald G. Barnhouse, "The Errors of Fundamentalists," *Revelation* March 1935, 127.

105. One more example is worth noting. The Los Angeles Jail Workers Association, an organization of about 500 members, mostly poor and a mix of whites, blacks, hispanics of both sexes (some of whom had been in jail themselves), "taxed" themselves to support their work among the families of the inmates.

106. Sadly, Mark Noll, while declaring the intellectual and political bankruptcy of the historic fundamentalists during the Great Depression era, reduces all this compassionate social activity to one sentence in his *The Scandal of the Evangelical Mind*. "And throughout the country," he writes, "countless acts of kindness were being done in rescue missions, soup kitchens, and settlement houses by Salvationists, pentecostals, Baptists, Church of the Brethren, independents, and other evangelicals" (168). Why is "fundamentalists" such a difficult word to say when it comes to social compassion?

107. Hamilton, 2.

108.   Robert Lundin, *The Culture of Interpretation: Christian Faith and the Postmodern World* (Grand Rapids: William B. Eerdmans Publishing Company, 1993), 186. Eric L. Johnson of Nothwestern College agrees. In an unpublished paper, *Teaching First Principles: A Model for a Biblical Liberal Arts College*, Johnson writes:

...there has been a tendency towards increased professionalism which has sometimes worked against helping faculty to think Christianly. . . . When combined with a relatively uncritical openness to modern thought, the basically secular education of some Christian faculty has gradually shaped their pre-theoretical commitments, values, and assumptions, and provided first principles that are sometimes at variance with a Christian world-view (2, 3).

CHAPTER FOUR

Historic Fundamentalism Speaking Politically: The Duties and Passions of the Christian Citizen

It seems that the point ought to be yielded that the historic fundamentalists were more generous toward their fellow Americans, and more involved in seeking to ameliorate the economic/social trauma of the Great Depression, than their critics have been willing to concede. Certainly what they did deserves more than a passing comment grudgingly acknowledging an impulse or two of compassion. However, that still leaves the issue of their obvious political failings. Did they not argue that to be involved "in society actually denied rather than fulfilled the gospel?"[1] Actually the answer is no. Was not their political interest and political reflection at an all time evangelical low?[2] Here again, such a judgment is overblown. If the church was to avoid political entanglement, this was in no way to inhibit the individual fundamentalist from willingly performing the duties and responsibilities of conscientious citizenship.

In fact, this was an issue discussed in the journals of the historic fundamentalists. For example, in February 1935, *The Sunday School Times* printed a letter from one of its subscribers which stated that many ministers and laymen "refused to vote or do anything toward community improvement except to try and win individuals to Christ." "Should we go to this extreme," the writer asked, "and ignore the needs of the community, state or nation?"[3]

In reply, the editor observed that the New Testament did not prohibit Christians from participating in civic affairs, thus:

> In absence of any such Scriptural prohibition, there would seem to be good reason why the Christian should do everything in his power to secure good government in every legitimate way, by voting for the best candidates and by exercising other rights and duties of good citizenship.[4]

This included seeking to apply "the principles of Christ...in civic affairs." Both *Revelation* magazine and *Moody Institute Monthly* seconded this position.[5]

Dan Gilbert, an example of a historical fundamentalist *cum* political activist, and author of *The Biblical Basis of the Constitution* [6] (and who wrote on that subject for *The King's Business*), stated that all Christians owed "A duty to their Lord, as well as to their country, to exercise every effort to prevent from rising higher in our land the swelling tide of beastism, lawlessness, the rule of brute force, and organized violence."[7] Such a situation, he wrote, must not be allowed to overturn "constitutional government and democratically established law and order."[8] With the advent of the intense persecution of the Jews and Jewish Christians in Europe, and the first explosions of World War II shredding all illusions of "peace in our time," Joseph T. Britan, secretary of the Friends of Israel Refugee Relief Committee, extended this responsibility to global dimensions. "Christians in America, and in the world," he wrote, "have two responsibilities in the present crisis—to preserve the fundamental rights of men and to relieve the persecuted and oppressed." The church and all that it believed and stood for was under worldwide attack along with those "inalienable rights for which free men have ever fought and died."[9]

The Responsibilities of the Christian Citizen

Had the critics of historic fundamentalism's "political indifference" been in the auditorium on the morning of July 3, 1936, they would have heard James Congdon, D.D., deliver a passionate talk on "Christian Patriotism" to the student body of Moody Bible Institute. Any present day politically active evangelical would have been at ease with his reasoning. First he established the biblical basis for a Christian's involvement in civic affairs and concluded: "So far as I am able to remember, there is not a single passage in the Bible which would lead the most devout believer in the inspiration and authority of the Scripture, to refrain from performing all the duties required of a good citizen."[10] In fact, Congdon reminded his student audience that the "Christian patriot is interested vitally, always and everywhere in human welfare." He then criticized those who refused to participate "in any way in the affairs of [the] country" as well as those of the opposite approach, the Social Gospel, which ignored the need of personal salvation. "True Christian patriotism," Congdon stated, "lies between these two extremes." Concerning the latter group, he asserted that the Christian patriot "will not permit the godless, the theological liberal, or the crafty politician to manifest more concern for his neighbor's welfare than he...will manifest."[11]

As for the non-participants, Congdon stressed that the believer cannot stand by and "neglect undertaking the protection of the weak and helpless." No, the true Christian patriot will perform his duties and,

will hold up to the community the highest conceptions of personal and community righteousness. He will undertake to bring down condemnation upon the heads of evildoers, guilty of wrongs against the community, as well as point out the way of moral and civic righteousness.[12]

In closing, Congdon reminded the students that Peter's admonition to "honor the king" still held true. However, in America this was to be understood as the individual citizen being sovereign. "Every man and woman who votes is sovereign. We, who as citizens own the ballot boxes, are kings and we rule. If our government is corrupt, it is first corrupt at the ballot box where each American can express his sovereign rights."[13]

Admittedly, one might question Congdon's "Americanization" of I Peter 2:17, but nevertheless, these are hardly the words of one in whom political interest has gone into hibernation. A similar conclusion can be made regarding Paul Rood, who in 1936 was President of Biola and editor of *The King's Business*. Also addressing himself to the issue of citizenship, Rood declared that both the Social Gospel, which sought "to bring in a new social order," and the view that the believer "should refrain from all participation in civic affairs," were "extreme and unscriptural."[14] Clearly the fundamental task of the believer was to witness and win souls to Christ. Nonetheless, "God's messengers must protest against unrighteousness in the individual and in the nation as did the prophets of old." Christians must exercise their privilege of voting with a "Scripturally instructed conscience" and be ready to take a strong stand "when moral issues are involved."[15]

In fact, being a Christian should make one a better citizen, willingly performing his duty to vote and use his "influence against everything that is wrong and for everything that is right in the eyes of God." Rood concluded his editorial by declaring, "If there ever was a time when the Christians of the United States needed to function as citizens it was now. Subversive influences are at work that would destroy constitutional government. We need to be informed in order that we may pray and act intelligently."[16]

The editor of *Moody Institute Monthly* was of the same mind. In 1936, after the National Recovery Act was declared unconstitutional, he thought it was time to get rid of the politicians (i.e., lawyers [what else?]) in Congress and replace them with businessmen who understood problems at a practical level. (By businessmen, the editor explained, he meant both workingmen as well as business owners.) "If the political and economic catastrophe now upon us does not open the eyes of the voters," the editor queried, "is there anything that will do so?" It was time for the Christian citizen to be more diligent in his voting and "try to make better selections than hitherto."[17] In the same issue, *Moody* also reprinted editorial comments from the *United Presbyterian* which asserted that America's greatest peril was the "failure...of Christians to participate in politics." Christians must shoulder their responsibility as they were the only ones that could protect the country from evil and determined special interest groups.[18]

Along with the clear-cut proposition that Christians were to be involved as informed citizens of the political problems facing the country, these dispensational fundamentalists also believed that it was biblical-historical Christianity alone which could provide the moral character the American people needed to overcome their difficulties and exercise properly their political responsibilities. James Gray, for example, in a critical review of a book published by the Federal Council of Churches—a book advocating socialism—nevertheless agreed with its conclusion that only Christianity could prepare men to do the right thing socially. Of course, for Gray that meant biblical Christianity, that is, a Christianity which taught of the "indwelling Holy Spirit:"

> It is this Christianity and none other whose fundamental task is "to develop the kind of personality and character that can work social plans, use social tools and bring ideals into actuality." And this task true Christianity has performed again and again in the history of mankind, and is now performing it, whenever the gospel of the Son of God is proclaimed in power.[19]

Gray was obviously challenging the idea that a social gospel, shorn of this power, could ever do the needed work of preparation.

Clarence Benson, writing in *The Sunday School Times* claimed that the only thing that could save America from moral and spiritual disaster now upon it was the development of moral character in its people. But how could this be done? "To whom are we to look for this all important development of morality and character?" According to Benson, only to Christian leaders. But where are we to find them, who could produce these needed Christian leaders? Again, according to Benson, only in the fundamentalists' Bible institutes. If enough Christian leaders could be produced by these institutes, then "it may still be possible to stem the titanic tide of godlessness and lawlessness that threatens to overwhelm the nation." It may not be the churches' job to reform the nation, but it was its job to inculcate moral truths into those individuals who could and would. "Once multiply real Bible schools until they are as thick as schoolhouses, then righteousness and not rowdyism will rule the nation, and America will be restored to its former position of prestige and promise." A moral people was indispensable to economic and political recovery.[20]

Cautious, Cooperative?, Ambivalence Toward the New Deal

One reason why the historic fundamentalists were motivated to active participation in the political process was because they believed that America's civil liberties were fundamentally grounded in the Word of God. The "Constitution merely affirms and enforces the moral law as it has been revealed to us," wrote

Dan Gilbert. At heart, individual political rights were not the gift of government. Rather, "Our government is founded upon the Christian principle that individual rights are the gift of God...."[21] If this was true, than these "rights" must be protected by intense Christian involvement, not withdrawal.

By 1936, such thoughts were on the minds of many historic fundamentalists. At the inception of Roosevelt's first term, most were cautiously supportive of his efforts to solve the overwhelming social and economic problems burying America in despair and fear. Although doubts began to surface within the first few months, an article that appeared in *Moody Institute Monthly* at the close of 1933, probably reflected the prevailing attitude. It noted that a social and political revolution was taking place in America. This was not the direct fault of the Roosevelt administration. No, if collectivism was gaining favor, it was the fault of the community-at-large. Greed had brought about America's sad state of affairs. We were reaping what we had sown. Both employer and employee must share the blame—both had been selfish. Now the government was trying to make everyone "altruistic by law." Perhaps these were the first stirrings of an emerging dictator?[22] And considering the situation in Europe, the growing disillusionment with capitalism, and the agitating rhetoric bombarding the American public, this was not an unwarranted thought. As John Lewis Gaddis has noted in his *We Now Know: Rethinking Cold War History* (1997), "nightmares always seem real at the time—even if, in the clear light of dawn, a little ridiculous."[23]

Another indication of the historic fundamentalist's ambivalent but cautious support of FDR was reflected in their response to the National Recovery Act. Although some doubted its constitutionality and did not cooperate, others responded out of a sense of "patriotic" duty. *The Sunday School Times*, a prime example of this, declared that it was the duty of "every true Christian in America to stand with President Roosevelt and the government in their sincere effort to improve economic conditions and give everyone a chance to work." Showing its support, the magazine signed the Periodical Publishing Industry's code of fair practices and proudly displayed the Blue Eagle,[24] as did *Revelation* magazine.[25]

In the same edition of *The Sunday School Times* that displayed the Blue Eagle, an article by Louis Bauman appeared entitled, "The Blue Eagle and Our Duty as Christians." Bauman began by noting that many Christians were worried about cooperating with the anti-Christ as the apostasy in the church deepened. Therefore, they were leery of the "growing tendency among nations to use some mark, or insignia, for setting apart those who are the recipients of national favor." Russia, Germany, Italy and Japan all had such insignia and the question in many minds was, how does the Blue Eagle of the NRA fit into this trend?[26]

In response to this question, Bauman pointed out that, "It is only fair to President Roosevelt that we recognize the gigantic problems with which he grapples," whether all agreed with his methods or not. One thing the reader was not to forget was that communism and fascism thrived only "where economic distress is black and keen." The purpose of the NRA was, "to see…that every American citizen shall remain in his fundamental right to a job—the right to earn an honest living in the land of plenty." If this were the case, communism and fascism would not flourish. In this endeavor, "Our President should have the hearty support of every loyal American citizen. Such is a righteous war. And if the blue eagles are the insignia of the warriors of that war, then God bless the blue eagles."[27]

Bauman reminded his readers that Roosevelt and his administrators had stressed that the blue eagle meant "selflessness not selfishness." If the world's greatest democracy were "not to dim and disappear," it must be impressed upon the American people the need for sacrifice. "Undeniably," Bauman wrote, "democracy is on a sick-bed, terribly sick." The communists and fascists were hoping it would die. "And if President Roosevelt stands to thrust back the hungry wolves of Fascism and Communism, and maintain our heritage, then it is our supreme duty to stand by him in this hour."[28] Bauman's only regret was that the President and his advisors did not give public recognition "to the fact that the character of the sort demanded in American life to make the war of the blue eagle a success is founded on faith in, and fear of, God." If God were given proper recognition, he asserted, "we could have more faith in its ultimate success."[29]

"Proper recognition" of God was never forthcoming, however (and neither was the success of the NRA—it was declared unconstitutional by the Supreme Court in May, 1935—no connection, I am sure). By 1936, the historic fundamentalists were growing disillusioned with the New Deal and by 1938 the process was complete. A number of factors contributed to this disenchantment. One was the rising labor violence and the increasing class-war rhetoric emanating even from the Administration.[30] Louis Bauman quoted Harry Hopkins telling his subordinates in the W. P. A., "that the present status of affairs in America forms itself into 'a *fight* between those who have not and those who have,' " and the administration is on the side of the former. Bauman angrily opined that "our government" was no longer a government of all but only a government for the "have nots." "We have fallen on an evil hour," Bauman lamented, "when those in authority begin making their appeals for continuance of power to the passions and prejudices of particular classes rather than to the people as a whole." Class conflict will only give victory to a tyrant, he warned.[31]

Another "irritant", one I have mentioned before but as late as 1942 was still on the minds of the historic fundamentalists, was the wanton destruction of livestock and food by the New Deal in order to raise agriculture prices. In 1935 the historic fundamentalists were willing to attribute the dust storms to this "unconscionable" governmental action. However, by 1942, it was proposed as one of the reasons God had brought America into war with Japan.[32] Nor were many of the historic fundamentalists thrilled with the New Deal's alphabetic recovery program, fearing it might threaten the individual's constitutional rights. James Gray was of this mind. He opposed the NRA on the grounds that it went against the Constitutional principle of individual liberty. Citing the judicial appeal of a York, Pennsylvania manufacturer who had been convicted and sentenced "for violating the N. R. A. code," Gray believed the case "will be a test of the invasion of the liberty and right of a citizen to run his business without the interference of the government, the President, the Congress, or a code authority composed of business competitors to fix the wages paid by any manufacturer." Gray considered the upcoming Supreme Court decision one of the most crucial it would ever make. The issue, according to Gray, was not one of employee and employer, or capital versus labor, "but one of personal liberty, the birthright of American citizens...."[33]

Deficit spending also set off the alarm bells among the historic fundamentalists. As noted, *The Sunday School Times* had been an enthusiastic participant in the "Blue Eagle" experiment right from its inception. However, by 1936 it was challenging its readers to a greater zeal in order to preserve America, in part, "from the unprecedented radical legislation that threatens its foundations."[34] Louis Bauman acidly commented:

> America, after an unprecedented spending spree in which we have filched billions upon billions from the pockets of our children unborn, in an effort to create employment and restore prosperity, twenty million—a larger number than ever before—are still being fed on the dole. The best brains of the worst brains that ever directed our old ship of state candidly admit that the only way out they knew is through methods that the Supreme Court denounces as but little better than pillage.[35]

Even the dispensational theological journal, *Bibliotheca Sacra*, was moved to editorial comment. "Periodical literature," wrote editor Rollin Chafer, "is filled with articles dealing with America's problems, and all of them taken together indicate that something basic in the life of the country is radically wrong." And (naturally) everybody offered his or her own particular nostrum. However, the New Dealers offered the most "preposterous cure of them all, the uneconomic doctrine that it is possible for the government to spend us out of the Depression by piling up a high and ever increasing debt, and that the consequent burden of taxation will not endanger our American ideals and form of government...."[36]

Chafer believed the end results would be a loss of freedom. The question, then, was no longer just one of what was the best economic program to bring about recovery, but how that program was going to affect the very political structure of American society. The issue emerging was one of threatened civil liberties. Keith Brooks approvingly quoted the editor of the *Los Angeles Times*, who was disturbed at the way "the public has been deceived as to our national indebtedness" (thirty-four billion dollars), and wrote, "Nobody has ever seen anything like it; the deliberate, purposeful wrecking of Russian finances by the early Soviet regime, in order to steal capital from credulous investors abroad, is the nearest parallel. But in this case the capital that is being stolen for Socialistic schemes is the savings of the American people."[37]

Finally, of course, their growing disenchantment was fed by the perceived "socialistic" leanings of some of the President's advisors (including his wife). Louis Bauman listed Harold Ickes, Felix Frankfurter, Rex Tugwell, Harry Hopkins, Francis Perkins, and Elanor Roosevelt as among America's most outstanding socialists.[38] Keith Brooks, in a post 1936 election "meditation," scoffed at reports that President Roosevelt was a (closet) communist but he did consider him a fabian socialist. He also thought some of Roosevelt's closet advisors might be communist, or, at a minimum, a goodly "number of them were undoubtedly collectivists."[39]

In fact, after hearing Earl Browder, Secretary of the Communist Party, U.S.A., Brooks decided that Browder "was mild in his assertions" compared with comments [Rex] Tugwell had made in a Los Angeles speech. "Nor," Brooks continued, "was his appeal to class prejudice any more pronounced than that uttered by the President in his 'state of the union' address of last January."[40] Brooks also noted that the goal of the Communist Party—according to Browder—did not differ from that espoused by Rex Tugwell. In his Los Angeles speech, Tugwell was, according to Brooks, "openly urging that we do away with the," (and he quotes Tugwell directly), "sterile morality of individualism, and that all who disagree are tories, autocrats and enemies, and they must get out of the way with the moral system that supports them."[41]

Considering recent revelations about communist penetration of the Roosevelt Administration, and the obvious sympathy of New Deal fellow-travelers, the political "instincts" of the historic fundamentalists were not all that amiss. Arthur Herman, author of *Joseph McCarthy: Reexamining the Life and Legacy of America's Most Hated Senator*, points out that Harold Ickes was friendly toward communist and supportive toward communist front organizations.[42] And evidently the same held true for Mrs. Roosevelt. The authors of *The Venona Secrets: Exposing Soviet Espionage and America Traitors*—Herbert Romerstein and Eric Breindel—while emphatic that she was not a communist—do point out "she was extremely naïve and fooled" by them, and that this "naivete helped the Communists to exert influence."[43] However, the real shocker is Romerstein and Breindel's well reasoned charge that Harry Hopkins, Rooosevelt's closest and most trusted advisor, was a true soviet agent—agent 19, a traitor to his President and his country.[44] Herman is not willing to go that far. He believes that "Hopkins became the archetypal 'Communist dupe'—the well-intentioned liberal who believes every lie the Marxists tell him, with disastrous results."[45]

Jeremiads for the Rich

Without a doubt, most of the leaders of historic fundamentalism came down on the side of capitalism. It is not that they considered it sacrosanct; rather, they thought its elimination would be "to sacrifice the values which inhere in liberty, democracy, personal initiative and voluntary cooperation."[46] And considering the current alternatives, it was no contest. "Capitalism," as James Gray noted, "is bad enough, but socialism may be only out of the frying pan and into the fire." [47] (However, Gray also admitted that capitalism was no more Christian than socialism, and was doing its share in bringing on the anti-Christ.) By the end of 1933, Gray leaned toward the view that America was moving toward its own brand of fascism in which the government would limit both profits and loses while keeping both "under strict government direction and control." He believed that this was the "gist of the President's remarks to the American Bankers Association. Government must be the leader, 'the judge of the interest of all groups in the community, the outward expression of the common life of all citizens.'" That might be acceptable, Gray reasoned, under a "good government, but governments are not always good. Therefore, we still think the traditional American system is preferable, the system of a free competitive market, with as few governmental rules as may be compatible with good order."[48]

Though grumbling that foreign propaganda had so influenced the American public that anyone "who dares to say a word in defense of capitalism is likely to find himself unpopular in almost any group," Keith Brooks stilled weighed in with his analysis. While noting that the "capitalistic system is justly denounced for certain evils" (i.e., unfair concentration of wealth and oppression of workers), Brooks believed these could be corrected by law. "If history teaches us anything," he warned (echoing Gray), "it is that capitalism at its worst is better than socialism at its best."[49] It was capitalism, Brooks pointed out, that created the jobs and provided the taxes upon which governments feed. He was of the opinion that were America to abolish capitalism it would then end up with a government reflecting either fascism or communism. Either way we would lose our freedom.[50]

Brooks believed that it was "the spur of keen competition that makes for human progress." On the other hand, when there is no competition, and political bureaucrats are safely entrenched, government becomes "universally...less efficient and overwhelmingly" expensive. "When people work for themselves," Brooks reminded his readers, "they pay for their own mistakes. Bureaucrats (on the other hand) do their experimenting at the expense of the people."[51]

However despite favoring capitalism the historic fundamentalists had no qualms about castigating the rich for their greed. In fact, Donald Barnhouse placed a good portion of the blame for the on-going labor violence at their doorstep. When the depression hit, he charged, they laid-off employees in droves without any form of security while continuing to pay dividends. The results of this disparity "between the miseries of the masses" and the heaped-up wealth of the rich was a growing class-consciousness that was producing violence.[52] Louis Bauman agreed with Barnhouse's assessment of the situation and wrote in 1937 that,

> the greatest folly that the rich ever committed was committed a few years ago, when the great depression came. Instead of opening their storehouses and keeping up the music of the saw and hammer, instead of keeping the mills grinding, and the wheels rolling on the rails, they jammed their heaps of treasure into bank vaults, and let government power step in to do what they should have done. The moth on their garments and the rust on their dollars are the damnation of the rich.[53]

This is a rather harsh evaluation, but seemingly a common one. Five years earlier, *The King's Business* had taken to task "men with millions," who, seeing the "misery of millions," were unmoved to help. The real cause of the depression lay in the lack of work, food, housing, and clothing for millions while millionaires "are hoarding their 'frozen assets' and have not the charitable attitude that a time like this demands." There was plenty of money but, "the common people who are in need of the bare necessities of life do not possess it."[54] Interestingly, a year later, while the Roosevelt administration was churning up an alphabet of recovery programs, *The King's Business* offered up a novel recovery program of its own. The nation's leaders should consider instituting Israel's Sabbatical year and Jubilee year. If the Sabbatical year were instituted, the magazine reasoned, it would not be necessary to burn cotton. In fact, it would solve the problem of agriculture overproduction. And if the Jubilee year was enforced, "strangling" farm mortgages would be cancelled and America's farms would be unencumbered. Greedy landlords would have to give up all but their own homesteads. This, *The King's Business* concluded, was God's way of limiting wealth.[55] Obviously this suggestion never caught on.

Basically, the historic fundamentalists seemed to agree—some form of redistribution of wealth must take place. Louis Bauman noted that if the leaders of American industry would not wakeup to the fact that they could not cheat their fellow citizens then, "the political socialization of industry has come to stay." In fact, Bauman was willing to predict that a "capitalistic society in America...will not be tolerated [any] longer unless its prosperity is broadly shared."[56] The editor of *Revelation* wrote that labor violence was inevitable as long as there was such disparity between the wealthy employers and the poorly paid employees—capitalistic gain was always at the expense of the workers—and the editor's sympathy was with the employees. Basing his position on James 5:4, he emphatically noted, "We have, therefore, a definite right to say that it is distinctly Christian that labor should have a greater share in the profits of industry."[57]

Even James Gray, who often sided with business against the New Deal, agreed.

In an editorial response to the 1935 "Labor Sunday Message" issued by the Federal Council of Churches, Gray seconded the FCC's statement that the church could not be indifferent to the suffering and hardship being experienced by millions of Americans. "We have no reservations in saying this," he noted,

> or when we also express our agreement that some new way must be found to solve our maladjustment in distribution, and remove the anomaly of so great want in the midst of so great abundance. And above all, we agree. . .that "the churches. . .must stand always not only against exploitation but against the very desire to exploit...."[58]

The Fundamentalists Defense of Civil Liberties

At heart, though, there was a basic difference between the historic fundamentalists and FDR's New Deal that could not be surmounted. The historic fundamentalists believed it was men who had failed and brought on the Great Depression. Early in 1932, Vance Havner wrote:

> God is bringing the expert to confusion.... It is deeply significant that just when we become most mechanically efficient, most thoroughly standardized here in America, right then we turn the corner into the most baffling depression in history. A nation of experts and not one can explain or solve our puzzling dilemma.[59]

The FDR administration, on the other hand, at least as understood by the historic fundamentalists, held that the system had failed not men, and by tinkering with it a more promising alternative might be assembled. Historic fundamentalists, however, considered this approach a false hope. The problem was spiritual. Sin was too deeply entrenched in human life to be overcome "by a mere program of social improvement."[60] In fact, from the perspective of the historic fundamentalists, the New Deal programs seemed to "deny" what the historic fundamentalists believed was the biblical view of man ingrained into the American idea of government by law. The principle of government by law not only acknowledged that men were untrustworthy by restraining them, but at the same time also guaranteed them their liberties. This "rationale" permeated the Constitution. It was at this point, then,— the Constitution—that the historic fundamentalists stared with increasing alarm at the legislative tinkering of the New Deal.[61]

Many historic fundamentalists feared that the American government was beginning to reflect the worst features of European governments. Where communism and fascism had surfaced, godless dictators had arisen that had centralized authority, controlled the government through the auspices of a single, compliant party, ruled by decree, manipulated class hatreds and economic hardships to gain and hold power, persecuted the church, and placed themselves above any constitutional laws that may have existed. In 1935, J. Gresham Machen, who was not moved to political analysis based on prophetic speculation, exclaimed:

> Little did I think that a war supposed to make the world safe for democracy would be followed by an era in which Italy and in Germany, as well as in Russia, democracy and liberty would be openly despised and would be replaced by a tyranny far more crushing and soul-killing in many respects than the cruder tyrannies of the past. Little did I think that even in America the civil and religious liberty which was our dearest possession and won by our fathers at such cost would be threatened today.[62]

Machen was convinced that a great emergency was confronting mankind, an emergency that made it "perfectly clear to thoughtful people, whether they are Christians or not, that humanity is standing over an abyss."[63] And, indeed, it was. One more terrible than any but a very few could imagine.

Machen's comments marked a position fast solidifying in the thinking of the historic fundamentalists. For a few, this meant a sojourn into dingy and corrosive corridors that were sloganed with the rantings of an anti-Semitic, fascist sympathizing extremism. But such was not the case for the great majority of this group, especially among the leadership. And parallels did seem to be surfacing as the New Deal progressed. Roosevelt had a compliant, numerically superior Democratic Party that had given him extraordinary authority with hardly a murmur of protest. He chafed at the constitutional restraints placed on his programs by the Supreme Court, and he appeared to be stirring up class conflict to gain even greater power. A few months before the 1936 election, the editor of *Bibliotheca Sacra* voiced the fear that,

> in our land…we note a distinct swing in governmental circles toward a greater realization of centralized power at Washington, and there seems to be a more or less blind acceptance of the radical principle underlying the changes by a considerable portion of the citizenry of the country.[64]

Following the 1936 electoral triumph by FDR, the editor of *The King's Business* sourly prophesied:

> In the United States, the overwhelming victory for the New Deal indicates that the plan of the members of the so-called "brain-trust" to repudiate our cherished national principles has met with enthusiastic approval of the voters. During the next few years we can expect that attempts will be made to reconstruct the Supreme Court and to curtail the freedom of the press and to centralize power.[65]

When Roosevelt held true to form with his proposal to "pack" the Supreme Court, *The King's Business* bitterly reflected that he wanted second-rate judges "who will do their master's bidding and will allow the White House to dominate not only the working of our laws but also the interpretation of these laws." This was the essence of dictatorial lawlessness and a direct threat to the traditional American concept of government under law.[66] Prophetic speculation might incline the historic fundamentalists to see the possibility of a dictator emerging, but so did current events.

A few months later, disturbed by this trend, *The King's Business* published an article by Dan Gilbert that reiterated, in part, his arguments presented in *The Biblical Basis of the Constitution*. Titled "The Christian View of the Constitutional Government," it was obviously written to stimulate the reader to reflect on the thrust of current political thinking at the highest levels of American politics in light of international events. If everything said about the historic fundamentalists being apolitical and all wrapped up in their own personal piety and prophetic speculations were true, Dan Gilbert would be the proverbial exception that proves the rule. Along with a well-received book about the influence of the Bible upon the Constitution (and a number of articles along the same vein—such as the one reviewed below), he also took on atheism, communism, and the "ism" of evolution in his home state of California. In 1938, he circulated an initiative to have atheism/communism barred from the public classroom. "If the schoolroom is to be barred against Christ," (which, he noted, was happening), "let it be barred against his enemies." It appeared, he wrote, that "academic freedom" was reserved for those opposed to Christianity; "certainly, under the present system, there is no academic freedom for either Christian teachers or Christian students."[67]

Gilbert began his above mentioned essay by claiming that the "Founding Fathers" believed all political authority should be under God's authority, and that the same God had granted men certain "inalienable rights." Government was to make sure these rights were secured, but this was only possible if government itself "adhered to divine moral law upon which these rights are based."[68]

Man's God-given rights were the right to life, and the right to honestly acquired "property for the nurture and benefit of himself and his family." To safeguard these rights, God gave men His moral law embodied in the Ten Commandments. The Constitution both recognized these divine rights and protected them by enforcing the moral law "upon the government itself." Neither state nor federal government could deny any American his right to life, liberty, or property without "due process of law." In fascist or communist countries it might be "legal" for the government to take a citizen's property as it wished, but under "our Constitution" this was considered stealing. For Gilbert, this was the essence of what he termed "Americanism."[69]

Gilbert contrasted his "Americanism" with the fascist and communist governments of Europe. These governments denied God-given rights and God-given moral law, and, in fact, "refuse to recognize the authority of God." They were dictatorships that reserved for themselves the right to decide what would be the moral law, and when and how the individual would be deprived of his life and property. They did not acknowledge "the right or wrong of an act of government." "Such a system of government," Gilbert noted, "is sheer lawlessness: it is organized violence. It respects neither the demands of justice nor of morality. It is based, not on divine law, but rather upon the will and whim, the ego, of the dictator."[70]

And as far as Gilbert was concerned, a dictatorship was a dictatorship whether it consisted of one man, a minority of men, or a majority of men. Whenever the moral law was denied and force employed in such a way as to deprive a man of his life or property, a dictatorship existed. Theft and violence were wrong no matter who exercised them. The Ten Commandments applied to men collectively as well as to individuals. "They are binding on a government of the majority, just as they are binding on a government of a minority." Certainly the Constitution recognized majority rule but only in accordance with the "moral law" and never at the expense of the individual. "The Constitution deliberately denies to majority-rule government any right and any power to restrict individual liberty." No majority could vote in an administration, even if it desired to do so, that would convert our democracy into despotism. Public officials, like all other citizens, were under the Constitution and thus under "divine moral law."[71]

No matter how sincere politicians might be, Gilbert cautioned, no group of people could, over the long run, really improve their situation "by giving any politician or groups of politicians power to override the Constitution and moral law." He concluded his essay by affirming—and warning:

> Ours is a government "of laws not of men." The highest law of our government is the Constitution, and the fundamental law of the Constitution is the divine moral law. The Constitution enforces and expresses those individual rights and principles of liberty and justice which are derived from our Creator. We must not substitute for God-given principles, for divine moral law, for a system of government that recognizes Deity— we must not substitute for these, as our supreme authority, the will and judgement and moral standards of any man, or group of men, or majority, however large or well intentioned.[72]

To do something so foolish would be to forfeit the greatness that had come to America because she had remained under God in past years. Without a doubt Gilbert's reasoning would find a ready response among many Christians of all persuasions in the opening decade of the twenty-first century.[73] It expressed a well accepted American, Protestant view of republican government and civil liberties.

In its immediate context, Gilbert's essay was a "fundamentalist" rebuke to the New Deal's attempt to extend presidential authority through heavy-handed power politics. It also expressed an underlying apprehension historic fundamentalists harbored toward their own future civil status as an unpopular "religious minority" under a government whose reform efforts Donald Barnhouse characterized as a form of "godless humanitarianism."[74] Machen articulated this unease when he wrote:

> Civil and religious liberty is being treated openly as though it had been merely a passing phase in human life, well enough in its day, but now out of date . . . Everywhere there rises before our eyes the specter of a society where security...will be attained at the expense of liberty, where the security that is attained will be the security of fed beasts in a stable, and where all the high aspirations of humanity will have been crushed by an all-powerful State.[75]

With this in mind, Machen was moved to rhetorically ask, "Is this a time when we ought to be contented with things as they are?"[76]

Keith Brooks (whose *Prophecy Monthly* at times read as much like a "Current Events Digest and Commentary" as it did a religious monthly), although no "friend" of the Roosevelt presidency, and as noted above, was willing to consider that there existed "subtle tendencies toward setting up infallible masters here," was not as pessimistic as some other historic fundamentalists. Reviewing the book, *Two Worlds in Conflict* by Hamilton Fish Armstrong in July 1937, Brooks noted "the great gulf" between "European dictatorships and American democracy." Quoting freely from Armstrong, he drew attention to the fact that the "two systems" held radically incompatible views of mankind, and though using the same words, meant entirely different things by them. (How very postmodern.) Art, music, literature, philosophy, science, and the media were all subsumed by dictatorships for self-justifying propaganda purposes. And, he noted, "people live according to the rules... 'revealed' to infallible men...and enforced by decrees and bullets...." Such was not [yet] the case in America.[77]

"Obviously our own government is not ideal," he wrote, "for it shelters many narrow and selfish individuals, yet we still have a semblance of freedom. We do not allow any one man to set himself up on high where his aberrations can destroy the comfort, security and even the lives of millions of men and women."[78] Brooks' main concern was over the gullibility of the public in general and Christians in particular—especially regarding Hitler.

"Is it possible," he queried, "that intelligent people of the United States should swallow the glowing reports of what Hitler has done spiritually for Germany?" Is there anyone, Brooks wondered, who does not realize that if any German newspaper editor or any citizen were to utter words of doubt about "the infallibility of the regime," such a person would immediately end up in prison or even dead? "Under such conditions," he asked rhetorically, "do we not expect to find a deadly uniformity?"[79] "Yet," Brooks revealed, with more than a touch of frustration and disgust in his words,

speeches have only recently been made from church platforms in the city of Los Angeles in defense of Hitler, the "facts" from which we could easily show were put together with scissors and paste from mimeographed releases coming from the official propaganda bureau—and many good Christian people gulped it down, nodding approval at one another.[80]

One Man's Passionate Plea in Defense of Civil Liberties

Donald Barnhouse, writing in *Revelation* magazine in September 1938, also addressed these fears over civil liberties being curtailed. However, he did so from a more down-to-earth perspective. He, too, defended the "rights" of the individual against an overbearing authority. But his essay, which can only be labeled "amazing" in light of the criticism repeated hurled at the historic fundamentalists for their reputed "political indifference," was aimed more at his fellow fundamentalists than others, calling on them to practice what they preached in the arena of civil liberties. It is noteworthy that Barnhouse, who was one of the most "notorious" prophetic practitioners of the 1930s, leaves prophetic comparisons and possibilities out of this essay. It is a completely political discussion.

He began by reminding his readers that Americans still enjoyed a tremendous amount of liberty compared to what others around the world enjoyed, especially in eastern and central Europe. The Constitution still ensured the right of freedom of press, though he foresaw "encroachments upon this principle." And there was still free speech even though Barnhouse believed it "is curtailed in several important respects." Freedom of worship was still enjoyed by all, "though there are important enemies of this principle." Yes, rights and liberties were still in place, rights and liberties "theoretically guaranteed to all, without respect of race, sex, income, or religion."[81] But....

Barnhouse was deeply troubled. What was happening in Europe seemed to be beginning in America. This moved him to warn the believer that it was "extremely important that Christians in this country be on the lookout to war against every attempt at lessening our liberties, because the destruction of minor liberties is ALWAYS followed by the destruction of liberties of proclaiming the Christian faith."[82]

Barnhouse was convinced numerous attempts were taking place in America to suppress the liberties of unpopular groups, groups with whom even Christians strongly disagreed, and thus "some Christians, at least, may be guilty of participating in this curtailment," while others were simply indifferent toward such actions. This was wrong. Barnhouse admitted that in saying this he might be accused of not understanding (for example) the racial issues of the South. On the contrary, he did understand, "not only from travel, reading, and conversation with people who have been touched by these matters, but by seeing the other side of the problem also."[83] Barnhouse reminded those who would commit a "little wrong...in order to nourish a great right," that they might bring about a situation, "which in turn will destroy the very rights for which [they] once compromised."[84]

He went beyond generalities and gave specific examples, "right out of our own American life," with which his fundamentalist readers could grapple. There was, for example, the Jehovah Witnesses. They taught their children that to salute the American flag was blasphemous. There were "patriots," members of local school boards and town councils who then barred "these poor deluded children" from going to school. Barnhouse called this a "clear violation of the Constitution of the United States." To allow such a violation to go uncorrected endangered everyone's "right of worship." He had seen the fanatical crowds in Germany salute the Swastika flag and Hitler, and considered it better that a few children be able to abstain from saluting the American flag in a classroom "than to unleash movements which might make us all salute some banner," which would indicate the death of all freedoms.[85]

Barnhouse pointed his readers back to an incident that had occurred in 1917 as an example of what he was protesting. A group of Boston pacifists, "The Association to Abolish War," not only was continuously spied on by the federal government but "when they gave to their printer the text of the Sermon on the Mount to be printed in a leaflet by itself without comment, the United States government authorities refused permission to have it printed on the grounds that it was anti-American propaganda."[86]

Surprisingly, he also "heartily" believed in the work of the American Civil Liberties Union. Despite their radicalism and communist connections, he believed they were doing a good work. "They are right," he wrote, "in rushing to the defense of the defenseless." In raising money "to defend the right of a lone communist to distribute a political tract, they have been preserving my rights to distribute a religious tract."[87] And he praised the Supreme Court's decision that upheld this right of unmolested distribution, calling it "a just and needed verdict."[88] Why such passion on Barnhouse's part? Why was he, as he put it, "strongly prejudiced in favor of this particular Communist who was in jail in the South for passing out leaflets?" Because, as he reminded his readers, he had been to Germany:

> I have stood in the room where a multigraph was printing secret leaflets in favor of the freedom of the pulpit of Pastor Niemoller, and knew that some who circulated these very leaflets, which were in favor of liberty and justice, would go to prison and death for passing them on.... I do not want anything in America to take us even one step on the road that leads in that direction.[89]

Yet he did see America beginning to move down that road, being led in part by public officials—including the President. He believed Roosevelt had undermined civil liberties by doing nothing when unions seized control of factories through sit-down strikes. Barnhouse was not against labor's right to organize, but he also strongly favored an open shop, because, as he wrote, "to force a man into a Union with whose principles he may heartily disagree is an intolerable condition" that needed to be corrected if "our labor difficulties" are to be solved. And factory owners had rights, too. "The property of the employers is theirs. The machines do not belong to the workers, nor does an incompetent worker have a vested right to his job." Instead of defending the Constitutional rights of the owners, the President had remained silent. Why? Because, as Barnhouse cynically commented, "presidents need votes, and elections are always approaching," and then noted:

> Some men's votes are bought for a glass of whiskey, or the promise of a job. Other men's votes are bought by a sacrifice of some of the liberties which belong to us all, without realizing that they, who have sold their votes for such a price, may be the chief victims some day.[90]

For the same reason—votes—he believed the President had remained silent in the face of the "fascistic" actions of Frank Hague, Mayor of Jersey City, New Jersey. Here was a situation that clearly rankled Barnhouses' high view of civil liberties, and he believed it should do so for all believers. "Christians must realize the importance of the struggle in Jersey City, and be concerned about it," he warned, because

> every suppression of Christianity in fascist states had begun exactly in the manner in which Jersey City authorities have moved in recent months. The Gospel has always flourished where civil liberties flourished and the Gospel is always ultimately persecuted where civil liberties are curtailed.[91]

What had happened in Jersey City? What had Mayor Hague done to so arouse Barnhouse's civic ire? First he had declared himself "the law" in his city, and then had taken upon himself (evidently with the aid of his heavy-handed police force) the right to deny Labor the right to picket during a strike. When "lovers of civil liberties" came to the city to protest Hague's arrogant actions, including the socialist Norman Thomas, they were sent packing by the Jersey City Police. As Barnhouse dramatically wrote, "A former candidate for the Presidency of the United States was hustled away by a few officers, armed with blackjacks, and ignominiously thrust upon a departing ferry boat."[92] And Roosevelt, who could have "showed a world of mad dictators the real greatness of democracy," did nothing because (according to Barnhouse) Hague was Vice-Chairman of the Democratic National Committee and a close friend of James Farley who dispensed "federal patronage for modern New Jersey, controlling the WPA for that third of the state."[93]

Outraged, two Congressmen, Jerry O'Connell and John Bernard, vowed they were going to challenge Hague by speaking in Jersey City's Journal Square. On the evening they were to speak, a large "pro-Hague" crowd gathered and the police cordoned off the area, preventing the Congressmen from speaking. Frustrated, they went home, as did the New York newspaper reporters. However, the evening was not over yet and at this point in his essay Barnhouse began to liberally quote from the account of one of the reporters, Donald B. Robinson.[94] According to Robinson, a group of reporters were in the Jersey City subway station sometime after 11 p.m. when a gang of thugs invaded the station and began beating up "Semitic-looking men." Robinson described one such beating as follows:

> We heard the first scream. We ran up the (tube) stairs. A slugger gang was at work. Eight or ten of them, hard, strong, some wearing sweaters: the Jersey City Athletic League. They were thumping a little fellow, obviously a Jew. The Jew was sobbing, "Please, please, I'm a sick man." But they kept on swinging, gouging. He broke away, rushed down a staircase to the platform. They followed at a run. "Catch that G__ d___ Jew," one yelled at me as he ran by. They caught him and knocked him down. They punched and kicked him—in the eye, the mouth, the stomach, the groin. Blood streamed across the tube platform, dripped down the side. "Leave me alone," the little Jew begged. "I didn't do nothing." Two station guards stood nearby, [but they] did nothing. We reporters were sick, but what could we do? Cowards, of course, all of us....[95]

Robinson briefly described other beatings that had also taken place. His experience moved him to cry, "don't talk to me about the possibility of Fascism in these United States. I saw Fascism, Nazism, anything you want to call it, in all its beastiality. I heard the cry I've expected but dreaded hearing in this country: 'Kill the Jew Bastard!' "[96]

Robinson concluded with these words: "We reporters were quiet on the train, scared inside us. Not by blood. We've seen too much of that. It was by the premonition of what this scene may mean."[97] Barnhouse was of the same mind and reminded his fundamentalist audience that "that fear should be in the minds of true Christians everywhere."[98] He closed his essay on civil liberties by once more mentioning that he had been in Europe and had witnessed the demise of liberties over there. He wanted none of it at home. Then, with intense passion, he concluded:

> Any Christian who fails to cry out against these same tendencies while they are at work in the United States, *even though their victims be the enemies of our truth*, is an enemy of the liberty of the Gospel of Jesus Christ. Not only may he have to answer for that weakness some day, but he may be the cause of much suffering on the part of those who have stronger consciences than he, and who will stand to the death against the infringement of the rights and liberties of all men.[99]

Yes, strong and admirable words from the pen of a historic fundamentalist during the Great Depression. Indisputably they belie any charge of political indifference. And he still speaks, "even though he is dead." At times Barnhouse's essay startles us with its graphic language and anecdotes, making us shamefully reluctant to embrace our past. It is passionate, it is imposing, it is disturbing. This is *my* American history? Perhaps it ought to be required reading, even today, especially by those evangelicals who wish to impose prayer in our public schools, or those patriots who wish to make flag burning a violation of the Constitution, or those university intellectuals who, under the name of "political correctness," are seeking to stifle dissenting voices. The word picture of the beating of Jews in a Jersey City subway station is as vivid in the mind as are the television images of the black civil rights marchers in Selma, Alabama being attacked by clubs and police dogs and fire hoses—and just as sickening and offensive. How deep has been the American people's bondage to the sin of racial hatred, a bondage even many evangelicals have willingly submitted to.

Nor did Barnhouse, or his fundamentalists allies, fall silent on this issue after this one outburst of "political reflection" and protest. In 1940, when the Supreme Court ruled 8 to 1 that the children of Jehovah Witnesses who refused to salute the flag could be expelled from school by local school boards, many historic fundamentalists protested. *Moody Monthly*, for example, reprinted a scathing editorial from the *Christian Union Herald* which concluded by noting that "this ruling of the highest court of the land ought to give all who cherish the supreme rights of conscience serious concern," and then heatedly asked: "Is America going to resign her position as defender of the rights of small religious minorities? Are world conditions going to induce a wave of hysteria among us which will let us in for a new and sinister form of witch-hunting?"[100]

Barnhouse considered the decision "the first bad decision against freedom of religion," and in 1942, when the Supreme Court ruled 5 to 4 to allow local communities to tax tract distributors (i.e., Jehovah Witnesses), and even to "revoke the right to distribute literature at any time—even after tract distributors have paid the tax—'without cause, notice or hearing,' " he called it "a decision that is directly against all the nation is fighting for." Incensed over such a restriction, not only on religious freedom, but also freedom of speech and press, Barnhouse took pen in hand, noting that "the matter is so important that we feel it proper to give more space to it than we would to a usual editorial."[101]

Although stressing his opposition to the doctrines of the Jehovah Witnesses, he also emphasized that he had "great sympathy with their right to religious freedom" because it was his freedom, too. In support of his position, Barnhouse quoted Chief Justice Harlan Fiske Stone, who authored the minority opinion (that "a way has been found for the effective suppression of speech and press and religion despite constitutional guarantees"), and Justice Murphy (a Roman Catholic, Barnhouse noted), also part of the minority opinion, who wrote that "if the Court is to err in evaluating claims that freedom of speech, freedom of the press and freedom of religion have been invaded, far better that it err in being over-protective of these precious rights."[102]

Barnhouse, who evidently wanted to show he was not alone in his indignation, also quoted from a St. Louis *Post-Dispatch* editorial (which stated that to restrict the Constitutional rights of one "sect" opened the door to restrict other "sects"), and a New York *Times* editorial which noted (much to Barnhouse's approval):

> The minorities whose civil rights are threatened are always small and, to many, obnoxious . . . Yet their treatment is the test, and will always be the test, of the sincerity with which we cling to the Bill of Rights. If those of us who belong to the larger groups do not defend the rights of persons with whom we disagree, and whom we may actually detest, we are confessing that we hold our own rights on sufferance, or by our numbers, or by our political or other power.[103]

If written words could shout, then Barnhouse's bellowed when he wrote: "With these writers we agree. The Editor of *Revelation* holds that the majority of the Justices of the Supreme Court did most grievously err in handing down this decision." (Evidently the Court came to "agree" with Barnhouse for it reversed itself the following year.)

But in August 1942, not knowing the future of this item, Barnhouse found himself wondering how anyone would believe what was written in the Atlantic Charter, "when at the same moment our own Supreme Court is finding a loophole" that would allow local suppression of religious freedom. Under the ruling, he reasoned (perhaps yielding to hyperbole), a Catholic dominated locality could exclude the distribution of Protestant literature, a Jewish local Christian literature, and a "Ku Klux municipality in Alabama" Catholic tracts. Anger etched his words as he concluded his essay:

> This decision is nefarious, un-American, un-Christian, and should be resisted by all right-thinking men. The same law that gives a Russelite the right to spread his tracts gives you the right to spread yours, and the same law that takes away his right takes away the rights of all men except the clique which rules. This is sheer Nazi-ism.[104]

Considering the fact that when Barnhouse wrote this editorial America was in the midst of white-hot, righteous patriotism, he is to be commended for his bold advocacy of the civil liberties of the Jehovah Witnesses who appeared very unpatriotic to many Americans.

No doubt Barnhouse's essays on civil liberties put him at odds with some historic fundamentalists. But it also put him at odds with many beyond fundamentalism, including some of the political leaders of the day—especially those who promoted the "Brown" scare. One will look long and hard for more impassioned pleas for civil liberties by anyone during those cheerless decades, or one that places them in such salvific dimensions—one is an enemy of the gospel if one supports the suppression of Constitutional liberties, or a Nazi sympathizer, which, at that time, amounted to the same thing. Considering how open and vocal the historic fundamentalists were in this area, it is something of a mystery as to how such forceful and clear concerns for protecting the civil liberties of the least liked among us, during decades when the fascist and communist mind-set appealed in varying degrees to many Americans of all social classes and races, have been overlooked by historians, especially evangelical historians. [105]

NOTES

1. John D. Woodbridge, Mark A. Noll, and Nathan O. Hatch, *The Gospel in America: Themes in the story of America's Evangelicals* (Grand Rapids: Zondervan Publishing House, 1979), 241.
2. Mark A. Noll, *The Scandal of the Evangelical Mind* (Grand Rapids: William B. Eerdmans Publishing Company, 1994), 168.
3. "Notes on an Open Letter: Should Christians Vote?" *The Sunday School Times*, February 23, 1936, 122.
4. Ibid. At the same time, this same editor could seemingly contradict himself. In answer to a letter asking *The Sunday School Times* to "arouse the people" to boycott periodicals that printed "indecent and degrading" cigarette and liquor advertisements, the editor, while sympathizing with the letter writer, nevertheless answered: "But do we find any commands or injunctions in the New Testament that Christians in this present age should attempt to deal with the world as such—that is, the unsaved world—concerning these matters? This does not seem to be the duty or mission of the church."

    The editor did concede that there may be times when "some gross immorality" or some serious threat to the community that would endanger families might arise and thus "it may be proper for Christian people to appeal to the 'powers that be.' " But this was an exception. As far as the editor was concerned, there was nothing in either the gospels or the epistles that gave credence to the belief that the church was to "deal in a large or general way with the sins of the unsaved world about us," or even it would seem, "attempt to change such conditions in any way or...to remonstrate against them." ("Notes on Open Letters: Should Christians Try to Reform the World," *The Sunday School Times*, June 29, 1935, 430.)

    That the above seems to contradict what is quoted in the text by the same editor of the same magazine leaves one puzzled. (It may be the editor is distinguishing between the church as such and the individual believer, but this is far from clear in this particular response.) It also apparently contradicts what *The Sunday School Times* published in 1938; that is, a petition to be submitted to Congress to stop, "so far as possible by Federal law, the great advertising campaign for the sale of alcoholic beverages now going on by press and radio." The petition was sponsored by a consortium of 27 organizations including among others, the W. C. T. U., the Anti-Saloon League, the International Society of Christian Endeavor, and the Presbyterian Church, U. S. A. (R. H. Martin, "A Crusade to Stop Liquor Advertising," *The Sunday School Times*, July 30, 1938, 532.)

5. The editor of *Revelation* stressed that every Christian should, by voting and personal interest, do all he can for society ("Tomorrow: Class Struggle," August 1934, 319.) In another article he took to task those who opposed all schemes of social betterment simply because they were proposed by social gospelers. A true Christian should have a compassionate "attitude toward every work which can in any wise alleviate human suffering" ("Errors of Fundamentalists," *Revelation*, March 1935), 126, 127. Also see " Businessmen for Congress," *Moody Institute Monthly*, July 1936, 506.

6. *The King's Business*, in introducing Gilbert to its readers, wrote that his book had been widely reviewed "by the great city newspapers as a unique contribution, resulting from deep research into the spiritual and moral forces which underlie America's Constitutional ideals." *Moody Institute Monthly* gave it a brief but favorable lead review in its "Book Notices" section, July 1936.

7. Dan Gilbert, "The Rise of Beastism in America," *Moody Monthly*, September 1938, 14.

8. Ibid.

9. Joseph Taylor Britan, "The Continuous Cry of the Persecuted," *The Sunday School Times*, October 14, 1939, 714.

10. James Edward Congdon, "Christian Patriotism," *Moody Institute Monthly*, November 1936, 111, 112.

11. Ibid, 112.

12. Ibid.

13. Ibid. This, of course, is as true today as it was in 1936. Also see, "The Stay at Homes," *Moody Institute Monthly*, November 1935, 110. This editorial quoted extensively the Rev. M. P. Boynton who pastored Chicago's Woodlawn Baptist Church. Boynton agreed with Congdon on the ballot box reflecting the political health of the nation. He charged that "the stay at home vote is the major menace to our Republic," and that "the stay at home citizen is in league with every evil troubling America." Pretty strong words.

14. Paul Rood, "Citizenship," *The King's Business*, July 1936, 252.

15. Ibid.

16. Ibid.

17. "Businessmen for Congress," *Moody Institute Monthly*, July 1936, 252.

18. "Our Greatest National Peril," *Moody Institute Monthly*, July 1935, 526.

19. "Our Economic Life in Light of Christian Ideals," *Moody Institute Monthly*, July 1933, 481.

20. Clarence H. Benson, "Shelving the Bible in America," *The Sunday School Times*, May 5, 1934, 291. So much, then, for the myth that the historic fundamentalists did not believe "that Christians must build moral principles into society...." (*The Gospel in America*, 241).

21. Dan Gilbert, "God and the Constitution," *The King's Business*, July 1936, 254, 255.

22. "Reaping What We Sow," *Moody Institute Monthly*, December 1933, 146. (But then, this thought was on the minds of many that were not historic fundamentalists.) See Leo P. Ribuffo, *The Old Christian Right: The Protestant Far Right from the Great Depression to the Cold War* (Philadelphia: Temple University Press, 1983), 19ff, 180-185, and T. H. Watkins, *The Hungry Years: A Narrative History of the*

Great Depression in America (New York: Henry Holt and Company, 1999), 313-321.

23. John Lewis Gaddis, *We Now Know: Rethinking Cold War History* (New York: Oxford University Press, 1997), 188.

24. "Editorial Comment," *The Sunday School Times*, September 16, 1933, 583.

25. "Editorial: The Blue Eagle," *Revelation*, September 1933, 329.

26. Louis Bauman, "The Blue Eagle and Our Duty as Christians," *The Sunday School Times*, September 16, 1933, 583.

27. Ibid, 584. It is interesting to note that Bauman evidently believed that having a job was a "fundamental [individual] right," (i.e., something the government should try to guarantee).

28. Ibid.

29. Ibid. In a second article on the NRA, considering its prophetic significance, Bauman also considered its political implications. The NRA, he wrote, symbolized a failure of democracy, and was an indication of the extent of lawlessness abroad in society. Despite this, he believed it sought "to recover to every man that inalienable right that is his—a decent job at an honest wage." Bauman went on to note that, "In the tremendous effort our government is now making to provide millions with the work that means food, shelter, and clothing for them and their little children, every true Christian should lend a strong hand." ("N. R. A., the Sign, and Its Spiritual Significance," *The King's Business*, November, 1933), 379.

    These comments, appearing in a prophetic article, apparently are a reminder to the readers not to become so futuristic minded that they are of no earthly good to their country in a crisis. They also confirm the possibility that prophetic articles served as "vehicles" for historic fundamentalist's political commentary.

30. The historic fundamentalists were quite concerned about the class-war rhetoric (in part fed by the New Deal) and the labor violence that was increasing as the Depression continued. See, for example, "Returning Sanity," *Moody Institute Monthly*, February 1935, 263; Rollin T. Chafer, "Editorial: Economics and the Lord's Work," *Bibliotheca Sacra*, April-June 1938, 135. Chafer pleaded with government, business, and labor to sit down together and make peace. "It is impossible to fight one another into prosperity," he wrote. Also see "Breakdown of Law in America," *The King's Business*, April 1937, 176.

31. Louis Bauman, "1935 - Prophetic Review (Part I)," *The King's Business*, April 1936, 129.

32. Clarence E. Mason, Jr., "The Pearl Harbor Disaster," *The Sunday School Times*, April 18, 1942, 307.

33. "Editorial: The Code vs. Liberty," *Moody Institute Monthly*, March 1935, 314.

34. Clarence H. Bensen, "Why Has Crime Come in Like a Flood in America," *The Sunday School Times*, May 9, 1936, 327.

35. Louis Bauman, "In 1935—A Prophetic Review, (Part I)," 91.

36. R. T. Chafer, "Editorial: What is Wrong?" *Bibliotheca Sacra*, October-December 1937, 385.

37. "The Epoch of Intellectual Dishonesty," *Prophecy Monthly*, June 1936, 27.

38. Louis Bauman, "A Remarkable 'Horse and Buggy' Days Prophecy Fulfilled," *The King's Business*, April 1937, 129.

39. "A Post-Election Meditation," *Prophecy Monthly*, December 1936, 29.

40. "Why Not Put Browder in the Brain Trust?" *Prophecy Monthly*, May 1936, 8.

41. Ibid, 9. Also see "Tugwell's Trinity," *The Sunday School Times*, July 14, 1934, 453 (front page).

42. Arthur Herman, *Joseph McCarthy: Reexamining the Life and Legacy of America's Most Hated Senator* (New York: The Free Press, 2000), 67, 68, 74.

43. Herbert Romerstein and Eric Brendel, *The Venona Secrets: Exposing Soviet Espionage and America's Traitors* (Washington, D. C.: Regency Publishing, Inc., 2000), 173, 181. Also Herman, 74.

44. Ibid, 210-219.

45. Herman, 75, 76.

46. "Our Economic Life in the Light of Christian Ideals," 481.

47. F.W. Haberer, "Socialism and First Century Christianity," *Moody Institute Monthly*, July 1933, 482. This article favored a "Christian" form of socialism, but nevertheless was published by Gray, who, as editor of *Moody*, often aired both sides of a particular political or theological issue.

48. "What Will Pull Us Out," *Moody Institute Monthly*, December 1934, 152.

49. "Shall We Kick Out Capitalism," *Prophecy Monthly*, February 1937, 4, 5.

50. Ibid, 5.

51. Ibid, 6.

52. "Tomorrow: Class Struggle," 318.

53. Louis Bauman, "The Death Struggle of Two Tyrannies," *The King's Business*, January 1937, 10. Elsewhere in this article, Bauman speculated that the clash between the rich and the worker was a conflict that, "will bring just judgment to the rich, many of whom, on the wages of the toilers, kept back by fraud, have lived wantonly," 12.

54. "The Cure for the Depression," *The King's Business*, April 1932, 156.

55. "Government and National Prosperity," *The King's Business*, July 1933, 210.

56. "N. R. A., The Sign and Its Spiritual Significance," 380.

57. "Tomorrow: Class Struggle," 318. Barnhouse was also upset that the Supreme Court had overturned New York's minimum wage law. The decision, he wrote, allows "unscrupulous employers" to continue to "exploit" workers for starvation wages. The Bible, he warned, quoting Malachi and Paul, condemned such men ("A Window on the World," *Revelation*, August 1936), 324. He also criticized those who voted against child-labor laws ("Editorial: Social Gospel," May 1938), 194.

58. James Gray, "Labor Sunday Message: Editorial," *Moody Institute Monthly*, September 1935, 5. It is interesting to note that Gray republished in the July 1935 issue of *Moody* an editorial book review ("Twenty Years at Hull House") which had first appeared in the July 1911 issue of what was then known as the *Christian Workers Magazine*. The reviewer in that editorial accorded Jane Adams and Hull House "every mead of praise," calling her a philanthropist without equal and a true patriot. The editor had little sympathy with the unintelligent demagogue, "political or religious," who would call her a socialist or anarchist. "In her chosen sphere criticism is shamed to silence. As for ourselves, her shoe lachet we are 'not worthy to unloose.' "

59. Vance Havner, "Specialists or Seers," *Revelation*, January 1932, 5. Others seconded Havner's criticism. Louis Bauman had toured the country in 1931 and had witnessed first-hand the closed factories and fields full of rotting produce. He had also seen

the long bread lines in the cities where families were haunted with the possibility of starvation. Those who had shaped the modern world—men of learning, science and commerce—now seemed totally inept in dealing with the Depression. "We cannot help but have a haunting fear," he wrote, "that these modern intellectual gods of the world of science and commerce have been taking advantage of us...." All things considered not an unwarranted suspicion. ("The Sad Failure of 'Men of Renown,' " *The Kings Business*, November 1931), 486.

60. Joseph Edwin Harris, "Sin, Satan and the Social Gospel," *Bibliotheca Sacra*, October-December 1934, 451. What the historic fundamentalists were criticizing was not the efforts designed to deal with the obvious pressing social and economic wrongs (though they might disagree with the means). What troubled them was the political philosophy motivating such legislation, as well as the purported end—the perfectly just, compassionate and righteous society. Having lived through the New Deal, Fair Deal, and the Great Society with its "War on Poverty," the historic fundamentalist's theologically grounded cautions do not seem at all out of place.

61. Here, then, was what deeply troubled many historic fundamentalists—the idea that a viable, economically sound democracy could be constructed by substituting for God's guidance and words, government regulation and manipulation.

62. J. Gresham Machen, *The Christian Faith in the Modern World* (Grand Rapids: Wm. B. Eerdmans Publishing Co., 1936, 1970), 3, 4.

63. Ibid.

64. R. T. Chafer, "Centralized Power," *Bibliotheca Sacra*, April-June 1936, 130.

65. "On the Threshold of a New Year," *The King's Business*, January 1937, 4.

66. "Breakdown of Law in America," *The King's Business*, April 1937, 126.

67. Dan Gilbert, "How Can We Combat Atheism in Our Schools," *The Sunday School Times*, August 6, 1938, 550, 551.

68. Dan Gilbert, "The Christian View of the Constitutional Government," *The King's Business*, November 1937, 424.

69. Ibid.

70. Ibid, 425.

71. Ibid.

72. Ibid, 458.

73. When the *New York Times* declared that evangelical involvement in politics posed "a greater threat to democracy than was presented by communism," Richard Land, President of the Christian Life Commission of the Southern Baptist Convention responded, in part, by going to history:
    In 1798, John Adams, the nation's second President said: "We have no government armed in power capable of contending in human passions unbridled by morality and religion. Our Constitution was made for a moral and religious people. It is wholly inadequate for the government of any other." ("A Threat to Democracy," *Light*, March-April 1996, 2.)

74. Donald Barnhouse, "The Errors of Fundamentalism," *Revelation*, March 1935, 127. Also Oliver E. Williams, "Spiritual Recovery First," *Moody Institute Monthly*, November 1935, 126. Williams complained that "the theory of the New Deal seems to be that of reformation—reform capitalism, reform democracy, reform business. It leaves God out."

75. Machen, 9, 10. Machen's fears cannot be limited to the Depression era. Nor, considering all that was unfolding during that period, can we call him paranoid.
76. Ibid.
77. "An Impossible Gulf Between Democracy and Dictatorships," *Prophecy Monthly*, July 1937, 32, 33.
78. Ibid, 32.
79. Ibid.
80. Ibid, 33.
81. "Tomorrow: Current Events in Light of the Bible—The Decline of Civil Liberties," *Revelation*, September 1938, 378.
82. Ibid, 396.
83. Ibid.
84. Ibid.
85. Ibid, 397.
86. Ibid. Barnhouse could have justifiably mentioned how some had falsely accused the premillenial dispensationalists of being in Germany's hire during the First World War.
87. Ibid, 397, 398. *Moody Monthly* agreed with Barnhouse on this issue of unhindered tract distribution, and for the same reason. See "The Right to Distribute Tracts," September, 1938, 4. Also see "American Liberty—and Tracts," *The Sunday School Times*, January 7, 1939, front page, for its amen and appreciation of the *Christian* liberties "we still have in this beloved land."

    It should be noted, however, that Barnhouse believed that communists should be forbidden from holding any government office, as well as being forbidden from occupying any pulpit ("Communists and Preachers," *Revelation*, April 1938, 146.)
88. Ibid.
89. Ibid. Carpenter, in *Revive Us Again*, is aware of Barnhouse's visit to Germany, (93), as well as some of the Historic Fundamentalists' responses to the New Deal, (100, 101, 106, 107). Yet he sees no political motions or reflection in their statements, and can still claim "Fundamentalists had little reason to believe that their voices could be heard in the arena of public affairs in the 1930s, so it seemed practical for them to steer clear of such activity," 107. It is difficult to understand how Carpenter can make such a statement.
90. Ibid.
91. Ibid. At this point in his essay, Barnhouse inserted an implied "political" criticism of the Catholic Church's fascist sympathies, remarking:
    > Jersey City is a predominantly Roman Catholic city. The Catholic Church is imbued with the idea that it must fight "communism" today above every other enemy. It is blind to the fact that what it needs to fight is the suppression of civil liberties fostered under both communism and fascism. The dictatorship in Italy smiles upon the Church at present because the Church has blessed its Ethiopian moves and has, some authorities say, bought Italian government bonds by the millions in order to uphold the credit of Italy. But the dictatorship in Germany…has steadily fought against the rights of the Church. Rome has not yet awakened to the fact that she must fight principles and not movements, since dangerous principles can crop up even in friendly movements, (398).

92. Ibid. This was not the first time Thomas was sent summarily packing. T. H. Watkins records a similar incident in his book, *The Hungry Years*. In March 1935, Thomas was about to speak to a few hundred sharecroppers (under the auspices of the Southern Tenant Farmers Union), in Birdsong, Arkansas. Suddenly they were "surrounded by a gang of thirty or forty armed thugs." One of them shouted, "there ain't going to be no speaking here. We are the citizens of this county and we run it to suit ourselves. We don't need no G___ D___ Yankee Bastard to tell us what to do!" At that point, Thomas and his companions "were seized, forced back into their car, and told to leave the county forthwith. They left" (386).

93. Ibid. Barnhouse, despite his prophetic "pick-ups" from the politics of his day, also appears cynically familiar with the political machinations going on around New Deal patronage.

94. Ibid, 399. Barnhouse does not mention which New York City newspaper Robinson worked for.

95. Ibid.

96. Ibid.

97. Ibid.

98. Ibid.

99. Ibid.

100. "Fanatics Must Salute the Flag," *Moody Monthly*, October 1940, 87.

101. "Danger to Liberty," *Revelation*, August 1942, 351.

102. Ibid.

103. Ibid.

104. Ibid. Also see, Barnhouse, "Tomorrow: Motives of Judgment," *Revelation*, November 1947, 478.

105. Other political and social problems also attracted the attention of the historic fundamentalists which will not be pursued in these pages—Social Security, Mercy Killing (euthanasia), the Townsend Plan, the evil of the United States trading with Japan while it was raping China, the spiritual causes of WW II, etc.

CHAPTER FIVE

Historic Fundamentalism Post World War II: The Evangelical Obligation to Save America

Recently, within a two-day span, I listened as two evangelicals scholars publicly repeated the hoary cliché that the historic fundamentalists withdrew into the closet of personal piety and ignored the world during the 1930s. Both times I had to restrain myself from leaping to my feet and embarrassing one and all by shouting, "It wasn't necessarily so!" But I said nothing (out loud), having noticed that those who hold to this cliché have trouble processing any information that might expose it as less than absolute. Few things are as popular among activistic evangelical academics today as reminding each other of that doleful "pietistic time."

The conventional wisdom is that the awakening of evangelical political life and reflection, and its own brand of an evangelical social gospel began with Carl Henry's *The Uneasy Conscience of Modern Fundamentalism* (1947).[1] And Henry's book did indicate a new and more militant direction he and his fundamentalists allies wanted to go. He rejected the spiritual church concept that had dominated historic fundamentalists' thinking in the 1930s (as well as the extreme separatist, Anabaptist type stance that some historic fundamentalists had adopted) and advocated instead a cultural mandated activism derived from covenant theology. It was time, he declared, for the historic fundamentalists to get "political," to develop so to speak, their own "social plan" and put it into practice. I put the phrase in quotes because Henry was clear in cautioning evangelicals not to discard their foundation or move toward liberalism, and certainly he stressed there "was no need for fundamentalism to embrace liberalism's defunct social gospel."[2] Sadly, it must be admitted that as we enter the twenty-first century, a great many evangelicals seem to be ignoring this wise advice.

Henry (and associates) believed the evangelical church possessed the answers a desperate, atomically frightened world needed in 1947. Only the Christian view of man, sin, and God's redemptive message was "the adequate key to the door of Fundamentalist world betterment."[3] However to accomplish this not only worthy but mandated goal, fundamentalists were going to have to change their errant ways.

Basically Henry had four criticisms of the way fundamentalists were functioning that needed to change if they were not going to be marginalized into a cultic, inconsequential movement.

Eliminate the Negative

First, it lacked a social program to practically deal with acknowledged social evils, or even the "social" passion to take on such a task. The "gospel," Henry lamented, "stands divorced from a passion to right the world" and evangelicals stood, for the first time in history, "divorced from the great reform movements." Christian "social imperatives," he concluded, "were in the hands of those who understood it in sub-Christian terms."[4] Henry was aiming directly at the dispensationalists. Personally, he favored a form of non-dispensational premillennialism that did not exclude working for some Kingdom "trophies" here and now. "Christian civilization," he reasoned, "does not argue against an effort to win as many areas as possible by the redemptive power of Christ."[5]

This led to Henry's second criticism. Fundamentalisms' "prophetic cheerlessness," he charged, made it impossible to have a world-changing message, that its "despairing view of world history" severed the "relevance of evangelicalism to the modern global crisis." Such pessimism had caused many fundamentalists to lose their humanitarianism. And some fundamentalist "workers," Henry fumed, substituted "a familiarity with the prophetic teaching of the Bible for an aggressive effort to proclaim Christ as the potent answer to the dissolution of world culture." Telling people that only Christ's second coming would solve the world's problems caused many of them to turn from the church to humanism for answers needed now.[6]

Third, Henry chided, fundamentalists not only did not involve themselves in reform movements, but they attacked groups that did, such as the Federal Council of Churches or the World Council of Churches which were energetically trying to defeat "social ills." Henry was willing to admit that the American Council of Christian Churches, the National Association of Evangelicals, and the Southern Baptist were making some attempts at social action, but on the whole "the Fundamentalist opposition to societal ills has been more vocal than actual." At one point, Henry harshly compared fundamentalism with the priest and Levite in the Parable of the Good Samaritan (Luke 10:25-37), and noted that when fundamentalists were moved to social action, it was "spotty and usually of the emergency type." In fact, Henry held that not to support attacks on social evils being sponsored by non-evangelical groups put an evangelical in the place of opposing his Savior, who would "unhesitantly condemn" such evil.[7]

This somewhat harsh evaluation set the stage for Henry's final criticism. How is it, he queried, "that a world changing message narrowed its scope to the changing of isolated individuals?" Fundamentalist sermons, Henry complained, only preached against personal sin, not social sin. He did admit that such preaching indirectly attacked social evils (e.g., preaching against drinking did indirectly attack the liquor industry, "even though it does nothing to curb the menace itself" which was, of course, what Henry wanted).[8] "Modern Fundamentalism," he explained, "does not explicitly sketch the social implications of its message for the non-Christian world...." Just what did Henry mean by this? His answer was somewhat surprising: "It does not challenge the injustices of totalitarianism, the secularisms of modern education, the evils of racial hatred, the wrongs of current labor-management relations [or] the inadequate bases of international dealings."[9]

Accentuating the Positive

Evangelicals must, Henry asserted, offer their solution to the world's most pressing problems because "its redemptive message" was germane "to the global predicament." He was convinced that fundamentalists must affirm "two great convictions...if" they were going "to express the genius of Christian tradition." First, they must take a stand against all evil—both individual and social, and (second) they "must never be represented as in any way tolerant of such evil." Along with this, Christians must insist that "the redemptive work of Jesus Christ and the regenerative work of the Holy Spirit" were the only real way to overcome every expression of evil.[10] In fact, Henry believed it was right and proper for the "unregenerate" to live under Christian standards for "they are more easily reached for Christ than those who have made a deliberate break with Christian standards, because they can be reminded that Christian ethics cannot be retained apart from Christian metaphysics."[11]

Henry also believed "that without a transcendent spiritual ground in the living Redeemer no government can surmount the threat of disintegration," or put another way, "no political or economic system has utopian promise if the essential redemptive ingredient is missing from it." Due to the primacy this point had in Henry's thinking, he could write: "A redemptive totalitarianism is far preferable to an unredemptive democracy; a redemptive Communism far more advantages than an unredemptive Capitalism, and vice versa. But the very element which is abstracted from currently proposed solutions is this redemptive element. The evangelical task will be to reproclaim it."[12] (One can almost sense Roger Williams turning over in his grave.)

Along with adamantly declaring redemptive government as the only best solution to the world's social and political ills, Henry also called upon evangelicals "to discard elements of its message which cut the nerve of world compassion as contradictory to the inherent genius of Christianity" (i.e., a focus on prophecy) and "recapture its rightful leadership in pressing for a new world order." And most importantly, they must begin speaking with one voice. The FCC spoke for liberal Protestants. Likewise, "protestant evangelicalism too needs a single voice," and he urged the ACCC and the NAE to (somehow) come together.[13] "A single voice that speaks for Jesus in our global conferences," Henry enthused, " can be a determinative voice...a single statesman with the convictions of Paul would echo the great evangelical affirmations throughout world politics."[14]

Finally he called upon evangelical/fundamentalists to be willing to cooperate with others. "The evangelical ought to be counted upon," he urged, "in the war...against every wrong." Even if evangelicals could not achieve their own goals, they could still cooperate with others for the common good, even when the solution proposed may not be the very best possible—provided, of course, they gave "appropriate warnings" of the limitations and lack of stability in purely human solutions. This latter was an important caveat for Henry. On the one hand, in cooperating with others, evangelicals could not "maintain silence when evils are condemned by others." On the other hand, fundamentalists must not abandon their redemptive position. If they were in a majority within a mixed group, they should always "press the claims of Christ" as the only answer. If in a minority, they should join with others in condemning social evil but also issue a minority report, as it were, "insisting upon the regenerative context as alone able to secure a permanent rectification of such wrongs." Henry insisted though, that in working with non-evangelical groups, evangelicals must have the right "to witness to the redemptive power of Jesus." If they were not allowed to offer "a redemptive reference as a live option for the achievement of good ends," then they must leave the group and act independently—but "action there must be if evangelicalism is to recapture the spirit of its evangel."[15]

Expectations Seeking Confirmation

In looking back, one is taken by how idealistic, how optimistic, and, yes, even naïve Henry sounds. He tries to justify his case for evangelical political activism by appealing to Scripture and history, but in retrospect his arguments are surprisingly weak. He rightly points out that the Old Testament prophets spoke out against social injustice but fails to mention that they did not form political action committees. Next, when he tries to have John the Baptist, or even Jesus speak a "social message," he comes up woefully short. The best he can do with John the Baptist is speak of "the social spirit of John's preaching...."[16] He basically does the same with some of the things Jesus said, using as an example Jesus' answer to John's disciples' question as to whether Jesus was the expected Messiah after all.[17] Jesus' answer, according to Henry, makes it "difficult to find room for a gospel cut loose entirely from non-spiritual needs." Henry does admit, though, that Jesus did not offer a program for world peace, or the redistribution of the world's goods, or even a formula for how nations are to "carry on international relations." "But," Henry was quick to add, "He is not on that account disinterested in the nations and in the global man." Jesus' answer to the world's problems, however, was a redemptive one. "There is not a problem of global consequences but that, from the viewpoint of Jesus, redemption is a relevant formula. It is offered as the only adequate rest for world weariness...."[18] (Of course, it might be asked that when Jesus said, "come unto me...and I will give you rest," to whom was he speaking—individuals, or nations, or societies, or economic systems? Henry avoids the complication.)

Next Henry tries to solicit the support of the Apostle Paul to his crusade for an activistic, politically intrusive, Protestantism. "Paul's position" was also one of "ethical universalism," proving, Henry claimed, he was interested "with more than individual morals." Paul's message of Christ did not divide humanity but rather presented Christ as the only "Lord of humanity," the only true "relief for man's needs." This, too, proved, according to Henry, that Paul proclaimed "a social, as well as a personal, Christianity." Furthermore, Paul's missionary zeal nullified any idea "that he conceived of a believer's life as an exclusive privilege to be lived in monastic privacy; rather he was spiritually aflame to bring the whole world to the feet of Jesus."[19] But despite Henry's strivings, he offers no Scripture to support his "Pauline" interpretation. Although he implies the possibility, Henry does avoid claiming Paul was offering a program for solving the world's social evils. As for Paul "being aflame to bring the world to the feet of Jesus," well, so were the historic fundamentalists as their constant missionary and evangelistic efforts attested. Neither did many of them live in "monastic privacy." Many historic fundamentalists believed in separatism regarding church purity, but they lived and worked in the world in a variety of places and positions, and frequently, and even irritatingly, witnessed to their neighbors or fellow workers.

After Paul, Henry appealed to the early church, a church filled, he wrote, with a "world-changing zeal," a church "not embarrassed" over being accused "of turning the world upside down." Again, though, Henry admits: "This does not mean that early Christianity charted a course for moral reform; rather, it furnished the basic principles and moral dynamic for such reform, and concentrated on regeneration as the guarantee of bettered conditions."[20] One is hard pressed to see how the early church's ignoring of social activism and focusing on "regeneration as the guarantee of bettered conditions" differed from the position of the historic fundamentalists Henry was being so harsh toward. Nor do I think he would have appreciated someone quoting Tertullian at this point: "All zeal in pursuit of [political] glory and honor is dead in us. So we have no pressing inducement to take part in your public meetings. Nor is there anything more entirely foreign to us than the affairs of state."[21]

It is only when Henry arrived at the Zwinglian and Calvinistic reformations, did he find the comforting support he has been trying to extract from Scripture and church history:

> The Zwinglian Reformation in Switzerland, however, became more articulate about the civil and moral implications of regeneration, and the Calvinistic Reformation moved toward a truly catholic view of the Christian life. Calvin felt that the Hebrew-Christian tradition historically involved an articulate statement not only of dogmatics but of the social implications of redemption.[22]

It is in covenant theology, then, with its cultural mandate that Henry rests his case for a politically engaged evangelicalism. In doing so, however, he ignores the Anabaptist movements and the treatment meted out to them by the Reformers. He also ignores any subsequent history (e.g., the early Baptists in England or America, or Roger Williams) that might question his social/political ambitions for the post-war fundamentalists. Instead, he writes: "Today, Protestant fundamentalism although heir-apparent to the supernatural gospel of the Biblical and Reformation minds, is a stranger, in its prominent spirit, to the vigorous social interest of its ideological forebears."[23]

Responses Pro and Con

Despite its weaknesses, Henry's book was well received by such leading fundamentalists' journals as *The Sunday School Times* and *Moody Monthly* which began its review by declaring, "Dr. Henry sends out a ringing appeal for action, which his fellow fundamentalists can ill afford to ignore if evangelicalism is to make the impact upon the world which the times so desperately need." This magazine concluded its review by noting, "There is a pungent, tonic quality to this book that should commend it to all who long and pray for a mighty gospel offensive."[24] Keith Brooks, editor of *Prophecy Monthly*, gave the book a two and a half page review, drawing attention to the fact that, "He writes as an evangelical, born-again Fundamentalist, and if he finds some things among his Fundamentalists brethren that need correction or improvement, his attitude is that of an insider, and his suggestions are constructive rather than destructive."[25]

Nevertheless, even though Brooks agreed with Henry that fundamentalists may not have done all they could have done in the civic realm, and did have some duties in this world, he also believed there were a number of "questions on which many a pastor and layman would like to have a clearer light," but that Henry's book "does not seem to provide them."[26] Brooks' problem with Henry was probably widespread—how much time and effort was to be given to the political at the expense of the spiritual? Should church services be given over to advocates of civic and moral reform:

> Where shall the line be drawn? Shall church members devote time and energy to these movements to the neglect of church services and duties? Is any moral reform work of enduring character and should Christians engage in any such activities except where they have a definite opportunity to witness for Christ? . . . These are pertinent questions. There is a great need for spiritual discernment regarding these issues and this must have its basis in the New Testament.[27]

Perhaps the best critical response came from a young and still conservative Bernard Ramm, who by the mid-1960s was going to be one of neo-evangelicalism's shining scholars. Published in the *United Evangelical Action* in response to that magazines open query on whether "Dr Henry was right," Ramm, reiterating the thoughts of the historic fundamentalists of the Great Depression, began by asking the most basic of questions: *"For whom is Christian ethics?"* If it "is for governments, nations, and economic systems" then Christianity indeed has a social as well as a spiritual "task," Ramm conceded. However, he cautioned, Christian ethics rests upon "the *Christian doctrine of redemption.*" That meant, Ramm concluded, that Christian ethics applies to, and can only be practiced by, believers. We cannot expect other people, governments or "economic systems to practice Christian ethics" because they are not on redeemed "territory."[28] Ramm also frowned upon the idea of believers' cooperating with "liberals and non-Christians" because it would create confusion and be detrimental to churches.

Ramm next posed the question, *"What is the nature of Christian ethics?"* By nature, they are not political, social, or economic, not, that is, if one takes the New Testament seriously. Rather they are "the quality of life that arises from the redemptive experience of the gospel." As far as Ramm was concerned, there were no economic, political, or social systems found in the New Testament, but there was found there a *"body of principles* which characterize the true man of God."[29] It follows then, that while one may encourage non-Christians to practice "Christian principles" (because society will function better that way), yet "the Christian ethic is only *imperative*" in the believer's life. Or put another way, "A Christian citizen practices in his citizenship those principles that apply to him," even if others do not, be he or she a senator, mayor, labor leader or businessman.[30]

Ramm was of the opinion that neither the Lord nor Paul advocated a social Christianity. Obviously, he noted, a Christian is "grieved in the presence of [social] unrighteousness." But, he enjoined, we "must be an Abraham and look for the city whose maker and builder is God. Hence the spirit of detachment—not asceticism nor monasticism—must characterize our walk as Christians." This does not mean we do not groan aloud when we see the "infamy" of man collectively "exhibited" before us, nor does it mean we do not burn with "indignation when the oppressor runs high." Ramm concluded by writing, "I too am uneasy about the mess we are in. But I find no injunction in Scripture for me to follow but to (1) evangelize, and (2) keep my spiritual life at the right level. Doing this I am salt and light to the world in which I live."[31]

On Paper It Looked Good—But?

While Ramm may have had the better of the argument from a biblical standpoint, Henry had the better of the flow of history. Many historic fundamentalists of the post-war period wanted to be politically involved to save America from what they perceived as a possible fascist or communist future. Looking back, though, this political involvement may not have been all that salutary.

It could be pointed out that Dr. Henry's hope for a united evangelical community that would dominate America's political landscape came up considerably short. Protestant evangelicals/fundamentalists did not then and *do not* now speak with a single voice. Nor can we say that a good portion of American society welcomed then nor welcome now evangelical participation in politics, or wanted to then nor want to now work with them in solving social evils, or even agrees with them on what constitutes a social evil, or (especially this one) wants to live under or admit that the evangelical "redemptive motif" is desirable or necessary.

As noted earlier, Henry had five areas of social evils in which he believed the historic fundamentalists had failed to stand up and be counted: "the injustices of totalitarianism, the secularisms of modern education, the evils of racial hatred, the wrongs of current labor-management relations, the inadequate bases of international dealings."[32] However, there seems to be no one evangelical answer to these issues (and there may not be any), any more than there is a Christian economic system that wins the support of all fundamentalists and evangelicals. We are still caught between a rock and a hard place in this regard, as either some form of capitalism or socialism, or some ghastly hybrid is our Hobson's choice. And the Bible, of course, supports one or the other, depending on your evangelical political economics.

Nor would all fundamentalists/evangelicals have agreed with Henry that "a redemptive totalitarianism [short of the millennial kingdom] is far preferable to an unredemptive democracy" and a "redemptive Communism [an oxymoron if there ever was one] far more advantages than an unredemptive Capitalism...."[33] But can there be such a thing as redeemed Capitalism? (Did not Walter Rauschenbush imagine this once also?) Looking back 50 plus years, we can take note of the meager, yet deeply flawed, results of Henry's challenge to historic fundamentalism in 1947. As Ian Murray has noted, "More than one commentator on the contemporary evangelical scene has noted how a policy which was expected to lead to so much has instead produced so little."[34] The answer may be found in

Steven Keillor's book, *This Rebellious House* (1996), where he wrote: "Christianity was not designed to accomplish a human purpose such as integrating a culture, a polity or an economy."[35] Such words, of course, may be sacrilege to the ideological heirs of Henry's vision. However, one thing has remained constant as David Moberg's *The Great Reversal*, and Mark Noll's *The Scandal of the Evangelical Mind* make clear—those historic fundamentalists are still to blame for neo-evangelicals' coming up short. But it is difficult not to see this as finger pointing at its most immature. They are hardly to blame that the slogan "cooperation without compromise" turned out to be hollow. They are hardly to blame that evangelicals are dividing over doctrines the historic fundamentalists guarded with great, if often pugnacious, fidelity: the verbal, plenary, inerrant Scripture, the meaning and purpose of the atonement, the eternal state of the unbeliever, the sovereignty of God over history and the actions of people and nations, and even the meaning of who, or what, is an evangelical.[36]

However, questions remain that need to be asked and answered regarding *The Uneasy Conscience of Modern Fundamentalism*. First, was Henry being fair in his criticisms of the historic fundamentalists. Granted, "fair" is difficult to define in this context but we will attempt one shortly. Second, why did some of the historic fundamentalists emerge from the war so militant or aggressive regarding political involvement? Was it just that they suddenly discovered "cultural mandatism" in Scripture and were acting out their repentance, or were there other factors? Third, was Henry asking too much and expecting too much of American evangelicalism given the make-up, problems, and theological divergences of that community in the late 1940s, and the make-up of American society as a whole? (The answer to this latter question is, of course, an obvious yes.) One could editorialize endlessly about neo-evangelical shortcomings—from its embrace of secular psychology to its setting aside of evangelical distinctives to be allowed into the academy—but space prohibits such a lengthy but inviting analysis. And finally why did Henry seem to think that Americans would be grateful for evangelical solutions to pressing social and political difficulties?

The Fairness Question

It is obvious Henry had an agenda when he wrote *The Uneasy Conscience of Modern Fundamentalism*. However, was he fair in his criticism of those he chides? What do I mean by fair? First, giving credit for what was done and said prior to 1947—even if he did not think it went far enough. Second, acknowledging that there are sincere theological differences on what is the purpose of the Church in this world that ought to be respected even if not agreed with. Henry did neither of the above and thus set the stage for even harsher criticism down the road that came from the pens of David Moberg and Mark Noll.

There were roughly three views on the purpose of the Church current among the historic fundamentalists at the time Henry wrote. One was the radical separatists view; the Church is not here to save the world in any political sense but was to preach the gospel and bring into the Church those that responded. Neither the Church nor the individual believer has any obligation to reform the world. Another was the "spiritual church" view. I have covered this in some detail in Chapter Three so it is not necessary to repeat myself here. Suffice to say the Church as such was not to be involved in trying to reform the world. However, it was to be compassionate toward those in need, and the individual believer was encouraged to be involved in community needs and reform. The third view was one Henry and associates brought over from the Reform community. This view insisted that the Church was mandated not only to preach the gospel but also to redeem the social order. This meant intense involvement in social and political issues on the part of the Church as such, as well as the individual. (Remember, Henry wanted evangelicals to unite and speak with one voice on political, social and economic problems.) In pushing the latter view, Henry was, in essence, rejecting out of hand the other two with their dispensational eschatology. Premillennial dispensationalism simply could not provide the motivation necessary to recapture America. Evidently many dispensationalists agreed.

The Fairness Question—Totalitarianism

As stated above, Henry was not as successful as he had hoped. Mark Noll's *The Scandal of the Evangelical Mind*, written almost fifty years later, and in which he bemoans the baleful influence historic fundamentalism still has upon today's evangelical thinking, supports this conclusion. Part of the reason may have been that Henry was not that convincing. As Keith Brooks noted, many pastors wanted guidance on the question of how involved the church should be, but Henry's book did not provide them with the answer. And he was not always fair in his accusations concerning fundamentalist failings. Consider, for example, his charge that they failed to "challenge the injustices of totalitarianism." It is difficult to understand why Henry would make such a statement when one considers the vocal and unrelenting opposition of the historic fundamentalists toward communism and fascism both at home and abroad. It is fair to say that until about 1938, the historic fundamentalists considered Stalin's communism a greater menace than fascism.[37] Still, they gave ample coverage to fascism's nefarious activities prior to that date.[38] In 1941, months before Pearl Harbor, Keith Brooks wrote an editorial which, by his many quotations from others, evidently reflected the conclusion of a great number of the historic fundamentalists—that the United States must do whatever is necessary to help defeat the forces of evil incarnate in Nazi fascism. If this could be accomplished by providing unlimited aid to England and Russia, fine. But if it meant that the United States must enter the war, than it must do so. "It is our profound conviction," he wrote, "that we have reached the point where the responsibility of Americans is inescapable." Brooks understood the situation well, noting, "We in America are going to rise or fall with those who fight to stop the aggressors who seek to take the Word of God from all men."[39]

It also might be pointed out that much of the opposition the historic fundamentalists exhibited toward Roosevelt's New Deal was based on their fear that it was beginning to reflect too many of the characteristics of European dictators (i.e., the end justifies the means) and thus endangered the individual American's constitutional freedoms.

The Fairness Question—Peace, Peace, but there is no Peace

Even in the area of "the inadequate basis of international relations," Henry seems to overstate his case. It is true the historic fundamentalists often related international events to the possible nearness of the Second Coming, but their point in doing so was the same as Henry's, though from a different perspective—that is, that without recognition of the need for God's divine assistance through the redemptive work of Jesus Christ, any attempt to construct a lasting international peace was folly and hubris.

However, there is no better example of the historic fundamentalists' take on international relations than the series that appeared in *The Sunday School Times* in the Spring of 1934. Noting the rumors of war and preparations for war taking place, the magazine announced a ten-part series by Joseph Taylor Britan entitled, "The Program for Peace." The series was to consider such questions as "why is the world on the verge of another war, will internationalism cure the ills of the world, why must nations go to war when they don't want to, should the United States enter the League of Nations, is God for nationalism or against it," and finally (of course), "what is Armageddon, and when will it come?" *The Sunday School Times* promised that one would not find "hackneyed observations" in Britan's series but rather "vigorous and compelling truths that bear on the survival of civilization and the human race."[40] Britan was a Presbyterian premillennial dispensationalist and his evaluation of the international situation, then, is written from that perspective. He began his ten-part essay by observing:

> Never has the race heard so many arguments for peace. Never have the nations considered so many proposed remedies for war. Never have men faced so many incontrovertible proofs of the utter insanity of war. Yet never has the Lord of earth and

Heaven looked down upon so many men in arms in time of peace. Never have such extravagant preparations for war been made. Never have the dangers of war been so great as at the present moment.[41]

Britan's main points can be summarized as follows:

1. No matter how much mankind wants to avoid war it will not be able to do so because it fails "to acknowledge the fact that the cause of war is supernatural" to its great harm. Expanding on this failure, Britan pointed out that (a) "war has its origins, not only in the lusts and hatreds of men, but primarily in the evil mind and purpose of Satan,"[42] and that (b) "not once, so far as I know, have the blessings and wisdom and guidance of God been invoked on the deliberations [of men] in their quest for peace."[43] For this reason, then, "the world is full of fear…" and "men despair for civilization and the future of the race."[44] And for this reason wars would continue, including war in a Europe "chafing under the restraints and unnatural fellowships imposed by the treaty of Versailles…."[45]

2. The reason men will not call upon God to help them resist the demonic influences that compel them to war is that mankind is in rebellion against God. "What we are witnessing today over the face of the earth is a veritable revolt against God and his Christ."[46] As Britan sarcastically noted, the "progressive" thinkers of the world think "it were far better that the modern world should fall into the ditch rather than we turn back to believe the ancient doctrines of a personal Devil who is manipulating national affairs and to look for the supernatural interference of almighty God in the affairs of men."

3. Because of mankind's rebellion and determination to build its own kingdom, Britan accused it of trying to rebuild the tower of Babel, so to speak, through international organizations such as the League of Nations—a united world competent, powerful and at peace without God.[47] Although he believed that "internationalism is championed principally by those who have declared war on God and his Church," Britan was not oblivious to the more mundane reason internationalists were clamoring for a world government:

> In the advocacy of internationalism there are few who base their theories on any other than economic reasons. Internationalism is demanded today, we are warned, because of the demands of trade and commerce. . . . Until the "disease of nationalism" is eradicated, there can be no restoration of economic health to the world.[48]

This, Britan noted, was exactly what the communists wanted "world revolution and world unification of government."[49] And economic arguments notwithstanding, behind internationalism were the enemies of God and his

Church—reason enough to reject it. "We are witnessing a strange experiment among the nations today," he warned:

> If history has any lesson for our age, written in letters of doom across the scroll of time, it is that the decline and fall of nations begins always with religious apostasy. Religious apostasy is followed in turn by political corruption, social chaos, and ultimate oblivion.[50]

4. Yet, Britan pointed out, not everybody was enthralled with the idea of a "centralized superpower" that would erode "national life and ...responsibility." These opponents of internationalism simply did not have the trust in "unknown and unproved men sitting in a governmental capacity thousands of miles removed from them" to yield over "their most vital earthly and eternal interest."[51] Obviously Britan favored nationalism over against internationalism. He gave three reasons for his position. First, sin had dissolved "the fundamental unity of the [human] race...." "And it is sin," Britan wrote, "...that makes the progress of the League of Nations so slow or impossible."[52]

Next, Britan pointed out in good biblical fashion, "Human nature being fundamentally and essentially sinful, government by states and nations is required" or any orderly society would be impossible.[53] Britan considered local governments (states and even more, their subdivisions) the best place for these restraints on sin to be exercised "The ultimate...authority in human government...must of necessity be local, available to the governed and conversant with the conditions, needs, and demands of each community and nation."[54] "National life," Britan emphasized, "was ordained by God" and thus he found it "difficult to imagine any real blessing coming to any nation by substituting internationalism for nationalism—remote control for local governments."[55]

Third, and this was the most important point for Britan, he believed "*there is a deep and abiding necessity for nationalism today.*" National loyalties, which take precedent over international governments, are "not a blind and unreasoning instinct..." but have their "origin and purpose" in God's plan of redemption. What was (and is) that purpose? Britan found it in Acts 17:26, 27 ("God hath 'made of one [blood] every nation of men to dwell on the face of the earth, having determined their appointed seasons, and the bounds of their habitation; that they should seek God'"). It was God then, who sent some nations into oblivion and created others, who determined their historical length and whether they would be great or small—"all for the one great purpose of leading them to Himself"[56]

It follows, then, that those who favor uniting nations under one government operated by unregenerate men are in serious rebellion against God, because they are seeking to overthrow God's redemptive providence—something Satan desires to do also.

5. This revolt by mankind "against God must lead to judgment; and when this revolt assumes world-wide proportions then the judgments of God must be world-wide in extent. Thus the whole world is unconsciously preparing for Armageddon."[57]

Given his position on internationalism and understanding of the state of the world, what did he think about international cooperation and the need for world peace in those tense, middle years of the 1930s? What was to be the Christian's position? "We believe," he wrote, "in every attempt to promote peace and concord among the nations; we call upon all to cultivate the 'peace complex,' to promote justice and fair dealing among individuals and races...."[58] He expanded upon this thought in the fifth supplement of his series:

> In enumerating some of the dangers that lie along the pathway of world federation and world government we do not overlook the fact that the world has in effect become one vast community with identical problems and similar interests. . . . We should even go so far as to say that, under the present system of commerce and communications, no nation lives unto itself and that in the future national isolation will probably become more and more impossible.
>
> We should be, therefore, most heartily in accord with every attempt to cultivate national friendship and conciliation. We believe in making every possible attempt to prevent war. . . . We believe in cultivating the "will to peace," in promoting honest and just commercial and diplomatic relations with all reputable nations on earth. But all this is far from believing in, or advocating, the surrender of our national sovereignty and merging our identity in a government of all nations.[59]

Britan was also clear that it was not the church's mission to bring about world peace. As noted, Britan did not oppose international peace treaties but advocated supporting them. However, Britan believed what his Bible said about the heart of man and knew that in this present age Christians can no more bring about lasting world peace than can the pagan.[60] Short of advocating that evangelicals write all peace treaties, it is difficult to see how Henry could have improved upon Britan's position.

The Fairness Question—Liquor

Again, one is surprised to read Henry criticizing the historic fundamentalists for their failure to take on the liquor industry. For one finds in the pages of their journals a constant flow of articles criticizing that business, as well as the cigarette and movie industries. Even before it took place, the historic fundamentalists were appalled by the movement at the highest level of government to repeal Prohibition.[61] They laid part of the blame for the rise of crime during the Great Depression to this very fact.[62] As the editor of *Moody Monthly* heatedly wondered five years after repeal, and drawing attention to a series of robberies, rapes, and murders committed by minors under the influence of alcohol: "Where are the people who assured us that moral conditions would be much improved with the repeal of prohibition? The liquor industry is always lawless. If it cannot be suppressed under prohibition, it cannot be controlled under license."[63] Not only did *Moody* consider the liquor industry lawless, but it also labeled it "vile" and "vicious," and in the harshest of terms noted: "If there is one part of hell hotter than another, it seems to us it must be reserved for those who are not satisfied to make their living from the weaknesses of the old, but in their thirst for profit are willing to debauch youth."[64] In the same year (1938) *Moody* editorially congratulated the Gannett newspaper chain for its act of "costly courage" by refusing to accept liquor advertisement. Gannett recognized that the whole family read their papers and they were sure Moms and Dads did not want their children reading liquor ads.[65] (Where, one is compelled to ask, is that kind of integrity and concern today?)

The historic fundamentalists had no illusions by the late thirties that they were going to be able to reverse the repeal of Prohibition, although they continued to talk about the issue within their own ranks. However, indirectly they sought to limit the influence of the liquor industry by seeking limits on its ability to advertise. (Back to the future indeed.) Toward this end, the National Temperance and Prohibition Council agreed "in making the one project for united action for the coming year [1938/1939] the suppressing of liquor advertising over the radio, in newspapers, magazines, and by other means." The Council hoped to achieve this goal through a massive protest campaign aimed at advertising sources plus a petition drive to get Congress to outlaw liquor advertising.[66] This confrontational approach toward the liquor industry (and the administration's "friendliness" with that industry) continued throughout the war and into the postwar period.[67]

It is plain that Henry was not being fair or giving credit to those historical fundamentalists who during the Great Depression had taken a strong and public stand against the selling, use, and advertising of liquor in America. And in retrospect one must see the neo-evangelical campaign to restrain the liquor industry (if there ever was one) a dismal failure. Not only do Americans continue to swill-down enormous amounts of liquor and advertise the same, but now one must add to that use enormous quantities of "recreation drugs," creating an international lawlessness that is even endangering national governments.

The Fairness Question—Public Education

Nor does Henry's charge that the historic fundamentalists failed to challenge the secularization of modern education carry enormous conviction. The historic fundamentalists were perfectly aware of the nature of the secular attack taking place in the nations colleges and universities and were meeting the challenge. A booklet published by Frank Gaebelein—*From A headmaster's Study* (1940)—written for parents, contained the following analysis:

> No sensible Christian parent would expect a state university or a non-sectarian college to teach Bible Christianity. The most that he could reasonably expect is a neutral attitude that rules out discussions of such matters, or a truly liberal point of view that accords to both Modernism and Fundamentalism...an equal hearing. And that is just what the American university today does *not* do. In thousands of classrooms...there is being carried on a subtle atheistic propaganda... by the cynical professor of English, or the brilliantly ironical lecturer in Philosophy, or the sardonic psychologist who is doing them damage.[68]

And one also needs only to recall the continuous efforts and numerous writings of Dan Gilbert[69] that were very popular to realize Henry was not giving due credit to evangelical efforts to counteract secularization. Even before Henry wrote, a Christian school movement was under way that had its roots in the pre-war years.[70] The continuous addition of evangelical colleges and seminaries[71] during the twenties and thirties (and beyond), and the ever increasing enrollment of these institutions, is another indication of the historic fundamentalists' response to the modern secularization of American education. Evangelical student organizations were up and functioning before the start of World War II. The Students Foreign Missions Fellowship, an evangelical/fundamentalist campus movement was formed in 1936 and Inter-Varsity Fellowship entered America in 1939 and was formally organized in 1941. By 1945 there were almost 200 campus chapters in place. The two campus organizations merged in 1945.[72] Even if Henry had never written his book, a fundamentalist response to educational secularization was well under way and had been for years. Henry, of course, may have dreamed of a great evangelical crusade to recapture the universities for evangelicalism. If so, it never materialized.

Looking back, though, not a great deal has changed in the secular onslaught over the last fifty years or so. If anything, the public school system is more secular than ever. The same holds true for public colleges and universities. Evangelical organizations must threaten, and even use, the legal system to continue to function on some public university campuses. In fact, though we have a plethora of Christian scholars (some quite outstanding) and over five score Christian liberal arts colleges and universities that were supposed to have lifted us above the historical fundamentalist dark age, it appears that secularism is having a greater impact on the Christian academician and academy than the other way around. The great neo-evangelical challenge to the secularization of public education, though full of sound and fury, never became very great after all.

The Fairness Question—Labor/Management

I have covered to some extent in the previous chapter the views of the historic fundamentalists concerning business and labor. One could add that they were alarmed at the communist influence within the CIO, the seeming endless labor violence and the increasing ability of a handful of labor leaders to mercilessly bring the country to its economic knees. They considered the open-shop as compatible with their own understanding of individual rights and freedoms, and they clearly wanted the Wagner Act revised so that it was not so pro-labor.[73] However, it must be admitted they had "no plan" to solve the "wrongs of current labor-management relations."

Yet when the intense labor strife of the post-war period became "detrimental to the welfare of the entire nation," and the Executive Committee of the Board of Administration of the National Association of Evangelicals issued a statement on the issue—"Christ and Class Strife"—one is hard pressed to see any difference between it and what one of the historic fundamentalists might have preached in the pre-war years. The Committee, noting that "class-strife" was threatening the well being of society, declared that "it behooves Christians to speak and exemplify the Divine message with great clarity and force so that all involved will give heed."[74]

Acknowledging that in a labor-management dispute neither side has a monopoly on right, the Committee made it clear it was not taking sides: "Therefore, it is not for the Christian to make partisan pronouncements."[75] However, if they were not taking sides or offering an economic solution, what was the Committee's message that was to compel both sides to "give heed." It was "for both management and labor" to first get right with God:

> None of the good ends both seek can be gained apart from God. . . . Unless vertical righteousness between man and God is experienced there can be no horizontal righteousness between men. Let the individuals involved in this dispute kneel humbly together before God! Then let them heed the words of His prophets....[76]

And the prophet the Committee pointed management to was James, who warned that God had heard the cry of the defrauded workers and that management's ill-gotten riches were going to become a cancer witnessing against them and eating their "flesh as it were fire" (James 5:3, 4). Turning to labor, the Committee cautioned employees to "heed the message of John the Baptist," and quoted to them Luke 9:14: " 'Do violence to no man, neither accuse any falsely and be content with your wages.' " The Committee closed its statement by reminding both parties (presuming, of course, that they had humbled themselves before God) that they were not to hold grudges toward each other because God was at the door ready to judge them both (James 5:9).[77]

Although one can appreciate the sincerity and truthfulness of the statement—that men must be reconciled to God through Christ—yet it seems unrealistic in its approach to the issue and from a practical standpoint not very helpful. (The committee does not even offer to mediate.) It is quite possible many in the dispute were already Christians but were still at loggerheads over who is to blame and what should be done. The supposed "right wing" historic fundamentalists' (such as Dan Gilbert and Keith Brooks) demand for a modification of the Wagner Act seemed far more politically realistic and to the point concerning part of the problem (even if partisan)—that is, that the Wagner Act, by unduly favoring unions, was allowing certain labor bosses to gather into their hands enormous amounts of political and economic power that threatened democratic institutions and processes. It is doubtful that anyone on either side paid too much attention to the NEA pronouncement. But the Wagner Act was modified by the Taft-Hartley Act in 1948.

The Fairness Question—Race

Only when he mentions race relations does Henry zero-in on an area in which the historic fundamentalists exhibited *serious, serious* failings. America was a blatantly racist culture in the 1930s and many in the ranks of historic fundamentalism were tainted, if not outright infected, with this evil. The close of World War II brought the issue dramatically to the fore, forcing them to begin to confront the problem. Certainly they were a long way from offering leadership. As one Jewish Christian (Fred Kendall) wrote in 1948:

> It is tragic but true that orthodox believers have largely left this work [of dealing with race hatred] to the liberals. The voice of fundamentalism is almost silent when it faces this Frankenstein. What makes us even more culpable is the fact that our ranks are by no means free of this deadly poison…one must admit that in many places modernists put us to shame by simulating more of the spirit of Christ than fundamentalists express. *Here and there among those who shout their orthodoxy the loudest, and their dispensationalism the boldest, race propaganda is lent wings with religious fervor.*[78] (Italics added.)

"Can a born again believer be an anti-Semite or Negro hater?" Kendal was forced to admit, "with a sickened heart," that the answer was yes. Seeing in the bible the means "to deliver man from this demon" loosed "from hell," he wanted his fellow historic fundamentalists to "face the race issue" within their own numbers "and wrestle through with their Bibles" until "their prejudices are lost in the love of Christ."[79]

Still, it is only fair to point out that in the 1930s and 1940s leadership of the historic fundamentalists took a strong stand against anti-Semitism in America and denounced in no uncertain terms the Nazi persecutions in Europe. Those within their ranks who embraced anti-Semitism, such as Gerald Winrod, found themselves isolated and discredited.[80] But the same attitude was not extended to the Black community. They accepted with little protest the segregated American society with all its inequities. It could be said they were against racial hatred and violence but not separation.

Donald Barnhouse was somewhat of an exception to the above. In the early thirties he spoke out against all racial slurs, declared there was no inferior or cursed race, and that there are no favored classes in the body of Christ. He denounced such terms as "Gentiles only" or "Christian Community" used in national advertising. These terms fostered racial prejudice and suffering and should not, therefore, have a place in one who truly followed Christ. He also spoke out against secret societies that sought to oppress the foreign-born, Catholics, Jews or Blacks. Barnhouse believed that those who joined such organizations were not true Christians.[81]

Interestingly, Dan Gilbert, in his favorably received *The Biblical Bases of the Constitution* (1936), praised the Supreme Court for upholding the "due process" clause of the Constitution against those who would use it to enforce racial prejudice and deprive a Chinese American or Black American of that which was his by virtue of his labor. The "due process" clause (which Gilbert believed rested on the Commandment not to steal) was "a death blow to race hatred expressed and enforced through discriminatory [local] legislation...."[82]

However, there is very little written and even less leadership provided to confront the blatant, often mean-spirited and violent, discriminatory segregation that faced Black Americans during the Great Depression.

As the war concluded, a renewed interest in the racial problem is evident in the journals of the historic fundamentalists. And one finds in their writings a sincere though limited attempt to face racial prejudice. For example, in its January 1944 issue, in the "Notes on Christian Endeavor," *The King's Business* published the lesson for Sunday, February 13. The topic was "My Neighbor" and covered three groups; the Negro, the Jew, and the Japanese. The gist of the lesson was that these people are our neighbors and we are to love them accordingly, doing them good and seeking their salvation.[83] A year later, again appearing in the Christian Endeavor section, *The King's Business* published the lesson for February 11 entitled, "The Myth of Racial Superiority." The conclusion of this lesson is worth noting:

The enemies of the United States are using the American discrimination against colored people as powerful propaganda against us.

They are saying to the Philippines, China, and India, "Look at the Americans; will white men give you equality?"

As Christians, let us avoid any semblance of racial prejudice, and help to destroy the attitude of racial superiority.[84]

In the May 1945 edition of *Revelation*, Donald Barnhouse published an important article on the increasing racial tensions in America. Its purpose was basically to "record the fact of the problems existence and discuss its roots and cause." However, in the process of doing so he revealed his own limitations, seeing it only from a "white" perspective. He began by acknowledging the "present" racial anger:

In California returning Japanese have found themselves in great difficulties. Houses have been burned...dark warnings issued to get out and stay out. Negroes have been killed in the streets of Detroit and have retaliated, killing many white people. Jews have fallen in the parks of Boston at the hands of young Irish mobsters. In almost every part of the country thoughtful people are saying there is going to be a great deal of race trouble when the war is over and the Negroes have no more high wages, or when the Japanese wish to return to their lands on the Pacific Coast.[85]

Barnhouse followed the above by trying to show both the cause of racial conflict and the root of racial hatred which he extracted from Scripture. Although he briefly discussed anti-Semitism and hatred of the Japanese, Barnhouse devoted the greater portion of his article to the "Negroes."[86] First noting how the war had given the Negro a new economic freedom, he then examined the results. (In doing so he makes clear he was for limited mixing, opposed to interracial marriages, and expressed doubt that the recently passed New York State anti-discrimination law would work. Given the nature of the natural man, he mused, "the law will run afoul of practical realism" and will no doubt, "cause a great deal of trouble.")[87]

Barnhouse approvingly pointed out that many Negroes had used their economic freedom wisely. Negro colleges were "crowded as never before," they were purchasing homes in record numbers, and some had even moved into largely white neighborhoods and integrated successfully—"if they had sympathetic comprehension and did not seek to force themselves beyond the toleration of cultural bonds," and, thus, "in general, [they] have the freedom of any human being moving in the limits of his economic and social place."[88]

Others, however, under the preaching of labor unions, "city political machines and left-wing political parties" (which had made such a "point of racial 'equality' " that some Negroes had become "intoxicated" with the idea), had become "trouble makers...who have sought liberties which would not have been accorded to white men in similar situations." Barnhouse gives a number of these examples provoked by the trouble-makers including recent racial brawls in the New York City high schools.[89]

With the above in mind and considering the status of the "natural heart," Barnhouse gloomily concluded that there was no solution to the ongoing racial tensions short of the Second Coming. In the meantime, however, "Christian people should be very tolerant, very sympathetic, and very loving with the love of the Lord Jesus Christ." He also suggested his readers read "two recent publications." One was by Richard Wright, a well-known Negro author, who, in his recent book, *Black Boy*, had written of his experiences growing up in Memphis and Mississippi. Barnhouse quoted from a favorable *New York Times* reviewer of the book, who called it "explosive" and that it "aroused anger and sympathy," and finished his review by declaring that "if enough such books are written, if enough millions of people read them, maybe some day, in the fullness of time, there will be a greater understanding and a more true democracy."[90] The second reading recommended was an article entitled "What if the South Should Be Right?" which had appeared in the December 1944 issue of *American Mercury*, and was, Barnhouse noted, "a vigorous defense of the Southern methods of handling the race problem."[91] One gets the impression that in offering these two publications to his readers, Barnhouse believed they would emerge from the experience more sympathetic to Black Americans.

Still, Barnhouse was of the opinion that there was no longer "any first best method of dealing with the 'Negro question.' " As he confessed, "our forefathers violated the laws of God in stealing black men from their homes in Africa and transporting them across the sea as slaves." And because of their unlawful actions, "The children of those forefathers must reap the consequences."[92] The concluding paragraph of his article is worth quoting in full (and, perhaps, was somewhat prophetic):

Again we say, there is no final solutions for these problems short of the return of the Lord Jesus Christ. We record the fact of the problem's existence. We believe we see race riots and race hatreds on an unprecedented scale just around the corner in our national future. We agree that the situation is scandalous, but it is a situation that exists. The attitude of the true Christian will be one of great sympathy, broad tolerance, a true Christian love for all men, a recognition of the common rights of God's creatures, a careful recognition of the bounds of race, and, above all, an application of the knowledge which we have that the only real method of dealing with the problem lies in the application of the Gospel of salvation to the individuals. And if we acknowledge our national sins and the sins of our fathers, perhaps our Lord will spare us from some of the troubles which seem, from the human point of view, to be inevitably near.[93]

The following year an article, written by the visiting instructor of anthropology at Wheaton College, George R. Horner, appeared in *Moody Monthly*. The article, entitled "A Christian View of Race," evidently was published to establish *Moody's* position on the race issue. Starting with the premise that "neither the Bible nor science recognizes racial superiority, inferiority or prejudices (racism)," Horner launched into a scientific discussion on the issue of race, more or less debunking popular racial views that attempted to justify racial superiority—especially Darwinian anthropology.[94] "This kind of thinking," Horner wrote,

> in practice, led to the extinction of the aboriginal Tasmanians, and the enslavement of the Negro race by the evolutionary superior white race. Our superiority made it ethically legal! Nietsche's superman is also a result of this kind of thinking, which led to the might-is-right philosophy of the Nazis.[95]

Horner also discussed the biblical view of race—namely that there is none. "All the Bible teaches," Horner believed, "is the dispersion of three family groups and *not* the origin of three separate races."[96] As far as Horner was concerned, the Bible identifies people by language and not by race. He considered "the results of racial thinking" was racial hatred or racism. "Today," he noted:

> Our papers are full of racism examples: Negro hatred in the North and South; house-burning of the unwanted American-born Japanese, whose sons covered themselves with blood and glory on the battlefields for all our freedoms; Jewish persecution in many parts of our country; and all-to-easy names "wop," "Polack," "Nigger," used by so many of us.[97]

After discounting attempts to justify racism in emotional, social, or psychological traits, Horner spoke approvingly of the anti-discrimination legislation that had been recently passed in New York and New Jersey, pointing out "equal opportunity with another race does not mean…equality in marriage. It does mean that, given the same educational chances, plus personal initiative, all men ought to have the same social rights to become what they want to become."[98] Taking note of all the racial prejudice abroad in the nation, he challenged Christians to "make a definite stand against such attitudes" with Christian love. "Only by this love—'the love that passeth all understanding'—can men of different 'races,' cultures, social groups and attitudes meet on a common ground to settle recognizable differences."[99]

The following year, Keith Brooks found the ideal opportunity to state his position on the issue. He printed a letter from a woman who was part Indian and part Negro, complaining that "some fundamentalists" (along with others), "say we Negroes were intended by God to be inferior and servants of others" because of the curse on Ham. Such teachings, the writer complained, "makes for much bitterness among our people." Obviously frustrated, the good woman wanted Brooks to tell her "where such a doctrine is found [in the Bible]?"[100]

In response, the first words he penned were, "We can find no justification either from the Bible or science for any notion of 'white supremacy.' " Although he believed that race was a "God-given birthright," Brooks believed God divided mankind into two groups—"regardless of race"—those who are saved in Christ and the unsaved who "are the children of Satan...." Brooks was also of the opinion "that neither antedeluvean or post-deluvian man was fair skinned." "Can it be," he wondered with heavy sarcasm, "that some of our lily-white brethren are laboring under the impression that Adam and Eve were white folks whose descendents got sunburned?"[101]

Brooks also believed (once more with sarcasm) that too many fundamentalist Bible teachers got their understanding on race "from Christian calendar pictures," and would probably be shocked to realize that both Moses and Abraham married black women.[102] As far as Brooks was concerned, skin color had nothing to do with anyone's "mental or spiritual" capacity. "So far as general human characteristics are concerned, given like environment and opportunity, the Negro has no trouble to make good."[103] Brooks acknowledged that there would be times when "certain racial groups" would prefer to worship by themselves so they would not be criticized for their worship styles. Nevertheless, he concluded by writing: "But when it comes to any notion of 'white supremacy' or any feelings of spiritual superiority among believers because of skin color, we want no part of it. The real answer to such problems of course, is a more vital experience of the grace of God and a real apprehension of I Cor.13."[104] (However, Brooks offered no comment on "fairness" legislation or how to end segregation as such.)

It goes without saying that the historic fundamentalists were divided over how— or even if they should—end racial segregation, as well as divided over the best means to do so. Perhaps the division within the fundamentalist/evangelical community is best illustrated by a "pronouncement on racial discrimination," issued and signed by seventeen evangelical educators and an editorial that appeared five months later in *United Evangelical Action* highly critical of the Fair Employment Practices Committee. The seven point pronouncement called upon legislators at the state and federal level to pass laws that would establish "equal opportunity for all Americans regardless of racial background." The pronouncement in its entirety reads as follows:

> In view of current discussions of racial discrimination, the undersigned, as evangelical Christians, united for common witness and common action, state, as the testimony of their Christian consciences, the following propositions:
>
> 1. Equality of opportunity in education, vocation, and religion for all persons, regardless of racial or creedal background, should be guaranteed by state and federal law to every citizen.
> 2. This equality of opportunity cannot exist side by side with compulsory segregation

based, as it is, upon racial ancestry. The demand, by the "superior" race, that minorities be kept "in their place" by social pressure, is contrary both to the spirit of Christ and to the principles of a theistic democratic state; it is a violation of the Golden Rule.

3. These convictions are implicit in the second commandment and are in no wise indebted to the ideologies of humanism and communism.
4. It is expressly understood that the removal of racial discriminatory legislation does *not* commit one to an advocacy of "one world, one race, one creed."
5. It is also understood that an encouragement of intermarriage between races does *not* follow from an advocacy of human rights.
6. In view of these considerations we urge our representatives in state and federal governments to promote legislation designed to guarantee equality of opportunity for all American citizens, regardless of racial background.
7. It follows that Christians, corporately and individually, should give evidence of a concern that minority groups should be encouraged, rather than frustrated in their desire for a more abundant life in this world as well as in the next. This is simply an application of the Golden Rule. Our churches should give leadership in the Christianizing of this area of American life.[105]

The above appeared in the May 1, 1949 *United Evangelical Action.* Five months later, in the same magazine, a major editorial was printed highly critical of the Fair Employment Practices Committee for the danger it presented to American evangelicals. It is worth quoting a couple of paragraphs from the editorial to understand evangelical fears, no matter how unfounded they may seem today. Paragraph five reads as follows:

Evangelicals especially need to beware of FEPC. By a combination of certain minority blocs whose ideals are the very antithesis of ours an insidious, long range program could be undertaken which would destroy our testimony. Under the guise of promoting fair-practices for minorities we could be eliminated from radio broadcasting rights, our journals…denied postal privileges, our institutions and organizations…crippled, our church extension programs…blocked and our testimony…denied voice in the press. There are a hundred and one ways in which this could be accomplished…, all of which would be aided and abetted by the FEPC.[106]

If the editor sounded like he expected a knock on the door any minute now, the seventh paragraph reinforces this impression. Added to the fears of the FEPC was the threat of the United Nations' "universal declaration of human rights" possibly superceding America's own "Bill of Rights," thus threatening American's individual liberties. It was not hard, then, for the editor to conclude:

It would take little imagination to envision what could happen to evangelical Protestantism in America under such conditions. The tremendous influence of Roman Catholicism as a world power, the subtle machinations of World Jewry, or the ruthless invasions of Russian communism could be aimed at our destruction.... The very laws designed for the prevention and punishment of genocide would thus become the instrument for the mass destruction of Protestantism.[107]

Why the editor of *United Evangelical Action* felt so besieged is difficult to fathom, particularly over the issue of a government guarantee of fair employment. However he did. He insisted evangelicals must get involved as American citizens to preserve the "Constitutional form of government" under which Protestants had thrived. If this were accomplished, than there would be "more hope for American racial, political, and religious progress than in any subversive secular, politically motivated social legislation, however high-sounding its idealism."[108] It is obvious though, in retrospect, that American did not want an evangelical Protestant solution to its great pressing racial problems despite Henry's hope that it would.

The reason for this, of course, was that Fred Kendall was right when he wrote "it is tragic but true that orthodox believers have largely left this work to the liberals," and that within the ranks of the historic fundamentalists "are [many] by no means free of this deadly poison."[109] In other words, the liberals had the high ground on this issue, at least as far as the minorities were concerned. Evangelicals did not speak with one voice, nor even, at times, with a biblical voice. But Kendall wanted to do something to change that. He proposed a course of action he believed would allow evangelicals to take the lead. He wanted his fellow fundamentalists to "seize the race issue, and make it an occasion to inject the Gospel antidote into the hearts of men." Kendall proposed, and had already participated in, a "good will" team to go to various colleges, rallies, and other Christian venues—a team made up of a "born-again Jew, a born-again Negro, and a born-again Gentile, joined in the flame of the love of Christ." Such meetings, Kendall believed, would provide "opportunity for the display of the grace of God." "The possibilities," he concluded, "of such a testimony are boundless."[110] Sadly, though, the fundamentalist/evangelical community did not seize these possibilities in a cohesive, united manner that allowed it to provide a model that others could admire and copy.

NOTES

1. See Mark A. Noll, *The Scandal of the Evangelical Mind* (Grand Rapids: William B. Eerdman Publishing Company, 1994), 221.
2. Carl F. H. Henry, *The Uneasy Conscience of Modern Fundamentalism* (Grand Rapids: Wm. B. Eerdmans Publishing Company, 1947), 85.
3. Ibid, 27.
4. Ibid, 36, 45. Also see 16, 17.
5. Ibid, 69. Also see 55, 56.
6. Ibid, 30-32, 20, 50.

7.   Ibid, 17, 18, 80.

8.   Ibid, 26, 21.

9.   Ibid, 45.

10.   Ibid, 68, 57, 45.

11.   Ibid, 72. However, as history has shown, this possibility does not daunt the secularists.

12.   Ibid, 73.

13.   Ibid, 57, 76, 81, also see 70.

14.   Ibid, 70.

15.   Ibid, 78-80, 85.

16.   Ibid, 40, 41.

17.   See Mathew 11:2-6 and Luke 7:18-23.

18.   Henry, 41, 42.

19.   Ibid, 42, 43.

20.   Ibid, 43.

21.   David W. Bercot, ed., *A Dictionary of Early Christian Beliefs* (Peabody, MS: Hendrikson Publishers, Inc., 1999), 502.

22.   Henry, 44.

23.   Ibid, 44, 45.

24.   "Book Notices," *Moody Monthly*, August 1947, 853.

25.   "The Uneasy Conscience of Modern Fundamentalism," *Prophecy Monthly*, August 1947, 6.

26.   Ibid, 9.

27.   Ibid.

28.   Bernard Ramm, "Is Dr. Henry Right? No!" *United Evangelical Action*, July 15, 1947, 5.

29.   Ibid, 5, 16.

30.   Ibid, 16. Note that Ramm was not denying a Christian had duties to uphold as a citizen, nor was he denying a Christian may serve in a public leadership position.

31.   Ibid.

32.   Henry, 45.

33.   Ibid, 73.

34.   Ian Murray, *Evangelical Dividing: A Record of Crucial Change in the Years 1950 to 2000* (Carlisle, PA: The Banner of Truth Trust, 2000), 305.

35.   Steven J. Keillor, *This Rebellious World: American History and the Truth of Christianity* (Downers Grove: Inter Varsity Press, 1996), 21.

36.   David F. Wells, *No Place for Truth: Or Whatever Happened to Evangelical Theology?* (Grand Rapids: William B. Eerdmans Publishing Company, 1993). Certainly no fan of historic fundamentalists, nevertheless David Wells acknowledged, "their commitment to the formal and material principles of Protestantism was unyielding" (128). He also noted that today, "for both the liberals and evangelicals...the search for 'essence' has been a tactical retreat. It is not the kind of retreat that the Fundamentalists engineered, preserving their view of the world by separating themselves from the unbelieving world outside. The evangelical form of a separation is as real as that of the Fundamentalists; it is simply not as effective, and it is much more damaging to the Protestantism of which the are heirs" (131). See pages 127 through 136 for an extended discussion along these lines.

37. On the front cover of the September 1938 issue of *Prophecy Monthly* (two months
    before *Kristallnacht*) Brooks quoted from an editorial by Barnhouse which had
    appeared in the August issue of *Revelation*:

    > The menace of Fascism is more real in the United States today than is the
    > menace of communism. We may be in the same position as Pastor Niemoller
    > before many years have passed. The development of the dictator spirit sweeps
    > the world. It already exists within denominational organizations, and men with
    > the outlook of the bishop and would-be bishops would be ready collaborators
    > with a dictatorial mind in politics.

    Also see, "Buffaloed by the Bluffer of Berlin," *Prophecy Monthly*, November 1938,
    8-11. The leaders in the historic fundamentalist's community were contemptuous of
    Chamberlain's Munich sellout and did not believe it would stop Hitler. Birger Pernow,
    director of the Swedish Israel Mission, wrote in the Spring, 1950, *The Hebrew
    Christian*, "it is well known that although persecution of the Jews began in 1933 in
    Germany, it first became a real catastrophe when on March 13, 1938, Hitler marched
    into Vienna." ("Comfort them that are in Trouble," 9.)
38. See Chapter Seven in this regard, pp 190-196.
39. "Keep Freedom's Flag Flying!" *Prophecy Monthly*, July 1941, 3, 4, and "Why Aid
    Russia," *Prophecy Monthly*, November 1941, 20, 21. In late Summer 1940, at a
    "patriotic service," Moody Bible Institute drew up "a pledge of loyalty to the United
    States of America." All faculty and staff signed it. Those who "were conscientiously
    opposed to personal participation in war…were not asked to violate conscience"
    but could decide on their own to just what "extent" they would "participate if the
    nation ever engaged in war." The pledge read as follows:

    > I solemnly promise, in the sight of God, that I will be loyal to the United
    > States of America and I pledge every necessary personal sacrifice for the
    > defense of its flag, its form of government, its constitution, and its territory.

    ("A Loyalty Pledge," *Moody Monthly*, September 1940, 3.)
40. "Winston Churchill Urges Preparedness for War," *The Sunday School Times*, March
    17, 1934, 170.
41. Joseph Taylor Britan, "The Problem and Program of Peace," *The Sunday School
    Times*, March 24, 1934, 191.
42. Ibid. Elsewhere Britan wrote: "Indeed we may go so far as to say that no program
    of national procedure, no philosophy of national life, is worth a moments
    consideration which does not take into account not only the sinful tendencies of
    men but the actual presence and tremendous power of satanic influence which are
    superhuman and which must be fought with superhuman forces." ("The
    Unconsidered Factor in World Peace," *The Sunday School Times*, March 31, 1934,
    209.)
43. Ibid.
44. Ibid. "The fundamental weakness of the League of Nations," Britan wrote, "lies in
    its ignoring of God and his claims upon the race for obedience and honor and worship.
    And because these claims of God are ignored in all the plans of men for peace, 'God
    has a controversy with the nations,' and never, until men and nations repent of
    individual and national sins and turn in humility to and surrender to God and his
    Christ, can this old world know peace and rest." ("Rebuilding the Tower of Babel,"

The Sunday School Times, April 7, 1934, 223.)

This type of "fundamentalist" thinking carried over into their view of the United Nations. Wilbur Smith was alarmed by the atheistic tendencies of UNESCO (United Nations Educational, Scientific and Cultural Organization.) because Julian Huxley was elected its general director. As Smith noted, "He is definitely not only an enemy of the Christian faith, and really a bitter opponent of the Bible, but he is an outspoken denier of the existence of a living and personal God." Observing that Huxley advocated evolution as the "philosophical basis of UNESCO," Smith contrasted this with the fact that "in our Declaration of Independence, we began by recognizing God. In the Preamble for the Constitution of UNESCO, God is never mentioned, but it begins with a recognition of the goodness and sufficiency of man." This moved Smith to angrily wonder if it was "not time that our great congressional legislative bodies rise up together in a powerful protest against the non-Christian aspects of this entire vast program of world education." ("We'er Footing the Bill for Atheism," *Moody Monthly*, July 1947, 747. This article was an excerpt from Smith's new book, *The Increasing Peril* [1947].) Also see, "A. C. C. Resolutions: The Prayerless Conference," *The Baptist Bulletin*, June 1945, 5.

45. Britan, "Revolt Against God—the Final War," *The Sunday School Times*, May 19, 1934, 330.
46. Ibid.
47. Britan, "Rebuilding the Tower of Babel," April 7, 1934, 203.
48. Ibid.
49. Ibid.
50. Britan, "Is Internationalism the Cure?" *The Sunday School Times*, April 28, 1934, 272.
51. "Rebuilding the Tower of Babel," 234.
52. Britan, "Nationalism—Is It Right or Wrong?" *The Sunday School Times*, April 14, 1934, 240.
53. "Is Internationalism the Cure?" 272.
54. Ibid. It is worth noting that Britan draws upon the works of Abraham Kuyper ("statesman, philosopher, and theologian of Holland") to support his arguments for points one and two.
55. Ibid.
56. "Nationalism—Is It Right or Wrong?" 241.
57. Britan, "Approaching Armageddon," *The Sunday School Times*, May 26, 1934, 343.
58. "Rebuilding the Tower of Babel," 224.
59. "Is Internationalism the Cure?" 273.
60. See "The Unconsidered Factor in World Peace," 208, and "Approaching Armageddon," 343.
61. See for example, Melvin E. Trotter, "Is Life Worth Living," *The King's Business*, September 1932, 385, 386, and three articles by Louis Bauman also appearing in *The King's Business*; "The Despair of the President," October 1932, 434, "Lawlessness in High Seats—A portent," June 1933, 181, and "N. R. A., the Sign, and its Significance," January 1934, 14.
62. "The Saloon Again," *Moody Monthly*, July 1938, 560.
63. Ibid.

64. Ibid.

65. "Our Best Wishes to a Newspaper Chain," *Moody Monthly*, May 1938, 451.

66. R. H. Martin, "A Crusade to Stop Liquor Advertising," *The Sunday School Times*, July 30, 1938, 532.

67. See, for instance, H. J. Ockenga, "The N. A. E. U. A. and the Nation," *United Evangelical Action*, October 1, 1942. This article contains a blistering attack on the Liquor traffic in America and the government for allowing young soldiers access to alcohol. "We have not forgotten," Ockenga wrote, "that the same President who now asks us to sacrifice our blood, our money, our comforts, and our loved ones is the one who introduced repeal which initiated this orgy of drinking, nor can we forget that at the Stalin, Churchill, Harriman conference the celebration was described by the leading Toronto papers as one great joviality in which twenty-five toasts were drunk. This is far from calling on the Lord for our Leadership" (2). Also see Clarance E. Mason, Jr., "The Pearl Harbor Disaster," *The Sunday School Times*, April 18, 1942, 307; "The Bible in the News: Truth in Advertising," *The King's Business*, August 1947, 19; "Wasted Grain," *Moody Monthly*, November 1947, 166. Many more articles could be listed.

68. Quoted in Wilber Smith's *Therefore Stand* (Grand Rapids: Baker Book House, 1945), 121.

69. I have previously mentioned Gilbert's efforts to float an initiative in California to ban the teaching of atheism/communism in the state's colleges and universities. He also wrote a number of tracts/booklets exposing the secular "sins" threatening students in the public schools. And he toured under the auspices of the World's Christian Fundamentals Association in this regard. ("Encouraging Students Through Defense of the Faith," *The Sunday School Times*, February 11, 1939, 106.) Also see, V. C. Oltrogge, "Book Review: The Mind of Christ by Dan Gilbert," *The Baptist Bulletin*, November 1941, 11, and "Educational Reactions," *The Sunday School Times*, March 18, 1944, 193. This editorial begins by charging, "Lawlessness has been fostered by modern theories of evolution."

70. "Where Do We Go from Here?" *Moody Monthly*, April 1948, 609, 610. This article was written in response to the Supreme Court decision banning Bible classes in public schools.

71. The Master's College is an example of this. Started in 1927 as the Los Angeles Baptist Seminary (to establish a fundamentalist Baptist presence on the west Coast) the liberal arts college was added in 1953. The college achieved accreditation in 1975 and changed its name to The Master's College in 1985 and became non-denominational. In 1959 there were 69 students. Today there are over 1,000, yet the college has adhered very closely to its original conservative evangelical roots and faith commitment.

72. Joel A. Carpenter, *Revive Us Again: The Reawakening of American Fundamentalism* (New York: Oxford University Press, 1997), 183.

73. See, for example, Dan Gilbert, "Views and Reviews of Current News," *The King's Business*, June 1939, 213, and from the *Prophecy Monthly*, "The Bed-Fellows of John R. Lewis," September 1937, 21-23, "Ultimatum," July 1946, 19, and "Shall It Ring Again," July 1946, 3, 4.

74. "Christ and Class Strife: A Statement Adopted by the Executive Committee of the

Board of the Administration of The National Association of Evangelicals, Washington, D. C.," January 24, 1946, *United Evangelical Action*, February 15, 1946, 11.

75. Ibid.
76. Ibid.
77. Ibid.
78. "Conservatism and Race," *United Evangelical Action*, February 1, 1948, 2, 23.
79. Ibid.
80. Nowhere is this better exemplified than in a letter written to Louis Bauman by Gerald S. Pope of the Defenders of the Christian Faith. Dated December 2, 1939 (shortly after Bauman came out with his influential *The Time of Jacob's Trouble)*, it is a smarmy, whining letter berating Bauman for siding with Keith Brooks who was attacking fine, upright servants of the Lord (i.e., Winrod and associates), and threatening him by claiming that the Defenders had something embarrassing on Bauman which they might publish, claiming that the Jews controlled the "news channels" and were using them to try to destroy Dr. Winrod, that opposing such "lying propaganda" was not anti-Semitism despite what Bauman thought, and finally, charging that Bauman had "been rather severe in the language [he] used against others." To prove this latter point, Pope quotes from a letter he supposedly received from a pastor in Ohio. This unnamed pastor claimed that Bauman's "writings... invariably bristle with *hatred* for anyone who dares to suggest that Jews have anything to do with Communism." He also accused Bauman of having "absorbed the spirit of Jewish hatred for Gentiles, for he speaks about 'the putried (sic) carbuncles on the anatomies of the Gentiles.'" The Ohio pastor's criticism of Bauman concluded by stating, "It is in such terms that Dr. Bauman refers to his fellow Fundamentalists. What a beautiful spirit of love this is! And how magnanimous of Mr. Brooks to endorse Dr. Bauman's book, "The Time of Jacob's Trouble" and then pass this sweet phraseology on to the public." Obviously, neither Bauman or Brooks were too popular with the Defenders of the Christian Faith.
(I am indebted to Jim Lutzweiler of Wake Forest, who is of a like mind when it comes to the historic fundamentalists, for supplying me with a copy of this letter as well as assisting me in a number of other ways that made my research less burdensome.)
81. See *Revelation*, "Editorial: Tolerance," October 1932, 408; "The Three Sons of Noah: The Black Man," July 1932, 289, and "A Window on the World," August 1936, 324.
82. *The Biblical Basis of the Constitution* (San Diego: The Danielle Publishers, 1936), 37-41. In 1938, Gilbert wrote, *Our Chameleon Comrades: The Reds Turn Yellow!* It was a mocking booklet on the American Communist Party's attempt to avoid persecution by cleaning up its image and presenting a more reasonable face to the public. This included injecting itself into sensitive racial issues, especially in the South, "recasting...," Gilbert wrote, "a victim of *racial* injustice in the role of a Communist casualty of *capitalist* injustice and class war." Gilbert charged that by insisting on 'defending' the Negroes in Southern courts the communist were making it impossible for them to get a fair trial. But that is what the communist wanted—martyrs. "It might be funny," Gilbert complained,
      if it were not so tragic—; this contemptible exploitation of unfortunates by

Communists, who wax fat so long as they can land in jail or in the morgue a convincing number of martyrs to serve as "object lessons" of capitalist injustice and, therefore, of the need for revolution. This trading upon human misery, ...this pimping upon the slave trade of racial injustice, ...this is about as low a profession as a political racketeer can stoop to. The Reds are assuming the role of *agent provocateur* of racial outrages and injustices. By identifying the struggle for racial justice with the fight for Revolution, the Reds have tied the hands of all sincere friends of the colored people. . . . They have encouraged racial injustice, that they might personally profit and advance politically thereby.

Gilbert went on to charge that the communists, by encouraging the Negro to revolt and set up their own "Soviet Black Republic," were embittering race relations and creating the possibility of another reign of K. K. K. terror. "And when they [the communists] tie up their plan for 'Negro liberation' with all reasonable demands for Negro rights," Gilbert angrily wrote,

they make it appear that every step taken toward improvement of the living
conditions of Negroes is really a step toward a Black revolt against white 'rule.'
The Reds have put the Negroes in the position where they cannot ask for common justice, for equal opportunities, without laying themselves open to the charge of moving toward Revolution.

...The Reds have made the Negro a prey for every form of baiting and badgering. (*Our Chameleon Comrades* [San Diego: The Danielle Publishers, 1938], 146, 147.)

Also, the editor of *The King's Business* agreed with a black pastor when he rebuked an "all white" private club. "We applaud the rebuke," the editor wrote, "as a justifiable reminder that *character* not *color* is the true gauge of a man...not *race* but *regeneration* that is of paramount importance," ("Color or Character," April 1939, 132).

83. "My Neighbor," *The King's Business*, January 1944, 27-29.
84. "The Myth of Racial Superiority," *The King's Business*, January 1945, 29, 30.
85. "Tomorrow: Racial Difficulties," *Revelation*, May 1945, 199.
86. As the word "Negro" was the common term for Blacks or African-Americans during this period, I will conform to this term when discussing the content of Barnhouse's essay as well as other historic fundamentalists' articles on the subject of racial equality.
87. "Tomorrow: Racial Difficulties," 227. In May 1945, the American council of Christian Churches passed a resolution unequivocally opposing the New York anti-discrimination legislation and any extension of it to the national level. The ACCC believed such legislation would "actually foster ill will between various groups and destroy certain inalienable rights of minorities...." ("A. C. C. C. Resolutions: The Ives-Quinn Bill," *The Baptist Bulletin*, June 1945, 5.)
88. Ibid, 226.
89. Ibid.
90. Ibid, 227.
91. Ibid.
92. Ibid.
93. Ibid.
94. George R. Horner, "A Christian View of Race," *Moody Monthly*, August 1946, 734.

95. Ibid. Horner is unwilling to identify Southern evangelicals as implicated in slavery, which was entrenched in America long before Darwin wrote.

96. Ibid, 777, 778.

97. Ibid, 778.

98. Ibid.

99. Ibid.

100. "Correspondence and Comments," *Prophecy Monthly*, November 1947, 30.

101. Ibid, 30, 31.

102. Ibid, 31.

103. Ibid, 30, 31.

104. Ibid, 31.

105. "Educators Issue Word on Racial Relations," *United Evangelical Action*, May 1, 1949, 21. Those who signed the resolution were Claude H. Thompson, Harold B. Kuhn, David Paul Smith, J. Harold Greenlee, C. B. Hamann, George A. Turner, James D. Robertson, W. C. Mavis, Bob Schuler, Jr., W. C. King, D. C. Corbit, Byron S. Lamson, J. Paul Ray, Albert T. Puntney, Lawrence M. Arksey, Jay B. Kenyon, Gilbert James, and Paul F. Abel.

106. "Editorial: Threats to Freedom," *United Evangelical Action*, October 1, 1949, 11.

107. Ibid.

108. Ibid.

109. Kendall, 2.

110. Ibid, 23.

CHAPTER SIX

Historic Fundamentalism Post World War II,
Part II:
Saving Protestant American Democracy from
Roman Catholicism

Why, at the end of World War II, did many historic fundamentalists adopt a more militant, activistic, even interventionist approach toward government? Why did they embrace a seemingly covenant view of church and state in practice if not in principle or eschatology? Part of the answer is realizing that despite their understanding of the "spiritual church," despite their dispensationalism, many of the historic fundamentalists saw America as an evangelical Christian creation and responsibility. They simply did not want to stand by and see it destroyed or perverted. They might want to see Jesus return and they might expect the world to get worse and worse, but they did not want America to be a part of that—contradiction or no contradiction. Events of the 1930s and 1940s (and even as far back as the 1920s) agitated their souls and left them frustrated and disquieted. The humanism of the New Deal and the universities, the threat of communism with its record of brutality toward Christians in Russia, the failure of the German church to effectively oppose Hitler and the Nazis and their Holocaust,[1] all helped to convince many historic fundamentalists that they must take action to prevent something similar from happening in America. As Greg Singer, chairman of the Wheaten College history department, warned in a "call to arms" article printed in the July 1947, *Moody Monthly*: "An awakening is imperative. Either our government will be administered according to the political concepts inherent in the Word of God, or it will be subjected to political theory stemming from deism or humanism. There will then be no place for the Christian Church, nor for a Christian world and life view."[2]

Thus we had Carl Henry's plea for evangelical unity, plans, and actions to solve America's (and even the world's) political, economic, and social evils and inequities—beginning right now. In so doing, of course, he held out the possibility that the gospel would become more attractive to unbelievers. That what he was proposing was impossible considering the divergent viewpoints within the fundamentalist/evangelical community did not seem to deter him and his allies. Fundamentalists/evangelicals must come together to redeem what they could of the American culture. It was that or an ignoble marginalization. Nor in his enthusiasm did he reveal how one would know when any particular part of the culture had achieved redeemed status.

Embracing a Reformed View of the Christian and the State

However, when one of the premier dispensational journals—*Moody Monthly*—published a strong Reform historian's understanding of the state and the Christian, one senses that "times they are a changing." C. Gregg Singer's essay, "Are We Forgetting Our Government," parallels Henry's, *The Uneasy Conscience of Modern Fundamentalism* in even stronger Reform terms. The uncompromising totalitarian (and seemingly anti-Christian) strain which appears inherent in all current liberal political thought—the intrusive, humanistic, managerial, authoritative state, justifying its actions on the hubris of the "expert," which is the end result—created considerable unease among those historic fundamentalists and other evangelical who believed in a "dual citizenship" and that righteousness was for nations as well as individuals.

Singer was sure (and somewhat prophetic) when he warned that continued "indifference" toward things political on the part of evangelicals would not only give "humanistic" political thought greater and greater influence in American politics, thereby isolating the church (which in turn would move those in authority to ignore the church), but would also put believers "more and more on the defensive." In turn, this would result in "less freedom of expression and action than before."[3] Either American evangelicals must reverse their way of thinking or an anti-Christian "political hierarchy" would come to power which would be "distinctly hostile to the Church and all forms of Christian activity."[4]

Roughly half of Singer's essay was spent decrying the historic fundamentalists supposed withdrawal from American politics during the previous seventy-five years. In doing so, he politely refrained from identifying by name the premillennial dispensationalists as the main culprit. However, he, too, gave somewhat of an "edited" version of the historic fundamentalists supposed betrayal of what he called a "Christian world and life view," which in turn had encouraged "the growth of the very liberalism they opposed." Such a result was inevitable, however, because the historic fundamentalists had failed "to preach the whole truth of the Bible." Thus, despite the problems brought about by America's industrialization, problems demanding solutions, there "was a growing insistence within fundamentalist circles that it was not the duty of the church to offer any formulas for the solution of such problems and that Christians should separate themselves from all world problems."[5] This separation, Singer believed, caused Americans to distrust the church and turn to humanism for help. In a statement that ought to surprise anyone familiar with the calvinistic view of the unsaved, Singer concluded:

> It was too much to expect the American people to accept the judgment of some fundamentalists that apart from the return of Christ there could be no solution to their problems therefore none should be attempted. They concluded that if there could be no approach within the framework of Christianity, they would seek one elsewhere.[6]

And that "elsewhere," Singer pointed out, was in the "humanism of modern democracy" which taught man could bring about his own utopia.[7]

There are, of course, two objections to Singer's indictment that one would think even he would have been aware of. Objection number one was the idea that if the fundamentalists had offered the American people a "biblical" solution (presuming one existed) to their economic and political anxieties, they would have embraced it. However, such a proposition flies in the face of a theological premise Singer must have believed himself—the mind of the unbeliever is at enmity with God, therefore he will not and cannot submit to His will (Romans 8:5). If this is so, is it fair, then, to hold the historic fundamentalists at fault for America going secular? All one needs to do is note the almost hysterical reaction of today's secularist to any possibility that evangelicals might have their way, or even have an influence, in national politics to verify my objection.

Second, while some fundamentalists may have promoted the idea that nothing should be done, as I have shown, the mainstream fundamentalists' leaders advocated that the individual should be concerned with political issues, and more than once said no true Christian should oppose political and economic programs meant to alleviate human misery. Singer had to be aware of this as well as the fundamentalists' political activities in the 1920s to limit the effects of humanism.

Nevertheless, many historic fundamentalists, along with many other evangelicals, emerged from World War II in something of an alarmist mode and were determined—embracing as they did the myth of a Protestant formed Christian America—to somehow bring the country back under the sway of Protestant Christian political and moral thought. "The Church," as Singer put it, "must return to the world and life view embodied in the Scripture." This included "a Christian approach to government" and a "Christian political philosophy" that would yield nothing "to evolution, socialism or communism on the one hand, and involves no retreat from orthodoxy on the other."[8] (In this regard, Singer was a poor prophet.)

While basing the Christian understanding of government on the overall "organic unity" of Scripture, Singer especially focused on Romans 13:1-7 as resting on "the absolute sovereignty of God in human affairs," and that this sovereignty was exhibited in both His common and special grace. This led Singer to claim in good,

400-year-old Reform fashion that,

> human government, in general, exists for the maintenance of civil order and for the
> creation of a society in which God may carry out His program of salvation through the
> church. . . . It exists to enforce the moral law of God, to repress evil and to encourage
> good works.[9]

Even for those historic fundamentalists who were restless for political action such
a claim must have given them pause. Evidently, however, they swallowed hard
and nodded agreement. Others, of course, would have been mightily vexed. They
were among those whom Singer singled out for their "erroneous" view of
government—that is, that it is only " a necessary evil to be tolerated, but not worthy
of support" from one who was a citizen of heaven. Singer held such fundamentalists
wrong in their view of government, wrong because they possessed a "poor
theology." National righteousness must rest upon the submission of people of any
country to "the laws of God."[10]

The implications of the Christian doctrine of government were two-fold for the
believer. One was obedience to civil government and "obedience to human law."
Singer doubted that "a Christian should be [a] party to any revolutionary movement"
unless those in authority sought to force him "to violate his own Christian
conscience." Still, Singer hedged a bit noting that it might be possible for a Christian
to participate in "some revolutions" though he does not specify exactly what type
"some" might be.[11]

Second, Christians ought to, and in fact, must "participate in human government
and that none but Christians should hold public office." If, Singer reasoned, the
purpose of government is to promote public righteousness, then it follows that
"civil rulers are to enforce the law of God regarding questions concerning the
Sabbath day and its observance, marriage, divorce, and punishment for various
crimes."[12] Singer admitted that what he was advocating might seem "strange to
many present day [1947] evangelicals." However, he claimed it was the position
of the Scripture and the practice of Protestants up until the nineteen century, and,
in fact, some "state constitutions [had prohibited] all but Christians to hold public
office."[13]

In conclusion, Singer stressed that Christians must reverse their habit of ignoring
political issues because it had permitted "the secularization of the American
government," something all evangelicals now regretted: "Citizenship and the
obligations of office holding on the part of Christians must once more be proclaimed
as part of the whole counsel of God, if the Church of Jesus Christ is to remain true
to her divine mission and calling."[14] Again, it must be noted how radical it was for
Singer's article to appear in *Moody Monthly*. One cannot help but suspect that
James Gray would have been very uncomfortable with it.

The Menace of Roman Catholicism Under "Hitler's Pope"

However, there seems to have been one other reason why the historic fundamentalists/evangelicals became so politically alarmed and militant. A reason that would make today's Evangelical and Catholics Together, or evangelical scholars seeking academic cross-fertilization from all scholars of "good will," cringe.[15] That "reason" was the Roman Catholic Church and its pope, Pius XII (Eugenio Pacelli). The historic fundamentalists might appear to be focused on secularism, but the far more ominous specter looming behind it was Roman Catholicism. Henry addressed this fear in the preface of his book writing: "It is a sober realism, rather than undue alarm, that prompts the fear that, unless we experience a rebirth of apostolic passion, Fundamentalism in two generations will be reduced either to a tolerated cult status or, in the event of Roman Catholic domination in the United States, become once again a despised and oppressed sect."[16] The historic fundamentalists believed two things characterized the Roman Church: it was (and had been for some time) friendly to fascism, and it wanted to dominate the United States government to the detriment of Protestants and others. And they believed they had ample evidence to back-up their misgivings.

In fact, they probably would have agreed with John Cornwell's, *Hitlers Pope: The Secret History of Pius XII* (1999). Perhaps the only thing they would have disagreed with was the word "secret" in the title. They considered the Pope's fascism an observable fact. Cornwell's damning appraisal of Pius XII's relations with Germany under Hitler, his apparent anti-Semitism, his failure to speak out against the Nazis' final solution for the Jews, as well as his desire to protect and extend Papal power and reach[17] add up to a telling indictment of the "Holy Father." "We are obliged," Cornwell writes, "...to seek not only whether the institution of the papacy was inadequate to the challenge of the Final Solution, but also whether in some shocking way it was hospitable to Hitler's plans from as early as 1933."[18] Cornwell answers his own question in the harshest of terms:

His complicity in the Final Solution through failure to register appropriate condemnation was compounded by a retrospective attempt to portray himself as an outspoken defender of the Jewish people...[and]...revealed him to be not only an ideal Pope for the Nazi Final Solution but a hypocrite.[19]

Cornwell's condemnation of Pius XII (who evidently is yet another candidate for Catholic sainthood) brought swift imprecatory responses, three of which appeared in the pages of the Catholic oriented *First Things*. All three drew attention to the high praise Pius XII received from the Jewish community at the end of the war for all he had done to try and save Jewish victims of Nazi hatred—something Cornwell virtually ignores.[20] William D. Rubenstein, author of *The Myth of Rescue*, while not ignoring Catholic anti-Semitism tries to soften it by pointing out the high rate of survival of Jews in Europe's Catholic controlled countries (Poland excepted—[which is a pretty big exception]), and then wondered if Pius XII's policy of silence was not "the most effective possible, given Hitler's obsessive and overriding intention to kill every Jew in Europe."[21]

Rubenstein follows the above with a salient critique of postmodern historiography regarding the Holocaust (which also has some bearing on historic fundamentalists' historiography as will be seen in chapters seven, eight, and nine). "For too many historians," Rubenstein charges,

> the Nazis appear in accounts of the Holocaust as some inexplicable force of nature whose destructive powers it is pointless to question, while criticism focuses on the alleged inadequacies of those who could not prevent the slaughter. That this is utterly unfair should be evident, yet library shelves are filled with works on the "failures" of the allies, as there are with works critical of Pacelli.[22]

He concludes with a telling expose of the moral bankruptcy of this type of historiography: "At the very best such books deflect attention from the real criminals; at worst they imply a moral equivalency between mass murderers and those who tried, whether effectively or not, to stop them."[23] In Rubenstein's estimation, Cornwell's book is simply a smear of Pius XII.[24]

Michael Novak's response in *First Things* was one of conservative Catholicism. He places Cornwell among Catholic "progressives" whose purpose seems to be to not only to smear Pius XII but also "to discredit John Paul II and his ilk, that is, popes speaking as solitary moral voices...."[25] Unlike their parents and grandparents, "A few Jewish spokespersons today both in America and elsewhere, have also turned on Pius XII." Why? Novak believes it is out of frustration. Because those who engineered the Holocaust were so effective, many today are asking why no world leaders (including the pope) interfered or sounded the "alarm" or condemned the Nazis' actions.

Pointing out that the Pope was totally dependent on the Italian government of Mussolini for services and supplies, and that Italian and Nazi intelligence had penetrated the Vatican, Novak claims that "among world leaders, none was more at the mercy of surrounding Axis powers for the entire period of the war than Pius XII." Nevertheless, Novak claims the pope was outspoken, had rescued numerous Jews, and provided relief to millions of refugees. "He was," according to Novak, "as steady and courageous as he was cool and analytical."[26] And if he was silent, Novak contends, it was because of principle, "not out of fear."[27] Those who condemn the Pope because he never gave "a no-holds-barred...condemnation of unprecedented evil...offer nothing but speculation about what would have followed from such a statement."[28]

Somewhat contemptuously, Novak places Pius XII's critics into two categories: secular Jews and "others" who resent or are in rebellion against the "law of God".

He concludes by charging that "this new establishment resents the imputation that what it blesses as moral is contrary to the law of God and hence immoral. The critics of Pius XII are deflecting attention from themselves; for this new establishment, it is convenient to discredit the messenger."[29]

The third response to Cornwell comes in the form of a book review written by John Jay Hughes (a priest and a church historian) of Ronald J. Rychlak's tome (548 pages), *Hitler, the War and the Pope*. Rychlak's book, which begins in the 1920s and concludes with the death of Pius XII, "presents the judgment of the Pope's contemporaries in rich detail," judgments Rychlak considers right and true—the Pope was a friend to the Jews and an enemy of fascism.[30] Hughes, who charges the *New York Times* with being one of the leaders in "propagating the myth of Pius XII's 'silence,' " offers some snippets of headlines (taken from Rychlak's book) dating from the 1930s and 1940s, from the same newspaper praising the Pope for his courage in speaking out against the Nazi atrocities and protecting the Jews.[31]

Both Hughes and Rychlak attribute the turning against the Pope to "the rebellion against authority" which was surfacing in the West in the early 1960s. "The demonization of an authority figure revered by millions was welcome to an age proclaiming the death of God and rejecting the pretensions of those claiming to speak in His Name."[32]

Almost half of Hughes lengthy review is given over to Rychlak's refutation of Cornwell's thesis in *Hitler's Pope*. In essence, Rychlak accuses Cornwell of lying about wanting to write a book favorable to the Pope but the evidence forced him to change his mind. He also accuses Cornwell of being shallow in his research, and of either misunderstanding or misinterpreting, and even misrepresenting what Pius XII said, wrote, and did.[33] Hughes calls Rychlak's "refutation of the Black Legend...impressive" but doubts it will "change many minds" because "deeply held beliefs seldom yield to facts."[34] He closes his review with words similar to those written by Rubenstein:

> In the face of six million dead, no one can claim enough was done. To claim however, that nothing was done—or that the failure to do more was the result of cynicism or indifference—is a grave falsification of history. When the victim of this falsification is a person of demonstrable moral greatness, it is shameful.[35]

However, like the cat that kept coming back, this is an issue that refuses to go away. Hughes admits as much when he writes, "already an Israeli member of the panel charged with evaluating the eleven published volumes of wartime documents from the Vatican archives has called Pius XII 'complicit in Germany policy.' "[36] Hughes' irritation was aimed at a report issued in late 2000 by a six member committee of scholars, half Jewish and half Roman Catholic, "asking the Vatican to answer questions about its response to the Holocaust and urging the Holy See to give the group greater access to Vatican archives from that era."[37] The six scholars had spent a year perusing " 'the eleven volumes of works detailing the Vatican actions during World War II' " and came away dissatisfied.[38] A study of " 'these volumes,' " they wrote, " 'does not put to rest significant questions about the role of the Vatican during the Holocaust....' "[39] The official Vatican position of course, is that Pius XII "refrained from any harsh condemnation" of Hitler and the Nazis so as to not stir them to greater fury against the Jews.[40]

American Hebrew Christian Fundamentalists and Pius XII

The Jewish Christians of the Hebrew Christian Alliance of America would have strongly aligned themselves beside the committee of scholars disturbed by Pius XII's silence. They had no doubts as to the Pope's and the Roman Church's anti-Semitism. As early as 1932, Morris Zeidman, a leader within the HCAA cabled Pope Pius XI the following appeal (and by doing so highlighted Catholic anti-Semitism):

> As a Hebrew Christian, I appeal to you on behalf of three million Jews in Poland, and intercede in the name of Jesus of Nazareth, the King of the Jews, that you direct the clergy of the Roman Catholic Church of Poland to instruct their people to cease barbaric and anti-Christian persecutions against the Jews and enjoin them to love their neighbors as themselves.
>
> The eyes of Christian and enlightened America are not only on Poland, but on the Vatican, to see what action your Holiness is going to take in this matter. Acquiescence may be interpreted as consent.[41]

Zeidman closed his cable by reminding the Pope of the Abrahamic curse and blessing, pointing out that such could be applied to Poland.

The December 1936 issue of *The Jewish Era* took note of the fact that the Vatican opposed Jewish emigration to Palestine and the establishment of a Jewish state. Claiming its opposition was toward Zionism not the Jews as such, a report emanating from the Vatican claimed, " 'Never can the Holy See agree to this process opposed to the fundamental dictates of justice of a minority asserting itself over the natives by means of immigration and special privileges.' "[42]   There was, of course, a terrible irony to the Vatican report, for it failed to apply the same standard to Mussolini's invasion of Ethiopia. Be that as it may, the above Vatican opposition was enough to condemn the papacy in the eyes of the Jewish Christians. As the article noted in conclusion: "The Vatican cannot prevent the restoration of the Jews to Palestine. What God has said will stand despite secular or clerical opposition."[43]

The Winter 1938 issue of the *Hebrew Christian Alliance Quarterly* carried a major article, also written by Morris Zeidman (now the unpaid general secretary of the Alliance), denouncing Roman Catholicism and especially the Pope for dangerous political ambitions and anti-Semitism. He began the article by noting that Italian newspapers "declared that Fascism" had three enemies—Protestants, Masons, and Jews. These also were the enemies of Roman Catholicism, Zeidman claimed, and its press was trying "to prove that the Jews are plotting the destruction of the world." This, however, was a ruse on Rome's part to cover up their own [Jesuit] plot to once again "enslave the world as once before they enslaved it during the Middle Ages:"[44]

> That the Vatican with the aid of Fascism and Catholic Action, is engaged in such an attempt is very clear to all intelligent readers of newspapers as well as to those of us who have of late made the Papacy and Roman Catholicism a special study.[45]

To support his claim, Zeidman scornfully offered three examples: "The rape of Ethiopia," "the civil war in Spain where the baby butcher Franco...is hailed as the 'Defender of Christian Civilization,' " and Japan's invasion of China which had Mussolini's open support "and the secret aid of the Pope...."[46]

The rest of Zeidman's article is, in all frankness, a bitter tirade against the papacy, reciting evils past and present, and agreeing with the Reformers that the Pope is the anti-Christ. He concluded by asserting that fascism was not the great foe of democracy. "Fascism is a mere phase," he claimed, "used at the present by the Pope as a useful instrument to further" his ambitions. Yes, the real enemy of democracy was the papacy:

> Forget about the war of Fascism against the Democracies of the world. The evil lies far deeper and in another direction—it is the **Papacy against Democracy**. And peace will never reign in Europe until the Vatican is abolished, its wealth confiscated and given to the poor, and the Pope sent to Devil's Island....[47]

Zeidman was convinced that the "Jesuit Hierarchy" was covering its own tracks by promoting "suspicion against the Jewish Nation." Nothing could be more ludicrous, Zeidman pointed out, than that "Jews should be picked out as the danger to civilization." Everywhere in Europe and among the Arabs of Palestine he was harassed—"hunted, persecuted, reviled and mocked.... Only in the United States and the British Empire did he find safety and refuge...."[48]

"The implacable foe of Democracy" was the Vatican, Zeidman concluded. "The Papacy," he wrote, "is against Democracy, because the Papacy is the crudest, the cruelest, the most ancient Dictatorship in Europe.... The genius of Roman Catholicism is Dictatorship both in Church and State." On the other hand, "The genius of Protestantism is Democracy, in church as well as in State." If Democracy was to be saved, the Papacy had to be destroyed.[49]

Nothing changed during the war that softened the Hebrew Christian Alliance's view of the papacy. In the Summer 1945 edition of the HCA *Quarterly*, editor Aaron J. Kligerman noted that while "writers, politicians and some preachers have almost frightened us to death with... 'hear come the Communist,' what Americans really needed to fear...is not communism but the growth of the Catholic Church."[50] To support his "alarm," Kligerman referred his readers to a "series of articles in THE CHRISTIAN CENTURY on the Growth of the Catholic Church in America...." It was, according to Kligerman, an eye opener. "The Jews are not less fearful, even though not much is being said about it. Our experience with the Catholic System through the centuries cannot be so easily erased."[51]

Victor Buksbazen, director of the Friends of Israel Missionary and Relief Society[52] and editor of *Israel My Glory*, also wrote a section for the *Hebrew Christian Alliance Quarterly* as the war was coming to a conclusion called, "Happenings in Israel." There would appear in this section, along with a variety of items covering events in and politics about Palestine, an occasional item on the Roman Catholic Church's cooperation with fascism during the war. Three are worth reviewing for the light they shed on Jewish Christian animosity toward the Vatican. The first—"Czechoslovakia: Catholic Prelate Follows Hitler"—began by declaring that "where you find Catholicism you find persecution of the Jews." From this premise, Buksbazen went on to note: "It is not surprising then to find priest-led [Father Tiso] Slovakia even outdid other Catholic countries like Austria, Poland and Hungary in its persecution of the Jews, for it was more directly dominated by the Vatican." After briefly reviewing the fate of the Jews in "Father Tiso's puppet republic, Czechoslovakia," Buksbazen concluded by pointing out that "Father Tiso was singled out by Hitler himself as the first ruler in Europe who made his country 'Judenrein.' "[53]

The second item—"France: The Vatican and Anti-Jewish Laws"—appeared in the Spring 1947 edition of the HCAQ. It was in large part a reprint from *The Jewish Chronicle* [no date given] which in turn had reprinted an article that had appeared in the *La Monde Juif* of Paris. *La Monde Juif* had reproduced without "editorial comment" a lengthy "confidential report on the Vatican's alleged attitude" regarding Marshall Petain's anti-Jewish legislation. Supposedly written by the Vichy ambassador to the Vatican, one M. Leon Berard, and dated September 2, 1941, the report evidently set at ease any unease Petain may have had that Pius XII would condemn such action. Berard informed "Petain not to worry about the consequences of anti-Jewish legislation; there had never been any protest on the part of the Papal authorities, who he [Berard] claimed, actually favored 'charitable' discrimination against the Jews."[54] A direct quote from Berard's report "claimed that the pontifical authority shows no sign whatever of ever having paid the slightest attention to this gesture of French policy," and went on to assert that while the church "has condemned Racism," where the Jew was concerned the "Church makes mental distinctions and provides for nuances which are worth noting."[55] The above is, of course, third-hand information. Nevertheless, it was believed without qualification, and added one more bit of evidence that convinced the Jewish Christians of the HCAA that Pius XII was indeed "Hitler's Pope."

This conclusion was further reinforced by the third item appearing under Buksbazen's by-line—"Cardinal Mindszenty"—in the September 1949 HCAQ. Noting the "world" presses' outrage over the arrest and imprisonment of the Hungarian Cardinal, and acknowledging that the charges may have been "all trumped up against the Cardinal as a political maneuver of the Reds to attack the hated Catholic Church,"[56] Buksbazen drew attention to Pope Pius XII's harsh protest against the Cardinal's sentence, and his excommunication of "all those who had a hand in his [Mindszenty's] imprisonment and in his trial." However, Buksbazen turned this against the Pope by asking, with obvious bitterness, why the Pope had not been willing to do the same toward the persecutors of the Jews during World War II:

> But Christians will find it very hard to understand why "His Holiness" did not express his condemnations of Hitler and his satanic partners who murdered 6,000,000 Jews. . . . Why has he never excommunicated Hitler who was a Roman Catholic, nor…Goebbels, also a Roman Catholic? Why did he not excommunicate Benito Mussolini when he launched out on a war of extermination against the helpless Ethiopians? At that time the world would have respected the Pope for using the moral weapon of excommunication, but when he raises his voice in defense of a "Prince of the Church" somehow the Christian finds it hard to work up righteous indignation.[57]

Gentile Fundamentalists and Pius XII

That Gentile fundamentalist foe of anti-Semitism, Keith Brooks, was also a foe of Roman Catholicism, matching step for step the fervor of his Hebrew Christian brethren in this regard. He needed no convincing that the papacy was fascist friendly. His prime evidence in this regard was the papal embrace of Francisco "Baby Butcher" Franco of Spain. Brooks kept a running account of Franco's war on Protestant missionaries and indigenous evangelists, pastors, and churches, as well as the Vatican's support of his actions.[58] Brooks was, interestingly, sympathetic to the republican side in the Spanish civil war. He believed the Hearst papers exaggerated the "red atrocities" while ignoring the fact that Franco was persecuting Protestants at an alarming rate and closing down or destroying their churches while "restoring the property and status of the Roman Church" and placing all education under its control.[59] Drawing on the English *Churchman's* magazine (among others), Brooks concurred with its statement that the "persecution of Protestants in Spain is worse than at any time since the Inquisition."[60] He pointed out that when the

Spanish republic was founded the "Roman hierarchy condemned that charter of liberties and set out to regain Rome's lost control. All the bishops in Spain signed the manifesto against democracy because it provided for separation of church and state and religious freedom for the people for the first time in centuries."[61]

Brooks was not alone, of course, in reporting the massacres of Franco, his anti-Protestantism, and the silence and support of the Pope who was reported to have called Franco's regime a "happy restoration…which we have been watching day by day…[including] its continuous demonstrations of piety. We have seen Christ triumph and *the Christian spirit penetrate the laws, the institutions, and all the manifestations of official life.*"[62] Also the Pope's complicity in Ethiopia's conquest drew a great deal of notice and harsh condemnation. The historic fundamentalists were not about to forget what Rome did to the Protestant missions in that country, or the brutal treatment meted out to indigenous evangelicals by Catholic "missionaries," or the failure on the part of the Vatican to protest when the Italian army massacred thousands of Ethiopian civilians.[63] Nor were they unaware of the Roman Catholic Church's influence and involvement with Vichy France, or the horrors of Croatia's Catholic Church's slaughter of its Orthodox Serbian population and seizure of Orthodox church property.[64]

The historic fundamentalists were convinced that Pius XII was pro Mussolini, pro Franco, and worst of all pro Hitler. Donald Barnhouse made no attempt to hide his opinion.[65] As far as he was concerned, the Pope was pro German. "During the war," he editorialized, "the sympathies of the Vatican were always with Germany. If Germany and Italy had won the war Protestant England and Communist Russia would have been delivered, wrapped and tied, to the Papacy."[66]

Brooks, too, noted the German tilt of Pius XII. In the November 1941 *Prophecy Monthly*, he quoted liberally from an article that had first appeared in the *Churchman* magazine. The editor of that journal was concerned that the papacy was angling for a voice at the peace table. "Why does not Pius XII excommunicate Hitler and Mussolini," the *Churchman* asked, "instead of trying to dictate terms of a peace he has done nothing to win?" Citing the fact that the previous Pope had excommunicated the leaders of the new Spanish republican government in 1933, the *Churchman* surmised the present Pope's actions were a way of camouflaging his anti-British, anti-Protestant leanings. "The Roman Church," the article concluded, "is still the foe of our faith and liberties as much as the dictators who were reared in the Roman cradle."[67]

When President Roosevelt's envoy to the Vatican, Myron C. Taylor, returned from there without a declaration that "the fight of Great Britain and Russia against Germany" was a "just war," Brooks turned to Herbert L. Matthews of the *New York Times* for an analysis. According to Brooks, Matthews reduced the Pope's uncooperative reply into three simple answers, one of which was that because theoretically there is no such thing as a "just war," the papacy could not take sides.

Brooks found the Pope's position on the "just war" theory hypocritical in the extreme because "Franco had the Pope's blessing."[68]

In mid-1944, "when the Soviet newspaper, *Izvestia*, made a few plain statements on the 'servility of the Vatican toward Fascism' and the Vatican approval of many notorious acts of aggression by Fascist powers," Brooks gave them his blessing. While stating he harbored no love for the "Reds" (which was certainly true), he still had to admit that "what [*Izvestia*] said about the Vatican was nevertheless the unvarnished truth, although the propaganda agencies of Romanism on this continent hotly denied every charge."[69] When the New York State legislature, in response to *Izvestia*'s charges, "passed a resolution condemning as untrue" that the Vatican was pro-fascist, Brooks quoted from a Barnhouse editorial in *Revelation*:

"They might as well pass a resolution against snow in the winter and the law of gravity operating, or a resolution that we do not grow. It is notorious that the Roman Catholic Church is behind Franco, behind Mussolini and behind Hitler. The documents have been set forth by Harvard University professors in "What to do With Italy?" by Salvamini and La Piana. All the resolutions by the New York State legislature or anybody else will not change the facts."[70]

In December 1944, *The Baptist Bulletin* published an article which came "from London and is datelined SEPT 20." The article covered some angry remarks by the Bishop of Chelmsford, Dr. Henry Wilson, and directed toward the Pope who had evidently asked "that Londoners should show Christian sentiments of charity, forgiveness and mercy towards the Germans." Apparently the Pope's plea caused the good bishop to "go ballistic" and he angrily retorted: " 'It is difficult to remember one single word from the Pope in condemnation of the Nazis when they swept London with destruction.' "[71]

Kenneth R. Kinney, who authored the article for *The Baptist Bulletin*, found Bishop Wilson's logic irrefutable. The Pope had been silent while the " 'Beasts of Berlin' " bombed "Protestant England" at will. Even the most fanatical "Roman zealot" could not deny it. "On the other hand," Kenney continued, "his tearful appeal to 'spare the cities and people of Germany' when the shoe was on the other foot is so well known that none can deny it, as it was carried by our American papers as well as those in Britain."[72]

The historic fundamentalists' belief in the Vatican's fascist sympathies, a belief, present day protests to the contrary, not without some merit, made them especially sensitive to Roman Catholic activities in the United States which appeared aimed at increasing its influence and power to the point that Catholicism would become "the state religion." And for once, in one of those inexplicable oddities of history, the Federal Council of Churches and *The Christian Century* agreed with, and were on the same side as the historic fundamentalists.[73] In an address given at Moody Memorial Church in the spring of 1945, and published in *United Evangelical Action*, and in a similar sermon given at his own Park Street Church in Boston, and published as a three-part series in *The Sunday School Times*, Harold J. Ockenga—leading the charge—accused the Roman Catholic hierarchy in America of wanting to destroy America's Protestant culture (with its "insistence on the liberties and rights of man") and instead "make America Roman Catholic."[74]

And, as Donald Barnhouse noted, quoting Gaetano Salvemini, a Harvard University professor, "The Pope is very powerful; not in Rome, however, but in the White House."[75] This was, of course, a sentiment widely shared in the historic fundamentalist community. Roman Catholic moves in three areas especially alarmed and incensed the historic fundamentalists: attempts by the Roman hierarchy in America to block Protestant missionaries from South America by denying them passports and visas, its opposition to religious freedom, and its attempt to gain dominance over public education in America.

American Roman Catholic Bishops Oppose Protestant Missionaries

In April 1945, a brief column appeared in *The King's Business* drawing attention to the growing controversy between Protestants and Catholics over "the plans of the Roman Catholic Church concerning this country and the whole Western Hemisphere." Part of those plans included shutting down Protestant missions in South America. The writer concluded with thankfulness to God "that many sleeping Protestants are apparently awakening to the need for earnest prayer and for united action in order to press the battle against the entrenched forces in these darkened lands."[76]

A year and a half later, an editorial in *The King's Business* broached the subject once more. Claiming that there had been "considerable political intrigue," the editor noted that missionaries wanting to go to Latin America were either being denied passports or having them held up without explanation. Apparently this was happening because the "Roman Catholic hierarchy [in America] whose representatives are well entrenched in…[the] State Department" was blocking the issuance of the needed documents. When confronted over the issue, "these religious politicians have explained that since South America is almost entirely Catholic and satisfied with its present religion, it does not want any proselyting on the part of Protestants."[77] That, of course, was simply not true, the editor charged, and by way of example offered up the religious statistics printed by the Chilean government. According to those statistics, "Chile was not 90% Catholic as it was popularly believed to be" but rather 70% free thinkers, 25% Catholic and 5% Protestant.[78]

It was Harold Ockenga, though, who exposed the issue in detail in the second part of his three-point series that appeared in *The Sunday School Times* (August 1945). He drew attention to the fact that in November 1943 the American Roman

Catholic hierarchy had met in Washington, D. C. and issued a manifesto that claimed (1) the people of Central and South America were brother Catholics, and that efforts "made to rob them of the Catholic Religion or ridicule it is deeply resented by the people of these countries and by American Catholics," and (2) these efforts were undermining "our international relations" (i.e., "sabotaging the Good Neighbor policy"). Therefore, the manifesto concluded, Protestant missionaries should not be given permission by the U. S. government to go to Latin America.[79]

Rather than respond in his own words to what he believed was Roman Catholic nonsense, Ockenga summarized the joint statement put out by the Federal Council of Churches and its Foreign Missions Council and Home Missions council. The Joint Statement accused the Roman hierarchy of doing "violence both to historic truth and contemporary fact," and "deplored the pretensions" of the hierarchy which sought to limit the religious freedom of Protestants while exclusively proclaiming their own. "We can imagine no policy more certain," the Joint Statement read, "to project into the new world the baneful intolerance which is now producing such tragic consequences in the contemporary life of Spain."[80] The statement concluded by affirming (1) support for religious liberty and protection of "the rights of religious minorities in the United States and throughout the world," (2) they would stand by the Protestant churches in Latin America "whose numerous members are loyal and patriotic citizens of the countries where they dwell...," and (3) the Protestant work in Latin America was not undermining good relations and in fact were "regarded with great favor by governments and peoples in the countries where they are located."[81]

Next, Ockenga quoted from the remarks of the well known liberal, Dr. H. P. Van Dusen, which, in essence boiled down to the charge that Catholics were claiming the right to persecute Protestants and that that claim "must be resisted."[82] Ockenga agreed wholeheartedly with Van Dusen's criticism, noting "that this is the settled policy of the Roman Catholic Church is shown by the history of that church in Spain...in Ethiopia...[and] in Poland before it was overrun by Germany, where the priest instigated persecution against Protestant minorities, which I witnessed with my own eyes as I was preaching in Poland."[83] The Roman Catholic position, as far as Ockenga was concerned was one of expediency: " 'When we are a minority we claim freedom in the name of your principles; when we are a majority we refuse it in the name of ours' " (George Veullet).[84]

Additional proof of this was to be found in George P. Howard's *Religious Liberty in Latin America* (1944). Again, Howard was a liberal but evidently just as incensed as any historic fundamentalist over the high-handed political moves by the American Catholic hierarchy. "Dr. Howard," Ockenga pointed out, "after seeing the attitude of the American hierarchy, journeyed through all of the South American countries, interviewing lawyers, editors, legislatures, authors, educators, and leading persons in every walk of life to ask them their opinion upon this matter of religious liberty."[85]

The results were anything but favorable to the position of the Catholic hierarchy in America. The overall consensus was that the Roman Catholic Church in South America was given over to "magic" rather "morals," that it was "pagan," "autocratic," "monopolistic," "undemocratic," and that "the American State Department has favored dictatorships, autocratic government, and Catholic interests in South America under the hierarchical influence."[86]

Ockenga was convinced, because of its favoring of Catholic interests, that the State Department was subservient "to the influence of the Roman Catholic Church." He was also convinced that for political considerations, the same held true for President Roosevelt. The evidence substantiating this was Roosevelt establishing diplomatic relations with the Vatican despite the fact that it was an "affront to millions of Americans and is a violation of the cardinal principle of the separation of church and state, basic to American history."[87] "Clericalism," Ockenga ominously concluded, "...is a greater menace than communism. A new portent, sinister and ugly, has made its appearance in American affairs."[88]

American Roman Catholic Leadership Opposes Freedom of Worship

Behind the Latin American issue, though, was a far more important issue in the minds of the historic fundamentalists, and that was the issue of religious freedom. On this point more than any other, the historic fundamentalists both feared and fought Roman Catholicism. They were convinced, not without cause, that Rome not only opposed religious liberty, but where the Catholic Church dominated society and the state it suppressed such liberty. This, they believed, was also the goal of the Roman Catholic hierarchy in America.

Charles G. E. Chilton, editor of the *United Evangelical Action*, published an editorial on this subject early in January 1945 in response to an article that had appeared in the *Boston Herald* on December 5, 1944. The *Herald* article had declared that Catholics, Protestants, and Jews were all opposed to Nazi paganism, "the reign of might, the apotheosis of the State, the suppression of minorities, and the oppression of small nations." Without mentioning Catholicism by name, Chilton pointed out that Protestants in Spain and South America, a minority group, were being suppressed. "Any group (or institution)," Chilton wrote, "which is essentially autocratic in its claims, and dictatorial in its power can hardly be said to be against the suppression of the minorities."[89]

By contrast, Chilton reminded his readers, where evangelical Christianity is found there is found a "zeal and passion for Liberty," and that "where the Bible goes liberty is sure to follow." Chilton selectively raised the banner of Roger Williams as proof of his assertion. He closed his editorial with a brief rebuff to the *Harold*:

There are those who speak of religious toleration, and refuse to see that religious toleration is miles from religious liberty. It follows, therefore, that the claim of any group, in its championship of freedom, must be demonstrated in its everyday life and translate into terms of human life and experience.[90]

The Roman Catholic Church, as far as the historic fundamentalists were concerned, failed in this regard, and failed badly.

Kenneth Kinney, writing in *The Baptist Bulletin* (July 1944), was not as circumspect as Chilton. Drawing attention to an article written by New York's Cardinal Spellman in the "current issue of *American Magazine*" which denounced bigotry of any kind, Kinney noted his own incredulousness. For no other church had a worse record of bigotry than did the Roman Church. To support his point, Kinney quoted from an article written by Father Francis Connell on the faculty of the Catholic University in Washington, D. C. Father Connell's article had appeared in the October 1943 issue of *The Ecclesiastical Review* and covered the issue of religious freedom. Noting that freedom of religion was one of the "four freedoms" Americans were fighting for, Connell wrote:

> Beyond doubt, the expression "freedom of worship" is ordinarily understood by our non Catholic citizens, when they advocate the "four freedoms," in the sense that everyone has a natural, God-given right to accept and to practice whatever form of religion appeals to him individually.[91]

Kinney put the following words by Connell in capital letters to emphasis how deadly was Catholic opposition to the above interpretation of freedom of religion:

NO CATHOLIC CAN WITH CONSCIENCE DEFEND SUCH AN IDEA OF FREEDOM OF RELIGIOUS WORSHIP. FOR ACCORDING TO CATHOLIC PRINCIPLES, THE ONLY RELIGION THAT HAS A GENUINE RIGHT TO EXIST IS THE CATHOLIC RELIGION that God revealed and made obligatory on all men.[92]

"America has risen to its greatness," Kinney exclaimed, "LARGELY because of being pre-dominantly PROTESTANT, for DEMOCRACY is the child of PROTESTANTISM. Let us keep BOTH alive."[93]

The following year, Donald Barnhouse came out with a lengthy article in his *Revelation* magazine that went into greater depth the issue raised in Kinney's article—that the Roman Catholic Church not only believed it was the only true church, but also "that it is the right of the church, wherever it is in control, to exterminate false ideas." Barnhouse supported his position by quoting from Francis Connell's pamphlet, "Freedom of Worship—The Catholic Position," and from volume three of *A Companion to the Summa* by Walter Farrell, a noted Catholic scholar of the day. Their view of religious freedom allowed Barnhouse to charge that Catholics in the armed forces were "fighting for a debased concept of freedom.... The freedom of worship for which they fight" along with the rest of America's Catholics, "is a freedom for themselves but chains for all others."[94]

Barnhouse closed his commentary with an angry and bitter denunciation of Roman Catholicism in America:

> The pamphlet by Connell and the book by Farrell demonstrate that the Roman Catholic Church is a sinister and bitter enemy of Protestantism, Jewry, Liberalism, Humanism, in short, all that is not Roman Catholicism. It demonstrates itself to be un-American in the highest degree for we believe that Americanism stands for the right of any man to believe as he pleases.
>
>   Over twenty million people among us are sworn to destroy that Americanism. Let us not forget it.[95]

Six months later Barnhouse was again beating the drum of alarm. He was convinced by two articles that had appeared in two major magazines that something nefarious was afoot. The first article appeared in the January 1946 *Collier's* magazine and was, Barnhouse surmised, an "epistle written by the Pope himself to America." The second article appeared in *Life* magazine [same year but no date given] and was a fawning piece about the importance, savvy, and brilliance of New York's Cardinal Spellman. Together, both articles pointed to the fact (Barnhouse believed) that the Roman Catholic Church was making "her greatest bid for power in all her history,"—that is making Roman Catholicism the dominant religious power in the United States, and the United States the protector of the Vatican from communism. Quoting the following sentence from *Collier's*, (or the Pope as far as Barnhouse was concerned), "The American people have a genius for splendid and unselfish action, and into the hands of America, God has placed the destinies of afflicted humanity,"[96] Barnhouse responded by writing: "Without any violence to the thought of the Vatican we might read: Into the hands of America the Vatican is placing the destinies of an afflicted Papacy."[97] "On several occasions," he continued, "we have pointed out in the pages of REVELATION that there is no such thing as four freedoms or any kind of freedom for anyone who has anything to do with Rome."[98]

Toward the end of his own rather lengthy "epistle," in which he discussed the less than honorable course of Vatican political thought and history regarding state and church affairs, Barnhouse tied the Pope's words in *Collier's*—"into the hands of America, God has placed the destinies of afflicted humanity"—with a quotation from the biographer/author of the article on Cardinal Spellman that appeared in *Life*:

> "In the present state of world affairs the Vatican looks to the United States, and its 24,000,000 Catholics,...for a number of indispensable things including moral support,

political and diplomatic cooperation, healthy, aggressive personnel to carry on the Church's missionary work around the world, food for the starving people of Europe—and money."[99]

What this meant, Barnhouse opined, was that the United States was to provide the funds whereby the Catholic Church brought the nation under its control. America was to have the dubious honor of "holding the stirrup for the whore to mount the beast."[100] Rome was moving on America with ill intent, Barnhouse again gloomed. "The lines of conflict are laid down. Anyone familiar with history and Papal strategy can plot the course of Rome's advance. The shadows grow darker."[101]

James DeForest Murch, in the same month of the same year (March 1946) also sounded the alarm in an editorial in the *United Evangelical Action*, listing six reasons why he considered Roman Catholicism a threat to American religious liberties. First on the list was the Catholic doctrine of church and state that always led to the state being dominated by the church. Next was the on-going attempt by the American Catholic hierarchy "to extend its political domination in the United States as it had done in Spain...." The third reason was the Roman teaching that denied religious freedom to religious minorities where it dominated. Fourth was the willingness "to weaken the American constitutional principle and practice of separation of church and state." Fifth was Murch's belief that no church or religion should be recognized as both a church and a state. Last but not least, was Roman Catholic "pressure on American institutions—radio, newspapers, etc.—which cripple freedom of speech and undermine our civil and religious liberties."[102]

Finally, there appeared in the August 1948, *Moody Monthly*, an editorial which printed an extensive quote from the Roman Jesuit publication, *La Civilita Cattolica*. In America the quote had originally appeared in *The Christian Century* and *Moody* picked it up from there. It is quite lengthy but the editor believed that it would "once for all give the lie to any claim that the ascendancy of Romanism in America would not do away with religious freedom guaranteed under our political democracy."[103] And because it originated with "high Jesuit officials in Rome" *Moody* believed it was to be taken with all seriousness:

"The Roman Catholic Church, convinced, through its divine prerogatives of being the only true Church, must demand the right to freedom for herself alone, because such a right can only be possessed by truth, never by error. As to other religions, the Church will never draw the sword, but she will require that by legitimate means they shall not be allowed to propagate false doctrine.

Consequently, in a state where the majority of the people are Catholic, the Church will require that legal existence be denied to error, and that if religious minorities actually exist, they shall have only a de facto existence, without opportunity to spread their beliefs. If, however, actual circumstances, either due to government hostility or the strength of the dissenting groups, make the complete application of this principle impossible, then the Catholic Church will require for herself all possible concessions, limiting herself to accept, as a minor evil, the de jure toleration of other forms of worship. In some countries, Catholics will be obliged to ask full religious freedom for all, resigned at being forced to cohabitate where they alone should rightfully be allowed to live. But in doing this, the Church does not renounce her thesis.[104]

The above was reason enough, then, for the historic fundamentalists, and modernists, to be militantly wary of Roman Catholicism.

American Roman Catholic Leaders Threaten American Public Education

One other area of Roman Catholic assertiveness alarmed the historic fundamentalists—public education. Even before the February 10, 1947 Supreme Court decision upholding a New Jersey statute which allowed the use of state funds to pay for the transportation of Roman Catholic children to their parochial schools, the historic fundamentalists were horrified at Roman Catholic incursions into public school systems. Harold Ockenga, in his three-part series in *The Sunday School Times*, gave an example from his own state and city—Boston, Massachusetts—that must have instantly grayed the hair of many a historic fundamentalist.

According to Ockenga, Massachusetts already had a law on the books [1945] allowing public funds to be used to bus parochial students to their church schools. However, it was the Boston school system itself that Ockenga considered a prime example of Catholic subversion:

Every member of the School Committee is Roman Catholic. Nearly one hundred percent of the principals of the schools in the city are Roman Catholic. The majority of the teachers are Roman Catholic. The archbishop entered the public schools of the city in his full robes, explaining them as an object lesson for the children, had the teachers come to kiss his ring, distributed publicly pictures of himself to all who would take them, and then dismissed the schools at noontime on the day of his visit. In one public school of metropolitan Boston, medals of Mary were passed out to the Children, and they were urged to go to the Roman Catholic Church to make a novena just proceeding Easter 1945.[105]

It was the Supreme Court's 5 to 4 pro-Catholic vote that really aroused the historic fundamentalists to fever-pitch opposition. Murch wrote a blistering editorial critical of the decision in *United Evangelical Action* that began by declaring: "February 10, 1947, will go down in the annuals of the U. S. Supreme Court as one of the darkest days for religious liberty on record. By a five to four decision, the court ruled constitutional the New Jersey law permitting payment from tax funds for the transportation of pupils of Roman Catholic schools...."[106] Some, Murch thought, might consider the issue "trivial," but, he warned, "the decision may well precipitate serious religious strife and eventually destroy all our cherished freedoms."[107] (In retrospect, the majority opinion does seem disingenuous when it claimed "that the issue of the separation of church and state was not involved" and that if it were the majority "would never consent to such a union," or that "such state aid...was not 'support' of religious education in the strict meaning of the law," or "that such aid was for a public purpose and the promotion of the general welfare.")[108] Surprisingly, Murch noted Judge Jackson's somewhat risqué (minority) response to such reasoning, writing, "Justice Jackson, slyly remarked that the decision reminded him of Julia, who according to Byron's reports, 'whispering, "I will ne'er consent"—consented.' "[109]

In fact, Murch was fulsome in his praise of the minority justices Jackson and Rutledge. They "neatly exploded the idea," he reported, "that such aid was for a public purpose." Murch was especially taken with the concluding words of Justice Rutledge's opinion,

> that this seeming "inconsequential matter" was in reality a grave matter of principle—"to keep separate the separate spheres (of church and state) as the First Amendment drew them; to prevent the first experiment upon our liberties; and to keep the question from becoming entangled in corrosive precedents."[110]

In the "Window on the World" section of *Revelation*, Barnhouse printed the response of the Joint Conference Committee on Public Relations for the Baptists of the United States:

> We feel that the majority opinion must be acknowledged as turning back the hands of the clock as far as religious liberty and separation of Church and State are concerned in these United States. . . . As Baptists of the United States, we are resolved that the struggle for religious liberty, in terms of the separation of Church and State, must be continued. Having lost the battle, we have not lost the war.[111]

The King's Business took note of the growing dissent. The Supreme Court's decision had aroused "a storm of protest," it wrote and listed a few of them: "The Pennsylvania Supreme Court has upheld the directors of a school district in refusing to provide transportation for parochial school students;" the state of Maine Senate had killed a bill that would have provided such transportation; "a resolution has been introduced [in Congress] to amend the constitution, prohibiting the giving of aid to any educational institution under sectarian control;" in states all across the country "there are debates...as to what to do with this very involved problem."[112]

An extensive and critical evaluation of the Supreme Court's decision appeared in the pages of *The King's Business* in June 1947. It was a two-part discussion by the reverend David W. Ewart, a transplanted Scotsman who had an unfeigned love for his adopted country. It had, he wrote, "the best form of government on the face of the earth, so good, in fact, that we are still just learning how to live up to it."[113] In the second part of his discussion, Ewart began by quoting the President of the Southern Baptists to the effect that "a great and terrible cloud" may be drifting over the land "to darken the torch of religious liberty." Ewart then briefly summarized the argument of the Court majority: "That the law authorizing such payments is basically social legislation for the benefit of students and their families, with benefits to the church merely incidental! Justice Black argued that no person may be denied the benefit of such a law by reason of his religion."[114]

Declaring himself "appalled" by such convoluted logic, Ewart built his response around the words of four critics of the Court's majority opinion. The first was the editor of the *Watchman-Examiner* who called the Court's decision " 'the stiffest blow at the great American principle of separation of church and state since the Bill of Rights became law.' " However, the *Watchman-Examiner* also pointed out that "if sufficient numbers of Americans now tell the Supreme Court and their representatives in Congress what they think of this destructive decision, a way may be found to change it."[115] Ewart was especially taken with the conclusion the editor of the *Watchman-Examiner* wrote, one he called courageous:

"There remains, however, the tortuous and expensive course of correction, which is always difficult. *It will require some patriotic citizen to refuse to pay his school tax on the ground that he is made to support a religion in which he does not believe....* It is inconceivable that in this country a citizen shall be compelled to pay taxes to build a religious sectarian privilege which will not merely live off him, but in the end overmaster him and take away his rights."[116]

Ewart next quoted the words of dissenting Justice Robert Jackson, words that he was "quite thrilled to read!" In essence, Jackson opined that to support Catholic schools with tax funds, was to support the Catholic Church itself:

"We know that such schools are parochial only in name—they, in fact, represent a world-wide and age old policy of the Roman Catholic Church . . . Catholic education is the rock on which the whole structure rest, and to render tax aid to its Church schools is indistinguishable to me from rendering the same aid to the church itself."[117]

And if the state could aid " 'religious schools,' " Jackson concluded, " 'it may therefore regulate them.' "[118]

Ewart followed Jackson's words with those of another dissenting Justice, Wiley Rutledge, which had appeared in the February 22, 1947 issue of *Time* magazine. Justice Black, who had written the majority opinion, had evidently quoted from the writings of Thomas Jefferson to support his case. Rutledge took umbrage at this, and taking the same quotation—" 'To compel a man to furnish contributions of money for the propagation of opinions which he disbelieves, is sinful and tyrannical' "—concluded the following: " 'I cannot believe that the great author of these words...could have joined in [the majority] decision. Neither so high nor so impregnable today as yesterday is the wall raised between church and state. . . . Thus with time, the most solid freedom steadily gives way before a continuing corrosive decision.' "[119]

Finally, Ewart turned to Clayton Morrison's "blast on the subject" (also thoroughly covered in the March 2, 1947 issue of *Time*) to round out his supporting cast. Morrison, aging editor of *The Christian Century*, considered the Supreme Court decision a wake up call for American Protestants " 'to the strategy of the Roman Catholic Church in its determination to secure a privileged position in the common life of this country....' " Morrison, however, blamed Protestants for the whole sorry mess. Far too many ministers considered the issue too trivial to get worked up about. " 'They were blind to the strategy of the Roman Church in using these apparently insignificant matters as the thin edge of the wedge which would ultimately crack open the Constitution.' "[120] Morrison closed with a warning that if Protestants " 'passively' " tolerated compromises of religious liberty, " 'it sealed its own doom,' " which would be, " 'in the end, a minority sect existing on the margins of American life.' "[121]

The great question for America, Ewart reasoned, is what is to be its destiny. There were only two possible answers. "Shall we continue in the footsteps of our political and spiritual forefathers," he rhetorically queried, "or shall we betray them by going back to religious tyrannies of medieval Europe?"[122] And if any were of the opinion that the Catholic Church changed and was no longer a threat, Ewart reminded them that that church was still the same church that had "massacred French Huguenots."[123]

To prove his assertion, Ewart gave four examples from the recent past. The first was Archbishop Stepinac of Croatia who was tried as a Nazi collaborator and persecutor of thousands of Orthodox Serbs. Because of America's dislike of Yugoslavia's Tito, Ewart noted, we forget that he [Stepinac] really was "a tyrant, responsible for the death of many people on politico-religious grounds." Next on Ewart's list was the anti-Semitic Father Tiso of Hungary.[124] "He was one of Hitler's most efficient murderers and is on trial for his crimes." Ewart's third witness to Roman Catholic incorrigibility was Antonescu of Romania—"a murderer and persecutor...." When he was at the height of his power, Ewart pointed out, "when he was the darling of the then triumphant Nazis, he was called to the Vatican and presented with a medal of honor. This man, whom the present Pope saw fit to honor, was recently tried by a people's court and shot." Finally, Ewart drew attention to the fact that while the Pope excommunicated "Tito and all who participated in the trial of Archbishop Stepinac," he did not do the same to Hitler, "an indisputable Catholic." Even the *New York Times*, Ewart stressed, "In its first coverage of the Tito excommunication story, happened to mention how unprecedented this was and stated that not even Hitler had suffered this punishment."[125]

No, the Roman Catholic Church had not changed, Ewart believed, and "Protestants would not be so naïve if they would read a little history!" He insisted he was not against Catholics exercising the same freedoms he exercised. What he was opposing was a standard that gave the Roman Catholic Church privileges it had garnered "for itself more by political coercion than by moral grandeur." "In short," he wrote, "I plead for fair play. I ask nothing for Protestants that I am not willing to concede to Roman Catholics."[126]

In closing, Ewart expressed his "deep conviction that the wall which separates church and state is crumbling," and pleaded with his readers "to dedicate" themselves "to the task of strengthening the wall." He admitted Americans had "a lot of faults," even "grievous sins" and that "in some things we will have to change," nevertheless, he cautioned,

> The basic principles of our government must not be tampered with, and for anyone to imply that a small deviation from these principles is warranted to please any religious group, is sheer folly. There can be no *small* deviations in the First Amendment. Any deviation is significant[127]

And with an emotional Protestant patriotic flourish, he finished by proclaiming, "I say these words with deep feeling, words which must never be trite, 'Long may our land be bright with freedom's holy light.' "[128]

Summing Up

Henry and Singer might bemoan the inroads secularism was making into "Christian America," and loudly exhort their fellow fundamentalists to get "political" or lose their country to the ungodly, but evidently the secularist easily morphed into a far more deadly Catholic prelate. So much so that even though Keith Brooks admitted "that we would far rather risk a soul with the Roman Church than with a Modernist bloodless cult,"[129] the historic fundamentalists were still willing to find common cause with the dreaded secularist to stop the political ambitions of the Roman Catholic Church. Thus James D. Murch enthusiastically supported the "clarion call" issued by the Protestants and other Americans United for Separation of Church and State "for Americans of all faiths to defend" their religious liberty granted by the Constitution.[130] Although Murch disapproved of the word "Protestant" appearing in the title "of the new organization" and considered it even "more unfortunate that its officiary is so heavily weighed with 'liberals,'" (because it was not just a "liberal" or "Protestant" battle), nevertheless he supported it, and hoped that the yet to be appointed Advisory Council would be broadly representative of all elements of American society "who love freedom and will fight for it:"

> It should represent every denomination, every undenominational movement, every inter-denominational organization and reach down to every local church, every preacher, every layman. It should represent the Jews, the Mormons, the Unitarians, the atheists, the lodges, the civic welfare organizations, the public schools and *all the rest.*[131]

In looking back, there is a certain irony to the historic fundamentalists' position of opposition, for now it is evangelicals who are asking for government assistance in the form of vouchers that would pay for private evangelical schooling out of tax funds or government funds for faith based organizations. And now we have Catholics and evangelicals making common political cause against the secularists who presently control public education, the media and the social services of the nation, and through these have waged war against Christianity. Ruefully, pragmatism sweeps all evangelicals before its conquering tide.

NOTES

1. I have already written a great deal about the historic fundamentalists views on the New Deal and communism. C. Gregg Singer's remarks about the German Church, then, are worth quoting for the collapse of German Christianity weighed heavily on the minds of the historic fundamentalists as well as other evangelicals:
    > The problem of their relations to the state confronted German Christians after the rise of Hitler in 1933 in a startling manner, and with a magnitude unprecedented for the Church in the land of the Reformation. But until the nature of the Nazi philosophy of life made it impossible [any] longer to ignore its threat, the church paid little or no attention to this vital problem. In looking back, it is clear that the failure of the German church clearly to define the responsibilities of its members accentuated the crisis confronting German Christians after 1933. ("Are We Forgetting Our Government?" *Moody Monthly*, July 1947, 745.)
2. Ibid.
3. Ibid.
4. Ibid. Singer goes on to predict that a "more severe restriction if not total abolition, will be placed on Christian radio. Missionary enterprises will be seriously restricted. There were signs of such a trend during the recent war and they are not absent today." Though Singer proved wrong regarding Christian radio and missions, in other areas, such as the public schools or the mainstream media, a distinct anti-Christian hostility exists and is practiced.
5. Ibid.
6. Ibid.
7. Ibid.
8. Ibid, 747.

9.   Ibid.
10. Ibid, 795.
11. Ibid.
12. Ibid.
13. Ibid.
14. Ibid.
15. See Mark A. Noll, *The Scandal of the Evangelical* Mind (Grand Rapids: William B. Eerdmans Publishing Company, 1994), 245, 246. To a certain extent, Noll reminds one of Erasmus, who thought education and knowledge the key to curing what ailed the Church and Christendom. In the process Erasmus rejected that which was must essential—regeneration by the power of the Holy Spirit through the preaching of the Word.
16. Carl F. H. Henry, *The Uneasy Conscience of Modern Fundamentalism* (Grand Rapids: Wm. B. Eerdmans Publishing Com., 1947), npn.
17. John Cornwell, *Hitler's Pope: The Secret History of Pius XII* (New York: Viking Penguin, 1999). See pages 248-260 ("Catholic Croatia's Atrocious Regime") for a good example of this. Even after the Croatian Roman Catholic Church stopped persecuting the Serbian Orthodox in Croatia, it confiscated Orthodox property and churches.
18. Ibid, 294. Also see, David P. Gushee, "Rescue Those Being Led Away to Death," *Books and Culture*, March/April 2002, 22, 23, 40-42. This is a review of a number of new books which deal critically with the Vatican over its response to the Jews and the Holocaust.
19. Ibid, 297.
20. William D. Rubenstein, "The Devils Advocate," *First things*, January 2000, 39; Michael Novak, "Pius XII as Scapecoat," *First things*, August/September 2000, 20; and John Jay Hayes, "Hitler's Pope," *First Things*, October 2000, 66.
21. Rubenstein, 42.
22. Ibid.
23. Ibid.
24. Ibid, 39.
25. Novak, 20.
26. Ibid, 22.
27. Ibid, 21.
28. Ibid, 22.
29. Ibid.
30. Hughes, 66, 67.
31. Ibid, 67.
32. Ibid, 67, 68.
33. Ibid, 69, 70.
34. Ibid, 71.
35. Ibid.
36. Ibid.
37. "Religion in Brief: Vatican Asked for Holocaust Answers," *Los Angeles Times*, Saturday, October 28, 2000, B3.
38. Ibid.

39.   Ibid.
40.   Ibid.
41.   "Notes and Comments by the General Secretary," *Hebrew Christian Alliance Quarterly*, April-June 1932, 8.
42.   "Palestine Notes: Vatican Opposition Futile," *The Jewish Era*, December 1936, 127. Also see Elli Wohlgellernter, "Pope Pius's 1943 letter against Jewish statehood revealed," *The Jerusalem Post: North American addition*, July 9, 1999, 6. The article reports on a letter written by Pius XII and sent by A. G. Cicognani, the Pope's special representative to the United States, to Roosevelt's papal emissary, Myron Taylor. It is dated July 22, 1943. A quote from the letter reads as follows:

   It is true that at one time Palestine was inhabited by the Hebrew Race, but there is no axiom in history to substantiate the necessity of a people returning to a country they left nineteen centuries before.

   If a "Hebrew Home" is desired, it would not be too difficult to find a more fitting territory than Palestine. With an increase in the Jewish population there, grave, new international problems would arise.

   Wohlgelernter follows the above with Rabbi Marvin Hier's interpretation of Pius's remarks. (Rabbi Heir is the dean of the Simon Wiesenthal Center.) The letter, Heir is quoted as saying, " 'is an indictment of Pius XII, because it basically says that when the pope wanted a point of view expressed about how he clearly felt, he said it clearly. Where is a similar letter to Adolf Hitler telling Hitler that the Vatican finds his policies against the Jews repugnant? But at the height of the Holocaust, the Vatican knew how to oppose the State of Israel.' "
43.   Ibid.
44.   M. Zeidman, "The Jewish Peril," *Hebrew Christian Alliance Quarterly*, Winter 1938, 23. (The Winter 1938 issue really covered the last quarter of 1937—October through December).
45.   Ibid.
46.   Ibid.
47.   Ibid, 27, 28.
48.   Ibid, 28.
49.   Ibid, 29.
50.   A. S. K., "Across the Desk: America's Future Problem," *Hebrew Christian Alliance Quarterly*, Summer 1945, 18.
51.   Ibid.
52.   At the very beginning of 1943, the Friends of Israel Refugee Relief Committee changed its name to the Friends of Israel Missionary and Relief Society because, in the words of Joseph Britan, "There were no more refugees." With the change in name and emphasis, the FOIMRS hired a full time director, Victor Buksbazen. Buksbazen was a native of Poland, a Jewish Christian refugee, himself, and also one who lost family in the Holocaust.
53.   Victor Buksbazen, "Happenings in Israel: Czechoslovakia: Catholic Prelate Follows Hitler," *Hebrew Christian Alliance Quarterly*, Fall 1945, 25, 26.
54.   Buksbazen, "France: The Vatican and Anti-Jewish Laws," Spring 1947, 26, 27.
55.   Ibid, 27. However, this report is offset somewhat by a brief item that appeared in the Spring 1942 issue of the *Jewish Missionary Magazine*. "According to a usually

reliable source in Vichy," the item begins, "the Papal Nuncio protested to" Marshall Petain "against the 'inhuman arrests and deportation' " of the Jews in the Nazi occupied zone of France "to Silesia and occupied parts of Russia." The item goes on to note that the Nuncio insisted that Petain give serious attention to the Pope's protest "in view of the 'Christian precepts involved.' " Petain allegedly did respond by petitioning Pierre Lavel, "Chief of Government at that time in Paris," that the deportations be cancelled. However, according to the news item, Lavel's attempt to bring this about "was unavailing, except, possibly, regarding an agreement 'for the moment to confine deportation to non-French Jews.' " The news item concluded on an ominous note: "The first trains carrying Jews to concentration camps in Poland and Russia left Paris on August 4th." ("Jewish Notes: Papal Plea," 127.)

56.   Buksbazen, "Cardinal Mindszenty," *Hebrew Christian Alliance Quarterly*, September 1949, 26.

57.   Ibid, 26, 27.

58.   See the following articles from *Prophecy Monthly*: "Information from Missionaries," June 1937, 17; "Protestant Work Paralyzed by Spanish Rebels," June 1937, 28, 29; "What Franco Victory Means for Spain," March 1939, 10; "Rome's Role in the European Chaos," July 1940, 14-17; "Door is Closed," May 1941, 41; "Modern Martyrs," April 1944, 22, 23; "Protestantism Under Franco," May 1945, 6-8; "New Light on Franco's 'Holy War'," May 1946, 14, 15.

59.   "What Franco's Victory Means to Spain," *Prophecy Monthly*, March 1939, 10. Also from *Prophecy Monthly*, "Protestants Out," November 1939, 37, and "Modern Martyrs," April 1944, 23.

60.   "Protestants Suffer," *Prophecy Monthly*, September 1941, 22.

61.   "Well What About Spain Now," *Prophecy Monthly*, December 1944, 11. Also "New Light on Franco's 'Holy War'," May 1946, 15.

62.   Ernest Gordon, "A Survey of Religious Life and Thought," *The Sunday School Times*, March 18, 1944, (5) 197. Also see "A Survey of Religious Life and Thought" for October 23, 1937, 747, March 12, 1938, 191, June 12, 1943, 401, and June 14, 1947, 589. In addition see "Starving Spain," *Prophetic Word*, January 1943, 22-25, "Window on the World," *Revelation*, February 1945, 67, and Ockenga, "II. The Roman Catholic Hierarchy Challenges Protestant America," *The Sunday School Times*, August 18, 1945, (3) 627.

63.   See "Tomorrow: The Shock of Peace," *Revelation*, July 1945, 287; "A Window on the World," *Revelation*, for February 1945, 95, and August 1945, 333; Harold Ockenga, "II. The Roman Catholic Hierarchy Challenges Protestant America," *The Sunday School Times*, August 18, 1945, (3) 627; "Ockenga Charges Roman Church As A Menace To American Religious Freedom," *United Evangelical Action*, Saturday, May 19, 1945, 3; Ernest Gordan, "A Survey of Religious Life and Thought," *The Sunday School Times*, for March 12, 1938, 192, August 9, 1941, 641, and December 21, 1946, 1178; "Tables Turned," *Prophecy Monthly*, March 1945, 42, "Rome Don's the Garb of True Liberalism," *Prophecy Monthly*, May 1944, 11, 12.

64.   See Ernest Gordon, "A Survey of Religious Life and Thought," *The Sunday School Times*, for December 19, 1942, 1037, June 10, 1944, 418 (6), and May 22, 1943, 418; "Notes on Open Letters: Catholic Persecution in Croatia," *The Sunday School Times*, February 20, 1943, 146, 152; "Flashes," *Prophecy Monthly*, April 1947, 26.

Also see Cornwell's *Hitler's Pope*, 248-260 for his account of "Catholic Croatia's Atrocious Regime."

65. "Editorial: Effect and Cause," *Revelation*, March 1945, 105.

66. "A Window on the World," *Revelation*, July 1947, 335.

67. "Pope's Predicament," *Prophecy Monthly*, November 1941, 22, and "Vatican-Hitler," *Prophecy Monthly*, December 1942, 21. Also see "The Pattern of Nazi Militarism," which appeared on pages 8 and 9 of the February 1945, *Prophecy Monthly*. It was a reprint of a (probable) letter to the editor of the Utica, New York, *Press*, written by a couple of clergymen in response to a press release put out by the Catholic Information Society in the Press. Dated November 21, 1944, the press release claimed that "the pattern of Nazi militarism derives from the political tactics employed during the [Protestant] Reformation." Not so, declared the offended clergymen. Nazi fascism was "totalitarian in pattern" and mimics Catholicism, not Protestantism which is democratic in pattern. The clergymen then went on to charge:

> The Vatican State has blessed and co-operated with every Nazi, Falangist, Sinarquist order, in the old and new world. It has drafted amazing pacts with Nazism and Fascism in the form of Concordats. The Roman Catholic historians, Blood-Ryan (sic), declare concerning this treaty with the Nazis, "Thus the Catholic Church won a great victory over Protestantism...." And Koeves in his biography of Franz von Papen says: "The Concordat was a great victory for Hitler. It gave him the first moral support he received from the outer world."

In addition, the irate pastors pointed out, Hitler, Himmler, Goebbels, and Von Papen were all reared as Catholics and Von Papen had "received the highest Papel decoration as Defender of the Faith." These were hardly Reformation "patterns." They closed their letter by charging, "the Roman Catholic Church and the Vatican State cannot at this late hour escape the liabilities of having made peace treaties with the enemies of Democracy, the Nazi, the Fascist, Clerical-Fascism states of the world, while we were at war with them." The letter was signed by the Rev. A. L. Keller and the Rev. R. S. Brown.

68. "Vatican Mission," *Prophecy Monthly*, December 1941, 14.

69. "Rome Dons the Garb of True Liberalism," *Prophecy Monthly*, May 1944, 10.

70. "Dust Cloud," *Prophecy Monthly*, September 1944, 12. Brooks had a section labeled "Flashes," in which he placed brief news items regarding the war with Japan and the Nazis, Jewish persecutions, anti-Semitic happenings in America, and any items about the Vatican that might lend support for his view that the Pope was pro-fascist. The following item appeared in the "Flashes" section of the November 1943, *Prophecy Monthly*, 22, 23: "The Grand Cross of the Order of Pope Pius XII was recently conferred on Mihail Antonescu, Hitler's puppet premier of Rumania, according to an Associated Press dispatch in the *New York Times* [dated] July 15."

71. Kenneth R. Kinney, "Some Protestants are Awakening," *The Baptist Bulletin*, December 1944, 10.

72. Ibid.

73. Harold Ockenga, in "I. The Roman Catholic Hierarchy Challenges Protestant America," *The Sunday School Times*, August 11, 1945, 607, refers to a series of articles by Harold E. Fey ("Can Catholicism Win America") that appeared in *The Christian Century* and the book, *Religious Liberty in Latin America* (1944) by George

P. Howard. (Fey's articles appeared between November 29, 1944 and January 17, 1945 and Ockenga thought so highly of them that he believed they should "be read by every American.") Both Fey and Howard were liberal Protestants. David Ewart, in an article in *The King's Business*, "blasting" the Supreme Court for allowing Catholics to receive state tax funds to bus their children to parochial schools, quotes liberally and approvingly from the words of Clayton Morrison, aged editor of *The Christian Century*. William Ward Ayer does the same in his, "Protestanism: Guardian of Religious Liberty," which was printed in the April 1948, *Revelation*, 148, 184. And James D. Murch, editor of the *United Evangelical Action*, approved of, and supported, the liberal laced Protestants and Other Americans United for Separation of Church and State, an organization determined to counter the growing Roman Catholic influence in America.

74. Ockenga, 607, and "Dr. Ockenga Charges Roman Catholic Church as a Menace to American Religious Liberty," *United Evangelical Action*, May 19, 1945, 3.
75. "A Window on the World," *Revelation*, February 1945, 95.
76. "The Bible in the News," *The King's Business*, April 1945, 133. Also "A Window on the World," *Revelation*, October 1946, 479.
77. "Editorial Speaking," *The King's Business*, November 1946, 2.
78. Ibid.
79. Harold John Ockenga, "II. The Roman Catholic Hierarchy Challenges Protestant America," *The Sunday School Times*, August 1945 (3) 627.
80. Ibid.
81. Ibid.
82. Ibid.
83. Ibid.
84. Ibid.
85. Ibid.
86. Ibid, 627, 628.
87. Ibid, 628.
88. Ibid.
89. Charles E. Chilton, "An Answered Required," *United Evangelical Action*, January 2, 1945, 8.
90. Ibid.
91. K. R. Kinney, "Will Protestants Fall For This Drivel?" *The Baptist Bulletin*, July 1944, 34.
92. Ibid, 34, 36.
93. Ibid, 36.
94. "Tomorrow: Distorted Freedom," *Revelation*, September 1945, 367, 368, 394-396.
95. Ibid, 396.
96. "Tomorrow: Rome's Vast Expansion," *Revelation*, March 1946, 108.
97. Ibid.
98. Ibid.
99. Ibid, 136.
100. Ibid.
101. Ibid, 137. Also see William Ward Ayer, "Protestantism: Guardian of Religious Liberty," *Revelation*, April 1948, 148, 184. Ayer considered that religious liberty

had two enemies; communism and the Roman Catholic Church, and in America it was the latter who was the greater threat.

102.   "Murch: Is This Intolerance?" *United Evangelical Action*, March 1, 1946, 14. Murch replaced Chilton as editor of *UEA*. Nevertheless, Murch ended his editorial by declaring that he would "fight to guarantee all Roman Catholics in America the enjoyment of their opinion, their right to express it, their right to worship God according to the dictates of their conscience, and every other right guaranteed them by the Constitution…and the fundamental principles of the Christian faith."

103.   "Catholics on Religious Freedom," *Moody Monthly*, August 1948, 858.

104.   Ibid.

105.   "III. The Roman Catholic Hierarchy Challenges Protestant America," *The Sunday School Times*, August 25, 1945, (5) 649.

106.   "Murch: Threat to Liberty," *United Evangelical Action*, March 1, 1947, 12.

107.   Ibid.

108.   Ibid.

109.   Ibid.

110.   Ibid.

111.   "A Window on the World," *Revelation*, May 1947, 209.

112.   "The Bible in the News: Rising Storm," *The King's Business*, November 1947, 5.

113.   David W. Ewart, "The Christian's Warfare," *The King's Business*, June 1947, 18.

114.   Ibid.

115.   Ibid.

116.   Ibid.

117.   Ibid, 17.

118.   Ibid.

119.   Ibid.

120.   Ibid.

121.   Ibid.

122.   Ibid.

123.   Ibid, 18.

124.   Ewart mistakenly wrote Hungary when he should have written Slovakia. Regarding Stepinac, Barnhouse included the following item in his June 1948 section, "A Window on the World," in *Revelation*: "It is a well established fact that the late Roman Catholic Archbishop Stepinac was a Nazi collaborator during the war, and that he did everything possible to throw the weight of the Roman Catholic Church in favor of Germany. He was arrested and tried as a war criminal and executed by the Yugoslav Government. Early in November Cardinal Spellman laid the cornerstone for a new high school at White Plains, New York, to be called the Archbishop Stepanic School" (257).

125.   Ewart, 18.

126.   Ibid.

127.   Ibid.

128.   Ibid.

129.   "For Tolerance," *Prophecy Monthly*, March 1944, 21.

130.   "Murch: Defend Religious Liberty," *United Evangelical Action*, March 1, 1948, 12.

131.   Ibid.

CHAPTER SEVEN

Historic Fundamentalism and the Jews:
Responding to European Anti-Semitism

With apologies to Ernest Sandeen, it can be said that the fate of historic fundamentalists/Jewish relations, historiographically, "has been worse than its lot in history."[1] As with other aspects of historic fundamentalism during the 1930s and 1940s, this topic, too, has come under recent scrutiny by some scholars. And its fate in this regard is little better than the supposed non-existent political, economic and social activities and thoughts of that movement. As I noted at the beginning of the book, it is better to be condemned outright than be damned by faint praise. Unfortunately, however, the historic fundamentalists get both when it comes to their concourse with the Jews.

The Secular Critic

The secular historian can waste little time and few words over the historic fundamentalists' relation with the Jews, and in the process can appear to have little concern for distinctives or accuracy. Leonard Dinnerstein (author of *Antisemitism in America* [1994]), for example, calls William Dudley Palley, founder of the American fascist organization, the Silver Shirts, one of fundamentalism's "most prominent...antisemite."[2] However, Palley, who consorted with spirits, was roundly condemned as pagan by the historic fundamentalists. It would not have taken much effort on Dinnerstein's part to verify this. What is disturbing, though, is not his misidentification of Palley, but rather his brief but harsh and poorly researched characterization of the historic fundamentalists' concern for the Jews under the Nazis. "In later years [circa 1939/1940]," he writes, "Protestant religious journals, and the fundamentalists press in particular, reported Hitler's persecution of the Jews but they generally failed to convey the horror of Nazi pogroms, were indifferent to the plight of the Jews, believed the Jews partly responsible for Nazi attacks, or saw the tragedy as the fulfillment of God's judgement."[3] This quotation by itself (and this seems to be the sum and substance of his opinion of the historic fundamentalists), makes them seem calloused and uncaring.

Dinnerstein leans in part on Robert W. Ross' *So It was True: The American Protestant Press and the Nazi Persecution of the Jews* (1980). Although Ross gives passing marks to the historic fundamentalist publications he surveyed for reporting the details of the Jewish persecutions in Europe, he also concluded that because they tended to discuss "the persecution of German Jews in a rather specialized way" one could not help but conclude "that the writers had no feeling for the Jews as persons" but only as a group being used by God to fulfill prophetic Scripture.[4]

He specifically repeats this charge when discussing the writings of Louis Bauman. While acknowledging that Bauman gave some of the best "documentary" reports on Jewish persecution, these reports were "weakened" because they were only illustrations to lend support "to the prophetic analysis of contemporary events."[5] From Ross' perspective, then, "Writers such as Bauman conditioned readers" to become "spectators" as it were, to unfolding events:

> In this context, it was much easier for the reader to see persecution of the Jews in Germany as part of what God was supposedly doing through the Chosen People to bring about the "end of the ages" than to deal with the fact that individual Jews and Jewish families were suffering terribly under Hitler and the Nazis.... For the readers, the Jews of Germany were thus depersonalized...they became objects to be manipulated as part of prophetic schemes not persons to be helped or sympathized with in their hour of need.[6]

Though Ross admits that the details of the persecutions were clearly recorded, he sees this as only creating a paradox "that compounded the tragedy." In fact, Ross was willing to entertain the possibility that this was just another "all too familiar," form of anti-Semitism, one that taught that Christians "should only approach Jews" with the intent to convert them.[7]

Toward the end of his book, however, Ross does relent somewhat and even seems to contradict himself, admitting that though he considered Bauman's main interest in the Jewish plight was prophetic, nevertheless, "he did react with horror and dismay at what he read and reported." Ross even extends a unique compliment to Bauman:

> But regardless of his primary objective...Louis S. Bauman over an eleven year span provided American Protestant Christians with continuous, substantive information about what was happening to Jews under Hitler and the Nazis in the several periodicals in which his articles and editorials appeared, including reports of the existence of the death camps. *For this he is to be commended.*[8] (Italics added.)

Evidently Dinnerstein missed this compliment when he read Ross. Ross, himself, is willing to concede, when the evidence was tallied, that Bauman cared after all. It is interesting to note that while the historian can almost casually accuse the historic fundamentalists of lacking any real feelings for Jews as suffering human beings (even when there is evidence to the contrary) because of their prophetic beliefs, the historian seems to have a like problem with the historic fundamentalists—of seeing them as real people and not just incorrigible caricatures. As such, then, the historic fundamentalist is depersonalized and deserving of the scorn and dislike directed his way.

The Evangelical Critic

It must be admitted, however, that it is not just the secularist who trashes the historic fundamentalists over the "Jewish Question." In fact, some evangelical scholars almost out-do their secular counterparts in this regard. For example, in his *Armageddon Now* (1977), Dwight Wilson first noted how Arthur D. Morse, author of *While Six Million Died* (1967), grieved over "the lack of any moral outcry by Christianity against" the Nazis' persecutions. Then, with this as his platform, Wilson makes the astonishing accusation that "among the premillenarians there was seen no need for moral indignation against the persecution, since they had been expecting it." A few sentences later, he expands upon this canard by writing "that any moral outcry against Germany would have been in opposition to God's will. In such a fatalistic system, to oppose Hitler was to oppose God."[9]
A few pages more and he writes:

> The irony of the "Hands Off" attitude was that it resulted in closing the eyes or looking the other way as the German "final solution" of Jewish extermination developed. Pleas from Europe for assistance for Jewish refugees fell on deaf ears . . . because of a residual anti-Semitism, because persecution was prophetically expected, because it seemed the beginning of the Great Tribulation, and because it was a wonderful sign of the imminent blessed hope.[10]

Finally, in the epilogue of his book, Wilson recklessly charges that

> they have expected and condoned anti-Semitic behavior because it was prophesied by Jesus. Their consent (even given while spewing pro-Zionism out of the other side of their mouths) makes them blameworthy with regard to American as well as Nazi and Soviet anti-Semitism. Neither as a body nor as individuals has their cry against such inhumanity been more than a whimper.[11]

Joel Carpenter, while far from Wilson's viciousness, nevertheless charges that the historic fundamentalists had a "propensity to become entangled in *unsavory* speculation about the Jewish people...."(italics added).[12] Now, unsavory can mean "morally offensive" or simply "distasteful to consider." Which is meant here? It is difficult to tell as ambiguity obscures intent. He also charges that they

> found it difficult to rise above common prejudice. Even their praise of the Jewish people partook of the familiar stereotypes; Jews were usually ambitious, intelligent, and adept at making money. But more to the point, fundamentalists' dispensational theology could fortify their suspicion as well as their affection toward the Jews.[13]

Carpenter goes on to note "some fundamentalist leaders were slow to repudiate anti-Semitic views," and offers William Bell Riley as a prime example. Riley held strong feelings toward non-believing Jews, charging they were "vicious atheists" as well as "intolerable communists." How could someone who claimed to be pro-Zionist, Carpenter wonders, and hold such outlandish views? Apparently, Carpenter concludes, fundamentalists like Riley (and Arno C. Gaebelein), were convinced "that non-believing Jews in particular were prominent in a Communist world conspiracy." Without commenting on whether or not there was any justification for their conviction, Carpenter concludes, moving from specific historic fundamentalists to all historic fundamentalists:

> Their dispensationalist views greatly enhanced fundamentalists' propensity to look for great conspiracies behind human affairs. And the Jews, whom they thought would have a central role in the end times, were easily linked to such theories. *What is surprising, then, is not that some fundamentalist leaders held such* [anti-Semitic?] *views, but that only a minority of them did.*[14] (Italics added).

Carpenter does acknowledge, also using Ross' study of the Protestant religious press, that the historic fundamentalists were probably the most informed group in America regarding the Jewish plight in Europe, and that unlike the liberal Protestant *Christian Century*, "most fundamentalist leaders expressed a great deal of interest and concern."[15] Nevertheless, as if compelled to offset any compliment with a greater criticism, Carpenter denigrates the response of the historic fundamentalists by writing:

> Yet for all of the attention they received in print, the Jewish people held a rather low priority on fundamentalists' agenda. The many expressions of sympathy and outrage produced very little positive action. There were a few gestures of solidarity against anti-Semitism, such as a rally of Gentiles and Jews at the Hebrew Christian Alliance's annual conference at the Moody Memorial Church in 1936. There were some refugee relief efforts as well, most of it mobilized by Jewish missionary boards, and at least one clandestine effort early in the war by American missionaries in Belgium and Portugal to help Jewish fugitives escape the Nazis. But one looks in vain for any further action

on behalf of persecuted Jewry.[16]

If one senses that Carpenter has put the historic fundamentalists in an impossible quandary, one senses right. As far as he is concerned, the historic fundamentalists come up short. "For most fundamentalists," he writes, " 'the time of Jacobs trouble' was a portent of things to come, rather than an evil to be resisted. Sympathy mingled with suspicion in fundamentalists' perception of the Jews, but in the end, both were offered with a measure of detachment."[17] Seconding Ross' spectator thesis, Carpenter editorializes that considering the extent of the world's suffering during the 1930s and 1940s, "One would have hoped to have seen a measure of compassion from the prophetic diviners. Glimpses of broken-hearted pity appeared now and then, but more common was a detached mood, akin to staring out the window on the world's pain."[18] Of course, how one can express "a great deal of interest and concern" but at the same time be largely detached from those suffering and show little pity is a situation that could use some explanation. Carpenter offers none.

Timothy Weber is still another evangelical historian who has spent a considerable amount of words (many negative) evaluating the historic fundamentalists' relationship with the Jews in America, and especially their involvement with *The Protocols of the Learned Elders of Zion*. Because of this latter emphasis, his criticisms will be dealt with in greater depth in Chapter Nine. However, in a recent article in *Christianity Today*, Weber, while acknowledging that the historic fundamentalists were "among the first to warn the world of the coming catastrophe" regarding the Jews, and knew what was going on in the concentration camps way "before most people realized what the Nazis were capable of," still declares that "dispensationalism had a dark side that grew out of its beliefs about the Jews' complex role in prophecy."[19] Now "dark side" is another ambiguous phrase that can connote "evil" or "negative" or "dismal" or "gloomy." But it is not clear which Weber intended to convey.[20]

Years earlier, in his *Living in the Shadow of the Second Coming* (1979), Weber conceded on the one hand that "premillennialists...were fierce opponents of anti-Semitism in any form," yet on the other hand, he charged that because of their "peculiar" understanding of the Jews in this "present age," the Jews also "deserved their *scorn*...as well as their sympathy" (my italics).[21] Weber went on to add: "Accordingly, at times premillennialists *sounded* anti-Semitic. Despite their claims that anti-Semitism was a gross and inexcusable sin against God, some leaders of that movement *acted* like representatives of American anti-Semitism" (italics added).[22]

These statements by Weber brought a heated response in the pages of the *Journal of the Evangelical Theological Society* from the biographer (and apologist) of Arno C. Gaebelien, David Rausch. Weber responded, to which Raush wrote a rejoinder, to which Weber wrote a surrejoinder.[23] (Thankfully it ended there or we might still be getting replies to replies). No matter the apparent complimentary statements, Rausch was convinced that Weber was accusing the historic fundamentalists in general, and Gaebelein in particular, of *being* anti-Semitic. Weber replied that "sounding" like and "acting" like is not the same as being anti-Semitic (perhaps straining credulity in the process). In using the terms as he did, Weber stated, he believed he was making this clear. I have, of course, only touched the surface of their debate.[24]

It is All in How You Say It

But Rausch did raise one insightful point that is worth developing further. As noted above, the critics of historic fundamentalism do have a way of wording their criticisms (and even their praises at times) in such a way as to leave a question mark hanging invisibly above the statement—and the heads of the historic fundamentalists.[25] For example, to step out of our immediate context, William Tollinger, Jr., in his book on William Bell Riley (*God's Empire: William Bell Riley and Midwestern Fundamentalism, [1990]*) states that "the fundamentalists *believed* that the modernists had gutted orthodox Christianity of its traditional dogmas" (italics added).[26] Carpenter, in his *Revive Us Again*, makes a similar comment: "The supernatural character of Christianity was under attack, fundamentalists *believed*, so they counterattacked by upholding doctrines that defied naturalism and historicism" (italics added).[27] Fundamentalists believed?—well did they believe correctly or was this just their opinion? Is there some doubt that the modernists sought to destroy biblical/historical Christianity and reinterpret it in more acceptable, contemporary terms? Why, then, the reluctance to say that the historic fundamentalists understood clearly what was happening?

Or consider this sentence by Carpenter: "Another product of fundamentalists *professed* love for the Jews was their sense of duty to present the gospel 'to the Jew first,...' " (italics added).[28] Professed, of course, can mean "pretend," "alleged," or "sincere." Which one did Carpenter intend? Considering some of his remarks, it is not out of line to think he intended to question the depth or nature of the historic fundamentalists' affection for the Jews. It is as if someone was to write (in good tabloid headlines) **"The fundamentalists thought they loved the Jews— But did they really?"**

This is not to nit-pick over words, except to say that how one says something (or writes it), the words he or she uses, sets the "tone" of the article or essay for the reader or hearer. It leads them subtly to the writer's side. Add to this the thoughtful comment by historian John Lukacs that "the choice of words [the historian uses] is not only a matter of accuracy, not only an aesthetic choice; it is a moral choice,"[29] and perhaps the reader will understand what is troubling me (and troubled Rausch). There are, then, some interesting problems with the way the critics handle the historic fundamentalists that when taken together add up to a troubling redundancy. The question cannot help but arise as to whether the critics of the historic fundamentalists want to make them seem as deviant from historic evangelicalism as possible?

This possibility is reinforced by an example from *Revive Us Again*, where Carpenter compares the historic fundamentalists with past radically heretical cults:

> Even though dispensational views profoundly informed fundamentalists' outlook, the result was different from that of earlier millenarian movements. Unlike the movements that erupted in medieval and early modern Europe, there were no fanatical self-identification with the Lord's avenging host. Unlike the founder of the Mormons, no leading fundamentalists claimed to be the Almighty's prophet and revelator. Unlike the founder of the Shakers, none claimed to be united with the Godhead itself. By comparison, twentieth century fundamentalists followed a much more restrained, rationally argued form of millenarianism.[30]

By comparison!? Well, one is, of course, certainly relieved to know that the historic fundamentalists, while they *may* have possibly—kind of—been sort of cultic like, were mild-mannered and relatively harmless—even if appearing as somewhat anti-Semitic, unsavory, apathetic spectators who hardly raised a whimper of protest at cruelty and brutality. But one wonders why such a comparison with Shakers, Mormons, and Munsterites should be made in the first place? Was the mildness of the historic fundamentalists' "millenarianism" the real difference between them and the truly heretical cults mentioned by Carpenter? Nothing else? Nothing, say, more theologically important in nature?

Then, of course, there is the accusation that the historical fundamentalists' understanding of history and the end-times is unbiblical. Dwight Wilson charges that "the record has amply demonstrated the premillennial philosophy of history to be deterministic," which meant "the direct manipulative action of a personal God in history," that is, "it depicted God's plan as embodied in the whole of history."[31] Wilson concludes, then, that premillennial dispensationalism is an enormous heresy—especially if one takes into account their attitude toward Israel:

> Although it is difficult to prove from direct statements, when one analyses the premillenarians' responses to Israel, the inescapable conclusion is that their philosophy of history in many cases is equivalent to the antinomian heresy…if every action is preordained, then there is no need to measure one's actions by moral law, since the decision to obey or disobey the standard has already been made.[32]

When applied to Israel, "ordinary rules of international law (morality) do not apply to God's chosen people; and there is no absolute standard by which they can be judged." Wilson concedes this is not part and parcel of the premillennial understanding of prophecy but where Israel is concerned, "this is how things work out."[33]

Timothy Weber also accuses premillennial dispensationalists of being unbiblical in their understanding of God's sovereignty over history and end-times:

> As Christian history makes clear, in the *wrong hands* the doctrine of providence, divine sovereignty and eschatology become fatalism; and fatalism takes the significance out of human actions. If the future is fixed, people are merely playing out their assigned roles, with no ability to alter the direction or outcome of the divine drama. If one is privy to the process, one can identify the players, evaluate the performance, and make judgments about them. When one knows how the drama is going to end, there are no surprises. At times, then, dispensational prophecy can be quite fatalistic.[34] (Italics added).

However, were historic fundamentalists really deviants from "sensible," historical evangelicalism? Were they fatalistic—which is pagan thinking not biblical thinking? If the historic fundamentalists were fatalistic, they were in good Christian company. And if the historic fundamentalists were fatalist, then so were Isaiah, Ezekial, Daniel, John, Paul and even Jesus Christ. And, of course, looking back through history one could add Ireneaus, Lactantius, Augustine, Wycliff, Luther, Calvin, many a Puritan, and Jonathan Edwards, who wrote concerning those who vigorously waved the banner of man's rational free-will in the face of God (and thus, as Sydney Ahlstrom commented, "make an absurdity of the biblical teaching of an omnipotent, omniscient God") the following:

> In such a situation God must have little else to do, but to mend broken links as well as he can, and be rectifying his disjointed frame and disordered movements, in the best manner the case will allow. The supreme Lord of all things must needs be under great and miserable disadvantage, in governing the world which he has made, and has the care of, through his being utterly unable to find out things of chief importance, which hereafter shall befall his system, which if he did but know, he might make seasonable provision for.[35]

However, despite Edwards' sarcastically humorous rejoinder to the free-wheeling free-willers, and my lapse in bringing it to everyone's attention, it is not my intent to get into a theological debate over the problem of man's free-will versus God's absolute sovereignty—mainly because I am always at a disadvantage in arguing with God. But it is apparent that the historic fundamentalists are being blind-sided with a theological opinion that evidently presumes a "limited" sovereignty on God's part and a radical freedom for man to shape the future. What is disturbing is that it is presented in such a way as to make the historic fundamentalists seem once more to be the odd man out, that they have little in common with historical Christianity. That, however, is simply not the case. Why, then, is their view presented in such a negative light? Why do Weber and Wilson think it necessary to present the historic fundamentalist view of history as an unbiblical oddity? Again, such [editorial] opinions are put forward, I am convinced, to make them seem as deviant as possible from historical evangelicalism, and because they are deviant deserving of the "unsavory" criticism attached to them. It is more than Mark Noll who has made the historic fundamentalists a favorite "whipping boy."[36]

Of Pitfalls and Prejudices

The above discourse on how the chosen word, not historical evidence, can shape our historical opinions of others is given to lay the foundation for consideration of the charges made against the historic fundamentalists concerning anti-Semitism and Jewish persecutions. Some of the charges against them are serious and need to be addressed. Were they really just spectators to a cruel and evil historical episode of human depravity? Can they really be held responsible for Russian, German, and American anti-Semitism because of their eschatology? Was their biblical understanding of the Jews future truly "unsavory?" If so, why? However, before examining the accuracy of the charges against them, and comparing that with what they actually did say and do regarding anti-Semitism and the persecution of the Jews in Europe, I would like to mention three things that affect the configuration of the discussion to follow.

One is a comment from John Lewis Gaddis' *We Now Know* (1997): "It would be the height of arrogance for historians to condemn those who made history for not having availed themselves of histories yet to be written."[37] Or, for that matter, for not anticipating in 1933 what was going to take place in 1938 in Vienna, or at Buchanwald in 1943. And as Martin E. Marty, in defending the liberal *Christian Century* from charges of anti-Semitism in the 1930s and 1940s, has noted: "We have to see the past not only by hindsight but in the conflict of the possibilities then open to people."[38] Next, there has developed, as Marty points out, a canon of literature by those involved in Holocaust studies which seemingly condemns or severely criticizes anyone and everyone in America for not doing more to rescue the Jews in Europe.[39]

Finally, there is the problem of how the term "anti-Semitic" or "anti-Semitism" is used or defined. William Buckley noted that it is seldom defined and perhaps difficult to do so, despite its association with the Holocaust. It evidently can range from a mild, personal dislike that carries no public consequences to a full-blown hatred that seeks to harm the Jews in any way possible, including their total destruction. (And as I have noted, even sharing the gospel with a Jew is equated with anti-Semitism of the worst rank.) But does every criticism of a Jewish organization, or, say, Israel's policies, constitute anti-Semitism? Is it anti-Semitic to speak of Jewish group characteristics or Jewish political influence? Does every criticism by the historical fundamentalists of the "free-thinking" Marxist embracing Jews in the 1930s represent anti-Semitism? And, of course, the charge of anti-Semitism can be used as a weapon to silence legitimate criticism or stifle needed discussion, or even to stigmatize those who are disliked, such as the historic fundamentalists. As columnist Joe Sobran angrily noted, after having been accused of such for his criticism of Israel's foreign policy lobbying in Washington, "The word 'anti-Semitism' is more potent than most of the charges of bigotry that are flung about these days. It carries the whiff of Nazism and mass murder. 'It means,' as a friend of mine puts it, 'that you ultimately approve of the gas chamber.' "[40]

Letting the Historical Fundamentalists Be Themselves

And, in addition to the above cautions, it is necessary that the historian respect, in an academic/historical context, the prophetic speculations of the historic fundamentalists regarding the Jews. This is, sadly, seldom the case. Too often editorial dislike replaces historical evaluation. Yet, it was an essential element of their world-view. They interpreted Scripture literally. If Scripture said Jesus fed thousands beginning with two loaves of bread and five small fish, then that is what really (historically) happened. It was not an allegory or a lesson on sharing one's lunch with his neighbor who forgot to bring one. They carried this literalism over into prophetic Scripture, especially those portions concerning Old Testament Israel, that is, the Jewish people. Israel was the chosen people of God, who through consistent disobedience to God's Law and the rejection of His promised Messiah, had been "temporarily" set aside, as God's unique nation, by God Himself. Yet as history draws to a divinely ordained close, they would be gathered back to their original home—Palestine—where, at the end of the Tribulation period, when Jesus returns to the earth, they would accept Him as their messiah/savior. (It is not necessary to go into greater detail as the position of the historic fundamentalists in this regard is well known.)

Because they did take Scripture literally (and with the utmost seriousness), they believed the curses enunciated against Israel (if it failed to keep its covenant of obedience with God) in Deuteronomy, chapter 28, were being, and had been, literally fulfilled in the history of the Jewish Diaspora since the destruction of the second temple in A. D. 70. This does not, *ipso facto*, make them anti-Semitic. It means they believed Scripture is to be believed. Because one does not believe the Bible is true does not give one the right to axiomatically label those who do anti-Semitic. As one Jewish essayist has written:

The Hebrew scripture portrays God as ordering the Israelites to do things His way or He will wipe the floor with them. . . . Now comes a bifurcation. If one is a believing Jew or Christian, God would appear to have followed through on his threat; the Jews did not observe the law too well, and they have accordingly been punished. This is a classic instance of fulfillment of Biblical prophecy. Jewish suffering at the hands of others is divinely ordained.[41]

All Christians, if they take the Bible seriously—that is, believe God has "written it" so to speak, also believe God has set aside the Jews as a peculiar nation exclusively representing God. Where the historic fundamentalists differed was in believing such a setting aside was not permanent. In fact, their understanding of the gospel impelled them to evangelize the Jews as vigorously as other people-groups, while at the same time their understanding of prophetic Scripture impelled them to support the restoration of the Jews to Palestine. Also, as is well documented, that while they considered Jewish persecutions a fulfillment of God's Word, they also considered anti-Semitism a sin God would punish. The nation that succored the Jews would be blessed by God and the nation that persecuted them would be punished by Him. As the editor of *Bibliotheca Sacra* unequivocally wrote: "The Abrahamic covenant has never been abrogated.... God will judge the nations for their unreasoning anti-Semitism in all its inhuman and ugly manifestations. This God has declared."[42]

While on the one hand, the historic fundamentalists were firm in holding the Jews proximately responsible for the crucifixion of their Messiah,[43] they rejected the label "Christ killers" being attached to the Jews because they believed and taught that all men, both Jew and Gentile, because of sin, were responsible for the necessity of Christ's death on the cross.[44] And ultimately, behind the mundane, were the machinations of the prince of evil, Satan, who hates anyone God loves and has hatefully set himself at opposites with God's purposes for mankind in general, and the Jews in particular (because of the place the Jews play in God's plan of salvation—both in the past as well as in the future).[45] The problem with many secular scholars, and perhaps particularly some secular Jewish scholars may not be the supposed anti-Semitism of the historic fundamentalists because they believed Jewish persecution is ordained by [the] God [of the Bible] as a result of disobedience to [the] God [of the Bible], but rather their own atheism regarding this possibility. Having rejected the actuality of their own spiritual history (as written in Scripture) they are apparently intolerant and even hostile toward anyone who does believe it. It is not, then, a mark of insightful scholarship to call the historic fundamentalists anti-Semitic (no matter how kindly they may have been disposed toward the Jew) because they believe the Bible, but rather an indication of the historical critics own (resentful?) feelings and thoughts toward those who take the biblical view of history seriously.

Also, there is another perspective. Rather than viewing the historic fundamentalists' prophetic understanding of the Jews as "unsavory," or "dark," or anti-Semitic, Yaakov Ariel, in his recent book, *Evangelizing the Chosen People: Missions to the Jews in America,1880-2000* (2000), observes: "The theology that motivated the movement to evangelize the Jews conceived of that people not as a rival religious community but as a remnant of an ancient people who carry a special mission and are predestined to help bring the drama of Christian salvation to its conclusion."[46] This, Ariel notes, "created a missionary movement that has demonstrated a great amount of goodwill and appreciation for the Jews and their cultural heritage...."[47] Ariel goes on to conclude:

> The theological perceptions that inspired the movement were extraordinary. In no other case has one religious community assigned a predominant role to another religious community in its vision of redemption or claimed the other group held a special relationship with God.[48]

Keeping Things in Context

Now, the time has come to look closely at the charges leveled against the historic fundamentalists that seem at times so harsh, unfair, and even based on ignorance. And because we can only study them in the context of the times, it needs to be remembered that in the 1930s Americans struggled with the frightening economic hardships of the Great Depression. Americans also were largely isolationists regarding involvement in another European conflict or even Europe's refugee problem.[49] In this regard, the historic fundamentalists were no different than the rest of America. For example, as late as June 1939, Dan Gilbert chided Congress for wasting time on foreign affairs while "the great needs of the hour" remained unresolved. He listed six such "needs" all of them domestic.[50] Also in the Fall of 1939, Jacob Bernheim, field representative for the American Hebrew Christian Alliance wrote: "In the present world crisis with so many uncertainties convulsing Europe, we humbly pause before God and pray that our country may not be drawn into the holocaust of war." He then went on to assert: "With the Dictator madmen of Europe plunged into the cesspools of hatred, our hearts bleed for our unfortunate brethren of the household of Israel, who are caught in the waves of persecution that have made life so bitter for them."[51]

When the war spirit did come, as it suddenly did on December 7, 1941, and isolationism vaporized almost instantaneously,[52] the war that came was not fought directly to end the persecution of the Jews. It was fought to defeat the tyranny inherent in Nazism and Japanese imperialism (and to make sure America survived, as well as England).

However, beyond the difficulties of the Great Depression and the fear of war, followed immediately by the great obligations of a two front war on the part of

America, the historic fundamentalists found themselves with more than the Jewish persecutions on their minds. One of the problems with focusing excessively on the European persecutions, and especially the Holocaust, is that one tends to forget there were other extremely serious events happening, even life and death events, with which people had to grapple. If we start with 1933, Stalin's persecutions in Russia (including the starvation of millions of Ukrainians) and the civil wars and famine in China were as much on the minds of the historic fundamentalists as were events in Germany. Through the mid-thirties the situation remained basically the same. Vying for the attention of the historic fundamentalists and off-setting events in Germany was the Italian invasion of Ethiopia, the Spanish civil war, and the brutal Japanese invasion of China, typified by the rape of Nanking, all of which were devastating to the missionaries as well as the indigenous believers, and brought famine and unimaginable hardship to millions of people.[53] Only after 1937 does it seem that events in Europe began to take a greater share of the concerns of the historic fundamentalists. Although the Jews held a unique place in their eschatology, the whole world was their commission, and as has been shown, there was suffering in many places that called out for their attentive love.

Nevertheless, from the early 1930s on the anti-Semitism in Germany, as well as the struggles of the Confessing Church, attracted the attention and brought forth numerous comments from the historic fundamentalists. So many, in fact, that the accusation that they were indifferent to the plight of the Jews or did not convey the real horror of the Nazi persecutions seems outlandish at best.

J'accuse: Sterotypes

Altogether, the various accusations posted against the historic fundamentalists can be numbered at eight. One (that of believing in the prophetic Scriptures) has been dealt with above. A couple of them seem frivolous, such as the charge that they used sterotypes.[54] It is true, of course, they did—especially the Hebrew Christians among them. In noting how difficult it was to get Jewish Christians to work well together, Jacob Peltz, general secretary of the American Hebrew Christian Alliance, claimed that "The Jew is independent in his thinking...bubbling over with ideas," and while holding on to his own "traditions and ideas" sought to "change the existing order of things so as to improve them." Finally, he noted, the Jew wants to be the leader whether he is capable of the task or not—"he wants to be at the head of the parade." Peltz lamented he had seen "these Jewish characteristics and human deficiencies...at work in the inner councils of our Alliance" to its harm.[55]

Frederick Aston, director of the New York Jewish Evangelization Society, writing in the *Hebrew Christian Alliance Quarterly* (Fall 1939), listed a number of possible causes of anti-Semitism in America. Among those listed were five Aston believed were "clearly the fault of the Jew." Today, of course, Aston would be condemned as politically incorrect in the extreme. And he would probably be the first to admit that he was generalizing and that not every Jew fit this list. First on the list was "unethical business practices;" next was "personal loyalty rather than loyalty to principle;" third, "Jewish discrimination against other Jews;" fourth, "excessive insistence on his own rights, coupled with carelessness of the rights and sensibilities of others;" finally, "supersensitiveness and lack of self-criticism." Aston also added, "restlessness and over ambition," though he did not hold Jews "directly culpable" for this trait.[56]

What should be said about all this stereotyping? Were Peltz and Aston self-loathing Jews trying to please their Gentile supporters? Knowing how outspoken they could be, this hardly seems the case. Perhaps a few words from Manfred Weidhorn will help put it in perspective:

> The agonizing over whether group characteristics are essential or accidental can be disposed of rather peremptorily. People possessing a linguistic, religious, and cultural tradition are certainly going to have a set of vices and virtues in common. As long as two conditions are met, nothing is wrong with observing that the Scots are thrifty, the Irish dreamy, the Jews studious and money-conscious, the Hispanics laid back, the New Englanders laconic and puritanical.[57]

In other words, stereotyping groups is not automatically a sign of prejudice. What are the two conditions that serve as a caveat on the above? The first is that we understand such characteristics are environmentally generated not genetically imprinted. "The second caveat," he writes, "on the use of group characteristics is that they not be applied mechanically and that each individual must be judged on his/her own." Weidhorn considers such a "using of group traits," as a kind of "early science, a lazy man's attempt to make sense of the multiplicity of facts." Nevertheless, Weidhorn stressed, "the individual" always "comes first."[58] Using "familiar stereotypes" (i.e., "Jews were unusually intelligent and adapt at making money"), then, may not necessarily be evidence of exhibiting "common prejudice" but simply noting group characteristics that even the Jews of that day acknowledged. (And, of course, stereotyping is still used with abandon as the histories of the historic fundamentalists testify—even Carpenter's.)

J'accuse: Unsavory and Dark

The charge that the historic fundamentalists' understanding of the Jews' place in God's prophetic plan for history was "unsavory speculation" (Carpenter) or had a "dark side" (Weber) is more disturbing than the above. Even if Weber meant dismal or pessimistic rather than bad or mean, and even if Carpenter meant distasteful rather than morally offensive, the ambiguity of the words is questionable, as is the conclusion. From the perspective of the historic fundamentalists, the "good news" was a word of hope in a dark world in bondage to sin and Satan. The Jew was not barred from hearing and believing the gospel. It was for him first as well as the Gentile, and during the 1920s and 1930s, and even into the 1940s, there was a sizable ingathering of Jews into the evangelical fold.[59] Also, by emphasizing that while man is lost in sin he can be redeemed in Jesus Christ, the historic fundamentalists were proclaiming that the individual was not inescapably locked into the natural order of things as taught by the secularist—that is, that "evil" is just a natural part of the evolutionary order, that even our best efforts cannot prevent "bad" things from happening for no apparent purpose to seemingly innocent people. That is the way things are. This, then, is the true "dark" side—that there is no hope of deliverance from such a nihilistic and meaningless world without end.

The same holds true concerning the persecution of the Jews. Was it just another inexplicable evil in an apparently meaningless universe? The historic fundamentalists did not think so. And the cursings and blessings of Deuteronomy 28 offered a door by which they could explain the reasons for the persecutions and allow them to offer Jesus to the Jews as their Messiah.[60] The Holocaust was not a meaningless, mocking evil that drove them into unrelenting existential despair or bitter nihilism. From their vantage point, it revived the doctrine of the depravity of man to a generation of humanist and liberal Christians who wanted to admit no evil. It literally drove millions of very reluctant Jews to see the necessity of a Jewish homeland and embrace eretz Israel as that place.[61] In addition, unnumbered Jews found Jesus as their Messiah through the testimony of their Jewish Christian brothers and sisters who shared with them in the suffering and degradation and death of the concentration camps.[62] Nor is it pessimistic to point out that those who deliberately sought the destruction of the Jews are no more as the historic fundamentalists predicted. Certainly it is not unsavory to hold that God, the God of the Bible, keeps His word. To those who believe in Him nothing is more comforting. Of course, believing that God keeps His word, even regarding history and its conclusion, is providentialism, (an anathema today to even many evangelical scholars) and evidently to others, determinism. But given the circumstances, the historical fundamentalists had ample reason to read history from a providential perspective.

Exactly why the historic fundamentalists' understanding of the Bible regarding the Jew is "unsavory speculation" is not clear. Open to question is how are we to take the phrase—as morally offensive or simply distasteful? And to whom is it unsavory? What or whose criteria are we to use? Millions of evangelicals did not find it unsavory, nor did many orthodox Jews in the 1930s. They saw the persecutions as a sign the messiah was near.[63] In what way is it unsavory to warn the world of a coming judgment, and that people's only salvation is in Jesus? Is it unsavory to believe in the imminent return of Jesus, his promised Second Coming, and that this will have (to say the least) profound implications for both Jew and Gentile? Is it unsavory to believe that the Jews are still favored by God and sustained by God and have been given their land by God, or that the day is coming when all Jews will accept Jesus as their messiah? This unsavory speculation speaks of a glorious conclusion to Jewish history. If the historic fundamentalists' speculations concerning the meaning of the Jewish persecutions and the restoration of Israel derived from their literal interpretation of Scripture is unsavory, what can be said of alternative interpretations? Is the view of some Christians that God has permanently rejected the Jews (a view that has engendered so much vicious anti-Semitism throughout history) savory? Or is the Nazi interpretation preferable? Or perhaps pointless evil and existential psychological speculations on why man does what he does are more satisfying? But do these alternate explanations really explain anything or give meaning to anything? Of course any talk of history having meaning in a postmodern academy makes for night-sweats and bad dreams, and hostile books attacking metanarratives. However, bleak nihilism and bitter denunciation of people who lived through that era for not seeing what we see are hardly a satisfaction for the craving of the soul for meaning.

Museums of tolerance may remind us of past evils of great magnitude, but they have not and cannot prevent them, or explain why people willingly participate in them. We may be repulsed by man's inhumanity to man but we seem incapable of preventing it. Nor can anyone gainsay the historic fundamentalists' prediction that a greater anti-Semitic uprising awaits in the future. We may not appreciate such prophetic realism about man and history (and in that sense find it "unsavory") but no one can say it will not happen. Considering the present hatred toward the Jews in the Arab world, nothing can be denied. Given the gospel that the historic fundamentalists preached—even to the Jews—it is they that seemed to have offered concrete hope, both in the present and for the future, in a "dark" world given over to unremitting evil and which many thought was without end. If that is unsavory, then I support it.

J'accuse: Indifferent and Unfeeling

Two more serious charges, closely related, must now be discussed. One is that the historic fundamentalists, though they wrote a great deal about the persecutions, failed to convey the horror of the Nazi pogrom, and second (so very close to the first), they were indifferent to the plight of the Jews.[64] I have already noted how Robert Ross charged them with being little better than spectators lacking personal feelings for the Jews.[65] Dwight Wilson charges that the historic fundamentalists issued no outcry of moral indignation against Jewish suffering (because it was ordained by God), closed their eyes to the final solution, and that whatever "noise" they did make never rose above a whimper.[66] As I write these words, I have before me *hundreds* of articles and items from a few lines to many pages, from various historical fundamentalist publications, covering the period 1933 through 1948, in which the Jewish persecutions are covered and the Nazi brutalities exposed. (And I did not copy all the articles published or research all the journals available or use all the articles in my own files.) The articles also express a wide range of emotions from anger to horror to compassion to disgust at the depths of depravity to which human beings could sink. It is inconceivable that such an abundance of material could be so easily missed or overlooked but apparently it has.

Wait—did they not often relate what was taking place to end-time prophetic interpretation? Yes they did and in doing so they resorted to scriptural terminology which can be emotional at times, judgmental at times, even gory at times and biased in God's favor. Overall, though, it is descriptive; that is it tells what is going to happen. However, such is the nature of prophetic Scripture—it is basically descriptive. When one reads the Olivet discourse, there is little personal, emotional concern for those going through the tribulation expressed on the part of Jesus. His language is descriptive. Did he not care? The answer is obvious. When one reads the book of Revelation, little concern is expressed for those experiencing God's wrath. What is important is that God is just and right in his judgments, and that his enemies, who hate him, are getting theirs. Heaven rejoices. Does God care about sinners? Yes—for God so loved the world that he gave his only begotten Son, that whosoever believes in Him will not perish but have everlasting life. Did the historic fundamentalists care about the Jews despite their "unsavory speculation" concerning the end-times? Of course they did—that is why they preached to the Jew first and then the Gentile. The historic fundamentalists believed everyone—Jew or Gentile— needed Jesus Christ as their personal Lord and Savior in order to have one's sins forgiven and escape God's wrath. The historic fundamentalists' enormous mission enterprise was an act of ongoing compassion. They used no force (though force was often used against them), only words to tell people God loved them.

The Jewish Christian Fred Aston saw evangelization of the Jews as part of the Christian's duty. Noting the rising anti-Semitism, he saw the responsibility of the Christian in America as two-fold—comprehension and action. Comprehension included a biblical understanding of the purpose of Israel ("to be a spiritual people, a missionary nation to teach the Gentiles") and its future ("they are to go back to Palestine in unbelief"). Comprehension also included taking seriously what the newspapers were saying about persecution and the increasing anti-Semitism. Aston pointed out that in his conversations with "refugees from Germany" he had "noted the apparent agreement of all that in the early days of Nazi propaganda few people took it seriously." They called it "selch unsin," (such nonsense) and never dreamed

Hitler would come to power. The people of America must not let the same thing happen here.[67]

Christian action included, first, "opposition to all forms of anti-Semitism." Aston made the interesting observation, based on Matthew 18:7 (offenses must come but woe to him by which they come) that "although for the present the Lord allows the forces of evil to persecute the Jews, it is no part of that plan that His church should be either [an] accessory to that persecution or neutral." Opposing anti-Semitism was a form of true patriotism, helping "save America from the divine wrath that will fall upon all who harm Israel."[68] Second, the "primary concern" of the Christian should be "the evangelization of Israel." As he wrote, "the Lord is using the present sorrow to soften the hearts of the Jewish people, and never in all the long years since the tragedy of Pilate's hall and Golgotha have they been more receptive to the gospel message."[69]

How Can They Believe Who Have Not Heard

There were three levels by which information on Jewish persecutions was disseminated throughout the historic fundamentalists' community, other than the secular press and radio. First, through the major journals such as *Moody Monthly*, *Revelation*, *The King's Business*, *The Sunday School Times*, or *Prophecy Monthly*. Second, through individual mission publications such as *The Jewish Era*, bulletin of the Chicago-Hebrew Mission; the *Chosen People*, voice of the America Board of Missions to the Jews; or the *Jewish Missionary Magazine*, publication of the New York Jewish Evangelization Society. These secondary publications were marvelous sources of information on Jewish persecutions in Europe. Their contents were available to those beyond their own constituencies (which numbered in the thousands) for they usually had exchange agreements with other fundamentalist magazines.[70] The third way was via personal letter, word of mouth, sermons, visiting missionaries, and conferences such as Palestine Week in Chicago, which was an annual event at Moody Memorial Church. Jacob Peltz, who became general secretary of the International Hebrew Christian Alliance in 1935, called such joint Jewish Christian/Gentile Christian gatherings an excellent "antidote" against anti-Semitism.[71]

As early as 1931 Donald Barnhouse, editor of *Revelation*, was drawing attention in that magazine to Hitler's attitude toward the Jews in Germany and how he and his fellow fascists wanted to ghettoize them.[72] In March of the following year, he wrote that "Germany is pledging herself to Hitler," noting that Hitler wanted to expel all the Jews and was blaming them for Germany's misery.[73] In a September editorial, he reminded his readers that everyone (you and me), not just the Jews were responsible for Christ's death. Only inquisitors from Rome, the ignorant and unregenerate pushed anti-Semitism—true Christians, he claimed, loved the Jews.[74]

In 1933, Barnhouse devoted at least four major articles to the issue of anti-Semitism. In the January issue of *Revelation*, an editorial appeared drawing attention to the rising persecution of Jews in Eastern Europe. In light of this information, he stressed again that the Christian must "show every way possible that the true spirit of Jesus Christ is one of real love for the Jews."[75] In May, another editorial and a major article were included once more concerning the "Jewish Question." In the editorial, entitled "Love the Jews," Barnhouse stressed yet again, because of the growing anti-Semitism, that Christians must go out of their way to speak kindly to the Jew. The article ("Tomorrow: Jewish Travail") dealt with the increasing acts of anti-Semitism in Germany, which, because they were so widespread, had to have the approval of the government. The article also debunked the truthfulness of letters from German Jews asserting "all is well." In addition, the May issue carried an item in its "The Editor's Scissors" section commending H. R. Knickerbocker's article in the *New York Evening Post* because it revealed what was really being done to the German Jews by Nazi Storm Troopers.[76] In the September issue, an editorial was included which predicted that the same fate that was meted out to Haman would be meted out to Hitler and others for their persecution of the Jews, and just as the Jews had survived previous persecutions so they would survive Hitler.[77]

In addition to occasional articles and editorials,[78] all through the 1930s *Revelation's* "Window on the World" section carried information on the Jewish persecution by the Nazis and their allies.[79] Nor did *Revelation* "fail to convey the [personal] horror" of the Nazi pogrom. For example, in one of his editorials, Barnhouse related the story of a Hungarian Jewish couple trying to flee Austria but unable to do so, and the feelings of hopelessness and fear that overwhelmed them.[80] In an earlier article, detailing the Nazi persecutions in Austria, Barnhouse is quite vivid about the havoc and terror circulating in the Jewish community.[81] And L. Sale-Harrison writing for *Revelation* in late 1938, related his conversations with Jewish Refugees in England, noting that they included stories of indecencies "too awful to publish."[82]

If *Revelation* made known the plight of the European Jews, Keith Brooks' *Prophecy Monthly* did so to, to an even greater degree. Brooks was a vigorous opponent of anti-Semitism. Beginning in the first half of 1933, even before he completely freed himself from Gerald Winrod's Jewish conspiracy influence, Brooks was reporting on the Nazi persecutions in Germany, noting, "in spite of denials from Germany, the half has not been told concerning the atrocities perpetuated by the Nazis of Germany against the Jews."[83] Brooks also took note of the rising suicide rate among German Jewish professionals,[84] the proposed laws to destroy the Jewish community,[85] and the deliberate, libelous lies that issued forth from the Nazi propaganda machine[86]—and this is just in 1933 (and is only a sampling). This type of unrelenting and straightforward reporting on the persecution of the Jews in Germany and other places in Europe, continued in *Prophecy Monthly* throughout the Great Depression and into the war years.[87] Nor did Brooks soft-peddle the horror and grim results of Nazis hatred. For example, an account of what was happening in the Nazi concentration camps appeared in the article, "Behind the Gates of a Nazi Camp." The information came to Brooks in a letter from a "trusted missionary" friend in China, who in turn had received it from two Jewish refugees, themselves victims of the Nazi concentration camp described. Brooks' friend wrote: "We wept [as we] listened to them relating some of their experiences in a concentration camp in Germany. I want to pass on some of the things they said which show that all we have read about the Nazi treatment of Jews is truly senseless and brutal."[88] The following is one of the incidents recorded in the missionary's letter. It is not for the squeamish:

> On one Christmas eve all those in the concentration camp were called out and were made to stand in a ring. The prisoners didn't know what to expect—perhaps a treat for all they knew. What do you suppose the treat was? The Mayor of the town came and announced that because of the Jews' treatment of the Nazis, they would have special celebrations, so they chose one of the Jewish prisoners, put a rope around his neck, strung him up where all could see him and while he was dangling in the air, the Nazi orchestra was playing the latest Jazz music. This afforded amusement for the Nazis, and if any of the prisoners would shut his eyes to try and hide that awful scene from his sight he would get a good stiff biff that would keep him looking. This was Nazi concert entertainment for Christmas eve.[89]

Brooks' friend closed with the most fervent desire of all true believers of that wretched era—"May the Lord Jesus come soon!" (One cannot fault the historic fundamentalists for wanting to see Christ's millennial reign "appear" as the ultimate good to come out of the Holocaust.)

As early as October 1930, *The Sunday School Times* took note of Hitler's anti-Semitism and warned that he had better be careful and take heed of the national penalties outlined in Scripture for persecuting the Jews.[90] Ernest Gordan, in his regular column in that magazine, "A Survey of Religious Life and Thought," (and writing after Hitler had assumed the Chancellorship of Germany) also commented on the continuing persecution of the German Jews and wrote that "it has the marks of a permanent policy...," which, he believed, made "it [all] the more sinister."[91] The following year, *The Sunday School Times* published an in-depth and thoughtful three-part series on Germany and the Jews by Will Houghton. Houghton was visiting that country and talked at length with many Germans—both Jew and Gentile. "The persecution has been very real to the Jews of Germany," Houghton wrote, "however lightly the German Christians may esteem them. Tales of genuine suffering are heard everywhere. The separation of dear ones in the breaking up of families has occurred. Once again the Jew has become a wanderer."[92] Turning to the personal, Houghton went on to describe the effects Nazi policy was having on a young woman he had meet—one quarter Jewish—who had hoped to become a doctor. "What will become of this charming cultured girl—about the age of our own daughter," Houghton wondered. "May God guard her and guide her!"[93] Houghton closed his second article with a poem that would be reprinted many times in the historic fundamentalists' journals:

> Say not a Christian ere would persecute a Jew;
> A gentile might; but not a Christian true..
> Pilate and Roman guard that folly tried,
> And with that great Jew's death an empire died.
> You read a Bible passed to you with age,
> A Jew wrote this, and that, and each succeeding page.
> The book where Moses had so much to say,
> That law he gave, makes statute books today.
> The poet sang of shepherd's care so kind,
> Your Mother found that psalm a solace to her mind.
> Ah, David wrote for her far better than he knew,
> "The Lord my Shepherd"—written by a Jew.
> When Christians gather in cathedral, church, or hall,
> Hearts turn toward One—the name of Jesus call.
> You cannot persecute—whatever else you do—
> The race who gave Him—Jesus was a Jew.[94]

Charles Trumbull reported (as did most of the fundamentalists journals) on the vicious orgy of violence the Nazis visited upon the Jews following the shooting of its diplomat in Paris. In the same article he related an Associated Press report that told of a political cartoon that had been published in the Nazi newspaper, *Voelkischer Beobachter*. The cartoon portrayed Uncle Sam "weeping over the plight of the Jews in Germany." Standing next to the weeping Uncle Sam was a "smiling Nazi Storm Trooper patting [him] on the back and saying, 'don't cry, Uncle Sam, you can have all of them.' "[95] (Tragically, of course, as Hitler well knew, Uncle Sam would take only a few of them.)

In the December 3, 1938 issue of *The Sunday School Times*, an article appeared announcing the formation of a relief organization named "The Friends of Israel Refugee Relief Committee," with the sole purpose of providing funds to those Hebrew Christian mission organizations working directly with Jewish and Jewish Christian refugees.[96] Leading historic fundamentalists such as Louis Bauman, Lewis Sperry Chafer, Will Houghton, Harry Ironside, Mark Matthews, Robert McQuilkin, Harry Rimmer, Wilbur Smith, and Charles Trumbull endorsed the new organization. (It was, then, at heart, a dispensational relief agency.)

Written by Joseph Taylor Britan, Secretary of the new relief organization, the appeal got directly to the issue at hand:

> The Jew is being persecuted. A cruel tide of anti-Semitism is rolling over the face of
> the earth. . . . Hatred of the Jews has become a fetish with many pagan individuals and
> with some nations. Even so-called civilized peoples are influenced and are yielding to
> vicious propaganda of hate that is spreading over the world as a poison gas.[97]

After briefly surveying anti-Semitism throughout Europe (and especially in Austria)
and America, and warning that "anti-Semitism is anti-Christian," Britain turned to
conditions in Germany. "And who," he laments, "can describe the terrors of life
for the Jews in Germany!" Both Jews and Jewish Christians were unwanted, robbed,
prohibited from earning a living, in essence being economically annihilated and
"free only to end it by suicide—unless the Christians of the freedom loving portions
of the world come to the rescue."[98]

Ten months later, with the war in Europe now under way, Britan summarized
the unrelenting persecution the Jews faced and called on believers to help:

> At no time in their long and melancholy history has the future of the Jew loomed
> darker and more foreboding. . . . When we remember what men have done to the Jew
> in the past, often in the name of Christ and His church, we cannot wonder at the
> contempt and indifference with which many Jews have regarded Christ and His gospel.
> Today the Christian church, in its ministry to the Jew in his indescribable misery and
> loss, and its ministry to the Jewish Christian in their similar plight, has an opportunity
> to show the Jew the true spirit of Christ and the power of Christian love.[99]

In the March 16, 1940 issue of the same magazine, Britan up-dated the bleak
status of the Jews, covering the establishment of the ghettos in Poland, and quoting
from an advertisement placed by the London based Barbican Mission to the Jews
in *The British Weekly*. The ad made clear the horrors the German Jews were
experiencing:

> The White Paper, recently published by the British Government, proves that the
> treatment accorded to the Jews in Germany under the present regime is reminiscent of
> the darkest ages in the history of man. Jews tied by the wrists round trees and left
> hanging there. Innumerable inmates of concentration camps have died of exhaustion.
> Some rush to the live wires of the prison fence, or the rifle of the sentry to bring an end
> to their agony. One camp superintendent himself said: "You are coming into a
> concentration camp. This means that you are coming into hell."[100]

Overwhelmed by Excess

Lest excessive redundancy overwhelm, it is not necessary to continue to reference article after article from the journals of the historic fundamentalists. In addition to the above both *The King's Business*[101] and *Moody Monthly*[102] carried articles on the Jewish persecutions. And in addition to the articles, there were numerous full page advertisements which functioned as much as sources of current information on the persecution status of European Jews as they did for appeals for funds and information on what the organizations were doing to help. Throughout the 1930s, the American Board of Missions to the Jews ran full page ads detailing Jewish and Jewish Christian persecutions (as well as what it was doing in the way of relief) in *Moody Monthly, The King's Business, The Sunday School Times,* and *Revelation.*[103] Beginning in early 1939, The Friends of Israel Refugee Relief Committee also began running full page advertisements in the same journals,[104] and in 1940 the International Hebrew Christian Alliance did the same.[105] Using smaller ads, the Bethel Eastern European Mission likewise reported on its work in the Polish cities of Lodz and Warsaw.[106]

Also, as mentioned previously, continuous and often detailed information on the Jewish persecutions was found in the Jewish missions magazines. The *Chosen People, Jewish Missionary Magazine, The Jewish Era, The Bethel Witness, Israel My Glory* (which began publishing at the beginning of 1943 when the Friends of Israel Refugee Relief Committee changed its name to the Friends of Israel Missionary and Relief Committee), *The Hebrew Christian Alliance Quarterly,* and the increasingly read *The Hebrew Christian,* the quarterly of the International Hebrew Christian Alliance (headquartered in London), all carried moving articles on the persecution of the Jews and refugee suffering, and what they were doing to help. Although I have covered into the early 1940s, all of these magazines (and I have not included every one or even touched on denominational journals) continued to report on Nazi atrocities right through the war.

Time of Jacob's Trouble

Perhaps one of the most widely heralded anti anti-Semitic works to come out of the historic fundamentalists community was Louis S. Bauman's *The Time of Jacob's Trouble.* Originally published in early 1939, the booklet went through numerous printings.[107] (The fourth printing was for 5,000 copies, half of which were purchased by the American Board of Missions to the Jews to distribute in the New York City Jewish community.)

In his booklet, Bauman surveyed anti-Semitism and the terrible persecutions of the Jews in Europe, writing, "Everywhere the Jew is insulted, castigated, mutilated, assassinated, while his shops are broken, bombed, and burned."[108] In the midst of his survey of what specifically the Nazis were doing to the Jews in Germany, he passionately exclaims:

The most cruel, the most diabolical, the most bestial, the most pernicious, the most envenomed, the most dastard, the most inhuman, the most damnable, the most rotten—gentle reader, there simply aren't any usable adjectives that will properly designate the order that has just been issued by those denizens of the pit that has come to earth in human form and found reception in Berlin....[109]

The order Bauman referred to was the one issued on January 1, 1939, requiring Jews to carry a special I. D. card. "On these cards," Bauman wrote, "every male Jew must add the name 'Israel' to his given name, and every female must add the name of 'Sarah.' 'Israel' and 'Sarah'—what honored names, hated only in the regions of the damned."[110]

Bauman tied the attempt to destroy the Jews to both an attack on liberty—those who hate the Jews hate democracy—and an attack upon Christianity. "Let no Christian permit himself to be deceived as to this: *The foes of the Jew are inevitably the foes of the Christian.*" Reminding his readers that many Jewish Christians were also suffering, he encouraged Jews and Christians to support each other, and concluded, "It is ever the same—whenever the State deifies itself, both the Jews *and the Christians* become the object of its barbaric persecutions." [111]

Bauman also included a section that related the awful persecutions of the Jews in Austria following the recent Nazi takeover. And for those who think Bauman only saw the Jews abstractly as fulfilling God's plan for history and did not sympathize with them as a suffering people—well, they should read his imaginary but moving account of what it must have been like to be a Jewish mother living under such grotesque circumstances. "Imagine yourself a Jewish mother in Vienna," he begins, whose husband had been taken away by the Nazis. He then tries to imagine the horror, the helplessness, and the desperation she must feel with no one to assist her, or protect her and her children.[112]

The thoughts and feelings of the average historic fundamentalist might be gauged by a sampling of letters written to Joseph Hoffman Cohn, director of the American Board of Mission to the Jews, and a poem that appeared on the cover of *The Jewish Era* magazine. "My heart bleeds," wrote one correspondent to Cohn, "as I read what the Jews are going through." Another wrote, "I must lay my paper down, for the tears keep pouring out of my eyes and can't stop." Another, finding articulation in Scripture, wrote, "We can only cry out, 'How long, oh Lord, how long.' " As Cohn explained, "These are samples of what the Lord's people are writing us these days, and they show how tender is the heart, and how responsive the conscience, of the one who has been truly baptized into the one Body, the Church of the Lord Jesus Christ."[113] There is ample evidence to give credence to Cohn's assurance.[114]

The poem, by Clara Bernhardt, was originally written for the *Christian Witness*. It appeared on the front cover of the January 1940 edition of *The Jewish Era*, voice of the Chicago Hebrew Mission. It was titled, "For Israel's Peace:"

Not just today, but everyday
For the Peace of Israel we must pray.
Driven and homeless, and lonely too,
Their only crime to be born a Jew
Across our world sounds the cry
Of a stricken race which can not die.
Through centuries the nations fall,
But Jews still weep at the Wailing Wall.
O Father above, the debt we owe
To this race should cause our prayers to flow
In a daily stream of faith that they
Shall find release from hatred's flay.
Give us the vision, Lord, to see
That love for Jews is love for Thee.[115]

In Summing Up

Given just the small sampling reviewed above, the judgmental shibboleths must fall. Dinnerstein's charge that historic fundamentalists failed to convey the horror of the Nazi persecutions or were indifferent is untenable, as is Ross and Carpenter's charge that historic fundamentalists were conditioned to be spectators by their prophetic interests. As for Wilson's bizarre accusations (that they raised no moral outcry because it would have placed them against God's will, that they looked the other way as the Nazi "final solution" of Jewish extermination developed, and that they were apathetic and unwilling to offer assistance), they are, to be brutally frank, unsavory nonsense. The evidence of the historic fundamentalists' concern for the Jews of Europe is so abundant that ignorance of it, or the deliberate ignoring of it, or an unwillingness to investigate it, is inexcusable. Many of today's evangelical scholars decry the supposed lack of scholarship among the historic fundamentalists. Well and good—a point humbly taken. Now we have an abundance of evangelical scholars. How, then, do we explain this obvious and at times seemingly almost deliberate by-passing of historical information that gives a far more accurate picture of how the historic fundamentalists really reacted to Jewish persecutions in Europe?

NOTES

1. See note #1, Notes for Chapter One.
2. Lenord Dinnerstein, "Antisemitism in the Depression Era (1933-1939)," in *Religion in American History: A Reader*, eds. Jon Butler and Harry S. Stout (New York: Oxford University Press, 1998), 419.

3. Ibid, 420. Interestingly, William D. Rubinstein, in his, *The Myth of Rescue: Why the democracies could not have saved more Jews from the Nazis* (New York: Routledge, 1997), writes: "Most recent historians of American anti-Semitism and American attitudes toward the Jews in this period have simply ignored the wealth of positive indices of overwhelming American hostility to Nazi anti-Semitism: for example, Lenord Dinnerstein's, *Anti-Semitism in America* (Oxford, 1994), which systematically exaggerates the amount of anti-Semitism throughout American history by ignoring all evidence of philo-Semitism" (228, endnote 133). In *Beyond Belief*, Deborah Lipstadt writes, "The *Christian Science Monitor* was not the only representative of the Protestant press to suggest the Jews were responsible for their suffering or to express a subtle animus toward Jews and Judaism. The *Reformed Church Messenger*, *Lutheran Companion*, *Moody Bible Institute Monthly*, and other publications echoed these views." (*Beyond Belief: The American Press and the Coming of the Holocaust 1933-1945* [New York: The Free Press, 1986], 44 and endnote 10, page 291.) Ms. Lipstadt was basing her statement on what Robert Ross wrote in his, *So It was True*, pp 33-36, and evidently not from any personal research of her own.

4. Robert W. Ross, *So It was True: The American Protestant Press and the Nazi Persecution of the Jews* (Minneapolis: University Press, 1980), 38. Ross' selection of historic fundamentalists' journals is somewhat limited and he misses some important ones. He never refers to articles that appeared in *Revelation, The Sunday School Times, Prophecy Monthly*, or the *Chosen People*, which was the publication of the American Board of Missions to the Jews. The ABMJ was by far the largest Jewish mission organization in America in the 1930s and active in Europe. Thus the circulation of the *Chosen People* would have greatly exceeded that of the American Hebrew Christian Alliance *Quarterly* that Ross used. The same holds true for *The Sunday School Times* which had the largest circulation of any historic fundamentalist journal during the 1930s (close to 70,000 with a readership of approximately 200,000).

5. Ibid, 47.
6. Ibid.
7. Ibid, 47, 48.
8. Ibid, 280, 281. However, the American Protestants Bauman informed were mostly those in the historic fundamentalist's community. It is doubtful that those who read *The Christian Century* also read *The King's Business*.
9. Dwight Wilson, *Armaggedon Now! The Premillenarian Response to Russia and Israel Since 1917* (Grand Rapids: Baker Book House, 1977), 94. One cannot help noting how Wilson's accusation echoes the theme of Albert Camus' *The Plague*.
10. Ibid, 96, 97. If premillenarians *really* believed the last three (3) things, it is very doubtful they would be apathetic about events taking place around them. And, of course, they were not. It might also be worth noting Rubenstein's insightful observation at this point. He notes that once Hitler controlled Europe and began his "final solution," the Jews of Europe were no longer refugees but prisoners who could not be rescued. *The Myth of Rescue*, 79, 80.
11. Ibid, 97.
12. Joel A. Carpenter, *Revive Us Again: The Reawakening of American Fundamentalism* (New York: Oxford University Press, 1997), 107.

13. Ibid, 98. However, if dispensationalism fortified the historic fundamentalists' suspicion of the Jews, how do we explain non-dispensational evangelical suspicions or even outright anti-Semitism during the same period. And how do we explain Catholic anti-Semitism? Such accusations based on dispensationalism alone are unconvincing.

14. Ibid, 99.

15. Ibid. In this regard, one might want to read Martin E. Marty's correction on the supposed indifference of *The Christian Century*. ("The Century and the Holocaust: Setting the Record Straight," *The Christian Century*, April 10, 1985, 350.)

16. Ibid, 99, 100.

17. Ibid, 100.

18. Ibid, 95, 96.

19. Timothy Weber, "How Evangelicals Became Israel's Best Friend," *Christianity Today*, October 5, 1998, 43.

20. In a recent article in the Winter/Spring 2001 edition of *Fides et Historia*, Paul Spickard uses the same phrase in a similar fashion. He does so in the context of what he considers to be equally oppressive actions taken on the part of an evangelical, a Mormon, and a communist university. "There is a dark side to these religiously inflected universities," he warns (darkly), "that I would be remiss to ignore: each practices enforced conformity and institutional hegemony over what many of us would regard as people's private lives." He goes on to describe some of the "private" conduct and how those involved were punished by their respective institutions. He concludes his "dark side" expose` by writing: "whatever was done or said within the confines of one's home or intimate friendships was fair game for those who would police individual behavior." ("Its All Religious Education," 140/141.) It is obvious that the author intended "dark side" to mean "bad," "wrong," or even "evil" or perhaps "unsavory."

21. Weber, *Living in the Shadow of the Second Coming: American Premillennialism, 1875-1925* (New York: Oxford University Press, 1979), 154.

22. Ibid.

23. See David A. Rausch, "Fundamentalism and the Jew: An Interpretive Essay," June 1980; Timothy P. Weber, "A Reply to David Rausch's 'Fundamentalism and the Jew,' " March 1981; David A. Rausch, "A Rejoinder to Timothy Weber's Reply," March 1981; Timothy P. Weber, "A Surrejoinder to David Rausch's Rejoinder," March 1981. All, of course, printed in the *Journal of the Evangelical Theological Society*.

24. In his rejoinder, Rausch did resort to heated argumentation, accusing Weber, for example, of "a lack of depth and accurate scholarship," and elsewhere of being "insensitive and inaccurate," and of substituting "psychological fantasy" in place of "solid research." (See his rejoinder, pages 75 and 76.) Of course, I must admit that Rausch was right about some of the strong biases of the critics of historical fundamentalism. And these biases have affected the way they have assembled their material and written about the movement.

25. See Rausch's "A Rejoinder to Timothy Weber," 73 and 74 for his examples.

26. William Vance Trollinger, Jr., *God's Empire: William Bell Riley and Midwestern Fundamentalism* (Madison: The University of Wisconsin Press, 1990), 66.

27.   Carpenter, 70.
28.   Ibid, 97.
29.   Donald A. Yerxo, "Remembering the Past: The Historical Philosophy of John Lukacs," *Fides et Historia*, Winter/Spring 2001, 134.
30.   Carpenter, 107, 108.
31.   Wilson, 143.
32.   Ibid.
33.   Ibid.
34.   Weber, "How Evangelicals Became Israel's Best Friend," 49.
35.   Sydney E. Ahlstrom, *A Religious History of the American People* (New Haven: Yale University Press, 1972), 306.
36.   Philip Yancey, "Fixing Our Weakest Link," *Christianity Today*, July 9, 2001, 65. Marsden rightly notes that the historic fundamentalists' way of looking at history "had long been basic to Western historical thought." He goes on to point out that "even in the nineteenth-century America, widely held views of history, influenced by postmillennial theology, were often dominated by such categories. Certainly any Christian interpreter of history from Augustine to Edwards would easily have understood the dispensationalist's approach." (George M. Marsden, *Fundamentalism and American Culture* (New York: Oxford University Press, 1980), 63, 64.)
37.   John Lewis Gaddis, *We Now Know: Rethinking Cold War History* (New York: Oxford University Press, 1997), 188.
38.   Marty, 352.
39.   Robert H. Abzug, in his *America Views the Holocaust, 1933-1945*, gives a brief historical survey of this literature of inclusive "blame," (beginning with Hannah Arendt's *Eichmann in Jerusalem* [1962]) that has been published over the last forty years. He takes note of the recent swing of the pendulum to a more modified analysis of America's response to the Holocaust, one less judgmental and that takes into consideration all of the complexities, difficulties, and limitations that people and governments faced during the Great Depression and World War II. Evidently the blame game started early among the American Jews (see, Victor Buksbazen, "USA, A Startling Revelation," *Hebrew Christian Alliance Quarterly*, Spring 1945, 24). Also see William D.Rubenstein's, *The Myth of Rescue: Why the democracies could not have saved more Jews from the Nazis* (1997), 4-11. This book is a devastating attack on the "everybody is guilty school" of Holocaust writing. One also might want to read William D. Rubenstein's balanced and informative review of Norman Finkelstein's *The Holocaust Industry: Reflections on the Exploitation of Jewish Suffering*, in *First Things*, December 2000. Rubenstein closes his review with these words:

       "Indeed the problem with the Holocaust as a meaning and a metaphor today is precisely that it is too powerful, an ever expanding black hole of consciousness that invariably swallows up everything in its path. To millions, it is perhaps the only real contemporary religious event; for hundreds of thousands of Jews, it has served to define their Jewish identity, taking the place of everything else. It is at the heart of many contemporary forms of political correctness, and of many remaining academic and intellectual taboos. Its automatic moral authority is such that it allows charlatans and hucksters to flourish unchallenged. The great importance of Finkelstein's work, flawed though it is, lies in breaking those taboos and exposing the charlatans" (43).

40. Quoted in William F. Buckley's provocative, *In Search of Anti-Semitism* (New York: Continuum, 1992), 10. At the beginning of his book, Buckley writes:

> It is probably never too early to distinguish the kinds of anti-Semitism we run into in the world. The apocalyptic kind was, of course: The Holocaust; and I'll be asking whether the shadow of the Holocaust is being made to stretch too far in contemporary politics. This is different from denying that the Holocaust is, and will always be, one of the great historical ventures in denatured human barbarism. There are Jews who continue to fear that the fires that lit the Holocaust might one day be rekindled. But there are also Jews, who, comfortable with the protocols built up around Auschwitz, are disposed, so to speak, to prolong the period of de-nazification indefinitely (4).

Finally, a personal note. I was shaving one morning shortly after the Orlando, Florida Holy Land Experience theme park opened. It was being discussed on the radio but I was not listening too closely until a rabbi came on who compared a Christian's attempt to convert a Jew to a Nazi SS guard at Auschwitz cremating a Jew. I must admit I "lost it" at that moment. Here was a venomous anti-evangelical hate statement that would have done proud any radical anti-Semite.

41. "An Essay by Manfred Weidhorn," in Buckley, 145. Weidhorn leaves out of his truncated version that the Israelites willingly entered into this covenant with God, agreeing to keep his commands and statutes in exchange for being His particular people. Also see, "England: The Price of Transgression," *Hebrew Christian Alliance Quarterly*, Fall 1945, 26. This is a reprint of a fascinating letter that appeared in the London *Jewish Chronicle* (no date given). It was evidently written by an Orthodox Jew and is clearly worth quoting in full for the support it gives to the historical fundamentalists understanding of Deuteronomy 28:

> In reply to the points raised by Lt. John Rayner, I would like to point out that the conception of national suffering as a form of Divine punishment is the constant theme of Divine revelation, throughout the Torah and the prophetic writings. If this principle is not understood by your correspondent, this does not constitute it a heresy. If our people have been punished as a community, this has been because they have failed in their mission and duties as a community. Guilt attaches to the members of a community not only for there sins as individuals, but also for their connivance at the sins of others, and their failure to carry out their communal duty of upholding truth and justice. "He who fails to oppose the commission of a sin is accounted a sinner" (Shabbat 55a).
>
> "All Israel bears responsibility for one another" (Shevuot 39a). It runs counter to the letter and spirit of the whole of Jewish teaching to suggest that the suffering of our people are merely the result of arbitrary forces, such as anti-Semitism. In truth, they are the direct expression of Divine judgment, whose object is not merely the punishment of the guilty, but the repentance of the survivors. "As a man chasteneth his son, so the Lord thy God chasteneth thee" (Deut. 8:5). The right attitude to the Torah does not lie in the selection of a few high-sounding principles, and the rejection of anything that does not appeal to us or does not fit in with our preconceived idea of what the Torah is in its entirety, combined

with a sincere and humble attempt to discover the meaning of that which we do not understand.

42.   Rollin Chafer, "Editorial: Dwelling in the Tents of Shem," *Bibliotheca Sacra*, April-June 1939, 133.

43.   "Shall We Laud the Jews or Save Them?" *The Sunday School Times*, February 6, 1932, 69, 70. Also see, "Why, Why, Why?" *The Jewish Era*, July 1944, 89 and James Vaus, "What's Wrong in Jewry," *Prophecy Monthly*, January 1947, 10.

44.   See for example, Barnhouse, "Editorial: King of Kings," *Revelation*, September 1932, 368, 369 and Louis Bauman, *The Time of Jacob's Trouble* (Long Beach, NP, 1939 [1943]), 106.

45.   See for example, Bauman (above), 107, 108 and "Satan Breaking Loose in Germany," *Jewish Missionary Magazine*, May-June 1933, 67-73, and in the same magazine, "Editorial Notes: Oppressors of Israel," September-October 1936, 129.

46.   Yaakov Ariel, *Evangelizing the Chosen People: Missions to the Jews in America, 1880-2000* (Chapel Hill: The University of North Carolina Press, 2000), 287.

47.   Ibid.

48.   Ibid.

49.   A September 1939 *Fortune* magazine poll showed a strong isolationist current among Americans. In answer to the following question—"If France or England got into a war against the dictator nations, should we send our Army and Navy abroad to help them immediately, or only if it is clear they are losing, or not at all"—3.1% answered "immediately," 24.5% answered "only if losing," 6.8% had no opinion, and 65.6% answered "not at all (84)."

50.   Dan Gilbert, "Views and Reviews of Current Events," *The King's Business*, June 1939, 213. According to Gilbert, the six great domestic needs were 1) a fair and equitable revision of the Wagner Act, 2) sweeping adjustments of our lop-sided and burdensome tax structure, 3) a determined effort in the direction of a balanced budget, 4) a new and adequate agriculture set-up, 5) a new approach to the whole relief problem, and finally, positive legislation to promote recovery.

51.   Jacob Bernheim, "Report of the Field Representative," *Hebrew Christian Alliance Quarterly*, Fall 1939, 18.

52.   Gaddis, 35, 36.

53.   Consider, for example, the November, 1938 issue of the *Prophecy Monthly* which on page 28 contained an article entitled, "Modern Refinement of Cruelty," and was a description of some of the horrors of internment at Buchenwald as reported to Keith Brooks by Samuel Wilkinson of the Mildmay Mission to the Jews. Wilkinson would not relate in mixed company some of the horrors suffered. On the opposite page (29) is an article with the title, "Horrors witnessed by the Missionaries," and begins with these words: "If there is anything that should stir our hearts to pray: 'come Lord Jesus', it is the inhuman atrocities committed by the Japanese against the Chinese people. According to word that reaches the American Prophetic League, from trusted friends in China, the cruelties are of such a revolting nature and on such a colossal scale that the mind is benumbed."

      Also consider Ernest Gordon's column, "A Survey of Religious Life and Thought," for May 16, 1942, in *The Sunday School Times*, (394). He reported on various incidents of Jewish suffering in Europe, (taken from the *Hebrew Christian Alliance*

Quarterly) including the statement that "it is calculated that nearly two million Jews have lost their lives since the Nazi persecutions began in 1933. They have been driven like dumb beasts from Germany, Austria, and elsewhere, into ruined Poland, and interned in the Warsaw Ghetto with its eight-foot-high cement wall. Here conditions are terrible, some fifty men and women being crowded into one large room. Drinking water has to be bought! Since July there has been no bread, only insufficient quantities of potatoes."

This is followed by an excerpt taken from a letter written by E. A. Brown, a Presbyterian missionary in Suchowfu, China. "Today," he begins, "I have been getting acquainted with David, Samuel, and Moses, three as fine little fellows as you want to see, aged from two to ten. Two days ago their father was bayoneted by Japanese soldiers in this little church-yard before their eyes and the eyes of their mother." Brown goes on to give a brief biography of the murdered Chinese pastor, noting that "Mr. Feng was one of our most faithful preachers, holding this lonely and dangerous outpost for nine years." Gordon closed his excerpt from missionary Brown by quoting these poignant words from his letter. "They gave me Mr. Feng's well-worn Bible. It had been drenched in blood, for he held it under his arm as the soldiers stood him up against the wall." Gordon follows this episode with a review from *The Presbyterian Survey* describing the terrible persecution thousands of Christian leaders in Korea were enduring at the hands of the Japanese "because they would not bow at Shinto Shrines." He then singled out one of these pastors—Choo Kichui—whom he calls the John Hus of Korea, and details the gruesome suffering he and his family and his congregation were experiencing.

54. Carpenter, 98.
55. Jacob Peltz, "Editorial Notes and Comments," *The Hebrew Christian Alliance Quarterly*, October-December 1933, 12. Max I Reich, one of the founders of the Hebrew Christian Alliance in America and teacher at Moody wrote in 1936: "Intercine strife and the tendency to disintegration have been the tragedy of Jewish history.... This feature has haunted the Jewish people till our day...and it has not stopped yet" (*Hebrew Christian Alliance Quarterly*, Fall 1936, 1). Also see Haim Genizi's *American Apathy: The Plight of Christian refugees from Nazism* (Israel: Bar-Ilan University Press, 1983), 43, 72, 73, for comments about infighting and competition between Jewish refugee agencies during the 1930s and 1940s.
56. Frederick A. Aston, "The Menace of Anti-Semitism in America Today," *The Hebrew Christian Alliance Quarterly*, Fall 1939, 8, 9. This article also appeared in two parts in Aston's own magazine, the *Jewish Missionary Magazine*, in November 1939, 145-150 and December 1939, 162-169. Nathan Levison, vice-president of the International Hebrew Christian Alliance, wrote the following in October 1944: "I admit that there is something about us Jews that is unlovable; we will not assimilate, we are proud and may be arrogant, though I think the arrogance is due to an inferiority complex ingrained during centuries of persecution and suffering. Among the orthodox Jews I have seldom come across a loud type, only humility, coupled with spiritual pride, one of our besetting sins" ("Editorial," *The Hebrew Christian*, October 1944, 43).
57. Buckley, 150.
58. Ibid, 150, 151.

59. Mitchell L. Glaser, President of the Chosen People ministries, extensively surveyed Christian (evangelical) missions to the Jews throughout Europe and concluded, "the greatest movement of Jews to the Messiah came in the second and third decades of the 20th Century." He goes on to state "nothing...could compare with the numbers of Jewish people who became believers in Jesus between the wars." Glaser believes that "the number of Jews who became Christians during the first third of the 20th century may have been upwards of 230,000...." "These figures," he writes, "are staggering. Since they can be corroborated in report after report from various sources, including those of the Jewish community itself, one cannot but affirm the integrity of these figures." ("A Survey of Missions to the Jews in Continental Europe 1900-1950." [Ph.D. diss. Fuller Theological Seminary, (1998)], 407, 408.) Glaser's conclusions agree with what was appearing in the historic fundamentalists' journals except they indicate conversions continued through the 1930s and 1940s. See, for example, "Jewish Notes: Jews in the Fatherland," *The Jewish Era*, October 1935, 103; "News and Notes: Germany," *The Hebrew Christian*, October 1935, 102; "No Man Careth for My Soul," *Prophecy Monthly*, September 1936, 23, 24; "Awakening Among the Jews," *The Sunday School Times*, June 3, 1939, first page (339); Bartlett L. Hess, "Are the Jews Turning to Christ?" *The Sunday School times*, May 3, 1941, 356, 357; *Hebrew Christian Alliance Quarterly*, Summer 1945, 15, for an extensive quote on Jews converting to Christianity in Budapest written by George Knight in the *International Review of Missions*, April 1944; Harry Bucalstein, "Converts from Judaism Flow 'Like a River,' " *United Evangelical Action*, April 1, 1946, 8. Quite often these articles quoted Jewish sources that admitted large numbers of Jews were converting, much to the consternation of the Jewish leaders.

60. "Praying and working: Our Ministry to the Jews," *Jewish Missionary Magazine*, January 1939, 13; James A. Vaus, "What's Wrong in Jewry," *Prophecy Monthly*, January 1947, 8-10; "Report from Baptist Jewish Mission," *The Baptist Bulletin*, January 1944, 24; "Why, Why, Why?" *The Jewish Era*, July 1944, 89, 90.

61. See, for example, L. Sale-Harrison, "Has God Forgotten His Covenant? Or The Anti-Semitism of the Nations," *Moody Monthly*, May 1939, 487. "It is noteworthy," he wrote, "that since the war [WW I] more than 400,000 Jews have entered Palestine from other nations, and millions more are eager to return, for the anti-Semitism of today is acting as a divine broom to sweep these people back to the land promised to their fathers."

62. See for example, Otto Samuel, "My Experience in Nazi Germany," *The Hebrew Christian*, April 1945, 14-18; "News and Notes," *The Hebrew Christian*, July 1945, 24; Erna Samuel, "Reunion—1946!" *Jewish Missionary Magazine*, August 1946, 97-100; Ernest Gordon, "A Survey of Religious Life and thought," *The Sunday School Times*, September 13, 1947, 880; Lydia Feinstein, "Days of Terror in Jassy," *The Hebrew Christian*, April 1948, 10-14; Birger Pernow, "Comfort them that are in Trouble," *The Hebrew Christian*, Spring 1950, 9-13; "Editorial: Nazi Furnace—God's Refining," *The Bethel Witness*, Vol. 9 (1945), No. 3, 3. It is estimated that 250,000 to 300,000 Jewish Christians died in the Nazi persecutions.

63. See, for example, Will Houghton, "Jewish Pangs," *Moody Monthly*, July 1940, 592; Keith Brooks, "Jacob's Trouble," *Prophecy Monthly*, November 1941, 24, and Louis Bauman, "Socialism, Communism, Fascism," *The King's Business*, March 1935, 120.

64. Dinnerstein, 419.
65. Ross, 47 and Carpenter, 95, 96.
66. Wilson, 94, 96, 97.
67. Aston, 29.
68. Ibid, 30. Also Vous, "In the Jewish World," *The King's Business*, January 1934, 16.
69. Ibid. Also see his "The Present Plight of German Jewry," *Jewish Missionary Magazine*, February 1939, 23; Albert Hughes, "The Church's Task: The Evangelization of the Jew," *The Hebrew Christian Alliance Quarterly*, Winter 1936, 29, and Agnes Scott Kent, "Let My People Go," *The Jewish Era*, July 1933, 79.
70. *The Jewish Era*, for example had exchange agreements with *The Advent Witness, The Evangelical Christian, The King's Business, Moody Monthly, Our Hope, Prophecy Monthly, The Prophetic News, Israel's Watchman, Revelation, The Sunday School Times*, and *The Voice*. This seems to have been standard practice among the various historic fundamentalist journals.
71. Jacob Peltz, "News and Notes: Palestine in Chicago," *The Hebrew Christian*, July 1937, 50. Also see, "Reports from Hebrew Christian Alliance Branches," (*Hebrew Christian Alliance Quarterly*, April 1935, 29). This report detailed "a mass meeting of Jews and Christians" at the Moody Memorial Church on March 24, 1935, to demonstrate "friendliness on the part of Christian people toward their Jewish fellow citizens, and as a Protest against Anti-Semitism and Racial Discrimination." A letter was sent to every Rabbi in Chicago which stated in part: "We should like you to know we are deeply grieved at the calamities that have befallen the Jewish people in Germany and in other lands, and we desire to give public expression to that feeling." An estimated 3,000 people attended the meeting, approximately 600 of which were Jews.

At the 25th annual conference of the Hebrew Christian Alliance in St. Louis in 1940, another mass meeting of Christians and Jews was held. Leon Rosenberg, founder of the Bethel Eastern European Mission and having only recently arrived in America from Poland, spoke of the situation in that country. Jacob Peltz, general secretary of the International Hebrew Christian Alliance, spoke on the "Plight of the Jewish Christian Refugees," ("News from America," *The Hebrew Christian*, July 1940, 632). At the 1942 gathering of the Hebrew Christian Alliance held in Ashville, North Carolina, another Jewish-Christian rally was held. At that meeting "a refugee told of the horror...of the unprovoked torture outside and inside the Concentration camps...." There was also another report on the Jews in Poland. "The hearts of all were deeply moved on behalf of the sufferers. There was however a note of encouragement in the account of Christians—Gentile Christians—who loved the Jews and accompanied their stricken neighbors to the Camps, not forsaking them in their distress." (Margaret Wiesenberg, "Hebrew Christians Hold a Conference in Ashville, N. Car," *The Hebrew Christian Alliance Quarterly*, Fall 1942, 11, 12.)

Finally, while browsing through the archives of The Church of the Open Door, I came across a bulletin called the Kappa Chi News: Official Publication of the Combined Young People's Organizations of the Church of the Open Door. On page one of the bulletin was a paragraph entitled, "What Has Happened to the Jews of Germany." The paragraph noted "of the 650,000 Jews who lived in Germany in 1933, 200,000 have fled the country, 30,000 are in concentration camps, 20,000 have committed suicide, 8,000 have been murdered, and 90,000 have died. These figures have been gathered from official sources by the Jewish Missionary Magazine." The date of the bulletin was November 1941. So even the Sunday School children knew in fundamentalist circles.

72.   Donald Barnhouse, "Tomorrow: Future Events in the Light of the Biblical Prophecy," *Revelation*, February 1931, 70.
73.   "Tomorrow: Which Way Germany," *Revelation*, March 1932, 104.
74.   "Editorial: King of Kings," *Revelation*, September 1932, 368, 369.
75.   "Editorial: The Jew Again," *Revelation*, January 1933, 10.
76.   "Editorial: Love the Jews," 169; "Tomorrow: Jewish Travail," 170; "The Editors Scissors," 178. All appeared in the May 1933 edition of *Revelation*.
77.   "Editorial: Hitler's Cake," *Revelation*, September 1933, 329. The following poem was printed in *The Hebrew Messenger*, December 1933, 15. It had originally appeared in the *Jewish Times*. During the 1930s and 1940s it would be reprinted in a number of historic fundamentalist publications. Written by Philip M. Raskin, whom the editor of *The Hebrew Messenger* called "America's Jewish poet laureate," the poem, *A Jew to Hitler*, was, the editor wrote, "a proud answer to Hitler's war against the Jews:"

> Hitler, we shall outlive you,
> As we outlived the Hamans before you;
> Hordes of slaves may crown you chief,
> Throngs of fools—adore you.
> One day you shall fall from your tower of might,
> From Pride's uppermost steeple,
> With the brand of Cain carved on your brow,
> And the curse of an innocent people.
> The Torquemadas of all time,
> The Tituses and the Neros,
> Cursed is their vanity and might—
> Their martyrs are hailed as heroes.
> We are the deathless sons of the Earth,
> Life is our God-given charter;
> And what is another auto-da-fe
> To a race—an eternal martyr?
> Hitler, we shall outlive you,
> However our flesh you harrow;
> Our wondrous epic shall only add
> The tale of another Pharoah.

78.   See, for example, "Tomorrow: The Jews in Poland," *Revelation*, April 1937.
79.   See, for instance, "Window on the World" sections in the following issues February 1936, 61; March 1936, 102, 103; September 1936, 370, 371; September 1937, 380; March 1938, 106; July 1938, 290; December 1938, 506, and October 1938, 415.
80.   "Editorial: Men in Traps," *Revelation*, November 1938, 462.
81.   "Tomorrow: Jewish Travail," *Revelation*, June 1938, 248, 263-265. Barnhouse quoted extensively from the *New York Times* in this article and yet again stressed that "Christians must be very tender toward Israel." Also in the June 1938 issue was a

full-page advertisement (back cover) by the American Board of Missions to the Jews relating the terrible Austrian persecutions and the plight of Jewish refugees in Paris.

82. L. Sale-Harrison, "Tomorrow: Europe in Conflict," *Revelation*, October 1939, 343, 412, 413. In a follow-up article, he described with a great deal of pathos the frantic efforts of terrorized Jewish families trying to enter Belgium. He apologized to his readers for publishing such graphic details but believed it necessary for people to know the truth of what was happening to the Jews so that people would be moved to sympathize and help. ("The World's Anti-Semitism Amongst the Refugees," *Revelation*, November 1939, 430, 456, 457.)

83. "Spirit of the Beast Sweeps Germany," *Prophecy Monthly*, May 1933, 1.

84. "Terrible Toll of Suicides Among German Jews," *Prophecy Monthly*, July 1933, 16.

85. "Proposed German Laws Terrify Jews," *Prophecy Monthly*, June 1933, 10.

86. "Hitlerites Resurrect the Ritual Murder Lie," *Prophecy Monthly*, May 1933, 11.

87. See, for example, "Jews in Germany Sitting on Powder Keg," July 1934, 10; "Has Anything Happened in Germany?" January 1935, 34; "Brutality That Can No Longer Be Denied," November 1935, 21, 22; "Why We are Compelled to Oppose Hitler," January 1936, 17-20; "Reprisals for Anti-Nazi Actions in the U. S.," June 1937, 13, 14; "Intensification of Terror in Germany," December 1937, 28, 29; "Will World Jewry Be Annihilated?" June 1938, 11-14; "The European Crisis and the Jews," May 1938, 10, 11; "Dark Ages," June 1939, 39; "Modern Haman—Migration Mad," March 1940, 16-18. Numerous other articles could be added. See "Notes by the General Secretary: American Prophetic League," *Hebrew Christian Alliance Quarterly*, Fall 1941, 14, 15. This article offers both praise and thanks to Brooks for his efforts on combating anti-Semitism in America and in the fundamentalist community.

88. "Behind the Gates of a Nazi Camp," *Prophecy Monthly*, June 1940, 13. The following item appeared in the February 1946 issue of the *Prophecy Monthly* ("Flashes," 25): "My father made 40 prisoners available for me on my birthday to teach me shooting. I shoot until all the prisoners lay dead. Otherwise I can't say anything against my father." A statement made by the "15 year old son of an SS commander at Mauthausen concentration camp, Germany." Also see the *Story of a Secret State* by Jan Karski (Boston: Houghton Mifflin Company, 1944), 332, 333 for a similar incident that he witnessed in the Warsaw ghetto, and "The Jewish Agony," *The Jewish Era*, November 1943, 121.

89. Ibid, 15. Also see, "Three Million Souls Being Starved Out," May 1936, 31; "Modern Refinement of Cruelty," November 1938, 28 (this article is a reprint of a letter Brooks received from Samuel Wilkinson of the Mildmay Mission to the Jews and begins with these words: "The refinement of cruelty carried on in the concentration camps in Germany is such that I dare not give details where woman are present."); "By the Waters of Babylon," May 1938, 7, 8; "Europe's Herds of Terrorized Jews," January 1940, 13-15. Again, many other articles could be listed.

90. "The Perils of Anti-Semitism," *The Sunday School Times*, October 4, 1930. Also, "Him That Curseth Them," *The Sunday School times,* March 11, 1939, front page. This was a reprint of a Charles Trumbull editorial that had appeared in the *Toronto Globe* in 1933.

91.   Ernest Gordon, "A Survey of Religious Life and Thought," *The Sunday School Times*, August 19, 1933, 524.
92.   Will H. Houghton, "The Truth About Germany and the Jews," *The Sunday School Times*, August 18, 1934, 523.
93.   Ibid, 527.
94.   Ibid. In the third article in his series, Houghton concluded that the only satisfactory solution to the Jewish problem was to give them their own land. He reminded his readers that "the Christian must look with great sympathy and understanding upon the Zionist hopes of the Jew, and must do his best to make the Jew understand that the spirit of persecution is not of Christ. Pray and work for the peace and welfare of Israel." ("The Jewish Problem in Europe," *The Sunday School Times*, August 25, 1934, 539.) Houghton also did an article promoting the establishment of a Jewish homeland in Palestine (writing, "The Jews can have a homeland and a voice in the councils of the nations") for the August 1934 issue of the *Pro-Palestine Herald*, voice of the Pro-Palestine Federation of America which was evidently a pro-Zionist organization made up of largely liberal Christian clergy and educators who supported the establishment of a Jewish state in Palestine. (See *American Protestantism and a Jewish State* by Hertzel Fishman [Detroit: Wayne State University Press, 1973], 64-68.)
95.   "German Brutally Fulfills Prophecy," *The Sunday School Times*, November 21, 1938, front page. Also see, Bauman, "Europe's Triumvirate of Beasts," *The Sunday School Times*, July 20, 1940, 581.
96.   The Friends of Israel refugee Relief Committee was formed out of the initial efforts of Paul Berman, of the Board of National Missions, Presbyterian Church, U.S.A. Berman attended the 1937 Vienna Meeting of the International Committee on the Christian Approach to the Jews and saw first hand the suffering taking place. He returned to America determined to do something to help. Out of this effort came the FOIRRC. All its officers served without pay and the office space had been donated free of charge. Only an office secretary was paid a salary. It eventually became the second largest evangelical mission to the Jews in America. Today it is simply known as Friends of Israel.
97.   Joseph Taylor Britan, "An Appeal for Persecuted Israel," *The Sunday School Times*, December 3, 1938, inside the front cover.
98.   Ibid. Both *Moody Monthly* and *The King's Business* reprinted Britan's appeal.
99.   "The Continuous Cry of the Persecuted," *The Sunday School Times*, October 4, 1939, 713.
100.   "Continued Persecution of the Jews in Europe," *The Sunday School Times*, March 16, 1940, 216. Also see "Desperate Need in Belgium," *The Sunday School Times*, May 25, 1940, front page and Joseph Taylor Britan, "The Ministry of the Persecuted," *The Sunday School Times*, June 28, 1941, 526, 527.
101.   See, for example, Bauman, "Gog and God and 1937," April-May, 133; "The Jews in Germany," June 1933, 171; Bauman, "Present Day Fulfillment of Prophecy: Hitlerism," 224; Bauman, "The Great Red Dragon and the Woman child—1934," March 1934, 93 and May 1934, 79; Thomas Chalmers, "The Present Situation in World Jewry," June 1934, 216; Bauman, "Socialism, Communism, Fascism," March 1935, 120; Bauman, "The Old Serpent Crawls On," July 1937, 246, 247; Britan,

"Cry of the Persecuted Jews," "Day of Prayer for Israel," "Plea on Behalf of the Jews," all in the December 1939 issue and all on page 491; Bauman, "The Jews Darkest Hour—and the Dawn," August 1941, 300, 301; Hess, "Will the Refugee Find Christ in America," November 1941, 414, 415.

102. See, for example, "The Nazi and the Jew," January 1934, 208; "Christian Jews in Germany," August 1934, 539, 540; "The Jews in Germany," December 1934, 151, 152; "Conrad Hoffman's World Report on the Jews," December 1934, 167; "Book Notices: The Missionary Review of the World," July 1935, 544; Britan, "An Appeal for Persecuted Israel," February 1939, 316, 345; "The Present Plight of German Jewry," April 1939, 441; "World Jewry," June 1939, 558; "Witnessing to European Jews," July 1939, 610; "Unparalleled Sufferings of Jewish Refugees," December 1939; "A Flickering Light in Poland," August 1941, 712; Britan, "Persecuted for Righteousness' Sake," October 1941, 83.

103. See, for example, its advertisement in the *Moody Institute Monthly*, February 1934 ("Shout It From the Housetops: Its Time to Help the Jews"), inside back cover; this ad mentions persecutions in Russia and Germany, and the increase of anti-Semitism in America; in *The Sunday School Times,* April 30, 1938, 328 "Is Suicide A Sin." This ad describes the horrors visited upon the Jews in Austria. This one also was placed on the back cover of *The King's Business,* and *Revelation,* June 1938. In *The Sunday School Times*, December 1938, inside back cover, "Daughters of Jerusalem! Weep Not for Me, But Weep for Yourselves and Your Children!" This ad gives a report on *Kristallnacht.* It also appeared on the back cover of *The King's Business,* January 1939.

104. The Friends of Israel's advertisements generally surveyed the Jewish and Jewish Christian predicament country by country, mainly focusing on the hunger and homelessness faced by hundreds of thousands. See, for example, their ads in *The Sunday School times* for March 9, 1941, inside front cover, June 29, 1940, inside front cover, and March 29, 1941; *Revelation* for October 1940, inside front cover, and December 1940, first page; and *Moody Monthly*, September 1940, 25 and December, 1940, inside front cover. An ad appearing in the July 8, 1939 *The Sunday School Times* reprinted a letter from Jacob Peltz, general secretary of the International Hebrew Christian Alliance, thanking the FOIRRC for their gift of $1500 (approximately $18,000 by today's measure) and pleading with it to bear the expense of a hostel for refugee mothers, young women, and children, "destitute victims of Nazi terror." A full page ad appearing in the same magazine on May 11, 1940 listed the exact amount FOIRRC had received since it's founding in December 1938 through January 1940. It was $14,971 (by today's measure approximately $175,000). Another ad, a Thanksgiving appeal, was a 1600 +/- word essay by Joseph Britan surveying the wretched condition of the European Jews, and pleading with believers not to despair but to serve Christ through aid to the Jews (*Moody Monthly*, November 1940, inside front cover). Finally, in *Revelation* (April 1942), the FOIRRC inside front cover ad related the work of Berger Pernow in Vienna. Pernow was the director of the Swedish Israel Mission and in that capacity engineered the rescue of about 3,000 Jews and Jewish Christians, one-third of whom were children.

105. In 1940, Jacob Peltz, general secretary of the International Hebrew Christian Alliance, returned to America to raise funds specifically for the IHCA. He was enormously

successful, raising just under $200,000 between 1940 and 1947. (By today's measure that would approximate $2,100,000.) With his return, full page ads appealing for relief funds for the IHCA began appearing in historic fundamentalist magazines. While on the whole they were general in nature, they were more specific in their details of Jewish and Jewish Christian suffering than those of FOIRRC. Peltz also included mention of the hardship faced by the IHCA workers in London due to the Nazi bombardments. See, for example, its ads in *Moody Monthly*, November 1940, 145 and *The King's Business*, also November 1940, 149; *Moody Monthly*, April 1941, 473 and *The King's Business*, April 1941, 149; "Israel's Darkest Hour," *The Kings Business*, October 1941, 339; *Revelation*, October 1941, 457; *The Sunday School Times*, "Jewish Misery and Christian Indifference," November 15, 1941; "The Jews in this World Crisis: the Christian Approach," *The King's Business*, February 1942, 63.

106. Bethel Eastern European Mission operated orphanages and mission centers among the Jews in Lodz and Warsaw, Poland. Because it was a native Polish mission it was allowed to operate in a limited way for most of the war. When the Jews were forced into the ghettos, Bethel went with them, operating soup kitchens and their orphanages as long as possible. Tragically, all the orphans and orphan workers perished at the hands of the Nazis. All this information appeared in abbreviated form in their advertisements in the major historic fundamentalists journals and in greater detail in their own *Bethel Witness*. Usually a quarter to one third page in size, the ads showed up in *Moody Monthly*, *The King's Business*, and *Revelation*.

107. A review of his book in the *Hebrew Christian Alliance Quarterly*, spring 1939, copied from *Prophecy Monthly*, called it a book that "has exerted a tremendous influence in Christian circles" (32).

108. Louis S. Bauman, *The Time of Jacob's Trouble* (no publisher, 1939, [1943], 4th edition), 14. Also see Keith Brooks' *The Jews and the Passion for Palestine in Light of Prophecy* (1937) for an account of Nazi persecutions and anti-Semitic propaganda (31-36).

109. Ibid, 26.

110. Ibid, 28.

111. Ibid, 44-46.

112. Ibid, 53-57.

113. J. Hoffman Cohn, "Re-Affirming God's Method: January 1939," *Beginning At Jerusalem* (New York: American Board of Mission to the Jews, 1948), 131. This book is a collection of editorials written for the January editions of the *Chosen People* through the Great Depression and World War II.

114. In *The Bethel Witness*, journal of the Bethel Mission of Eastern Europe, one finds a number of letters from contributors. One (from N. I. E.) reads: "The conditions in Europe are terrible. My heart goes out to all those poor suffering people. I only wish that they could get out of that awful trouble" (October-December 1940, 15). Another couple wrote telling how the husband had just lost his job, but then added that this was only "a 'speck' compared to the sorrows and heartaches you know so well." They sent $25 (January-March 1942, 13). Another wrote: "My sister who died many years ago had a gold ring given her by her brother, and just this week I sold it and I am sending the money to help feed the hungry Jewish refugee children

in Europe. My heart aches for all such" (January-March 1943, 10).

One letter from *Israel My Glory* is worth quoting for its eloquence:

> Greetings in the Risen Savior's Name; By his grace sending you again a little offering for your blessed work of giving help to the helpless, hope to the hopeless and cheer to the cheerless. I read the appeal for help in the Evangelical Christian and The Sunday School Times and my heart is breaking and bleeding for their misery and suffering, but at the same time we are thankful that there is a little door open through which help may be sent, be it ever so small. We cannot but pray that these days of their suffering might be shortened, and the Lord Himself would wipe away their tears and give joy in the place of sorrow, and heal their broken hearts and spirit (June 1943, 14).

115.   Again, as I have noted elsewhere, it is difficult to read through the hundreds of accounts of persecution, in this case Jewish and Jewish Christians, without being moved to anguish—as must have been the even more intense response of those who first read these stories. Many of the more personal stories were not known until after the war. One wishes they might all be shared. I must share one. I debated over whether to tell of the elderly Romanian Jewish Christian pastor who was arrested, torn from his family, shoved into a cattle truck with 140 other Jews—so many in fact that men could only stand and barely breath. The heat and stench were unbearable. The elderly pastor was dying, held up only by the press of bodies, but nevertheless he witnessed to his brethren from the Old Testament on the Messiahship of Jesus until he expired where he stood. Then I thought of sharing the story of the Gestapo officer who was assigned to attend the services of the church of Pastor Krakiewitc in Warsaw. Under the pastor's preaching he came to a saving faith in Christ and one day confessed before his fellow Gestapo officers and a family that belonged to Krakiewitc's church (who thought he had come to arrest them) "I will now follow Christ as my Savior" and embraced the father. He was never seen again. Instead, I will share the story of the death of the Lubtshanksis family, a Jewish Christian family executed by the Nazis. The details of their execution were related by Rev. Najmilowski of the Polish Baptist Church:

> I was invited, shortly before they fell victims at the hands of the Nazis, to partake of the Lord's Supper with them. I could not forget what the father said to his only child when they were on their knees. "Dear Elizabeth, they will shoot us, but do not be afraid. As soon as you hear the shooting, we will be with the Lord Jesus."
>
> I was eager to have the details of the execution. This is what I was told by a friendly policeman who was one of the guards at the place. He related the story about this Jewish couple with a little girl of eight or nine years. The father of the child pleaded with the officers to permit him to die together with his wife and child. He said, "We are Hebrew Christians. We belong together." This tragic plea was granted. The father stood on one side, the mother on the other, both holding the hands of their darling, Elizabeth. At the open grave, they bowed their heads in prayer. While still praying, they were machine-gunned, and the three fell into the grave. ("The Last Hour of the Lubtshanksis," *Bethel Witness*, Vol. 11, No. 1, 1947, 18.)

Before we take the high road morally in the face of such beastly behavior by men, let us say to ourselves, "but for the grace of God go I." It is more than a cliché, it is the mercy of God toward us. Given the same situation, pressures, education, society, (the same Sitz em Leben) I cannot say I would do better, the same, or perhaps even worse. Those who condemn the atrocities of others have been known to commit their own. It is right and necessary to condemn the evil of the Nazis. It is also right and necessary to do it with humility.

CHAPTER EIGHT

Historic Fundamentalism and the Jews:
Is this Suffering Nothing to You Who Pass By?

Perhaps the unkindest cut of all is the accusation that the historic fundamentalists did nothing concrete to help the Jews of Europe (Wilson), or, if they did do something, it was minimal in magnitude and consequence considering the theological and historical importance the historical fundamentalists attached to the Jews as a people/nation. This is the gist of Carpenter's remarks in *Revive Us Again*:

> Yet for all of the attention they received in print, the Jewish people held a rather low priority on fundamentalists' agenda. The many expressions of sympathy and outrage produced very little positive action. There were a few gestures of solidarity against anti-Semitism, such as the rally of gentiles and Jews at the Hebrew Christian Alliance's annual conference at Moody Memorial Church in 1936. There were some refugee relief efforts as well, most of it mobilized by the Jewish missionary boards, and at best one clandestine effort early in the war by American missionaries in Belgium and Portugal to help Jewish fugitives escape the Nazis. But one looks in vain for any further action on behalf of persecuted Jewry.[1]

As mentioned in the last chapter, Carpenter does not leave the historic fundamentalists much latitude with his analysis, or even much respect with his "one looks in vain for any further action on behalf of persecuted Jewry." Of course, if one down plays all someone *could* do and then condemns one for not doing more, one has to wonder where fairness comes in.

Although not as extreme as Wilson's "hands off" accusation, the whole tenor of Carpenter' comment does amount to a statement of denigration. Again, we are back to how history is worded so as to create a particular attitude about the subject on the part of the critical historian. Therefore his comment needs to be carefully "parsed." Consider, for example, the statement that "the Jewish people held a rather low priority on fundamentalists' agenda." The problem with this charge is that I am not sure exactly what a, or the, historic fundamentalists' agenda was.

They never announced one that I am aware of. Historic fundamentalism was a movement not a vast denominational bureaucracy or formal, centralized political or religious organization that could demand or confiscate people and funds for a particular project, or even an over-arching guiding council. Its many colleges, Bible schools, mission agencies, and charitable organizations were, on the whole, dependent on voluntary giving and a good deal of voluntary serving. Missionaries served in a particular place because this is where the "Lord led them." If there was anything that might be called an agenda it would have been worldwide evangelism (Jews included), followed by faithful adherence to certain doctrinal truths derived from and including an inerrant Scripture. But this seems more of a given than an agenda as far as the historic fundamentalists were concerned. Individual believers and individual churches would have different interest in whom or what faith mission to support. Again, it was as the Lord led. So exactly what agenda the historic fundamentalists had drawn up that put the Jews low down on the list of people to help is difficult to discern. Carpenter owes the reader an explanation he does not provide.

Following close on the heels of the above is the implication that they really did not do much, certainly not as much, evidently, as they could have or might have or should have done. From this position Carpenter denigrates by unspecified, unmentioned comparison, what the historic fundamentalists did do—they wrote a lot about the suffering of the Jews, held a few anti anti-Semitic solidarity rallies, did some relief work to help the refugees, and tried a couple of rescue efforts—"but one looks in *vain* for any further action on behalf of persecuted Jewry." (Italics added).

Having dismissed the value of what they did do, Carpenter leads us into an opinion of historic fundamentalists that portrays them as neglectful at best and less than caring at worst, a group holding at arms length a suffering people. However it is not unfair to ask Carpenter to inform us of what more the historic fundamentalists could have done or should have done for suffering Jews *that they were capable of doing* given the world and domestic problems that were so much a part of the 1930s.[2] (As we have discussed these in some detail in Chapters Three and Seven, it is not necessary to repeat them here.) What did they fail to do that we can point the finger of criticism at them and say "shame," or "hypocrite?" It is incumbent on Carpenter; indeed, I believe he has a moral obligation, having implied a gap between words and actions, to explain what he meant by writing, "One looks in vain for any further action on behalf of persecuted Jewry."

Timothy Weber, who parallels Carpenter in his almost palatable dislike of the historic fundamentalists' scriptural understanding of the Jews, in his 1998 *Christianity Today* article, "How Evangelicals Became Israel's Best Friend," leans heavily upon the prophetic interests of the historic fundamentalists in Israel, and covers their debate over the *Protocols* yet again ignoring any compassionate activities they may have engaged in on behalf of the European Jews. At one point in the article, evidently questioning the priorities of the historic fundamentalists, he notes that in 1939 "dispensational leaders called for an international day of prayer for the Jews. Interestingly, the organizers did not advise people to pray for the persecutions to stop, only that Jews might turn to Christ in their despair. The best thing people could do for the Jews under the circumstances was send them more New Testaments and missionaries."[3] (One might surmise from Weber's comment that taking the gospel of God's love toward sinners to sinful Jews facing terror, death, and eternity was a poor choice on the part of the historic fundamentalists.)

Serving the Jews: The Imperative of the Gospel

However, rather than starting with Carpenter's and Weber's obvious bias, I want to start with the simple premise that what they thought they could do, and what they thought they ought to do, the historic fundamentalists tried to do. It is true, of course, that they fervently desired the conversion of the Jew, and this was particularly true for the Jewish Christian evangelists among them. The Great Commission was the "prime directive," not saving societies, rescuing refugees, or stopping dictators. They might support and participate in such things, but not at the expense of the gospel. In addition, they believed they were indebted to the Jews for both Scripture and Jesus, so to speak, and longed for the Jews to experience the eternal fullness of their own heritage in Messiah Jesus. The desire of the historic fundamentalists for the Jews to accept Jesus as their Messiah-Savior was not born of anti-Semitism but philo-Semitism. It is not surprising, then, that as anti-Semitism increased and persecution against the Jews turned more cruel and brutal, and as the world as a whole and Europe in particular slouched rough-beast-like toward the new world order of blood and war and slaughter, the historic fundamentalists were anxious that the gospel go forth with greater intensity—and rejoiced at the greater response to it. Max I. Reich, a leading American Jewish Christian, teacher at Moody, president of the Hebrew Christian Alliance of America, and poet, expressed this sentiment in the following poem:

1941
"DEUTE PROS ME—Hither To Me
Matthew 11:28

They are coming to His cross
Out of shame and bitter loss,
They are coming for the healing in His blood;
Jew and Gentile, east and west,

With their aching hearts seek rest,
Which is found alone in harmony with God.

From the voices of deceit
They still gather round His feet,
Where the erring hear the Word that makes them sure;
For our spirit's anchor-ground,
And the Truth, in Him are found,
And the Teaching which makes learners trebly pure.

For our world has lost its way—
In this dark and cloudy day,
And like scattered sheep we wander in our quest;
But a voice of tender love
Still pursues us from above:
"Come to me, your Friend and Lover, and find rest!"

Come, ye broken men and bruised!
Haste, ye captives, to be loosed!
For His power now, as ever, is the same;
He will hush your storm-tossed heart,
And the peace of God impart;
There is heaven in the music of His Name![4]

More than economic, political, and physical persecution was involved. We may argue endlessly about who should have done what circa the late 1930s, but one thing was inescapable—eternity loomed large and immediate for many a Jew. And as the horrors of the persecutions increased, so, too, it seemed, did the Jews' interest in Jesus as their Messiah.

Timothy Weber, again, perhaps somewhat skeptical, writes: "Sometimes dispensationalists took comfort in *their belief* [italics added] that persecution made Jews more susceptible to the gospel. Moody Institute president Will Houghton *claimed* [italics added] that Jewish youth in Warsaw turned to Christ *en masse* in the summer of 1939, immediately before the Nazi invasion."[5]

There are two very strong objections with Weber's characterization of the historic fundamentalists' "faith" in the gospel among the Jews. The first is that Houghton did not "claim" that the Jewish youth of Warsaw were turning to Christ in large numbers. Actually he was reporting what was printed in a major Jewish newspaper—to wit:

Just before the breaking up of Poland, *The Morning Journal* [N.Y.] which is the official organ of Jewish orthodoxy in America, published a cable from Warsaw, which said, "The spread of Christianity among the Jewish school youth in Warsaw is truly assuming proportions of a masse movement." [6]

Unless Houghton made the above up out of whole cloth or the paper was printing a bogus story, he had good reason to be joyful. It would have been helpful, and certainly fairer, had Weber included the above information on the source of Houghton's "claim."

The second objection stems from Weber's comment that "sometimes dispensationalists took comfort in their *belief* that persecution made Jews more susceptible to the gospel" (italics added). Did the historic fundamentalists "believe" correctly or were they deluding themselves? Were Jewish missionaries exaggerating numbers so that people would be more willing to give? As noted in the previous chapter, the evidence is overwhelming that an unusually large number of Jews were turning to Christ in the late thirties and early forties, and an even larger number were open at least intellectually to discussing "Jesus of Nazareth."

For example, a few years after World War II, Birger Pernow, director of the Swedish Israel Mission, related the experiences of its mission in Vienna shortly after the Nazis marched into that city and began their reign of terror. His article appeared in the Spring 1950 issue of *The Hebrew Christian* and is both moving and memorable. The Nazi invasion, he noted, brought to the Jews a true realization "that they were sentenced...and of this they had no illusions." Even the SIM mission was temporarily closed and its funds seized by the Gestapo. However, as Pernow put it, "by God's merciful help we were able to obtain...[Gestapo] permission to start our mission work again with a sermon on the following Sunday:"

> For the first time not only the chapel but even the big entrance hall was crowded by Jews of the highest rank and education and by the poorest as well, now all eager to listen to the Gospel of salvation and life everlasting. None of us will ever forget that service, not only because of the spirit resting upon the congregation, but because it began a wonderful revival, which lasted summer and winter until June 1941 when the Gestapo forbade the preaching of the Gospel to the Jews.[7]

But the Nazis were too late for the harvest had been gathered:

> During that time hundreds of Jews in Vienna were converted and became believing Christians; many of them had to suffer even death for Christ and thus won the crown of glory. The hunger for the Word of God was so great that at the outbreak of the war in September 1939 we had to double the morning service every Sunday.... Thus these our fellow Christians received strength of belief so desperately needed in the times ahead.[8]

The Bethel Witness also spoke of crowded services at its mission stations in the Polish ghettos of Litzmonstadt and Warsaw, which was "greatly blessed with a spiritual awakening among the Jews."[9] A like report came from Barbican Mission to the Jews in Czechoslovakia,[10] and also from Shanghai, China,[11] and France.[12] Even in America there seemed to have developed a new willingness to hear the gospel among both Jewish citizens and recently arrived refugees.[13] As for the Jews in Nazi occupied territory, they derived no political benefits from converting to Christianity. They were still Jews in the Nazis' eyes and unless they were able to escape, they still went to the death camps.

As hinted at above, something that is almost always ignored when discussing the plight of the Jews in Europe during this period is that they were being brought face to face with enormous spiritual questions of eternal magnitude. More than vicious anti-Semitism was in contention. As Harvey Phelps of the European Christian Mission noted during his brief stay in a refugee camp in France, "There were several Jewish refugees in our camp, and I had no difficulty in making their acquaintance and engaging them in conversation about spiritual things. Everybody seemed more susceptible to the things of God than ever before and was open to talk about his personal need."[14] And the conservative Protestant missions were in a strategic position to offer this needed spiritual help. The Jews were now subjected to the merciless mercies of fallen and hate filled, even demonically driven men. Only God would listen to them now. The missions, then, were places of compassion and hope in a wicked and endless sea of hate.

Perhaps the following poem by Si Tannhauser, a Jew who occupied "the position of stationmaster on an Eastern railroad in the U. S. A." as the introduction informed, expressed the tentative and uncertain but pleadingly hopeful relationship the Jews in a whirlpool of chaos and fear would have toward their crucified Messiah/King. It is a passionate and movingly poignant confession and plea:

A Jew's Heart-cry

> We've torn the perils from the sky,
> The secrets from the sod;
> We've chained the lightning to our wheel,
> And called the man-thing God.
> On heights we stand, while at our feet
> We watch the storm-clouds roll;
> But, oh, Thou thorn crowned Nazarene,
> Have mercy on our soul!
>
> The zero hour of despair
> Is mine, and mine alone;
> All mine the darkness of the pit,
> The glory of the throne;
> All mine, my life, to make or mar,
> To conquer or to fail;
> And none but I own equity
> Where I, myself, break trail.

Through trackless seas I plough my way,
By nameless stars I steer;
A broken rudder keeps my course,
My mates are Doubt and Fear;
No Pilot guides my chartless drift,
No compass holds me true;
Oh, Captain of the portless ship,
Have mercy on the crew!

There is no fountain filled with blood
To wash my sins away;
There is no Comforter by night,
No shadowed Rock by day;
I wander through the desert land
Where shapes affrighted stroll;
And thou—Oh, Thou—who know'st me not,
Have mercy on my soul!

There is no face in pity bent
When by the way I fall;
No anxious, loving Shepard comes
In answer to my call;
There are no tender eyes that seek,
No gently arms to hold,
No nail-pierced hands to take me up
And bring me to the fold.

And when on naked bleeding feet,
To Calvary I go,
And stagger, crushed, beneath the Cross,
There's none to heed or know;
There's none to lift the cruel weight,
There's none to even share;
Thou, Who did'st climb the Hill before
Look down and help me bear.

Thou, Who did'st fear, yet drained the cup
Of valed Gethsemane,
Who hung from torn and bleeding palms,
And died, like that for me;
Oh, Thou, if Thou can'st understand,
Forgive, forgive, atone,
Unto my outcast soul that drifts
Alone—alone—alone!

By scales that weight the universe,
By rule that measures time,
By law that knows no compromise
With blood, not love, nor rhyme,
By lead that plumbs the spaceless void'
By reason's shackles rive,
Oh, Thou—Oh, Thou—whom we deny,
Have mercy and forgive![15]

Were the dispensationalists "comforted" by their belief the Jews were more receptive to the Gospel! Yes, yes they were—because the Jews really were more receptive. The evidence in this regard is irrefutable. In the midst of a century and a culture of death without equal, many a Jew found abundant life in Jesus the Messiah. Thus gas chambers and crematoriums, instead of being instruments of implacable hate and unfathomable existentialist despair, became gateways into the presence and peace of their Messiah, the Lord of Glory. If historians wish to fault the historic fundamentalists for this emphasis on "Christ in you, the hope of glory" in the midst of persecution, wickedness, and death, so be it.

Serving the Jews: Pray Without Ceasing

"Prayer," wrote the author of the article, "Call to Prayer," "is the greatest power in the world" and "the quickest and surest method of averting the great calamity of anti-Semitism in our land."[16] The historic fundamentalists believed this without qualification. Prayer was not a psychological placebo to make them feel better or important. Rather it was central in their belief system. Whatever else they might do for the Jews, prayer was perhaps the greatest of these. This may be difficult for the secular historian to grasp. However, it is impossible to understand the historic fundamentalists if one discounts this crucial aspect of their life. Not to pray was concrete evidence of unbelief. Not to pray was not to care about people or that God's perfect will be done. Not to pray was to leave people at the mercies of men and Satan—it was to make the situation worse. And the most important thing to pray for was the salvation of individuals no matter who he or she was, or the circumstances they were in.[17] When the editor of *Moody Monthly* wrote that he hoped that the day of prayer set for January 1, 1939 would "find many Christians on their face before God on behalf of God's people," he did so in the confidence that such would be the case.[18]

Although there were scattered calls to pray for the Jews within the historic fundamentalist community prior to 1938,[19] it was in that year a regular program of prayer days for God's chosen people was put in place. The idea for such a day stemmed from the concern of a Jewish evangelistic worker named Ella Mae Canney of Los Angeles, California. On a cross-country tour during which she spoke to "hundreds of Jews" and was invited into many synagogues to show "her Palestine pictures and speak of the Old Testament prophecies now being fulfilled,"

> she found the Jews everywhere expressing fear of pogroms in America, as in other countries, because of the widespread anti-Semitic propaganda backed by foreign money, attributing to Christians in general the contempt for the Jews expressed by a few local Christian leaders. She was amazed to find Jew-hate so widespread in some eastern states, even some pastors outspokenly anti-Semitic.[20]

Returning to Los Angeles spiritually shaken, she came up with the idea of a "special day of prayer" to both save "the Christian testimony to Israel" and ward "off serious bloodshed."[21] With the support of a few leading historic fundamentalists, March 27, 1938 was announced as a "special day of prayer for Israel."[22] The idea caught on immediately. When the appeal was published in *The Sunday School Times* it was noted that it was "also endorsed by the Executive Committee of the Philadelphia Fundamentalists."[23] *Moody Monthly* also endorsed the appeal, writing: "There is a rising tide of Jew-hate not only in Europe, but also in America, and Christians are everywhere called upon to share a little of Christ's own love for His brethren and Paul's longing for their salvation."[24]

The prayer call listed three items the believer should bring before God. First, that the "rising tide of Jew-hate" in the country would be stemmed and that God would convict those Christians guilty of anti-Semitism of "the dangers of such a course, in view of the definite warnings of the Word of God." Second, that all Christians would show love toward the Jews and deeply long for their salvation. And finally, to "pray for the peace of Jerusalem: they shall prosper that love thee." The historic fundamentalists believed that "if the Palestine issue [could] be settled fairly, a great step will be taken toward relief of a distressing situation for persecuted Jews of many lands."[25] (It should be noted that prior to the invasion of Poland, the Nazi policy toward German Jews was to force them to emigrate.[26] When England issued its 1939 White Paper severely restricting Jewish immigration to Palestine, the historic fundamentalists were both grieved and angered—not only because Britain was turning its back on the Balfour policy, but also because it meant many Jews would be trapped in Europe.)[27]

This first day of prayer was so successful (the response was overwhelming) that an increased number of historic fundamentalists proposed such a day every three months. Thus one read in the published appeal that appeared in *The Sunday School Times* that the undersigned (14 of the leading premillennial dispensationalists in America) "gladly lent their names to the appeal for a special day of prayer for Israel on the first Sunday of July and October, 1938, and January and April, 1939; with the suggestion that pastors arrange if possible to give special messages dealing with the subject on the same Sunday."[28]

This second call for extended prayer listed the same three suggestions for prayer as the first, but added an additional request that people pray "Israel will look to God and not to nations for her help in this hour of deep distress," and that "American Christians will have a share in the care of Jewish people who are being driven from European countries" (many of whom were Jewish Christians).[29] Those issuing the appeal also hoped that their appeal would inspire many to "daily intercession for those who so sorely need the knowledge of the great love of the Redeemer for them."[30]

The above season of prayer was followed by an appeal for an International Day of Prayer for Israel on December 1, 1939.[31] The purpose of this day of prayer, unlike the previous ones, was to specifically pray for the salvation of the Jews. Those who issued the call believed with good reason that the persecutions "and the ever-increasing anti-Semitism through-out the world" had made Jews more open to the gospel due to their longing "for security and rest."[32]

Evidently unaware of the five previous days of prayer that had occurred since March 1938, and ignoring as well the fact that those promoting the December 1, 1939 day of prayer specifically and clearly stated its sole purpose was to pray that the Jews would come to Christ, Timothy Weber writes:

> "Later that same year [1939] dispensational leaders called an international day of prayer for the Jews. Interestingly, the organizers did not advise people to pray for the persecutions to stop, only that Jews might turn to Christ in despair. The best thing people could do for the Jews under the circumstances was to send them more New Testaments and missionaries.[33]

By omission, Weber, like Carpenter, places a question mark over the heads of the historic fundamentalists' actions. Were they unsympathetic spectators only interested in proselyting? Or, because they believed the persecutions were God ordained, were they unwilling to pray against them lest they be at opposites with God? We are left to supply our own answer but its range seems clearly limited. Of course, as shown, the historic fundamentalists would have heartily agreed with Weber's conclusion; the best thing to give anyone, at any time, in any place, under any circumstances, was the good news found in Christ Jesus their Lord.

Interestingly, shortly after the news of the Nazis systematic wholesale execution of the Jews was verified by the State Department in December 1942, the Great Commission Prayer League called for three days of fasting and prayer for the Jews during the Feast of Purim, March 19, 20, 21, 1943. According to the front page announcement that appeared in *The Sunday School Times*, Christians were to be mindful of "the intense suffering of the Jews under the merciless heal of cruel dictators" and "pray for the alleviation of Israel's physical distress," keeping "in mind the necessity for the re-birth of the Scattered Nation." Christians were also to pray "that the testimony of God's Word may be effectively given to every

Israelitish heart at this time...." The call also encouraged believers to "pray now for suffering Israel, and prepare for the special season of prayer and fasting on the days of the feast of Purim."[34] (Weber was evidently also unaware of this call to prayer.)

The Jewish Era published the League's call verbatim and the last paragraph is worth quoting in full:

> *Prayer even with fasting* during the Jewish "Feast of Purim" is urged upon all Christians as a privilege and obligation. When wicked Haman sought to destroy Israel with his oppressive measures, *prayer and fasting* were honored of God in the nation's deliverance. At this hour of unparalleled distress of Israel, surely all who know Christ should cry to God in deep united prayer for her deliverance and salvation as well as for the world-wide benefits which are most certainly attendant upon the blessing of Israel.[35]

Serving the Jews: Giving to Help the Refugee

The historic fundamentalists had no organizational or political power that might impact international affairs or stop the persecutions in Europe, nor even any political clout with which to influence the Roosevelt Administration's emigration policy. However, they could speak out against what was happening and they did. They could bring the matter before the throne of Grace, which they did fervently and frequently. They could also share the gospel with those who had come to realize that man and his ways was a vain and frail foundation upon which to build hope and peace. This, too, they did continuously in love. And, of course, they could contribute to the relief of the refugees, which they did with a generosity that marked so many among their numbers.

Exactly how much money flowed from individual historic fundamentalists' wallets or church coffer's to help the Jewish refugees is probably impossible to determine. There were so many avenues through which to channel funds—denominational agencies, Jewish agencies, organizations such as the FCC's, American Christian Committee for German Refugees (later the American Christian Committee for Christian Refugees) or the Quaker's American Friends Service Committee, or even the American Red Cross or the Salvation Army.[36] Then there were the independent agencies that were fundamentalists friendly such as the European Christian Mission or the American European Fellowship or the Belgium Gospel Mission. Finally, of course, were the specifically Jewish Christian missions, both foreign and domestic, such as the Mildmay Mission to the Jews [England] or the American Board of Missions to the Jews. All of the above and more ministered to the Jewish refugees to one degree or another.

Quite often financial records no longer exist or were simply beyond reach. And in some cases logistical difficulties made it impossible to scour archives for buried data. For example, the Mildmay mission evidently had a large constituency in America during the 1930s. When England became involved in the war with Hitler, money could not be sent outside that country. Thus the Chicago Hebrew Mission, which Mildmay had helped get off the ground in the late nineteenth century, became the repository for American contributions to Mildmay, and distributed the funds as Mildmay directed. Yet no amounts are ever mentioned in the pages of *The Jewish Era*, the journal of the Chicago Hebrew Mission.

Nevertheless, there were and are a few Jewish Christian mission agencies for which I was able to obtain some financial information concerning aid to Jewish refugees in the 1930s and 1940s. They are the Hebrew Christian Alliance of America, the International Hebrew Christian Alliance, the Friends of Israel Refugee Relief Committee (later the Friends of Israel Missionary and Relief Society), the New York Jewish Evangelization Society, the Bethel Mission of Eastern Europe, and the American Board of Missions to the Jews.

During the height of the Great Depression, the Hebrew Christian missions across America (with the exception of the American Board of Missions to the Jews) experienced serious budgetary problems. The president of the Hebrew Christian Alliance, in his opening address to the 18th conference [1932] remarked how the conference almost had to be cancelled because of the economic situation which had caused giving to plunge drastically.[37] At the beginning of 1934, the general secretary (Jacob Peltz) resigned in order that funds might be available to pay the organization's missionaries and debts.[38] Giving for the period from June to December 1933 was $2,000 less than the same period the previous year and thus the Alliance was running "a large deficit."[39] Total income for the Hebrew Christian Alliance of America for the period April 29, 1931 to May 10, 1932 was $13, 077. For the period June 1, 1933 to June 1, 1934, it dropped to $8,950. It would not be until the fall of 1937 that the HCAA would be out of debt, back-salaries paid, and a small surplus left over.[40]

The same experience plagued the Chicago Hebrew Mission. Income plunged 50% between 1929 and the beginning of 1933. The following year was even worse as income was only 37% of pre-Depression levels. Some workers had to be dismissed and the mission Superintendent noted that some of the areas churches would not open their doors to the CHM to present its ministry due to Depression conditions.[41] The mission's remaining workers took approximately a 33% cut in salary for the years 1932 through 1935 in order to keep the mission solvent.[42]

Also facing financial straights was the New York Jewish Evangelization Society. By the autumn of 1932 the Society was in debt over $2,000 because of depressed income. And its income continued to fall during the hard years of the Great Depression. In 1932 income was $16,800. By 1935 this had dropped to $10,500 and in the following year to $10,000. The next year (1937), income climbed to $11,000, and in 1938 inched up some more to $12,500. Finally, in 1939 income exceeded the 1932 amount, reaching approximately $17,000. Finances were definitely looking up. However, in the next two years income dropped below $15,000 and would not exceed $17,000 again until 1942. From that point on the Society's income grew and it was back on firm footing once more.[43]

Like other missions in the cities across America, the Hebrew Christian missions, as well as the Hebrew Christian Alliance, operated as "rescue missions" in the Jewish communities where they were located. They fed the hungry, helped the poor, and tried to find work for those desperately needing it.[44] As with most missions, the primary function of these organizations was evangelism. Thus, despite the Great Depression and assistance extended to the needy, the Hebrew Christian Alliance sent a Jewish Christian couple to work among and evangelize the growing Jewish community in Buenos Aires, Argentina. Similarly, the Chicago Hebrew Mission, despite salary shortages and budget constraints, opened a mission in Milwaukee, Wisconsin to evangelize the Jewish community of that city.[45]

The Hebrew Christian missions were largely dependent on voluntary giving from various historic fundamentalists' churches or individuals (though some also received funds from denominations). This meant they had to compete with scores of other missions for limited Great Depression funds. The Hebrew Christian Alliance, despite the implication of its title, directly represented at the most only a few hundred of the estimated 20,000 Hebrew Christians in America (circa 1935), although its influence extended well beyond its ranks, and its journal was widely read within the historic fundamentalist community.[46] Also, because not all Christians believed in specifically evangelizing the Jews, or believed that God still looked with favor upon Israel and had promised to restore it to its biblical homeland, it was difficult at times to raise funds as easily as other mission agencies. As Jacob Peltz once complained: "For while other worthy causes get succor and relief from thousands, yet our cause appeals only to the chosen few who have learned to pray for the peace of Jerusalem and who believe sincerely in the need of Israel's reconciliation to the Messiah."[47]

Giving: The Hebrew Christian Alliance of America

Because it was a Jewish Christian organization, and part of the International Hebrew Christian Alliance, the members of the American Hebrew Christian Alliance were extremely sensitive to the rise of anti-Semitism in Europe and particularly in Germany. By mid-1933, the Hebrew Christian Alliance *Quarterly* was covering and protesting events in Germany[48] and announcing the establishment of a special fund to assist German Hebrew Christians, who, they believed, were having a more difficult time than their Jewish counterparts.[49] However, funds were slow in coming. The financial report for the year May 10, 1932 to June 1, 1933 showed only $120

($1,500) to the relief fund and $89 ($1,100) distributed. How much of that went to help the German refugees is not reported.[50] The following year (June 1, 1933 to June 1, 1934) the relief fund received $382 ($5,000) and distributed $30 ($400) at home and $300 ($3,900) overseas for German refugee relief.[51] The next year (June 1, 1934 to June1, 1935) $440 ($5,500) was received into the relief fund and almost $400 ($5,000) given toward European refugee relief.[52]

In 1936 the executive committee of the HCAA decided to "send our gifts and contributions direct to the needy persons, instead of through the International Alliance. We, however, are cooperating, and informing the International of our endeavors in this direction."[53] This change in policy may reflect what was to become an ongoing tension between the American Alliance and the International Alliance that would continue into the war years. The International Alliance, mainly focused on Europe and increasingly involved with the Jewish refugees flooding into England, obviously believed American Christians in general and Hebrew Christians in particular, were not sufficiently concerned with the troubles being heaped upon the Hebrew Christians of Germany as the 1930s progressed.[54]

On the other hand, the American Alliance had its own agenda which, while it included awareness and concern for the German Jewish Christians,[55] did not absorb all its activities (which included expanding missionary activities in South America, Poland and Palestine). In 1935, Jacob Peltz, who had been the general secretary of the American Alliance until scarcity of funds had eliminated his paid position, was brought to London, England to become general secretary to the International Alliance. Clearly it was an unspoken attempt to bring the American Alliance into a deeper involvement with the German Jewish and Jewish Christian refugee problem. If that was the intent, it was not very successful. And in late 1939, when Peltz was required to return to America, he also carried with him the assignment to raise funds for the International Alliance in America and Canada. This, of course, exacerbated the tensions between the two Alliances, as they now would be competing for funds from the same constituency.

In the financial year ending June 1, 1936, receipts for the Hebrew Christian Alliance of America totaled $8,650 ($112,400) of which only a meager $380 ($4,850) was given to the relief fund. Of this amount, $150 ($1,950) was sent to Germany, $25 ($325) to England, and $110 ($1,430) was used at home.[56] For some unknown reason, the next financial report covered a period of seventeen months. However, again, only a scant $425 ($5,350) was given to relief of which $175 ($2,200) was distributed. The following financial period covered eight months (September 11, 1937 to May 23, 1938) but showed $1,000 ($12,600) given for relief of which $60 ($750) went to Poland, $50 ($625) each went to Germany and Austria, and $600 ($7,500) went to the International Alliance. By 1938, the American Alliance began to take note of the Jewish and "non-Aryan" refugees showing up in America and began diverting some of its relief fund to minister to this group. In 1939, the annual meeting petitioned President Roosevelt "to use his good influence to allow persecuted and suffering Hebrew Christians to come to our shores to occupy and cultivate the many acres of land which are lying waste and unproductive."[57] Between May 23, 1938 and April 20, 1939, the relief fund received $2,830 ($35,400)—up considerably from the previous year (perhaps reflecting the impact of *Kristallnacht)*—and distributed $1,770 ($22,000) to "England, St. Domingo, U. S. A., etc."[58]

Between April 20, 1939 and May 25, 1940, with carry-over from the previous year and gifts, the relief fund totaled $2,670 ($33,100) of which $2,240 ($27,800) was distributed "to Europe, China, [and the] United States."[59] In late 1940, the Hebrew Christian Alliance took on a new refugee project; assisting "the hundreds of [refugee] Hebrew Christians who are interned in prison camps [by the English government] in Canada," and willingly helped find sponsors so that the young interns (under 21) might go to school outside the camps.[60] The following financial year (May 25, 1940 to May 31, 1941) $2,825 ($34, 800) was given for relief of which $2,200 ($27,300) was distributed "at home and sent to England."[61] Finally, for the financial year June 1, 1941 to July 25, 1942, the year in which the refugee stream dried up because all of Europe was under the Nazi heel and the final solution was beginning, and more and more of the financial burden for supporting the Jewish and Jewish Christian refugees in England was being taken up by Americans, the relief fund received $2,140 ($25,700) of which $2,000 ($24,000) was distributed.[62]

Overall, between 1933 and mid-1942, the Hebrew Christian Alliance of America, though a small organization, raised approximately $13,200 for refugee relief, or approximately $164,000 by the 2001 value of the dollar, by far the greater portion given between 1939 and 1942. And as mentioned, this was not the only project funded by the Alliance. In 1942, besides the relief fund, the American Alliance had sixteen other funds it financed. The largest of these other than the general fund was the evangelism fund followed by the home fund, which was a fund to finance a headquarters building and small dormitory for refugees newly arrived in the United States. It needs to be remembered that the American Alliance functioned as a sending missionary and educational organization as well as an American Hebrew Christian fellowship, not primarily as a refugee relief organization. Still, as Max I. Reich, president of the HCAA, commented in a speech at the June 1941 annual conference: "Many *needy Hebrew Christians* have been succored financially and the pressing claims of the *refugees* in this country and abroad have not been unheeded by us. We have helped as far as we could."[63] Not reflected in the dollar amounts, of course, is the assistance given in finding housing, jobs, paying passage and extending loans and grants to those starting anew in this country, and providing affidavits so that those waiting to enter America might do so.

Giving: The International Hebrew Christian Alliance

The International Hebrew Christian Alliance, headquartered in London, consisted of various national alliances (mostly European) and the Hebrew Christian Alliance of America, but in many ways functioned as an independent organization. Like the HCAA, it financed a number of funds including one which contained $90,000 [1937] to purchase land in Palestine to establish a Hebrew Christian colony (a dream never realized). However, because its main focus was European Jewry, the IHCA found itself drawn more and more into trying to assist them as their persecutions and sufferings multiplied. A special German Relief Fund was established, separated from its regular relief work and in a short time absorbed the greater portion of it funds.

The IHCA is a good example of an overseas organization that was working directly with Jewish and Jewish Christian refugees and once the war was underway, received large contributions from America—most of which came from the historic fundamentalists. Interestingly, like so many missions of this period, the IHCA listed every donation received each quarter as well as a detailed end of the year financial report. As to be expected, most of the IHCA income was listed in pounds and shillings. However, mixed in among these was an occasional dollar contribution. This occasional contribution became a torrent of American money as the war took hold in Europe and 50,000 or more European Jewish refugees found sanctuary in England.

From the end of September 1934 until the end of September 1935, The International Alliance received $635 ($8,000) from America, the greater portion of which went to the German Relief Fund.[64] The following financial year that dropped by nearly 50% to $340 ($4,270).[65] (Of course, it is possible that more than the dollars listed was contributed by Americans. Some may have converted their dollars into British currency before sending them over but there is no way to confirm this—but see below.) In 1937, the dollar amount "jump" back up to $713 ($8,900)[66] However, as the totals for the IHCA Relief and German Relief Funds amounted to $22,000 in American dollars, historic fundamentalists seemed at this point to be contributing very little indeed.[67] When Max I. Reich, president of the American alliance, proposed a plan to help the children of Hebrew Christian refugees from Germany (a scheme, sadly, that never got beyond the paper it was written on), Jacob Peltz wrote (with barely contained frustration), "We are indeed thankful to God that at least some of the Christian leaders in America are becoming concerned over the problems of the victims of the Nazi persecutions, and that something will be done for the innocent children of the Hebrew Christian sufferers."[68]

Still, despite the fact that the above scheme (and others like it) never made it from paper to practice and that "in the matter of giving aid to the countless numbers of Hebrew Christians in distress, American Christians have not been so generous,"[69] Peltz looked on the brighter side. "There are encouraging signs," he wrote in the January 1939 IHCA quarterly, "of an awakening Christian conscience in America in respect to the plight of Jewish Christians," and then graciously concluded, "We have also been heartened by the many encouraging letters of sympathy and gifts for our work received from our members and Christian friends in America."[70] And things were looking up. Before the year [1939] was over, the IHCA would begin to receive increasing amounts of money for refugees from both the American Alliance and the newly formed Friends of Israel Refugee Relief Committee, while Peltz himself would return to America to begin raising funds directly for the IHCA.[71] As for 1938, $1,183 ($14,200) came from America into the relief coffers of the IHCA.[72] Nevertheless, this was still only a minute portion raised not only for the Relief Fund and the German Relief Fund, but also for the newly established Hostel Fund and the Refugee Settlement fund. The following year, which covered the period from December 1, 1938 to November 30, 1939, the four above mentioned funds received the American equivalent of $68,000 of which $2,840 ($34,000) is listed on its contribution lists as coming from America. However, this figure cannot reflect all the money received from America in 1939. For example, Harcourt Samuel mentioned in the July, *The Hebrew Christian,* that the IHCA had already received "more than $4,500 from" the FOIRRC. As the FOIRRC came into existence in December 1938, the $4,500 ($55,000) would have been sent in the first six months of 1939. There are two possible explanations. The first is that the FOIRRC converted American money into British currency before sending it over to the IHCA, or it is possible that the IHCA simply did not list large gifts from other organizations in its contributions lists. Either way it would appear that American giving to the IHCA easily *exceeded* $7,340 for the year 1939. It should also be noted that in 1939 the British government began matching pound for pound monies raised by refugee relief agencies, including the IHCA.[73] The 1939 figures show an increasing flow of largely historic fundamentalists' dollars to the IHCA. Even more generous days were ahead.

As mentioned, in December 1939, Jacob Peltz returned to America. Although his return was required by State Department regulations, the IHCA saw it as an opportunity to reach the American Christian public directly for desperately needed refugee funds. Knowing that such a project might cause additional resentment and tension with the American Alliance and its supporters, the IHCA sent an open letter addressed to their "Brethren of the American Hebrew Christian Alliance and Dear Friends." Drawing attention to the fact that "events in Europe have…upset all our plans" and that "the dreadful war in which we are at present engaged has made things very difficult," the IHCA asked the HCAA for "help in affording him [Peltz] every possible opening in order to make our work known in your country."[74] Acknowledging the "splendid work" the HCAA was doing and the "large heartedness" it had shown "toward all suffering folk," the IHCA expressed confidence that the HCAA would want to be a part of "the cause which we represent and for which we labor unceasingly."[75] However in asking for their cooperation, the IHCA tried to assure the HCAA that it was not trespassing on its domain:

> We are sure that you will not look upon our action in asking Mr. Peltz to spread information of the work we are doing, as an intrusion upon your own work, but rather as an opportunity of widening your own interest, and aiding a world-wide effort in the name of our Lord Jesus Christ. We desire your wholehearted co-operation and we are sure that our brother will seek that in all love and good fellowship. As he is intimately acquainted with every phase of our work and knows the situation in the world, we leave this task to him with full confidence. We emphasize the fact that he will not trespass upon any other interest but seek in every way to co-operate with the Christian Churches, and especially with the American Hebrew Christian Alliance, and all other Hebrew Christians who are working for the salvation of Israel.[76]

The letter was signed by Arnold Frank, president of the International Hebrew Christian alliance, himself a refugee from the Nazis' persecution, and Harcourt Samuel, the Recording Secretary, who would take on his shoulders much of the duties Peltz had once carried. But despite the assurances tensions did exist and that may be the reason why the IHCA backed a proposal by the HCAA (which had an extensive missionary work among the growing Jewish refugee community in Argentina) to establish a Jewish refugee agriculture colony in that country. The IHCA pledged five thousand dollars when the colony was finally established, "provided it had been fully consulted as to details and approves them."[77] Needless to say the colony never came into existence.

Making Chicago his headquarters (where he became president of the Chicago branch of the HCAA), Peltz would travel the length and breadth of America and Canada many times over during the war years, and as noted earlier, by 1947 had raised just under $200,000 ($2,100,000) for IHCA refugee needs.[78] Peltz evidently hit American soil running for the April 1940 issue of *The Hebrew Christian* took note of a letter received from him which related the "finding of many opportunities of widening our circle of friends both in the United States and Canada, everywhere eliciting a warm-hearted response." He also sent "a cheque for [$900 ($11,250)] which came to hand the other day [and] represents the first fruits of his labors."[79]

Full page advertisements soliciting funds for the IHCA also began appearing in 1940, advertisements accurately portraying the appalling conditions in Europe and the hardships in England for Jewish refugees. And because money could not be sent out of England due to the war, Peltz directed relief funds from his Chicago office, including funds (as long as possible) for the Hebrew Christian Alliances in Romania and Hungary.[80] Only funds to be used exclusively in England were directed there. In addition to raising funds, Peltz also labored to secure affidavits for Jewish refugees waiting in England who had obtained permission to emigrate to America. He was pleased to report he was successful "in a number of cases."[81]

The effectiveness of Peltz's efforts is reflected in part by the surge in giving from America—$13,200 ($164,000) is listed as America's 1940 contributions. The Refugee fund showed $2,015 received directly from Peltz's deputation and the Refugee Settlement Fund, $2,500.[82] Again, it is doubtful this reflects all the giving from America. And probably due to paper rationing, quarterly contribution lists were not printed on a regular basis. However, the year-end financial statement ending on September 30, 1941, showed $1,115 ($14,000) received from Peltz's deputation into the Refugee Fund and $3,130 ($39,450) received into the Refugee Settlement Fund.[83] The following year (1942) the Refugee fund received $1,020 ($11,900) and the Refugee Settlement Fund $11,345 ($132,750) from Peltz's tireless efforts.[84] Finally, in the financial year ending on September 30, 1943, Peltz sent to the Refugee Fund $4,615 ($49,000) and to the Refugee Settlement Fund $8,340 ($89,000).[85]

Because of the incompleteness of financial records during the war years it is difficult to ascertain exactly how much money went from America to the IHCA in London. As mentioned, Peltz handled some funds from America. In addition, some organizations such as the FOIRRC sent money to the IHCA directly rather than through Peltz. However, Peltz claimed that between August 1, 1940 and March 31, 1947, he raised $196,297.75 (about $2,100,000) in contributions from Canada and the United States with probably 90% coming from America.[86] (And approximately $100,000 of this was sent between the years 1940 and 1944.) It cannot be said that all of it came explicitly from historic fundamentalists. However, considering that the IHCA advertisements appeared almost exclusively in historic fundamentalist journals and that most of the churches Peltz spoke in could be classified as conservative or fundamentalists, it would not be out of line to suggest that the greater portion of the almost $200,000 came from the wallets and purses of the historic fundamentalists.

From 1935 through 1940, $18,900 ($233,000) in aid was sent to the IHCA, most of it, of course, coming from the HCAA and the FOIRRC. The years 1941, 1942, and 1943 saw at a minimum an additional $29,565 ($336,000) given to the IHCA in England. Between the years 1935 through September of 1943, then, at the very least $48,500 ($570,000) was raised for refugee assistance being administered by the IHCA in England. (And I would not be surprised that if all the contributions could be uncovered, that figure would swell to approximately $65,000 [$770,000].) Whatever the total, the greater bulk of it was sent after 1938. As Harcourt Samuel, Recording Secretary and Treasurer of the IHCA commented, "the bulk of the contributions" during the war years for the relief funds came "from the American deputation."[87]

Giving: The Friends of Israel Refugee Relief Committee

Perhaps no other organization (with the exception of the American Board of Missions to the Jews) represented historic fundamentalist giving to aid Jewish and Jewish Christian refugees than did the Friends of Israel Refugee Relief Committee.[88] FOIRRC was organized through the energy and concern of Paul Berman, Field Secretary, Board of National Missions, Presbyterian Church, U.S.A. Berman was also a member of the Hebrew Christian Alliance of America. He had attended the International Mission Conference on the Christian Approach to the Jews that met (deliberately it seems) in the SIM mission facilities in Vienna, Austria in 1937. The purpose of the gathering, in part, was to discuss the plight of the Jewish Christian refugees, which apparently was more extreme than that of their purely Jewish counterparts. Moved by their plight and the lack of interest shown by the American Church, Berman returned to Philadelphia determined to do something about the problem. The result was the FOIRRC, whose "formal" debut was announced in the pages of the December 3, 1938 issue of *The Sunday School Times*. The announcement—"An appeal for Persecuted Israel"—was written by Joseph Taylor Britan, who was secretary of the new organization and evidently its unofficial public spokesman.[89] The article, the first of many to follow,[90] carefully rehearsed the rise of world-wide anti-Semitism, and the suffering inflicted upon the Jewish people as a whole by the Nazis. However, Britan also singled out the Hebrew Christians in Europe as desperately needing assistance due to the neglect of their brothers and sisters. "The entire Jewish population of Europe," he wrote, "is more or less in danger of death," and about one million of these were Christians who are also being "dispossessed and defrauded," and who "are slowly being exterminated:"

> These are our Christian brethren. Their backs are bowed under a burden heavier than men and women can bear for long without breaking. Their faces are sad with the thoughts of a future that is filled with cruelty and pitiless persecution. Patiently they are living amid the ruin of all that they hold most dear, their life at least a thing of shreds and patches. They are looking to us daily for help, for only we can help them. Our gifts are the means by which they live.[91]

Britan highly praised the Jews for their relief efforts: "To the everlasting credit of the Jews of America, they have from the first persecutions organized for the relief of their brethren in Europe." Christians, however, had not done the same and, as "one Christian minister, who had recently returned from Europe" claimed, "unless the Christians of America come to their rescue, and at once, thousands will perish."[92]

The officers of the new organization served without pay in order that "all money contributed will be used for the purpose of relieving the sufferings of the Jews and

Jewish Christians in Central Europe, unless otherwise directed." Recognizing the enormity of the work, the leadership of the FOIRRC asked "for the prayers of God's people. This work is entirely too great for human wisdom and human power. Pray for the persecuted and persecutors. And then will you give?"[93] (And to their credit, thousands did both.) At the conclusion of the article was a list of layman and ministers who supported the FOIRRC appeal and served the purpose of an advisory committee. The majority of names were familiar in the historic fundamentalist's community: Bauman, Biederwolf, Chafer, Houghton, Ironside, Johnson, McCartney, Matthew, McQuilkin, Wilber Smith, and Trumbull.[94]

Once announced, funds were quickly received. The February 3, 1939 issue of *The Sunday School Times* printed a thank you letter from the FOIRRC reporting that by January 20, 1939, the organization had received $3,600 ($43,200) and had dispensed $1,500 ($18,000). Britan promised "the balance will be mailed soon to other organizations. The money is being spent on Jews, Jewish Christians, and Gentile Christians who are married to non-Aryans and who, because they will not divorce their husbands who are Hebrew Christians, have been deprived of everything and are counted as Jews."[95]

By the end of June 1939, Britan gave another report in the pages of *The Sunday School Times*. Nine thousand ($110,000) had been received to date and $4,550 ($56,000) distributed for relief. Seventeen hundred ($20,400) had gone for expenses and advertising, and $2,700 ($32,400) was yet to be allocated. "Your committee well knows," Britan informed his readers, "that the work is full of tragedy and cruelty and oppression and carnage."[96] Sadly, these words were all too true. Stories of suffering and persecution were so common and so appallingly numerous that it is easy for one to become inured to bestial behavior from that period.

Another FOIRRC financial accounting appeared in the February 22, 1941 issue of *The Sunday School Times*. Part of the reason for doing so was a U. S. Government report that inaccurately portrayed what the FOIRRC was sending overseas:

> It might be well to say just here [Britan wrote] that in the report of the United States Government concerning the activities of philanthropic organizations sending moneys abroad the Government is interested in, and prints only, the *amount sent by its permission to belligerents.* Thus the amount of money sent by our committee during any years to refugees abroad is never fully indicated by the Government report, for the reason we sent money for refugees to other nations than those designated as belligerent.[97]

Actually, for 1940 the FOIRRC received $15,900 ($199,000) in contributions (although income from other sources plus carry over would probably raise available funds close to $20,000). Of the $15,900, $2,100 ($26,300) was spent on refugee relief in America, and $9,900 ($123,000) overseas. And, Britan added, "of the $5,200 ($62,400) in the bank [as of] January 1, 1941, $4,200 ($52,500) has been allocated and pledged to suffering refugees as this is written January 29, 1941.

These amounts spent for refugee relief work do not include office and advertising expenditures, which were covered by the balance left from 1939."[98]

By the end of 1942, the FOIRRC was supporting, among other projects, a number of refugee children boarded in various English homes, a hostel for refugee mothers and their children operated by the International Hebrew Christian Alliance, and sending $750/month ($8,450) to the Swedish Israel Mission which, because of Sweden's neutrality, was allowed to operate in Nazi occupied Europe for most of the war. From December 1938 to December 1939, 941 contributors gave a total of $15,400 ($191,000). Along with other sources of income and carry over, FOIRRC received a total of $16,300 ($202,000) and gave out in relief in America, Europe, and Canada, $7,200 ($160,000).[99] The following year, as noted above, $15,900 ($199,000) was received from 1989 contributors with total receipts around $20,000 ($250,000). Of this amount, $12,000 ($150,000) was given for relief.[100] In 1941, total income was approximately $33,000 ($409,000) and refugee giving was approximately $15,600 ($193,400).[101] In 1942, 1289 individual contributions totaled $12,260 ($143,400). Those plus carry over and other sources of income gave the FOIRRC receipts of $35,350 ($413,600). Of this, $14,000 ($163,800) was given for refugee relieve.[102]

Overall, between December 1938 and December 15, 1942, the FOIRRC received $81,000 ($973,000), spent $70,000 of which $49,000 ($588,000) went directly to refugee relief. And a balance of eight or nine thousands dollars was sitting on the books to be used for the coming year. At the conclusion of 1942, FOIRRC changed its name to the Friends of Israel Missionary and Relief Society, hired a full-time director, Victor Buksbazen, began publishing a monthly magazine, *Israel My Glory*, and added missionary activities along with its relief work. Beginning in 1943, the newly named FOIMRS began setting aside 20% of its income for a post-war relief and reconstruction fund. Even so, in 1943, with an income of $35,600 ($377,400), $11,500 ($122,000) was given toward relief.[103]

In the inaugural edition of *Israel My Glory* (December 1942), there was an unsigned editorial of sorts (probably written by Buksbazen) titled, "A Glimpse Into the Future." It began by lamenting, "each day brings us a new message of the unspeakable horrors, which have become their [Jews] lot." However, this may only be the prelude, the author surmised, to even greater suffering when the war concluded—a challenge which would tax Christians to the uttermost limits of their faith:

> But what misery, what unspeakable suffering shall we face once the war is over.... It will take all the faith and all the self-sacrificing love that Christians can muster, to heal the wounds, feed the hungry and to bring the light of Christ into the darkness of their sorrowful lives. There will be scars left on the souls of men: burned in by the wickedness of their oppressors, which no power on earth will be able to erase from the memories of the victims, nothing except the power of Christ.[104]

Giving: The New York Jewish Evangelization Society

The New York Jewish Evangelization Society was a "Mom and Pop" organization whose income was devastated by the onset of the Great Depression and England's entrance into the war.[105] Although the mission always maintained a benevolence fund of sorts, during the Great Depression it seldom exceeded $100 per year. But beginning in the year 1939, it started a German Relief Fund as well to assist the Jews and Jewish Christians suffering under Hitler's relentless attempt to force the Jews out of Germany. In that first year, the German Relief fund received $269 ($3,360) and the Home Fund $102 ($1,275).[106] (However, by this time, the Home Fund was being used for refugees arriving in America, and probably this was true for some of the German Relief Fund as well. In 1940, the German Relief Fund was up to $800 ($10,000) while the Home fund remained static at $100 (1,250).[107] In 1941, the German Relief Fund actually saw a considerable decline in its income (as did the mission income as a whole). Only $435 ($5,435) was given to the German Relief Fund while $200 ($2,500) was given for the Home Fund.[108] However, this was the last year of meager contributions—comparatively speaking. In 1942, $2,500 ($29,250) came into what was now called the German and Polish Relief Fund because food packages were being sent to Jews captive in the ghettos of Poland through the Red Cross of Switzerland.[109] The following year (1943), $4,000 ($42,500) was contributed to what was now called a General Refugee Fund.[110] In 1944, the giving slightly exceeded that of 1943 with $4,100 ($41,000) given for refugee relief.[111] Along with sending money overseas to such organizations as the Swedish Israel Mission, the International Hebrew Christian Alliance, or the British Society for the Propagation of the Gospel among the Jews, the NYJES secured affidavits for refugees waiting in England to emigrate to the United States, and offered assistance to those already here who needed work or other forms of aid.[112] The NYJES may have been small and financially limited, but it served and gave from its heart and to the extent of its abilities to help Jewish and Jewish Christian refugees.

Giving: The Bethel Mission of Eastern Europe

There was one mission that secured funds for the persecuted and ghettoed Jews of Poland. Studying the Holocaust through the pages of the Jewish mission journals can be at times, even today, a difficult exercise—emotions still well up and gloom shrouds the landscape of one's thoughts. The reports of those ministries nearest the center of this enormous, almost incomprehensible evil bear true witness to the demonic levels men and women can sink when what is vile is honored in society and God is exiled. All the politically correct, postmodern multiculturalist's attempts to relativize cultures, and who wallow in moral equivalency come up dumb and blind before the bestiality of a Pol Pot or a Hitler. Sometimes the simplest remark can carry the starkest revelation of the extent of the horror. Such was the comment made by Berger Pernow of the Swedish Israel Mission in a letter to Victor Buksbazen, director of the Friends of Israel Missionary and Relief Society, and printed in its September 1944 issue of *Israel My Glory*.

After discussing in his letter the general work his mission was doing among the thousands of Jewish refugees in Sweden, he then wrote: "Our extensive relief work among deported Jews and Hebrew Christians in Poland is ended, to our deepest regret. *Most of these people no longer exist*" (italics added).[113] I have never forgotten that sentence from the day I first read it. In a way, the reality of the Holocaust is capsulated in those seven terrible words—"most of these people no longer exist."

No mission agency in America experienced more directly or more personally the reality of the Nazi hatred of the Jew than did Leon Rosenberg's Bethel Mission of Eastern Europe. Rosenberg operated in Lodz, Poland both an orphanage and a mission center. When the Nazis closed down the Jewish missions in Germany and forbade the giving of funds to Jewish mission organizations, the Bethel Mission of Poland (as the mission was then known) lost a great deal of its support.[114] In desperation, Rosenberg turned to American evangelicals.

Rosenberg's Bethel Mission of Poland was already known to some extent to the historic fundamentalist community. As early as January 1936, *Moody Institute Monthly* had carried an article introducing the mission's work among the children of the ghetto of Lodz.[115] And in a visit to America in 1937, he addressed the delegates to the 23rd Annual Conference of the Hebrew Christian Alliance of America on conditions of the Jews in Poland and his mission in Lodz.[116] Rosenberg returned to America in the summer of 1938 and along with crisscrossing America speaking in scores of churches (with the friendly support of H. A. Ironside opening doors),[117] he again addressed the Annual Conference of the Hebrew Christian Alliance of America meeting in Baltimore, Maryland.[118] He also formed an American advisory council and branch named the Bethel Society of Friends of Israel in America.[119]

Rosenberg returned to Poland in August 1939. His efforts had paid off to a certain extent. For the year 1938, $10,700 ($134,500) came from America and Canada to the mission in Lodz.[120] One month after Rosenberg returned to Poland, Hitler invaded and the mission, though still able to function because it was an indigenous organization, found itself isolated from the outside world and its source of financial support. In fact, America was going to become the sole means of support for the beleaguered Jewish Christians of the Bethel Mission of Poland. This new situation was reflected in the fact that only $7,600 ($96,000) was contributed in 1939 to the mission from America and almost nothing from any other source.[121]

Faced with a war situation, financial disaster, and increasing persecution (the orphanage's buildings were confiscated by the Nazis, forcing the children and orphanage workers to crowd into the already cramped mission building in Lodz), the workers and members of the Hebrew Christian fellowship at Lodz voted unanimously that Rosenberg return to America and plead Bethel's plight there.[122] He did as requested and left for America. Going first to Holland, he somehow obtained a permanent visa to this country and made arrangements for his wife to follow. But events intervened before Mrs. Rosenberg was able to leave and it would be seven years before the couple was again united. Trapped in Poland, she was to witness first hand Nazi atrocities and conveyed them to her husband as best she could under the thumb of Nazi censorship.[123]

Arriving in America on March 19, 1940, Rosenberg set about raising funds to send back to his occupied homeland. He pleaded with Christians to be generous as a way to show the compassion of Christ to the persecuted Jews of Poland, for this was "a time of trouble, the most disastrous they have yet experienced in their sad, eventful history. A tide of virulent, ruthless, relentless persecution is now sweeping over Central and Eastern Europe. Rarely has the sun looked down upon such a pitiful spectacle of human sorrow and despair."[124]

Rosenberg faced a number of obstacles in trying to raise money for his mission in far-off, Nazi dominated Poland. First, he was coming late on the American scene asking for relief, relief for a specific, not overly well known mission. Second, the American Neutrality Act made it difficult to send money to "belligerent" countries. He had to secure a special license from the Treasury Department as well the State Department. After the United States entered the war, sending funds became even more difficult if not impossible. (He was able to get some money into Poland by first forwarding it to either Fred Settler of the American European Fellowship, who was located in Switzerland, or Berger Pernow of the Swedish Israel Mission.) Third, inflation in Poland ate deeply into the value of the money that did get through—the dollar had only 12 cents purchasing power in Lodz by late 1940.[125] Nevertheless, Rosenberg was able to get at least food packages to his wife until early 1944.

Year by year financial records are missing but some information is available. In 1940, income was $12,000 ($148,800) of which $8,100 ($100,400) was sent to the Lodz mission. In addition, $150 ($1,900) was sent directly to Mrs. Rosenberg.[126] At the conclusion of 1944, the next available financial report, income was $38,400 ($384,000). It was divided up as follows: $10,000 ($100,000) was set aside for salary reimbursement for mission workers or their surviving family members, ("Because of the war," Rosenberg noted, "the Treasury Department would not let these monies to be sent"); $7,000 ($70,000) was set aside for the rehabilitation of mission properties after Poland was liberated—sadly, though, the communists of

Poland never let Bethel continue; $5,000 ($50,000) was set aside for the orphanage and $1,000 ($10,000) for immediate relief.[127]

What is found in the archives of the American European Bethel Mission (the present name for the old Bethel Mission of Eastern Europe) are photo copies of letters pleading with the Treasury Department to grant licenses so that money might be sent to the Polish ghettos, copies of the granted licenses, and copies of money orders and receipts. Cut off from personal contact with his wife and children and other relatives and friends, there is a poignancy and desperation to these documents for most of the recipients died at the hands of the Nazis. One such document is an application for permission to send $1,030 ($12,700) to 12 individuals who either worked with the orphans at Starochowice or in the mission/soup kitchen at Litzmanstadt. All but one, Rosenberg's wife, were killed by the Nazis.[128] Included also in the archives is a letter from the Red Cross of Portugal, dated June 1943, notifying Rosenberg that the orphanage "is in terrible distress—suffering great need of medicine, food and clothing" and that he needed "to come to their aid immediately."[129] It is doubtful Rosenberg needed to be reminded of his duty in this regard, but it must have been like a knife thrust into his lonely and anxious heart.

It is impossible, then, to determine how much money the Bethel Mission of Eastern Europe received from the historic fundamentalists, but the fact that the mission's income went from $12,000 ($148,800) in 1940 to $38,400 ($384,000) in 1944—a three-fold increase—shows a generous, even sacrificial group of donors, particularly when one considers how many mission agencies were competing for historic fundamentalists' dollars. Perhaps a fair estimate might be in the neighborhood of $100,000 ($1,125,000) for those five years. Roughly 60-65% went into relief funds or restoration funds, and as much as was legally possible and could be delivered was sent overseas.

However, despite his best and singularly devoted efforts, the Nazis executed a beastly retribution upon Bethel. As Rosenberg lamented at the war's conclusion:

> We have suffered heavy losses, humanly speaking, in precious lives. Our group of workers, missionaries and believers, in Lodz, in the ghetto of Litzmanstadt, including boys and girls of our orphanage, were wiped out with the exception of one brother. The experience of Mrs. Rosenberg in the orphanage at Starochowice, were no less appalling. We lost many of our dear orphans, who fell victim to the inhuman atrocities of the Nazis.[130]

In fact, over 200 Bethel orphans were slaughtered by the Nazis, as were all their caretakers. Others, the older orphans, were forced into labor gangs to dig trenches on the front lines or work in the mines. Few of them survived. Leon Rosenberg personally lost his brother and his brother's wife, his wife's brother and his wife and their three children, his daughter Helen and her husband, Samuel Oster. The story of his daughter's arrest is especially heart wrenching. One of the orphans— age 14—after being taken away by the Nazis escaped and made his way back to Helen Oster. She did only what her heart would allow her to do; she tried to hide him. Somehow the Gestapo tracked the youth to her place. There, in her presence, they killed him and then took her away to a concentration camp from which she never emerged (her husband had already been arrested).[131] Despite his personal losses, Rosenberg's faith was unshaken. "We cannot understand God's ways in his dealings with his people," he wrote, nevertheless, he was convinced that the Holocaust was used by God to bring many Jews to Messiah Jesus through the testimony of Hebrew Christians who shared the sufferings of their brethren in the flesh, even, it seems, unto death.[132]

Giving: The American Board of Missions to the Jews

There was one other organization that was deeply involved in sympathetic relief of Jewry in Europe (as well as combating anti-Semitism in America) and that was the American Board of Missions to the Jews (now the Chosen People Ministries). It, too, was a classic historic fundamentalist mission organization. And like the Hebrew Christian Alliance of America, it spoke out early against anti-Semitism and the Nazi persecution of the Jews in Germany. However, unlike the HCAA and other Jewish missions in America, it did not suffer financially during the Great Depression. In fact, the ABMJ was an enormously successful organization that dwarfed in size and finances all other similar Jewish missions. Between 1933 and 1942 its budget actually increased 3-fold, from $84,500 ($1,014,000) to $254,000 ($2,800,000). Besides an extensive work in New York City, it helped support or operated Jewish missions in half a dozen other cities across the country. Its large General Fund alone averaged about 50% of its annual budget. It also supported a number of European Jewish missionaries and funded an extensive tract and Bible ministry as well as three monthly publications. During the 1930s and 1940s, there was simply nothing comparable to it among American Jewish mission organizations. Early on, also, under the energetic, often times controversial, and very independent leadership of J. Hoffman Cohn, who made numerous trips to Europe to view first hand the increasing crisis of the Jews,[133] ABMJ was giving aid to organizations assisting the Jewish refugees in Europe, providing affidavits for refugees waiting to come to the United States, paying steerage for some, finding work and giving medical assistance through its own dispensary to those that arrived, helping support a small orphanage in France, operating "soup Kitchens" in Vienna and Paris, and carrying the salaries of a number of European Hebrew Christian evangelists.[134]   Once it was closed out of Europe, it, too, sent funds to such organizations as the International Hebrew Christian Alliance and the Swedish Israel Mission.

Harold A. Sevener, in his centennial history of the mission, *A Rabbi's Vision* (1994) wrote: "From 1934 through 1948 the amount of relief sent by the American Board of Missions to the Jews to its foreign branches steadily increased. In 1936 the mission sent just over $14,000 [$176,000].... By 1948 the amount had increased to $127,000 [$1,088,000]...."[135] However, while it is true that funds going overseas did increase from 1934 on, it is not clear from ABMJ's yearly financial statement published in *The Chosen People* exactly how much was pure relief funds and how much was simply ongoing mission expenses. Other expenses, also, such as Cohn's travel expenses to Europe (which became an annual event by the late thirties) were included in the total amount spent abroad. In addition, allocations for overseas' expenses for the coming year were included in the previous year's budget.

Despite this "messiness," the amounts expended overseas were considerable as the 1930s progressed and the argument could be made that by the late 1930s any European expenses could be related to relief of Jewish refugees as these people occupied more and more of the missionaries time and energies. There were two channels by which ABMJ's funds helped the refugees; its Poor Fund and its Overseas Work fund. The Overseas Work fund distributed $1,447 ($18,400) in 1933 "for Jerusalem, Soviet Russia, Poland, Riga, other European fields."[136] No relief funds as such are included in the 1933 total. The following year, however, the Overseas Work began to reflect ABMJ's concern for the German Jews. Disbursement increased four-fold to $5,550 ($73,800) designated "for Jerusalem, Soviet Russia, Poland, Riga, other European fields, *Special Relief Funds,* expenses of European visit" (italics added).[137] In 1935 $6,350 ($82,100) was distributed through the Overseas Work "for Jerusalem, Soviet Russia, Poland, Riga, other European fields, Special Relief Fund, expenses of [the] Palestine Trip."[138]

The year 1936 saw another large increase in the Overseas Work to $14,200 ($178,900) designated for "Jerusalem, Soviet Russia, Poland, Riga, other European Fields, Special Relief Fund." Also listed under the General Fund of that year was $15,000 ($189,000) allocated for "1937 Overseas Expenses and German Refugee Disbursement."[139] In 1937 the Overseas Work was allocated $26,770 for "Jerusalem, Soviet Russia, Warsaw, Germany, Paris, other European fields, Special Relief Funds, including appropriations for 1938 distribution."[140] As appropriation for the following year always seemed to have been $15,000, the actual amount distributed in 1937 was $11,770 ($147,000). This conclusion is reinforced by the 1938 Overseas Work distribution. Divided into two sections, one section was for work in "Jerusalem, Soviet Russia, Warsaw, Germany, Paris, other European fields, Special Relief Funds" and totaled $16,350 ($196,200). The other section was an "allocation for 1939 Overseas Relief Work and Colonization" and totaled $15,000 ($180,000).[141] Also not mentioned in either the 1937, 1938, and 1939 Overseas Work fund were the extensive European trips Cohn made in each of those years. As the expense of these trips are mentioned nowhere else in the year-end financial statement, they probably came out of the Overseas Work monies. (The colonization mentioned above was a scheme involving a number of Jewish mission agencies to buy land in Ecuador and settle 100 Jewish refugee families on it. Once there, they would become farmers. Only about ten families were settled before the plan collapsed into a pile of impracticality.)

However, also appearing for the first time in the 1937 financial summary was a Resettlement Fund which was identified as "expenses in resettling German Jewish refugees." The amount disbursed through this fund in 1937 was $2,030 ($25,375).[142] In 1938, $1,328 ($16,000) was allocated to this fund.[143]

In 1939 the Overseas Work fund received $34,800 ($426,300) for "Jerusalem, Soviet Russia, Belgium, Poland, Germany, France, other European fields, Special Relief Funds, including appropriations for 1940 distribution." Again, presuming the last mentioned was $15,000 ($217,000), the actual amount distributed for 1939 would be $19,800 ($235,350). The Resettlement Fund showed an almost five-fold increase to $6,000 ($73,500) to cover "expenses in resettling German Jewish refugees"—usually to South America.[144] In 1940, the Resettlement Fund vanished leaving only the Overseas Work fund. That fund showed an allocation of $41,000 for "Jerusalem, Soviet Russia, Belgium, Poland, Germany, France, other European fields, Special Relief funds, including appropriation for 1941 distribution."[145] Assuming that the 1941 appropriation was still $15,000 ($187,000), the actual amount distributed would be $26,000 ($325,000). Additionally, the General Fund listed $2,500 ($31,250) used to establish and renovate a house to be called the Menucha Home for Refugees and $11,000 ($137,500) to renovate Hebron House which was to become a fellowship center for Jewish Christians.[146] Both of these projects reflect the growing presence of German Jewish and Jewish Christian refugees in New York City.

The 1941 Overseas Work fund reflected the reality of Europe at war. The name of the fund was changed to Overseas Work and Refugee Relief and $27,600 ($339,500) was allocated to it for "Jerusalem, Belgium, Poland France, other European fields, special relief funds."[147] (No appropriations for the coming year were included.) Nineteen forty-one was the peak year for the distribution of relief funds in Europe. The following year, with Europe securely under Hitler's boot heel, the refugee stream choked off, and the final solution under way, the ABMJ allocated $22,800 ($253,000) for its Overseas Work and Refugee Relief fund for "Jerusalem, France, South America, other European fields, special relief fund."[148] Also put aside in the General Fund was approximately $20,000 ($222,000) for post war reconstruction in Europe. A like amount, $20,000 ($210,000) was set aside the following year for the same purpose. And in 1943, with the United States now embroiled in total war, and overseas funds under government scrutiny and regulation, the Overseas Work and Refugee Relief fund dipped to $14,100 ($148,000) distributed to "Jerusalem, France, South America, and other European fields, special relief funds."[149]

As noted above, in addition to the relief money going overseas, the ABMJ operated a relief fund at home for the poor. Although in the early thirties the fund was used to help the unemployed and destitute, it is apparent that after Hitler's takeover of Austria and Czechoslovakia, and certainly after *Kristallnacht*, the poor fund reflected increased aid to the almost penniless Jewish and Jewish Christian refugees flowing into New York City from Europe. Thus in 1934 the fund totaled $1,800 ($24,000), by 1937 it had risen to $2,600 ($32,700), by 1940 to $3,700 ($46,200), and by 1943, $4,400 ($46,200).[150] Considering the fact that by 1943 the American economy was up and humming, the best explanation for the increases in the Poor Fund was the assistance being extended to the newly arrived European Jewish refugees.

If we only consider monies sent overseas from 1936 through 1942, the ABMJ disbursed through its Overseas Work fund, $139,000 ($1,675,000). Even if we deducted 30% of this amount for expenses not directly related to the relief ministry (such as Cohn's numerous trips to Europe), it would not be out of line to suggest approximately $98,000 ($1,172,000) went toward relief ministries. Add to this the $9,350 ($114,400) disbursed through the Resettlement Fund and the money spent on the Menucha Home for Refugees ($2,500 [$31,250]), and the total rises to $109,850 ($1,317,650). If we also presume that 75% of the Poor Fund between 1939-1942 went to assist Jewish Refugees—$10,725 ($129,000)—then it would not be a distortion to estimate that between 1936 and 1942, seven very crucial years, the ABMJ allocated approximately $120,500 ($1, 447,000) for Jewish and Jewish Christian relief—all of it coming voluntarily from individuals and local churches that would be designated as fundamentalist.

A Generous People Serving the Jewish Refugees

When one considers the above review of the monetary giving of the historic fundamentalists (which, as mentioned, is far from exhaustive), to assist Europe's Jewish and Jewish Christian refugees, and taking into consideration all other responsibilities they carried, Carpenter's remark that "there was some refugee relief as well" seems almost churlish, the raising of a disdaining eyebrow at the widow's penny. People who sell an heirloom ring, or donate their paper-route earnings, or forsake a vacation and give the money to help the suffering, or pick raspberries in the hot sun so they might help strangers with the money they earn, should not be treated with disdain. Historic fundamentalism was a movement with both faults and virtues open to public scrutiny and, oh my, how it has been scrutinized—with a vengeance so to speak—especially its faults! Historic fundamentalists were a people who acknowledged they were sinners who had been redeemed by the blood of Jesus Christ. They were, then, as Luther noted, "sinners yet not sinners." Some were more faithful than others, some more quarrelsome than others, some more legalistic than others, some more perceptive than others, some more involved in the world's turmoil than others, some more generous than others, but on a whole, bearing their faults as they did, they tried to live out their faith which included helping those in need. Being unable to see into their hearts or their wallets, I can only report what I have uncovered in their surviving records. Compared to the amounts raised by Jewish organizations such as the Joint Distribution Committee, or the FCC's American Christian Committee for Christian Refugees or the Quaker's American Friends Service Committee (both of whom, interestingly, received funds from Jewish organizations) their giving seems small.[151] However, neither did they receive millions in government refugee funds as did these other groups. All things considered, then, the historic fundamentalists were a caring and generous people, and a great many even sacrificial in their giving. However no relief was truly relief, as far as the historic fundamentalists were concerned, without the eternal relief provided by the good news of redemption in Jesus Christ—to the Jew first and also to the Gentile.

Serving the Jews: Believing in and Supporting Eretz Israel

There is one other way by which the historic fundamentalists assisted the Jews, and that was in their support of Jewish migration to Palestine and the establishment of the nation of Israel. Generations of Sunday School children had been taught that some day God intended for the Jews to return to Palestine and reestablish Israel as a nation. And then it happened just as they were taught it would. Hardly an issue of a historic fundamentalists journal was published between 1933 and 1948 that did not have some reference to Jewish emigration to Palestine, or once there, what they were doing.[152] They followed political events in Palestine and about Palestine with a "religious" fervor. The pre-war Arab resistance,[153] the 1939 British White Paper restricting Jewish emigration just as the Nazi persecutions were increasing,[154] the fascist influence and assistance to the Mufti of Jerusalem and other anti-Jewish Arab leaders,[155] schemes to partition Palestine,[156] British and Arab resistance to allowing the surviving European Jews to emigrate to Palestine and the Jewish response,[157] where the American public, Congress and Presidents Roosevelt and Truman stood on the same issue,[158] and, of course, the birth of Israel and its victory over the Arabs,[159] all were given ample coverage in their journals. And always, always they were on the side of the returning Jews. Other than the Zionists themselves, eretz Israel had no better friend. A poem by Max I. Reich captured this Zionist longing, a longing the historic fundamentalists apparently understood and sympathized with:

Heart-Longing for Eretz Israel

Land of our sires, remembered still
Where the Shekinah dwelt
For centuries our home-sick hearts
Thy mystic spell have felt.

Eating the bread of tears we dream
Still of thine azure skies
Thy lily-covered hills appear
Before our hungry eyes.

Lost fatherland! thy love of thee,
Thy olives and thy vines,
Thy fig trees and thy pomegranates,
Its tendrils round us twines.

Have we not kept thy harvest feasts
At the appointed time?
And celebrated vintage joys—
Midst ghetto gloom and grime?

We visualize thy beauteous stars—
Night's anodyne for pain—
We know, midst changes, they, unchanged,
Still shine o'er Mamre's plain.

Of Abram's seed the symbols they,
Thy seed preserved to prove
The ancient promises made good,
Thy covenant of love.

Thy homeless children seek at last
The shelter of thy breast;
Where else but where their fathers dwelt,
Can Zion's sons find rest?[160]

Granted, they saw the return of the Jews to Palestine as the fulfillment of prophecy and a sign that the Lord's return was near. However, they also supported the Holocaust generated thesis that the Jews, after all they had suffered, and in light of the realistic admission that anti-Semitism was not going to disappear, deserved a country they could call their own. By this time (post war 1940s), Palestine was the only acceptable geographic location for the vast majority of surviving Jews in Europe, and in America the choice of both Zionist and non-Zionist Jews, the majority of the American Public, with the exception, of course, of some liberal Protestants and the Catholic hierarchy which followed the Papal line in this regard.[161]

A Critic Answered

Mark Noll, in his, *The Scandal of the Evangelical Mind* (1994), indicts all historic fundamentalists for their support of the Jews return to Palestine solely on the basis of prophetic Scripture:

> A few evangelists, inspired by dispensationalism's focus on the role of the Jews in the latter days, were easy prey for conspiratorial anti-Semites. Many times more were enthusiastic proponents of the Zionist movement. In both cases, however, the stance toward the Jews arose from prophetic interpretation much more than from contemporary analysis or more general theological reflection on nations, international justice, or the recent history of the Middle East. These illustrations come from self-conscious fundamentalists in the North, but they are representative of the most visible political commentary of any sort from evangelicals during the 1930s.[162]

We have, in past chapters, dealt with some of what Noll lays out against the historic fundamentalists. For instance, his claim that dispensationalism's "focus on the role of the Jews in the latter days" primed some evangelicals to become "easy prey for conspiratorial anti-Semitism," is a charge often made, almost to the point of becoming a yawn inducing cliché, but never, as far as I can discern, rationalized. There is nothing inherent in dispensationalism *per se* that lends itself to "conspiratorial anti-Semitism." In fact, one thing the historic fundamentalists stressed was that if one were a true premillennial dispensationalist he or she could not be anti-Semitic. Perhaps, then, the source of one's anti-Semitism, even if a dispensationalist, might be found in other than the dispensationalism's "focus on the Jews."

It has also been shown that the "Northern" historic fundamentalists had quite a bit to say about political issues in the 1930s, so it is incumbent on Noll to explain just what he means when he claims that the historic fundamentalists support of the Jews was "representative of the most visible political commentary of *any sort* from evangelicals during the 1930s" (italics added). Evidently he has a definition that would exclude a great many people and a great deal of what they said.

However, it is his criticism of the reason why the premillennial dispensationalists supported Israel—prophetic interpretation—that needs a response. He considers this a weak reed to lean on when developing a "stance toward the Jews," rather than "from contemporary analysis or more general theological reflection on nations, international justice, or the recent history of the Middle East." As Noll gives no explanation on how I am to understand and apply these concepts or why or how these will help me develop a better, or more proper "stance toward the Jews" than does prophetic Scripture interpreted in a dispensational context (and he by-passes the Holocaust altogether), the reader is left clutching ephemeral intellectual constructs rather than having to face concrete historical realities.

It is true that the historic fundamentalists were adamant in their belief that God intended to bring the Jews (still his chosen people) back to their biblical homeland— British White Paper or no British White Paper, Arab opposition or Arab favor, Zionism or no Zionism, United Nations support or lack of the same. It did not matter. What God had ordained for Israel would come to pass. Whether one agrees that God brought the Jews back to Palestine or not, the historic fundamentalists proved right—the Jews did return and established the nation of Israel. It should not be necessary to remind one and all (but I will anyway) that the historic fundamentalists did not create, or contribute, or approve of (Dwight Wilson not withstanding) the virulent anti-Semitic pogroms of Russia and Eastern Europe at the turn of the twentieth century. They did not create Zionism though they approved of it. They did not bring about the Balfour Declaration though they rejoiced in it (and perhaps some British officials may have been influenced by premillennial dispensationalism's view on Israel's return). They did not bring Hitler to power or establish the Nazi regime, or give birth to its horrible anti-Semitism (again, Dwight Wilson not withstanding).[163] They did not promote or cause the Holocaust and despised those involved with it, considering them to be demonically inspired. They had no control over Jewish emigration to Palestine in the 1930s though they were happy to see it occur. They had no power to stop the implementation of the British 1939 White Paper, or the implementation of the Nazi "final solution." They did not control or even have influence over British, American, Arab, or United Nations policy toward the post-war Jewish refugees, or the refugee's "illegal" attempts to get into Palestine, or the fate of the Jews already in Palestine or the establishment and recognition of the state of Israel. (It is possible that Truman was influenced by Biblical prophecy, and, of course, the historic fundamentalists made known their support of Israel to both him and Congress.) Nor did they have any means to restrain Arab hatred of the Jews or help the Israelis survive the seemingly deadly Arab onslaught of May 15, 1948, which aimed to mimic Hitler's "final solution" in Palestine.

However, the new state of Israel did survive and even emerged victorious. David once more defeated Goliath. Against all odds, scenarios, historical probabilities and national oppositions, the Jewish State of Israel came into existence. God, it could be argued, vindicated the historic fundamentalists' prophetic interpretation, much to the discomfort of all who mocked them. (And even evangelicals who do not agree with the premillennial dispensationalists, but who do believe God oversees history, raising nations up and putting them down, and who causes even the wrath of men to praise Him, must admit it evidently was in God's purpose that a Jewish state should come into existence in 1948 and continue to exist until the present.

Whether it signals the approach of the end times and Jesus' second coming, well, one will just have to wait and see—hopefully on the right side.)

Contemporary analysis, general theological reflections on nations (whatever this means regarding the establishment of Israel in 1948), international justice, and recent history of the Middle East, all have to be understood and interpreted in light of the Holocaust and the "recent" history of anti-Semitism in Europe. British leaders and many in America's State and Defense Departments were openly pro-Arab because of the Arab world's oil reserves (and perhaps some "closet" anti-Semitism of their own). The Muslim Arabs, one with the German fascists in their hatred of the Jews and opposed to any partition whatsoever, were not just opposed to the Jews having a state in Palestine because it would displace fellow Arabs, but also for religious reasons—which included *their* interpretation of the Old Testament relationship between Abraham, Isaac, and Ishmael, and which encouraged anti-Jewish hatreds. The same holds true for Catholics, Orthodox, and many Protestants who believed that the Jews had been set aside permanently by God when they crucified Jesus Christ. The Church was now the true Israel of God. This, too, led to severe anti-Semitism throughout history.

In other words, many others beside the historic fundamentalists were (and are) influenced in their "stance toward the Jews" by their own religious and/or biblical interpretations, not by "general theological reflection on nations." Perhaps this is true even for Noll himself. Even Zionism, a secular organization, based its zeal for Palestine on the Old Testament history of Israel. Nor can we say that those who favored the Arabs, and maybe harbored some anti-Semitism of their own, were moved by principles of international justice. One is inclined to see their actions based more on national interests pure and simple. (And in Britain's case, a considerable amount of resentment toward Jewish terrorists who had singled out British leaders in Palestine.) Some American Protestants opposed the formation of a Jewish state because they were involved with Arab Christians who also opposed Israel and did not want to jeopardize that relationship.[164] Richard Niebuhr favored a Jewish state, believing the Jews needed one to survive. At the same time, he admitted, "There was no perfectly just solution for the conflict of rights between the Arabs and the Jews in Palestine." But he also pointed out that "the Arabs have a vast hinterland in the Middle East, and the fact that the Jews have nowhere to go, establishes the relative justice of their claims and of their cause.... Arab sovereignty over a portion of the debated territory must undoubtedly be sacrificed for the sake of establishing a world [Jewish] homeland."[165]

Nahum Levison, one of two vice presidents for the International Hebrew Christian Alliance, also took a position similar to Niebuhr's (before Niebuhr). Levison had been raised in Palestine, been on friendly terms with his Arab neighbors, and had not favored Palestine as the Jewish homeland because "it meant the replacement of four Arabs by every Jew who came into the country.... I felt that the Jewish wrong ought not to be righted at the expense of the Arabs."[166]   However, the Holocaust had caused him to change his mind. "I cannot see," he wrote, "how any self-respecting Jew can want to remain in any of the countries that have shown themselves so utterly cruel and ruthless towards his flesh and blood, nor can I see many who have been fortunate enough to escape...wanting to go back to the countries that have treated them so inhumanly."[167] The only answer, then, was a homeland in Palestine, despite the fact that it would displace many Arabs. Levison argued as follows:

> We have for nearly two thousand years given mankind in every corner of our dispersion the benefit of our brawn, brain, and blood, and now we ask for a very small portion of the land of our fathers. I still love and sympathize with the Arabs of Palestine, but they have such a large portion of the Middle East—can they not give us a little bit for the resting in peace of our weary bodies and souls? I believe in their generosity; we are of the same family; they have never failed in hospitality and large heartedness. I have said nothing about the Scriptural aspect of the matter, for I am painfully aware that that argument no longer calls forth any response. I have become a national Zionist because it is the only answer from God to the Jewish problem, and it is the least that the world can do for the remnant of Israel.[168]

The Anglo-American Committee of Inquiry seems to have agreed with Niebuhr and Levison as it concluded in April 1946 that the British 1939 White Paper be abrogated and 100,000 Jewish refugees be allowed to immediately emigrate to Palestine.[169] The United Nations also agreed, for it voted in late 1947 to partition Palestine (and in the process perhaps coming as close to international justice as possible in a fallen world). For the Arabs, of course, the U. N. decision was not only rejected but was a signal to begin preparing for a bit of "Judenrein" themselves.

Considering all the various motives that moved individuals and nations to oppose or support a Jewish state in Palestine, one which would accept the tens of thousands of European Jewish refugees, it seems somewhat specious to single out the historic fundamentalists because they based their ultimate support for Israel on their understanding of prophetic Scripture. After all, even Noll admits that history has a spiritual dimension that cannot be ignored if we are to properly understand the meaning of it all.[170] Others opposed Israel on similar grounds, and still others opposed on far less noble suppositions. It may sound academic and wise to speak of basing one's decisions regarding Israel on "contemporary analysis or more general theological reflection on nations, international justice, or the recent history of the Middle East," but there are two problems with this reasoning. First, it would subject Israel to the conclusions of the "expert" and one is moved to conclude that it is doubtful Israel would ever have been given birth in such a court. Even contemplating such a possibility is depressing for nothing is to be more feared than the tyranny of the "expert."[171] But more important, at heart, these academic considerations played little or no part in the cauldron of international passions, national self-interest, religious convictions, desires for a safe refuge, and personal ambitions that were given birth by the aftermath of the Holocaust and the remaining Jews' plea for compensation in the form of a homeland. It seems Noll would place a burden on the historic fundamentalists no one else is asked to carry.

A Closing Word

All things considered it seems unfair of Carpenter to imply the historic fundamentalists should have done more, or were capable of doing more, or were unwilling to do more. He offers no evidence that they ignored possibilities of further action. (And the same could be said concerning the criticisms of Weber and Noll, that is, they lack the necessary ingredient of fairness.) In fact, considering the nature of the movement and its voluntarily shouldering of worldwide obligations, the historic fundamentalists showed much concern and love toward the suffering Jews (as they did for others in other parts of the world), and rejoiced in the creation of Israel. Admittedly, they saw it as a sign that the second coming could not be far off. However, it does not mean they were not glad that the Jews now had a place they could call their own. Yet to claim, as Carpenter does, that "for most fundamentalists, 'the time of Jacob's trouble' was more a portent of things to come rather than an evil to be resisted," is to callously equate a prophetic forecast with the historic fundamentalist's reaction toward the actual anti-Semitism they encountered in the 1930s and 1940s. Such a comparison seems biased and unnecessarily thoughtless. The same seems true of his following comment that "sympathy mingled with suspicion in fundamentalists' perception of the Jews, but in the end both were offered with a measure of detachment."[172] The evidence just does not support his less than convincing conclusion.

NOTES

1. Joel A. Carpenter, *Revive Us Again: The Reawakening of American Fundamentalism* (New York: Oxford University Press, 1997), 99, 100.
2. When Roosevelt established the National War Fund in December 1942 to assist various refugee agencies with enormous expenditures of tax dollars, not a penny of it found its way into the treasuries of the historic fundamentalists' refugee organizations. (See Ham Genizi, *American Apathy: The Plight of Christian Refugees from Nazism* [Jerusalem, Israel: Bar Ilan University Press, 1983] 111-134.)
3. Timothy Weber, "How Evangelicals Became Israel's Best Friend," *Christianity Today*, October 5, 1998, 44.
4. Reich's poem appeared in the Winter 1941 issue of the *Hebrew Christian Alliance*

Quarterly, 9.

5.   Weber, 43, 44.

6.   "Jewish Pangs," *Moody Monthly*, July 1940, 592.

7.   Birger Pernow, "Comfort them that are in Trouble," *The Hebrew Christian*, Spring 1950, 10. Also see, Mitchell A. Glaser, "A Survey of Missions to the Jews in Continental Europe 1900-1950" (Ph. D. diss., Fuller Theological Seminary, 1998), 300-308.

8.   Ibid.

9.   See, "Letter from a Missionary," *The Bethel Witness*, January-March 1941, 10 and "Editorial: Echoes of Blessed Service," *The Bethel Witness*, October-December, 1941, 3.

10. "A Window on the World," *Revelation*, February 1939, 55.

11. "Jews in China Calling for Christ," *Hebrew Christian Alliance Quarterly*, Fall 1939, 14.

12. Bartlett L. Hess, "Are the Jews Turning to Christ?" *The Sunday School Times*, May 3, 1941, 357. Also see "Awakening among the Jews," *The Sunday School Times*, June 3, 1939, front page.

13. Ibid, 356, 357. This seems to have been especially true when the speaker was talking about the persecutions in Europe, or the speaker was a Hebrew Christian who had spent time in a Nazi concentration camp. Also see, "Jewish Notes," *The Jewish Era*, September 1940, 95; "Taking Refuge With Us," *The Prophetic Word*, February 1942, 17-19; "Changing Jewish Estimates of Jesus," *The Jewish Era*, January 1942, 11, and Frederick A. Aston, "The Challenge of Current Trends in Jewish Thought, Part II" *Jewish Missionary Magazine*, October 1938, 130-133.

14. Harvey L. Phelps, *God's Deliverance from Nazi Hands* (Brooklyn: European Christian Mission, 1943), 55, 56.

15. Tannhauser's poem appeared in the January 1940 issue of *The Hebrew Christian*, 170. Louis Bauman quoted two stanzas of the poem in an article that appeared in the March 1934 issue of *The King's Business* ("The Great Red Dragon and the Woman's Child—1934", 93).

16. "A Call to Prayer for the Jewish People," *The Sunday School Times*, July 30, 1938, 541.

17. Pernow, 10. Pernow described how the Jewish converts in Vienna were taught to pray for their enemies. " 'To love one's enemy in an evangelical sense,' " their pastor/teacher Ivarsson instructed them, " 'is to offer earnest prayer for his or her salvation.' " "This explanation solved the whole question [of mistreatment by the Nazis]," Pernow wrote. "The most moving experience from our Vienna congregation at that period was to listen to their prayers for Hitler and his gangsters."

18. "Prayer for Israel," *Moody Monthly*, January 1939, 243.

19. See, for instance, *The Jewish Era*, of October 1939, 114 wherein the Chicago Hebrew Mission announced October 7, 1933 as a day "of prayer for the persecuted Jews in Germany" and that they would turn to Messiah Jesus; "Sunday, May 20, 1934: A Call to All Christian People to United Prayer for the Jews," *Jewish Missionary Magazine*, May-June 1934, 82-84; "A Call to Conference and Prayer," *The Jewish Era*, October 1934, inside front cover; Jacob Gartenhaus, "Israel Needs Prayer," *Hebrew Christian Alliance Quarterly*, Fall 1938, 14. Also at meetings such as the

annual Palestine Week at Moody Memorial Church and the annual Conference of the American Hebrew Christian Alliance there would be intercessory prayer for the persecuted Jews.

20. "An Appeal for a day of Prayer in Behalf of Israel," *The Sunday School Times*, March 12, 1938, 206.

21. Ibid.

22. Ibid, 206, 207. The original signers were Keith L. Brooks, H. A. Ironside, Louis S. Bauman, and Louis T. Talbot.

23. Ibid, 207. The president of the Philadelphia Fundamentalists was Merrill T. MacPherson and the vice-presidents were Charles G. Trumbull and Schuyler English.

24. "Day of Prayer for Jews," *Moody Monthly*, March 1938, 370.

25. "An Appeal for a Day of Prayer in Behalf of Israel," 206, 207.

26. See Haim Genizi, *American Apathy: The Plight of Christian Refugees from Nazism* (Jerusalem, Israel: Bar-Ilan University Press, 1983), 18-20. William Rubenstein, in his *The Myth of Rescue*, points out "*fully 72 percent* of German Jewry escaped from Nazi Germany before emigration became impossible, including *83 percent of German Jewish children and youth.*" (See pages 16-20.)

27. " 'Palestine True Index of Entire Program of World Reconstruction,' " *The Jewish Era*, April 1944, 43-45. Also see the articles listed in note 154 below.

28. "A Call to Prayer for the Jewish People," *The Sunday School Times*, July 30, 1938, 541. Those signing the appeal were Barnhouse, Bauman, Ironside, Talbot, Brooks, Albert Johnson, pastor of the Hinson Memorial Baptist Church in Portland, Oregon, Briton Ross, vice president of the American Prophetic League, Norman B. Harrison, author and Bible evangelist, T. Marshal Morsey, editor of the *Harvest Messenger*, J. Oliver Buswell, president of Wheaton College, Allen MacRae, president of Faith Seminary, Bernard B. Sutcliffe, president of Multnomah School of the Bible, Bob Jones, president of Bob Jones College, (surprisingly) Conrad Hoffman, secretary (or director) of the International Committee on the Christian Approach to the Jews, and the Seattle Christian Business Men's Committee, N. A. Jepson, chairman. Also see, "October 2 for Intercession," *Prophecy Monthly*, October 1938, 30, (Brooks confessed the Jewish problems "were beyond human solutions"), "Pray for Israel," *Moody Monthly*, January 1939, 243. Will Houghton, the editor, declared that he was "deeply in sympathy" with such a prayer appeal, and hoped "the day will find many Christians on their face before God on behalf of God's ancient people."

29. Ibid.

30. Ibid. The July 1940 Prophecy Conference that assembled at Moody Bible Institute issued a Statement and Call summarizing its conclusions. Seventy leading prophetic teachers had been invited by Will Houghton and 50 were able to attend. No public meetings were held. Interestingly, the Statement and Call was not released to the press until mid-October. Article six of the Statement and Call reads as follows:

> As Christians we must stand unalterably opposed to all forms of racial hatred, including hatred of God's ancient people Israel, believing these things to be contrary to the mind of Christ. We compassionately urge the Jews to turn to Jesus Christ, their Savior and their Messiah, of whom Moses in the law and the prophets did write. We join with the rabbis in urging tolerance and consideration, and at the same time plead that they and all Jews manifest the same consideration

toward Jews who become Christians.

31. "A Day of Prayer for Israel on December 1," *The Sunday School Times*, November 4, 1939, 790. The signers were Ironside, Trumbull, Talbot, Max I. Reich, Coulson Shepherd, Houghton, Charles Fuller, Barnhouse, L. Sale-Harrison, and George T. B. Davis. Also see, "A Day of Prayer for Israel," *The Jewish Era*, December 1939, 162; "A Day of Prayer for Israel," *Jewish Missionary Magazine*, December 1939, 1; and "Praying and Working," *Jewish Missionary Magazine*, December 1939, 170.

32. Ibid.

33. Weber, 44.

34. "Special Prayer for the Jews," *The Sunday School Times*, February 13, 1943, 125.

35. "A Call For World-Wide Prayer for Israel," *The Jewish Era*, March 1943, inside the front cover. In January 1943, the National Jewish Mission, an affiliate of the European Christian Missions, published "An Urgent Call," in the *Prophetic Word* calling on believers to pray "for a minute or more a day to deliver Jews from extermination by Hitler: let every lover of Israel make this resolve now." Convinced that "prayer is the only certain means of deliverance for the Jews," the mission feared that if Hitler was not stopped millions of Jews would be murdered within another year. "Pray we must that God will rescue the Jews in the countries which Hitler rules," the mission implored.

36. Fundamentalists were not against appeals for refugee aid from the Federal Council of Churches. See, "Our Brethren in Germany," *Moody Institute Monthly*, March 1935, 314; "Surely We Will Not Fail These," *Prophecy Monthly*, January 1937, 24-26, and "Christian Cash Offered Jews," *The Jewish Era*, February 1939, 19. Of course, they would usually get a flood of protesting letters.

37. "Report of the Eighteenth Annual Conference," *Hebrew Christian Alliance Quarterly*, July-September 1932, 14, 25.

38. "Resignation of Paid General Secretary," *Hebrew Christian Alliance Quarterly*, January 1934, 32.

39. "Financial Report," *Hebrew Christian Alliance Quarterly*, January 1934, 40. Two thousand dollars was a considerable sum in 1933. Today's equivalent would be close to $30,000.

40. See the following from the *Hebrew Christian Alliance Quarterly*: "Financial Report of Hebrew Christian Alliance of America April 29, 1932 to May 10, 1932," July-September 1932, 40, "Financial Statement of Hebrew Christian Alliance from June 1st, 1933 to June 1st, 1934," July 1934, no page number, and "Notes by the Hon. General Secretary" and "Debts Wiped Out," Fall 1937, 11.

41. See the following from *The Jewish Era*: "Praise the Lord," April 1933, 55-57, "Gleanings Near and Far," April 1934, 53, "Treasurer's Report for the Year 1933," April 1934, 59, and "Hitherto Hath the Lord Helped Us," February 1939, inside front cover. The old Chicago Hebrew Mission is now the American Messianic Fellowship. Wes Tabor, president of AMF, and his staff were most cooperative in helping in my research. AMF made copies of the *Jewish Era* from 1933-1948 and mailed them to me. I greatly appreciated their assistance.

42. "Finances," *The Jewish Era*, April 1936, 42. As late as the last six months of 1939, missionaries were still not receiving anywhere near full salary ("Earnest Prayer Request," *The Jewish Era*, January 1940, 10.) For an indication of the type of relief

work Mildmay Mission was involved in among the German Jewis, in part financed by American funds, see, "Jewish Notes: Mildmay Mission Helps German Jews," *Jewish Missionary Magazine*, November-December 1936, 183, 184.

43.   The figures listed are taken from the annual financial reports published in the *Jewish Missionary Magazine*. Although most mission organizations began to recover during World War II, some, such as the American European Fellowship never recovered from the financial shock of the Great Depression. During the mid-1920s its income was approximately $25,000 per year. When the Depression came its income fell by 50% and stayed at that level right through the war and beyond.

44.   Every month, *The Jewish Era* listed non-monetary contributions to the Chicago Hebrew Mission. For example, contributions for April 1934 included large quantities of canned food, bags of flour and sugar, lard, honey, men's, women's, and children's clothes, shoes, socks, underwear, etc. In Baltimore, Aaron J. Kligerman's Neighborhood House did the same. It also had an agreement with the General Baking Company which enabled the mission to distribute hundreds of loaves of unsold bread free ("Relief Work," *The Hebrew Messenger*, December 1933, 12). Also see from the *Hebrew Christian Alliance Quarterly* the following articles: "The Plight of the Hebrew Christian," January-March 1932, 3, "Notes and Comments by the General Secretary," April-June 1932, 8, "An Appreciation and an Appeal," April-June 1932, 5, "Our Appeal," June 1933, 7, "Notes by the Hon. General Secretary," Summer 1935, 7. Also see "Cold Weather Incidents," *The Jewish Era*, April 1936, 46, 47, and "Our Experience In a Jewish Mission," *Prophecy Monthly*, May 1936, 34, 35.

45.   See, "Our Missionary to Argentina," *Hebrew Christian Alliance Quarterly*, January 1934, 28. Also, "Another Objective," *The Jewish Era*, December 1936, 131 and "Milwaukee and the Prospective Branch Mission," *The Jewish Era*, October 1937, 114.

46.   F. A. Aston, "Consolidation of Hebrew-Christian Forces," *Hebrew Christian Alliance Quarterly*, Fall 1935, 7, 8. Aston noted that many Jewish Christians simply did not want to be known as Jews, while others did not want to join because they believed it was putting back up the wall the New Testament had taken down. Aston also noted that many did not want to join because of the lack of harmony within its ranks and between the various Jewish missionary agencies.

47.   "An Appreciation and an Appeal," 5. However, there were numerous Faith missions competing for scarce funds during the 1930s. At the end of the decade *The Sunday School Times* listed 120 mission agencies that had its approval. But it admitted its list was not exhaustive. (See, "Suggestions for Your Christmas Giving," December 7, 1940.)

48.   See the following articles from the *Hebrew Christian Alliance Quarterly*: "Editorials: the Plight of Jews in Germany," June 1933, 3, "From W. Bell Dawson, M. A.," January 1934, 5, "Editorial Notes: No Let-Up for Judah," 2, and "Victims of Anti-Semitism In and Out of Germany," 3, July 1934.

49.   "Hebrew Christians in Germany are Suffering," *Hebrew Christian Alliance Quarterly*, January 1934, 8. Also see, "The Persecution of Hebrew Christians in Germany," *The Hebrew Messenger*," September 1933, 6.

50.   "Financial Report...May 10, 1932 to June 1, 1933," July-September, 1933, 40. Dollar

amounts in parenthesis reflect approximate dollar equivalents in 2001, rounded off. It is interesting that in the financial year April 27, 1931 to May 10, 1932, the relief fund was given $524 ($5,700) and $480 ($5,300) distributed. Probably most of this was for home relief as an International Fund received $400 ($4,400) and that amount was forwarded to the International Hebrew Christian Alliance in London. The next year the International Fund disappeared from the financial report. Perhaps one of the problems was that the American Alliance had too many special funds that made it difficult for money to be reallocated.

51. "Financial Report...June 1, 1933 to June 1, 1934," *Hebrew Christian Alliance Quarterly*, July-September 1934, inside back cover.

52. "Financial Report...June 1, 1934 to June 1, 1935," *Hebrew Christian Alliance Quarterly*, Summer 1935, inside back cover.

53. "Report of the Hon. General Secretary," *Hebrew Christian Alliance Quarterly*, Spring 1939, 21.

54. See the following articles from the *Hebrew Christian Alliance Quarterly*: "Notes By the Hon. General Secretary: Delegates from Great Britain," Spring 1939, 17; "International Delegation Coming," Summer 1939, 17, and "How Can We Help in America," Summer 1939, 28, 29.

55. See the following articles from the *Hebrew Christian Alliance Quarterly*: "Editorial Notes: Victims of Anti-Semitism In and Out of Germany," July 1934, 3, 4; "These German Refugees," Winter 1936, 10, 11; "German Relief Work," Fall 1937, 1, 2; "Help German Refugees," Winter 1937, 16; "Sorrow and Despair," Spring 1938, 13, 14, and "We Must Help," Spring 1938, 14.

56. "Financial Report...June 1, 1935 to June 1, 1936," *The Hebrew Christian Alliance Quarterly*, Summer 1936, inside back cover.

57. See the following articles from the *Hebrew Christian Alliance Quarterly*: "Reception for Refugees," Winter 1938, 17, and "Hebrew Christian Refugees," Summer 1938, 13, 14. (Actually, the Winter edition of the *Quarterly*, although designated 1939 or 1940 etc. really covered the last quarter of the previous year. Thus Winter 1939 really covered the period October-December 1938). Also see, "Minutes of the 24th Annual Conference of the H. C. A.," Summer 1939, 30.

58. "Financial Statement...May 23, 1938 to April 20, 1939," *Hebrew Christian Alliance Quarterly*, Summer 1939, 31.

59. "Financial Statement...from April 20th, 1939 to May 25th, 1940," *Hebrew Christian Alliance Quarterly*, Summer 1940, 32. Also see from the same quarterly, "A Message from Shanghai Hebrew Mission to the Alliance," Spring 1940, 19, 20.

60. See the following articles from the *Hebrew Christian Alliance Quarterly*: "Pray for Interned Hebrew Christians," Winter 1941, 17; "The General Secretary's Report," Summer 1941, 23, 24; "Interned Hebrew Christians," Winter 1941, 15, 16, and "The Release of Refugees," Winter 1942, 16.

61. "Financial Report...May 25, 1940 to May 31, 1941," 32. In addition, $67 ($825) was contributed to the Bethel Mission of Eastern Europe, and $56 ($700) to the Shanghai mission.

62. "Financial Report...June 1, 1941 to July 25, 1942," *Hebrew Christian Alliance Quarterly*, Fall 1942, 30.

63. "The Annual Address of the President of the H. C. A. Given at New York, June 10,

1941," *Hebrew Christian Alliance Quarterly*, Summer 1941, 1.

64. See the Contributors list for April 1935, 43f; July 1935, 92f, October 1935, 146f, and January 1936, 193f of *The Hebrew Christian*, quarterly journal of the International Hebrew Christian Alliance.

65. See the Contributors list for April 1936, 46f, July 1936, 107f, October 1936, 150f, and January 1937, 194f of *The Hebrew Christian*.

66. See the Contributors list for April 1937, 40f, July 1937, 85f, October 1937, 130f, and January 1938, 172f of *The Hebrew Christian*.

67. "The International Hebrew Christian Alliance Receipts and Payment Accounts and Summary of Balances—30th September 1937, *The Hebrew Christian*, January 1938, npn.

68. Jacob Peltz, "News and Notes: for Refugee Children," *The Hebrew Christian*, January 1938, 138.

69. Peltz, "News and Notes: America," *The Hebrew Christian*, January 1939, 148. Peltz went on to almost bitterly note that "the Jews in America have done nobly in contributing more than [$25,000,000] for the relief of their suffering brethren, but the Christian churches in America have thus far been unmoved by the appalling suffering of a million Christians in Germany with Jewish blood in their veins, known as non-Aryans, who are the victims of the Nazi terror in common with the Jews" (148).

70. Peltz, "News and Notes: Awakening American Conscience," *The Hebrew Christian*, January 1939, 148.

71. In the "News and Notes" section of the April 1939 issue of *The Hebrew Christian*, Peltz acknowledged receiving $1,000 ($12,400) from the newly organized FOIRRC: "He (Paul Berman) tells us that the 'Sunday School Times' and 'Moody Monthly' have been generous in giving publicity to the appeal…especially grateful are we to the anonymous 'Sunday School Times' reader for designating five hundred dollars for Jewish relief." The July 1939 *Quarterly* noted that the amount contributed from the FOIRRC now exceeded $4,500 ($55,000). (Harcourt Samuel, "America and the Refugee," *The Hebrew Christian*, July 1939, 68.)

72. See the Contributors list for April 1938, 39f, July 1938, 85f, October 1938, 127f, and January 1939, 177f of *The Hebrew Christian*.

73. See the Contributors list for April 1939, 38f, July 1939, 93f, October 1939, 128f, and January 1940, 171f of *The Hebrew Christian*. Also, "The IMJA: A Short History; An Interview with the Late Rev. Harcourt Samuel, O. B. E. 1986," *Messianic Jewish Life*, July-September, 1999, 26. See note #71 above for Peltz's and Samuel's comments on funds received from the FOIRRC in 1939.

74. Harcourt Samuel, "News and Notes: The General Secretary," *The Hebrew Christian*, January 1940, 139, 140.

75. Ibid, 140.

76. Ibid. As late as 1944 problems over fundraising were drawing attention. The Fall 1944 issue of the *Hebrew Christian Alliance Quarterly* carried (yet again) a "special notice" mentioning that complaints had been received over the similarity between the names of the organizations, and that donors needed to be careful to get the name correct when sending a gift, ("Special Notice, Please," the *Hebrew Christian Alliance Quarterly*, Fall 1944, 17.)

77. Samuel, "News and Notes: The American Alliance," *The Hebrew Christian*, October 1940, 79, 80.
78. Out of the funds raised by Peltz came his expenses and advertising budget. However, he claimed these were minimal compared to other organizations. If the giving to the FOIRRC is any indication, roughly 90% of the total given was from American sources.
79. Samuel, "News and Notes: In the Field," *The Hebrew Christian*, April 1940, 6. Because of publishing schedules and mailing difficulties, it can be surmised that the check was probably received in early March.
80. Samuel, "News and Notes: Overseas," *The Hebrew Christian*, January 1941, 111. Exactly how much money went from Peltz's Chicago office to other countries besides England is not discernable. And like many other organizations, the IHCA sent money to the Swedish Israel Mission, which continued to operate in German occupied Europe long after other mission organizations were forced out or closed down. The money had to have been sent from Peltz's office though.
81. Peltz, "News from America," *The Hebrew Christian*, October 1940, 96. Also see *The Hebrew Christian*, July 1940, 63. Every immigrant, in addition to his visa permitting him or her to migrate to America, also needed an affidavit from an American family guaranteeing that the immigrant would not go on public welfare.
82. See the Contributors list for April 1940, 38f, July 1940, 69f, October 1940, 102f, January 1941, 139f, and February 1941, 22f of *The Hebrew Christian*.
83. See "The International Hebrew Christian Alliance Receipts and Payments Accounts for Year Ended 30th September 1941," *The Hebrew Christian*, January 1942, npn. The total on these two funds is $4,245. However, the contribution list for the three-month period March through May showed almost $3,900 contributed by Americans. Of the 281 contributions listed, the greater majority of them are $10 and under with most of these only $1 or $2 gifts. Only nine exceeded $100 or more with the largest being a gift of $300 and the total amount of these nine gifts being $1,433. It is obvious, then, that the IHCA was not listing all the gifts being received from America in dollar amounts in its annual report or even on its contributors list.
84. See "The International Hebrew Christian Alliance Receipts and Payments Accounts for Year Ended 30th September 1942," *The Hebrew Christian*, January 1943, npn.
85. See "The International Hebrew Christian Alliance Receipts and Payments Accounts for Year Ended 30th September, 1943," *The Hebrew Christian*, January 1944, 75f.
86. "Minutes of the Seventh International Conference of the International Hebrew Christian Alliance," *The Hebrew Christian*, October 1947, 68.
87. Ibid, 67.
88. I am exceedingly grateful to the Friends of Israel ministry for its unstinting hospitality when I visited its New Jersey headquarters. Not only was I given a room on the compound, but every pesky question I could think to ask was answered and I was given unrestricted access to its archives.
89. Joseph Taylor Britan, "An Appeal for Persecuted Israel," *The Sunday School Times*, December 3, 1938, inside front cover.
90. Within weeks the appeal was also printed in *Moody Monthly* and *The King's Business*, although *The Sunday School times* remained the primary publication used by the FOIRRC.

91. Britan, inside front cover.
92. Ibid, 895.
93. Ibid.
94. Ibid, 896.
95. "A Letter of Thanks," *The Sunday School Times*, February 11, 1939, 106.
96. "Will You Continue to Help the Jews?" *The Sunday School Times*, June 24, 1939, 438.
97. "Relieving the Sufferings of the Jews," *The Sunday School Times*, February 22, 1941,152.
98. Ibid.
99. "Minutes of the Meeting of the Executive Committee of the Directors, 28 April, 1940."
100. "Relieving the Sufferings of the Jews," 152, and "The Minutes of the Meeting of the Executive Committee of the Directors, 28 April, 1941."
101. "Minutes of the Meeting of the Executive Committee of the Directors, 31 October, 1942" and the "Minutes of the Meeting of the Directors, 6 January, 1943." There was some overlap in the financial reports of 1941 and 1942 as well as an absence of the break down of financial giving for the last quarter of 1941. This makes it difficult to determine exactly how much was given in 1940 and how much was given in 1941.
102. "Minutes of the Meeting of the Friends of Israel Refugee and Relief Committee, January 6, 1942." Again, the figures of 1942 are somewhat misleading. In an attempt to rescue John Rottenberg from the Nazi clutches in Holland (he was a renown Jewish Christian leader and scholar who translated the New Testament into Yiddish), Paul Berman raised over $14,000 to "bribe" Rottenberg out of Holland. However before the rescue could be consummated, Rottenberg was arrested and sent to a concentration camp from which he never returned. The $14,000+ had to be returned to the donors. All of it or almost all of it evidently passed through the FOIRRC. Thus on "Receipts" is listed $7,075 as a return of money sent out for refugee aid. If this amount is deducted from the total receipts, the balance is only $28,275. On the "Expenditures" side is an item listed as return of relief funds, $8,100. If this amount is deducted than expenditures really only come to $19,000 of which $14,000 was actually spent on refugee relief. (For a detailed and touching account of John Rottenberg and the attempt to rescue him, see Berman, "The Reverend John Rottenberg—The Jewish Missionary Martyr," *Israel My Glory*, September 1945, 6-9.)
103. "Minutes of the Annual Meeting of the Friends of Israel Missionary and Relief Society, May 19, 1943," and "Minutes of the Annual Meeting of the Friends of Israel Missionary and Relief Society, February 1944."
104. "A Glimpse Into the Future," *Israel My Glory*, December 1942, 5, 6.
105. The New York Jewish Evangelization Society derived "a substantial part of its income from friends in the British Empire, but through wartime regulations this source of support" had "been cut off." ("An Urgent Appeal," *Jewish Missionary Magazine*, October 1941, 1.)
106. "Financial Report of the New York Jewish Evangelization Society...for the Year Ended December 31, 1939," *Jewish Missionary Magazine*, March 1940, 48.

107. "Financial Report of the New York Jewish Evangelization Society...for the Year Ended December 31, 1940," *Jewish Missionary Magazine*, February 1941, 32.

108. "Financial Report of the New York Jewish Evangelization Society...for the Year Ended December 31, 1941," *Jewish Missionary Magazine*, March 1942, 48.

109. "Financial Report of the New York Jewish Evangelization Society...for the Year Ended December 31, 1942," *Jewish Missionary Magazine*, February 1943, 32.

110. "Financial Report of the New York Jewish Evangelization Society...for the Year Ended December 31, 1943," *Jewish Missionary Magazine*, April 1944, 64.

111. "Financial Report of the New York Jewish Evangelization Society...for the Year Ended December 31, 1944," *Jewish Missionary Magazine*, May 1945, 80.

112. See, "Notes by the Director: Our Refugee Work," *Jewish Missionary Magazine*, March 1942, 40, and "Relief for Refugees in Poland," *The Sunday School Times*, February 28, 1942, 164 (8).

113. "Report from Sweden," *Israel My Glory*, September 1944, 11. On the other hand, there are stories of the unshakable faith of Hebrew Christians that bring to mind the real and vibrant words of the old hymn, "Faith is the Victory that Overcomes the World." Such is the story of a young man named George, a Jewish convert at the SIM mission in Vienna in 1939. He wanted to become a missionary to his people and God granted that request in a way George never anticipated. He was arrested and shipped off to Riga where he joined 10,000 other Jews 'all bound for execution.'" (This story, too, comes from the pen of Berger Pernow, so I will let him finish the narrative):

> "As soon as the situation was clear to him [George] he began to go from one barrack to another reading from his New Testament and singing his hymns. But as death by starvation was too slow for the Nazis, gas chambers and crematoria were erected, and every morning in the dawn some hundred Jews were chosen for death. Then George put himself in the front of the procession, singing his most loved hymn by Neumark. But at the barbed wire fence he had to stop, because he had not yet been selected for death. There he stood singing his hymn again and again as loud as he could until the gas chamber door was closed behind the very last Jew. So he went on day after day, but he was spared to the very last batch. Then he was allowed to enter the gas chamber singing,
>
>> If thou but suffer God to guide thee
>> And hope in Him in all your ways,
>> He'll give thee strength, whatever betide thee,
>> And bear thee through the evil days;
>> Who trusts in God's unchanging love
>> Builds on rock that naught can move
>> Only be still, and wait His leisure
>> In cheerful hope, with heart content
>> To take whatever Thy Father's pleasure
>> And all-discerning love have sent;
>> Nor doubt our inmost wants are known
>> To Him who chose us for His own.
>
> Thus he had accompanied all those Jews in song in their death march. Only one was found alive on the liberation the following morning, and he brought the

greetings from George, a young hero of Christ." "Comfort them that are in Trouble," *The Hebrew Christian*, Spring 1950, 12, 13.

114. "News and Comments," *The Bethel Witness*, April-June, 1938, 6.

115. "Feeding the Lambs in Poland," *Moody Institute Monthly*, January 1936, 258.

116. "Minutes of the 23rd Annual Conference," *Hebrew Christian Alliance Quarterly*, Fall 1937, 25.

117. Vera Kuschnir, *Only One Life: A Story of Missionary Resilience* (Broken Arrow, OK: Slavic Christian Publishing, 1996,) 268ff. Vera Kurchnir is the granddaughter of Leon Rosenberg, founder of the mission. The mission is now known as the American European Bethel Mission and Kurschnir is its director. She, too, welcomed me to her small mission, answered my numerous questions, and gave me unlimited access to the mission's archives. For this courtesy, I am most grateful.

118. "Minutes of the 24th Annual Conference," *Hebrew Christian Alliance Quarterly*, Summer 1938, 28.

119. Kuschnir, 268ff and *The Bethel Witness*, April-June 1938, 13.

120. Financial report located in the archives of the American European Bethel Mission, Santa Barbara, CA., Rosenberg File.

121. "Audit Report for 1939," *The Bethel Witness*, January-March 1940, 16, 17.

122. See, "Be My Witness," *The Bethel Witness*, April-June 1940, 5-11.

123. Ibid, 9. Also see, Kuschnir, 274. As all correspondence from the Jewish ghettos was censored, the Rosenberg's always ended their letters with a hidden quote from Scripture. As the Nazis had no idea this was what they were doing, it passed censure. An excellent example of this is the last letter anyone was to receive from Samuel Oster. It was sent to his brother-in-law Sievert in Holland and described the abrupt, cruel, and heartless way the Nazis forced the orphanage to vacate its quarters in Ludz and shipped it off to Starochowice. The letter ended with the sentence, "Our friend David gave us nice word—he is 68 on the twentieth or twenty-first." (Psalm 68:20, 21: "Our God is a God who saves; from the Sovereign Lord comes escape from death. Surely God will crush the heads of his enemies, the hairy crowns of those who go on in their sins." NIV) A copy of the letter is found in the archives of the American European Bethel Mission, Rosenberg file.

124. "Editorial," *The Bethel Witness*, October-December 1940, 1.

125. Ibid. Also "Letter from Helen," *The Bethel Witness*, January-March 1941, 7; "A Wise Arrangement," *The Bethel Witness*, Vol. 11 [1947], No. 1, 6, and also, "Editorial: Nazi Furnace-God's Refining," *The Bethel Witness*," Vol. 9 [1945], No. 3, 7.

126. "Total Cash Receipts and Disbursements, Bethel Mission of Eastern Europe for the Year 1940," *The Bethel Witness*, January-March 1941, inside front cover.

127. Financial report located in the archives of the American European Bethel Fellowship, Santa Barbara, CA, Rosenberg File. After the war concluded Rosenberg went to Poland in 1946 where he dispensed $12,300 ($118,000) in cash and $7,500 ($44,250) in "commodities." (Minutes of the Board Meeting of the Directors of the Bethel Mission of Eastern Europe held in Minneapolis, Minn., March 18, 1946.) Also see, "The Ministries of Bethel Mission in Devastated Europe Countries," *The Bethel Witness*, Vol. 10 [1946], No. 1.

128. There is no date on the application but internal evidence suggests late 1940 or early 1941.

129.   Letter in the archives of the American European Bethel Mission, Rosenberg File.

130.   "Editorial: Appalling Reports," *The Bethel Witness*, Vol. 9 [1945], No. 4, 3.

131.   Ibid. Also Kuschnir, 276, 277, and "The War Barometer," *The Bethel Witness*, Vol. 11 [1947], No. 1, 6, 7. The Nazis seemed to have taken special delight in murdering Jewish orphans. We have previously mentioned how they destroyed the work of Trodis Christofferson in Warsaw. Another Warsaw orphanage founded and run by a Dr. Kortchak, and evidently well known outside of Poland, was also destroyed by the Nazis. When the Nazis came to take the children, Dr, Korchak and his staff refused to be separated from their charges and thus were murdered along side the youngsters they loved. ("The Agony of Israel," *Israel My Glory*, September 1943, 6).

132.   "Editorial: Nazi Furnace-God's Refining," 3.

133.   In 1933, Keith Brooks and Cohn teamed up and from that time on Brooks was an ardent supporter of the ABMJ and defender of Cohn. Brooks joined the ABMJ advisory board and was appointed the honorary treasurer for the Pacific Coast. Articles covering Cohn frequent rips to Europe and his descriptions of the plight of the Jewish and Jewish Christians on that Continent (and ABMJ relief efforts) appeared frequently in *Prophecy Monthly*. See for instance, "Joseph Cohn Goes to Help of Refugees," August 1934, 6, 7; "Mr. Cohn on Another Missionary Tour," July 1937, 26, 27; "Pray That God May Use This Man," July 1938, 41, 42; "If Christ Does Not Soon Come—What?" September 1938, 25-27; "Prayer Needed," August 1939, 30, 31; "We Must Pray as Never Before," October 1939, 27, 28.

134.   See *A Rabbi's Vision: A Century of Proclaiming Messiah* (Charlotte: Chosen People Ministries, Inc., 1994), 181-190, 208-211, and Glaser's unpublished Ph.D. dissertation, *A Survey of Missions to the Jews in Continental Europe 1900-1950* (1998), 264-267, 295-307. Also see, "Refugee Work," February 1939, 43, "Refugee Work," September 1940, 27; "Day of Missionary Heroism," December 1940, 15, 16, and "Jewish Relief," February 1941, 30, all from *Prophecy Monthly*. Also see a full-page ABMJ advertisement ("Pearl Harbor Shuts the Door") in the *Sunday School Times*, February 14, 1942, inside the front cover.

135.   Ibid, 184.

136.   Annual Financial Report, American Board of Missions to the Jews, Inc. [1933].

137.   Ibid, [1934].

138.   Forty-first Annual Financial Report, American Board of Missions to the Jews, Inc. [1935].

139.   Forty-Second Annual Financial Report, American Board of Missions to the Jews, Inc. [1936].

140.   Forty-Second (sic) Annual Financial Report, American Board of Missions to the Jews Inc. [1937]. This should have been the forty-third report but was misnumbered.

141.   Forty-Fourth Annual Financial Report American Board of Missions to the Jews, Inc. [1938].

142.   See the 1937 financial report.

143.   See the 1938 financial report.

144.   Forty-Fifth Annual Financial Report American Board of Missions to the Jews, Inc. [1939].

145.   Forty-Sixth Annual Financial Report American Board of Mission to the Jews, Inc.

[1940].

146. Ibid.

147. Forty-Seventh Annual Financial Report American Board of Missions to the Jews, Inc. [1941].

148. Forty-Eighth Annual Financial Report American Board of Missions to the Jews, Inc. [1942].

149. Forty-Ninth Annual Financial Report American Board of Missions to the Jews, Inc. [1943].

150. See the ABMJ financial statements for those years.

151. For example, the FCC's American Committee for Christian Refugees had an overall budget of $226,214 for 1940. Of this amount only $35,551 was raised from FCC churches (15.7% of the total). The rest came in the form of grants and loans from other organization. The American Federation of Labor donated $30,000, the United Jewish Appeal donated $125,000, and the Jewish Distribution Committee loaned $5,000, to the ACCR. (See Genizi, *American Apathy*, 122-124, 342.) By way of contrast, the Friends of Israel Refugee Relief Committee and the Bethel Mission of Eastern Europe (both direct relief agencies in 1940) had combined budgets of $32,000. In addition, the Hebrew Christian Alliance of America budgeted $2,860 for relief in 1940, the New York Jewish Evangelization Society $900, and the American Board of Missions to the Jews $26,000. The grand total for these five historic fundamentalist faith missions in 1940, then, is $61,760, all given freely by individuals or churches. None of their money came from other organizations or agencies or the government.

152. See "Growing Opposition to the Restoration to Palestine," *The Hebrew Christian Alliance Quarterly*, April-June 1932, 14-19; "Israel's Second Great Exodus—Now Before Our Eyes," *The Sunday School Times*, December 7, 1935, 811, 812; "Notes on Open Letters: Are the Jews Returning?" *The Sunday School Times*, May 18, 1935, 338; "Jews Prepare for Palestine Life," *Moody Institute Monthly*, February 1935, 285, 286; "Prophecy Fulfilled Under Our Own Eyes," *Moody Institute Monthly*, September 1937, 28, 29; "Palestine Haven for Refugees," *Jewish Missionary Magazine*, April 1941, 63; "Hitler's Gift," *Prophecy Monthly*, October 1942, 24; "Does Palestine Belong to the Jews or the Arabs?" *The Jewish Era*, September 1945, 100; "Tomorrow: The Jordan Valley Authority," *Revelation*, February 1945, 60, 61; "Let My People Go," *The Sunday School Times*, March 1940, 275-277, and "Palestine, Russia and Ezekiel," *The King's Business*, November 1947, 8, 9.

153. "From Our Palestine Evangelist," *The Jewish Era*, November 1936, 118; "Who Gained by the Palestine Strike?" *Prophecy Monthly*, November 1936, 18, 19; "Palestine Notes," *The Jewish Era*, October 1938, 121, 122; "News and Notes: Palestine," *The Hebrew Christian*, January 1938, 138, 139; "Palestine," *The Hebrew Christian*, April 1939, 14-16 and "The Munich State of Mind Prevails," *Prophecy Monthly*, May 1939, 9-11.

154. "Jewish Notes: Illegal Entry into Palestine," *Jewish Missionary Magazine*, June 1939, 95, 96; "Can Britain Back Out of the Balfour Plan," *Hebrew Christian Alliance Quarterly*, Fall 1939, 24-26; "Government Papers Can't Block God," *Prophecy Monthly*, August 1939, 18-20; "Appeasing the Arabs," *The Jewish Era*, March 1942, 39; "We Will Not Be Diverted," *Prophecy Monthly*, July 1943, 6, 7; "Book Reviews: The Forgotten Ally," *The Jewish Era*, May 1944, 57, 58, 64, and "The Murder of

Lord Moyne," *Jewish Missionary Magazine*, February 1945, 31.

155. "Lend-lease," *Prophecy Monthly*, January 1946; "Grand Mufti," *Prophecy Monthly*, March 1946, 39; "Hidden Hands in Palestine," *Moody Monthly*, December 1947, 264, 265, 285, 286; "The Near East," *The Hebrew Christian Alliance Quarterly*, Fall 1936, 5-12. Also see Arich Stav's book, *Peace: The Arabian Caricature* (2001) and the October 22, 2001 review of the same in *The Weekly Standard*, ("Semite and Anti-Semite: Hatred of Jews in the Arab World," by Carlo Romano, 37, 38). See also, "Gentiles Only," *HCAQ*, Winter 1941 [October-December 1940], 20.

156. "Arab and Jew," *The Jewish Era*, September 1937, 105; "Jehovah Hath Done Great Things," *Moody Institute Monthly*, December 1937, 178; "The Retreat from Palestine," *Hebrew Christian Alliance Quarterly*, Summer 1938, 2-6; "The Dilemma in Palestine: Is There a Way Out?" *The Hebrew Christian*, July 1938, 69-72; "Is British Mandate Breaking Down?" *Prophecy Monthly*, October 1938, 16, 17; "Jewish Notes," *The Jewish Era*, May 1945, 62; "Silver Condemns Divided Palestine," *Jewish Missionary Magazine*, August 1946, 111, 112; "Palestine," *The Hebrew Christian*, October 1947, 55, and "The Jews in the News: Partition Again," *Salvation*, November 1947, 10.

157. "Political Pressure," *Prophecy Monthly*, July 1944, 40, 41; Victor Buksbazen, "Let My People Go," *Israel My Glory*, March 1946, 6-12, 19; "Ferment in Israel," *United Evangelical Action*, July 15, 1946, 15; "British Perfidy," *Prophecy Monthly*, July 1946, 20; "Editorially Speaking: What About Palestine," *The King's Business*, October 1946, 2; "It's Illegal," *Prophecy Monthly*, October 1946, 38, 39; "We've Twisted the Lion's Tail," *Prophecy Monthly*, February 2, 1947, 16-19; "The Jews in the News: Bevin speaks Up," *Salvation*, April 1947, 16; "Happenings in Israel: Palestine," *Hebrew Christian Alliance Quarterly*, Spring 1947, 24, 25; "Terrorism in Palestine," *The Sunday School Times*, May 31, 1947, 538, 539; "Editorially Speaking: England's Problem," *The King's Business*, November 1947, 4; "Palestine Looms Large," *United Evangelical Action*, February 15, 1948, 3, 4; "A Survey of Religious Life and Thought," *The Sunday School Times*, February 21, 1948, 164, 165. In addition, also see, "The World's Unique Refugee Problem," *Prophecy Monthly*, April 1943, 15-18; "Editorial: Why I have Become a National Zionist," *The Hebrew Christian*, October 1944, 43, 44; "Jewish Notes," *The Jewish Era*, October 1945, 114; "Wandering Jews," *The Sunday School Times*, June 8, 1946, (1) 521; "Illegal Refugee Ship Arrives At Palestine Port," *Jewish Missionary Magazine*, July 1946, 93; "Israel's Travail in Returning to the Land," *The Sunday School Times*, November 16, 1946, 1049, 1050, 1060, 1061; "Jewish D. Ps.," *Prophecy Monthly*, October 1947, 39.

158. "A. F. of L. Resolution Asks Fulfillment of Balfour Pledge," *The Jewish Era*, January 1942, 10; "The Congressional Resolution on Palestine," *The Jewish Era*, April 1944, 45; "Shall We Liberate All But the Jews?" *Prophecy Monthly*, June 1944, 17-19; "Palestine in the News," *The Sunday School Times*, November 18, 1944, (1) 837; "Jewish Notes," *Jewish Missionary Magazine*, November 1944, 157, 158; "Disturbing Factors as to Palestine," *Prophecy Monthly*, August 1945, 5-8; "Editorially Speaking: Thank You Mr. President," *The King's Business*, December 1945, 454; "Observations on the Palestine Situation," *The Jewish Era*, January 1946, 3-5; "Editorials: the Jewish Problem," *Revelation*, February 1946, 54, 55; "Courageous Move," *Prophecy Monthly*, March 1946, 5, 6; "A Window on the

World," *Revelation*, May 1947, 209; "Information on the Palestine situation," *Prophecy Monthly*, May 1947, 13-15; "The Position of the Jew," *Salvation*, November 1947, 6, 7, 12; "Views on the Palestine Outlook," *Prophecy Monthly*, March 1948, 6-8; "The Switch on Palestine," *Hebrew Christian Alliance Quarterly*, Spring 1948, 6; "Bible Predicts Jewish State," *The Jewish Era*, July 1948, 88; "The Bible in the News: Republican Plank," *The King's Business*, September 1948, 5.

159. "Can the Jews Succeed in Palestine," *Moody Monthly*, June 1948, 724, 725, 762; "Jewish State Declaration of Independence," and "Eretz Israel: The Jewish State," *The Jewish Era*, July 1948, 87; "Tomorrow: Israel's Self-Inflicted Travail," *Revelation*, July 1948, 292, 293, 319, 320; "Happenings in Israel," *Hebrew Christian Alliance Quarterly*, Summer 1948, 28-31; "Editorially Speaking: Israel Is A Nation," *The King's Business*, August 1948, 4; "The New Year 5709," *Salvation*, November 1948, 13, 16; "Dr. Yuk's Diary," *The European Harvest Field*, November-December 1948, 11, 12; "The Steady March of Israel's Feet," *Prophecy Monthly*, December 1948, 12-14; "Happenings in Israel," *Hebrew Christian Alliance Quarterly*, Winter 1948, 25-27; "Christian Attitude Toward the New Jewish State," *The Jewish Era*, September 1948, 99, 100; "The World Scene: Progress in Israel," *Prophetic Word*, March 1949, 176-178; "Editorial," *Hebrew Christian Alliance Quarterly*, Summer 1949, 27, 28, and "Israel the New World Wonder," *The European Harvest Field*, May-June, 1950, 1.

160. Reich's poem appeared in the Spring 1937 issue of the *Hebrew Christian Alliance Quarterly*, 1.

161. See Hertzel Fishman's interesting study, *American Protestantism and a Jewish State* (1973), 68, 69, 72ff, 103, 152ff, 178-183. Also see "Pope Pius's 1943 letter against Jewish statehood revealed," *The Jerusalem Post: North American Edition*, July 9, 1999, 6, and "Rifts Over Holy Land Widen," *Los Angeles Times*, Saturday, July 28, 2001, B76. This article shows the continued liberal Protestant's policy of being critical toward Israel.

162. Mark A. Noll, *The Scandal of the Evangelical Mind* (Grand Rapids: William B. Eerdmans Publishing Company, 1994, 166, 167).

163. Why do I stress Dwight Wilson not withstanding? Because Wilson is especially condemnatory toward the historic fundamentalists when it comes to anti-Semitism. In the process of labeling premillennial dispensationalism deterministic, He writes:

> They have expected and condoned anti-Semitic behavior because it was prophesied by Jesus. Their consent (even though given while spewing pro-Zionism out of the other side of their mouths) makes them blameworthy with regard to American as well as Nazi and Soviet anti-Semitism. Neither as a body nor as individuals has their cry against such inhumanity been more than a wimper. (*Armageddon Now*, 217.)

I do not think I have come across a more vicious accusation against the historic fundamentalists. Hostility and dislike leaps from every jot and title. That such unfair accusations made it into print under the imprint of an outstanding evangelical publisher is surprising. That it has not been denounced by other evangelical historians is equally surprising. I have already disproved Wilson's comments about whimpering. The same seems hardly necessary for his accusation that the historic fundamentalists "condoned" and "consented" and are partially to blame for anti-Semitism in America,

Germany and the deceased Soviet Union. Nevertheless, let us consider the flow of Wilson's logic. The historic fundamentalists believed what Jesus said. Well, Jesus said there would be famines. The historic fundamentalists believed him. Terrible famines have marked the twentieth century. Therefore, the historic fundamentalists must have condoned and consented to them even while hypocritically raising money to combat them. They are, then, blame-worthy regarding the famines. Jesus also predicted wars, plagues, and apostasy and the historic fundamentalists believed him regarding these, too. And the twentieth century did not fail them in this regard either. So—see where all this leads? Wilson's reasoning is fallacious at best and slanderous at worst.

164.   Fishman, 94-98.
165.   Ibid, 79, 80, and also 68-70.
166.   N. Levison, "Editorial: Why I Have Become a National Zionist," *The Hebrew Christian*, October 1944, 43.
167.   Ibid.
168.   Ibid, 44.
169.   Fishman, 80.
170.   Noll, 169.
171.   Machen once wrote that the "tyranny of the experts is the most soul-crushing tyranny that could be set up." At the time he was responding to the public discussion advocating euthanasia for the "hopeless invalids" who, as the argument went, were of no use to themselves and society. (Yes, in America in 1936, just as in America today we are once more arguing the same issue—only this time it includes partial birth abortions. The historic fundamentalists opposed such "human" mercies just as evangelicals oppose them today.) In response, Machen angrily wrote: "This is very dangerous business—this business of letting experts determine what people will 'never be missed.' For my part, I do not believe in the infallibility of experts, and I think the tyranny of experts is the worst and most dangerous tyranny that ever was devised" (*The Christian Faith in the Modern World*, 123, 209). Considering what was coming out of the academies in Russia and Germany (and even in America), Machen and his fundamentalist allies were a light in an ever-darkening world.
172.   Carpenter, 100.

CHAPTER NINE

Historic Fundamentalism and Anti-Semitism: Refuting Undeserved Accusations, Reclaiming Sullied Reputations

I have covered in the two previous chapters, to a certain extent, part of the ground that will be explored in this chapter. But reiteration is a good teacher. Certainly (as has been shown) the accusation that the historic fundamentalists were indifferent toward the plight of European Jews has little support in fact. We have also covered some of the anti-Semitic accusations leveled against the historic fundamentalists and shown them to lack substance. However, anti-Semitism did exist in America and it did exist in the historic fundamentalist community, the evidence for which is always exhibit A—Gerald Winrod and his Wichita based Defenders of the Christian Faith. On this basis then, most secular scholars seem axiomatically to hold to an assumption that needs no verification—the historic fundamentalists were anti-Semitic.

Also as noted, some evangelical scholars who have investigated historic fundamentalists/Jewish relations seem to take a certain satisfaction in drawing attention to the accusation that historic fundamentalists, despite their prophetic insistence that the Jews were still God's chosen people—making anti-Semitism a great sin—exhibited just such a tendency. Historian Timothy Weber seems to have led the way in this regard when he wrote in 1979 that "at times premillennialists sounded anti-Semitic" and that "some leaders of that movement acted like representatives of American anti-Semitism."[1] As mentioned in Chapter Seven, this created a heated exchange between Weber and historian David Rausch in the pages of the *Journal of the Evangelical Theological Society*.[2]

Indirectly they continued their disagreement in subsequent publications; Rausch in his, *Arno C. Gaebelein 1861-1945, Irenic Fundamentalists and Scholar* (1983), and Weber in his expanded, 1987 version of *Living in the Shadow of the Second Coming*. While it is apparent Rausch has long since dropped out of the debate, Weber, it seems, has not.[3] In the October 5, 1998 edition of *Christianity Today* he appears more determined than ever to push and prove the rightness of his side of the argument. The article, "How Evangelicals Became Israel's Best Friend," has included within it a section—"The Protocols Conspiracy"—that briefly surveys the response of four historic fundamentalists to *The Protocols of the Elders of Zion* between the two wars, and what their reaction to this document possibly revealed about their anti-Semitic leanings.[4] This section of the *Christianity Today* article is an extremely truncated version of an article by Weber which appeared in the Summer 1992 *Fides et Historia* titled, "Finding Someone to Blame: Fundamentalism and Anti-Semitic Conspiracy Theories in the 1930s." (More on this article shortly.)

Wordsmithing a Dysfunctional Historic Fundamentalist Mindset

In his *Christianity Today* article, Weber charges that during the 1920s and 1930s, "a number of leading dispensational teachers promoted right-wing conspiracy theories and even fell prey to Nazi propaganda."[5] By this latter remark it is evident Weber primarily means the *Protocols* which did indeed become the prime document for "American anti-Semites," supposedly proving the Jews (as a whole) were plotting to destroy Gentile, Western civilization and rule it. While Weber does admit "not all dispensationalists were fooled by the *Protocols*," he gives them little coverage, focusing instead on those whom he believes were fooled—James Gray, Arno Gaebelein, Gerald Winrod, and William Bell Riley.[6] To support his accusation against Gray and Gaebelein, Weber uses words they wrote in the early 1920s. Both Gray and Gaebelein believed the *Protocols* reflected events that were unfolding in their day, offering confirmation for the validity of biblical prophecy interpreted from a dispensational perspective. Weber also includes a quotation from Gaebelein that showed deep antipathy toward "apostate Jews."[7]

To confirm Winrod's guilt, Weber does a one sentence review of Winrod's often expressed opinion which charged "that Jews were in charge of the world's banking system and responsible for World War I, the Great Depression, President...Roosevelt's New Deal, and just about everything else."[8] Likewise Weber does a quick take on William Bell Riley's *The Protocols and Communism* (1934) to exhibit his guilt as a purveyor of anti-Semitism. In his book, Riley charged, according to Weber, "that the same conspiracy that turned Russia communist was at work in Roosevelt's New Deal," and that Jews controlled the economy as well as the immoral movie industry.[9]

However, despite the above analysis which would seem to imply guilt, "Gray, Winrod, Gaebelein, and Riley strenuously denied that they were anti-Semites" but simply interpreting "events in light of biblical prophecy." By this time, however, (Weber writes) the majority of the historic fundamentalists had come to the conclusion this was bad form that put those "using such arguments" on the wrong side. By the time of the Great Depression, "*The Protocols*," Weber points out, "were identified with the peddlers of virulent anti-Semitism," which was, plain and simple, "a horrible sin against God."[10]

It would be difficult, given the way Weber chooses his words, not to conclude that three very highly respected, leading historic fundamentalists (circa 1930s), Gray, Gaebelein, and Riley definitely belong in the same category as Gerald Winrod, whom, by the mid-1930s practically all mainstream historic fundamentalists leaders considered pro-Nazi and anti-Semitic. According to Weber, *The Protocols* deeply divided the historic fundamentalists. Jewish Christians protested that acceptance of the *Protocols* as genuine would bring trouble down upon the head of "all Jews" not just apostate one's. "Others," Weber writes, "concluded that some of their colleagues had been duped by Nazi propaganda." Weber reinforces this conclusion by quoting something Harry Ironside wrote in early 1934 (though Weber does not date the quotation). Ironside "was grieved, Weber asserts," " 'to find that the *Protocols* are being used not only by godless Gentiles, but even by some fundamentalists Christians to stir up suspicion and hatred against the Jewish people as a whole.' "[11] Weber next brings in Keith Brooks as a witness for his position. Brooks, who had once been associated with Winrod but broke with him in late 1933, formed the highly respected American Prophetic League in 1938 to, according to Weber, "put as much distance as possible between dispensationalism and Nazi anti-Semitism."[12] Although this was not the only reason for forming the League, Brooks was responsible for circulating a manifesto in late 1939 condemning anti-Semitism within the historic fundamentalist community.[13] Within weeks, practically ever major leader of historic fundamentalism signed the manifesto. Weber concludes this section of his article by claiming that James Gray "swore off ever using *The Protocols* again" shortly before he died in late 1935 but that Riley and Winrod continued to use them. As for Gaebelein, it is apparent Weber considers him little better than a hypocrite. "Some time after the 'Manifesto' appeared," Weber writes, "Gaebelein tried to get his name added to the list of signers. The fact that he never told his constituency and continued to sell *Conflict of the Ages* until he died in 1945 made the gesture disingenuous."[14]

Writing History to Blame a Fundamentalist

There are, of course, a number of troubling problems with Weber's interpretation of these historic fundamentalists and American anti-Semitism, even taking into consideration the briefness of his survey in *Christianity Today*. Again, the issue is one of how history is narrated, the words chosen, the information included or left out. However, before analyzing Weber's *Christianity Today* article, it would be best to review what he wrote in more depth in his 1992 essay, "Finding Someone to Blame," and include it with the above. My concern is two-fold. First I am personally disturbed with Weber placing James Gray and Arno Gaebelein, two of the most honored historic fundamentalists of the period under question, on a level with Gerald Winrod. Winrod "earned" the anti-Semitic label pinned to him, especially after he visited Germany in the summer of 1935. He returned pro-Nazi and even carried and sold Nazi material. However, even Ribuffo, author of *The Old Christian Right*, (1983) which gives a fairly in depth look at this anomaly within historic fundamentalism, noted that Winrod's brand of anti-Semitism was relatively mild compared to what was being espoused in the 1930s:

> Nevertheless, Winrod's denial of ethnic animosity does show the limits of his anti-Semitism. Unlike Pelley, he never wrote long disquisitions on racial inferiority, never mocked the accents of immigrants, and never proposed stripping Jews of constitutional rights. Furthermore, Winrod's stereotypical portraits of Jews, like his social and economic views, were subordinated to an overriding theological system. On the one hand...Winrod's religion contributed to his belief in *The Protocols*. On the other hand, firm adherence to doctrine softened his anti-Semitism. He admitted that Zionist Elders were fulfilling a "predestined purpose," recalled that Jesus had appeared "in the garb of a Jew," and continued to insist that a "Faithful remnant of Israel" would someday enjoy divine grace.[15]

As for William Bell Riley, I simply am not familiar enough with him and his work to have an opinion. In fact, it is surprisingly noteworthy how little Riley is mentioned for any reason in the mainstream historic fundamentalists magazines during the 1930s. William Vance Trollinger, Jr., in his *God's Empire: William Bell Riley and Midwestern Fundamentalism* (1990), offers a strong case that Riley was anti-Semitic.[16] Weber and Carpenter simply echo Trollinger along these lines. Interestingly, the FBI kept a slim file on Riley but there is no indication that Riley was ever a candidate for indictment as was Winrod.[17]

Also of interest is Yaakiv Ariel's brief overview of Riley in his, *Evangelizing the Chosen People* (2000). Ariel considers Riley's attitude toward Jews much more ambivalent and complicated than one of Riley's principle critics of the day, J. Hoffman Cohn of the American Board of Mission to the Jews, cared to admit or understand. In fact, Ariel implies that Cohn himself is partially to blame for Riley's anti-Jewish attitude. It is obvious there was, on a personal level, bad blood between the two men.[18] Ariel also notes that despite his anti-Jewish (and anti-Cohn) sentiments, Riley remained a true-blue premillennial dispensationalist who understood the Jews to be God's chosen people, destined to return to Israel. "Yet," Ariel admits, "Riley's messianic outlook did not guarantee an admiring view of the Jews. He shared a *common notion* among some fundamentalist thinkers during the period that, since the Jews had not accepted Jesus as their Savior, they were spiritually and morally depraved and thus susceptible to distorted ideologies such as socialism."[19] Still, Ariel seems to go almost out of his way to avoid labeling Riley an out and out anti-Semite as that term is usually understood. Perhaps what is needed is a more nuanced and in depth study of this aspect of Riley's thinking.

This brings me to my second concern—balance, or as I prefer, fairness. I do not think there has been a fair presentation of historic fundamentalist/Jewish relations in America during the 1930s and 1940s done by anyone. It is my conviction that Weber, Wilson, Carpenter, and others have consistently presented a mostly biased, negative, one-sided, and incomplete narrative of this aspect of historic fundamentalism.

A Blame Game Gone Awry

As Winrod and Riley are not central to this book or chapter, I will largely ignore what Weber writes about them in his essay, "Finding Someone to Blame." My concern is with Gray and Gaebelein (and how they related to other historic fundamentalists) during the 1930s. What Weber wrote about these two circa the 1920s in his *Christianity Today* article is true as far as it goes. But that is the problem, he does not go far enough. It would have been fairer to Gray, for example, if Weber had added, after writing that "In 1921, James M. Gray...called *The Protocols* 'a clinching argument for premillennialism and another sign of the possible nearness of the end of the age,' " Gray's follow-up comment that "Anti-Semitism is evil and has no place in our Christian civilization." Weber did add this statement by Gray in his 1992 essay, "Finding Someone to Blame." Why he left it out of his *Christianity Today* article is a puzzle.[20]

In his 1992 *Fides et Historia* article, Weber contends that beginning in 1933 "a number of prominent fundamentalists went public with new charges that Jews were engaged in a *Protocols*-inspired conspiracy to take over the world" prior to the Second Coming. He attributes this interest to the then prevailing world conditions—the Great Depression, the New Deal, the teaching of evolution, the "Red Scare," and other vexing world and national problems. Someone or someones, the fundamentalists believed, had to be behind this anti-Christian, anti-Western civilization attack, and the world-wide Jewish conspiracy as outlined in the *Protocols* became the prime suspect.

Winrod was the first to propose this scenario when he published his *Hidden Hand*. (A work, interestingly, Keith Brooks initially approved and recommended every fundamentalist read.)[21] Winrod's book was followed many months later (October 1933) by Gaebelein's well received, *The Conflict of the Ages*. In this book, Gaebelein traced what he believed was an anti-God, anti-Christian, "humanist conspiracy" through history with special focus on the period beginning with the Enlightenment and French Revolution up to and including the communist revolution in Russia. Gaebelein included a brief section on the *Protocols* and the part it was possibly playing in this plot. "While he could not be sure of its authorship," Weber writes, "he was certain that the document was no 'crude forgery.'" Gaebelein was convinced a large number of apostate Jews were involved in the Russian revolution as well as with the rise of humanism in general, and "amassed extensive evidence" of such involvement to support his charge. However, Weber is careful to point out that Gaebelein did not claim "all Jews were involved in the conspiracy, though 'bad' Jews outnumbered 'good ones.'" According to Weber, Gaebelein "liked Orthodox Jews" but "disdained" apostate Jews (including Reform Jews) who were presently "involved in the *Protocols* conspiracy" and would be aligned with the "Anti-Christ at the end of the age."[22]

Finally, in 1934, Riley came out with his, *The Protocols and Communism*, which charged that the Jews controlled the American economy, had an undue influence within the Roosevelt administration, and that the communists were at work within the New Deal. (As we now know, Riley was right about one thing. Communist were at work within the Roosevelt administration.)

"Few fundamentalists considered such views" particularly extreme according to Weber, noting that *The Conflict of the Ages* received sterling reviews in the pages of many of the leading historic fundamentalist magazines, and indeed it did as we shall see. Weber goes on to draw a connection between those "who used the Protocols" and zealous, anti-communist, "political extremists." However, the worst he tags Gaebelein with is that he "quoted freely from the *National Republic* magazine" which Weber labels "a leading right-wing journal," and that Gaebelein once lent his name to an advisors list for the Paul Revere Society when it was first organized.[23]

Weber offers additional support for his position by asserting "the fundamentalists connection to the political right could be seen in their *confused* reaction to the rise of Hitler" (italics added). The reason for this, Weber believes, was due to Hitler's anti-communism and that he supposedly limited his activities against the Jews to "Jewish criminals" and Jewish communist.[24] Weber fits Gray into this "confused" category because Gray took a wait-and-see attitude toward what was really happening within the German church and to German Jewry. "Accordingly," Weber charges, "he published propaganda pieces from German clergy who credited Hitler with bringing peace and harmony to the nation by cracking down on Social Democrats and Marxists and justified the election of a Nazi Reichsbishop to minister church life." However, Weber also fairly points out that Gray spoke out against "'German Christians'" for expelling Jewish Christians from the churches and banning the use of the Old Testament.[25]

Although the pro-*Protocols* conspiracy fundamentalists expected approval from their fellow fundamentalists, including (and particularly) Jewish Christians, they received instead "a strong rebuke from their own camp." Interestingly, Weber casts a wide-net at this point, writing, "By late 1933, the *Hebrew Christian Alliance Quarterly*...openly criticized the *Moody Bible Institute Monthly*, *The Sunday School Times*, and *Revelation* for promoting the *Protocols*, and other forms of anti-Semitism."[26]

More to the point in Weber's opinion was the attack of a few leading Jewish Christian fundamentalists upon Gaebelein for publishing *The Conflict of the Ages*. Specifically, Weber points to Joseph Hoffman Cohn, head of the American Board of Missions to the Jews. Cohn used the rather vituperative writings of Elias Newman in attacking Gaebelein. In a book review published in *The Chosen People*, Newman sought to refute in detail Gaebelein's implication that possibly some communist, apostate Jews may have had something to do with the Protocols and that they had been numerous in revolutionary Russia, and were still influential in the same circa 1933. (Newman also accused Gaebelein of spreading anti-Semitism.)[27] In addition to Newman's book review, Cohn also published an article by Harry Ironside which Weber believes was in part, at least, aimed at Gaebelein. Weber only quotes one sentence from Ironsides' article. "He was grieved 'to find,'" Weber writes, " 'that the Protocols [were] being used not only by godless Gentiles, but even by some fundamentalist Christians to stir up suspicion and hatred against the Jewish people as a whole.' "[28]

Weber concludes that the historic fundamentalists seriously divided over the genuineness of the *Protocols*. Weber contends that a number of historic fundamentalists rejected the *Protocols* from the beginning "while others who had endorsed their authenticity early on backed away from them because of the mounting criticism by fundamentalists and non-fundamentalists alike." Weber places what he terms a "frustrated James Gray" in this latter category.[29]

Gaebelein took a different tack according to Weber—one of silence. In April 1934, Gaebelein called the attacks on *The Conflict of the Ages* " 'unfair and unjust' " and vowed to never mention the subject [of the *Protocols*] again in the pages of his magazine, *Our Hope*. Evidently he kept that promise, though, as Weber notes, "he continued to worry and write about the threat of communism and its connection to apostate Judaism." Weber's almost open contempt toward Gaebelein comes across in the following sentences:

> When Gaebelein *ostensibly* repudiated the *Protocols* by belatedly adding his name to Brooks' "Manifesto to the Jews," he never informed his own constituency that he had done so . . . Evidently Gaebelein never saw himself as part of the problem. He continued to advertise *Conflict of the Ages* in *Our Hope* and to distribute it through the magazine's office until his death in 1945.[30] (Italics added.)

Weber concludes his survey of the writings of Gaebelein (and Winrod and Riley) by charging that fundamentalists such as these three "were too quick to accept what appeared to be corroborating evidence," that their interpretation of prophetic

Scripture was the right one. Thus, Weber contends, they latched hold of "the idea of an international Jewish conspiracy" because it dovetailed with their pre-conceived conclusions. However, according to Weber:

> It did not work. As many of their fellow dispensationalists eventually recognized, one could not legitimately condemn all forms of anti-Semitism and promote the arguments of anti-Semitism at the same time. The likes of Winrod, Riley, and Gaebelein wanted to have it both ways; but other fundamentalists would not let them. Wrapping themselves in the prophetic pages of Scripture did not absolve them from taking responsibility for what they taught. Using dispensationalism to justify their conspiracy theories did not make them any less anti-Semitic. During the 1930s one had to be terribly naïve to think that one could sound like a Nazi and not be criticized.[31]

There is a proverb that reads, "The first to present his case seems right, till another comes forward and questions him," (Proverbs 18:17, NIV). This has been the case, as has been shown again and again in this book, among those who write about the historic fundamentalists. Much gets left out that ought to be included and when included—amazingly they do not look so terrible after all. Such would be the case, for example, of James Gray. I have no doubt the historic fundamentalists of the 1930s, including the vast majority of Jewish Christian fundamentalists, would have been shocked in disbelief with the way Weber has treated Gray. There is, then, more to the story than Weber (and others) have related.

Again, we need the historical context. As mentioned elsewhere, in 1933 the historic fundamentalists considered Stalinistic communism a greater menace to America than Hitler and his Nazism. Still, they were aware of Hitler's anti-Semitism and were very critical of it and him,[32] but communism was much more on their minds because of the inroads it was making in America and the bloody narrative of Christian slaughter associated with the Soviet Union. And as noted in Chapter Two, the historic fundamentalists were right on target in their suspicions of a Moscow generated conspiracy to subvert America—the right-wing "red-baiters" as they are called, were largely right after all regarding communist penetration of the Roosevelt administration and the academy. Nowhere do the critics of historic fundamentalism acknowledge this. Also, Weber's assertion that "it is easy to identify fundamentalists who used the *Protocols* with political extremists because as fervent anti-communist, they often endorsed and promoted their positions" simply cannot hold up. Keith Brooks, for example, who was anything but friendly to the *Protocols* and Winrod by the end of 1933, was very supportive of Elizabeth Dilling's *The Red Network* in 1935, and noted that she distanced herself [at that time] from anti-Semitism.[33] Practically all the historic fundamentalists, no matter what their position on the *Protocols*, were vigorous anti-communists and believed it was working evil in America and the FCC, which, of course, it was.

The Protocols and the Historic Fundamentalists

Perhaps the best way to deal with the many criticisms and accusations is to evaluate them with the historical sequence and context always in the foreground. We need to begin in 1932 at the annual conference of the Hebrew Christian Alliance of America meeting in Boston, Massachusetts between May 16 and 19. That meeting took serious note of a movement among liberal Jews (ironically known as the "Good Will" movement), in cooperation with the Federal Council of Churches, to "slander" Hebrew Christian Missions and accuse Hebrew Christians of taking bribes to convert to Christianity. This joining of liberal Jews and Christians also denied that the Jews needed Jesus as their Messiah and rejected the idea of evangelizing the Jew. In protest to this liberal Jewish attack, the HCAA passed a resolution and forwarded it to the FCC, "the press and the editors of the leading religious papers."[34] The resolution read as follows:

> Be it therefore resolved that we, the officers, members of the Hebrew Christian Alliance of America and heads of missionary organizations assembled at our eighteenth Annual Conference in the City of Boston, Mass., do hereby earnestly protest and in the interest of religious liberty appeal to the Executive Committee of the Federal Council of Churches of Christ to stop lending its support and approval to a movement aimed at the integrity of Hebrew Christians and the efficacy of the transforming power of Jesus Christ.[35]

Elias Newman, who at this time worked for the HCAA, wrote in his "Report of the Pastor Evangelists," that Jewish Christians must remain "unswervingly loyal" to the Jewish people in their moment of trouble, but he also noted "with feelings" of pain and regret that Hebrew Christians were being subjected to "a wide-spread *conspiracy* to deprecate, malign, insult and misrepresent Jewish believers in Christ" (italics added). Continuing on in a hyperbolic vein, Newman charged that Hebrew Christians were "faced with the greatest campaign in history aiming at the destruction of the real religious liberty of Hebrew Christians and others desirous of making known the Gospel of our Lord and Savior."[36]

Newman went on to deprecate Reformed Judaism, which, he charged, spoke in "vague and impudent terms" about "its future mission on earth, when Christianity shall have become effete." Newman considered this a ridicules goal because Reformed Judaism was, in Newman's words, "utterly apostate from God" and could only offer "cold negations and abstractions" which was cold comfort to one's fellow man.[37]

Newman considered this work of Liberal Jews both a danger to the missionary efforts of Hebrew Christians and a danger "for the Jewish people themselves." Why? Because, Newman wrote, "It is tactics such as rationalistic Judaism is employing in America, which is in a measure responsible for provoking unenlightened Christians to join in the Anti-Semitic agitations."[38]

Jacob Peltz, in his "Notes and Comments by the General Secretary," also weighed in on this subject in even greater detail than Newman. It was "time for us to speak frankly," Peltz declared, "and take our Christian friends into our confidence in these matters even though we run the risk of being called anti-Semites." Peltz then drew attention to a three-part article written by the editor of the Boston *Jewish Advocate* at the conclusion of the HCAA conference. In his article, this editor called Hebrew Christians "renegades," "unprincipled scoundrels," "flotsam human driftwood," and "men without character." The editor concluded by claiming, " 'that he who forsakes Judaism for any other faith is either a hypocrite, a scoundrel, or a person of unbalanced mind.' "[39]

In light of what he considered a dangerous situation, Peltz announced the formation of a nondenominational (Gentile) Advisory Committee of up to fifty consisting of men of strong Christian character and a strong stand on the "fundamentals of our faith." Those named on the committee read in part as a who's who of premillennial dispensationalists. It was to be chaired by the highly revered James Gray. (And, it might be added, he was chosen for this honor by an HCAA fully aware of his position on the *Protocols*.)[40] In choosing Gray, Peltz wrote, "In him Hebrew Christians have found a friend who understands and sympathizes with the peculiar problems and sore trials of the Jewish convert to Christianity. Dr. Gray has also been a sincere and consistent champion...of Jewish evangelism. It was therefore natural for Dr. Gray to accept chairmanship of this important committee."[41]

1933—That Momentous Year

Nineteen thirty-three stands out in the annals of the history of the twentieth century. It truly was a momentous and portentous year. Hitler achieved absolute power in March of that year and began building his Third Reich, persecuting and imprisoning all who stood in his way. This included socialist, communists, and social and religious undesirables, as well as Jews.[42] And Nazi/fascism was beginning to find a welcome among many in America. Stalin was putting the finishing touches to his slaughter by starvation of six million Ukrainians even as his "brand" of communism was doing nicely in America; being lovingly embraced in the academy, masterfully seducing religious liberals in the Federal Council of Churches, and even "moling" its way into the Roosevelt administration. March 1933 was also the month that Roosevelt became President of the United States, launching his alphabetically addicted New Deal and installing his "Brain Trust," all in hopes of alleviating American's fears, hunger, and unemployment.

All three of these governments occupied the interest and concern of the historic fundamentalists. To a certain extent, this concern was reflected in their reaction to the rising anti-Semitism in both Germany and the United States. In 1933, Gerald Winrod began his decade long action of promoting the *Protocols* as genuine evidence of an all-inclusive Jewish plot to take over the Gentile world. However, outside of his circle few leading historic fundamentalists agreed with his extremism, or if they momentarily did (such as Keith Brooks), it was only momentary. As soon as they realized the true anti-Semitic thrust of his ministry and his pro-Nazi disposition, they isolated him like a man spreading bubonic plague.

Outside of Winrod's circle, the historic fundamentalists carried a variety of nuanced opinions regarding the *Protocols*. Most of the Hebrew Christians among them branded the *Protocols* a forgery and insisted there were no Elders of Zion or a Jewish conspiracy to take over Gentile civilization or governments. They were alarmed by what was happening in Germany and the increasingly display of mean-spirited anti-Semitism in America. They thought that the *Protocols* were playing a leading role in this regard. They were also angered at those who generalized that communism equaled Jewry and vise versa. Some also denied apostate, materialistic, communist Jews (or any Jews for that matter) had anything to do with assembling the *Protocols*. It is apparent that this latter charge made them nervous for there was a large number of apostate, free-thinking Jews associated with communism even in America. Hitler and the Nazis gave them a valid excuse for sidetracking this embarrassing problem.

The Gentile fundamentalists, as noted in Chapter Seven, took early notice of Hitler and his anti-Semitism, and this included Gaebelein.[43] A few, like James Gray, expressed uncertainty about the extent of Hitler's anti-Jewish activities—were all Jews being persecuted or only the criminal/communist Jewish element? Nevertheless, Gray, along with the rest of the leadership of historic fundamentalism, condemned anti-Semitism at home and abroad.[44] As for the *Protocols*, there was, interestingly, despite Weber or other historians' words to the contrary, a considerable amount of agreement. None of them circa 1933 (Winrod's group excluded), for example, believed there was a world-wide (inclusive) Jewish conspiracy led by the Elders of Zion aimed at taking over the world. None of them were advocates or sympathetic to any form of anti-Semitic activities. Almost all of them seemed to have agreed that what was outlined in the *Protocols* was indeed unfolding historically before them, especially in the Soviet Union. Most of them seemed to believe that radical/communist, apostate Jews may have had a hand in putting together the *Protocols*. On the whole they also believed that these apostate Jews played an important part in the Bolshevik revolution and were still somewhat influential in the upper echelons of Soviet Russia. They also believed that the same type of Jews were deeply involved in American communism, and that Jews (not necessarily communist but certainly socialists) were influential in the Roosevelt administration. And finally, they believed apostate Jews were involved in the pornographic and movies industries. Obviously such differences between some Jewish Christian fundamentalists and the Gentile fundamentalists created tensions, but on the whole they seemed to have kept them from causing acrimonious divisions.

Whether or not there was any reality to the historic fundamentalists concerns about communism and the part played by apostate Jews in the same is never addressed by Weber, Wilson, or Carpenter. Nor do they offer a definition of anti-Semitism. Too often, it is assumed that we all know what it means and easily recognize an anti-Semite when we see one (i.e., evidently any passing fundamentalists). However, we need just such a definition to guide us in our evaluation of the charges leveled against the historic fundamentalists, such as sounding like the Nazis. Perhaps the one given by Elias Newman, one of Gaebelein's harshest critics, will serve our purpose. It is taken from his, *The Jewish Peril and the Hidden Hand* (December 1933) which was written against Winrod and Palley. In the preface of his book, Newman charged that "it is a crime against humanity, against justice, thus to stir up the hatred of Gentiles against a race chosen of God but now in exile and therefore helpless." The rulers and nations that did this would be accountable to God.[45] He went on to write:

> An anti-Semite, therefore, in our case means an opponent of the Jews ('Judengegner'). It is not a question of whether the Jews, like other men, are sinners, but the Jew himself, from the sole of his foot to the crown of his head, his very existence, is an unpardonable crime. His very virtues are brought up as accusations against him, and the whole literature of the world, from the writings of Cicero, the ravings of Voltaire to the platitudes and paradoxes of Chesterton, are ransacked, and often misquoted, in order to prove that every Jew who has the impudence to live, has been nothing else than an unmitigated rascal, to whom all the woes which have come upon the uncircumcised are to be traced.[46]

Looking at the fundamentalists community, Newman charged that "A still greater responsibility rests upon the shoulders of those while styling themselves as Fundamentalists are helping forward the Anti-Semitic propaganda in this country, either by actual participation in movements against the Jews *or in silent acquiescence.*[47] (Italics added.)

This latter comment—supposed silent acquiescence—was apparently a deep irritant with Hebrew Christians such as Jacob Peltz. Thus Peltz, even as he was announcing his resignation as general secretary of the HCAA in the October (-December) 1933 issue of the *Hebrew Christian Alliance Quarterly*, took to task the editors of *Moody Institute Monthly, Revelation,* and *The Sunday School Times* ("and others") for not informing "the Christian public as to the true nature of the *Protocols.* Why do not these Editors...take up the defense of the Chosen people in these days when the poison of Anti-Semitism is being sown so widely by the enemy."[48] A number of sincere believers, according to Peltz, had asked him if the

Protocols were true, and if not, why had not the editors of these magazines said so. There was, however, one Gentile fundamentalist, Peltz noted, who was "not silent in these days of Israel's agony", and that Gentile was Thomas Chalmers. Chalmers was the founder and director of the New York Jewish Evangelization Society, a life long friend of Israel, and a strong advocate of Jewish evangelism. To prove his argument, Peltz reprinted in the Alliance *Quarterly* an article by Chalmers expressing doubt that the *Protocols* were authentic and that holding the Jewish people as a whole responsible for them was a great crime. Chalmers article had first appeared in the September-October 1933 issue of his own magazine, the *Jewish Missionary Magazine*.[49]

Chalmers condemned the *Protocols* as part of an anti-Semitic program "by the enemies of the Jews and foisted on them as the Jewish secret plan and purpose for world conquest." Any "true, Bible taught Christian," he wrote, should react to "such craftiness" with "a real revulsion of feeling...." It was, he declared, "a crime against humanity, against justice, thus to stir up the hatred of the Gentiles against a race chosen of God but now in exile and therefore helpless because of their sins."[50] He went on to comment that "it is worthy of adding that the subtle mind of Satan is clearly revealed in the forgery of the Protocols and in the work of the Russian Reds." In fact, Chalmers opened his article by noting "that the work of the Russian Revolution was so exact a reproduction of the methods outlined in the Protocols, that attention to them was worldwide and immediate." Chalmers considered this train of events a spur to the prophetic Bible student:

> There was in all their teachings and in the Bolshevist Revolution a prophetic note, which sent the student of the Word back at once to the great prophecies of the Old Testament. There one sees the foreshadowing of world unrest, the rise of democracy, the coming of the Lawless One and finally the supremacy of Israel under the government of the Lord Jesus Christ.[51]

Still, whatever the "connection" between Red Russia and the *Protocols*, Chalmers ultimately saw it as the work of Satan: "Thus we recognize the dark sinister spirit of Evil seeking to forestall God in all his plans of blessing for men. Satan would ruin Israel by turning the hatred of the whole world against the Jews."[52]

What then, was to be the Christians' response to what was happening? He or she should "seek the good of every Israelite and...protest against all injustice to the Jew." No true Christian should be content "while our brother Jews are hounded to death." The Christian must "by prayer and faithful witness...seek the welfare of Israel."[53] Chalmers closed his article, however, on a most interesting note. "If individual Jews or bands of Jews plot against their lawful rulers, let those rulers deal with them along just lines. Let them not condemn a whole people for the crimes of a few."[54]

Chalmers' article, while clearly exonerating the Jews as a people from a *Protocols* revealing conspiracy of world conquest, was not a carte blanc statement that there was no Jewish connection to the *Protocols* or communism. By implication he hints there may be some "bad" Jews involved in the world's troubles. His position in this regard was widespread among the historic fundamentalists, including, apparently, some Hebrew Christians. One of these was Max I. Reich of Moody Bible Institute and one of the founders (and long time president during the 1930s) of the Hebrew Christian Alliance of America. Also writing in the October (-December) 1933 edition of the HCA *Quarterly*, Reich bemoaned the situation in American Jewry:

> The situation in America is serious in all conscience. The second generation of our people who have sought the shelter of these hospitable shores is fast becoming dejudaised (sic) without becoming Christian. And I tremble for the dejudaised Jew. The Jew simply cannot live without the restraints and hold-fasts of religious faith and religious habits. The history of thousands of years is written in his brain, his heart, his nerves, his whole psychology. Without religion the Jew goes down, becomes worse than others, as "the corruption of the best is always the worst corruption." Better far that our people should continue "shut up under the law till faith come"(Gal III.23), than that they should be irreligious altogether.[55]

The synagogue could offer nothing that would "keep its children," Reich continued, so they were "drifting away from the ethical and religious ideals of their fathers, and the Rabbis can do nothing...that will put a brake on their descent into materialism and agnosticism...."[56] Again, Reich was not alone in expressing such concern among his fellow Hebrew Christians.

If Peltz hoped to provoke the editors under consideration into repentance, he was to be disappointed. Instead, he got a rebuking lecture.[57] Nor can it be said that Peltz was even speaking for the Hebrew Christian Alliance for in the very next *Quarterly,* when Morris Zeidman (now acting as general secretary) repeated Peltz's complaint that it was liberal clergy who were protesting the Nazi persecution of the Jews while "the more conservative and evangelical-minded pastors have been seized with a sudden silence," the editor injected a bracketed exception to Zeidman's accusation. "We have in mind," the editor injected, "Dr. Gray, Dr. Chalmers and one or two others who have voiced their indignation against Israel's oppressors."[58] Although one cannot doubt the sincerity of Peltz and Zeidman, their complaints did not square with reality. Barnhouse, for example, as detailed in Chapter Seven, had published a number of articles in *Revelation* in 1933 sympathetically covering the very subject Peltz (and Zeidman) claimed he had not.

Memo to Peltz—Not So!

In January 1934, the editors of *Revelation, Moody Institute Monthly*, and *The Sunday School Times*, after conferring, answered Peltz's accusation. Without actually saying so, they all pointed to their past history of support for the Jews and anti-Semitic denounciations to point out the absurdity of Peltz's accusation. Barnhouse began his editorial response in *Revelation* by noting that he had often been criticized for giving too much space and time "to the subject of prophecy in connection with God's people." But now, it seemed, the tables were turned and Gray, Trumbull, and he were being accused by Jewish Christians of laxity," that is, they were not informing people "as to the true nature of the Protocols."[59] Barnhouse doubted that his two colleagues needed anyone "to defend them against such a *false accusation* (italics added)." And all three, he went on, were reaffirming that they loved "God's people" and would continue to support Jewish evangelism and expound those "prophecies which effect Israel."[60]

Barnhouse reminded his readers that a Yiddish newspaper had taken notice of his interest in the Jews and had called him "their 'noted friend' " "In this case," Barnhouse wrote in a dig at Peltz, "unsaved Jews saw more clearly than some Christian Jews." The heart of the dispute was how one treated the *Protocols*. Barnhouse and the others believed that by not discussing them they were showing kindness to the Jews. He agreed that the *Protocols* was a forgery and that the true author of them would never be known. However, he also agreed with most other historic fundamentalists that "the events of history have paralleled the Protocol policy in a remarkable way."[61]

Barnhouse was just warming up. He went on to claim that "every descent Jew" would agree that there were "some renegade apostates" in their midst ("villainy does not follow nationality"). Barnhouse called such apostate Jews, "Jacob Jews," and that such "could easily be responsible for the Protocols, and it is certain that renegade Jews have done some of the things prophesied therein." Barnhouse's example A in this regard was their involvement in pornography that was flooding the newsstands. However, he went on to stress that "this does not alter the worth of the high thinking, high-minded Jew. For them we have the highest respect and honor." And because he held them in such regard, he felt duty bound to tell them that the time of their greatest "trouble" lay ahead when God was going "to send His Hunters to hunt them" out of the lands where they were hiding and force them back to their land [Palestine]. After this great tribulation they would accept Jesus as their Messiah and be restored "to a place of world-wide...glory."[62]

In the meantime, Barnhouse asserted, no "true man" would hold "a great people" responsible "for the acts of some of its scoundrels." "We have nothing but revulsion," he added, "for the acts of Hitler's government." If anyone thought that he was being inconsistent by saying this after claiming that God was going to send hunters "to feret" the Jews out of their "hiding places and return them to the land," Barnhouse quoted Matthew 18:7 in response: " 'Woe unto the world because of offense! For it must needs be that offenses come; but woe to that man by whom the offense cometh!' "[63]

Gray started his editorial response by also appealing to the magazine's (and thus his own) history of support for the Jews and Jewish evangelism. He also drew attention to the fact that the Institute maintained, at great expense, "a Jewish Missions Course for the free training of Hebrew and Gentile Christians to work among the chosen people in all lands." Gray also pointed out that Solomon Birnbaum and Max Reich, both of whom had written articles in the same issue of the HCA *Quarterly* in which Peltz "blistered" Gray, taught at Moody.[64]

As for the *Protocols*, Gray took the same slant as Barnhouse. "If by their 'nature' were meant their contents, then we question whether it would help the chosen people at this time or allay anti-Semitism if their contents were further spread abroad."[65] Gray agreed with Chalmers that no one knew who wrote the *Protocols* but that they did seem to mirror prophetic Scripture. He also agreed with Chalmers that it was "a crime against humanity" to stir up hatred of the helpless, scattered Jews, and that the leader or nation so guilty would suffer God's judgement.[66]

In agreement with both Barnhouse and Chalmers, Gray believed that unless the Jews accepted " 'Jesus as their Messiah they would suffer more terribly than ever[before]' and…that God would use the nations to bring them to Himself:"

> This also the MONTHLY has said time without number, and we believe that God is thus using Germany today. Mr. Chalmers says, "let Hitler consider," and we echo the words, but we note that Mr. Chalmers admits impliedly that "individual Jews or band of Jews" may be plotting against lawful rulers. Is it unchristian (sic) therefore, to withhold judgment until the truth in that particular appears?[67]

Gray also stressed his agreement with Max Reich—that is, that the irreligious Jew became the worst of the worst, creating thereby a bad social situation. Gray closed his editorial by reiterating a theme he continuously put forward in the *Protocols* controversy: let us put "aside politics national and international," and get on with evangelism—to the Jew first and also the Gentile.[68]

Trumbull's response was the shortest. He began his editorial response by posting a letter from "a Maryland reader" who had clipped out Peltz's critical editorial and sent it to Trumbull with the comment, "You are not antagonistic to God's people, I know." The Maryland reader knew correctly, Trumbull affirmed, because *The Sunday School Times* "has been an outspoken friend of the Jews" over the years and still was. And, Trumball emphasized, the *Times* deplores the tragic persecution of Jews in Russia and Germany, and wherever else it may occur, and calls upon God's people everywhere to befriend Israel."[69]

As to who was responsible for writing the *Protocols*, well, that was "a question,"

Trumbull wrote, "which equally true and devout Christians may honestly differ." All kinds of guesses had been put forward as to where they originated and who penned "this sinister volume," but as Chalmers and Gray had noted, nobody really knew. Nevertheless, Trumbull wanted it clearly understood that,

> the *Moody Monthly* and THE SUNDAY SCHOOL TIMES agree unhesitantly with Mr. Chalmers that "It is a crime against humanity, against justice, thus to stir up the hatred of Gentiles against a race chosen of God but now in exile and therefore helpless because of their sin." The ruler who does this wicked deed must answer for it before the judgment bar of God.[70]

Peltz's somewhat thoughtless attack on the Jewish Christian's best friends not only irritated Barnhouse, Gray, and Trumbull, and many of their readers but evidently placed him at odds with some of his fellow Jewish Christian brethren. For example, in the February 1934 issue of *Revelation*, a two column advertisement was placed by the American Board of Missions to the Jews thanking Donald Barnhouse for calling on Christians to speak kindly to the Jews, and to love them, particularly in this time of "a national campaign of Jew–hate."[71] The advertisement was referring to editorials written in 1933 by Barnhouse.

When James Gray resigned as president of Moody Bible Institute (at age 84), the editor of the HCA *Quarterly*, Aaron Kligerman, wrote an editorial in the October 1934 issue of that journal praising Gray's many achievements and concluded by writing:

> We of the Hebrew Christian Alliance of America are glad to learn that Dr. Gray's resignation as president of the institute will not interfere with his work as editor, teacher and counselor. His great interest in the cause of Jewish evangelization and in Hebrew Christianity will always stand out as a noble example of what a true Christian leader should be. May the Lord continue his usefulness till he come.[72]

As neither Gray, Trumbull, or Barnhouse had retreated from their position on the *Protocols*, it appears that a little damage control was possibly going on.

Interestingly, the young Peltz and the aged Gray sustained—or developed—a friendship through their disagreement. In the August 1935 edition of *Moody Institute Monthly*, Gray published excerpts from a personal letter he received from Peltz, then in London serving as the general secretary of the International Hebrew Christian Alliance. "Our Hebrew Christian brother," Gray begins, "...sent us an enthusiastic report of the Jubilee celebration in that metropolis last June." Gray thought the account "of an eyewitness, a newcomer" in England, "and an American citizen" would interest *Moody's* readers. He then proceeded to give a couple of quotations from the letter of "our brother." Gray concluded his "editorial note" by writing:

His [Peltz] chief interest naturally is in the great Hebrew Christian movement which the International Alliance represents, and which we are happy to say, is broadening in the Hebrew Christian Alliance in our own land. The Twenty-first Annual Convention of the last named was held in Buffalo, N.Y., in June and was an event of inspiration and blessing.[73]

Although it is apparent that Weber and Carpenter made more of Peltz's outburst than the broader context warrants, there were differences, as Barnhouse noted, over the issue of the *Protocols*. The first difference was over whether the *Protocols* reflected a real situation or only anti-Semitic fantasy. Keith Brooks quotes James Gray as saying, " 'If I am being quoted as saying the Protocols is a genuine document, it is an error. I know no more its source than anyone else of whom I ever heard' "[74] Neither Gray nor any other leading historic fundamentalists being discussed in this chapter believed there was an inclusive Jewish plot directed by a secret group of Jewish elders to take over the world. Still, that did not mean the *Protocols* did not reflect a real situation. This is what Gray was speaking about.

The other disagreement was over who actually wrote or assembled the *Protocols*. (It did contain a considerable amount of material plagiarized from earlier supposedly illuminati authors.) Evidently Peltz (and some others) wanted a blanket statement from friendly Gentile fundamentalists such as Barnhouse and Trumbull that no Jew of any strip had anything to do with the compilation of the *Protocols*. Rather they wanted these leaders to say the *Protocols* were the writings of those who hated the Jews and wanted to do them great harm. However, due to the perceived communist tilt of the *Protocols* and the obvious apostate Jewish involvement in communism, both at home and abroad, many Gentile historic fundamentalists were hesitant to offer such an unqualified denial. This difference is reflected in the flurry of articles and editorials dealing with the *Protocols* that began appearing in late 1933 on into 1935.

Joseph Flacks, for example, a highly respected Hebrew Christian Bible teacher, wrote an article that appeared in the January 1934 edition of the *Hebrew Christian Alliance Quarterly*. In his article, Flacks tried systematically to show how the Jews could not be responsible for writing the *Protocols*: the Orthodox Jew was only interested in the coming Messiah and his kingdom centered in Jerusalem; the reform Jew was too much of a capitalists to be associated with the communist aims supposedly contained in the *Protocols*; and the atheist Jew, though like all atheist "a menace to Society and an abomination to the Lord," was not responsible for the *Protocols* because he simple was not interested in Jewish nationalism or Jewish anything for that matter.[75]

Well, then, who was responsible for them? Playing on the stereotypical Jewish nose and accent (his own), Flacks asked, "whose nose and tongue shall we say it is?" Flack was convinced that it was "that of another race and religion"—in essence, it belonged to the pope! Catholicism was the plotter of "the plot of the protocols...."

He supported his position by posing a number of questions:

> Who, or what religious system is it that claims the RIGHT TO RULE THE WORLD? It is NOT the Jewish religion. Who is it that hates the Jew and charges him with having "killed his God?" What system of religion is it that hates the Masonic order as much as the Jews? What system is it that hates England perhaps even more than she hates the Jew or the Masonic order?[76]

The Loquacious and Irrepressible Anti, Anti-Semitic Keith Brooks

Keith Brooks, who became one of the most vocal and most persistent Gentile opponents of the *Protocols* and anti-Semitism, backed up Flacks' suspicion of Catholic authorship. Brooks' believed "the program set forth in the Protocols as that of world Jewry, *is none other than the program of Jesuitism and Illuminism.*" And the illuminati itself was only "a secret [program] of the Jesuits reaching a class of people unreached by them."[77] Still, least his arch-foe (Winrod) use it against him, Brooks closed his article by stressing that there *was* a communist plot and *"there are Jews in it."* Satan's troops, both Jew and Gentile, were coming together and the world was being "prepared for the anti-Christ." Let the Christian take notice.[78]

The above article by Brooks was only one of a series dating back to late 1933. In a major article appearing in the November 1933, *Prophecy Monthly*, Brooks, showed that the *Protocols* stemmed from earlier *illuminati* documents—thus it was a forgery—and were written to create anti-Semitism by blaming the Jews as a race for Bolshevism and world conditions. Nor, Brooks stressed, did he "hesitate to say that *others than Jews* have been involved in this world plot. It is a fact, however," he continued, "well known to authorities, that a large percentage of radical agitators in our country are Jews. The thing is ATHEISTIC. Its originators are *Christ haters.*"[79]

Still, the fact that the *Protocols* had nothing to do with the Jews as a people did not mean a conspiracy did not exist. When one noted what was taking place in Russia, or what the communist party was up to in America, or when the financial situation reflected *Protocols* teachings, one could not say a conspiracy was not in motion. It was wrong to blame the Jews, but "either they [the Protocols] are the results of a most unaccountable human foresight of world events, or they represent a deliberate plan that has been *powerfully backed up from somewhere.*"[80]

The following month, Brooks published a letter from a Hebrew fundamentalist who was deeply offended that—"to our great surprise"—it was now fundamentalists who were "in the lead of stirring the anti-Semitic spirit which does not need stirring at all."[81] Brooks assured his correspondent that there were still "thousands of true Christians who have not fallen" for anti-Semitic propaganda. And he took the opportunity to make his own position "clear." He did not believe the Jews were out to subject the Gentiles, or that the *Protocols* "revealed a plot" on the part of the Jews to "enslave the Gentiles," or that Jews controlled banking in the United States.[82] He did admit there were "plenty of Jewish communists and atheists", but compared to the number of Gentiles guilty of the same offense, "they are but a drop in the bucket."[83]

In January 1934, Brooks published his most thorough and important article to date on the *Protocols*. J. Hoffman Cohn of the ABMJ, with whom Brooks was affiliated, included this article as part of a packet he had assembled for ABMJ supporters refuting and exposing the *Protocols* and those pushing them. It repeats in part some of what has been covered above so I will only briefly summarize a few salient points.

First, Brooks posited his deep concern that "some...sincere and trusted fundamentalist leaders" had been so touting the "Protocols" that they were "contributing, perhaps unwittingly, to the rising tide of hatred against the Jews," and this was having a seriously negative effect on "Jewish evangelism." While Scripture speaks of Jewish suffering, culminating in the " 'time of Jacob's trouble,' " the Christian should have no "part in the persecution of any people."[84]

Next Brooks dealt with the claim of Jewish dominance of Soviet communism. He had seen the percentages that placed it as high as 75 to 80% but he believed such numbers were both outdated and suspect. "A short time ago," he wrote, "a check was made of the officials of the Moscow government and it was found that 18 percent were Jews." And, Brooks added, "these Jewish Bolsheviks are Communist first, last and always, never seeking favors for Jews as such." The rest of the Jews in Russia "were brought under worse oppression than ever." Brooks admitted, "that a number of Jews were transported" from America to Russia by Trotsky "to carry on Bolshevik agitation in" that country. Nor, Brooks admitted, could there be any doubt "that some prominent Russian Jews, thoroughly atheistic, held important positions."[85]

Brooks then turned to the question of the authenticity of the *Protocols* reflecting a Jewish conspiracy to take over the world. Appealing to Arno Gaebelein's *The Conflict of the Ages*, Brooks pointed out that the *Protocols* were simply a collection of previously written illuminati documents dating back to the mid-eighteenth century and were the product of Gentiles. As for how they came to the world's attention, Brooks noted that even here the story was mired in contradiction. Their main purpose, however, was primarily to "create anti-Semitism." Satan, Brooks warned, "is doing his best to block Jewish evangelism." As for the possibility of a Jewish (racial) conspiracy, Brooks concluded:

> So far as we can learn there are no officers of the Zionist movement known as "Elders."
> There is no one man or set of men that can even claim to be representatives of world

Jewry. The Jews have no bishops, cardinals or popes. They have no Sanhedrin. There is not a Chief Rabbi. There is no union in Jewry upon any point.[86]

And if people cannot agree, Brooks reasoned, they cannot conspire to take over the world.

Nevertheless, despite the fact that Brooks considered the *Protocols* a case of historical plagiarism, he also held to his conviction "that these documents are but an expression of the old international Communist plot, designed to put nations on an atheistic basis." Although they had their origins in the illuminati, when they were "codified by Marx, the Jew, his 'Communist Manifesto' became the basis of the Russian revolution and atheist and Communists everywhere made it their charter." During the ferment of Bolshevism "someone brought forth the Protocols" and blamed it on the Jews, thus covering their own aims behind a screen of anti-Semitism.[87]

Other Hebrew Christian Responses

One other article is worth mentioning and that is the one written by J. A. Vaus in the January 1934, *The King's Business*. In this one page article Vaus briefly surveyed the rising anti-Semitism taking place, the way God was using Hitler to extract the assimilated German Jew back to Palestine, how the *Protocols* were being accepted at face value by far too many ministers without questioning either source or accuracy (thereby aiding "the world-wide spread of the poison of prejudice...against the Jews"), and concluded by asking if Christians were now going to "join the ranks of Israel's enemies? Shall we let prejudice against the Jews make us unfaithful to our Lord's great commission? Shall we join hands with those who would indict the whole Jewish race for the faults of a few?"[88]

While one might reasonably conclude from Scripture, Vaus wrote, that God was using the present persecutions to bring the Jews back to Palestine, "God forbid that Christians...[who know that salvation is from the Jews]...should be numbered among the persecutors."[89] There also appeared on the same page as Vaus' analysis a list of reasons why the *Protocols* would never pass muster in a court of law. Eight reasons were listed which taken together showed there was "not a shred of reliable evidence" to support the notion 1) that there is "a Jewish World-conspiracy" 2) "that the *Protocols* were a part of the minutes of the first Zionist Congress," 3) that Jews wrote the *Protocols*, or 4) that they are genuine ("authentic"), 5) that the *Protocols* are in anyway connected to Masonry, 6) that they "were secured from a reliable source," 7) that there is a secret organization called the "Elders of Zion" which meets in secret to plan the overthrow of all Gentile governments and replace them with "a Jewish world government," and finally, "that the Jews as a nation are responsible" for the Great Depression.[90] Other Jewish Christian magazines reprinted these eight points in their own pages.[91]

As noted above, Elias Newman published his first edition of *The Jewish Peril and the Hidden Hand* in December 1933. It was written, according to the Preface, "in answer to many requests received by the author for a concise statement with regard to the lastest attacks upon the Jews by Anti-Semitism."[92] The book was a compilation of previously published articles with some new material added. It was an impressively thorough work that surveyed the rise of modern anti-Semitism, refuted a number of anti-Jewish libels, exposed the *Protocols*, and covered Hitler's anti-Semitic doings in Germany. Chapter Two, "Leading Charges Against the Jews," was aimed directly at Gerald Winrod and William Palley.

It is not my purpose to rehash all of Newman's book. However, there are one or two items worth noting that bear directly on the issues germane to this chapter. In response to the charge that Bolshevism was Jewish, Newman wrote: "The Jewish proletariat in America may be strongly infected with Bolshevism, but the Jew in general is not, nor will he ever be Bolshevik. The Jews who become Bolsheviks are apostates and renegades." According to Newman, only Trotsky, Zinovien, "and perhaps one more" were leading Jewish Bolsheviks "but that practically exhausts the list. The rest are gentiles." Any list that posted more Jewish names "is usually untruthful."[93] "The Jews . . . absolutely undeniably do not lead it in spite of all the millions of words saying that they do—they do not."[94]

Later, in the middle of a discussion on the Nazi persecution of the Jews, Newman inexplicably injected the following:

> We do not entirely excuse the Jews in their influence upon the present day degradation of morals. The new psychology was largely influenced by Freud, an apostate Jew of no religion. The theaters and movies of America have an almost exclusively been in the hands of irreligious Jews. The licentious and libertine novel of the present era has frequently been by a Jewish author.[95]

But despite this, Newman protested, one cannot blame the Jew for causing every hardship—such as the Depression. Nor did he control the banking houses of America.[96]

In April 1934, Newman came out with an expanded addition of *The Jewish Peril* which included a brief, supportive introduction by Ironside. In his preface to the second edition, Newman complained that only "here and there a lonely voice of protest is heard.... Some editors, in recent editorials have straddled the question by vague and ambiguous explanations. Keith L. Brooks, H. A. Ironside and Thomas M. Chalmers have been exceptions. They have uttered their protest against the protocol-mongers."[97]

In his section denying serious Jewish involvement in Bolshevism, Newman included two footnotes containing additional evidence from various writers supposedly supporting his contention.[98] And on pages 57 and 58 of the new addition, he added a footnote that in essence accused Gaebelein of using discredited anti-Semitic material in *The Conflict of the Ages*. (He would save for other writings his more savage attacks on Arno Gaebelein.)[99]

Arno C. Gaebelein—an Anti-Semitic Leader?

This brings us to Arno C. Gaebelein and his October 1933 publication of *The Conflict of the Ages*. It was the first of a trilogy (the other two being *World Prospects* [October 1934] and *Hopeless—Yet There is Hope* [October 1935]), dedicated to exploring "the mystery of lawlessness," through history but particularly in modern times (i.e., from 1900 to the 1930s), and how all this related to end-times prophecy. Gaebelein saw the beginning of modern lawlessness having its roots in the secret formation and workings of the Illuminati (circa 1750) and coming to full fruition in Soviet Communism.[100]

Because it is this book by Gaebelein that Weber uses to label him anti-Semitic and Nazi-sounding, it is important that what Gaebelein actually wrote, or even implied, (and how others responded to this) in *The Conquest of the Ages* be carefully evaluated. Weber basically follows Elias Newman's harsh criticisms of Gaebelein and seems to give them his stamp of approval.

It is clear that Gaebelein considered Soviet communism an "Evil Empire"— bloody, ruthless, repressive, and fanatically anti-Christian—and that the communist of Moscow were trying (with some success) to export it to the United States. He considered the Soviets to be a far greater menace than the Nazis in 1933, as did most of the historic fundamentalists. He spent a considerable number of pages detailing the persecution of Christians in Russia, the horrible repression, the imprisonment and murder of those opposed to Stalin, including the unimaginable Ukrainian starvation, and communist activities in the United States. And he did so, as we now realize, with a considerable degree of accuracy.[101] He also excoriated Modernism and Reform Judaism, considering both a form of rationalism and a part of the anti-Christ mindset of the age. (But then, so did Elias Newman.) He severely denounced the modernist Christian's embrace and espousal of Stalinistic communism while denigrating the American Constitution, American life, and the American economy.[102] However, what got Gaebelein in trouble with many Hebrew Christians, and historians such as Weber and Carpenter, was what he wrote about apostate Jewish involvement in the early phase of the Bolshevik revolution and government, as well as their continued presence in ongoing communist agitation. In relation to this Jewish involvement, Gaebelein briefly discussed the *Protocols*.

Gaebelein spared no feelings in making known his dislike of "the Jew Marx" as he referred to him. He was convinced "*Some* of the leaders of the Russian revolution of 1917-1918 and the years following" were Jews (Italics added). In fact, although he never actually gives a percentage, Gaebelein probably believed the percentage of Jews involved in the early years of the revolution was quite high (considerably more than a bare majority). He offered a number of sources to support his claim, including information from a personal friend—George Simons—who was in Russia during the revolution.[103] In the same section of the book, Gaebelein offers a brief discussion of the *Protocols*, concluding that "the most important fact is that throughout the twenty-four Protocols we have a *very pronounced re-statement of the principle thesis of Illuminism and Marxism*."[104]

Gaebelein duly noted that many leading Gentiles and Jews had declared the *Protocols* a forgery, and his own opinion was that no one would ever discover who wrote them. However, he did believe that the "destruction of Christian civilization" as outlined in the *Protocols* was being carried out "by the Revolution and Sovietism." Due to the match between the *Protocols'* claims and unfolding world events, Gaebelein believed that no matter who was responsible for them, they were "not a *crude forgery*." Behind the document were "hidden unseen actors, powerful and cunning, who follow the plan still, bent on the overthrow of our civilization."[105] After his brief discussion on the Protocols, Gaebelein offered his readers two and a half pages of various quotations from the document, urging them to pay close attention to what they were about to read.[106]

In chapter seven of *The Conquest*, a thorough chapter devoted to the workings of communism in America (this was the chapter that caught the attention of the secular press), Gaebelein drew attention to a statement in the Fish Congressional Report which claimed that "In the vicinity of New York City the Communist camps include a *very high percentage of Jewish boys and girls, estimated to be as high as ninety percent*."[107] Finally, in the last chapter of his book, Gaebelein included his view on the apostate, rationalistic Jew. Regretfully, he noted, "the greater part of Jewry has become reformed, or as we call it 'deformed.'" They no longer believed in the Scriptures, or a coming Messiah, or a "glorious future for Israel." They had, Gaebelein groused, sunk into infidelity, wanting only "material things and power," thereby becoming "a menace" while "the lower elements become lawless." He concluded by writing:

> As we have shown, these infidel Jews were prominent in the revolutionary propaganda during the nineteenth century. Karl Marx, the author of the "Communist Bible" was an infidel Jew; so was Laselle and hundreds of others active in the socialistic-anarchist and communistic activities. Trotsky and at least two score other leaders of the Russian revolution were apostate Jews. They make themselves felt in our country and in other civilized countries.[108]

Despite the emphasis I have placed on Gaebelein's view on apostate Jews and communism (the reason for which will be apparent below), in actuality, he only devoted about a dozen pages to the issue in a book of one hundred and seventy one pages. He spent many more pages denouncing and confronting modernists, either by name or as a group, and their embrace of communism. It is important to mention that Gaebelein did not consider all the Jews of Russia communists, only "some," nor by saying that the *Protocols* were "no crude forgery" was he thereby saying they were genuine, that is, that they were the product of the "Elders of Zion" or that the Jewish people as a race were involved in a world wide plot to take over the world from the Gentiles. Gaebelein simply did not believe in such a scenario. He probably believed, though he never says so directly, that the *Protocols* were in part written by communist Jews promoting international communist revolution.

The Conquest of Ages Draws Hostile Fire

Among the leading historic fundamentalist journals, Gaebelein's book was well received and highly recommended. Only two of them, *Moody* and *Revelation* even bothered to mention his comments on the *Protocols*, and that was limited to a sentence or two.[109] Weber, on the other hand, as noted above, claims there was a major reaction to *The Conquest*.[110] However, if there was a charge against Gaebelein, the ranks were pretty thin. Even J. Hoffman Cohn's West Coast and always faithful supporter Keith Brooks, refused to join. Weber also over emphasizes Gaebelein's reaction to Newman's review, as will be noted below. Still, it is worth evaluating the Cohn/Newman attack on Gaebelein so that the "rest of the story" can be told.

Cohn introduced Newman's review (which appeared in *The Chosen People*) by declaring the climax of Gaebelein's book was found in the fifth and sixth chapters, chapters which "deal with the now exploded myth and fantasy of the" *Protocols*. Cohn expressed surprise that Gaebelein was taken in by them let alone used them. Cohn then went on to deny that any such group as the Elders of Zion ever existed, or that any Jews were ever "involved in any such absurd plot as alleged in the even more absurd 'Protocols.' " Cohn next traced the plagiarized sources from which the *Protocols* were composed.[111] But Cohn was already off to a bad start. In chapter five of his book, Gaebelein never mentioned the *Protocols* and in the sixth chapter only four pages out of 26 are given over to discussing that document, and in those four pages he never espoused belief in a world-wide Jewish conspiracy as outlined by Cohn. Clearly, the more one delves into the issue, the more one concludes there was an overreaction on the part of Cohn/Newman that seems hard to justify by what Gaebelein wrote in *The Conquest of the Ages*.

Newman's so-called "scathing review" is more of an unreasonable polemic than a "point-by-point rebuttal of Gaebelein's book." He, too, begins by claiming (wrongly) that chapter five is the climax of the book "and here we see the sinister influence of the exploded 'Protocols.' " And he charges that these "have so powerfully influenced our brother that he now blames the Jews for what he once blamed the Gentiles."[112] The rest of his review is an embarrassment (explaining, perhaps, why so few historic fundamentalists followed his lead.) He constantly charged Gaebelein with contradicting himself yet no contradictions exist when one checks out Newman's accusations in this regard. He also repeated a charge he made in *The Jewish Peril*—that of the 20 Jewish Bolsheviks listed on page 97 of *The Conquest* one was a gentile and another six were not Bolsheviks at all.[113] (Of course, that leaves the other thirteen as Jewish Bolsheviks, otherwise Newman would have noted the error.)

Perhaps the most surprising part of Newman's review is his vigorous defense of Karl Marx. He excoriates Gaebelein for being so negative and using terms like "Marx the Jew," or "Marx the liar," but did not use such terms when speaking of Gentiles such as Weishaupt, the supposed founder of the Illuminati. (This is true— but Gaebelein did call Weishaupt "a seed of Satan" and accused him of Devil worship).[114] Newman follows this complaint by writing:

> So far can prejudice go, when once fired by the first fuse of misinformation, [that] Karl Marx, the son of Jewish Christian parents, misled by Gentile revolutionists, and advocating a Socialism that is mild as compared to our own NRA, is condemned as a rascal of the deepest dye![115]

Newman followed the above by a comparison between Marx and an "evil" Lenin— Marx favored democracy, Lenin oligarchy; Marx believed in universal suffrage, Lenin was against it and favored dictatorship; Marx favored "revolution by law," Lenin stood for "revolution by force."[116] At the conclusion of his review, Newman wrote that he was with Gaebelein in "his condemnation of Bolshevism but held no brief for the defense of Capitalism. It too had proven itself an unreliable, hopeless system and a failure."[117]

One cannot help agreeing with Gaebelein in his response, that Newman's review of his book "was unfair and unjust" in the sense that Newman consistently misrepresented what Gaebelein wrote. However, Gaebelein refused to get drawn into a "lengthy reply." He simply refuted a couple of glaring erroneous accusations made by Neuman. One was that he had used almost verbatim, Henry Ford's "International Jew." Gaebelein pointed out that he had never seen or used the book. Next, Neuman had accused Gaebelein of using "the exploded theories of Mrs. Webster in The Cause of World Unrest and rehash[ed] practically the whole material covered in the first five chapters of [that] lying Anti-Semitic production." In reply, Gaebelein wrote that he had only used this work once.[118] (He did make use, he noted, of Mrs. Webster' "most reliable" book, "World Revolution.") However, he claimed his chief sources were the *Congressional Records* "of the investigating committees of 1919 and 1930," and the *National Republic* which he deemed "a trustworthy magazine."[119]

Gaebelein stood by his "main argument," though, calling it unimpeachable, and noted that "The alleged contradictions mentioned in this criticism do not exist in the book at all, but are read into it by the reviewer."[120] As he concluded his response, Gaebelein touched on the crux of the issue: "Nothing is gained by an attempt to white-wash the atheistic-revolutionary Jewish elements which are so strong everywhere today."[121] He closed by apologizing to his readers for even writing a response to Newman's attack. "We are sorry, that we had to mention this matter in our pages. It will not be mentioned again."[122]

But Cohn was not about to let the issue die. Even before Gaebelein responded to Newman in the April issue of *Our Hope*, Cohn published an article by Harry Ironside in the March 1934 issue of *The Chosen People*. Weber implies that Ironside's article was a further "renunciation" of Gaebelein's *The Conflict of the Ages*. Yet a close reading of Ironside's essay does not seem to support Weber's interpretation. (As Ironside's article is rather lengthy, I will confine my use of it to its possible bearing on Gaebelein.) Now, it is true, as Weber notes, Ironside did write that he deeply "regretted" and felt chagrined as a lover of Israel, to "find that the Protocols are being used not only by godless Gentiles, but even by some fundamentalist Christians to stir up suspicion and hatred against Jewish people as a whole."[123] However, just before Ironside penned those words, he had written that the *Protocols* "in a rather remarkable way...[traced]the course of extreme Marxian activity...." This convinced Ironside that the *Protocols* were the handiwork "of sovietizing leaders" who intended to replace lawful governments with a Bolshevik one. Ironside then wrote: "No one questions so far as I am aware, the fact that some apostate Jews may have been associated with apostate Gentiles in the preparation of these remarkable documents."[124]

Later in his article, he commented that it was "wicked to try to make the Jews as a people responsible for the *Protocols* and that "whoever may have written these documents" it was not someone [among the Jews] "entitled to speak for the race." It was Ironside's opinion that "Christian teachers would do well to stress this fact" so that they not be guilty of putting on the Jews "a responsibility which does not belong to them," and thereby bring persecution on an innocent people.[125] Before he was through, Ironside stressed yet a third time that he could not say who wrote the *Protocols* but having read them he was convinced that they were not "the Protocols of Jewish leaders as such. As already intimated above," he wrote, "I quite recognize the fact that some Jews have been more or less connected with the group that produced them, but what I mean is they do not represent Jewish thoughts or Jewish schemes characteristically."[126]

Ironside's position was in line with the other historic fundamentalists, be they Gray, Bauman, Brooks, Barnhouse, Trumbull, or even Gaebelein. The question among these men was not are apostate Jews involved in promoting communism (which the *Protocols* seemed to be advocating), but rather how deeply are they involved (i.e., how important is their contribution), and how much should we publicly discuss this. It is of interest that Ironside did not say that fundamentalists should not discuss the *Protocols*, but that if they did they should stress they were not a product of the Jews as a whole plotting against the Gentiles nations.

And although Gaebelein said he was not going to bring up the issue again, it does seem he fudged a bit in this regard. Following his April rebuttal to Cohn/Newman, he wrote an additional "I told you so" in the May 1934 *Our Hope*. In this editorial he quoted liberally from an article that appeared in the January 29, 1934, *Time* magazine. The *Time* article related how " 'a smart, ruthless Jew' " named Kaganovitch had become the number two man behind Stalin, and that " 'another Jew, roly-poly Maxim Maximovich Litvinoff' " was to be honored for his excellent work during his visit to Washington. According to *Time*, Stalin, who ever since he had " 'ousted the Jew Leon Trotsky,' " had been against promoting " 'Jews into high Soviet office' " seemed to have changed his mind and was now " 'benignly pro-Semite.' "[127] Gaebelein considered the *Time* article a refutation of those who had "tried to discredit his book" and say that Jews "have nothing to do with Communism." Gaebelein then made his position quite clear: "We love true Jews. We never had, and never shall have any sympathy whatever with Anti-Semitism. Our sympathy is with them as a nation...but we can never sympathize with the atheistic, the communistic Jew. They are a menace to their own people as well as a disgrace...."[128] Gaebelein had difficulty in understanding "why Jewish missionaries" would be defending such renegades.[129]

The Attack on Gaebelein Becomes Even More Vicious

But Gaebelein's clarification notwithstanding, Newman was determined to label Gaebelein a leading American anti-Semite, and in the process indirectly labeled three other leading historic fundamentalists as aiding and abetting the enemy by their refusal to take a stand. In October 1934, Augsburgh Publishing House came out with Newman's *Fundamentalists' Resuscitation of the Anti-Semitic Protocol Forgery*, only this time there was no forward by Harry Ironside. Newman began by drawing attention to the fact that anti-Semitism had been on the increase in recent years due to the desire to find a scapegoat to blame for the "misery and misfortune caused by the depression," and "partly through the *alleged* prominence of Jewish leadership in the Bolshevik Revolution in Russia...." (italics added).[130] Much of the book was a reiteration of what he had previously written concerning the background and make-up of the *Protocols*. However, beginning on page eleven, Newman initiated what can only be described as a campaign to discredit Gaebelein in the eyes of his fellow historic fundamentalists and other evangelicals.

Newman opened by noting that while [Ford's] *The Dearborn Independent* was defunct it had been replaced by Pelley's *Liberation*, "and is it not pitiful," he continued, "to see fundamentalists like W. B. Riley, Arno C. Gaebelein, [Gerald] Winrod and others join in a campaign of Jew-baiting." "Fiery fundamentalists," he charged, "Bible teachers, clap-trap preachers and cheap evangelists have become the new instigators of religious hate in America."[131]

According to Newman, fundamentalists were dividing into three camps. Camp one was the good guys, "the leaders of the Anti-Protocolists." In this camp were Talbot, Bauman, Brooks, and Harry P. Morgan of the Buffalo Bible Institute. The second group, the leaders "of the Protocol-mongers," consisted of Gaebelein, Winrod, and Riley.[132] The third paring, the "middle of the roaders," consisted of Gray (*Moody Monthly*), *Revelation* (Barnhouse), and *The Sunday School Times* (Trumbull). Reaching back to 1921, Newman claimed that some of the comments Gray made then, and which had never been retracted, made the "protocolists" think Gray might be one of them. However, Newman admitted Gray denied any endorsement. "At the present time," Newman wrote, "while refusing to withdraw his former statements, Dr. Gray persistently refuses to make any emphatic denial of the Jewish authorship of the Protocols."[133] Perhaps sensing he was walking on thin ice, Newman then added:

> Dr. James Gray, a clear thinker, conservative and a man whom many Jews and Christians have learned to trust is not an anti-Semite. He could do much to clear the situation by a concise and unambiguous statement, but he has not done so. The editors of *The Sunday School Times* and *Revelation* are not of the anti-Semitic type either, and could do much to dispel the dark cloud of anti-Semitism hovering over many Fundamentalists, but to date their attitude regarding the Protocols has been one of silence.[134]

It was for Gaebelein, though, that Newman poured out his most vitriolic writing. Much of what he wrote was a repeat of what he had written in *The Chosen People* review. However, he did add some new material implying that Gaebelein had lied about his chief sources and that he had doctored some quotes so that he might place "all responsibility for Bolshevism upon Jews."[135]

In summing up, Newman placed Gaebelein with those who murdered Jews! "It was such campaigns as these being fostered today," he wrote, "by Winrod, Pelley, the Silver Shirts, the Friends of New Germany and aided by books such as *The Conquest of the Ages* that created pogroms." Although they may say they are giving "legitimate discussion" to a problem of great import, it was really "quite useless for Winrod, Gaebelein and Riley to pretend that their books and articles are not really anti-Semitic propaganda...."[136] People who were smart and honest would see right through such special pleading. No—there was only one reason why these three wrote what they did:

> The only possible object in view is to convince the people who read them that civilized

society and religion is threatened by a world-wide secret conspiracy of Jews and is being led by an "invisible government," to the end of bringing all governments, all industry and all commerce, under the absolute domain of the Jewish 'hidden hand.'[137]

Newman went on to charge that the end results—if successful—of Gaebelein's and Winrod's writings would be to stir up hate, suspicion, and intolerance on the part of Gentiles toward their "Jewish neighbors." Newman saw "no essential difference in the tactics" used by Gaebelein and those used by Pelley and Winrod. And there was no difference between the tactics of these three and those in the past who "let loose upon thousands and thousands of helpless and inoffensive people the most bestial and fiendish cruelty and hatred ever attained by beings called human."[138] Having compared Gaebelein to those in Russia who had slaughtered Jews in the Pale, Newman twisted the knife. "The wholesale burning of Jews in Spain," he wrote, "and the more recent pogroms of Tsarist Russia were invariably inspired by a false religious fanaticism similar to the brand now being propagated by the Fundamentalist anti-Semitic protocol-mongers."[139]

The above goes beyond hyperbole. It is vitriolic and vituperous language that is out and out slander. And all of this from eight pages in Gaebelein's *The Conquest of the Ages*. Did it fit Gaebelein, did Newman speak for the majority of historic fundamentalists in so castigating Gaebelein? Hardly. I know of no individual among the mainline historic fundamentalists, or anyone writing in their journals, that considered Gaebelein in such terms—or anything near them! Whatever he wrote was well reviewed and recommended. He was never compared even to Winrod, let alone a Pelley, nor was he isolated within the fundamentalist community as was Winrod. He continued to be invited to speak at Bible conferences and churches all over America. At this time in his life he spent his winters in Southern California and often spoke at Bauman's and Talbot's churches as well as to the student body at Biola. In 1940 he was slated to speak at Moody's Founders Week but bowed out on the advice of his doctor. In fact, he gave up all public speaking that year, as at the age of eighty it was too difficult physically. It is obvious that Newman was deliberately distorting Gaebelein's writings and this must have been obvious to the historic fundamentalists of the time. Why Timothy Weber seems to believe that Newman (and Cohn) spoke for the historic fundamentalists as a whole, or why he leans so heavily on Newman in labeling Gaebelein anti-Semitic is a puzzle only he can explain.[140]

Why Such Hostility Toward Gaebelein?

That there may have been more to this on-going animosity on the part of Newman/ Cohn toward Gaebelein than was revealed in their writing should be obvious.[141] Consider and compare, for example, the accolades directed toward Louis Bauman and the "curses" heaped upon Gaebelein. Newman named Bauman as one of the "leaders" of anti-Protocol forces. Yet Bauman came out with a book in mid-1934 that in some parts sounded far more anti-Semitic than anything Gaebelein ever wrote. *Shirts and Sheets or Anti-Semitism, A Present Day Sign of the First Magnitude* was the name of Bauman's book and was enthusiastically endorsed by Keith Brooks, who wrote in the August 1934, *Prophecy Monthly*:

> It does not spare the Jew and it shows the mistake of some who defend all Jews because they are "chosen people." He turns the light on subversive movements in which Jews have had a large part. On the other hand he strongly shows the danger of blaming the Jews for everything, denying them the right to live and driving them farther away from the Messiah....[142]

While the underlying thrust of Bauman's book was to condemn anti-Semitism, which he did in no uncertain terms, both in Europe and America, and declared no true Christian should have any part in such activities,[143] nevertheless he still made the following assertions: "that apostate Jews themselves sit in the blood-smeared seats of Russian power;"[144] that there was "a disposition on the part of some Christians to blind themselves to all the sins of Irael;"[145] that it was not "wholly without cause that the tide of anti-Semitism has arisen against the Jew;"[146] that out of all "proportion to his numbers, the Jew is the world's archtroubler;" that thanks to Karl Marx and Friedrich Engels the "death damp of communism...rests as a noxious effluvium upon the nations today;"[147] that the Jews controlled the stage and movies, which Bauman believed was "the foremost of the Satanic agencies for the world-wide demoralization of youth,"[148] and (finally) that the Jews may be responsible for "the present universal economic breakdown" through ("especially German Jews") gold manipulation.[149]

Bauman also drew from *The Cause of the World's Unrest*, a book Newman criticized Gaebelein for using, the comment that of the supposed 50 leaders of the Bolshevik revolution, 43 of them were Jewish. Bauman did write, "In simple justice to the great mass of Jewry, it should be stated that the Bolshevik Jew is of atheistic Jewry—not of orthodox Jewry." And the Bolshevik Jew, he continued, "is a sworn enemy of his own believing brethren."[150] Still, Bauman also believed that "unquestionably, the Jew exercises a power in the political affairs of the world's greatest nation, all out of proportion to his numbers" (i.e., the Roosevelt administration).[151] In retrospect, it is not difficult to read Bauman's remarks as far more intemperate than anything Gaebelein wrote in *The Conquest of the Ages*, yet no criticism of anti-Semitic leanings was expressed toward him.[152] Of course, Bauman did speak out against the *Protocols*—sort of. He pointed out that they were dividing the historic fundamentalists into two opposing camps; the "Protocolists and anti-Protocolists." There were sincere people on both sides, but sincerity did not keep one from being wrong. He then wrote:

What if a group of very cunning and far-sighted Jews did write that sinister document known as the "Protocols," laying down a world program whereby the Jews would conquer the nations of the earth? If nineteen million Jews can pit their wits against nineteen hundred million Gentiles and win, then the Gentiles deserved to be conquered! The Gentiles would do the same—reversing the situation. But no nineteen million Jews are pitting their wits—no, not even nineteen even think of so doing. If the "Protocols" are of Jewish origin there is a mere handful of Jews having inside knowledge of the scheme. *It is mighty poor sport, and a thousand poorer Christians, who will be party to the persecution, impoverishing, and destroying of ninety-nine innocents—even little children—for the crime of one plotter.*[153] (Italics added.)

However, Bauman went on to write that even if it was conceded that "designing" Gentiles forged the *Protocols* and cleverly blamed the Jews, that still would not change a "stiff-necked, Christ-rejecting Jew" into a "saint."[154] Considering the above, it is difficult to understand how Newman could claim Bauman as a leader of the anti-Protocol group and Gaebelein as a protocol-monger and vicious anti-Semite.

Gaebelein and the Elizabeth Knauss Brouhaha

In fact, Bauman was so appreciated by the Hebrew Christian community that his name appeared on the Hebrew Christian Alliance of America's advisory board listed in the January 1935 HCA *Quarterly*. Meanwhile, Gaebelein was accused of stirring up ill-feeling against the Jews through an article with which he was only remotely connected.

In the October 1933 and January 1934 issues of *The European Harvest Field*, a two-part article on communism appeared written by Elizabeth Knauss. It was the second part, "Communism: What is behind the System," that drew the wrath of some Hebrew Christians. In this latter section, Knauss gave a brief definition of communism, outlined its goal as one of subverting our government, taking away ownership of property, and destroying religion and the family. She next discussed the *Protocols*, writing that they purported "to be a plan, as outlined by a powerful group of *atheistic, renegade, and apostate Jews*, for the destruction of Gentile civilization." The plans outlined in the *Protocols*, Knauss believed, "are most surely being fulfilled in the Communist movement" headquartered in Soviet Russia.[155] She went on to note the strong Jewish element within the New Deal "brain-trust" and hinted that some of what was taking place seem to line up with some things mentioned in the *Protocols*. Knauss finished by tracing the roots of Marxism back to the illuminati.

She closed her rather brief article by asking that every effort be made to win the Jews to Christ for "therein lies there only hope." She then added: "Not all Jews are involved in this awful program of destruction, but those who are atheistic and apostate. May His Spirit be able to reach many Jewish people before it is forever too late! Surely this is the prayerful desire of every truly born child of God."[156]

Evidently Solomon Birnbaum, director of Jewish Missions at Moody Bible Institute saw the second part of Knauss two-part article, was offended by the association of apostate Jews with the *Protocols* and communism, so fired off a lengthy and heated letter to Gaebelein (who was listed as the editor of *The European Harvest Field*). First, Birnbaum, in essence, rebuked the magazine for even sullying its pages by publishing such an article and then attacked the validity of Knauss' assertion that apostate Jews wrote the *Protocols*. Birnbaum claimed the *Protocols* were much too theological to have been written by atheistic Jews. Besides, the Jews had nothing to do with the *Protocols* to begin with, nor were there any Elders of Zion. The whole thing was a plagiarized forgery from the mind of a "hate-crazed brain."[157]

As for Jews and their relationship with communism—well, "of course there are many Jews among the communist" but it did not follow that all "Communist are Jews." Still, Birnbaum seemed to reluctantly admit considerable Jewish presence in the Soviet communist leadership:

> If in proportion some discover more Jews than Russians among the Communists, it is not because their Judaism makes them so, but because the Jews suffered more from the brutality of Czarism and from the Godless and atheistic conduct of priests or popes of the Russian Orthodox Church than any other class of people.[158]

Birnbaum continued along this path for the reminder of his letter and then closed somewhat disingenuously by writing that he had no "suggestion to you as to what you should do in order to correct the false impression that was made...," however, he was sure the magazine would do what was right before the Lord.[159]

Birnbaum's letter was dated February 26, 1934, and when he did not receive a reply from Gaebelein by the time the April issue of the *Hebrew Christian Alliance Quarterly* was to go to press, he had it published in that journal, turning a private correspondence into an open letter. However, although Birnbaum did not immediately hear from Gaebelein, he did hear from the managing editor of *The European Harvest Field*, Herbert Hogg. In a letter to Birnbaum dated March 1, 1934, Hogg explained that Dr. Gaebelein was on the West Coast and that for all intents and purposes he, Hogg, was running the magazine. And it was he who had made the decision to print the Knauss series. In fact, Gaebelein had not even seen the article in question but Hogg was forwarding Gaebelein a copy as well as a copy of Birnbaum's letter for his perusal "and make any reply...he may wish to do."

Hogg's letter was a gracious reply to Birnbaum. He explained the reason behind the Knauss articles, and admitted that, yes, some of her argument was based on the

Protocols. However, he also pointed out that in one place she did leave the "genuineness of them…open to question." More germane for Hogg was the problem of radical Jews. He believed it was necessary to acknowledge that such existed and that "the recognition and condemnation of such groups in the Jewish and Gentile press and in Christian circles would [not] foster anti-Semitism…." Rather, Hogg thought, the opposite would occur. If people understood that those associated with radicalism had "left the wholesome values that reside in orthodox Judaism," they would not blame all Jews.[160]

Hogg closed by noting that *The European Harvest Field* seldom ventured into this field but if "we have transgressed" he was willing to make amends. "If after consideration," he wrote apologetically, "it shall be found well for us to make some explanation regarding Miss Knauss' article, we shall be glad to do whatever seems proper and best."[161] (It is obvious that Hogg was offering Birnbaum an opportunity to respond and give him guidance.) Hogged closed by thanking Birnbaum for his criticism, stating "it is our earnest desire that we shall do nothing detrimental to the welfare of your people."[162]

If Hogg was holding out an olive branch to Birnbaum, Birnbaum [rudely] ignored it and Hogg's gracious letter, and Hogg himself. Birnbaum evidently wanted Gaebelein and rather than thank Hogg for clearing up the situation, he sought to embarrass Gaebelein publicly when Gaebelein did not respond in a way he expected. And it must be admitted that publishing his letter in the April 1935 *HCAQ* did, indeed, get a response from Gaebelein. In a letter dated May 27, 1934, Gaebelein gave a short and somewhat abrupt reply to Birnbaum's published letter. He began by expressing his displeasure that Birnbaum had gone public and gave a number of reasons why. Included in the list was Gaebelein's protest that he had never seen the Knauss articles until after they were published, that although he was listed as editor on the masthead, Mr. Hogg really ran the magazine, and finally that Hogg's letter, written at the urging of Gaebelein, had been ignored. As far as Gaebelein was concerned, he had been done a personal injury.[163]

"I am widely known as a staunch friend of Israel. There is NOT a drop of anti-Semitic blood in me," Gaebelein angrily protested, and pointed to his early years of Jewish evangelism and relief work. Gaebelein concluded by accusing his "Hebrew Christian brethren" of having a bad attitude that did not help their image "among true Gentile believers." Then (for some reason) he briefly defended *The Conquest of the Ages*, writing: "There is no question that ungodly Jews have much to do with the communist agitations. But nowhere do I say the Protocols are of Jewish origin. I state definitely in my book that their authorship cannot be ascertained."[164]

On June 7, Hogg , writing for both Gaebelein and himself, asked the editor of the *Hebrew Christian Alliance Quarterly* to print their respective replies to Birnbaum in "the next issue…, so that this matter may be fully understood."[165]

Not sure their request would be granted, Hogg also published their replies in the October 1934 edition of *The European Harvest Field*. Opening with a brief review of the controversy, he justified what he was doing "so that our constituency might know that Dr. Gaebelein's interest in Israel has been a most practical one" and that the American European Fellowship supported Jewish evangelism without qualification "and would not want to do anything inimical to the interests of Jewry."[166] Hogg then printed his and Gaebelein's reply to Birnbaum, in that order, and closed by holding out an olive branch once more:

> We have felt that, if the different leaders seeking to promote the testimony to Israel would unite on a basis of earnest prayer and conference as to the best ways of bringing about an effective message to Israel, there could be found a basis whereby constructive presentations could be given, in a loving way, and anything detrimental to these people, to whom we owe so much in the Scripture and in the person of our Lord, could be avoided. We have every desire to give ourselves to such an end, rather than promote controversy, strife, and something that savors of anti-Semitism.[167]

However, the *Hebrew Christian Alliance Quarterly* did publish Hogg's and Gaebelein's letters, albeit reluctantly and not without an acid follow-up commentary. According to E. S. Greenbaum, president of the HCAA, they "were both grieved and ashamed to receive such replies." Both he and Birnbaum believed they were entitled "to something quite different from those who stand for Bible truth and are actively interested in the evangelization of the Jews."[168] Greenbaum brushed aside Hogg's olive branch as insincere, noting somewhat sarcastically, "Well, friend Hogg, if you have still Col. Sanctuary on your board, you have deprived us even of the poor consolation that you have not gone as far as others. He certainly goes the limit, and is the treasurer of your organization."[169]

Having dismissed Hogg, Greenbaum responded to Gaebelein's letter point by point. In essence he defended Birnbaum for addressing his letter to Gaebelein and chided him for allowing his name to be listed as editor yet not really overseeing *The European Harvest Field*. He then placed the blame for Gaebelein's injured feelings on Gaebelein himself because Gaebelein had not personally answered in a timely fashion Birnbaum's letter.[170]

Greenbaum insisted that Birnbaum's letter had avoided casting "reflection on you personally." People like Gaebelein, who took a strong stand on the Bible had always been considered "the best earthly friends that God had given "sin-laden Israel." This is why Hebrew Christians were so frustrated and disappointed in Gaebelein—he was not matching up to what people knew to be his true position. Finally, Greenbaum exhibited some hurt feelings of his own. Taking umbrage with Gaebelein's "you Hebrew-Christians" admonition, Greenbaum (rhetorically) demanded to know what was wrong with the HCAA's attitude? "That spirit," he wrote accusingly, "is the one manifested by all who find fault with the Jewish people. Whenever an individual Jew hurts or insults them they wish to take it out on the whole people."[171]

It is interesting to note that despite the rather tense exchange, neither Birnbaum or Greenbaum accuse Gaebelein of being anti-Semitic, or in any way compared him or linked him with Winrod or Palley, or charged him with being a "protocols–monger." Even more interesting is Solomon Birnbaum's review of a 16 page tract Gaebelein wrote titled, *Shadows from the Talmud*. The review appeared in the June 1934 *Moody Institute Monthly* and was most laudatory:

> A little booklet of quotations from the Talmud revealing the thoughts and longings of the rabbis for the Messiah. It is refreshing at the present time, when there is so much hostile criticism of the Talmud as the source of great evil, to find that *an outstanding Bible teacher, Dr. Gaebelein*, has discovered in its pages such wonderful Jewels.... We cordially recommend this *excellent* little tract to the Christian reader.[172] (Italics added.)

It is to be doubted that if Birnbaum considered Gaebelein a protocols-monger along with Palley and Winrod, he would have written the above. In fact, if Gaebelein was really the anti-Semitic ogre Newman was painting him to be, it is doubtful Gaebelein would have written the tract in the first place.

It is of additional interest that the Winter 1936 (i.e., October-December 1935) issue of the *Hebrew Christian Alliance Quarterly* contained a brief but praiseworthy review of the last book in Gaebelein's trilogy on the history of lawlessness— *Hopeless, Yet There is Hope*:

> This is Dr. Gaebelein's *third great book on world conditions*. A historical review of 1900-1935. The great war. The insipid League of Nations. The blunders of our unbalanced administration. The Russian recognition and its disastrous results. The hopeless European situation. What will the future bring?[173] (Italics added.)

Again, it has to be asked if the Jewish Christian reviewer was not in agreement with much of what Gaebelein wrote, including what he wrote in *The Conquest of the Ages*, would he write "third great book?" Many Hebrew Christians may have been upset with Gaebelein over his position on the *Protocols* but that does not mean they agreed with Elias Newman, nor does it mean they disagreed with Gaebelein's take on history or even (for that matter) over the extent of Jewish influence within communism. They just did not like to talk about it publicly.

The Brooks-Gaebelein Friendship

This last, I admit, is my speculation. However, one of the best evidences that

Gaebelein was not held an anti-Semite and co-laborer in this regard with Winrod by historic fundamentalists was the friendship that blossomed between Keith Brooks and Gaebelein. Although he was affiliated with Cohn and the American Board of Missions to the Jews, and stood by Cohn through thick and thin (and at times it became pretty thick), nevertheless, when it came to Gaebelein, Brooks would not follow Cohn's lead.

Brooks had an ongoing denunciation of anti-Semitism and the "protocol-mongers" in the pages of his monthly journal, *Prophecy Monthly*.[174] This was especially true when it came to Gerald Winrod. From the time he broke with his former friend (late 1933) until Winrod's federal indictment in mid-1942, Brooks had an unending journalistic war with the Nazi-sympathizing, *Protocols* hawking editor of the anti-Semitic *Defender*.[175] It was just the opposite with Gaebelein. There friendship increased over the years. Even when he disagreed with him, such as over the issue of how deeply the Jews were involved in communism or the *Protocols*, Brooks still made sure there was no personal animosity between them. In the February 1934 issue of *Prophecy Monthly*, Brooks endorsed *The Conflict of the Ages*, noting the book had aroused "nation wide attention." But Brooks also wrote: "It is especially illuminating as to the sources of Communism and what may be expected along this line, *although, in our opinion, it is not altogether fair to the Jew*" (italics added).[176]

The next month Brooks wrote that Gaebelein's *Conquest*, "at some points" seemed "to be lacking in that deep concern for the Jewish people" found in his "earlier writings...." Brooks also opined that Gaebelein erred "in making the Bolshevik movement an entirely Jewish product."[177] Strangely, Brooks put forward the idea in this article that the educated Jews were "*literally forced*" by the Bolsheviks "to do there bidding." If they refused, they [the Jews] would be, Brooks dramatically related, "liquidated." Brooks also used figures from Newman's *The Jewish Peril* to show that Gaebelein was inaccurate about the number of Jews in Soviet leadership, and that communism was really the brainchild of atheistic Gentiles, not Jews.[178]

Brooks was almost contradicting himself at this point. In January, when he had written his important article on the *Protocols*, he had admitted that a number of apostate Jews (about 18%) were in leadership positions in Soviet Russia.[179] At the end of the year (December 1934), in an article titled, "The Real Root of World Disorder," he concluded by emphasizing that "THERE IS A COMMUNIST PLOT. *There are Jews in it.*"[180]

In September 1938, in his article, "Bombastic Lies Swallowed by Millions," he admitted, "No one can deny that the Jews have played important roles in Russian Bolshevism, or that Communist Jews of the most radical kind have been identified with the movement in the United States and elsewhere."[181] However, having said that, he then spends a considerable amount of ink contending for just the opposite—

that the Jews did not really have that much to do with the Bolshevik revolution. He quoted Russian communist party statistics from 1918 which claimed 124,000 members of which only 2% were Jewish.[182]

When a Swiss court declared the *Protocols* a forgery propagated for the purpose of creating hatred against the Jews, Brooks rejoiced and covered the case extensively (as well as the reaction to the verdict) in the pages of the *Prophecy Monthly* and in his book, *The Jews and the Passion for Palestine In Light of Prophecy*.[183] When the America Board of Missions to the Jews put out "A Manifesto and a Call" (and paid for it to be advertised in a number of historic fundamentalist magazines), a manifesto that denounced anti-Semitism as both un-American and anti-Christian, and rejoiced that a Switzerland court had declared the *Protocols* "forgeries, obvious plagiarism, immoral, and manifestly prepared for the purpose of inciting popular passion against the Jews," Brooks' name was on it along with the names of 31 other historic fundamentalists.[184] Brooks also published an edited version in his *Prophecy Monthly* (while taking a hard swipe at Winrod in the process).[185]

Why does Brooks seem to be on both sides of the issue—a kind of yes, there is a problem, no there is not, well, yes there is but too much is being made of it, position? One reason is that he did not want to give Winrod any ammunition to further his pro-Nazi, all Jews are communist, anti-Semitic propaganda. Second, he was allied with J. Hoffman Cohn and the ABMJ and wanted to offer support. Third, he was afraid the controversy would hurt efforts at Jewish evangelism. However, Cohn and Newman basically denied any major Jewish involvement in radicalism and were not above using the "race card" to stifle any discussion on the subject. Brooks knew this was not the position of the great majority of the historic fundamentalists and at heart it did not seem to be his position. He certainly did not agree with Newman's (and Cohn's) continued attempts at trying to discredit Gaebelein and appeared to go out of his way to cultivate a friendship with Gaebelein. Not only did continue to recommend *The Conquest of the Ages* despite his reservation,[186] but when *World Prospects* was published, he commended it to his readers "for immediate reading." He did the same for the last book of Gaebelein's "Great" trilogy, writing: "We feel urged to call it to the attention of our readers…. The book gives no consideration to the Protocols and the Jewish 'world plot' theory."[187]

When Winrod tried to claim Gaebelein as an ally, Gaebelein made it clear he wanted no part of such an arrangement, much to the delight of Brooks.[188] By 1936, Brooks was referring to "our good friend Dr. Gaebelein (whose books we sell)…" and would refer to his writings whenever the occasion allowed.[189] In 1939, the last year Gaebelein did any itinerate preaching and teaching, Brooks arranged his winter, West Coast speaking engagements.[190] Following that last trip to the West Coast, in May 1940, Brooks wrote: "It has been a rich treat to the editor of *Prophecy* to have fellowship with him [Gaebelein] on two occasions in the home of his son during his stay in Los Angeles. His wise counsel and encouragement has meant much in a period of many burdens."[191]

There also appeared in the August 1939, *Prophecy Monthly*, the reprint of a short letter (or a portion of a letter) that must have given Brooks tremendous satisfaction. It was a letter, I believe, written by Gaebelein. Although Brooks omits the name of the correspondent, the internal evidence points to his older friend and mentor.[192] Brooks introduced the letter by noting that "the editor of a well known Christian journal, who was at one time influenced by the Protocols propaganda, wrote us recently…," and then printed an extensive quotation from the letter. It is worth quoting in full:

> I am profoundly thankful for your stand and your forceful handling of the Jewish question. The Protocols fell into my hands years ago. I was led to believe that they were authentic. I even published portions of them as late as seven years ago. Then I began to see the awful storm of anti-Semitism arising, and although, as far as I could see, the Protocols might be genuine, I resolved never to refer to them again because of the incitement of hatred of all Jews that would inevitably result. I dreaded to think of contributing in the slightest measure to the frightful movement I could see coming. I never dreamed then that it would be so terrible as what we are seeing today. We pray for God's constant blessing upon your great work.[193]

Now, it is interesting that if this was a correspondence from Gaebelein, he did not say he no longer believed the *Protocols* were genuine, remembering, of course, that genuine for Gaebelein would be a document probably produced by Russian communists which would include communist Jews. But by 1939 this was a moot point. Those Americans that were pro-Hitler continued to promote the *Protocols* and unrelenting anti-Semitism. Looking back, Winrod's attempted embrace may have served as a wake up call to Gaebelein as to what was unfolding. And his apparently deepening friendship with Brooks may have also contributed. Though Brooks disagreed (somewhat) with Gaebelein, and even at one point generalized unfairly Gaebelein's position, he did not agree with the vicious attacks made by Cohn and Newman on the aging fundamentalist leader. He never implied that Gaebelein was anti-Semitic let alone a leader of the protocol-mongers.

A Second Manifesto Condemning Anti-Semitism

In October 1939, there appeared in *Prophecy Monthly* a manifesto against anti-Semitism. It was a word for word replica of the one sponsored by the ABMJ in 1936. When Brooks had printed an edited version of the 1936 manifesto, he had commented "that many other Christian leaders would have signed the Manifesto had they been given the chance."[194] This time Brooks was in charge and there was no restriction on who could sign it. The title of the Manifesto is really not so much a title as it is a purpose statement: "America's most honored Fundamentalists hereby REGISTER THEIR PROTEST against anti-Semitic propaganda in a guise of Fundamentalism. BEWARE of any who use Scripture as an excuse for such an attitude while they preach the protocols and associate with known Nazis. Note carefully the names of the Gentile Christian leaders."[195]

The manifesto went on to declare that lying and slandering Jews was a sin condemned by Scripture but over the last two or three years such had been taking place in America. The signers of the manifesto opposed such as both un-American and unchristian and called upon "every Christ-honoring child of God to show kindness to the Jews," and pray for them and their salvation. The signators expressed their desire to be "worthy of the Gospel of Christ" so that Jews might know the true Christian from the pretender. They also upheld in prayer those involved in Jewish evangelism.

Further more, those signing declared their sympathy for the Jew—remembering that Jesus, whom they "loved most" and to whom they owed all, was a "Jew after the flesh." And they "yearned that everyone of you might share with us the blessing of eternal life through Jesus Christ our Lord." They also stressed that they had "no part in the stirring up of base passions against you. And we want you to know that those who are guilty do not express the love which the Lord Jesus Christ has commanded us to show you." The manifesto closed with a note of rejoicing that a Swiss court had found the *Protocols* " 'forgeries, obvious plagiarism, immoral, and manifestly prepared for the purpose of inciting popular passion against the Jews,' " and a looking toward the day when all of Israel would be saved.[196] It is an important document in the history of fundamentalists/Jewish relations. Within weeks every major fundamentalists leader had signed it and it circulated widely even outside the fundamentalist community.

When originally published, the document had fifty-seven signatures (21 of whom were from the West Coast). The following month Brooks notified his readers that he had asked Dr. Mark Matthews if he might "add his name to the Manifesto" and Matthews had replied: " 'Yes, you may add my name. Why ask me? I started the fight in defense of the Jews and shall continue to fight against this anti-Semitism.' "[197] The next month (January 1940) Brooks once more wrote about his manifesto, this time answering queries about some leading historic fundamentalists whose names were *not* listed on the manifesto. "Our attention has since been called to the omission of the names of several prominent Evangelicals and this has led to queries as to their position on the matter. In nearly every instance the omission was due to *our* failure to contact these men" (italics added).[198]

Brooks then listed eleven more men who had been asked and had agreed to have their names added to the manifesto. The first name mentioned was "Dr. A. C. Gaebelein, editor of *Our Hope*," who wrote, " 'You may add my name to the

Manifesto against anti-Semitism' "[199] In "Finding Someone to Blame," Timothy Weber places this information in footnote 61, and gives it an anti-Gaebelein twist by writing, "Winrod, Riley, and Gaebelein names were not found in the original 1939 list, though the next year Gaebelein asked to have his name added," and on page 33, where Weber writes:

> When Gaebelein *ostensibly* repudiated the *Protocols* by belatedly adding his name to Brooks's "Manifesto to the Jews," he never informed his own constituency that he had done so or even acknowledged Brooks's crusade against those who had been taken in by Nazi propaganda. Evidently Gaebelein never saw himself as part of the problem. He continued to advertise *Conflict of the Ages* in *Our Hope* and to distribute it through the magazine's office until his death.[200] (Italics added.)

In his *Christianity Today* article, "How Evangelicals Became Israel's Best Friend," Weber comes across even more condemnatory, concluding: "some time after the 'Manifesto' appeared, Gaebelein tried to get his name added to the list of signers. The fact that he never told his own constituency and continued to sell *Conflict of the Ages* until he died in 1948 made the gesture disingenuous."[201]

It is difficult to understand Weber's position and interpretation of Gaebelein's actions considering what has been disclosed above. Gaebelein did not *try* "to get his name added" to the manifesto. And while "next year" may be technically correct, it does not reflect the true chronology between when the manifesto was first published by Brooks and Gaebelein giving permission to Brooks to add his name to it. Gaebelein, along with a number of other important historic fundamentalists, was *invited* to sign by Brooks. This is a point that Weber never mentions. One can only imagine Brooks' amazement to discover his "good friend," Dr. Gaebelein, was being "disingenuous" in signing the manifesto at Brooks' invitation. And Gaebelein's constituency was the historic fundamentalist community at large which never saw him as a protocol monger, or anti-Semitic, or pro-Nazi.[202] Nor did he try to "repudiate" the *Protocols* in the sense implied by Weber. Everyone knew who signed the manifesto as not only were tens of thousands of copies of it distributed to fundamentalists churches across America, but in February 1940, *The Sunday School Times* published the manifesto with all 67 names listed, including, of course, Gaebelein's. (Interestingly, the paragraph mentioning the Swiss courts finding on the *Protocols* was omitted from *The Sunday School Times* copy of Brooks' manifesto without any protest from Brooks.)[203]

Nor was there any reason why Gaebelein should have stopped selling *The Conflict of the Ages*. It was part of a trilogy that sought to trace the increasing spirit of lawlessness through history, seemingly finding a home in Soviet communism and its attempts to export revolution—particularly to America. It reflected the world of 1933 when communism was seen as far more of a menace than Nazism, and, of course, it was. Although overshadowed in the late 1930s by Nazism and then

World War II, the menace of communism was no less dangerous because of the turn of events. Most historic fundamentalists believed there would have to be a day of reckoning with the Soviets once the fascists were defeated. Gaebelein's view that apostate Jews played an important part in the founding of Soviet Bolshevism and in American communism was a view widely held among fellow historic fundamentalists—and it was not an inaccurate one. And, in fact, Orthodox Jews, like Christians, were suffering far greater persecution in Soviet Russia than they were in Germany at the beginning of the Great Depression.[204] Weber's comment that "During the 1930s one had to be terribly naïve to think one could sound like a Nazi and not be criticized," is not only grossly unfair, faulting people in 1933 for not anticipating what the Nazis would be doing or saying in 1938, or even 1935 (and no one did), but it simply cannot find support in the historic fundamentalists community of that period.[205]

There is, of course, room to criticize Gaebelein in his relation with Col. E. N. Sanctuary. And this may shed some light on why Cohn, at least, was so harsh toward Gaebelein. Sanctuary was treasurer of the American European Fellowship during Gaebelein' tenure as president of that organization. Sanctuary, along with Dilling and Winrod, was indicted by the United States government in mid-1942 for his pro-Nazi activities. He also was very negative toward the American Board of Missions to the Jews. In October 1935, Sanctuary was scheduled to speak at a pro-Nazi rally in New York City. Cohn learned of it and went to Dr. Gaebelein asking if the Fellowship was aware of Sanctuary's activities and attacks on the ABMJ. As a result of this meeting, Gaebelein called together the American European Fellowship board which passed "a resolution...instructing Col. Sanctuary that he must cease his attacks" on the ABMJ. Cohn sent a thank you note to Gaebelein for AEF's action.[206]

However, Sanctuary, after a brief pause, was back to bad-mouthing the ABMJ and continuing his pro-Nazi activities.[207] More resolutions were issued by the AEF board warning Sanctuary but it was not until 1939, when Sanctuary published an anti-Semitic edition/commentary on the Talmud (and used the address of the AEF, implying, of course, that he had the approval of the AEF) that Gaebelein forced him to resign as treasurer and sever all ties with the mission.[208] Why it took Gaebelein so long to deal with Sanctuary is difficult to explain. There was a long association between the two that went back to the beginning of the AEF when it was supplying relief for Russian refugees fleeing the Soviet communist regime. Nor did Sanctuary's anti-Semitism show up in his work for the AEF or in anything he wrote for *The European Harvest Field*. This long association may have made it difficult for Gaebelein to sever ties. And apparently Sanctuary's anti-Semitism became more extreme as the 1930s progressed. Nevertheless, Gaebelein can be justifiably criticized for his reluctance to break with Sanctuary as well as protect the AEF's reputation.[209]

The Jew and Communism—How Intimate?

One question that is never raised when discussing Gaebelein's writings (or other historic fundamentalists writings for that matter) is, was he right about the involvement of apostate Jews with and in communism—both in Russia and America? Was Gaebelein caught up in an anti-Semitic fantasy or was there, and is there, substance to Gaebelein's charge that a considerable number of Jews were prominent in the Bolshevik revolution and in communism in America during the 1930s and 1940s?

I have covered in the pages of this book studies written over the past decade that have shown the deep penetration of communism within both the Roosevelt and Truman administrations, as well as within the academy. However, interestingly, not a great deal of attention has been given over to whether there was a strong radical Jewish component in all of this. Evidently there was. Arthur Liebman, in his *Jews and the Left* (1979), took note of this, commenting in his Preface that as he pursued his education in sociology and politics, he "gained the impression that many leftists or Marxists were Jews or persons of Jewish parentage." He also found that many of his associates—"sociologists-socialists" —did not want to deal with the subject, that they were "reluctant to subject our own movement to the questions we asked of others in our research." In fact, Liebman writes, "the question of the relationship of Jews to socialism" was one that was deliberately ignored by "all concerned."[210]

Liebman sees Jewish influence and involvement with the left as considerable.[211] While Liebman is clear in emphasizing that the Jewish involvement with the left was always "a minority of the American Jewish population in any given period,"[212] he still notes that "as with the SP [Socialist Party], Jewish individuals and organizations provided the Communist Party with a disproportionate amount of its political backing and internal leadership." Liebman believes there is sufficient evidence ("indirect, partial, and circumstantial") to show that "the Jews were present to a disproportionate degree within the ranks of the Communist Party." He estimates that 50% of the membership of the CP from the mid-1930s through the late 1940s" was Jewish. This was the period of the American Communist Party's greatest strength. In Los Angeles, membership in the CP is estimated by Liebman to have been as high as 90% during the late 1920s and early 1930s.[213]

Jews also contributed a substantial minority, and at times even a majority, "of the Communist party's activists, cadres, and leaders." And, it seems, they "led all the Communist demonstrations at Union Square" as well as providing "most of the Communist leadership at the colleges."[214] Although the top leadership tended to be mixed during the 1930s, at the secondary level Jews predominated. Liebman also asserts that "Jews were so large a proportion of the party's 'permanent' membership and leadership, that their role was even more important than the total numbers indicate."[215] He also points out that the evidence shows "that Jewish voters constituted a major proportion of whatever electoral support the Communist party was able to win, either directly or indirectly, throughout most of its history." However, Liebman hastens to add that the vast majority of Jewish voters voted either Democratic (90% by the 1940s) or Republican "even in New York State."[216]

Robert S. Wistrich, in his *Revolutionary Jews from Marx to Trotsky* (1976), makes an observation similar to Liebman's regarding the percentage of Jews involved in European leftism. "What concerns us here," he writes, "is the indisputable fact that Jews have from the outset played a part out of all proportion to their numbers in the development of modern socialism."[217] Expanding on this theme, Wistrich not only points out the prominent role Jews played in the "short-lived Munich Soviet Republic" as well as the "inter-war" Hungarian communist party (among others), but goes on to note:

> Jews were *extremely* prominent at the side of Lenin when the October Revolution in 1917 brought into being the Soviet regime. Apart from Leon Trotsky, who planned and executed the armed insurrection, Sverdlov, Kamenev, Zinoviev, Radek, Joffe, Ryazavov, Uritsky, and Litvinov were leading figures in the Boshevik party.[218] (Italics added.)

Wistrich repeats this conclusion on page 175 of his book, again listing nine names, two of whom—Lozovsky and Volodarsky—were not listed above. He closes this second list with an "etc." implying, of course, that many more names could be added.[219] ("Ironically," he adds, "few of them were to survive Stalin's purges of the Old Guard in the 1930s.")[220] Wistrich also takes cognizance of the prominence of Jews elsewhere in the Revolutionary government:

> The prominence of other Jews not only in the Bolshevik political leadership in the period from 1917 to 1922 (15-20 percent of the delegates at party Congresses were Jews) but especially in the Cheka [Secret Police].... Jews were suddenly conspicuous as local Commisars, bureaucrats, and tax officers, as well as secret police officials. Trotsky himself appeared to have been worried at this, and favoured (sic) a greater number of Jews at the battle front—to counter "chauvinist agitation" among Red Army men.[221]

Finally, Jacob Miller, writing in *The Jews in Soviet Russia Since 1917* (1978), comments that,

> in early communist Russia the state may again have appeared to be in danger of becoming Jewish, this time because of the number of actual Jews in positions of power, locally as well as centrally, and this again may have influenced both official and popular thought throughout the Soviet period.[222]

In an accompanying footnote (1), Miller notes that despite the fact that the "proportion of Jews in the revolutionary movement, and in the senior ranks of the ruling party until the purge of 1937, was certainly high," it is wrong to conclude that Russian communism was an all-Jewish affair. Miller agrees with the communist historian M. N. Pokrovsky, "that Jews comprised from a quarter to a third of the organizer-stratum of all the revolutionary movements."[223]

Where, then, did the idea originate that Bolshevikism was a Jewish affair? This "mythology," Miller relates, "arose from two sources:"

> The high proportion of Jews amongst prominent senior members, and the influx of Jews into the party from the left wing of the Bunds, and other revolutionary or extremist groups. Many of the Jewish communists…tended to go further in administrating the new order than their gentile colleagues. The Jewish masses probably suffered more from this than did the gentiles, since revolutionaries staffed the state and party organizations administering Jewish affairs, but the idea of Jewish communist bosses went wide and deep.[224]

Gaebelein Vindicated

In light of the above, one would have to say that Gaebelein (along with other historic fundamentalists such as Bauman, Barnhouse, Gray, and Mark Matthews[225]) was considerably closer to the truth than Elias Newman and J. Hoffman Cohn, who denied any serious Jewish involvement in the Bolshevik government and blasted Gaebelein for daring to say otherwise. Actually, as noted above, Gaebelein never gave a number or percentage, simply writing in *The Conquest* that "*Some* of the *leaders* of the Russian revolution of 1917-18 and the years following were Jews" (italics added).[226] However, by quoting lists that indicated a high number of Jews were involved in the upper echelons of the revolution, it is obvious he considered the percentage of Jews in leadership quite high.

The fact that communism was anti-religious, especially anti-Christian, anti-family, and anti-democratic and anti-civil liberties made it a natural enemy of the American loving historic fundamentalists. That apostate Jews were deeply involved in this God-hating movement was doubly troubling to the historic fundamentalists. They saw the Orthodox Jew as the true Jew and an ally of sorts in the battle against the encroachments of humanism that was invading both religions. That any of God's chosen people would turn from the faith of their father's to passionately embrace atheistic communism was doubly shocking to the historic fundamentalists, far more so than the gentile modernist who were doing the same. It may have had prophetic significance but that did not make it any less disturbing. By end of 1938, of course, the origin of the *Protocols* and Jewish communists became secondary to German Nazism and its cancerous anti-Semitism, and the historic fundamentalists, as noted in previous chapters, gave more and more attention to opposing and denouncing what they considered at heart to be Satanically inspired anti-Semitism.

A Vindication for James Gray

As lengthy as this chapter has become, it cannot be concluded without an exoneration of Dr. James Gray. Again, as with Gaebelein, one finds Weber's treatment of Gray in his 1987 edition of *Living in the Shadow of the Second Coming* basically even handed regarding Gray's hesitancy over the extent of Hitler's early persecution of the Jews.[227] Yet in his 1992 article, "Finding Someone to Blame," he accuses Gray of publishing "propaganda pieces from German clergy who credited Hitler with bringing peace and harmony" to both the state and the church.[228] And in his *Christianity Today* article he charges that "During the twenties and thirties, a number of leading dispensational teachers promoted right-wing conspiracy theories and even fell prey to Nazi propaganda." It is obvious in this article that Weber includes Gray among the prey.[229]

Personally, Gray was uncertain about the extent of the Nazi governments persecution of the German Jews and thus tried to present both sides of the issue in the pages of *Moody* magazine. He wanted to suspend judgment until all the facts were known as Weber duly noted in *Living in the Shadow*.[230] Exactly why Gray was so hesitant is not entirely clear. He seems to have had a deep distrust of the press that may have stemmed from the press printing British propaganda about German atrocities during World War I. Personal contacts with German Christians may have also played a part. Certainly the German church was far from unanimous in its position on Hitler. (Of course, it could also be pointed out that even German Jews failed to take Hitler's anti-Semitism seriously in the early days of his regime.) Gray may have also been somewhat sympathetic toward Germany because of the harsh and very unfair way it had been treated under the Versailles Treaty. Of course, Gray was not alone in such hesitancy. *The King's Business*, while condemning anti-Semitism, backed Gray's position on not making hurried judgments about what was happening in Germany.[231] Even Thomas Chalmers, while denouncing the "crimes" and brutal treatment aimed at German Jews by "Nazi stormtroopers," and calling on the German people to "show their opposition" to the Hitler regime's actions, still wrote: "There may well have been some justification for taking measures against economic oppression of German tradesmen and others by the unscrupulous element in Jewry...."[232]

Others beside some historic fundamentalists also exhibited ambivalence about the Jewish situation in Germany. Conrad Hoffman, director of the International Committee on the Christian Approach to the Jews, while deploring the attempt "to 'cleanse' Germany of the Jews"—an attempt he compared to the Russian communists cleansing "Russia of the bourgeoisie"—still thought that had Hitler confined his program "to the Jews who have migrated to Germany from Eastern Europe," and were not yet citizens, "one could possibly excuse measures to expatriate such Jews."[233] Hoffman went on to stress that no true Christian could support the "unreserved persecution of any people." However, he drew attention to the fact that Jews in Eastern Europe had suffered "violent persecution" and there had been no protest. And, he noted, non-Jewish pacifists, socialists, and communists were experiencing persecution, "oftimes even worse than the Jews but we have not included them as victims of persecution in our protests." Hoffman considered this unfair.[234]

Others concurred with the above. Charles Pickett, for example, Executive Secretary of the American Friends Service Committee in 1933, and Richard L. Cary, who headed up the AFSC's Berlin office both believed, as Pickett put it, that while persecutions of minority groups had "been going for a long time in Europe...we have made little protest." Pickett went on to wonder if the AFSC should not be showing more "active concern with regard to those who are imprisoned and are being persecuted for conscience sake?" Cary, in turn, wrote that he believed the worst had passed regarding Jewish persecution (this was mid-1933) but also wrote that while the Jews resentment was understandable it could not be approved. "They are helping to perpetuate the hostility from which they suffer."[235] This was not an isolated opinion. Even Robert E. Asher, a "German-American Jew," who became "a distinguished social scientist...,"[236] agreed with Cary, as did Louis Bauman in his 1934 *Shirts and Sheets*.[237]

As late as 1939, Conrad Hoffman, writing in the *Hebrew Christian Alliance Quarterly* (which would imply some agreement with Hoffman by the Jewish Christian editors), wrote: "No one, not even a Jew, will deny that there are Jews who help to provoke anti-Jewish feelings by their attitudes, actions and activities." Hoffman, who worked tirelessly on behalf of the Jewish and Jewish Christian refugees in Europe, backed up his assertion by quoting both Rabbi Abba Hillel Silver and the *London Jewish Chronicle* both of whom severely criticized some fellow Jews for behavior that justifiably caused "provocation against the Jews." "Such individual objectionable Jews," he wrote, "do undoubtedly help to format anti-Jewish feeling but the real causes of anti-Semitism are much more fundamental and general and, while ofttimes latent, become active in times of great crisis and national stress." Hoffman went on to chastise Christians for protesting loudly but doing little else to help Jewish refugees.[238]

In the last issue of *Moody Institute Monthly* that James Gray edited, the October 1935 issue, (he had died the previous month), there appeared—"without comment"—a pro-Hitler letter from an elderly German woman living in Maryland. This elderly woman claimed she was "a devout Christian who prayed regularly" for Jesus' second coming. In her letter she claimed Hitler studied the New

Testament, that her evangelical relatives "loved Hitler, prayed for him, and refused to believe everything his enemies said against him." She also mentioned she had just returned from Germany herself where "she witnessed complete freedom in the church to preach Christ." This old woman labeled Hitler "a very good son."[239]

Weber is critical of Gray for insensitively allowing such "a blatantly pro-Hitler letter" to be published in *Moody* and concludes: "Either Gray had quite a sense of humor, or he was not as 'enlightened' as he should have been in 1935"[240] Of course, neither need be the case. The letter appeared in the "Letters to the Editors" section of *Moody*. By placing it there, Gray may have simply been drawing attention to the fact that many German-American evangelicals, rightly or wrongly, clearly did not see Hitler as an evil menace in the mid-thirties. Interestingly, Donald Barnhouse, following his visit to Germany in 1937, noted that among the Germans he spoke to "almost all" of them "of whatever party" admitted that Hitler had done some things that were beneficial for Germany. Chief among these were that he had stopped the communists and stabilized the economy. The majority also expressed regret at the treatment the Jews were receiving, and wanted more freedom than Hitler was allowing. But a great many that Barnhouse spoke to also voiced their irritation at the way Germany was being treated in the world press because of the Jewish persecutions when Soviet Russia was treating Christians far worse yet seemed to receive a pass.[241]

Even Keith Brooks, who once complained about "the vacillating policy of some of our orthodox editors" on the question of Jewish persecution in Germany and "the Protocols,"[242] responded in a kindly and patient manner when he received a critical letter from an "earnest" German-American pastor. Brooks, the pastor wrote, seemed unable to " 'find a single redeeming feature' " regarding his homeland. This pastor also took note of Brooks' " 'warm sympathy expressed toward the Jews....' " He had trouble understanding " 'WHY?' " True, there may have been " 'some instances' " when the Jews had " 'received unfair treatment.' " In most cases, though, " 'it was their own fault. They misused their privileges and controlled in economics, politics and finances.' "[243]

The pastor went on to claim that Hitler was not a tyrant, that he had seen " 'and heard him,' " that he was " 'sincere and upright' "—just the type of leader Germany needed. " 'It took a man of his type to save Germany from Communism.' " In addition, the pastor went on, Hitler, to his credit, was a man of clean habits. The German people " 'almost worship him.' " Why could not Brooks " 'write with an unbiased mind like Brother Gaebelein who never allows prejudice to run away with him.' "[244]

Brooks began his response by writing, "We can readily sympathize with this brother," however, there were times he just had to report on things that were "unpleasant to read, yet necessary for God's servants to know." He had tried, Brooks explained, "to give Hitler" his due for stopping Communism in Germany, and he had also brought to his readers attention Hitler's abstemious and "clean" habits as well as "the fact that the Nazis have cleaned up many social evils."[245]

Brooks admitted that he tended to mute "this side" because "two Fundamentalists papers" had been "lauding" Hitler and Nazism and mentioning nothing about the anti-Semitism and paganism emanating from the Nazis. Brooks reminded his critic and his readers that Hitler had written a book—"Mein Kampf"—which revealed "Hitler's bitter hatred of all Jews." In addition, Hitler "had associated himself with, and exalted to power, men who are carrying on a world-wide campaign to exterminate Jews."[246]

Brooks readily admitted he was on the side of the persecuted Jews. "We certainly have no sympathy with Communism, nor have we any desire to protect Jewish offenders against law and order. Our position on anti-Semitism is determined by Scripture alone."[247]

Brooks pointed out to his German brother, surely with a certain degree of satisfaction, that even his "good friend Dr. Gaebelein [considered unbiased by the German pastor] ...*although himself a German*, says in his latest book ('Hopeless, Yet There is Hope'[October 1935]): '*no sane person, not to speak of a Christian, can have any sympathy with the fostering of anti-Semitism. No political leader who is an anti-Semite will succeed.*' " Brooks went on to give a lengthy quotation from Gaebelein's book excoriating the "Aryomaniacs" for their attempts to paganize the German church and institutionalize their hatred of the Jews.[248] Brooks closed by asking how he could "do otherwise than oppose with all the means we have, such a movement as this, especially when it is being encouraged by Christian (?) papers with tremendous circulation?"[249]

Again, it is worth noting the courteous way Brooks responded to his German-American "brother". His goal with this pastor seems to have been persuasion rather than condemnation, evidently understanding how conflicted many believing German-American evangelicals were over what was happening in their homeland.

Adding Back in What has been Left Out

Reaching back to an editorial Gray wrote in 1921, Weber claims (in *Living in the Shadow of the Second Coming*) "Gray believed that the *Protocols* were the actual secret plans of Jewish conspirators." Next, Weber states that toward the end of 1933 "Gray was under increasing pressure to repudiate the *Protocols*." However, the only "pressure" Weber discusses is the editorial outburst by Jacob Peltz in the October 1933 *Hebrew Christian Alliance Quarterly*.[250] As I have discoursed upon this at length above, there is no need to cover the same ground again. Suffice to say that Weber believes Gray's response to Peltz was a failure, as it did not put an end to the controversy. According to Weber:

Accusations of anti-Semitism kept coming. By the beginning of 1935, Gray was fending off charges from the *American Hebrew and Jewish Tribune*, the *Bulletin of the Baltimore Branch of the American Jewish Congress*, and even *Time* magazine that persons connected with Moody had been actively distributing the *Protocols*. Gray defended the Institute in an address over MBI's radio station and eventually published his remarks in the Institute's magazine. Gray *never categorically denied the charges*; but he did say that he deplored their dissemination from any source.[251] (Italics added.)

Weber does draw attention to the fact that in the same editorial Gray denounced in no uncertain terms all anti-Semitism.

Weber concludes that the "growing criticism," some even from brother fundamentalists, brought Gray to the realization that "using the *Protocols* had become more of a liability than an asset." Weber claims that Gray did not mind using them as long as they seem to confirm the dispensational take on history but decided to dump them when it made him appear anti-Semitic. "As an opponent of anti-Semitism in all its forms," Weber writes, "Gray decided to do without them. Though he never quite repudiated their reliability, he suggested that the Bible, after all, contained all the information about the Jews that Christians needed to know."[252]

In "Finding Someone to Blame," Weber places Gray among those "who had endorsed their [the *Protocols*] authenticity early on" but had "backed away from them because of the mounting criticism by fundamentalists and non-fundamentalists alike."[253] Giving way to hyperbole, Weber writes:

> Attacked by everyone from the *American Hebrew and Jewish Tribune* to *Time* magazine for being an anti-Semite and turning the institute into a major distribution center for the *Protocols,* in early 1935 he decided that enough was enough. He denied all charges and declared that the *Protocols* were expendable. Interested persons did not need them to find out what the Jews were up to: they could learn everything they needed to know from the Bible alone.[254]

In his *Christianity Today* article, the "Great Gray *Protocols* Bailout" scenario, which had covered two paragraphs in *Living in the Shadow of the Second Coming* and slightly less than one paragraph in "Finding Someone to Blame," becomes the incredible shrinking story covering all of one half of one sentence—"Before his death in 1935, Gray swore off ever using *The Protocols* again,...."[255] However, brief as it is, it, too, manages to convey the impression that James Gray once "used" the *Protocols*.

There is, though, a great deal to the James Gray and the *Protocols* narrative that did not make it into Weber's accounts. Once more it is all in how you "wordsmith" your history. And Weber seems to have overlooked some important words that had they been included would have changed one's impression of James Gray's supposed use of the *Protocols* that is absent in Weber's interpretation.

For example, Weber claims "Gray believed that the *Protocols* were the actual secret plans of Jewish conspirators." However, this accusation is also somewhat vague and misleading. As noted, neither Gray nor any other leading historic fundamentalists believed the *Protocols* represented an inclusive Jewish conspiracy (led by Elders of Zion) to take over the Gentile nations. As also noted, Gray may have believed some apostate Jewish communists were involved in the compilation of the *Protocols*, yet he was not dogmatic in this matter. In his editorial response to Peltz, he declined to finger the authors, and Keith Brooks, in the October 1934, *Prophecy Monthly*, quoted Gray as saying that he had no idea who wrote the *Protocols* and that he had never said they were genuine.[256]

Again, after Gray responded to Peltz's accusation that he was not doing enough to squelch the anti-Semitism emanating from the circulation of the *Protocols*, Weber writes, "Accusations of anti-Semitism kept coming." However, this, too, is misleading and an exaggeration to put it mildly. Peltz was not accusing Gray of being, or of propagating, anti-Semitism nor did any other Jewish fundamentalists. And, in fact, again as noted, the next issue of the *Hebrew Christian Alliance Quarterly* contradicted Peltz's and praised Gray. Even Elias Newman, who also criticized Gray for not coming out and declaring the *Protocols* a forgery written by the enemies of the Jews, stressed at the same time that Gray was not an anti-Semite but just the opposite. As far as I can discern, no one in the fundamentalists camp, Jew or Gentile, ever accused Gray of being anti-Semitic or encouraging the use of the *Protocols*.

Of interest, following his January 1934 response to Peltz, Gray had published an important article on anti-Semitism in the February 1934 issue of *Moody* that has been ignored by historians. It was written by pastor Frederick Erdman of Philadelphia and had probably been prepared as a part of Gray's response to both Peltz and the rising anti-Semitism. In the January issue of *Moody*, Gray had announced: "Our February issue will contain a strong and enlightening article on Anti-Semitism, Past, Present, and Future...."[257] It is obvious the article had Gray's imprimatur stamped upon it.

What is most notable about Erdman's essay is the absence of any mention of the *Protocols*. However, this was in line with a constant emphasis of Gray's; no matter what you think of the *Protocols*, drop using them and discussing them, and let us get on with the evangelization of the Jews. The controversy over the *Protocols* was damaging this task. Erdman's message was typical premillennialism—those who persecute the Jews will suffer God's wrath. Still, some of his comments are worth noting for how the relate to the current affairs of the period.

Erdman drew attention to the fact that historically all who persecuted the Jews had been punished, so to speak, by God. "The Russian czars tried anti-Semitism," he related, "and the Jewish communists have triumphed." Turning to Germany, he wrote: "Hitler is trying to destroy the Jews of Germany and also Germany. Jew-haters never learn anything from history."[258] He went on to warn that it "is futile because it is fighting against God." In fact, Erdman went so far as to insist, "the Jewish people are indistructable."[259]   However, he went even beyond this and asserted "the Jew determines most of the thinking of the world." He [the Jew] had divided the "thinking of the Christian Church." Some believed in the necessity of preaching the gospel to the Jews no matter the consequences while others— liberals—flattered the Jews and "encouraged" them in their "unbelief." "Even now," Erdman continued, "when the world is getting away from religion, it is still the Jews who leads the thinking of the world, which is divided for or against the communism of the Jew, Karl Marx."[260] Erdman was convinced that,

> if the world rejects the blessings which come from the Jew through Christ, it will receive the curse of communism which also comes from the Jew. *Jews will always be leaders, whether in religion, or in politics, or in the business world, or medicine, science, or art.*[261]

Was it not "strange," then, that believers, who know that salvation is only "through the grace and mercy of a crucified Jew, can be guilty of hating Jews?"[262] Erdman even asserted "Human society is impossible without some observance of the Ten Commandments and the prosperity of a nation increases with the degree of its observance of the Ten Commandments."[263]

Erdman also made the interesting observation that "anti-Semitism is commonly a frank admission of inferiority to the Jew," and turning to Germany once again, wrote: "Anti-Semitism as seen in Germany is a result of the fear of the Jew's greater abilities, in commerce and in all professions." Erdman considered that one's "attitude toward the Jew classifies him at once, as to his knowledge of the history of the Bible, of Christ." If one was really "an actual anti-Semite" then he not only showed his incorrigibility regarding history but was also "a menace to the world and himself."[264] Erdman closed his essay by once more affirming that "human history revolves around the Jew." Without a doubt his last two sentences summed up the premillennial dispensationalist's understanding of the Jewish people. "The Jew is God's promised channel of blessing to the world. What then is anti-Semitism?"[265]

An additional example of Weber's biased and uneven treatment of Gray may be seen in a comparison between what he wrote in *Living in the Shadow of the Second Coming* (1987) and "Finding Someone to Blame" (1992). In the former, Weber wrote, "by the beginning of 1935, Gray was fending off charges from the *American Hebrew and Jewish Tribune*, the *Bulletin of the Baltimore Branch of the American Jewish Congress*, and even *Time* magazine that persons connected with Moody had been actively distributing the *Protocols*." In "Finding Someone to Blame," Weber writes: "Attacked by everyone from the *American Hebrew and Jewish Tribune* to *Time* magazine for being an anti-Semite and turning the institute into a major distributing center for the *Protocols*, in early 1935 he decided enough was enough."

A comparison of the two statements shows Weber listing three paper/magazines criticizing Moody institute for allowing someone "connected with Moody" to actively distribute "the *Protocols*" in *Living in the Shadows of the Second Coming* to implying in "Finding Someone to Blame" that there were multiple magazines/papers accusing James Gray of being "an anti-Semite and turning the institute into a major distribution center for the *Protocols*...." That is quite a transformation in only five years—for both James Gray and Weber's take on the issue. Gray goes from allowing someone to distribute the *Protocols* to becoming an anti-Semite and turning Moody into "a major distribution center for the *Protocols*...." I have not seen what the *Bulletin of the Baltimore Branch of the American Jewish Congress* or the *American Hebrew and Jewish Tribune* wrote, but the totality of *Time* magazine's comment is found in a footnote and reads as follows: "Last week the *American Hebrew & Jewish Tribune* named among others the following as current distributors [of the *Protocols*]: William Dudley Pally of the Silver Shirts of America; Representative Louis T. McFadden from Pennsylvania; The Order of 76; the Friends of New Germany and Moody Bible Institute."[266]

Gray replied to the accusation from the *American Hebrew and Jewish Tribune* and *Time* in a radio broadcast over MBI sometime in November and the script of that broadcast was published in the January 1935, *Moody Institute Monthly*. The reason he went on the radio, according to Gray himself, was "to correct an error recently promulgated by" the two above mentioned publications. Gray noted that the accusation made by the *American Hebrew and Jewish Tribune* and repeated by *Time*—that Moody Institute distributed the *Protocols*—was "erroneous and entirely without foundation." (This does seem like a categorical denial).

Gray went on to point out (and what follows is extremely important) that a similar charge had been made the previous March by "another Jewish journal, known as the *Bulletin of the Baltimore Branch of the American Jewish Congress*," and as soon as it came to the Institute's attention, the editor, Rabbi Israel, had been contacted and informed of his error. Rabbi Israel "promised to give publicity to our disclaimer." Although Gray did not check to see if Rabbi Israel did as he had promised, Gray had "no reason to doubt that he fulfilled his promise...." And Gray, always the Victorian gentleman, was not sure that the editors of the *American Hebrew and Jewish Tribune* and *Time* knew of this incident, "hence we are holding both of these journals free of wrong intent until the information now broadcast is made known to them."[267]

However, *what is of vital interest*, and never mentioned by Weber or any other historian, is that when Gray informed the Baltimore Jewish *Bulletin*, "the communication...to Rabbi Israel was supported by evidence from the Anti-Deformation League, and that evidence carried the names of Rabbi Samuel Freshof, D. D., and Mr. Samuel Livingston, chairman of that league."[268] In other words, it was not just Gray's denial against Rabbi Israel's accusation, *but the Chicago Anti-Defamation League supported Gray's denial*—Moody Institute did not distribute the *Protocols*. No wonder Rabbi Israel was willing to publish Gray's disclaimer.

One might wish for the same courtesy from at least evangelical historians. Douglas Wilson, in *Armageddon Now*, implied *Time* must have had some good reason for publishing its accusation.[269] And somehow the above *essential* information never makes it into any of Weber's accounts. In fact, Weber, in *Living in the Shadow of the Second Coming*, (1987) goes so far as to erroneously claim that Gray "never categorically denied the charge...."[270] In 'Finding Someone to Blame," he backs away somewhat from this mistake and writes: "He denied all charges and declared the *Protocols* expendable."[271] But no where does he ever mention that Gray's denial was valid and affirmed true by the Chicago Anti-Defamation League. It is also worth mentioning that evidently none of the publications accusing Moody Institute bothered to contact Moody to verify for themselves if the rumor was true that Moody did indeed circulate the *Protocols*. Nor was the point raised by historians mentioning this incident that publications that were hostile to fundamentalism might not be reluctant to publish material that would put the fundamentalists in a bad light—whether said material was true or not.[272] It is always, it seems, the historic fundamentalists who are axiomatically guilty unless overwhelming proof can be offered to the contrary, and even then apparently, it can be ignored.

In his editorial response, Gray continued in his disclaimer by asserting that his "present disclaimer...might not be regarded as adequate, did I not go further and affirm, that Moody Bible Institute deplores the distribution of the Protocols from any *Christian* source."[273] Gray refused to pass judgment on any one's motives for doing so, nor would the "Institute assume to control the opinions of its staff or its student body on the truth or falsity of any statement" found in the *Protocols*. However, he "strongly" doubted that it showed wisdom for believers to be distributing them "at this time when the public mind throughout the world is being inflamed against the Jewish race." Gray once again condemned anti-Semitism in the strongest of terms—"its spirit and language" were not only "alien and hostile to our republic," but also "alien and hostile to the Bible, and to God."[274] With great sincerity and emotion, Gray added that he "would tremble to be guilty of fomenting an uprising against the Jews, not merely because I fear the law, but because I fear God."[275]

Gray did not deal with the issue of the *Protocols* "genuineness." It is doubtful if his view had changed in this regard. He implied as much when he wrote: "that no matter who its human author or authors were, back of them was *one* author, a superhuman one, and his name is 'that old serpent, called the Devil and Satan, which deceiveth the whole world' (Rev. 12:9)." He closed his editorial with his now familiar request: "Meanwhile let us do all we can by testimony and by prayer to preach the gospel 'to the Jew first' (Rom. 1:16), as we are commanded to do, that we may 'by all means save some' (I Cor. 9:22)."[276]

The following month, there appeared on the Table of Contents page of *Moody Institute Monthly*, a one column advertisement placed by the American Board of Missions to the Jews, thanking Dr. Gray for writing that he would tremble to think he had fomented hate toward the Jews because he feared God, and that the Jews were God's chosen people who must by all means hear the gospel.[277] But one should not be surprised by this. J. Hoffman Cohn held Gray in the highest regard and always considered him a friend of the Jew par excellence.[278]

A Closing Comment

Considering all that has been discussed, and I admit it has been considerable, and all the evidence scrutinized, also considerable, it is indeed a puzzle of immense proportions why any historian would conclude that James Gray or Arno C. Gaebelein were anti-Semitic in any manner, or supported anti-Semitism in any way, or promoted the *Protocols* as a genuine document reflecting a Jewish (racial) conspiracy against the Gentile nations, or even sounded like a Nazi. Unless we are going to define anti-Semitism as any criticism of any particular Jewish group for ideas we may think are destructive to the well being of the commonweal or biblical Christianity (and such a definition would be extremely self-serving for those who would promote it), the weight of the evidence forbids such a conclusion regarding these two influential and honored historic fundamentalists. Nevertheless, there seems to be a number of historians, even some evangelicals, who seem determined to trash the historic fundamentalists even if it means they will produce less than fair, in what otherwise might have been commendable, histories. This is uncalled for and a great disservice to the evangelical community. It gives us a distorted and untrustworthy understanding of our spiritual, and for some according to the flesh, real, grandparents.

NOTES

1.   Timothy Weber, *Living in the Shadow of the Second Coming: American Premillennialism 1875-1925* (New York: Oxford University Press, 1979), 154.
2.   See Chapter Seven, 177-178 and notes 23 and 24.
3.   Weber, "Finding Someone to Blame: Fundamentalism and Anti-Semitic Conspiracy Theories in the 1930s," *Fides et Historia*, Summer 1992, 53. In footnote 67 on page 53, Weber claims that Rausch "never interacts with the material presented here."
4.   Timothy Weber, "How Evangelicals Became Israel's Best Friend," *Christianity Today*,

October 5, 1998, 42, 43.

5. Ibid, 42. Overall, Weber's portrayal of the historic fundamentalists is excessively unfair. For tens of thousands of *CT* readers, then, who know little or nothing about the movement, Weber's "introduction" cannot help but give them a warped impression.

6. Ibid, 43.

7. Ibid. However, as we shall see, Gaebelein's antipathy toward apostate Jews was one generally held in the historic fundamentalist's community, whether by Jew or Gentile Christian.

8. Ibid.

9. Ibid.

10. Ibid. This statement, though, is so broad both chronologically and so vague specifically as to be almost meaningless.

11. Ibid.

12. Ibid.

13. Ibid. Although anti-Semitism was mentioned in the by-laws as a reason for organizing, inside the cover of each issue of *Prophecy Monthly* there appeared a purpose statement that read in part as follows: "...dedicated to the promoting of a closer fellowship between those waiting for the appearing of our Savior, the dissemination of vitally important information bearing upon the signs of the times and Biblical problems, the granting of Biblical material to missionaries and needy Christian workers as funds permit, the aiding of reliable missionary enterprises and the furtherance of research along the lines of significant world movements."

14. Ibid.

15. Leo P. Ribuffo, *The Old Christian Right: The Protestant Far Right from the Great Depression to the Cold War* (Philadelphia: Temple University Press, 1983), 114, 115. Interestingly, the ACLU was divided over the "rightness" of the government's indictment of Winrod, et al (198f, 218).

16. William Vance Trollinger, Jr., *God's Empire: William Bell Riley and Midwestern Fundamentalism* (Madison: The University of Wisconson Press, 1990), 69-82.

17. I obtained a copy of Riley's file from the FBI through the Freedom of Information Act. The file only contained two pages with some of it blacked out including the name of the informants. Additional material was withheld. Basically the file gives the report by (name withheld) accusing Riley of being anti-Semitic and "viciously anti-communist" to the point of being fascistic. He even called Roosevelt a communist.

18. Yaakov Ariel, *Evangelization the Chosen People: Missions to the Jews in America, 1880-2000* (Chapel Hill: The University of North Carolina Press, 2000), 118.

19. Ibid, 118, 119. It should be mentioned that most Hebrew Christians held a similar view of freethinking Jews.

20. Weber, "Finding Someone to Blame," 45. Lack of space in *CT* seems an inadequate reason.

21. See, "Winrod Reveals a Hidden Hand," *Prophecy Monthly*, February 1933, 20. Brooks later admitted he had recommended the book without having actually read it. See, "Ye Editor—Protector of Gory Criminals," *PM*, September 1934, 6. See this article and "Sad Spectacle," *PM*, September 1942, for Brooks' account of why

he broke with Winrod and his regret for ever having assisted him. Also Weber, "Finding Someone to Blame," 45.

22. Weber, "Finding Someone to Blame," 47.

23. Ibid, 48. Weber is not clear whom "such views" include. Does he mean just Gaebelein's or Gaebelein's, Winrod's and Riley's? And "right-wing" is or can be a pejorative term. In the 1930s it implied fascist tainting. Weber tends to use too many generalizations and clichés in his writings on the historic fundamentalists.

24. Ibid, 48, 49.

25. Ibid, 49. Again, Weber seems to be criticizing Gray for not having his [Weber's] insights. What appears as Propaganda in 1992 might not have appeared as such in 1933.

26. Ibid, 50. However, this is not quite accurate, as Peltz did not accuse Gray, Barnhouse or Trumbull of promoting the *Protocols* or other form of anti-Semitism. And as their replies indicate, they were dealing with the *Protocols* in a manner they believed was most helpful to the Jews.

27. Ibid.

28. Ibid. However, whether Ironside was aiming his article at Gaebelein either directly or indirectly is open to question. It would seem far more likely he had Winrod and Riley in mind.

29. Ibid.

30. Ibid.

31. Ibid. The last sentence of this quotation is extremely prejudiced, and again, so chronologically broad as to be meaningless. It is in need of serious clarification and substantial verification.

32. This would include Gaebelein who wrote against Hitler and his anti-Semitism long before Hitler came to power. See, David A. Rausch, *Arno C. Gaebelein 1861-1945: Irenic Fundamentalist and Scholar* (New York: The Edwin Mellen Press, 1983), 162, 163.

33. In the June 1934 issue of *Prophecy Monthly* Brooks gave his stamp of approval to Dilling's *The Red Network*, and implied she was courageous in publishing it ("Keeping You in Touch with Good Things," 7). When she was accused of suppressing Jewish involvement in American communism, Brooks quoted Dilling as replying: "To start suspecting every Jew of being a Communist is idiotic. Most Jews, like most Gentiles, are ignorant of Communist intentions." She refused "to list people simply because they are Jews...." Brooks considered her position "a sound one." ("Mrs. Dilling on the Jewish Question," *Prophecy Monthly*, February 1935, 13-15.) When Dilling joined the anti-Semitic crowd, Brooks criticized her as vigorously as he did Winrod. And when she published the *Octopus* under an assumed name, he not only condemned the book but relentlessly helped expose her as the author.

34. "Excerpts from the Minutes of the Eighteen Annual Conference of the Hebrew Christian Alliance of America," *Hebrew Christian Alliance Quarterly*, July-September 1932, 31, 32.

35. Ibid, 32.

36. Elias Newman, "Report of the Pastor Evangelist," *Hebrew Christian Alliance Quarterly*, July-September 1932, 29. Also see, Joseph Hoffman Cohn, "Shearing

Samson's Locks," *Beginning at Jerusalem* (New York: American Board of Missions to the Jews, 1948), 76-79.

37. Ibid.

38. Ibid. Also see Aaron Judah Kligerman's "Christ, the Alpha and Omega of Good Will," *Hebrew Christian Alliance Quarterly*, Winter 1938 [October-December 1937]. In this article Kligerman discusses FCC churches that are closing their doors to missionaries from the HCAA least their Jewish rabbi associates become offended. "What do these things mean?" Kligerman answered: "They mean that because of these un-holy associations" Christ's church is abandoning its calling, while the very "Jewish leaders who call upon the Christians to be tolerant and liberal, are themselves most intolerant when it has to do with the Christian faith." Kligerman listed three areas where this was exhibited: they [the Jews] were against the Bible being "in our Public Schools," they wanted the crucifixion story revised "and insist that ministers do not teach it to Sunday School children," and third, they "are against Jewish missions" (3).

Also see, "Jewish Intellectuals and the De-Christianization of American Public Culture in the Twentieth Century," by David Hollinger, in *New Directions in American Religious History*, Harry S. Stout and D. G. Hart, eds. (New York: Oxford University Press, 1997), 462-484. Hollinger admits that discussing how "Free-thinking" Jews played a leading role in transforming universities to secularism "could be construed as a criticism of Jews, and as grist for the mill of T. S. Elliot's ideological descendents" (473). In addition, see Irving Kristol's essay, "On the Political Stupidity of the Jews," in *Azure: Ideas for the Jewish Nation*, Autumn 5760/1999, 47-63. Kristol severely criticizes the American Jews for trying to de-Christianize present day American society. "Such arrogance, is" he writes, "I suggest, a peculiarly Jewish form of political stupidity" (61).

39. Jacob Peltz, "Notes and Comments by the General Secretary," *Hebrew Christian Alliance Quarterly*, July-September 1932, 4-8. The persecution of Jews who converted to Christianity by their fellow Jews was often mentioned and much lamented by both Hebrew Christians and gentile evangelicals. See, Will H. Houghton, "A Conference on Prophecy," *Moody Monthly*, September 1940, 22; Max I. Reich, "Notes and Comments," *Hebrew Christian Alliance Quarterly*, Fall 1936, 2. "The Jewish people writhing under the lash of Gentile persecution," Reich wrote, "have not been and are not yet clear of the spirit of persecution themselves. They are often fanatical persecutors of their own flesh and blood when such confess the Name of Him whom they will not own as 'the glory of Israel,'...." See also, Ernest Gordon, "A Survey of Religious Life and Thought," *The Sunday School Times*, August 1932, 424, and the same Gordon column in *The Sunday School Times*, March 16, 1940, 219; Nadine Warner, "Faith of a Jewess," *The King's Business*, September 1944, 294, 295, 318; "What About It?" *Prophecy Monthly*, December 1947, 42, and the same magazine for May 1948, "Zionist Intolerance," 9.

The most shocking case of Jewish persecution of Jewish Christians I came across in my research occurred during the latter part of World War II. It was reported in *The Hebrew Christian*, July 1944. Harcourt Samuel received a cable from Pernow of the Swedish Israel Mission notifying the International Hebrew Christian Alliance that the SIM missionary in Romania could rescue up to 200 Hebrew Christian adults and children if certificates for Palestine could be procured for them. Pernow begged the IHCA to move immediately on this. Samuel did so but his attempt to obtain the certificates was blocked by the Jews. Samuel wrote:

> We made contact also with the office of the High Commissioner for Palestine, only to learn that the Jewish Agency did not consider that Hebrew Christians come under the mandate and that all their certificates for Palestine must be [for] Jews by religion as well as by race, who will be likely to settle in Zionists colonies.

With typical British understatement, Samuel consider the above "unfair," but rather than argue about it—lives were hanging in the balance—the IHCA went to the Colonial Office asking it to issue "additional certificates, specifically for Hebrew Christians." The issue was still up in the air at the time of the printing of *THC*'s July issue. Shortly thereafter, the overthrow of the pro-Nazi Romanian government rendered the request moot as official persecution of the Jews ceased. (See, "News and Notes: Roumania," *The Hebrew Christian*, July 1944, 24, 25.)

40. Ibid, 3,4.
41. Ibid, 5.
42. See, Stephane Courtois, et.al, *the Black Book of Communism: Crimes, Terror, Repression*, trans. Jonathan Murphy and Mark Kramer (Cambridge, Massa: Harvard University Press, 1999), 14. It should be kept in mind that the Holocaust simply was not in view in 1933, but what Russia was doing in the Ukraine was.
43. Rausch, 162ff.
44. See, for instance, the editorial, "Around the King's Table: The Jews in Germany," in *The King's Business*, June 1933, 171. Although the editor of *TKB* agreed with Gray about exercising caution about what was happening in Germany, he also condemned any and all anti-Semitism.
45. Elias Newman, *The Jewish Peril and the Hidden Hand: The Bogey of Anti- Semitism's International Conspiracy* (Minneapolis: The Hebrew Group, 1933), 10, 11.
46. Ibid.
47. Ibid, 15, 16.
48. Jacob Peltz, "Editorial Notes and Comments," *Hebrew Christian Alliance Quarterly*, October[-December] 1933, 7.
49. Ibid, 6, 7.
50. Thomas Chalmers, "Editorial Notes: The Protocols of the Elders of Zion," *Jewish Missionary Magazine*, September-October 1933, 130, 131. Also see his "The Present Situation in World Jewry," *The King's Business*, June 1934, 216.
51. Ibid, 131, 129.
52. Ibid, 131.
53. Ibid.
54. Ibid. Chalmers original article also contained a number of sentences condemning the Masonic Order as a conspiratorial organization with "immense influence in preparing the churches for the apostasy." He included in this section the following sentence: "Many Jews have been and are members of the Masonic Order"(130). Peltz, in reprinting Chalmers article in the *HCAQ*, edited out this section on Masonry.
55. Max I. Reich, "The Evangelization of Israel," *Hebrew Christian Alliance Quarterly*, October[-December] 1933, 5. Hyman Appleman, a popular Jewish Christian

evangelist in the mid and late 1940s agreed with Reich, stating: "You must remember the possibilities in the Jews for evil, for great evil." Thus the pressing need to convert them "or they will paganize us." (Ariel, *Evangelizing the Chosen People*, 117.) Keith Brooks also agreed with Reich's assessment. (See, "Millions of Jews Grope in Darkness," *Prophecy Monthly*, April 1934, 24.)

56. Ibid.

57. Weber and Carpenter (*Revive Us Again*, 104, 105) believe these men were embarrassed by Peltz's charge but I disagree. If anything, they were irritated with Peltz considering what he said inaccurate and uncalled for.

58. "Notes by the Hon. General Secretary," *Hebrew Christian Alliance Quarterly*, January 1934, 33, 34. Carpenter implies Peltz was speaking for the Alliance (*Revive Us Again*, 104) but this is obviously not the case. In the same editorial in which he criticized Gray, Barnhouse, and Trumbull (see note 48 above), Peltz also admitted, "those who are labeled as Fundamentalists" are "our best friends and the best friends of the Jewish people." Peltz was just disappointed in their gullibility.

59. Donald Barnhouse, "Fairness to the Jews," *Revelation*, January 1934, 6.

60. Ibid, 6, 7. One can almost read into Barnhouse's affirmation an additional thought: "despite Peltz's bumbling editorial."

61. Ibid, 7.

62. Ibid.

63. Ibid.

64. "Anti-Semitism and the Protocols: Editorial," *Moody Institute Monthly*, January 1934, 209.

65. Ibid.

66. Ibid.

67. Ibid.

68. Ibid.

69. "The Times and the Jews," *The Sunday School Times*, January 6, 1934, 2.

70. Ibid.

71. *Revelation*, February 1934, 75.

72. "Editorial Notes: Dr. Gray Resigns," *Hebrew Christian Alliance Quarterly*, October 1934, 2, 3.

73. "Editorial Notes: Good Cheer from England," *Moody Institute Monthly*, August 1935, 553.

74. "Voices of Protest Against Anti-Semitism," *Prophecy Monthly*, October 1934, 16.

75. J. S. Flacks, "The Plot and Plotters of the Protocols," *Hebrew Christian Alliance Quarterly*, January 1934, 11-17.

76. Ibid, 17, 18.

77. "The Real Roots of World Disorder," *Prophecy Monthly*, December 1934, 5.

78. Ibid, 7.

79. "Why Does Henry Ford Hold Aloof From N. R. A.?" *Prophecy Monthly*, November 1933, 4-8.

80. Ibid.

81. "A Paying (?) Business—Knocking the Jew," *Prophecy Monthly*, December 1933, 14.

82. Ibid, 15. This was a reversal on Brooks' part. In the April 1933 *Prophecy Monthly*,

he had written: "Wouldn't it be a strange thing if some of our bright legislators should actually wake up to the fact that a string of big banks (mostly Jewish controlled) has the world in its grip?" ("Sixteen Banks Have the Strangle Hold," 29.)

83. Ibid.
84. "Protocols (?): The Jewish Plot Bugaboo," *Prophecy Monthly*, January 1934, 1, 2.
85. Ibid, 2, 3.
86. Ibid, 4-6.
87. Ibid, 7, 8.
88. J. A. Vaus, "In the Jewish World," *The King's Business*, January 1934, 16.
89. Ibid.
90. Ibid.
91. See, for example, "The Protocols," *The Jewish Era*, April 1934, 36, and "The Jewish World: The Protocols," *Hebrew Christian Alliance Quarterly*, April 1934, 31.
92. Elias Newman, *The Jewish Peril and the Hidden Hand* (Minneapolis: The Hebrew Christian Group, 1933), 11. It was favorably reviewed in *Prophecy Monthly*, *Moody Institute Monthly*, and the *HCAQ* among others.
93. Ibid, 32.
94. Ibid, 33.
95. Ibid, 59.
96. Ibid, 59, 60.
97. Newman, *the Jewish Peril and the Hidden Hand, 2nd Edition* (Minneapolis: Augsburg Publishing House, 1934), 16. In the Preface of this second edition, Newman singles out Riley and Winrod without naming them by name. Other fundamentalists were guilty because they were "conspicuous by their silence." However, Newman is exaggerating to say the least.
98. Ibid, 41. Newman mentioned one list of twenty (supposedly Jewish) names "of alleged Bolshevists." He claimed six of those names "were not Bolshevists" and one of those named was a gentile. (Of course, that would still leave thirteen names as possible Jewish Bolshevists. But he says nothing about the remaining thirteen.) Of another "list of 50 alleged Bolshevists," Newman claimed 10 were not Bolshevists and "two were not Jews but Gentiles." That would still leave 38 as possible Jewish Bolshevists. It is difficult to see how Newman helped his argument.
99. Ibid, 57, 58.
100. Although Gaebelein believed in a conspiratorial view of history of sorts, he was not entirely wrong. The Soviet Union, for instance, in cooperation with American communists and fellow travelers, did conspire to undermine and subvert the United States government. And while one eschews a conspiracy theory per say, the triumph of secularism in our culture was not an accident.
101. Arno Clemens Gaebelein, *The Conquest of the Ages: The Mystery of Lawlessness: Its Origins, Historic Development and Coming Defeat* (New York: Publication Office "Our Hope," 1933), 103-108, 123, 124, 115-135.
102. Ibid, 125-135, 146-148.
103. Ibid, 94-98.
104. Ibid, 99, 100. This is exactly the same position Keith Brooks held.
105. Ibid, 100.
106. Ibid, 100-102. The quotations are filled with contempt toward gentiles.

107.   Ibid, 119.
108.   Ibid, 148.
109.   *The King's Business, Bibliotheca Sacra, Revelation, The Sunday School Times,* and *Moody Institute Monthly* all gave it high marks. *Prophecy Monthly* also gave it an endorsement even though Brooks believed Gaebelein was unfair to the Jews.
110.   Weber, "Finding Someone to Blame," 50.
111.   "Editorial," *The Chosen People,* February 1934, 7.
112.   Ibid.
113.   Ibid. Having read *The Conquest of the Ages* at least four times and some sections even more, and compared it with the Cohn/Newman editorial, it is difficult to square Newman's claims with what Gaebelein actually wrote.
114.   Ibid, 8. The term "the Jew so and so" was broadly used to designate leftist, radical Jews.
115.   Ibid.
116.   Ibid.
117.   Ibid, 9.
118.   That would be the footnote on page 97 of *The Conquest.* Newman gave almost a half of a page to discrediting the *Causes of World Unrest.*
119.   "Editorial Notes: An Unjust, Unfair Criticism," *Our Hope,* April 1934, 590.
120.   Ibid, 591.
121.   Ibid.
122.   Ibid. Weber seems to believe that Gaebelein was saying he was not going to discuss the *Protocols* again [Weber, "Finding Someone to Blame, 53]. However, it is not clear from Gaebelein's editorial that this is the case. He seems to be saying he will not refer to criticism of the book again.
123.   Weber, "Finding Someone to Blame," 50. Ironsides' article, "Are the Jews As a People Responsible for the So-called Protocols of the Elders of Zion," was not only published in the March issue of *The Chosen People* but also in the July 1934 edition of *The Jewish Era.* It is this latter magazine that I use here. 62.
124.   Ironside, 62.
125.   Ibid, 63.
126.   Ibid. It is difficult to see how Ironside's article constituted a repudiation of Gaebelein, although indirectly he may have been asking his friends to be judicious in their statements.
127.   "Jews Up," *Our Hope,* May 1934, 672. The words in quotation marks are taken directly from *Time* magazine.
128.   Ibid, 672, 673. "Jews Up," is followed in *Our Hope* by an article reviewing a *Los Angeles Times* story about "eleven alien agitators" who were waiting deportation and in the meantime were "continuing in their vicious propaganda against our government." Gaebelein listed the names of all eleven and pointed out that "eight of these are apostate, atheistic Jews." ("Awaiting Deportation Yet Still Active," 673.)
129.   Ibid. In the September 1936, *Our Hope,* Gaebelein published an extensive quotation from the London *Jewish Chronicle,* dated May 15, 1936. Gaebelein believed that the article furnished confirmation to what he had written in *The Conquest,* that is, that "Many of the Godless leaders in Russia are *apostate Jews* who are trying to

exterminate all forms of religion, including Judaism. They hate with a bitter hatred their former co-religionists." ("The Fight Against All Religion in Russia," 193).

130. Elias Newman, *The Fundamentalists Resuscitation of the Anti-Semitic Protocol Forgery* (Minneapolis: Augsburg Publishing House, 1934), 3.

131. Ibid, 11.

132. Ibid.

133. Ibid, 12.

134. Ibid. This, of course, is simply not true. Newman ignores what they had written, which was considerable—including their response to Peltz.

135. Ibid, 12-16. But Gaebelein had not placed all the blame on the Jews.

136. Ibid, 16. It is interesting to note how closely Weber follows Newman's position in the conclusion of his "Finding Someone to Blame."

137. Ibid, 17. Although Newman seemingly distorts Gaebelein's position (which undermines Newman's credibility), there was, of course, a conspiracy on the part of Russian communism to undermine western governments.

138. Ibid.

139. Ibid.

140. It is readily apparent that between the writing of the 1987 edition of *Living in the Shadow of the Second Coming* and the publishing of "Finding Someone to Blame," in *Fides et Historia* in 1992, Weber became much harsher and judgmental toward Gaebelein. In the book, after reviewing Gaebelein's "Jewish" views in *The Conquest of the Ages*, Weber admits that despite what he [Gaebelein] had written, "it would be misleading and facile to so label him [anti-Semitic]. His writings reveal a sincere love for Jews...." Although Weber believes "his writings also contain certain negative elements," nevertheless he admits Gaebelein "hated and condemned anti-Semitism. Before most people knew or seemed to care, he denounced with moral outrage the Nazi persecution of the Jews." However, on the downside, Weber believes that "by giving credence to tales of international Jewish conspiracies, he affirmed many of the arguments that anti-Semites used to justify their war against the Jews. In that way, Gaebelein was giving unintentional ideological support to the forces of anti-Semitism."

141. In January 1935 issue of *The Chosen People* (11, 12), Cohn inserted a number of brief quotations from various fundamentalists denouncing the *Protocols* as forgeries. He called it "A Symposium on the Protocols Humbug." Two of the eleven quotations were "slams" on Gaebelein although he is not mentioned by name.

142. "Shirts and Sheets'—and More Shirts," *Prophecy Monthly*, August 1934, 19.

143. Louis S. Bauman, *Shirts and Sheets or A Present-Day Sign of the First Magnitude* (Long Beach: NP, 1934), 13, 23, 26, 30, 37-42.

144. Ibid, 12.

145. Ibid, 19.

146. Ibid, 20.

147. Ibid, 21. Newman took umbrage at the Jews being called the world's arch troublemakers in *The Fundamentalists Resuscitation of the Anti-Semitic Protocols Forgery, 10.*

148. Ibid.

149. Ibid.

150.   Ibid.

151.   Ibid, 22-24. Bauman believed that should the Roosevelt administration fail to solve the Depression woes, the possibility of severe Jewish persecution would result because of heavy the Jewish influence on its programs. (See, "Socialism, Communism, Fascism," *The King's Business*, March 1935, 120.)

152.   Weber basically bypasses Bauman except to mention that he considered the *Protocols* an issue to eschew. (*Living in the Shadow....* [1987], 191.) Carpenter, on the other hand, writes that Bauman, along with Barnhouse, lead "the charge" against anti-Semitism within the evangelical camp. (*Revive Us Again*, 99.)

153.   Bauman, *Shirts and Sheets*, 17-19.

154.   Ibid, 19.

155.   Elizabeth Knauss, "Communism: What is Back of the System," *The European Harvest Field*, January 1934, 3.

156.   Ibid, 3, 4. George Hunter, the West Coast representative for the American European Fellowship also wrote a couple of articles in which he discussed the involvement of apostate Jews in Soviet Communism and attempts to export it to America. (See, "Radio Broadcast Over Station KREG," *The European Harvest Field*, May 1933, 14, and "Israel's Unfaithfulness and God's Faithfulness," *The European Harvest Field*, December 1934, 11-14.)

157.   "Prof. Burnbaum's Letter to Dr. Gaebelein," *Hebrew Christian Alliance Quarterly*, April 1934, 13, 14.

158.   Ibid, 14, 15.

159.   Ibid, 27.

160.   "An Explanation," *The European Harvest Field*, October 1934, 4.

161.   Ibid.

162.   Ibid, 5.

163.   Ibid.

164.   Ibid.

165.   "Communications," *Hebrew Christian Alliance Quarterly*, October 1934, 3.

166.   "An Explanation," 3, 4.

167.   Ibid, 4, 5. Hogg seemed genuinely disturbed and surprised by the controversy and wanted to do the right thing to prevent any future occurrence. Of the three, he alone showed a gracious, Christian spirit.

168.   "Some Remarks on the Letters By Dr. Gaebelein and Rev. H. Hogg Which Appeared in this Number of the Quarterly," *Hebrew Christian Alliance Quarterly*, October 1934, 5.

169.   Ibid. In retrospect, one wonders if Greenbaum, by being so rude to Hogg, did not miss a golden opportunity to help quench anti-Semitism among the historic fundamentalists and isolate the likes of Col. Sanctuary sooner.

170.   Ibid.

171.   Ibid. Hyperbole was not absent from Jewish Christian writers during this period. Again, they seemed especially touchy about Jewish involvement with and in communism. In part, perhaps, because it was quite extensive and they were embarrassed by it.

172.   "Book Notes," *Moody Institute Monthly*, June 1934, 532.

173.   "Books," *Hebrew Christian Alliance Quarterly*, Winter 1936 [October-December

1935], 22. The same issue reprinted from *Revelation* an extensive book review of *Rebirth: A Book Of Modern Jewish Though, An Anthology of Twenty-six Writers.* "We are grateful," wrote the editor of the HCAQ, "to the editors of 'Revelation,' the splendid Christian monthly, for permission to reprint this thought provoking article." ("Jewish Mind," *HCAQ*, Winter 1936, 20.) Also see "Books and Magazines," *Jewish Missionary Magazine*, November-December 1935, 191, for another laudatory review by Thomas Chalmers of Gaebelein's, *Hopeless—Yet There is Hope.*

174. One could list scores of articles. The following is just a small sampling from *Prophecy Monthly*: "A Paying (?) Business—Knocking the Jews," December 1933, 14, 15; "A Strange Attitude Concerning the Jews," May 1934, 15-17; "New York Nazis Start Persecuting Jews," November 1934, 12, 13; "Gentile Banking Firms Control International Loans," May 1935, 6, 7; "Jewish ritual Murder Tales," August 1935, 25-27; "National Socialist Movement Features Sanctuary," January 1936, 31, 32; "The Pyramidists, The Protocolists and the Peepers," March 1936, 10-12; "Bombastic Lies Swallowed By Millions," September 1938, 3-6; "Catching Up With Coughlin," February 1939, 8-10; "Propagandists," April 1939, 29; "The Christian and the Jewish Talmud," April 1940, 43-45; "Octopus," March 1941, 8, and "The 'Mein Kampf' of the Pellyite Preachers," March 1941, 9-12.

175. See, for example, in *Prophecy Monthly*: "Fundamentalists Contribute to Germany's Paganism," August 1934, 22, 23; "A Quotation and Challenge," September 1934, 3; "Be Sure You Know What the Issue Is," November 1934, 9, 10; "Wichita, Kansas, Linked to Nuremberg, Germany," September 1935, 23, 24; "A Defeated Political Messiah Explains Everything," October 1938, 9-11; "Cats Paws," August 1939, 31-33; "As We See It," July 1940, 45, and "Sad Spectacle," September 1942, 47, 48.

176. "Dr. Gaebelein's 'Conquest of the Ages,' " *Prophecy Monthly*, February 1934, 22. On the same page, Brooks reviewed Elias Newman's *Jewish Peril and the Hidden Hand.* He concluded the latter review by writing: "Mr. Newman rightly admits that many Jews have fallen in line with the Bolshevik movement but he denies that the Jew in general is, or ever will be Bolshevik. Only apostates and renegades will do so, he declares." ("Jewish Peril and the Hidden Hand," 22, 23.)

177. "Why So Many Jews in Soviet Jobs," *Prophecy Monthly*, March 1934, 14. Brooks was not being fair to Gaebelein at this point. Gaebelein never wrote that Bolshevism was an entirely Jewish affair.

178. Ibid, 15, 16.

179. "Protocols (?) The Jewish Plot Bugaboo," *Prophecy Monthly*, January 1934, 2.

180. "The Real Roots of World Disorders," *Prophecy Monthly*, December 1934, 7.

181. "Bombastic Lies Swallowed by Millions," *Prophecy Monthly*, September 1938, 3.

182. Ibid, 4, 5. Also see, *The Jews and the Passion for Palestine in the Light of Prophecy* (Los Angeles: Brooks Publishers, 1937), 41, for a similar comment.

183. See, "Swiss Nazis Have to Ask More Time," January 1935, 9, 10; "Newspapers Say Propaganda won't Stop," February 1935, 22, 23; "Bible of Anti-Semitism Proven Fake in Swiss Court," July 1935, 7-13; "Editorial—Comments Worth Pondering," September 1935, 31, 32, all in *Prophecy Monthly*. Also see *The Jews and the Passion for Palestine In the Light of Prophecy* (Los Angeles: Brooks Publications, 1937), 53-58. In addition, see "the Protocols were Forged," *Jewish Missionary Magazine*, May-June 1935, 87 and "Tomorrow: The Tanaka Secret Memorial," *Revelation*,

April 1935, 140, where Barnhouse mentions the Swiss Court's decision, a decision Barnhouse agreed with. However, he also noted that this decision did not excuse or absolve the acts of renegade Jews. Three years later, in an editorial—"Jewish Lies"— he listed various lies being circulated against the Jews and denounced them. This included anyone promoting the *Protocols* as authentic. Anyone doing so was a malicious liar. (*Revelation*, November 1938, 462, 463.) Also see his "Tomorrow: Anti-Semitism in America," *Revelation*, May 1936, 194, 228, 229.

184.   A copy of the "Manifesto and Call" appeared on the inside front cover of *Moody Institute Monthly*, May 1936, as a full page advertisement paid for by the ABMJ. Evidently those signing it had been specifically selected by J. Hoffman Cohn. Conspicuous by their absence are such leading historic fundamentalists as Barnhouse, Bauman, Mark Matthews, Trumbull, Houghton, and Talbot.

185.   "A Manifesto and a Call to Christians," *Prophecy Monthly*, June 1936, 8-10. The manifesto was also printed in its entirety in the Fall 1936 issue of the *Hebrew Christian Alliance Quarterly*, 3, 4.

186.   "Keeping You in Touch with Good Things," *Prophecy Monthly*, June 1934, 8.

187.   "An Arresting New Book by Dr. Gaebelein," *Prophecy Monthly*, December 1934, 22, and "A Prophetic Book We May Anticipate," *Prophecy Monthly*, September 1935, 11.

188.   "Ye Editor—Protector of Gory Criminals," September 1934, 4, and "In Fairness to Dr. Gaebelein," October 1934, 20, both in *Prophecy Monthly*.

189.   See all of the following in *Prophecy Monthly*: "Books Sparkling with Spirtual Help," February 1938, 17; "The Hope of All the Ages," December 1938, 19-21; "Real Food," August 1939, 40; "Dr. Gaebelein Tackles Prophetic Problems," January 1940, 15, 16; "Read This Now," October 1940, 26; "Moses 2nd Coming," January 1941, 36. Also see, "Good Reading," February 1940, 27. This article recommends four Christian magazines—*Our Hope, Moody Monthly, Revelation*, and *The King's Business*. In addition, also see in *PM*, "Why We are Compelled to Oppose Hitlerism," January 1936, 20; "Dark Ages," June 1939, 39, and "The Christian and the Jewish Talmud," April 1940, 43.

190.   "Engagements," *Prophecy Monthly*, August 1939, 13.

191.   "Dr. Gaebelein," *Prophecy Monthly*, May 1940, 40.

192.   "Satan's Work," *Prophecy Monthly*, August 1939, 33.

193.   Ibid.

194.   "A Manifesto and a Call to Christians," 10.

195.   "America's Most Honored Fundamentalists Hereby....," *Prophecy Monthly*, October 1939, 17.

196.   Ibid, 17, 18.

197.   "League Notes," *Prophecy Monthly*, December 1939, 32. Also see his tribute to Dr. Matthews following Matthews' death in early February 1940. ("Dr. Matthews," *Prophecy Monthly*, April 1940, 31.) Brooks especially mentions the Seattle Jewish community's high tribute to Matthews for his stand against anti-Semitism.

198.   "Our Manifesto," *Prophecy Monthly*, January 1940, 35.

199.   Ibid. The others, in order, were George T. B. Davis, Pocket League Testament, Mark Matthews, pastor of the First Presbyterian Church, Seattle, David L. Cooper, President of the Biblical Research Society, Rev. A. D. Weir, President of the Truth

for Students Movement, Rev. Carl C. Harwood, Western Evangelistic Fellowship and his brother, C. R. Harwood, Superintendent of the Denver Hebrew Mission, Dan Gilbert, General Secretary, World's Christian Fundamentals Association, L. Sale-Harrison, internationally known Bible teacher, Charles G. Trumbull, editor of *The Sunday School Times*, and the Rev. Lloyd T. Bryant, Director of the Christian Youth Campaign. Four more names were mentioned as added in the April 1940 issue of *Prophecy Monthly*: Donald Barnhouse, R. J. Leavengood of William Jennings Bryan University, Richard Lewis, editor of the *Biblical Digest*, and W. T. Reid of the Ohio Messianic Testimony. ("League Notes," 29.)

200.   Weber, "Finding Someone to Blame," 52, 53.

201.   Weber, "How Evangelicals Became Israel's Best Friend," 43.

202.   See *Our Hope* for November, 1943. It includes a section called "A Handful of Testimonies," (324-330). This article contained 35 brief testimonials congratulating *Our Hope* and Dr. Gaebelein on the Jubilee edition of that journal. They represent a cross-section of historic fundamentalists. One could look forever and never find such testimonials on behalf of Winrod.

203.   "A Manifesto to the Jews by American Fundamentalists," *The Sunday School Times*, February 10, 1940, 124, and "League Notes," *Prophecy Monthly*, April 1940, 29. One hundred and fourteen Lutheran ministers also adopted Brooks' manifesto in 1940 as their own (but also minus the sentences about a Swiss Court declaring the *Protocols* a forgery). "Manifesto to the Jews by American Lutherans," *Jewish Missionary Magazine*, November 1940, 153.

204.   See in *Prophecy Monthly*, "Hated Hebrews of Soviet Russia," August 1933, 21; "Why So Many Jew in Soviet Jobs," March 1934, 16; "Bombastic Lies Swallowed by Millions," September 1938, 4. Also see, David A. Rausch, *Arno C. Gaebelein, 1861-1945, Irenic Fundamentalist and Scholar* (New York: The Edwin Mellen Press, 1983), 121, 122, 125.

205.   Weber, "Finding Someone to Blame," 55.

206.   Harold Sevener, *A Rabbi's Vision: A Century of Proclaiming Messiah* (Charlotte: The Chosen People Ministries, 1994), 249, 250.

207.   Ibid, 250. Also see, "National Socialist Movement Features Sanctuary," *Prophecy Monthly*, January 1936, 31-33.

208.   Rausch, 269, 272, 273. Also see, "A New Treasurer Elected," *The European Harvest Field*, October 1939, 3; "Dr. Gaebelein Takes Up the Cudgels," *Prophecy Monthly*, September 1939, 45. In this notice, Brooks writes: "In this connection we desire to say that we have it on the highest authority that the splendid Mission Society, the **American-European Fellowship**, has absolutely no sympathy as an organization with the private activities of Col. Sanctuary and his propaganda which has borne the address of the Society's office without consent." In addition see, "The Christian and the Jewish Talmud," *Prophecy Monthly*, April 1940, 43, where Brooks mentions Gaebelein's denunciation of Sanctuary's Talmud writings in *Our Hope*.

209.   In this regard see, "Israel's Troubles," *Jewish Missionary Magazine*, July-August, 1939, 98.

210.   Arthur Liebman, *Jews and the Left* (New York: John Wiley and Sons, 1979), ix, xi.

211.   Liebman defines the term "left" to "designate a political ideology that in some way or to some significant extent [is] informed by Marxism," (1).

212.   Liebman, 1.

213.   Ibid, 55-59.

214.   Ibid, 60, 61. Also see pages 430, 463, 529, 535.

215.   Ibid, 61.

216.   Ibid, 66.

217.   Robert S. Wistrich, *Revolutionary Jews from Marx to Trotsky* (New York: Harper and Row Publishers, Inc., 1976), 1.

218.   Ibid, 2.

219.   Ibid, 175.

220.   Ibid. Both *Prophecy Monthly* and *Revelation*, quoting Jewish sources, mentioned the large number of Jews being "purged" in the Soviet Union in 1937.

221.   Ibid, 199.

222.   Jacob Miller, "Soviet Theory on the Jews," in *The Jews in Soviet Russia Since 1917* (3rd edition), Lionel Kochan, ed. (London: Oxford University Press, 1978), 47. Also see, Robert Wolfe, *Remember to Dream: A History of Jewish Radicalism* (New York: Jewish Radical Education Project, 1994), 135, 174-177, 182-187.

223.   Ibid.

224.   Ibid.

225.   In the July 1932 issue of *Revelation*, Mark Matthews' article, "The Place of the Jews," appeared. Among other items covered in this article, Matthews expressed the view that Jews were responsible for much of the infidel propaganda in the world, especially among the socialist and communist. In fact, Matthews' charged that "24 Jews were trying to control Russia." He closed his article by appealing to the Jews to accept Christ and abandon Spinoza, Marx, and other radical authors (307, 308).

226.   *The Conquest of the Ages*, 99.

227.   Weber, *Living in the Shadow of the Second Coming*, 1987 edition, 194-198.

228.   Weber, "Finding Someone to Blame," 49. Weber does mention Gray did speak out against attempts to dejudaize the church and "surprisingly" supported an FCC move to assist German pastors under harassment by the Nazis. However, this mention lacked the balance found in *Living in the Shadow*.

229.   Weber, "How Evangelicals Became Israel's Best Friend," 42, 43.

230.   Weber, *Living in the Shadow of the Second Coming* (1987), 198. See, for example, "the Nazi and the Jew," January 1934, 208; "Christian Jews in Germany," August 1934, 539; "The Jews in Germany," December 1934, 151, and "Conrad Hoffman's World Report on the Jews," December 1934, 167, all in *Moody Institute Monthly*.

231.   "Around the King's Table: The Jews in Germany," *The King's Business*, June 1933, 171.

232.   "Hitler and His Regime," *Jewish Missionary Magazine*, July-August 1933, 124.

233.   "Viewing Ourselves in Germany," *Jewish Missionary Magazine*, July-August 1933, 125.

234.   Ibid.

235.   Robert H. Abzug, *America Views the Holocaust 1933-1945: A Brief Documentary History* (Boston: Bedford/St. Martins, 1999), 26-33.

236.   Ibid, 36-40. (Asher wrote his, "A Jew Protests Against Protesters," for *Christian Century*, April 12, 1933, 492-494.)

237.   Bauman, *Shirts and Sheets or Anti-Semitism, A Present Day Sign of the First*

Magnitude, 20-24. Also see Bauman, "Socialism, Communism, Fascism," *The King's Business*, March 1935, 120.

238.   Conrad Hoffman, Jr., "Quo Vadis—Israel," *Hebrew Christian Alliance Quarterly*, Summer 1939, 4, 5. Interestingly, in this article Hoffman proposed that the U. S. government set aside some unoccupied land for an agricultural colony for Jewish refugees—up to 100,000 of them.

239.   "Letters to the editor: A Kind Word for Hitler," *Moody Institute Monthly,* October 1935, 69.

240.   Weber, *Living in the Shadow of the Second Coming* (1987), 197.

241.   Barnhouse, "Tomorrow: Seeing Straight in Germany," *Revelation*, December 1937, 520. Barnhouse spent considerable space in this article on the church crisis in Germany and the persecution the Confessing Church pastors were undergoing.

242.   "Joseph Cohn Goes to the Help of Refugees," *Prophecy Monthly*, August 1934, 6.

243.   "Why We are Compelled to Oppose Hitler," *Prophecy Monthly*, January 1936, 17, 18.

244.   Ibid, 18.

245.   Ibid.

246.   Ibid, 18-20.

247.   Ibid, 20.

248.   Ibid, 20, 21.

249.   Ibid, 21.

250.   Weber, *Living in the Shadow of the Second Coming* (1987), 189.

251.   Ibid, 190.

252.   Ibid, 190, 191.

253.   Weber, *"Finding Someone to Blame,* 51

254.   Ibid.

255.   Weber, "How Evangelicals Became Israel's Best Friend," 43.

256.   See "Anti-Semitism and the Protocols: Editorial, *"Moody Institute Monthly"*, January 1934, 209 and "Voices of Protest Against Anti-Semitism," *Prophecy Monthly*," October 1934, 16.

257.   "Anti-Semitism," *Moody Institute Monthly*, January 1934, 208. In the February issue, in his "Editorial Notes," Gray again strongly recommended everyone read Erdman's article. (See, "Hitler and the Jews," 252.)

258.   Frederick R. Erdman, "Anti-Semitism—Past, Present and to Come," *Moody Institute Monthly*, February 1934, 262.

259.   Ibid.

260.   Ibid.

261.   Ibid. If one is inclined to accuse the historic fundamentalists of stereotyping yet once again, consider the following by Richard John Neuhaus of *First Things:*
> Anti-Semitism—and there really are anti-Semites—think they have a corner on a dirty little secret. Their supposed secret is that Jews have a disproportionate influence in American society. But of course that is no secret at all: it is the obvious fact. About 2 percent of the population, a little over five million people, exercise an influence far out of proportion to their numbers. In certain sectors of American life—notably in the media, entertainment, prestige research universities, and to a lesser extent in finance—people in that 2 percent hold 20,

40, or even more than 50 percent of the positions of greatest influence. It is
quite astonishing. ("Whatever You Do, Don't Mention the Jews," *First Things*,
May 2002, 59.)
He reiterates this astounding conclusion toward the end of his essay:
> Among the peculiarities of this people is that they will almost certainly continue
> to exercise an influence dramatically disproportionate to their numbers. Those
> who think that influence inordinate must just get use to it. It should be viewed
> as a permanent feature of American life (63).

In between these two historic fundamentalists' sounding "bookends," Neuhaus
manages to echo yet another historic fundamentalists' conclusion:
> Jewish influence was viewed as a "Jewish problem" when Jews were
> conspicuously prominent in attacking what was taken to be the American way
> of life. This was the case with the Old Left in the first part of the last century,
> when Jews were portrayed as predominate in the leadership of communist and
> socialist movements, often because they were predominant (61).

262. Ibid.
263. Ibid, 243.
264. Ibid.
265. Ibid, 294.
266. "Religion: Protocols of Zion," *Time*, November 12, 1934, 33.
267. "The Jewish Protocols: A Radio Broadcast by the Editor-in-Chief," *Moody Institute
      Monthly*, January 1935, 230. Gray's editorial was reprinted in the January 1935,
      Hebrew Christian alliance Quarterly along with an admonition from Gray for gentile
      fundamentalists to do nothing that would increase hatred toward the Jews or impede
      in anyway Jewish evangelism. ("A New Year Message," 1, 2.)
268. Ibid.
269. Dwight Wilson, *Armageddon Now! The Premillenarian Response to Russia and
      Israel Since 1917* (Grand Rapids: Baker Book House, 1977), 97. Wilson writes:
      "*Time* magazine carried a report that the *Protocols* was being distributed by Moody
      Bible Institute. Although this was denied by the institute, apparently *Time's* editor
      believed it to be a credible possibility."
270. Weber, *Living in the Shadow of the Second Coming*, (1987), 190.
271. Weber, "Finding someone to Blame," 51.
272. The type of negative and even malevolent attacks the historic fundamentalists had
      to endure at the hands of the secular media is exemplified in an article published by
      a frustrated Keith Brooks in the May 1941, *Prophecy Monthly.* Brooks began by
      noting "that those known as Fundamentalists"—ten million people—were being
      "forced to bear the onus" of "anti-Semitic propagandist" because "of the activities of
      a half-dozen vocal leaders whose journals or radio voices travel far." He cites as
      exhibit "A" an article that appeared in the March 10, 1941, *New Republic.* Titled
      "The Battle of the Bible Belt," it implied "that Fundamentalists in general promote
      hatred of the Jews." Brooks pointed to the League's manifesto, signed by "the most
      influential orthodox leaders flatly oppose such propaganda."
            Exhibit "B" was a mean-spirited editorial that appeared in the Pasadena *Star
      News* on March 22, 1941. Most of Brooks' article is devoted to quotations and
      comments on what amounted to a vicious hit on fundamentalists. The editorial,

"Dangerous Religion," began by declaring that there " 'is no more blighting, demoralizing, devastating influence upon the individual or society than religion which is based upon ignorance, superstition, and fanaticism.' " (Of course, it does not take much imagination to guess whom the *Star News* has in mind.) What followed in the editorial is worth quoting in full from Brooks' article. It is indeed a bit of generalized, scurrilous slander:

> This country is experiencing today a revival of religion at its worst. It represents the nadir of intelligence and the zenith of fanaticism. The scene of its greatest influence is in the Midwest and Southland. Its converts are chiefly among Fundamentalists, of whom there are no fewer than 10,000,000 throughout the country. The leaders of this movement are ministers who were formerly devout Protestant Fundamentalists who believe in the most literal interpretation of the Bible.

The simple earnest faith of large numbers of these Bible literalists has become the snare of a political strategy in the hands of unscrupulous leaders which today commands the largest and most articulate single group of actual and potential Nazis in the United States.

This was pretty rank stuff. Brooks summarized the remainder of the *Star News* editorial which accused the Fundamentalists of a theology that tended "toward branding the Jew as a Christ-Killer and the cause of all the world's ills." In addition, they integrated the Bible with the " 'Protocols of Zion' " resulting in "a flaming fanaticism." The editor of the *Star News* did admit, Brooks acknowledged, that there were " 'many devout, sincere Fundamentalists' " who had nothing to do with such bigotry, "but the impression left is that 'hundreds of thousands' of the Fundamentalists are preparing the way for pogroms in America. That of course is simple hokum" (20, 21).

273.   "The Jewish Protocols....," 230.
274.   Ibid.
275.   Ibid.
276.   Ibid.
277.   "Dr James Gray Says," advertisement, *Moody Institute Monthly*, February 1934, 261.
278.   In January 1938, Cohn wrote that Gray "was among the truest and most loving friend the Jews of America ever had." "Salvation is of the Jews," in *Beginning at Jerusalem* (New York: American Board of Missions to the Jews, 1948), 138.

CHAPTER TEN

Historic Fundamentalism and the Supernatural: A Non-Conformist Historiography

Although the case has been made that the historic fundamentalists indeed had an interest in America's political, economic and social travails during the Great Depression, an interest that necessitated "serious [individual] Christian involvement," and that their interest and concern for the Jews of Europe and the suffering they were enduring brought forth an active, compassionate response, as well as a strong denunciation of anti-Semitism, it must also be admitted that they viewed or read everything through a vivid supernatural gird, an unapologetic biblical view of reality which under girded the turmoil of the mundane. Although often portrayed as an oddity unique to them, it actually placed them squarely in the mainstream of historic Protestant historiography. Only under the pressure of a new school of evangelical scholars who desire entrance into the secular academy as legitimate scholars of equal standing, has this central aspect of the Christian faith been academically muted and arguments praising and justifying the same advanced.[1]

This "new" position has been developing and gathering strength for some time now. For instance, D. W. Bebbington, in his 1979, *Patterns in History: A Christian View*, offers the following apology for his position. First, he writes, "a believer should not be a Christian and a historian but a Christian historian." Nevertheless, he also believes that the Christian must write the message according to the audience:

> If, however, he is writing for the general public or a university tutor, he must not put obstacles in the way of communicating with his audience. To describe an event as an expression of divine mercy...would be to surprise and perhaps annoy his readers. They would be likely to dismiss the Christian historian's case about human responsibility for an event along with his comments on divine participation.

Bebbington admits this may appear as an admission "that in the last analysis there is a gulf between technical history" (something all historians do) and history "on which the Christian meaning of history has been imposed." However, he refuses to accept such a conclusion. He believes that even if specifically "Christian allusions" are left out "the Christian vision of history can still have shaped its composition." Bebbington does not see this as a compromise or a contradiction. Rather, he writes:

> What is written will be a distinctively Christian product, but the Christian content will be implicit rather than explicit.... The Christian historian can discern God at work in the past without necessarily writing of him there.... The Christian is not obliged to tell the whole truth as he sees it in every piece of historical writing....[2]

Obviously, Marsden, Noll, Stafford, and many other present day evangelical historians have adopted Bebbington's position, perhaps even carrying it a step further, until it seems that this position reign's supreme among evangelical historians. However, uneasy lies the crown.[3]

Misunderstanding Historic Fundamentalism's Providentalism

The above may explain, however, why the historical fundamentalists' view of an active and easily discernable providence brings criticism from current evangelical historians. Mark Noll, for example, is especially unrelenting in this regard. Critical of what he labels "excessive supernaturalism," which he believes has had a negative impact upon evangelical political reflection, as well as its overall "life of the mind," Noll charges, "Dispensationalism promoted a kind of supernaturalism that, for all its virtues in defending the faith, failed to give proper attention to the world."[4] Elsewhere he writes, "Again, Fundamentalists were reading history as if they were inspired, like the authors of Scripture had been inspired, rather than as believers whom God had commissioned to participate in the ongoing nurture of the church in a time between times."[5]

Joel Carpenter makes a similar charge, writing, "fundamentalists tend to de-emphasize historical causation. They regularly read world events and their role in them from a divine angle of vision, as if they, like the authors of Scripture, are divinely inspired."[6] Using James Gray as an example, he notes that because the historic fundamentalists so highly prized religious activities, they tended not to take the "affairs of the secular world too seriously—at least on their own terms." Carpenter then claims:

> Leaders' discussions of public affairs quickly became attempts to correlate current trends with biblical prophecy or were turned into homilies about spiritual matters. James M. Gray briefly praised the development of the Social Security Administration in 1935, but then he launched into a discourse on the "eternal security" that came from knowing Christ as personal savior.[7]

In defense of Gray (and other leaders), as has been previously noted, he seems to have taken the "affairs of the secular world" with more seriousness than historians have credited him. It might also be worth noting (for the sake of fairness) what he actually did say about the passage of the Social Security Act.

Carpenter is slightly mistaken when he writes that Gray "briefly praised the development of the Social Security Administration in 1935" before launching into a homily on how in Christ we have eternal security. Carpenter cites a January 1935 editorial written by Gray that appeared in the *Moody Institute Monthly*. However, in that editorial, Gray was commenting on "the conference to promote social security" which had gathered "in Washington" the previous fall "to see what could be done to lessen fear, worry, and pain in the apprehension of deprivation and dependence in old age."[8]

And, true enough, after giving the meeting his nod of approval, he launched into a homily on how one could have eternal security through a personal faith in Jesus Christ. Why this represents evidence that Gray in particular and the historic fundamentalists in general did not take the "affairs of the secular world too seriously—at least on their own terms," is something of a puzzle. In fact, Gray was doing what pastor/teachers have done for centuries, and still do (present writer included)—use a current event as a launching pad to point people to the far more vital eternal. Such a teaching method was even used by Jesus.[9]

Carpenter is evidently unaware of an October 1935 editorial Gray penned following Congressional approval of the Social Security Act. In that brief editorial one gets the impression Gray was quite conversant with its content. Nor does he mention the eternal. He reviews the taxes that would finance the measure, and in conclusion, while being taken aback by the haste and "relative indifference" given to it before final passage, "devoutly" hoped that it would prove to be constitutional and "not become a social boomerang." Despite these misgivings, Gray declared that he,

> was glad the national heart is touched and the national conscience aroused, and that something real and practical is in the offering for these needy classes to some of which in the briefest time any of us may belong. In our earlier period of history we might have depended upon private charity to meet our needs, but the world seems to have grown too big for that.[10]

Perhaps even more revealing as to James Gray's response to "secular" issues "on their own terms," was his position concerning the Townsend Plan. In the May 1935, *Moody Institute Monthly*, Gray had published an editorial heavy with sarcasm toward Townsend and his plan. A deluge of critical mail had rained down upon his head in response. He printed one of the more "restrained and polite" responses, with his reply, in the August 1935, *Moody*. The letter, a vigorous defense of the Townsend Plan, accused Gray of unwarranted sarcasm and ignorance regarding the workings of Townsend's proposal. It closed with an admonition that Gray should "study the Townsend Plan thoroughly before you attempt to ridicule the movement." If he was not willing "to do this" then "for God's sake" do not say anything about it in the pages of *Moody*.[11]

Gray's reply began with an apology. He had reviewed "the offending editorial, and admit[ted] that from a Christian standpoint its tone gave justification for criticism." Gray apologized "to every devotee of the Townsend plan...."[12] On the other hand, he informed his critics, he was quite familiar with the details of Townsend's proposal. He had read "almost every word" of an 80 page "report of the hearing" Dr. Townsend (and his actuary Glen Hudson) had been granted before the House of Representatives' Ways and Means Committee. In fact, not only had he read "almost every word" of the report once but he had done so two or three times. In addition, he had also read the National Industrial Conference Board's evaluation "of the plan...to say nothing of the articles discussing it in current newspapers and periodicals."[13]

Having established his credentials, Gray briefly discussed his concerns over how the plan would be financed and the "fairness" in the way it would redistribute wealth, quoting Labor Secretary Perkins' comment to the effect that "the Townsend Plan 'would give 9 per cent of our population more than half the income of the country!' " "Where the justice or wisdom would be found in that adjustment," Gray wrote (almost sarcastically), "it is difficult to see."[14] Gray also feared that the Townsend Plan, were it to become law, would force the federal government to print, and print even more, money to finance the scheme. This would result in a hyper-inflation which would invite a repeat of the 1920s " 'German calamity.' " Without one reference to the eternal, Gray closed his editorial reply to his critics by apologizing once again. He admitted that he had been "so impressed...with the sincerity, the benevolence, and the patriotism" of Townsend and Hudson before the Ways and Means Committee, that he was not hesitant "in renewing our apology for anything in the way of ridicule we may have written."[15]

It would seem, then, if Gray is to be our example, that the historic fundamentalists could and did take seriously current affairs "on their own terms."[16]

A Place and a Purpose for Providentialism

It also ought to be kept in mind that the leaders of historic fundamentalism were not professional historians, sociologists, psychologists or anthropologists.[17] Nor were they writing for the secular academy or academic journals. They were pastors and teachers of the Word of God; it was their job to interpret things from "God's point of view" (Eph. 4: 11-15). An argument of sorts may be made for excluding the providential when functioning in a secular academic environment but no such argument can be supported for keeping it out of the Christian community. It has nothing to do with trying to be inspired as the authors of Scripture were inspired but rather being informed by Scripture on underlying realities that escape or are deliberately avoided by psychologists, sociologists, historians, and anthropologists who by nature eschew the frightening possibility that God may indeed be the Lord of history. What the historic fundamentalists were doing was no different than what prophets and preachers and apologists of the Word have been doing since the post-Apostolic age. Kenneth Monroe's "The Biblical Philosophy of History" is cut from the same cloth as Augustine's *City of God*, and both "start with the assumption that supernatural forces shape history."[18]

Evangelical historian Mark Noll believes that such a position leaves one "unprepared to countenance the complexity of mixed motives in human action, and uninterested in focusing seriously on the natural forces that influence human behavior."[19] However, the historic fundamentalists seemed quite aware of the human motives that stimulate people's actions. They simply founded those motives upon a deeper reason—a nature disposed to sinful rebellion against God. In saying this they did not seem particularly concerned over whether the academy approved of their position. And, if in fact the Bible is the revelation of God to man, and if, as a school of exegesis stretching back to the third century indicates, the best way to interpret Scripture is to interpret it literally, then one can see the historic fundamentalists' "supernaturalism" as a needed and welcomed corrective to the excessively secular historiography of the modern (and now postmodern) world. From their perspective, Noll could be accused of being so committed to modern historiographical methods that he does not give the spiritual nearly the attention it deserves.

The historic fundamentalists might also have noted that their position gave them the means of evaluating the "rightness" of what the secularists say about such things as human forces and mixed motives. While giving such their due, they may also have drawn attention to the fact that focusing on the "complexities of mixed motives" and "the natural forces that influence human behavior" may simply be a way of hiding from the truths revealed in Scripture and general revelation about God, man, sin, and history (such as those revealed in Romans 1:19, 20). In addition, they may have pointed out that the habits of the mind and social influences give an imperfect picture at best—deformed as they are by sin; that to leave out the spiritual will always lead to a wrong response due to a faulty analysis of man. The historic fundamentalists, as Carpenter himself acknowledges, refused "to accept the modern tendency to overpower spiritual consciousness with a matter-of-fact, this-worldly, secular outlook…they consistently subverted the assumption that current events and issues were of ultimate concern."[20] Their approach may have been at odds with a secularizing America, but not with Christian history or the Bible.

The Limits of Secular Historiography

Obviously modern historiography eschews any hint of a "theographic" interpretation of history. What else would one expect them to do? However, this now holds true for many evangelical historians as well. George Marsden, for instance, considers it wise for the Christian historian to hold back on making judgments about "what is properly Christian while he concentrates on observable cultural forces." By doing this, "he provides material which individuals of various theological persuasions may use to help distinguish God's genuine work from practices that have no greater authority than the customs or ways of thinking of a particular time or place." Marsden is willing, then, to conclude that "we may—and ought to—carefully identify the cultural forces which affect the current versions of Christianity."[21] Agreed—but....

Despite his confidence such an approach has its own limitations and imperfections. If this were not true, there would be no need to reconsider past interpretations of historical events. It is obvious that we may misread or exaggerate the impact of particular cultural forces upon historical events or persons, or inject our own interpretive preference (especially if we are as culturally imprisoned as the postmodernist claims). We might also ask why a Christian historian may not make judgments on what is properly Christian? In fact, one would think that such an historian's knowledge of history as well as a familiarity with great Christian thinkers and (hopefully) the Bible, would seem to be an advantage in this regard. Certainly "individuals of various theological persuasions" have no monopoly or special insights on "distinguish[ing] God's genuine work" in history. And seen from another perspective, the case could be made that the historic fundamentalists, as a people of a particular outlook, were looking at the cultural forces (a severe economic depression, theological apostasy, increasing secularization, and the bloody, carnal drift of political events and ideologies) and were compelled to conclude that a spiritual crisis existed, that God had a case against America (and other nations as well) and its people (and especially His Protestant church).

In addition, Marsden's approach leaves out the influence of the Bible on one who sees it as a word from God rather than simply another cultural item. Such a spiritual position may not be quantifiable, yet it can and is a powerful factor in how one conducts his or her life. One may study the "social" origins of a fundamentalist and then use these factors, along with other "cultural" constructs, to offer a secular interpretation on why that person became or is a fundamentalist. No doubt this would find ready acceptance in the academy. But if the influence of Scripture as understood by a fundamentalist—as well as his or her born-again experience—is left out, how accurate can such an interpretation be? It may satisfy the secular historian but it is inadequate as a viable interpretation. Cultural forces alone cannot begin to read the heart or what motivates it. As Iain Murray has pointed out, "But surely, to write the lives of eminent Christians with minimum notice of the things which meant *most* to them, and without which their lives cannot be understood, is to mislead?"[22]

For example, Marsden writes, "Fundamentalism appealed to some well-to-do, and some poor, but also and especially to the 'respectable' Protestant and Northern European working class, whose aspirations and ideals were essentially middle-class Victorian."[23] Not only do I believe that such catch-all phrases as "middle-class Victorian" are indeed shop-worn cliches that convey little real insight, except, perhaps the limits of the secular historian's "comfort zone," but from a biblical perspective there is something extremely dissatisfying about such a "cultural" reading on the source of a fundamentalist's conversion to Christ or his moral, ethical and social norms. Was there no conviction of sin under the preaching of the Word, no repentance, no amazing grace and no born again faith in Christ on the part of these people? The same criticism holds true for other "secular" interpretations, such as Douglas Frank's claim "that the wildfire growth of premillennialism in the decades after the Civil War really represented a bold move on the part of evangelicals to recapture their control of history."[24] (One is tempted, of course, to ask Frank just when and where these "bold" evangelicals met to make such a momentous decision.) Roger Lundin, for his part, wants to attribute it to alienation, leaning on Marsden for his support. Lundin believes that "the evangelical feeling of alienation was to lead, among other things, to the fundamentalist's embrace of dispensational premillennialism and to the definition of Christian life as an existence untainted by a short list of social vices."[25] All three of these gentlemen are evangelicals yet in the above analysis, they do not attribute one sincere biblical motive to the choice these past evangelicals made.

Joel Carpenter also fills his book *Revive Us Again* with much sociological and psychological interpretation, such as, "Fundamentalism has been ... one important way in which 'average Americans invested their lives with meaning.' "[26] And "Millions of otherwise ordinary Americans found it to be an attractive and empowering way of investing their lives in a larger purpose."[27]

Are these interpretations really the reasons millions of people became theologically conservative Christians holding passionately to a particular view of the Bible and the second coming of Christ—even to the point of being social pariahs in the eyes of America's influential classes and media? Such sociological purgation of historic fundamentalism moved one thoughtful reviewer of Carpenter's book to note:

> Above all else, fundamentalist preachers, evangelists, and ordinary people who tried to convert their neighbors spoke a message of personal sin, personal repentance, and personal salvation. Apparently this message made a lot of sense to a lot of people. . . . Perhaps, as Carpenter and so many other historians suggest, the rite of conversion and acceptance into the community of fundamentalism was more than anything a way for

people to bring order into their lives during unsettled times. Or maybe unsettled times had less to do with it than did unsettled lives.... Maybe one of the main forces driving the movement forward was that many Americans actually believed they were sinners in need of divine redemption, and to them, fundamentalist teachings about how one finds redemption seemed true.[28]

Believing the message wholeheartedly, they became wholeheartedly fundamental Christians. Was it a genuine supernatural regeneration, or a psychological catharsis that gave them a new direction in life? Why, for the sake of "professionalism," should one view be excluded from the academy simply because most secular historians do not want it there? Does this unpopularity make the "religious" interpretation wrong or even bad history? Hamilton's point is well taken—that there may be a valid alternative to the hackneyed secular explanation. Maybe what the historic fundamentalists believed the Bible taught was the primary motivating factor in what they did, said, and thought on a daily level. Sociological or psychological or economic interpretations are primary only insofar as one believes there is no theological dimensions (or there should not be any) to history, no Holy Spirit indwelling the new creation in Christ Jesus, or no Bible that deeply alters the way a person thinks and acts because he or she is convinced it is God's Word. If the interpreter factors out that which is most influential in a person's life simply because it is spiritual and substitutes his or her own secular reason simply because he abhors the spiritual, how can he arrive at anything but a truncated misrepresentation? Robert Wilken reminds the scholar:

Cut off from collective memory it is easy for scholars to construct an entire framework of interpretation that has no relation to actual human experience or aspirations. We need to be reminded that scholarship on the living religious traditions cannot exist in isolation from the communities that are the bearers of these traditions, as though those who transmit and practice the things we study have no say, indeed no stake, in the interpretations we offer.... The things we study, it is assumed, belong to no one; they are simply lying there waiting for whoever wishes to study them and in whatever way one sees fit.[29]

A Fundamentalist Insight: The Necessity of Providentialism

Interestingly, Noll admits, "The tumult of the 1930s no doubt reflect momentous spiritual realities; the trends could, in fact, not be analyzed satisfactory if the spiritual character of human beings was neglected." Noll, however, offers no such analysis himself nor does he offer any suggestions on how the historian can proceed along these lines. Having mentioned them, he is content to move on. Indeed, in the very next sentence he repeats his theme that "an excessive supernaturalism" damaged "evangelical political reflection."[30]

Yet if the 1930s truly do reflect "momentous spiritual realities" that should not be ignored, why are we faulting the historic fundamentalists for trying to identify and discuss them? If anyone was in a position to do this, and if anyone had an obligation to do this, was it not these Christians who believed so passionately in the authority of the Word of God and the providential view of history, and expended so much intellectual effort to defend their perspective?

Christianity is, after all, about the supernatural, not cultural forces. Evangelicals, of all people, must not ignore this. It was this that set the historic fundamentalists off from, and in opposition to, the Social Gospel. The issue was not the social, but rather the Gospel. Their insistence that man was lost in sin, that "every inclination of the thoughts of his heart was only evil all the time,"[31] (which in turn was an insurmountable obstacle to every effort on man's part to create utopia) was a needed correction to the secular, Darwinian, positivistic, blood-drenched, megalomania of the day. Only biblical-historical Christianity could offer an ultimate explanation for the madness about to burst loose at the end of the Great Depression decade. Only biblical-historical Christianity could witness to the reality of "the deep-rooted and protean nature of evil" in people's hearts, and that denial of this evil only increased the dreadful harm and reach of sin.[32] As Machen told his radio audience in 1935, "The distress of the world is due clearly to an evil that is within the soul of man."[33]

Likewise, the historic fundamentalists' insistence on the reality of the "evil one" made possible an understanding of the cosmic enormity of evil that secular historians were, and are, inadequate, and even unable, to explain. Is the academy really willing to think it can explain with a secular analysis of cultural forces the incomprehensible evil that is one of the hallmarks of the twentieth century, an evil that began with the slaughter of the Armenians and has ended with the "ethnic cleansing" of Kosovo by the Serbs and the murder of hundreds of thousands of Tutsis in Rwanda? And in between is an endless river of blood so deep and so wide and so evil that we can only "estimate" how many millions have died in its diabolically induced currents.

Tragically, and to the academies great intellectual deception, it thinks it can. This was recently driven home by an essay that appeared in *The Chronicle of Higher Education*. Written by historian Christopher R. Browning, the essay, "Human Nature, Culture, and the Holocaust," focuses on the central question of, "What allowed the Nazis to mobilize and harness the rest of society to the mass murder of European Jewry?"[34] Browning's approach is that the German people are really no different from the rest of us, that all of us are capable of doing terrible things. This moves Browning to ask his next question, "What really is a human being?" In other words, "we must give up the comforting and distancing notion that the perpetuators of the Holocaust were fundamentally a different kind of people because they were products of a radically different culture." It is his conclusion that if we ever hope to begin to understand "all those recruited into [Germany's] machinery of destruction" we must first investigate "human nature."[35]

For a brief moment one is tempted to think that Browning may be ready to move closer to where the historic fundamentalists stood: that human beings share a common nature that has an evil bent to it which is expressed in innumerable sinful common acts, habits, and cultural traits. But that hopeful thought is stillborn. "Here I think we historians," he muses, "need to turn to the insights of social psychology—the study of psychological reactions to social situations." These are the people, Browning believes, who can give us the necessary insight into "the relationship between legitimate authority, individual belief, and murderous behavior."[36]

Here, in glaring starkness is the prideful paucity of the secular. Imprisoned within the confines of historicism's supremely confident but obviously finite boundaries, secularism's historians can never seek solutions in transcendent answers no matter how inadequate their own. Even a secular critic such as Neal Postman understands the "wrong-headedness" of Browning's quest. In fact, this is what Postman label's "scientism," a "philosophy" of expertise he harshly condemns. "Social research," he writes, "can tell us how some people behave in the presence of what they believe to be legitimate authority. But it cannot tell us when authority is 'legitimate' and when not, or how we must decide, or when it may be right or wrong to obey."[37] With keen moral perception he reminds us that today we "call sin 'social deviance,' which is a statistical concept, and [we] call evil 'psychopathology,' which is a medical concept. Sin and evil disappear because they cannot be measured and objectified, and therefore cannot be dealt with by experts."[38]

It is of interest, and perhaps odd, that in an essay that seeks to explain why millions of ordinary citizens became supporters of the mass killing of millions of others, Browning never mentions the word "sin" or "evil" or even implies that such non-sociological conditions exist. His omission speaks volumes about the psychologized mindset of the modern and postmodern scholar. Indeed this tendency bears witness to the possibility that today's scholarship has, indeed (as Robert Wilken has noted), succumbed to the level of a " 'gray morass' of second order discourse," that divorced from religious memory, "the language of scholarship [especially in the social studies] is impoverished, barren, and lifeless, a tottering scaffold of secondary creations in which 'words refer only to words.' "[39] As Gertrude Himmelfarb sarcastically (and anxiously), has commented, noting the devastating effect deconstruction can have upon the writing of history, "Our professors look into the abyss secure in their tenured positions, risking nothing and seeking nothing save another learned article."[40]

More telling, though, is theologian David Wells' comment that modernity "has emptied life of serious moral purpose. Indeed it empties people of the capacity to see the world in moral terms, and this, in turn, closes their access to reality, for reality is fundamentally moral."[41] At this point, Wells is at least touching hands with modern evangelicalism's fundamentalist forebears. If nothing else one cannot argue that they did not leave us a recognition of the moral and spiritual dimensions of human nature and human history: man does have a nature prone to sin continuously, and Satan is the god of this age.[42] When Joseph Edwin Harris reminded his readers of this, he performed a greater service for his time than Browning has for this one. Scripture, indeed, had something to teach modern man, especially for those who were still foolish enough to believe that it was possible for humanity to bring in a Kingdom of some sort, the hellishness of the 1930s notwithstanding:

> Yet behind all the opposition to the gospel, behind all the evil rampant in this world, is that old serpent the devil. And what can man do to put him out of the way? What legislation can reach him? What program of social reform can cope with this invisible foe? The church is powerless to rid the world of him.[43]

No historian today, including, now, many evangelical historians, would be willing to touch Harris' analysis. However, that does not mean we should not, or that history is better for our having eliminated the "supernatural" from consideration, thereby making history exclusively "our history" at last. It may be we are bearing mute testimony to Albert Camus' dictum that modern man hates to be judged, even, it seems, the modern evangelical man. And, truthfully, there were not many scholars in Harris' own day, either, willing to accept his words, in part because many of them were too busy using their scholarship to try to destroy any influence biblical Christianity might still have in American society.[44] Nevertheless, he was faithful to his biblical and Reformation roots in refusing to ignore the biblical doctrines of sin and Satan and unredeemed man's bondage to both. The same must be said of Joseph Taylor Britan when he wrote, "What strange powers are they that compel governments to contribute to the damage and devastation of their own citizens rather than their joy and peace and well-being." The only obvious, sane answer, Britan concluded, to the growing "insanity" that ruled peoples and governments in the 1930s, was Satan and satanically inspired men.[45] And considering the magnitude of the slaughter perpetuated by the communist and fascists regimes, and the wars fought to stop them, bringing even more slaughter, the findings of the social psychologist appear justifiably anemic beside the conclusions of Scripture offered up by Harris and Britan.

What these " 'Fundamentalists,' these conservatives, these Christians" were doing, then, was identifying the "momentous spiritual realities" of their times. As far as they were concerned, Satan raged and howled and incited slaughter in the 1930s and 1940s. And Western man, unwilling to admit "the deep-rooted and protean nature of evil" resident in his own heart, and with Nietzsche, celebrating

God's demise, cast aside all the restraints that two-thousand years of Christianity might have imposed upon him and cooperated.[46] It is not the historic fundamentalists who testify to this. The unnumbered millions who were stripped of every shred of human dignity (a dignity the fundamentalists would have insisted was God-given), degraded beyond imagining, and murdered by the millions by Hitler's and Stalin's minions are testimony enough. Certainly it is a testimony that will be heard at the judgment bar of the Judge of all the Earth.

If all we have and can hope for to understand and restrain the horrendous evils which men seem compelled to perpetuate are revived neo-postmillennial, moralistic eschatologies, deconstructed histories, endless sociological studies, psychological pronouncements, political analyses of cultural forces, as well as unnumbered memorials and museums to the massive slaughters that have turned the earth (even Christendom's earth) into killing fields many times over in the twentieth century alone—if this is all we have, then the twenty-first century shall mimic the twentieth again and again and again. Here, then, the historic fundamentalist with his "excessive supernaturalism" has something to teach the ever-multiplying Christian scholars, who yearn for professional acceptance, a lesson they would do well to learn.

An Inescapable Calling—Even Today

Evangelical scholars ill-serve the world and ill-serve the academy if they set aside their inheritance, those great and momentous revelatory truths about God, man, and society they possess in Scripture (including the providential view of individual and corporate history) simply to participate on other-than-Christian terms in the dominant secular academy.[47] They will also ill-serve the evangelical community if they keep writing agenda-driven histories of fundamentalism that present it as a "dark-age" to be isolated from "normal" Protestant history. Historically, theologically, and in spirit, the historic fundamentalists were far closer and more faithful to their Reformation forebears than are many present day evangelicals, including some of their critics.[48]

It is not to be denied that historians must consider cultural forces (though they have come to place an exaggerated confidence in them), including Christian historians. No Christian's movement is free from cultural limitations, nor is the individual Christian pilgrimage through this life free from his or her cultural setting (though the Word of God does promise to wedge us free from a considerable amount of cultural blindness).[49] Neither the Bible, nor the historical record hides the weaknesses and prejudices of its heroes—nor should we. If we do, then we forget, as Edward Ulbach reminded his readers over a half-century ago:

Deep spiritual realities are seldom learnt by men without bitter wrestling with their own sins and sorrows, and that those who have gained faith and strength to do their duty in this life, will often retain much ignorant prejudice, and much narrow egotism to mar the nobility of their grandest deeds.[50]

On the other hand, as Iain Murray reminds us, "Scripture never stops at the sins and failures of believers; it goes on to show the triumph of God's purpose and grace in their lives."[51] So then, professionally, the Christian historian must be more than a pious agnostic, and must do more than acquiesce to the secular historian and his methodology. It is incumbent upon him or her to point out the limitations of all cultural interpretations on the one hand, while on the other remembering out loud that the spiritual is real and does impinge upon this world. They cannot, therefore, and should not avoid wrestling with the momentous questions of what God is doing through people or in events.[52] That does not mean they should answer with the irritating certainty of the historic fundamentalists. But neither should they avoid providentialism simply because secular historians detest the thought or would think ill of them professionally. If the general academy will not countenance such a "fundamentalist" approach then it does harm to itself. And if the academy will not let evangelical historians teach in its lecture halls, then they can preach at its gates. Either way the Christ of history and over history will be made known.

Historian Robert Wilken has emphasized that "*Dogma* and *truth* are not the kind of words that will pass the test of political correctness; yet—or perhaps therefore—they are most useful in helping us to identify precisely the distinctively theological task that lies before us." And that task, as he understands it, is that [all] "Christians must learn again to speak forthrightly about who we are and what we know of God."[53] The historic fundamentalists practiced this as they interacted socially, politically, economically and theologically with an increasingly secular, uncertain, Great Depression America, and a world hurtling once more into that unspeakable darkness which only the human heart is capable of producing. If present day evangelicals think they cannot learn from them, or must sacrifice the foundation that gave them their staying power and worldview, then it is we, with all our learning and scholarship, who will be unfaithful, not our spiritual grandparents.

NOTES

1. See, for example, Tim Stafford's glowing article approving this new evangelical way of writing history: "Whatever Happened to History," *Christianity Today*, April 2, 2001, 42-49.

2. D. W. Bebbington, *Patterns in History: A Christian View* (Downers Grove: InterVarsity Press, 1979), 187, 188. D. G. Hart thinks Christian historians should

adopt a kind of historical agnosticism when writing about historical events. See "History in Search of Meaning: The Conference on Faith and History," *History and the Christian Historian*, Ronald A. Wells, ed. (Grand Rapids: William B. Eerdmans Publishing Company, 1998), 85, 86.

When it was pointed out that there was no discernable difference between the way he wrote history and that of his secular colleagues, despite his evangelical stance, George Marsden was quick to defend himself. "My Christian perspective," he claimed, "helped shape every page" of *The Soul of the American University* ("Summing Up," *Academic Questions*, Spring 1996, 33). Still, his critics do seem to have a point.

As for the historic fundamentalists, they choose to interpret the Great Depression in theological terms because such dealt with ultimate reality. That does not mean they were unaware of how others were trying to interpret it in strictly cultural terms, or that these terms were not "true" on a mundane level and should not be studied. But neither were they willing to accept the position that in order not to offend their audience, they should so mute God's sovereignty over nations and history that God is hidden except to the writer.

3.   See, for instance, Edward J. Gitre, "History for Us: Who is writing the church's story?" *Christianity Today*, July 9, 2001, 52. "The academy's playbook is different than ours. Ours presupposes faith and trusts that God is at work in history. Pinpointing God's activity is no less difficult. Does that mean we write him out of the script? No. . . . Indeed, we would do well to question the church's consumption of histories written essentially for 'the world.'" Also see the symposiums in the Winter/Spring, 2002 *Fides et Historia*: "Rethinking the Framework of History" and "Revisioning History in Christian Scholarship." Not all Christian scholars are content with the idea of a history devoid of a discernable God.

4.   Mark A. Noll, *The Scandal of the Evangelical Mind* (Grand Rapids: William B. Eerdmans Publishing Company, 1994), 132.

5.   Ibid, 135, 136.

6.   Joel A. Carpenter, *Revive Us Again: The Reawakening of American Fundamentalism* (New York: Oxford University Press, 1997), xiii.

7.   Ibid, 64.

8.   "Social Security," *Moody Institute Monthly*, January 1935, 215.

9.   See Luke 12:13-21. One wonders whether it could be asked of Jesus if he was taking the economic affairs of the world on its own terms?

10.   "Social Security," *Moody Institute Monthly*, October 1935, 56.

11.   "Reviewing the Townsend Plan: Editorial," *Moody Institute Monthly*, August 1935, 555. Also see, "Can the Townsend Millennium Be Realized?" *Prophecy Monthly*, October 1935, 4-7.

12.   Ibid.

13.   Ibid.

14.   Ibid.

15.   Ibid. No doubt Gray would have agreed with the sociologist Philip Reif, that in a certain sense, "Political cures are always and entirely faithless," (*The Feeling Intellect: Selected Writings*, 360). Certainly he would have agreed with Kurt Schaefer that, "Just as leaders of the Reformation rejected the doctrine of *individual* 'perfectionism,'

so we need to reject the popular modern tendency toward *social* perfectionism" ("Creation, Fall, and What?" *Faculty Dialogue*, Fall 1992, 133).

16. Many historic fundamentalist leaders seem to have been quite conversant on the secular world's affairs "on their own terms." J. Oliver Buswell, for example, took graduate level courses wherever he worked. When he became President of the National Seminary in New York City, he continued his educational habit and was invited to participate in the Philosophy Club. ("The Philosophy Club Hears the Evidence for the Resurrection," *The King's Business*, June 1946, 243, 244.) Donald Barnhouse, to keep up on current affairs, read, on a regular basis, the *New York Times*, *Time*, *Life*, *Newsweek*, the Kiplinger News Service, *Harper's*, the *Atlantic Monthly*, the *Yale Review*, the *American Scholar*, and the *Foreign Affairs Quarterly*, and this is not a complete list. ("Tomorrow: Motives of Judgment," *Revelation*, November 1947, 478.)

17. Mark Noll makes this "lack" a major indictment of the historic fundamentalists, charging that they were intellectually sterile. Due to this sad state of affairs, Noll claims,

> the evangelical community gave birth to virtually no insights into how, under God, the natural world proceeded, how human societies worked, why human nature acted the way it did, or what constituted the blessings and perils of culture. To be sure, Fundamentalists...had firm beliefs about some of these matters— beliefs moreover that were backed up by citations from Scripture. Some of these beliefs were entirely correct. What even laudable scriptural beliefs lacked, however, was profound knowledge of the divinely created world in which those beliefs were applied. (*The Scandal of the Evangelical Mind*, 137.)

It is difficult to be more intellectually condescending than this. However, the historic fundamentalists, without denying the value of learning (critics to the contrary), might have stood Noll's charge on its head. All the "profound knowledge" in the world garnered from the wisdom of men that ignores the scriptural worldview, is not in submission to its authority, and/or ignores its teachings, will lead to profound ignorance about the true construction of reality, and has brought upon the world wordy scholarly hubris, and worse, endless social and individual tragedy. It is worth a moment's reflection to note that two of the intellectuals that have deeply influenced the postmodern movement (if I may call it that)—Nietzsche and Heidiegger—were Nazis. One a Nazi in spirit and was its "god-father," the other a true Nazi when the Nazis ruled Europe.

18. George M. Marsden, *Fundamentalism and American Culture: The Shaping of Twentieth-Century Evangelicalism 1870-1925* (New York: Oxford University Press, 1980), 63.

19. Noll, 141.

20. Carpenter, 64.

21. Marsden, 230. On the other hand, Walter A. McDougall, Alloy-Ansin Professor of International Relations and Professor of History at the University of Pennsylvania, believes that history has a moral function. He writes:

> If honestly taught, history is the only academic subject that inspires humility. Theology used to do that, but in our present era history must do the work of theology. It is, for all practical purposes, the religion in the modern curriculum.

Teachers with a true moral compass inevitable convey to their history students a sense of the contingency of all human endeavors and the yawning gap between intentions and consequences in all human action. If a course in history does not teach such wisdom, it is not history but something else. ("An Ideological Agenda for History," *Academic Questions*, Winter 1998-99, 34.)

22. Iain H. Murray, "Editorial Response," *The Banner of Truth*, March 1995, 11.

23. Marsden, 202. No attempt is made to show similarities and dissimilarities between "middle-class" values (in a country with a strong Christian component) and genuine Christian moral values developed from Scripture. Yet such an evaluation ought to be made.

24. Douglas Frank, *Less Than Conquerors: How Evangelicals Entered the Twentieth Century* (Grand Rapids: William B. Eerdmans Publishing Company, 1986), 68. Frank also caustically commented that, "When they did talk about social and economic realities, it was to express fear of whatever threatened the middle class society...."(98). Of course, a case could be made that historic fundamentalism was hardly a middle class movement. But even more disturbing is that Frank's comment denies to them any deeply held political or biblical values that shaped their viewpoint—all was ambition and self-interest.

25. Roger Lundin, *The Culture of Interpretation: Christian Faith and the Postmodern World* (Grand Rapids: William Eerdmans Publishing Company, 1993), 233. One has to question whether sincere fundamentalists would define the Christian life so briefly or so outwardly. Or that their embrace of premillennialism was a product of alienation rather than a conviction that this is what the Bible truly taught. To their credit, the fundamentalist's "short list of social vices" was a recognition that certain acts are not holy and can be a detriment to the Christian's walk with the Lord. They recognized that the "flesh" is weak and therefore needed to be kept in check through self-denial. This is difficult for an antinomian age to comprehend.

26. Carpenter, 88. As John Wilson writes, "the Fundamentalists...would not be satisfied with the assurance that they had 'invested their lives with meaning.' " ("The Secret History of Fundamentalism," *Christianity Today*, December 8, 1997, 48.)

27. Ibid, 243. However, Harry S. Stout, Jonathan Edwards Professor of American History, Yale University, characterizes the historical fundamentalists as "very angry people: angry at the prospect of a lost America; angry that the country no longer granted them respect; angry that science seemed to have passed them by; and most of all angry that their fellow Christian religionists refused to go along with their separatism...they felt and acted like losers who took their fundamentals and ran home...." ("Reviewers Reviewed," *The Banner of Truth*, March 1995, 10.) As Keith Brooks wrote over sixty years ago, "that of course is simple hokum."

28. Michael S. Hamilton, "The Hidden Years of Fundamentalism Revealed," *Evangelical Studies Bulletin*, Winter 1997, 4.

29. Robert L. Wilken, *Remembering the Christian Past* (Grand Rapids: William B. Eerdmans Publishing Company, 1995), 14, 15.

30. Noll, 169.

31. Genesis 6:5 (NIV).

32. Joseph Edwin Harris, "Sin, Satan, and the Social Gospel," *Bibliotheca Sacra*, October 1934, 451, 452. Harris believed that it was "a great weakness of the social gospel"

that it did "not take sufficient cognizance of the factor of human sin in its reckoning," (450, 451). Nor did Harris accept the premise that it was limiting the power of God to admit that the "social effectiveness of Christianity" was *only* partial. Realistically, he noted, the influence of Christianity had not eliminated wars, curbed crime and vice, or prevented the Great Depression (450).

33. J. Gresham Machen, *The Christian Faith in the Modern World* (Grand Rapids: Wm. B. Eerdmans Publishing Co., 1936 [1970]), 6.

34. Christopher B. Browning, "Human Nature, Culture, and the Holocaust," *The Chronicle of Higher Education*, October 18, 1996, A72.

35. Ibid.

36. Ibid.

37. Neil Postman, *Technopoly: The Surrender of Culture to Technology* (New York: Vintage Books, 1993), 162.

38. Ibid, 90.

39. Wilkin, 12, 15.

40. Gertrude Himmelfarb, *On Looking into the Abyss: Untimely thoughts on Culture and Society* (New York: Vintage Books, 1994), 26. Himmelfarb is responding to the deconstructionists and the way they have handled the Holocaust.

41. David F. Wells, *No Place for Truth: Or Whatever Happened to Evangelical Theology* (Grand Rapids: William B. Eerdmans Publishing company, 1993), 300. I recently heard a "public announcement" on the radio that referred to the violence in our public schools in California as a serious "public health" problem, as if stopping young people from killing each other is of the same nature as preventing a measles outbreak. A society that denies evil is evil and sin is sin, is a society in serious moral trouble—it forecasts its own doom by embracing euphemistic nonsense.

42. Wilbur Smith (desiring careful consideration "by every student of this problem of contemporary unbelief"), in his apologetic *Therefore Stand* (1945), quoted the great theologian James Denny on this subject:

> What sleepy conscience, what moral mediocrity, itself purblind, only dimly conscious of the height of the Christian calling, and vexed by no aspirations toward it, has any right to say that it is too much to call Satan "the god of this world"? (sic) Such sleepy consciences have no idea of the omnipresence, the steady persistent pressure, the sleepless malignity, of the evil forces that beset man's life (177).

43. Harris, 452, 453. Lest one think Harris is just being typically "fundamentalist" in scoffing at social reform, he also noted that not everyone who used the term "social gospel" was a modernist. Some used the term simply to point out the social dimensions and implications of the New Testament—and certainly these could not be denied. In fact, Harris believed the effects of the gospel witness "still remain all too limited and there is a crying need for the righting of many social need today," (448, 449).

Nevertheless, Harris considered the Social Gospel "another gospel," and doomed to failure because it would not recognize the reality of man's sinful nature and Satan's existence and dedication to inciting evil (451-458). Wilbur Smith, of one mind with Harris, and writing during the bitterest moments of World War II, wrote the following words of judgment on the tarnished vestments of the Social Gospel:

Charles Stelzle...whom all of us thought, a quarter of a century ago, was a prophet of God, once dared to say that Christianity was not "a scheme to increase the population of heaven...but to bring heaven down to earth...." Thirty years have gone by since Stelzle wrote this, and we are in the midst of hell on earth instead of heaven on earth! ... It seems almost as though God himself judged this social gospel, this idea of turning from Him and centering all our thoughts on the economic welfare of man, by really showing to the world, once and forever, what humanity can be when it turns from God, and how wicked and brutal and devilish man can be, when let loose in such a holocaust as this. (*Therefore Stand, 44*).

At about the same time Smith was writing, Shirley Jackson Case published his *The Christian Philosophy of History*, which, according to Bebbington, "was a Twentieth-Century echo of Turgot." Case wrote:

History to date is also reassuring. Even the casual observer realizes the tremendous spread of moral and spiritual interest over the earth over the last two thousand years. A gradual enlarging circle of mankind has learned to cherish ways of living the exemplify honesty, justice, and brotherly kindness. (Quoted in Bebbington's *Patterns of History*, [181]).

Wilbur Smith no doubt would have noted what Bebbington does: "Meanwhile the holocaust of Auschwitz was at its height." (Case also believed history should only take note of events..."at a natural level." Thus he "dismisses the possibility of belief in 'the capricious intervention of Deity' " (182).

44.   There is no better survey of this from a historic fundamentalists perspective than Wilbur Smith's *Therefore Stand*, especially the first chapter, "The Forces and Agencies Engaged in the Modern Attack Upon Christianity," 1-102, and the accompanying endnotes, 523-538.

45.   Joseph Taylor Britan, "What is Wrecking Morals and Governments Today?" *The Sunday School Times*, May 5, 1934, 252.

46.   Will Houghton wrote an editorial in the May 1938, *Moody Monthly* commenting on the despair overtaking the world. Noting the horror that was taking place in Vienna under the Nazi occupation, he wrote: "Whatever is possessing men to silently surrender all of the moral achievements of the ages? After all of the forces of education and religion have been at work these centuries, civilization has touched a new low." He then warned American about being smug in thinking it could not happen here. What was happening in Europe "never entered the imagination of historians or political economists." ("Pessimism and Despair," 451.)

47.   George Marsden, for one, desires to infuse the secular academy with a beneficial dose of properly constituted Christian theism. ("Why the Academy Should Include Religious Perspectives," *Academic Questions*, Spring 1996). He appeals to the secular academy to allow room for those of religious persuasion "to participate in constructive dialogue and debate that recognizes the realities of religious pluralism." He wants nervous secularists to realize that there are many "evangelicals or Catholics who are essentially traditional in their theological affirmations, but have little sympathy with the viewpoints of Fundamentalists and populist ideologues and politicians" (13, 14).

That clarified, Marsden is ready to bargain:

My practical suggestion for the mainstream academia is that even academics who are not themselves religious have some reason to welcome intellectually sophisticated and academically responsible religious viewpoints as an alternative to the more simplistic demands of dogmatic religious ideologues (14).

Not only is Marsden willing to jettison his less "intellectually and academically responsible" brethren, he is also willing to play by those rules necessary "for a pluralistic intellectual enterprise to operate." This, of course, would "include being willing to abide by standards of evidence and argument that can be assessed by their academic colleagues. That means…arguments cannot be settled by claims of special revelation" (16).

Marsden surrenders the heart of Protestant, Reformation rooted evangelicalism—the special revelation of Scripture. Discarded at the universities' gates, what then, do evangelicals bring to the academy that others cannot bring? Along these lines, Robert Wilkin reminds his readers of a comment T. S. Eliot made in 1939 in his *Christianity and Culture* (when evil and sin were obvious and permissible for even scholars to mention). Eliot, Wilken notes, thought it a " 'very dangerous inversion' for Christian thinkers 'to advocate Christianity, not because it is true, but because it is beneficial.' " (*Remembering the Christian Past*, 1995, 50.)

David Wells has noted "the evangelical church, whose taste for what is popular appears to be insatiable, is in danger of being destabilized by culture captivity of some of its popular 'thinkers,' as well as by the academic captivity of some of its scholars." (*Losing Our Virtue*, 1998, 11).

48. David Wells also notes in *No Place for Truth*, that except for their sometimes irritating ways of offending their opponents, the historic fundamentalists' "commitment to the formal and material principle of Protestantism was unyielding." An authoritative Scripture, the substitutionary meaning of Christ's death on the cross, and His miracles were all well defended. In addition, their unshakable

assertion that the Bible should be read literally not only signaled the Fundamentalists' intention to take it seriously but also, it would seem, to reject the whole raft of literary theory and critical chicanery that had made a mockery, in learned circles, of biblical inspiration. And when Fundamentalists insisted on the pre-millennial return of Christ…they were declaring their intention not only to understand biblical prophecy in a certain way but also to reject categorically the Liberal idea of the growing Kingdom of God on earth (128, 129).

49. Every great crisis in the church's history brings disruption, bitterness, militancy, and division. In this sense, the modernist/fundamentalist controversy was not unique. In fact, all things considered, the historic fundamentalists were a pretty mild bunch. Their great "crime" seems to be their often militant and sometimes nasty, "it is my way or the highway," speech; that their version of evangelicalism was the only right version—and they tended to readily separate from those they considered wrong, including their own. This got ugly at times and unnecessarily, even sinfully, disruptive. On the other hand, they burned no one at the stake, drowned no one, held no auto da fe, hanged no one, did not ram a hot iron through anyone's tongue or cut off anyone's ear, or otherwise torture those who disagreed with their theology. They sent no one into exile in the dead of winter, sold no one into slavery, branded

no one, burned no convents nor mobbed polygamists. Despite their intense opposition to communism, when one was arrested for passing out tracts, the editors of *Moody Monthly* and *Revelation* came to the defense of his constitutional right to do so.

50. Edward Ulbach, "The Reformers of the Sixteenth Century," *Bibliotheca Sacra*, July-September 1935, 318.

51. Iain Murray, "Editorial Response," 11.

52. Perhaps they should wrestle as well with the question as to whether the historic fundamentalists, with all their faults and foibles, were not raised up specifically by God to stand in the "breach" against the onslaught of modernism and secularism. In other words, was God uniquely with them and using them at that particular place and time (over and above the usual working of God's providential oversight modern evangelical historians are vaguely willing to concede)? As long as we approach them through the analysis of cultural forces, we can ignore or avoid that inappropriate (by today's historiographic standards) question. But at some point it must be answered by those who call themselves Protestant evangelicals.

53. Wilken, 50, 51. See *Therefore Stand*, 483-485, for a somewhat fuller and more militant and passionate appeal along these same lines by Wilbur Smith in 1945.

Addendum to Chapter Ten

The Unseemly Death of Providentialism At the Hands of Evangelical Historians

Should evangelical historians abandon providentialism as a component of their historical writings? (Perhaps this is already a moot question despite the symposium that appeared in the Winter/Spring 2002, *Fides et Historia*, which [unconvincingly] argued both sides of the issue.) D. G. Hart, Professor of Church History at Westminster Theological Seminary, supports such a position. In his essay, "History in Search of Meaning: The Conference on Faith and History," which appeared in *History and the Christian Historian*, (1998), Hart advocates that the Christian historian adopt a "historical agnosticism" when interpreting historical events, including those which have always been interpreted by evangelicals as clearly evidencing the unmistakable and direct intervention of God into the mundane course of daily events.[1] Hart specifically brings up the first Great Awakening in this regard, apparently to place himself on the side of Harry S. Stout (Jonathan Edwards Professor of American Christianity at Yale University) in Stout's confrontation with the Christian historian Iain Murray, editorial director of *The Banner of Truth* journal and author of *Jonathan Edwards: A New Biography* (1987).

Evangelical Stout's biography of George Whitefield (*The Divine Dramatist: George Whitefield and the Rise of Modern Evangelicalism*, 1991), written from a purely secular viewpoint, did not fare well in the pages of *The Banner of Truth*. Nor did his essay "George Whitefield in Three Counties," which appeared in *Evangelicalism: Comparative Studies of Popular Protestantism in North America, the British Isles, and Beyond 1700-1990* (1994), do any better.   In fact, *Evangelicalism* itself was severely critiqued by Murray. Murray's over-all criticism was that too many young evangelical historians have set aside their Christian worldview when writing religious history in order to be accepted as professional historians by the secular academy and their secular peers.[2]

The central criticism of Stout's biography of Whitefield, as noted by Murray, was that what was central to Whitefield's life was absent, and instead "the human and cultural" were made essential. In other words, Stout gave a strictly secular interpretation of Whitefield and the Great Awakening as a whole.[3] Stout defended himself by stating that he was not ashamed of his Christianity nor ashamed of writing about it, but that he is also a professional historian and "professional historians agree to settle for something less than ultimate explanations in the works that constitute our field...[and] to certain canons of evidence and interpretation that we all agree on." Stout admits that he finds such a situation "liberating in its capacity to bring diverse scholars together in a common discourse."[4]

Stout also noted that his "secular" approach to Whitefield had brought respect for Whitefield in the "professional academy" which Stout believes "means...that in some measure, they respect a self-proclaimed 'fool for Christ' in ways they were not prepared to do earlier."[5] Stout defends his position in rather stark terms:

> The stakes are simple. If there is no room for the Christian to write social and cultural history as *proximate history*, making no claims to its ultimacy or all-encompassing explanatory power, then there is no room for Christians in the secular academy. If, as Christian historians, we write only ostentatiously providential-based history, we are consigning ourselves to separatist ghettos.[6]

Stout wants nothing to do with such a "fundamentalist" scenario. However, despite his well-articulated response (and certainly he is not unreasonable in advocating the Christian historian's right to pen history "as *proximate history*"), Murray's insightful comment noted above still needs to be answered.[7] Murray agrees that, while it is not "To be denied that more attention to the *human* side of biography is often needed in Christian biography," he also wonders whether writing "the lives of eminent Christians with minimum notice of the things which meant *most* to them, and without which their lives cannot be understood, is to [surely] mislead?"[8]

Such was the situation into which Hart injected himself in order to support Stout. What is interesting, though, is that Hart seems to take a more rigid stand in this matter of "historical agnosticism" than does Stout.[9] For example, Hart addresses Murray's strong conviction that the first Great Awakening was clearly the work of the Holy Spirit in almost contemptuous terms. "But how does Murray know that the Great Awakening was the work of God?" he writes. "Did God tell him?"[10] Evidently Hart is unwilling to accept any circumstantial evidence (e.g., the conversion of thousands to a life-changing, deep faith in Jesus Christ) as proof that such an event is directly and unmistakably of God. To buttress his "agnostic" position, he notes that other Christians, such as Roman Catholics or "confessional Lutherans" may have an entirely different understanding of the Great Awakening.[11]

As an evangelical, of course, Hart does believe that God is providentially working in a general way in all historical situations. But, as he points out,

> to determine what God intended by a particular event is another matter altogether. In other words, without the special revelation God gave to the apostles and through the risen Christ, twentieth-century Christians, just like the early church, cannot know the meaning from God's perspective of any historical event, even the crucifixion.[12]

Just as the elders of a church cannot discern the heart of someone wishing to join their church (despite that person's confession of Christ), neither can the Christian historian, Hart reasons, discern the intent of God in any particular "political, economic, or cultural event." "One supposes," he concludes, "therefore, that discerning the actions of providence is not the appropriate test for a Christian historiography."[13]

It is obvious that Hart believes he has the better of the argument. Murray has been appropriately corrected. Christians simply cannot discern the direct and unmistakable hand of God in historical events anymore than anyone else, and it is poor history to try to do so. However, not only does Hart's demand for skepticism seem extreme for an evangelical, but his argument is also flawed. First, simply because Catholics or Lutherans may see the Great Awakening differently than evangelicals do is to beg the question as to whether it was clearly and unmistakably the work of the Holy Spirit. Not all interpretations of historical events are equally valid, or equally convincing, postmodern historiographic insistence notwithstanding. The weight of evidence should and can steer interpretation toward a particular conclusion.

Second, the basis for understanding the Great Awakening as a great and obvious work of God is based on Scriptural analogues. The New Testament writers themselves appeal to circumstantial evidence regarding the truthfulness of one conversion to Christ. For example, the Apostle Paul, who never met the Colossian Christians but had only heard of their "faith in Christ Jesus and of the love you have for all the saints," (Col. 1:3, 4 NIV), nevertheless assumes they are believers because it was reported to him that they "heard" the gospel and believed it, understanding "God's grace in all its truth," (Col. 1:16 NIV). Nowhere does Paul appeal to direct revelation to say he knows they really are born-again. Nor does he express any reservations or "agnosticism" regarding their historical status as God's immediate handiwork in Christ Jesus.

The same holds true with his direct experience with the Thessalonians. He accepts circumstantial evidence as sufficient. He believes they are truly Christians because when they heard the gospel preached they "accepted it not as the word of men, but as it actually is, the word of God" working in them (1 Thess. 2:13; also see 2 Thess. 2:13-15). Again, Paul makes no appeal to special revelation. In fact, at one point, he suffered such doubt that they might not have been truly converted that he sent his co-worker Timothy to check on them, because, as he later wrote to them, "I was afraid that in some way the tempter might have tempted you and our efforts might have been useless," (1 Thess. 3:5b NIV).

Other examples could be offered, such as Joseph's insightful interpretation of his experience of being sold into slavery by his brothers. "You intended to harm me," he said to them, "but God intended it for good to accomplish what is now being done, the saving of many lives," (Gen. 50:20 NIV). Nowhere in Scripture are we informed that this knowledge came to Joseph through revelation. Rather it seems this was his inescapable conclusion upon considering all that had transpired since that awful day, when as a young teenager, he found out just how much his brothers despised him. Even the Lord Jesus taught "All men will know that you are my disciples, if you love one another," (John 13:35 NIV). In other words, our attitude and actions toward each other is *prima-facie* evidence to the unbelieving world that we either are or are not true Christians.

It is evident, then, that Hart would deny to the Christian historian a means of discerning God's intent in historical events, whether acts of compassion or the conversion of many thousands of souls, that the writers of Scripture do not deny him.

Therefore, it seems to me, that if Iain Murray has noted that Whitefield's life and work conform to the examples and expectations given in Scripture, and understands from the same source that Jesus, who sent people out to preach His gospel, is the same today as yesterday, and knows that Satan never works to bring about anyone's true conversion to Christ but that God does, then he is justified in concluding that the Great Awakening (which saw thousands converted) is a historical event that exhibits specifically God's hand in a way superior to the vague generalizations that Hart approves.

In his biography of Jonathan Edwards, Murray quotes Edwards' reasons for believing the Great Awakening was a work of the Holy Spirit despite its excesses and foibles:

> The Spirit's true work can be distinguished from that which is false because we know that he always (1) causes a greater esteem for Christ (2) operates against the interest of Satan's kingdom...(3) promotes greater regard for the truth and the divinity of the Holy Scriptures (4) brings men to the light of truth (5) excites love to God and man, making the attributes of God, manifested in Christ, 'delightful objects of contemplation.'[14]

Neither Edwards nor Murray claim divine revelation for his conclusions. However, the circumstantial evidence they offer is weighty with Scriptural approving analogues, examples, and conclusions, and is open for all to consider.

Hart rhetorically asks, "Are Christian historians better able to discern the hand of God in history than non-Christians?"[15] Despite Hart's "no," I must respectfully disagree. In certain instances, such as the Great Awakening, I believe the answer can be "yes." Certainly such a conclusion is as good as, if not better than the assessment of those who would attempt to explain all events by "cultural forces" which are cued by the secular historian's bias, or are simply safer because they are more acceptable to one's peers.[16] The problem is not with the providential explanation but with historians who seem almost theophobic, who are obsessed with writing only "ostentatiously" secular wrought history, even when the event pleads for the assistance of something more, even something providential.

To deny that the Christian historian can ever discern the hand of God in history in a direct way is, to paraphrase a famous line from Hamlet, to have the gentleman protest *too much*. Though Murray may anger those evangelical historians who for professional reasons adopt the configuration of a secular historian, he is right—there is a price one pays for such "professional" acceptance. It may not be readily apparent now, but it will someday, for a dichotomy has appeared between who I am in Christ and how I write and teach as a "professional" historian in the academy.[17]

NOTES

1. D. G. Hart, "History in Search of Meaning: The Conference on Faith and History," in *History and the Christian Historian*, Ronald A. Wells, ed. (Grand Rapids: William B. Eerdmans Publishing Company, 1994), 85.
2. Iain H. Murray, "Explaining Evangelical History," *The Banner of Truth*, July 1994, 11, 12.
3. Iain H. Murray, "Editorial Response," *The Banner of Truth*, March 1995, 11.
4. Harry S. Stout, "Reviewers Reviewed," *The Banner of Truth*, March 1995, 8
5. Ibid. To this Murray replied: "We regret to say that we fear the 'new respect' you hoped you have gained for Whitefield is too largely dependent upon the elimination of those central aspects of his life and preaching which will always make Christianity offensive to the natural man," 11.
6. Ibid. It does not seem to have occurred to Stout that the ghetto works both ways. Though more numerous and more dominate in the academy than the Christian historian, the secular historian has also created an isolated community (and is quite contented in doing so) by excluding any mention of providence. Nor does Stout state why the academy must be exclusively secular.
7. Murray, "Editorial Response," 11.
8. Stout justified his position with these words:
   I knew that Christians would understand Whitefield on deeper devotional and

theological levels, and I knew they had all the information they needed in existing biographies. In case they did not, I prepared a separate biographical sketch for *Christian History* that was explicitly devotional and Christ-centered for the theological edification of Christian lay historians, ("Reviewers Reviewed," 8).

9. Hart, 85.
10. Ibid, 86.
11. Ibid.
12. Ibid.
13. Ibid.
14. Iain H. Murray, *Jonathan Edwards: A New Biography* (Edinburgh: The Banner of Truth Trust, 1987), 234.
15. Hart, 86. Even D. B. Bebbington, who believes that the Christian historian "can write of providence or not according to his judgement of the composition of his audience," 187, is willing to concede, "the task (of discerning God's providential hand in history) is not beyond us." In support of this claim, Bebbington offers Richard Baxter's belief that the restoration of Charles II to the throne in 1660, which took place " 'without a bloody nose' " was proof positive of God's direct intervention in history. "Surely," Bebbington comments, "in this instance Baxter had good grounds for discerning God at work," 173. He goes on to write:

> The evidence does suggest that the expected course of events had been diverted in a way which accords with the character of God as the author of peace. Baxter was expressing a faith that is reasonable. More than faith could hardly be expected.... But a reasonable faith can become aware of divine interventions. A claim to discern the hand of God in history need not be extravagant, (174).

(All quotations are from Bebbington's *Patterns of History: A Christian Perspective, 1979).*

Others are also willing to see the obvious hand of God in historical events. Stephen J. Keillor, for instance, in his, *This Rebellious House: American History & the Truth of Christianity* (1996), writes:

> American history is occasionally the story of how God's Spirit acted in redemptive ways when people least deserved it. Using church, gospel, Scripture and revival methods that were familiar to people, the Spirit acted autonomously. The Spirit's work was not shaped by the people's psychological state or by frontier conditions, nor did he sanctify the people's frontier lifestyle. He turned Kentucky upside down in the years 1797-1801, (122).

Marvin Olasky, editor of *World* magazine, sees God's direct providential care in the absence of nuclear war over the last 50 years. In the September 18, 1999 issue of *World* he forth-rightly states:

> Adult Americans have seen in international affairs many movements of God's hands, as when He swept the Soviet empire off the table 10 years ago. But the most impressive one of all may involve the road not taken, and the way God preserved us through so many dangerous nuclear intersections. ("God's Mercy: How Else have We Survived 50 Years of Potential Nuclear War?" 34).

(One could make the argument that Olasky's understanding of the demise of the Soviet empire is one with Baxter's understanding of the bloodless restoration of Charles II. If one exhibits the direct hand of God in history so does the other.)

16. Responding to those in his own day who considered the Great Awakening the product of human efforts, Jonathan Edwards wrote in 1742:

     They have greatly erred in the way they have gone about to try this work...in judging it...from the way that it began, the instruments that have been employed, the means that have been used, and the methods that have been taken and succeeded in carrying it on.... We are to observe the effect wrought and if, upon examination of that, it be found agreeable to the word of God, we are bound to rest in it as God's work; and we shall be like to be rebuked for our arrogance if we refuse to do so till God shall explain to us how he has brought this effect to pass, or why he made use of such and such a means in doing it.... (quoted in *Jonathan Edwards: A New Biography*, 158).

17. Regarding Stout's apparent bifurcation (see note #8), Murray writes:

     Still more serious, it is impossible for us to see how the Great Awakening is, as you say, chiefly to be understood in terms of Whitefield's success in "selling a product—the new birth," and at the same time to hold quietly that it was essentially an outpouring of the Spirit of God. ("Editorial Response," 11.)

EPILOGUE

The shibboleths crumble before the primary documentation. The infamous fundamentalist siege mentality with its supposed indifference toward things political, disengaged compassion, and even, if you will, its anti-Semitism, is less the product of history than the creation of the historians and critics of the movement. If Preston Jones is right—that it is especially incumbent upon the Christian historian "to be determined to get things right" and to be fair with the past—then when it comes to the historic fundamentalists some outstanding evangelical scholars seemingly fail this test.[1] It cannot be denied that some fairly obvious and convincing documentation, documentation that would call into question the present interpretations of historic fundamentalism has been either ignored, missed or explained away. The question, then, is why? Why has this happened over and over again?

The answer may be found in the almost inherent bias toward historic fundamentalism that many of today's evangelical scholars seem to exhibit. This has made them less than diligent in seeking out all the primary documentation and less than judicious in interpreting those documents, or even unwilling it appears to be fair in their use. Too often one gets the impression that the historic fundamentalists are judged by what the critic thinks they should have done or said or thought. But by imposing their own political position as the measure by which to judge them, the critic has deprived us of seeing the historic fundamentalists in their own context and measured by their own convictions.[2] The result is that the historian gives the impression that he has a point to make rather than a history to write.

In fact, when one reads histories of the historic fundamentalism, three things seem apparent (at least on the surface). First, there is a "dislike" of this movement, or at least a dislike of the way it handled the crisis it found itself in. Certainly there is dislike of its eschatology, and its attempts to "read" eschatological possibilities into present events. Second, present-day evangelical critics, apparently because they have scholarly ambitions that are at opposites with how they view the historic fundamentalists intellectually, almost of necessity seem compelled to portray them as the "bad guys" of American church history, or at a minimum as incompetent "losers." Obviously the secular critic will also portray them as the bad guys but this is due to irreconcilable worldviews. This has resulted in much misdirected socio/psychological analysis of the historic fundamentalists (which only muddies up the water) and the ignoring of their biblical c onvictions and "excessive" supernaturalism as primary motivating factors. Finally, the religious views and actions of the historic fundamentalists are often spoken of as if they are a historical anomaly, a bleak deviation, in Protestant history. Yet such, as has been demonstrated, is not the case. Theologically they revived Calvanistic views of man, sin, history, and the cross for a large portion of conservative evangelicalism, views that had fallen on decidedly hard times in the nineteen century (and seem to be falling on hard times again). In their defense of Scripture and historical Protestant doctrine, and even in their militancy, they were very much in touch with their Protestant roots. And in one sense, their eschatology acted both as a healthy corrective to the excessive postmillennialism that obsessed American Protestantism, as well as the American secularists, while injecting vigor into the great mission surge of the late nineteen century and the whole of the twentieth century.

Mark N oll bemoans the fact that the evangelical heritage from our historic fundamentalist's forebears makes us as "intuitive and populist as ever," and that prior to "our time" evangelicals exhibited "little evidence of any felt need for systematic theoretical reflection, for a theology applied self-consciously to politics, or for critical-historical studies in aid of political theory."[3] "Perhaps," though the evidence offered in this book may be an indication that this is a gross overstatement.

Considering their many p leas for thoughtful a nd w ell-informed Christian involvement a better word than intuitive might be "conviction." Their political positions seemed derived from deep convictions that were in part grounded in a deeper reverence for the S criptures as well as a sincere r espect for America's Christian roots a nd constitutional l iberties. C learly there w ere some historic fundamentalists who d id withdraw i nto a sa nctuary of p iety and n on-political involvement. Even here, though, fairness dictates that we recognize that such people followed Scripture as they understood it. But just as clearly, the historic fundamentalists referred to in this book, did not agree with them.

There are many things one might fault the historic fundamentalists for not doing or for not doing as well as they should have. Present-day historians have been more than adapt at uncovering these. (Children always see their parent's sins more clearly than their own.) For instance, politically and morally they are open to criticism for their acquiescence and even participation in America's blatant racial segregation. Also it seems clear that they were too deeply committed to the mythical idea o f "Christian America." Theoretically, this should have worked at cross-purposes with the logical thrust of their premillennial dispensationalism—yet it did not.[4] In this, they seemed to have d eparted from an earlier generation o f premillennial dispensationalists who would have largely agreed with S. H. Kellogg when he wrote, "Never does the Bible recognize what we call the Christianization of a nation as a conversion of that nation." Nevertheless, foibles and all, one simply cannot fault them for being politically silent, or for that matter, uninformed. It is more than evident they had not lost their prophetic voice of rebuke aimed at a selfish capitalism.[5] On the other hand, some of them could be extremely pessimistic, believing that America's wounds were beyond cure.[6] They were religious leaders writing in religious magazines concerning themselves mostly with religious issues (which were also of great historical significance). But their political convictions come through, convictions that seem for the most part derived from thoughtful, biblically framed considerations of the issues at hand. Despite their religious preoccupations and intense prophetic speculations, it is apparent many historic fundamentalists were also interested in the world around them, in history, in loving their neighbor, in active citizenship, and in being politically informed.

Yes, they were children of their times—but what times they were! Yes, their sins were many and often written large. Easily seen, then, by this generation of historians whom seem determined to write innumerable books and articles enumerating every one. However, words Edward Ulbach penned over six decades ago are worth repeating here: "that in all their wrestling with the ignorance of their times, and the weakness of their erring natures, they were animated by a leading idea of duty, and by a solemn recognition of something to be lived for beyond this world."[7] All things considered, then, they were workman that need not hide their faces before their peers or their progeny.

This study stands in support of this conclusion. It is a corrective to what has been written about (or perhaps it would be better to say not written about) the historic fundamentalists hither-to-fore. I gladly admit to an agenda—to set the record "straighter" because it has been bent scandalously beyond recognition. However, considering the political correctness of our day (yes, even in evangelical circles) I may be playing Don Quixote to the nearest postmodern windmill. One can still hope, though, that a study such as this will challenge historians to a greater diligence in their research and a greater balance (fairness) in their interpretations. After all, it is the historian's task, as much as is possible, to help us first know those who came before, before we construct self-satisfying caricatures of them.

NOTES

1. Preston Jones, "How to Serve Time," *Christianity Today*, April 2, 2001, 52.
2. To his credit, Joel Carpenter, in *Revive Us Again*, does make an effort to present the historic fundamentalists as a sincere people struggling with difficult decisions in difficult times. (See especially his concluding words on pages 242 through 246).
3. A good example of this is found in Mark Noll's *The Scandal of the Evangelical Mind*, pages 136 and 137. There he writes:
   Fundamentalist belief in the supernatural was by no means unique in Christian

history. But the way in which dispensationalism concentrated its energies upon the transcendent at the expense of the natural was distinct. When Lewis Sperry Chafer wrote, "the natural capacities of the human mind do not function in the realm of spiritual things," he defined himself and all those who followed after him as...an "enthusiast," for whom grace has destroyed nature. With such an orientation, not only was the exploration of nature and ordinary human affairs suspect, but every possible barrier had been erected against the attempts to let the deep riches of Christian theology guide human understanding of the world.

One might question, as this study does, Noll's historical conclusion that the dispensationalists were unique in their focus on the transcendent at the expense of the natural. But more germane is his attempt to isolate Chafer's understanding of I Cor. 2:12-16 from common historical exegesis of these passages. In interpreting these verses, Chafer was speaking only on the relation of the unbeliever to the Word of God. He was concerned with unregenerate scholars dictating "to the church what she shall believe." His actual words are as follows:

> There is a limitless yet hidden spiritual content within the Bible which contributes much to its supernatural character. This spiritual content is never discerned by the natural...or unregenerate man (1 Cor. 2:14), even though he has attained to the highest degree of learning or ecclesiastical authority. The natural capacities of the human mind do not function in the realm of spiritual things. The divine message is presented "not in the words which man's wisdom teacheth, but which the Holy Ghost teacheth, comparing spiritual things with spiritual" (1 Cor. 2:13), and the spirit has been given to the regenerate that they might "know the things that are freely given to us by God." (*Systematic Theology, Vol.* 1, 1947, vi.)

Now, in all honesty, it is hard to see how Chafer's words clash with traditional Protestant exegesis of these verses. In fact, Calvin wrote the following concerning these verses:

> Having shut up all mankind in blindness, and having taken away from the human intellect the power of attaining to a knowledge of God by its own resources, he now shows in what way believers are exempted from this blindness, by the Lord's honoring them with a special illumination of the Spirit. Hence the greater the bluntness of the human intellect for understanding the mysteries of God, and the greater the uncertainty under which it labors, so much the surer is our faith, which rests for its support on the revelation of God's Spirit, (*Commentary on the Epistle of Paul the Apostle to the Corinthians*, trans. By Rev. John Pringle, 1979, 110).

If Chafer is an "enthusiast" for his interpretation of I Cor. 2:12-14, what, then, is Calvin? If Chafer's "orientation" makes the "exploration of nature and ordinary human affairs suspect...," what of Calvin's? This type of isolation of the historic fundamentalists from their historical forebears not only fails to be fair with their theological and exegetical positions, but it also distorts their history in relation to Protestant history as a whole.

4.   S. H. Kellogg, *The Past a Prophecy of the Future and other Sermons*, (London: Hodder and Stoughton, 1904), p. 325. Kellogg held that the idea of a "Christian Nation" was simply foreign to the Bible. Again, Barnhouse was one who spoke out in the 1930s against the idea that America was such a nation. Such an idea was silly,

he believed, because only a small portion of Americans were truly believers, plus the country was filled with mob violence, child labor, peonage, divorce, drug addiction, lynchings and apostasy in the church. ("Christian America," *Revelation*, April 1932, p. 154).

5. Castigating selfish capitalism seems to have been a historic fundamentalists' tradition. For example, C. I. Scofield, speaking at Moody's Northfield Conference in 1895, (and obviously bearing in mind the bloody conclusion of the Pullman Strike), blasted those who place property rights above human life and labeled, "a monstrous national sin the complicity of courts and laws with the remorseless *greed* of corporations and of the rich. . . . We hear of the sanctity of vested rights and the inviolability of property. I tell you God cares more for one drop of human blood than for all your leagues of railway. I tell you that God is on the side of the sanctity of human lives, and the inviolability of human souls." ("National Sins," *Northfield Echoes, Vol. II*, (1895), p. 72.

   Scofield made similar harsh comments about the coal mining industry, (see "The Doctrine of the Last Things as found in the Prophets," *The Coming and Kingdom of Christ*, [1914], p.46).

6. A good example of this pessimism is M. H. Duncan's article, "Trends toward Liberalism in America," *Moody Institute Monthly*, November 1937, p. 118. Duncan bemoaned the fact that:

   > The friends of our American institutions have already waited too long to save them in their entirety from the inroads of the destructive philosophies that are more and more controlling our thinking. They have let the enemies of our life get into control of affairs, and about all they can do now is to wait for the end. Thousands who think, believe that we are witnessing the passing of old time Americanism and heading rapidly toward something that is new and foreign to us. They believe that we are headed, with the rest of the world, toward a dictatorship of communism or fascism, and what it will be may have to be decided by the force of arms.

   If we are inclined to think Duncan too pessimistic, let us remember how secular, even "politically-correct" and postmodern our universities have become, and that it was not until the last decade of the twentieth century that the issue of communist's world-domination was finally settled. And in an indirect way, it was "decided by the force of arms."

7. Edward Ulbach, "The Reformers of the Sixteenth Century," Bibliotheca Sacra, July-September 1935, p. 318. Ulbach was referring to the Reformers with these words. However, they can be applied equally well to many of the historic fundamentalists and he may have intended an implied comparison.

AUTHOR BIOGRAPHY

Coming into the academic community in his forties, Jim Owen is presently associate professor of History at The Master's College where he has taught for more than twenty-five years. His teaching focus is church history and historical research and writing. Along with an academic career, he has served as a chaplain in juvenile facilities, been involved in bible study ministries at alcoholic and drug rehabilitation centers, and pastored two churches during the 1990s. He has also authored one other book (now in its third printing) in the field of biblical counseling titled, *Christian Psychology's War on God's Word: the Victimization of the Believer* (1993). He and his wife, Roberta Jean, have been married for forty-three years and currently reside in the mountain hills of California.

INDEX